Strategic Information Management

Challenges and strategies in managing information systems

Second edition

R. D. Galliers, D. E. Leidner and
B. S. H. Baker

BUTTERWORTH
HEINEMANN

OXFORD   AUCKLAND   BOSTON   JOHANNESBURG   MELBOURNE   NEW DELHI

Butterworth-Heinemann
Linacre House, Jordan Hill, Oxford OX2 8DP
225 Wildwood Avenue, Woburn, MA 01801–2041
A division of Reed Educational and Professional Publishing Ltd

A member of the Reed Elsevier plc group

First published 1994
Second edition 1999
Reprinted 2000

British Library Cataloguing in Publication Data
A catalogue record for this book is available from the British Library

ISBN 0 7506 3975 X

Typeset by Graphicraft Limited, Hong Kong
Printed and bound in Great Britain by Biddles Ltd, *www.biddles.co.uk*

Contents

List of contributors   ix
Preface   xi
Introduction: The emergence of information technology as
a strategic issue   xv

1. **Developments in the Application of Information
    Technology in Business**   1
    Information technology in business: from data processing to
    strategic information systems
    E. K. Somogyi and R. D. Galliers

Part One: Information Systems Strategy   25

2. **The Evolving Information Systems Strategy**   31
    Information systems management and strategy formulation:
    applying and extending the 'stages of growth' concept
    R. D. Galliers and A. R. Sutherland

3. **Information Strategy**   61
    Assessment of information strategies in insurance companies
    M. T. Smits, K. G. van der Poel and P. M. A. Ribbers

4. **Information Management Strategy
    (Organizing the Information Systems Function)**   85
    Any way out of the labyrinth for managing information
    systems?
    B. R. Edwards, M. J. Earl and D. F. Feeny

5. **Information Technology Strategy**   102
    The role of the CEO in the management of change:
    the case of information technology
    E. H. Schein

6. **Change Management Strategy**   123
    Change agentry – the next information systems frontier
    M. L. Markus and R. I. Benjamin

Part Two: Information Systems Planning

157

7. **Information Systems Plans in Context:
   The Information Systems Planning Environment**   161
   Critical information technology issues in the year 2000
   R. I. Benjamin and J. Blunt

8. **Information Systems Plans in Context: A Global
   Perspective**   187
   Understanding the global information technology
   environment: representative world issues
   P. C. Palvia and S. C. Palvia

9. **Approaches to Information Systems Planning**   216
   Experiences in strategic information systems planning
   M. J. Earl

10. **The Information Systems Planning Process**   249
    Meeting the challenges of information systems planning
    A. L. Lederer and V. Sethi

11. **Evaluating the Outcomes of Information Systems Plans**   271
    Managing information technology evaluation –
    techniques and processes
    L. P. Willcocks

Part Three: The Information Systems Strategy–Business Strategy Relationship

291

12. **Information Systems and Business Strategy: An Overview**   295
    Information technology and corporate strategy:
    a view from the top
    S. Jarvenpaa and B. Ives

13. **Measuring the Information Systems–Business Strategy
    Relationship**   329
    Measuring the linkage between business and
    information technology objectives
    B. H. Reich and I. Benbasat

14. **Information Systems Strategy and Business Process
    Reengineering**   367
    Balance in business reengineering: fit and performance
    A. Huizing, E. Koster and W. Bouman

15. **Strategies in Response to the Potential of
     Electronic Commerce**   397
     Market process reengineering through electronic market
     systems: opportunities and challenges
     H. G. Lee and T. H. Clark

**Part Four: Information Systems Strategy and
the Organizational Environment**   427

16. **The Information Technology Infrastructure–
     Organizational Structure Relationship**   431
     Globalization and information management strategies
     J. Karimi and B. R. Konsynski

17. **The Information Technology–Organizational Design
     Relationship**   454
     Information technology and new organizational forms
     R. Lambert and J. Peppard

18. **Information Technology and Organizational
     Decision Making**   487
     The effects of advanced information technologies on
     organizational design, intelligence, and decision making
     G. P. Huber

19. **Information Technology and Organizational Culture**   523
     Understanding information culture: integrating knowledge
     management systems into organizations
     D. E. Leidner

20. **Information Technology and Organizational Performance** 551
     Beyond the IT productivity paradox
     L. P. Willcocks and S. Lester

Author index   573
Subject index   584

Contributors*

B. S. H. Baker, Virgin Direct (formerly with Warwick Business School, University of Warwick, Coventry), UK

I. Benbasat, University of British Columbia, Vancouver, British Columbia, Canada

R. I. Benjamin, Robert Benjamin Consultants, Rochester, New York and School of Information Studies, Syracuse University, New York, USA

J. Blunt, Information Technology Education Services, Waltham, Massachusetts, USA

W. Bouman, Centre for Innovative Technologies in Organizations, University of Amsterdam, The Netherlands

T. H. Clark, Department of Information and Systems Management, Hong Kong University of Science and Technology, Hong Kong

M. J. Earl, London Business School (formerly with Oxford Institute of Information Management, Templeton College, Oxford University), UK

B. R. Edwards, Brian Edwards & Associates and Oxford Institute of Information Management, Templeton College, Oxford University, UK

D. F. Feeny, Oxford Institute of Information Management, Templeton College, Oxford University, UK

R. D. Galliers, Warwick Business School, University of Warwick, Coventry, UK

G. P. Huber, University of Texas at Austin, Texas, USA

A. Huizing, Faculty of Economic Sciences and Econometrics, University of Amsterdam, The Netherlands

B. Ives, Louisiana State University, Baton Rouge, Louisiana (formerly with Edwin L. Cox School of Business, Southern Methodist University, Dallas, Texas), USA

S. Jarvenpaa, Graduate School of Business, University of Texas at Austin, Texas, USA

J. Karimi, University of Colorado, Denver, Colorado, USA

B. R. Konsynski, Emory University, Atlanta, Georgia (formerly with Harvard Business School, Boston, Massachusetts), USA

E. Koster, Faculty of Economic Sciences and Econometrics, University of Amsterdam, The Netherlands

R. Lambert, Cranfield School of Management, Cranfield University, Bedford, UK

* Where a contributor's institution has changed since the original publication of their article, both their current and former affiliations are listed.

A. L. Lederer, University of Kentucky, Lexington, Kentucky (formerly with Oakland University, Rochester, Michigan), USA

H. G. Lee, Department of Information and Systems Management, Hong Kong University of Science and Technology, Hong Kong

D. E. Leidner, INSEAD (European Institute of Business Administration), Fontainebleau, France

S. Lester, Lloyd's Register, London and Oxford Institute of Information Management, Templeton College, Oxford University, UK

M. L. Markus, Peter F. Drucker Management Center, Claremont Graduate School, Claremont, California, USA

P. C. Palvia, University of Memphis, Tennessee, USA

S. C. Palvia, Long Island University, New York, USA

J. Peppard, Cranfield School of Management, Cranfield University, Bedford, UK

K. G. van der Poel, Tilburg University, Tilburg, The Netherlands

B. H. Reich, Simon Fraser University, Vancouver, British Columbia, Canada

P. M. A. Ribbers, Tilburg University, Tilburg, The Netherlands

E. H. Schein, Sloan School of Management, Massachusetts Institute of Technology, Cambridge, Massachusetts, USA

V. Sethi, College of Business Administration, University of Oklahoma, Norman, Oklahoma, USA

M. T. Smits, Tilburg University, Tilburg, The Netherlands

E. K. Somogyi, The Farrindon Partnership, London, UK (formerly with PA Computers & Telecommunications)

A. R. Sutherland, Ess Consulting, Perth, Western Australia (formerly with Corporate Systems Planning), Australia

L. P. Willcocks, Oxford Institute of Information Management, Templeton College, Oxford University, UK and Erasmus University, Rotterdam, The Netherlands

Preface

This second edition of *Strategic Information Management: Challenges and strategies in managing information systems* (Galliers and Baker, 1994) shares with its predecessor an aim of presenting the many complex and interrelated issues associated with the management of information systems, with a likely audience of MBA or other Master's level students and senior undergraduate students taking a course in strategic information management or something similar. Students embarking on research in this area should find the book of particular help in providing a rich source of material reflecting recent thinking on many of the key issues facing executives in information systems management. Like the first edition, it does not aspire to familiarize the reader with the underlying technology components of information systems nor enlighten the reader on expected trends in emerging technologies. While readers of the first edition will recognize a number of the same readings, this second edition includes a large set of new readings included for two reasons: (a) to provide a coherent picture of the interrelationships of the major issues covered, and (b) to introduce the results of research undertaken since the first edition, thereby bringing our coverage more up to date. The concept of 'strategic information management' conveys manifold images, such as strategic use of information systems, strategic information systems planning, strategic information systems. . . . Our conceptualization of the term, and hence of the scope of the book, is presented in Figure 0.1.

The inner circle of the figure depicts the information systems strategy. Whether explicitly articulated or not – as appears frequently to be the case (Reich and Benbasat, 1996) – without an information systems strategy, the achievements of the IS in any given organization are likely to be more a result of hap and circumstance than a carefully guided intentional objective. The dimensions of IS strategy proferred in Galliers (1991), which builds on Earl (1989), form the major topics of the readings in the first section of the book – information strategy, information management strategy, information technology strategy and change management strategy.

The second circle in Figure 0.1, encompassing that of the IS strategy, depicts IS planning and forms the basis of the second section of the book. While the literature often associates strategic IS planning with IS strategy, we consider the topics as two: the plan produces the strategy. Included under the umbrella of IS planning are considerations of the IS planning environment, of

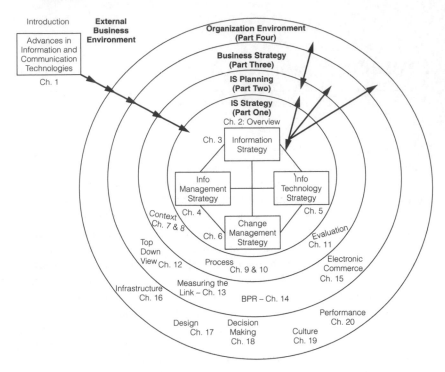

Figure 0.1 *Conceptualizing strategic information management*

the major issues of importance to IS planners, of the principal approaches used in developing IS plans, and of the evaluation of the success of IS.

The third circle in Figure 0.1 naturally forms the third section of the book, which considers the link between an organization's IS strategy (the inner circle) and the organization's business strategy. Because of the common substitution of IS planning for IS strategy in the literature, it was difficult to find articles that dealt explicitly with the IS strategy component as conceptualized in our figure. The topics forming this third section include the CEO's perspective of IS, measuring the IS–business strategy relationship, business process reengineering, and electronic commerce strategies.

The fourth circle then depicts the fourth and final section of the book which intends to offer some readings that examine the organizational outcomes of IS. The articles in this section deal less with IS strategy (as the underlying basis) but with IS arrangements and impacts (or in the case of the first article, IS structure). The reason behind the inclusion of this fourth section is that, ultimately, the aim of introducing IS into organizations is to achieve positive results on behalf of the organization and its various stakeholders. These articles consider the relationships of information technology to organizational structure; organizational design; organizational communication and decision making; organizational culture; and organizational performance.

The specific readings included in each section will be briefly summarized in the section introductions and hence will not be discussed here. It might be helpful to suggest that students prepare an analysis of the article using the following basic questions: (1) The research question: what is the major question, and why is this important? (2) The assumptions: what are some of the primary assumptions guiding the study, and are these valid in today's context? (3) The method: what method was used to investigate the questions (interviews, surveys, experiments, other), and how might the method have influenced, for better or worse, the results? (4) The results: what were the major findings, what was new, interesting, or unexpected in the findings, and what are the implications of the findings for today's IT manager? In addition, following each article, we offer some questions that could serve as points of departure for classroom discussion. We recommend additional readings relevant to the chapters in the introductions to Parts 1–4.

What we have attempted to achieve is to cover some of the more important aspects of each topic, while at the same time providing references to other important works. There is bound to be debate as to why a particular paper has been selected for inclusion as opposed to a number of other possible alternatives. There is also likely to be inquiry as to why certain topics – systems development, managing IT personnel, 'hot' topics such as the year 2000 problem – were not included. However, given the background research that informed the choice, and the fact that we have attempted to refer to some of the other important works in the field in the introductions to each section, we believe that we have covered as much of the ground as is possible in the available space. We hope you concur. The subject of strategic information management is diverse and complex. It is not simply concerned with technological issues – far from it in fact. The subject domain incorporates aspects of strategic management, globalization, the management of change and human/ cultural issues which may not at first sight have been considered as being directly relevant in the world of information technology. Experience, often gained as a result of very expensive mistakes (for example, the London Stock Exchange's ill-fated Taurus System), informs us that without due consideration to the kind of issues introduced in this book, these mistakes are likely to continue.

In selecting readings for this edition with the objective of covering the topics introduced in Figure 0.1, we observed a paucity of research related to the IS strategy topic. While writings on IS planning have been prolific and any number of outstanding pieces could have been substituted for those in Part 2, few articles were found that dealt explicitly with the content of information strategy itself. Likewise, while talk about the importance of linking

IT to business strategy has enjoyed longevity, the research on this link is primarily oriented toward process – again, articles discussing how to improve the planning process so that an apparent 'link' was achieved are numerous, yet research on the nature of the link, on evaluating whether indeed such a link is present, and from whose perspective (indeed there may be vastly different perspectives depending on whether one asks the CEO or the CIO) are relatively scarce. This is probably due to the difficulty of operationalizing the link. Finally, the academic community often bemoans the fact that organizational level impact studies of IT are eschewed by virtue of the diffculty of isolating the effect – such problems as the lag of IT implementation and impact, the isolation of only the IT impact exclusive of any other concurrent organizational change, and the definition of the IT itself, Indeed, few empirical studies of the organizational impact of IT were found, especially those that might be suitable for our target audience. Hence, we offer mostly conceptual pieces in this section. Despite the lack of extensive empirical work in this area, it is important to consider the organizational outcomes of IT so as to enable IS managers to make informed decisions on the basis of possible, but by no means given, organizational outcomes.

With this second edition, we hope that the reader leaves with a coherent framework for understanding the importance of information strategy to business strategy and to organizational performance. Moreover, we hope you will find this book both interesting and relevant to situations you will face in your own organizational context. Given the increasing importance of IT to the competitiveness of organizations in many industries today, managers can ill afford to be unaware of their organization's information strategy and the many, complex challenges associated with IT's use in and between organizations.

Happy reading!

Bob Galliers, Dorothy Leidner and Bernadette Baker

References

Earl, M. J. (1989). *Management Strategies for Information Technology*, Prentice Hall, London.

Galliers, R. D. (1991). Strategic information systems planning: myths, reality and guidelines for successful implementation. *European Journal of Information Systems*, **1**(1), 55–64.

Galliers, R. D. and Baker, B. S. H. (1994). *Strategic Information Management: Challenges and Strategies in Managing Information Systems*, Butterworth-Heineman, Oxford.

Reich, B. H. and Benbasat, I. (1996). Measuring the linkage between business and information technology objectives, *MIS Quarterly*, **20**(1), 55–81.

Introduction: The emergence of information technology as a strategic issue

Although information systems of some form or another have been around since the beginning of time, information technology (IT) is a relative newcomer to the scene. The facilities provided by such technology have had a major impact on individuals, organizations and society. There are few companies that can afford the luxury of ignoring IT and few individuals who would prefer to be without it . . . despite its occasional frustrations and the fears it sometimes invokes.

An organization may regard IT as a 'necessary evil', something that is needed in order to stay in business, while others may see it as a major source of strategic opportunity, seeking proactively to identify how IT-based information systems can help gain them a competitive edge. Regardless of the stance taken, once an organization embarks on an investment of this kind there is little opportunity for turning back.

As IT has become more powerful and relatively cheaper, its use has spread throughout organizations at a rapid rate. Different levels in the management hierarchy are now using IT where once its sole domain was at the operational level. The aim now is not only to improve efficiency but also to improve business effectiveness and to manage organizations more strategically. As the managerial tasks become more complex, so the nature of the required information systems (IS) changes – from structured, routinized support to *ad hoc*, unstructured, complex enquiries at the highest levels of management.

IT, however, not only has the potential to change the way an organization works but also the very nature of its business (see, for example, Galliers and Baets, 1998). Through the use of IT to support the introduction of electronic markets, buying and selling can be carried out in a fraction of the time, disrupting the conventional marketing and distribution channels (Malone *et al.*, 1989; Holland, 1998). Electronic data interchange (EDI) not only speeds up transactions but allows subscribers to be confident in the accuracy of information being received from suppliers/buyers and to reap the benefits of cost reductions through automated reordering processes. On a more strategic level, information may be passed from an organization to its suppliers or customers in order to gain or provide a better service (Cash, 1985). Providing a better service to its customers than its competitors may provide the differentiation required to stay ahead of the competition in the short term. Continual improvements to the service may enable the organization to gain a longer-term advantage and remain ahead.

The rapid change in IT causes an already uncertain business environment to be even more unpredictable. Organizations' ability to identify the relevant information needed to make important decisions is crucial, since the access to data used to generate information for decision making is no longer restricted by the manual systems of the organization. IT can record, synthesize, analyse and disseminate information quicker than at any other time in history. Data can be collected from different parts of the company and its external environment and brought together to provide relevant, timely, concise and precise information at all levels of the organization to help it become more efficient, effective and competitive.

Information can now be delivered to the right people at the right time, thus enabling well-informed decisions to be made. Previously, due to the limited information-gathering capability of organizations, decision makers could seldom rely on up-to-date information but instead made important decisions based on past results and their own experiene. This no longer needs to be the case. With the right technology in place to collect the necessary data automatically, up-to-date information can be accessed whenever the need arises. This is the informating quality of IT about which Zuboff (1988) writes so eloquently.

With the use of IT, as with most things, comes the possibility of abuse. Data integrity and security is of prime importance to ensure validity and privacy of the information being held. Managing the information involves identifying *what* should be kept, *how* it should be organized, *where* it should be held and *who* should have access to it. The quality of this management will dictate the quality of the decisions being taken and ultimately the organization's survival.

With the growth in the usage of IT to support information provision within organizations, the political nature of information has come into sharper focus. Gatekeepers of information are powerful people; they can decide when and if to convey vital information, and to whom. They are likely to be either highly respected, or despised for the power that they have at their fingertips.

Such gatekeepers have traditionally been middle managers in organizations. Their role has been to facilitate the flow of information between higher and lower levels of management. With the introduction of IT such information can now be readily accessed by those who need it (if the right IT infrastructure is in place) at any time. It is not surprising then that there is resistance to the introduction of IT when it has the potential of changing the balance of power within organizations. Unless the loss in power, through the freeing up of information, is substituted by something of equal or more value to the individuals concerned then IT implementations may well be subject to considerable obstruction.

Developments in IT have caused revolutionary changes not only for individual organizations but for society in general. In order to understand the situation we now find ourselves in with respect to IT, it is as well to reflect on their developments. This is the subject matter of Chapter 1. Written by Somogyi and Galliers, it describes how the role of IT has changed in business and how organizations have reacted to this change. They attempt, retrospectively, to identify major transition points in organizations' usage of IT in order to provide a chronicle of events, placing today's developments in a historical context. The chapter charts the evolution of the technology itself, the types of application used by organizations, the role of the DP/IS function and the change in the methods of system development. Such histories are not merely academic exercises, they can serve as a foundation for future progress, allowing organizations to avoid past mistakes and to build on their successes. A postscript has been added in order to bring the original article up to date, listing a number of key applications that have appeared over the past decade or so.

References

Cash, J. I. (1985) Interorganizational systems: an information society opportunity or threat. *The Information Society*, **3**(3), 199–228.

Galliers, R. D. and Baets, W. R. J. (1998) *Information Technology and Organizational Transformation: Information for the 21st Century Organization*, Wiley, Chichester.

Holland, C. (ed.) (1998) Special edition on electronic commerce. *Journal of Strategic Information Systems*, **7**(3), September.

Malone, T. W., Yates, J. and Benjamin, R. I. (1989) The logic of electronic markets. *Harvard Business Review*, May–June, 166–172.

Zuboff, S. (1988) *In the Age of the Smart Machine: The Future of Work and Power*, Butterworth-Heinemann, Oxford.

1 Developments in the Application of Information Technology in Business

Information technology in business: from data processing to strategic information systems

E. K. Somogyi and R. D. Galliers

Introduction

Computers have been used commercially for over three decades now, in business administration and for providing information. The original intentions, the focus of attention in (what was originally called) data processing and the nature of the data processing effort itself have changed considerably over this period. The very expression describing the activity has changed from the original 'data processing', through 'management information' to the more appropriate 'information processing'.

A great deal of effort has gone into the development of computer-based information systems since computers were first put to work automating clerical functions in commercial organizations. Although it is well known now that supporting businesses with formalized systems is not a task to be taken lightly, the realization of how best to achieve this aim was gradual. The change in views and approaches and the shift in the focus of attention have been caused partly by the rapid advancement in the relevant technology. But the changed attitudes that we experience today have also been caused by the good and bad experiences associated with using the technology of the day. In recent years two other factors have contributed to the general change in attitudes. As more coherent information was made available through the use of computers, the general level of awareness of information needs grew. At the same time the general economic trends, especially the rise in labour cost, combined with the favourable price trends of computer-related technology, appeared to have offered definite advantages in using computers and auto-mated systems. Nevertheless this assumed potential of the technology has not always been realized.

This chapter attempts to put into perspective the various developments (how the technology itself changed, how we have gone about developing information systems, how we have organized information systems support services, how the role of systems has changed, etc.), and to identify trends and key turning points in the brief history of computing. Most importantly, it aims to clarify what has really happened, so that one is in a better position to understand this seemingly complex world of information technology and the developments in its application, and to see how it relates to our working lives. One word of warning, though. In trying to interpret events, it is possible that we might give the misleading impression that things developed smoothly. They most often did not. The trends we now perceive were most probably imperceptible to those involved at the time. To them the various develop-ments might have appeared mostly as unconnected events which merely added to the complexity of information systems.

The early days of data processing

Little if any commercial applications of computers existed in the early 1950s when computers first became available. The computer was hailed as a mammoth calculating machine, relevant to scientists and code-breakers. It was not until the second and third generation of computers appeared on the market that commercial computing and data processing emerged on a large scale. Early commercial computers were used mainly to automate the routine clerical work of large administrative departments. It was the economies of large-scale administrative processing that first attracted the attention of the system developers. The cost of early computers, and later the high cost of systems development, made any other type of application economically imposs-ible or very difficult to justify.

These first systems were batch systems using fairly limited input and out-put media, such as punched cards, paper-tape and printers. Using computers in this way was in itself a major achievement. The transfer of processing from unit record equipment such as cards allowed continuous batch-production runs on these expensive machines. This was sufficient economic justification and made the proposition of having a computer in the first place very viable indeed. Typical of the systems developed in this era were payroll and general ledger systems, which were essentially integrated versions of well-defind clerical processes.

Selecting applications on such economical principles had side-effects on the systems and the resulting application portfolio. Systems were developed with little regard to other, possibly related, systems and the systems portfolio of most companies became fragmented. There was usually a fair amount of duplication present in the various systems, mainly caused by the duplication of interrelated data. Conventional methods that evolved on the basis of practical experience with developing computing systems did not ease this situation. These early methods concentrated on making the computer work, rather than on rationalizing the processes they automated.

A parallel but separate development was the increasing use of operational research (OR) and management science (MS) techniques in industry and commerce. Although the theoretical work on techniques such as linear and non-linear programming, queueing theory, statistical inventory control, PERT-CPM, statistical decision theory, and so on, was well established prior to 1960, surveys indicated a burgeoning of OR and MS activity in industry in the United States and Europe during the 1960s. The surge in industrial and academic work in OR and MS was not unrelated to the presence and availability of ever more powerful and reliable computers.

In general terms, the OR and MS academics and practitioners of the 1960s were technically competent, enthusiastic and confident that their discipline would transform management from an art to a science. Another general remark that can fairly be made about this group, with the wisdom of hindsight, is that they were naive with respect to the behavioural and organizational aspects of their work. This fact unfortunately saw many enthusiastic and well-intentioned endeavours fail quite spectacularly, setting OR and MS into unfortunate disrepute which in many cases prohibited necessary reflection and reform of the discipline (Galliers and Marshall, 1985).

Data processing people, at the same time, started developing their own theoretical base for the work they were doing, showing signs that a new profession was in the making. The different activities that made up the process of system development gained recognition and, as a result, systems analysis emerged as a key activity, different from O&M and separate from programming. Up to this point, data processing people possessed essentially two kinds of specialist knowledge, that of computer hardware and programming. From this point onwards, a separate professional – the systems analyst – appeared, bringing together some of the OR, MS and O&M activities hitherto performed in isolation from system development.

However, the main focus of interest was making those operations which were closely associated with the computer as efficient as possible. Two important developments resulted. First, programming (i.e. communicating to the machine the instructions that it needed to perform) had to be made less cumbersome. A new generation of programming languages emerged, with outstanding examples such as COBOL and FORTRAN. Second, as jobs for the machine became plentiful, development of special operating software became necessary, which made it possible to utilize computing power better.

Concepts such as multi-programming, time-sharing and time-slicing started to emerge and the idea of a complex large operating system, such as the IBM 360 OS, was born.

New facilities made the use of computers easier, attracting further applications which in turn required more and more processing power, and this vicious circle became visible for the first time. The pattern was documented, in a lighthearted manner, by Grosch's law (1953). In simple terms it states that the power of a computer installation is proportional to the square of its cost. While this was offered as a not-too-serious explanation for the rising cost of computerization, it was quickly accepted as a general rule, fairly representing the realities of the time.

The first sign of maturity

Computers quickly became pervasive. As a result of improvements in system software and hardware, commercial systems became efficient and reliable, which in turn made them more widespread. By the late 1960s most large corporations had acquired big mainframe computers. The era was characterized by the idea that 'large was beautiful'. Most of these companies had large centralized installations operating remotely from their users and the business.

Three separate areas of concern emerged. First, business started examining seriously the merits of introducing computerized systems. Systems developed in this period were effective, given the objectives of automating clerical labour. But the reduction in the number of moderately paid clerks was more than offset by the new, highly-paid class of data processing professionals and the high cost of the necessary hardware. In addition, a previously unexpected cost factor, that of maintenance, started eating away larger and larger portions of the data processing budget. The remote 'ivory tower' approach of the large data processing departments made it increasingly difficult for them to develop systems that appealed to the various users. User dissatisfaction increased to frustration point as a result of inflexible systems, overly formal arrangements, the very long time required for processing changes and new requests, and the apparent inability of the departments to satisfy user needs.

Second, some unexpected side-effects occurred when these computer systems took over from the previous manual operations: substantial organizational and job changes became necessary. It was becoming clear that data processing systems had the potential of changing organizations. Yet, the hit and miss methods of system development concentrated solely on making the computers work. This laborious process was performed on the basis of ill-defined specifications, often the result of a well-meaning technologist interpreting the unproven ideas of a remote user manager. No wonder that most systems were not the best! But even when the specification was reasonable, the resulting system was often technically too cumbersome, full of errors and difficult to work with.

Third, it became clear that the majority of systems, by now classed as 'transaction processing' systems, had major limitations. Partly, the centralized, remote, batch processing systems did not fit many real-life business situations. These systems processed and presented historical rather than current information. Partly, data was fragmented across these systems, and appeared often in duplicated, yet incompatible format.

It was therefore necessary to re-think the fundamentals of providing computer support. New theoretical foundations were laid for system development. The early trial-and-error methods of developing systems were replaced by more formalized and analytical methodologies, which emphasized the need for engineering the technology to pre-defined requirements. 'Software engineering' emerged as a new discipline and the search for requirement specification methods began.

Technological development also helped a great deal in clarifying both the theoretical and practical way forward. From the mid-1960s a new class of computer – the mini – was being developed and by the early 1970s it emerged as a rival to the mainframe. The mini was equipped for 'real' work, having arrived at the office from the process control environment of the shopfloor. These small versatile machines quickly gained acceptance, not least for their ability to provide an on-line service. By this time the commercial transaction processing systems became widespread, efficient and reliable. It was therefore a natural next step to make them more readily available to users, and often the mini was an effective way of achieving this aim. As well as flexibility, minis also represented much cheaper and more convenient computing power: machine costs were a magnitude under the mainframe's; the physical size was much less; the environmental requirements (air conditioning, dust control, etc.) were less stringent; and operations required less professional staff. The mini opened up the possibility of using computing power in smaller companies. This, in turn, meant that the demand grew for more and better systems and, through these, for better methods and a more systematic approach to system development.

Practical solutions to practical problems

A parallel but separate area of development was that of project management. Those who followed the philosophy that 'large is beautiful' did not only think in terms of large machines. They aspired to large systems, which meant large software and very large software projects. Retrospectively it seems that those who commissioned such projects had little understanding of the work involved. These large projects suffered from two problems, namely, false assumptions about development and inadequate organization of the human resources. Development was based on the idea that the initial technical specification, developed in isolation from the users, was infallible. In addition, 'large is beautiful' had an effect on the structure of early data processing departments. The highly functional approach of the centralized data processing departments meant that the various disciplines were compartmentalized. Armies of programmers existed in isolation from systems analysts and operators with, very often physical, brick walls dividing them from each other and their users. Managing the various steps of development in virtual isolation from each other, as one would manage a factory or production line (without of course the appropriate tools!) proved to be unsatisfactory. The initial idea of managing large computer projects using mass production principles missed the very point that no two systems are the same and no two analysts or programmers do exactly the same work. Production line management methods in the systems field backfired and the large projects grew manifold during development, eating up budgets and timescales at an alarming rate.

The idea that the control of system development could and should be based on principles different from those of mass production and of continuous process management dawned on the profession relatively late. By the late 1960s the problem of large computing projects reached epidemic proportions. Books, such as Brooks's *The Mythical Man Month* (1972), likening system development to the prehistoric fight of dinosaurs in the tar-pit, appeared on the book-shelves. Massive computer projects, costing several times the original budget and taking much longer than the original estimates indicated, hit the headlines in the popular press.

Salvation was seen in the introduction of management method that would allow reasoned control over system development activities in terms of controlling the intermediate and final products of the activity, rather than the activity itself. Methods of project management and principles of project control were transplanted to data processing from complex engineering environments and from the discipline developed by the US space programme.

Dealing with things that are large and complex produced some interesting and far-reaching side-effects. Solutions to the problems associated with the (then fashionable) large computer programs were discovered through finding the reasons for their apparent unmaintainability. Program maintenance was difficult because it was hard to understand what the code was supposed to do in the first place. This, in turn, was largely caused by three problems. First, most large programs had no apparent control structure; they were genuine monoliths. The code appeared to be carved from one piece. Second, the logic that was being executed by the program was often jumping in an unpredictable way across different parts of the monolithic code. This 'spaghetti logic' was the result of the liberal use of the 'GO TO' statement. Third, if documentation existed at all for the program, it was likely to be out of date, not accurately representing what the program was doing. So, it was difficult to know where to start with any modification, and any interference with the code created unforeseen side-effects. All this presented a level of complexity that made program maintenance problematic.

As a result of realizing the causes of the maintenance problem, theoreticians started work on concepts and methods that would help to reduce program complexity. They argued that the human mind is very limited when dealing with highly complex things, be they computer systems or anything else. Humans can deal with complexity only when it is broken down into 'manageable' chunks or modules, which in turn can be interrelated through some structure. The uncontrolled use of the 'GO TO' statement was also attacked, and the concept of 'GO TO-less' programming emerged. Later, specific languages were developed on the basis of this concept; PASCAL is the best known example of such a language.

From the 1970s onwards modularity and structure in programming became important and the process by which program modules and structures could be designed to simplify complexity attracted increased interest. The rules which govern the program design process, the structures, the parts and their documentation became a major preoccupation of both practitioners and academics. The concept of structuring was born and structured methods emerged to take the place of traditional methods of development. Structuring and modularity have since remained a major intellectual drive in both the theoretical and practical work associated with computer systems.

It was also realized that the principles of structuring were applicable outside the field of programming. One effect of structuring was the realization that not only systems but projects and project teams can be structured to bring together – not divide – complex, distinct disciplines associated with the development of systems. From the early 1970s, IBM pioneered the idea of structured project teams with integrated administrative support using structured methods for programming (Baker, 1972), which proved to be one of the first successful ploys for developing large systems.

From processes to data

Most early development methods concentrated on perfecting the processes that were performed by the machine, putting less emphasis on data and giving little, if any, thought to the users of the system. However, as more and more routine company operations became supported by computer systems, the need for a more coherent and flexible approach arose. Management need for cross-relating and cross-referencing data, which arises from basic operational processes, in order to produce coherent information and exercise better control, meant that the cumbersome, stand-alone and largely centralized systems operating in remote batch mode were no longer acceptable. By the end of the 1960s the focus of attention shifted from collecting and processing the 'raw material' of management information, to the raw material itself; data. It was discovered that interrelated operations cannot be effectively controlled without maintaining a clear set of basic data, preferably in a way that would allow data to be independent of their applications. It was therefore important to de-couple data from the basic processes. The basic data could then be used for information and control purposes in new kinds of systems. The drive for data independence brought about major advances in thinking about systems and in the practical methods of describing, analysing and storing data. Independent data management systems became available by the late 1960s.

The need for accurate information also highlighted a new requirement. Accurate information needs to be precise, timely and available. During the 1970s most companies changed to on-line processing to provide better access to data. Many companies also distributed a large proportion of their central computer operations in order to collect, process and provide access to data at the most appropriate points and locations. As a result, the nature of both the systems and the systems effort changed considerably. By the end of the 1970s the relevance of data clearly emerged, being viewed as *the* fundamental resource of information, deserving treatment that is similar to any other major resource of a business.

There were some, by now seemingly natural side-effects of this new direction. Several approaches and methods were developed to deal with the specific and intrinsic characteristics of data. The first of these was the discovery that complex data can be understood better by discovering their apparent structure. It also became obvious that separate 'systems' were needed for organizing and storing data. As a result, databases and database management systems (DBMS) started to appear. The intellectual drive was associated with the problem of how best to represent data structures in a practically usable way. A hierarchical representation was the first practical solution. IBM's IMS was one of the first DBMSs adopting this approach. Suggestions for a network-type representation of data structures, using the idea of entity-attribute relationships, were also adopted, resulting in the CODASYL standard. At the same time, Codd started his theoretical work on representing complex data relationships and simplifying the resulting structure through a method called 'normalization'.

Codd's fundamental theory (1970) was quickly adopted by academics. Later it also became the basis of practical methods for simplifying data structures. Normalization became the norm (no pun intended) in better data processing departments and whole methodologies grew up advocating data as the main analytical starting point for developing computerized information systems. The drawbacks of hierarchical and network-type databases (such as the inevitable duplication of data, complexity, rigidity, difficulty in modification, large overheads in operation, dependence on the application, etc.) were by then obvious. Codd's research finally opened up the possibility of separating the storage and retrieval of data from their use. This effort culminated in the development of a new kind of database: the relational database.

Design was also emerging as a new discipline. First, it was realized that programs, their modules and structure should be designed before being coded. Later, when data emerged as an important subject in its own right, it also became obvious that system and data design were activities separate from requirements analysis and program design. These new concepts had crystallized towards the end of the 1970s. Sophisticated, new types of software began to appear on the market, giving a helping hand with organizing the mass of complex data on which information systems were feeding. Databases, data dictionaries and database management systems became plentiful, all promising salvation to the overburdened systems professional. New specializations split the data processing discipline: the database designer, data analyst, data administrator joined the ranks of the systems analyst and systems designer. At the other end of the scale, the programming profession was split by language specialization as well as by the programmer's conceptual 'distance' from the machine. As operating software became increasingly complex, a new breed – the systems programmer – appeared, emphasizing the difference between dealing with the workings of the machine and writing code for 'applications'.

Towards management information systems

The advent of databases and more sophisticated and powerful mainframe computers gave rise to the idea of developing corporate databases (containing all the pertinent data a company possessed), in order to supply management with information about the business. These database-related developments also required data processing professionals who specialized in organizing and managing data. The logical and almost clinical analysis these specialists performed, highlighted not only the structures of data but also the many inconsistencies which often exist in organizations. Data structures reflect the interpretation and association of data in a company, which in turn reflect interrelationships in the organization. Some data processing professionals engaged in data analysis work began to develop their own view of how organizations and their management would be transformed on the basis of the analysis. They also developed some visionary notions about themselves. They thought that they would decide (or help to decide) what data an organization should have in order to function efficiently, and who would need access to which piece of data and in what form.

The idea of a corporate database that is accurate and up to date with all the pertinent data from the production systems, is attractive. All we need to do – so the argument goes – is aggregate the data, transform them in certain ways and offer them to management. In this way a powerful information resource is on tap for senior management. Well, what is wrong with this idea?

Several practical matters presented difficulties to the naive data processing visionary who believed in a totally integrated management information system (MIS) resting on a corporate database. One problem is the sheer technical difficulty of deciding what should be stored in the corporate database and then building it satisfactorily before an organizational change, brought about by internal politics or external market forces or both, makes the database design and the accompanying reports inappropriate. In large organizations it may take tens of person-years and several elapsed years to arrive at a partially integrated MIS. It is almost certain that the requirements of the management reports would change over that period. It is also very likely that changes would be necessary in some of the transaction processing systems and also in the database design. Furthermore, assuming an efficient and well-integrated set of transaction processing systems, the only reports that these systems can generate without a significant quantum of effort are historical reports containing aggregated data, showing variances – 'exception reports' (e.g. purchase orders for items over a certain value outstanding for more than a predefined number of days) and the like. Reports that would assist management in non-routine decision making and control would, by their nature, require particular views of the data internal to the organization that could not be specified in advance. Management would also require market data, i.e. data external to the organization's transaction processing systems. Thus, if we are to approach the notion that seems to lie behind the term MIS and supply managers with information that is useful in business control, problem solving and decision making, we need to think carefully about the nature of the information systems we provide.

It is worth nothing that well-organized and well-managed businesses always had 'systems' (albeit wholly or partly manual) for business control. In this sense management information systems always existed, and the notion of having such systems in an automated form was quite natural, given the advances of computing technology that were taking place at the time. However, the unrealistic expectations attached to the computer, fuelled by the overly enthusiastic approaches displayed by the data processing profession, made several, less competently run, companies believe that shortcomings in management, planning, organization and control could be overcome by the installation of a computerized MIS. Much of the later disappointment could have been prevented had these companies realized that technology can only solve technical and not management problems. Nevertheless, the notion that information provision to management, with or without databases, was an important part of the computing activity, was reflected by the fact that deliberate attempts were made to develop MISs in greater and greater numbers. Indicative of this drive towards supporting management rather than clerical operations is the name change that occurred around this time: most data processing departments became Management Services departments. The notion was that they would provide, via corporate databases, not only automated clerical processing but also, by aggregating and transforming such data, the information that management needed to run the business.

That the data processing profession during the 1970s developed useful and powerful data analysis and data management techniques, and learned a great deal about data management, is without doubt. But the notion that, through their data management, data aggregation and reporting activities, they provided management with information to assist managerial decision making had not been thought through. As Keen and Scott Morton (1978) point out, the MIS activity was not really a focus on management information but on information management. We could go further: the MIS activity of the era was concerned with *data* management, with little real thought being given to meeting management information needs.

In the late 1970s Keen and Scott Morton were able to write without fear of severe criticism that

> . . . management information system is a prime example of a 'content-free' expression. It means different things to different people, and there is no generally accepted definition by those working in the field. As a practical matter MIS implies computers, and the phrase 'computer-based information systems' has been used by some researchers as being more precise.

Sprague and Carlson (1982) attempted to give meaning to the term MIS by noting that when it is used in practice, one can assume that what is being referred to is a computer system with the following characteristics:

* an information focus, aimed at middle managers
* structured information flows
* integration of data processing jobs by business function (production MIS, personnel MIS, etc.), and
* an inquiry and report generation facility (usually with a database).

They go on to note that

> . . . the MIS era contributed a new level of information to serve management needs, but was still very much oriented towards, and built upon, information flows and data files.

The idea of integrated MISs seems to have presented an unrealistic goal. The dynamic nature of organizations and the market environment in which they exist forces more realistic and modest goals on the data processing professional. Keeping the transaction processing systems maintained, sensibly integrated and in line with organizational realities, is a more worthwhile job than freezing the company's data in an overwhelming database.

The era also saw data processing professionals and the management science and business modelling fraternities move away from each other into their own specialities, to the detriment of a balanced progress in developing effective and useful systems.

The emergence of information technology

Back in the 1950s Jack Kilby and Robert Noyce noticed the semi-conducting characteristics of silicon. This discovery, and developments in integrated circuitry, led to large-scale miniaturization in electronics. By 1971 micro-processors using 'silicon chips' were available on the market (Williams and Welch, 1985). In the 1978 they hit the headlines – commentators predicting unprecedented changes to business and personal life as a result. A new, post-industrial revolution was promised to be in the making (Tofler, 1980).

The impact of the very small and very cheap, reliable computers – micros – which resulted from building computers with chips, quickly became visible. By the early 1980s computing power and facilities suddenly became available and possible in areas hitherto untouched by computers. The market was flooded with 'small business systems', 'personal computers', 'intelligent work stations' and the like, promising the naive and the uninitiated instant computer power and instant solution to problems.

As a result, three separate changes occurred. First, users, especially those who had suffered unworkable systems and waited for years to receive systems to their requirements, started bypassing data processing departments and buying their own computers. They might not have achieved the best results but increased familiarity with the small machines started to change attitudes of both users and management.

Second, the economics of systems changed. The low cost of the small machines highlighted the enormous cost of human effort required to develop and maintain large computer systems. Reduction, at any cost, of the professional system development and maintenance effort was now a prime target in the profession, as (for the first time) hardware costs could be shown to be well below those of professional personnel.

Third, it became obvious that small dispersed machines were unlikely to be useful without interconnecting them – bringing telecommunications into the limelight. And many office activities, hitherto supported by 'office machinery' were seen for the first time as part of the process started by large computers – that is, automating the office. Office automation emerged, not least as a result of the realization by office machine manufacturers, who now entered the computing arena, that the 'chip' could be used in their machines.

As a consequence, hitherto separate technologies – that of telephony, tele-communication, office equipment and computing – started to converge. This development pointed to the reality that voice, images and data are simply different representations of information and that the technologies that deal with these different representations are all part of a new complex technology: information technology.

The resulting development became diverse and complex: systems develop-ers had to give way to the pressure exercised by the now not so naive user for more involvement in the development of systems. *End-user computing* emerged as a result, promoting the idea that systems are the property of users and not the technical department. In parallel, the realization occurred that useful sys-tems can only be produced if those who will use them take an active part in their development. Integrating the user became a useful obsession, helping the development of new kinds of systems.

It also became clear that a substantial reduction in the specialist manual activity of system development is necessary if the new family of computers, and the newly-discovered information technology, are to be genuinely useful. Suddenly, there were several alternatives available. Ready-made application systems emerged in large numbers for small and large machines, and *pack-ages* became a fashionable business to be in. *Tools for system development*, targeting directly the end user and supporting end-user computing, were developed in the form of special, high-level facilities for interrogating data-bases and formatting reports. Ultra high-level languages emerged carrying the name 'fourth generation languages' (4GLs) to support both professional and amateur efforts at system development.

For the first time in the history of computing, serious effort was made to support with automation the manifold and often cumbersome activities of system development. Automated programming support environments, sys-tems for building systems, analysis and programming workbenches appeared on the market, many backing the specialist methodologies which, by now, became well formulated, each with its own cult following.

New approaches to system development

In addition, new discoveries were made about the nature of systems and system development. From the late 1960s it was realized that the develop-ment of a system and its operations can be viewed as a cycle of defined stages. The 'life-cycle' view of systems emerged and this formed the basis of many methods and methodologies for system development. It became clear only later that, while the view of a life-cycle was the correct one, a *linear* view of the life-cycle was counter-productive. The linear view was developed at the time when demand for large-scale systems first erupted and most practitioners were engaged mainly in development. The first saturation point brought about the shock realization that these systems needed far more attention during their operational life than was originally envisaged. As the maintenance load on data processing departments increased from a modest 20 to 60, 70 and 80 per cent during the 1970s, many academics and practitioners started looking for the reasons behind this (for many, undesirable and unexplained) phenomenon.

It was discovered that perhaps three different causes can explain the large increase in maintenance. First, the linear view of the life-cycle can be misleading. Systems developed in a linear fashion were built on the premise that successive deductions would be made during the development process, each such deductive step supplying a more detailed specification to the next one. As no recursive action was allowed, the misconceptions, errors and omissions left in by an earlier step would result in an ever-increasing number of errors and faults being built into the final system. This, and the chronic lack of quality control over the development process, delivered final systems which were far from perfect. As a result, faults were being discovered which needed to be dealt with during the operational part of the life-cycle, thereby increasing unnecessarily the maintenance load. It was discovered that early faults left in a system increase the number of successive faults in an exponential way, resulting in hundredfold increases in effort when dealing with these faults in the final system.

Second, there are problems associated with specifications. The linear life-cycle view also assumed that a system could be safely built for a long life, once a specification had been correctly developed, as adjustments were unlikely to be required provided the specification was followed attentively. This view had negated the possibility that systems might have a changing effect on their environment, which, in turn, would raise the requirement for re-tuning and readjusting them. The followers of this approach had also overlooked the fact that real business, which these systems were supposed to serve, never remains constant. It changes, thereby changing the original requirements. This, in turn, would require readjusting or even scrapping the system. Furthermore, the idea that users could specify precisely their requirements seems to have been largely a fallacy, negating the basis on which quite a few systems had been built.

Third, maintenance tends to increase as the number of systems grows. It is misleading to assume that percentage increase in the maintenance load is in itself a sign of failure, mismanagement or bad practice. Progressing from the state of having no computer system to the point of saturation means that, even in a slowly changing environment and with precision development methods, there would be an ever-decreasing percentage of work on new development and a slow but steady increase in the activities dealing with systems already built.

Nevertheless, the documented backlog of system requests grew alarmingly, estimated by the beginning of the 1980s at two to five years' worth of work in major data processing departments. This backlog evolved to be a mixture of requests for genuine maintenance, i.e. fixing errors, adjustments and enhancements to existing systems, and requirements for new systems. It was also realized that behind this 'visible' backlog, there was an ever-increasing 'invisible', undocumented backlog of requirements estimated at several times the visible one. The invisible backlog consisted largely of genuine requests that disillusioned users were no longer interested in entering into the queue.

As a response to these problems, several new developments occurred. Quality assurance, quality control and quality management of system development emerged, advocating regular and special tests and checks to be made on the system through its development. Walk-throughs and inspections were inserted into analysis, design and programming activities to catch 'bugs' as early (and as cheaply) as possible.

The notion that systems should be made to appeal to their users in every stage of development and in their final form encouraged the development of 'user friendly' systems, in the hope that early usability would reduce the requests for subsequent maintenance. Serious attempts were made to encourage an iterative form of development with high user involvement in the early stages, so that specifications would become as precise as possible. The idea of building a prototype for a requirement before the final system is built and asking users to experiment with the prototype before finalizing specifications helped the system development process considerably.

By now, the wide-ranging organizational effects of computer systems became clearly visible. Methods for including organizational considerations in system design started to emerge. A group of far-sighted researchers, Land and Mumford in the UK, Agarin in the USA, Bjorn-Andersen in Denmark, Ciborra in Italy and others, put forward far-reaching ideas about letting systems evolve within the organizational environment, thereby challenging the hitherto 'engineering-type' view of system development. For the first time since the history of computing began, it was pointed out that computerized information systems were, so to speak, one side of a two-sided coin, the other side being the human organization where these systems perform. Unless the two are developed in unison, in conjunction with each other, the end result is likely to be disruptive and difficult to handle.

Despite these new discoveries, official circles throughout the world had successively failed to support developments in anything but technology itself and the highly technical, engineering-type approaches (Land, 1983). It seems as though the major official projects were mounted to support successive problem areas one phase behind the time! For example, before micros became widespread, it was assumed that the only possible bottleneck in using computers would be the relatively low number of available professional programmers. Serious estimates were made that if the demand for new systems should increase at the rate shown towards the end of the 1970s, this could only be met by an ever-increasing army of professional programmers. As a result, studies were commissioned to find methods for increasing the programming population several-fold over a short period of time.* Wrong assumptions tend to lead to wrong conclusions, resulting in misguided action and investment, and this seems to be hitting computing at regular intervals. Far too much attention is paid in the major development programmes of the 1980s to technology and far too little attention is paid to the *application* of the technology.

New types of systems

The 1980s have brought about yet another series of changes. It has become clear that sophisticated hardware and software together can be targeted in different ways towards different types of application areas. New generic types of systems emerged on the side of data processing systems and MISs. Partly, it was realized that the high intelligence content of certain systems can be usefully deployed. Ideas originally put forward by the artificial intelligence (AI) community, which first emerged in the late 1950s as a separate discipline, now became realizable. Systems housing complex rules have emerged as 'rule-based' systems. The expressions 'expert systems' and 'intelligent knowledge-based systems' (IKBS) became fashionable to denote systems which imitate the rules and procedures followed by some particular expertise. Partly, it was assumed that computers would have a major role in supporting decision-making processes at the highest levels of companies and the concept of decision support systems (DSS) evolved. When remembering the arguments about management information systems, many academics and professionals have posed the question whether 'decision support system' was a new buzz-word with no content or whether it reflected a new breed of systems. Subsequent research showed that the computerized system is only a small part of the arrangement that needs to be put in place for supporting top-level decision makers.

---

* This approach is reminiscent of the famous calculation in the 1920s predicting the maximum number of motor cars ever to be needed on earth. The number was put at around 4 million on the basis that not more than that number of people would be found to act as chauffeurs for those who could afford to purchase the vehicles. It had never occurred to the researchers in this case that the end user, the motor car owner, might be seated behind the wheel, thereby reducing the need for career chauffeurs. Or that technological progress and social and economic change might reduce the need for specialist knowledge and the price and might also change the economic justification, factors which all affect the demand for motor cars.

Manufacturers got busy in the meantime providing advanced facilities that were made available by combining office systems, computers and networks, and by employing the facilities provided by keypads, television and telecommunications. Electronic mail systems appeared, teleconferencing and videotex facilities shifted long-distance contact from the telephone, and – besides the processing of data – voice, text and image processing moved to the forefront. The emphasis shifted from the provision of data to the provision of information and to speeding up information flows.

Important new roles for information systems

The major task for many information systems (IS) departments in the early 1980s is making information available. The problems of interconnecting and exchanging information in many different forms and at many different places turned the general interest towards telecommunications. This interest is likely to intensify as more and more people gain access to, or are provided with, computer power and technologically pre-processed information.

As a result of recent technological improvements and changes in attitudes, the role of both data processing professionals and users changed rapidly. More systems were being developed by the users themselves or in close cooperation with the users. Data processing professionals started assuming the role of advisers, supporters and helpers. Systems were being more closely controlled by their users than was the practice previously. A new concept – the information centre – emerged, which aimed at supporting end-user computing and providing information and advice for users, at the same time also looking after the major databases and production systems in the background.

The most important result of using computer technology, however, was the growing realization that technology itself cannot solve problems and that the introduction of technology results in change. The impact of technological change depends on why and how technology is used. As management now had a definite choice in the use of technology, the technological choices could be evaluated within the context of business and organizational choices, using a planned approach. For this reason more and more companies started adopting a planned approach to their information systems. 'System strategy' and 'strategic system planning' became familiar expressions and major methods have been developed to help such activities.

It has been realized also that applying information technology outside its traditional domain of backroom effectiveness and efficiency, i.e. moving systems out of the back room and into the 'sharp end' of the business, would create, in many cases, distinct competitive advantage to the enterprise. This should be so, because information technology can affect the competitive forces that shape an industry by

- building barriers against new entrants
- changing the basis of competition
- changing the balance of power in supplier relationships
- tying in customers
- switching costs, and
- creating new products and services.

By the mid-1980s this new strategic role of information systems emerged. From the USA came news of systems that helped companies to achieve unprecedented results in their markets. These systems were instrumental in changing the nature of the business, the competition and the company's competitive position. The role of information systems in business emerged as a strategic one and IS professionals were elevated in status accordingly. At the same time the large stock of old systems became an ever-increasing burden on companies wanting to move forward with the technology.

More and more researchers and practitioners were pointing towards the need for linking systems with the business, connecting business strategy with information system strategy. The demand grew for methods, approaches and methodologies that would provide an orderly process to strategic business and system planning. Ideas about analysing user and business needs and the competitive impact of systems and technologies are plentiful. Whether they can deliver in line with the expectations will be judged in the future.

Summary

The role of computerized information systems and their importance in companies have undergone substantial transition since the 1950s. Over the same period both the technology and the way it was viewed, managed and employed changed considerably. The position and status of those responsible for applying the technology in various organizations have become more prominent, relevant and powerful, having moved from data processing, through management services, to information processing. At the same time, hitherto separate technologies converged into information technology.

As technology moved from its original fragmented and inflexible form to being integrated and interconnected, the management of its use in terms of both operations and system development changed in emphasis and nature. Computer operations moved from a highly regulated, centralized and remote mode to becoming more *ad hoc* and available as and when required. The systems effort itself progressed from concentrating on the programming process, through discovering the life-cycle of systems and the relevance of data, to more planned and participative approaches. The focus of attention changed from the technicalities to social and business issues.

Systems originally replaced clerical activities on the basis of stand-alone applications. The data processing department's original role was to manage the delivery and operation of these predominantly back-room systems. When data became better integrated, and more management-orientated information was provided, the management services departments started concentrating on better management of their own house and on making links with other departments and functions of the business which needed systems. This trend, combined with the increased variety and availability of sophisticated and easier to use technology, has led to the users taking a more active role in developing their own systems.

Lately, since it is realized that information is an important resource which can be used in a novel way to enhance the competitive position of business, information technology and information systems are becoming strategically important for business. Information systems are moving out of the backroom, low-level support position, to emerge as the nerve centres of organizations and competitive weapons at the front end of businesses. The focus of attention moved from being tactical to becoming strategic, and changed the nature of systems and the system portfolio.

It is evident that activity in the information systems field will continue in many directions at once, driven by fashion and market forces, by organizational need and technical opportunity. However, it appears that the application of information technology is at the threshold of a new era, opening up new opportunities by using the technology strategically for the benefit of organizations and businesses. It is still to be seen how the technology and the developers will deliver against these new expectations.

References

Baker, F. T. (1972) Chief programmer team management of production programming. *IBM System Journal*, Spring.

Brooks, F. R., Jr. (1972) *The Mythical Man-Month*, Addison-Wesley, Reading, MA.

Codd, E. F. (1970) A relational model of data for large shared data banks. *Communications of the ACM*, **13**, 6.

Galliers, R. D. and Marshall, P. H. (1985) *Towards True End-User Computing: From EDP to MIS to DSS to ESE*, Working Paper, Western Australian Institute of Technology, Bentley, Western Australia.

Grosch, H. R. J. (1953) High-speed arithmetic: the digital computer as a research tool. *J. Opt. Soc. Am.*, April.

Keen, P. G. W. and Scott Morton, M. S. (1978) *Decision Support Systems: An Organizational Perspective*, Addison-Wesley, Reading, MA.

Land, F. F. (1983) Information Technology: The Alvey Report and Government Strategy. An Inaugural Lecture. The London School of Economics.

Sprague, R. H. and Carlson, E. D. (1982) *Building Effective Decision Support Systems*, Prentice Hall, New York.

Tofler, A. (1980) *The Third Wave*, Bantam Books.

Williams, G. and Welch, M. (1985) A microcomputing timetable. *BYTE*, **10**(9), September.

Reproduced from Somogyi, E. K. and Galliers, R. D. (1987) Applied information technology: from data processing to strategic information systems. *Journal of Information Technology*, **2**(1), March, 30–41. Reprinted by permission of the publishers, Routledge.

Postscript

Since this chapter first appeared in March 1987 there have, of course, been many developments in information technology, some of which are covered elsewhere in this book, and the new era presaged in the final paragraph has most certainly dawned. Some of the most important developments occurring in the interim are discussed below. The intention here is not to be comprehensive, but to give a flavour of the kind of developments that have taken place and, more importantly, their impact on present-day organizations.

1   The *object-oriented concept* involves the groupings of data and the program(s) that use that data, into self-contained functional capsules called objects. These objects can be regarded as 'building blocks' which can be put together with other objects to create new applications or enhancements to existing ones. Unlike previous system development tools and techniques the object-oriented concept allows for *growth* and *change*. The reusing of objects for different applications will not only increase development productivity but also will reduce maintenance and improve the overall quality of the software being produced. In particular, the object-oriented concept has significant practical implementation on distributed processing. Rymer (1993) identifies four strategic benefits arising from such applications: development of distributed applications is greatly simplified; objects can be reused in multiple environments; distributed objects facilitate interoperability and information sharing; and the environment supports multimedia and complex interactive applications. It has to be said, however, that a fundamental change in mindset is required to support a move to object-oriented applications. Planning and commitment of top management are needed in the long term as returns from this approach are unlikely to be gained in the shorter term. Systems development staff must be retrained to cope with the new concept and to fully understand the benefits it can convey.

2 *Client-server architecture* is a distributed approach to the organization of the IT infrastructure in which two or more machines 'collaborate' in fulfilling a user's request. Although Benjamin and Blunt's chapter (Chapter 7) does discuss this concept they do so in passing; therefore a more detailed description of it and the management implications with respect to it are given here. The typical scenario is for workstations to be connected to local file servers and for these servers in turn to be connected to a central mainframe. The applications are divided between the client computer (i.e. the terminal and its end user) and the server (i.e. a dedicated machine running an application). However, at this time there is no standard or specific approach that identifies how the applications should be divided between the client and the server. This type of architecture enables resources to be more evenly spread across the network, improving response time for local requests by using the user's workstation to run part of the application. Besides the increase in user productivy gained through the improved response time, client-server architecture also provides ease of use with the performance, data integrity, security and reliability of a mainframe. This enables the information to be managed more effectively and provides greater flexibility (by allowing incremental growth) and control. One of the major problems, as with all new technologies or concepts, is the problem of implementation. There is a shortage of programmers who are skilled in network computing (Martin, 1992) and there is still a question as to the cost savings obtained despite some evidence that shows a benefit larger than initially expected (Cafasso, 1993). A distributed computing architecture often requires a complete reorganization of the IS function (LaPlante, 1992) because migration to a client-server architecture normally means downsizing or rightsizing. Therefore the transition must be carefully planned. The implementation of a client-server architecture will require not only retraining end-users, systems professionals and micro-oriented staff but also the overhauling of the data networks to provide the speed, integrity and reliability required by a distributed system.

3 *Data communications* form the backbone of modern computing networks. Local area networks (LANS) allow individuals to share information, printers and programs, improving the quality and accessibility of crucial information. Wide-area networks (WANS) allow communication of information between dispersed facilities (e.g. data centres or regional offices). There are two main problems associated with data communication between LANS and WANS: security and the management of local area network traffic across WANS. Encryption capabilities, public–private key algorithms and digital signatures are used to improve security helping to ensure that the information has not been tampered with during transmission. Integrated systems digital network (ISDN) promises to provide

unprecedented flexibility in the interconnection of networks. ISDN is a way of transmitting data over the public telephone network without having to convert it to sound. This allows vast amounts of data to be sent down a telephone line very quickly and with a high level of accuracy. However, to make enterprise networking a reality requires the interoperability between disparate computer systems and networks. Electronic data interchange (EDI) seeks to address the former while value-added networks (VANs) seek to address the latter. Communication between organizations is possible through EDI. This is the standard technique which enables computers in different organizations to send business or information transactions successfully from one to the other, reducing paperwork and costs, improving lead times and accuracy of transactions. VANs provide two main services: first, they provide connectivity between the different types of networks in different organizations, and second, they can provide different types of external information services to the organization, information that previously was too expensive and/or difficult for organizations to collect themselves which help management to make more informative decisions. The access to such external information has opened up new opportunities and threats that previously did not exist due to the cost barriers imposed by data collection. Management now not only have to think more proactively about the type of data that needs to be gathered from within the organization to make their decisions, but also what external information is available and how it should be exploited.

4 *Image processing* technology allows documents to be stored in the form of pictures or images. These images can be indexed for efficient retrieval and transferred from one computer to another. It can change the way firms support marketing, design products, conduct training and distribute information. Since image processing helps to improve work methods it can also play a key role in reengineering an organization (see Chapter 14), thereby improving customer service and increasing productivity. It has been reported that, in the UK, 95 per cent of all business information is still held on paper (Ash, 1991). Storing this information in digitized form (normally on optical disk) can not only save floor space but can reduce labour costs and the time needed to search for and retrieve documents, improve data security, allow for multiple indexing of documents and eliminate the problem of misfiled or misplaced documents. It is also easy to integrate these electronic documents with related information and, whereas paper documents must be processed sequentially, electronic documents can be processed in parallel. Ash (1991) reports improvements in transaction volume per employee by 25–50 per cent and reductions in transaction times of between 50 and 90 per cent. Other reported savings are in staff reduction of up to 30 per cent and a reduction in the storage space requirements of up to 50 per cent. Image processing, however,

suffers as do all of the areas mentioned in this section, from a lack of industry standards. In addition, there are legal issues that need to be resolved with respect to document authentication.

5 *Multimedia applications* combine full-motion video images with sound, graphics and text, and are based on the integration of three existing technologies, namely the telephone, television and computer. Besides offering users a more human interface with their data, multimedia applications enable organizations to improve their productivity and customer service through the incorporation of different types of data (e.g. video) into their organizational systems. Conferencing applications (e.g. video conferencing) will probably be the first to benefit from this technology, bringing people who are physically miles apart electronically together in the same room. The most sophisticated example of a multimedia application is called *virtual reality*. This application takes the use of multimedia to its extreme. Computer-generated, interactive three-dimensional images (complete with sound and images) are used to enable users to become embedded in the reality that is being created on the screen in front of them. Although most applications are still at the research and development stage (due to such limitations as adequate computer power and developments in networking) some are beginning to find their way to the market place. The opportunities open to business through this application will be vast. Virtual reality will be able to offer benefits to business in the areas of training, design, assembly and manufacturing. Products or concepts will be able to be demonstrated in a way that would normally be impossible due to cost, safety or perception restrictions. Electronic databases will be able to be manipulated by hand or body movements, network managers will be able to repair technical network error without even having to leave their chair Employees will be able to experience real-life situations within the training environment. These are just some of the applications of this technology. However, once again, one of the main problems with development in this area is the lack of standards.

6 A major development in recent years has been related to the whole question of *electronic commerce, the Internet and the World Wide Web (WWW)*. While electronic commerce applications began to appear on the scene in the early 1970s – with the electronic transfer of funds – we have witnessed many innovations in the period since the first edition of *Strategic Information Management* appeared in 1994, particularly with the advent of the Internet: 'Electronic commerce is an emerging concept that describes the buying and selling of products, services, and information via computer networks, including the Internet' (Turban *et al.*, 1998). Many different technologies enable electronic commerce, including electronic data interchange (EDI), smarts cards and e-mail, in addition to the Internet. There are very few medium to large organizations in the Western world

that do not have a home page these days, and most are very extensive. For example, 'in 1997, General Motors Corporation (www.gm.com) offered 16,000 pages of infromation that included 98,000 links to its products, services, and related topics' (*ibid.*).

References to postscript

Ash, N. (1991) Document image processing: who needs it? *Accountancy*, **108**(1176), August, 80–82.

Cafasso, R. (1993) Client-server strategies pervasive. *Computerworld*, **27**(4), 2 January, 47.

LaPlante, A. (1992) Enterprise computing: chipping away at the corporate mainframe. *Infoworld*, **14**(3), 20 January, 40–42.

Martin, M. (1992) Client-server: reaping the rewards. *Network World*, **9**(46), 16 November, 63–67.

Rymer, J. (1993) Distributed computing meets object-oriented technology. *Network World*, **10**(9). 1 March, 28–30.

Turban, E., Mckean, E. and Wetherbe, J. C. (1998) *Information Technology for Management*, 2nd edn, Wiley, New York.

Questions for discussion

1   What significance does the increasing rate and pace of advances in information and communications technologies have for organizations?
2   What are your predictions about the state of information and communication technologies, based on the past changes, for the coming decade?
3   Why is it important that we understand the developments that have been and are taking place with respect to IT?

Part One

Information Systems Strategy

We begin our discussion of key aspects of strategic information management by focusing on information systems strategy, the inner circle of our conceptualization of the term, reproduced as Figure I.1, and comprising:

- an information strategy
- an information management strategy
- an information technology strategy, and
- a change management strategy.

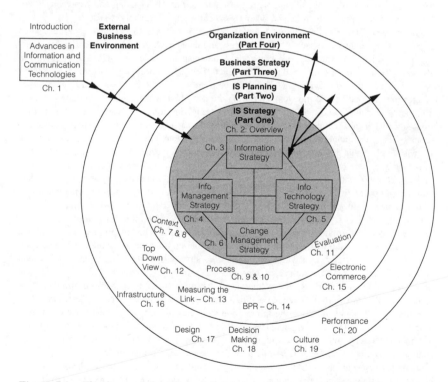

Figure I.1   *The focus of Part One: Information systems strategy in context*

Information systems planning, the process by which IS strategies are formulated and/or emerge, is the subject of Part Two.

In our search for articles that focus on these components of IS strategy, it became clear that some aspects of the topic receive more attention than others; that there are various definitions and conceptualizations of strategy relating to information systems; that there is some confusion between the terms information systems strategy and information systems planning; and that there is little to be found on the context of IS strategy. In this part of the book, we therefore set out to provide greater clarity as to the IS strategy domain, as well as to highlight key features and the results of recent research into the topic. Our overall orientation is to focus on the topic at a fairly general level rather than to look at the specifics, such as management of IS and the IS development process or the changing role and requisite capabilities/skills of IS managers and IS personnel generally. Useful sources of information covering these topics include Avison and Fitzgerald (1995) and Willcocks *et al.* (1997). Other important topics not covered in any depth here include infrastructural issues, sourcing IS services and lessons from implementation failures. Useful references here include Gunton (1989), Ward and Griffiths (1996), Kwon and Zmud (1987), Willcocks and Lacity (1997) and Sauer (1993).

We commence, in Chapter 2, with a general overview of the topic by reflecting on the so-called 'stages of growth' concept as applied to IS/IT, first articulated by Nolan (Gibson and Nolan, 1974; Nolan, 1979), following Greiner's (1972) broader consideration of evolutionary and revolutionary phases of organizational development. The 'stages' model has come in for considerable criticism as a means of predicting future developments, its overly narrow technological focus, the original concept's grounding in the database technology of the mid- to late-1970s, and its lack of empirical support (e.g. Benbasat *et al.*, 1984; King and Kraemer, 1984), but its intuitive appeal to both IS and business executives is remarkably robust.

Galliers and Sutherland's original intention in Chapter 2 was to extend the earlier Nolan frameworks to counter criticisms of their narrow, and dated, technological orientation, by focusing on a broader set of strategic, organizational and managerial issues, as well as those related to IS *per se*. Their work was informed by the so-called 'Seven-S' concept popularized by McKinsey & Co., with a view to providing a closer 'fit' between IS and the business, and by a range of 'stages' models that had been developed during the latter half of the 1980s (including, e.g. Earl, 1986 and Hirschheim *et al.*, 1988). Experiences of applying the framework in many organizations since its original development give credence to the earlier claim regarding its robustness, in terms of its general applicability and time independence. Note, however, that the authors would not wish to claim that the framework represents *reality*; rather, it can be used to considerable effect in raising questions and awareness regarding key IS strategy and IS management issues across a range of stakeholders – in assisting in providing some shared understanding as to what the key issues might be, and what might need to be done to move ahead. Further reading on applications of the framework may be found in Galliers (1991) and Galliers *et al.* (1994), for example.

Chapter 3, by Smits, van der Poel and Ribbers, is the closest we found to an article representing our view of information strategy, as depicted in Figure I.1. Our intention was to include a chapter which focused attention on the strategic information required to enable the implementation of business strategy, *and* which would provide strategists with information which would enable the questioning of assumptions on which that strategy was based. This would include information from the business and technological environment, and feedback information concerned with the impact (both intended and unintended) of the strategy once implemented.

Smits and colleagues describe the information strategies of three major insurance companies in the Netherlands. The chapter includes reflections on the various stakeholders involved in the information strategy process, and on aligning IT to business goals and processes. A major finding, contrary to the above comment regarding necessary feedback information (and in our experience common to most organizations) was that none of the companies studied assesses the effects of its information strategies at an organization-wide or business process level, and certainly not over time.

Chapter 4, by Edwards, Earl and Feeny, focuses on what we have termed the information management strategy, which is concerned with issues associated with the organization and provision of IS services. Again, it is our experience that only in a minority of cases do organizations consider such issues in the context of the overall IS strategy. As Edwards and colleagues put it: 'To judge by the behaviour of many complex organizations, management approaches towards structuring the information systems (IS) function look to be uncertain, diverse and sometimes downright contradictory.' From research into fourteen organizations in Europe and North America, the authors identify five types of IS organization, ranging from the centralized to the decentralized. Their analysis provides a justification for each model, and reactions (often adverse!) to each. Their analysis leads them to the conclusion that some kind of federal approach is most likely to be successful. They insist, though – quite rightly in our view – that this 'is no panacea': 'host organization characteristics should be the prime determinant of IS arrangements.' This chapter was written at a time prior to the lemming-like rush, in the early to mid-1990s, to IS/IT outsourcing, which often occurred as a result of decisions made in isolation from the IS strategy, and without the careful analysis proposed by the authors of Chapter 4. It is for this reason that this chapter has been retained from the first edition of *Strategic Information Management*. Further reading on the IS/IT outsourcing phenomenon, and responses to it, can be found in Lacity and Hirschheim (1995a, b) and Willcocks and Lacity (1998).

In Chapter 5, we turn to the topic of IT strategy. This is often considered in a fairly narrow, technogical sense, with attention being paid to hardware and software acquisition, infrastructural issues, and the like – often, unfortunately, in isolation from other key aspects of IS strategy, as conceptualized in Figure I.1. While these technological concerns are undoubtedly important, this chapter takes a more strategic stance, and attempts to provide a vision for IT and its potential role in organizations. Written by Schein, this chapter focuses on the key roles that CEOs might play in managing change (also a subject covered in Chapter 6), specifically with regard to IT projects. As a result of a series of interviews with almost 100 CEOs, Schein reflects on their assumptions about IT and their attitudes towards the issues associated with implementation and organizational change. The roles identified range from the IT 'skeptic' to the IT 'zealot'. What is important about this chapter is that the range of change agent roles identified may be applied to a variety of organizational change, including reorganization of work, authority relationships and management styles – a topic also considered by Pettigrew (1998).

The subject of managing change – a key feature in any IS strategy, as in any other strategy process (see e.g. Whittington, 1993) is taken up, in Chapter 6, by Markus and Benjamin. While strategy formulation (or formation) is one thing, implementation is quite another matter! The authors focus on the role of IS professionals in the change process, their motivation being to 'stimulate IS specialists' efforts to be come more effective – and more credible – agents of organizational change'. They describe – and critique – what they believe to be a commonly-held view of this role on the part of IS professionals, namely one which is embedded in technological determinism: a belief in 'the ability of *technology* (versus people) to cause change'.* Referring to the organizational design† literature, they propose two alternative models that might be more appropriate, and more successful, in the light of the rapidly changing nature and impact of modern IT: the 'facilitator' model and the 'advocate' model. As a result they propose new skills and career paths for IS personnel and IT managers, a revised research agenda for IS academics, and reform of IS educational curricula‡ to take account of the 'softer' skills necessary for the changed conditions pertaining in the late 1990s and into the twenty-first century.

---

* A point taken up by Davenport (1996) in his critique of applications of the BPR concept (see also Chapter 14).
† See, e.g. Cummings and Huse (1989), Schwarz (1994), Kanter *et al.* (1992) and Rogers (1995).
‡ Earlier calls for a more broadly-based approach to IS education can be found in Buckingham *et al.* (1987).

Chapter 6 brings Part One of the book, dealing with IS strategy, to a close. We trust that our treatment of this aspect of strategic information management has demonstrated just what a diverse and important topic this is – i.e. that it is much more broadly based than commonly assumed, often with the focus being little more than on information *technology* issues. Part Two then focuses on IS planning, the means by which this more broadly-based strategy may be developed.

References

Avison, D. and Fitzgerald, G. (1995) *Information Systems Development: Methodologies, Techniques and Tools*, 2nd edn, McGraw-Hill, London.

Benbasat, I., Dexter, A., Drury, D. and Goldstein, R. (1984) A critique of the stage hypothesis: theory and empirical evidence. *Commuications of the ACM*, **27**(5), May, 476–485.

Boland, R. J. and Hirschheim, R. A. (eds) (1987) *Critical Issues in Information Systems Research*, Wiley, Chichester.

Buckingham, R. A., Hirschheim, R. A., Land, F. F. and Tully, C. J. (eds) (1987) *Information Systems Education: Recommendations and Implementation*, Cambridge University Press on behalf of the British Computer Society, Cambridge.

Cummings, T. G. and Huse, E. F. (1989) *Organization Development and Change*, 4th edn, West Publishing, St Paul, Minnesota.

Davenport, T. (1996) Why reengineering failed. The fad that forgot people. *Fast Company*, Premier Issue, 70–74.

Earl, M. J. (1986) Information systems strategy formulation. In R. J. Boland and R. A. Hirschheim (eds) (1987), *op cit.*, 157–178.

Galliers, R. D. (1991) Strategic information systems planning: myths, realities and guidelines for successful implementation. *European Journal of Information Systems*, **1**(1), 55–64.

Galliers, R. D., Pattison, E. M. and Reponen, T. (1994) Strategic information systems planning workshops: lessons from three cases. *International Journal of Information Management*, **14**, 51–66.

Gibson, D. and Nolan, R. (1974) Managing the four stages of EDP growth. *Harvard Business Review*, **52**(1), January–February, 76–88.

Greiner, L. E. (1972) Evolution and revolution as organizations grow. *Harvard Business Review*, **50**(4), July–August, 37–46.

Gunton, T. (1989) *Infrastructure: Building a Framework for Corporate Information Handling*, Prentice Hall, New York.

Hirschheim, R. A., Earl, M. J., Feeny, D. and Lockett, M. (1988) An exploration into the management of the information systems function: key issues and an evolutionary model. *Proceedings: Information Technology Management for Productivity and Strategic Advantage*, IFIP TC8 Open Conference, Singapore, March.

Kanter, R. M., Stein, B. A. and Jick, T. D. (1992) *The Challenge of Organizational Change: How Companies Experience It and Leaders Guide It*, Free Press, New York.

King, J. and Kraemer, K. (1984) Evolution and organizational information systems: an assessment of Nolan's stage model. *Communications of the ACM*, **27**(5), May, 466–475

Kwon, T. H. and Zmud, R. W. (1987) Unifying the fragmented models of information systems implementation. In R. J. Boland and R. A. Hirschheim (eds) (1987), *op cit.*, 227–251.

Lacity, M. C. and Hirschheim, R. A. (1995a) *Information Systems Outsourcing: Myths, Metaphors and Realities*, Wiley, Chichester.

Lacity, M. C. and Hirschheim, R. A. (1995b) *Beyond the Information Systems Outsourcing Bandwagon: The Insourcing Response*, Wiley, Chichester.

Nolan, R. (1979) Managing the crises in data processing. *Harvard Business Review*, **57**(2), March–April, 115–126.

Pettigrew, A. M. (1998) Success and failure in corporate transformation initiatives. In *Information Technology and Organizational Transformation: Innovation for the 21st Century Organization* (eds R. D. Galliers and W. R. J. Baets), Wiley, Chichester.

Rogers, E. M. (1995) *Diffusion of Innovations*, 4th edn, Free Press, New York.

Sauer, C. (1993) *Why Information Systems Fail: A Case Study Approach*, Alfred Waller, Henley-on-Thames.

Schwarz, R. M. (1994) *The Skilled Facilitator: Practical Wisdom for Developing Effective Groups*, Jossey-Bass, San Francisco, California.

Ward, J. and Griffiths, P. (1996) *Strategic Planning for Information Systems*, 2nd. edn, Wiley, Chichester.

Whittington, R. (1993) *What is Strategy? – And Does It Matter?* Routledge, London.

Willcocks, L. C., Feeny, D. and Islei, G. (1997) *Managing IT as a Strategic Resource*, McGraw-Hill, London.

Willcocks, L. C. and Lacity, M. C. (1997) *Strategic Sourcing of Information Systems: Perspectives and Practices*, Wiley, Chichester.

2 The Evolving Information Systems Strategy

Information systems management and strategy formulation: applying and extending the 'stages of growth' concept

R. D. Galliers and A. R. Sutherland

Introduction

For some time, reason has held that the organizational growth with respect to the use of Information Technology (IT) and the approach organizations take to the management and planning of information systems could be conceived of in terms of various, quite clearly defined, stages of maturity. Whilst there has been some criticism of the models that have been postulated, many view the various 'stages of growth' models as being useful in designating the maturity (in IT terms) of organizations. Four such 'stages of growth' models are described briefly below, i.e. those postulated by: (a) Nolan (1979); (b) Earl (1983; 1986, as amended by Galliers, 1987a, 1989*); (c) Bhabuta (1988), and (d) Hirschheim *et al.* (1988).

The Nolan model is perhaps the most widely known and utilized of the four – by both practitioner and researcher alike. Despite its critics, by 1984 it had been used as a basis for over 200 consultancy studies within the USA by Nolan, Norton and Company, and had been incorporated into IBM's information systems planning consultancies (Nolan, 1984); Hamilton & Ives (1982) report that the original article describing the model (Gibson and Nolan, 1974) was one of the 15 most cited by information systems researchers.

---

* Galliers, R. D. (1989) The developing information systems organization: an evaluation of the 'stages of growth' hypothesis, paper presented at the London Business School, January 1989.

The Nolan model

Nolan's original four-stage model (Gibson and Nolan, 1974) was later developed into a six-stage model (Nolan, 1979), and it is this latter model which is most commonly applied. Like the models that followed it, it is based on the premise that the organizations pass through a number of identifiable growth phases in utilizing and managing IT. These 'stages of growth' are then used to identify the organization's level of maturity in this context, with a view to identifying key issues associated with further IT development.

Nolan posited that the growth phase could be identified primarily by analysing the amount spent on data processing (DP) as a proportion of sales revenue, postulating that DP expenditure would follow an S-curve over time. More importantly, however, it was claimed that this curve appeared to represent the learning path with respect to the general use of IT within the organization. As indicated above, the original four-stage model (Figure 2.1) was expanded into a six-stage model in 1979 with the addition of two new stages between 'control' and 'maturity', namely 'integration' and 'data administration'.

The six-stage model is illustrated in Figure 2.2. As can be seen, Nolan indicates that, in addition to DP expenditure, there are four major growth processes that can be analysed to identify the organization's stage of maturity with respect to IT use.

1   The scope of the *application portfolio* throughout the organization (moving from mainly financial and accounting systems to wider-ranging operational systems, to management information systems).
2   The focus of the *DP organization* (moving from a centralized, 'closed shop' in the early stages to data resource management in maturity).
3   The focus of the *DP planning and control* activity (moving from a primarily internal focus in the first three stages to an external focus in the latter stages), and
4   The level of *user awareness* [moving from a primarily reactive stance (reactive, that is, to centralized DP initiatives) in the first two stages, to being a driving force for change in the middle stages, through to a partnership in maturity].

Nolan argues that the information systems management focus is very much concerned with technology *per se* during the earlier stages of growth, with a transformation point occurring at the completion of stage three, after which the focus is on managing the organization's data resources, utilizing database technology and methods.

As indicated earlier, the model has been criticized because it has not proved possible to substantiate its claims to represent reality, either as a means to describe the phases through which organizations pass when utilizing IT, or as a predictor of change (Benbasat *et al.*, 1984; King and Kraemer, 1984). In

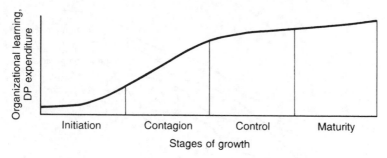

Figure 2.1 *Four stages of DP growth (amended from Gibson and Nolan, 1974; Earl, 1989, p.28)*

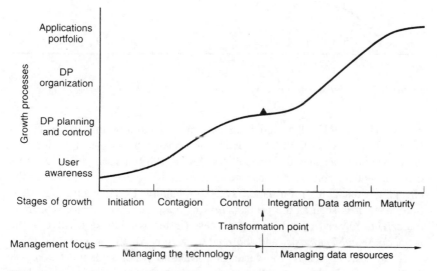

Figure 2.2 *Nolan's six-stage growth model (amended from Nolan, 1979; Galliers, 1989)*

addition, its focus on database technology clearly dates the model. Earl (1989), for example, argues that organizations will pass through a number of different learning curves with respect to *different* ITs, as illustrated in Figure 2.3. In addition, it is now clear that different parts of a single organization may well be at different stages of growth with respect to a particular IT.

The Earl model

Unlike Nolan's model, Earl's concentrates attention on the stages through which organizations pass in *planning* their information systems. First described

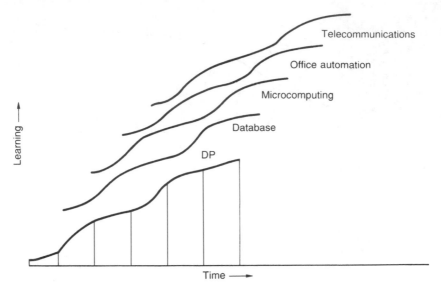

Figure 2.3   *Multiple learning curves (amended from Earl, 1989, p.31)*

in 1983 (Earl, 1983), the model has been revised on a number of occasions (Earl, 1986, 1988, 1989). The version presented here is based on the two earlier versions, as amended by Galliers (1987a, 1989), bearing in mind Earl's own subsequent changes. As can be seen from Table 2.1, Earl illustrates the changing agenda for information systems planning by concentrating attention on what is seen as the primary *task* of the process: its major *objective*, the *driving forces* of the planning process (in terms of those involved), the *methodological emphasis*, and the *context* within which the planning takes place. Following research on current information systems planning practice, Galliers adds to this a supplementary early stage of planning (which is essentially *ad hoc* in nature) and an additional factor, concerning the *focus* of the planning effort. In the latter context, he argues that the focus has tended to change over the years from a predominantly *isolated*, Information Systems function orientation, through an *organizational* focus, to a competitive, *environmental* focus.

Earl's argument is essentially that organizations begin their planning efforts by the first attempting to assess the current 'state of play' with respect to information systems coverage and IT utilization. Increasingly, the focus shifts to management concern for a stronger linkage with business objectives. Finally, the orientation shifts to a strategic focus, with a balance being maintained in relation to the make-up of planning teams (between information systems staff, management and users), environmental and organizational information (with the likelihood of inter-organizational systems being

Table 2.1 *Earl's planning in stages model (amended from Earl, 1986, 1988, 1989) and Galliers (1987a, 1989)*

Factor	Stages					
	I	*II*	*III*	*IV*	*V*	*VI*
Task	Meeting demands	IS/T audit	Business support	Detailed planning	Strategic advantage	Business-IT strategy linkage
Objective	Provide service	Limit demand	Agree priorities	Balance IS portfolio	Pursue opportunities	Integrate strategies
Driving force	IS reaction	IS led	Senior management led	User/IS partnership	IS/exective led; user involvement	Strategic coalitions
Methological emphasis	*Ad hoc*	Bottom-up survey	Top-down analysis	Two-way prototyping	Environmental scanning	Multiple methods
Context	User/IS inexperience	Inadequate IS resources	Inadequate business/IS plans	Complexity apparent	IS for competitive advantage	Maturity, collaboration
Focus	IS department		Organization-wide		Environment	

developed, cf. Cash and Konsynski, 1985), and the range of approaches adopted (with multiple methods being accepted).

The Bhabuta model

Based on earlier work by Gluck *et al.* (1980), which proposes a four-stage process of evolution towards strategic planning, and a somewhat similar model of IT assimilation and diffusion postulated by McFarlan *et al.* (1982, 1983), Bhabuta (1988) developed a model which attempts to map the progress towards formal strategic planning of information systems. This is illustrated in Table 2.2.

Underpinning Bhabuta's argument is the contention that strategies based on productivity improvement (and the information systems needed to support them) 'will become the dominant paradigm in the turbulent and fiercely competitive markets of the next decade' (Bhabuta, 1988, p.1.72). His model is more widely focused than either the Nolan or Earl models, in that it attempts to bring together elements of, for example, strategy formulation, information systems, and the mechanisms by which the information systems function is managed. The value systems associated with each phase of the model are also identified (cf. Ackoff, 1981).

In interpreting the Bhabuta model, it should be noted that the categories used are not distinct nor absolute. With the maturing of IT utilization, and managerial sophistication with respect to IT, it can be expected that some of the attributes associated with, for example, Phase 3 and 4 organizations will emerge within Phase 1 and 2 organizations. This point takes account of some of the criticism of the Nolan model (Benbasat *et al.*, 1984), which is itself based on earlier work by Greiner (1972), regarding the discontinuities that organizations experience in growth.

The Hirschheim *et al.* model

The Hirschheim *et al.* (1988) model also builds on the earlier work of Nolan (1979) and arises from research, undertaken during the first half of 1986, into the evolution and management of the IT function in a number of British organizations. As a result of this research. Hirschheim and his colleagues contend that in companies where top management had begun to realize that information systems are vital to their business, organizations move through three evolutionary phases in their management of the IS/IT function. The three phases are labelled 'delivery', 'reorientation' and 'reorganization' (see also Earl, 1989, p.197).

Table 2.2 *Bhabuta's model linking the evaluation of strategic planning with information systems and the organization of the information systems function (amended from Bhabuta, 1988, p.1.76; Sutherland and Galliers, 1989, p.10)*

	Phase 1	Phase 2	Phase 3	Phase 4
Evolutionary phases of strategic planning	Basic financial planning	Forecast-based planning	Externally oriented planning	Strategic management
Value System	Meet the budget	Predict the future	Think strategically	Create the future
Competitive strategy mechanisms	Operational level productivity and diffuse innovation	Focused (niche) innovation and operational/tactical level productivity	Focused innovation and strategic productivity (quality focus)	Systemic innovation and productivity
Lead by	Top management	Top and senior management	Entrepreneurial managers (top/senior/middle)	Corporate-wide employees
Application of IT/IS	Resource management Efficient operations Transaction processing Exception monitoring Planning and analysis	Effectiveness of divisional operations IT infrastructure Support key division makers	IT-based products and services Communications network Direct competitive tool	Inter-organizational IS (link buyers, suppliers, manufacturers, consumers). Facilitate organizational learning
Formalized IS and decision making	Processing of internal data	*Ad hoc* processing of external data	Systematic external data analysis	Link tactical/operational activities to external data analysis
Management of IT, location in hierarchy and scope	Technology management Individual projects Middle management responsibility	Formal planning of IS Data sharing and administration Focus on IT infusion Senior management responsibility	Couple IT and business planning IT planning at SBU/corporate level Senior/Top management responsibility	Systemic support of organizational processes IT planning at SBU/portfolio level Top management responsibility

The 'delivery' phase is characterized by top management concern about the ability of the IS/IT function to 'deliver the goods'. Senior executives have begun to take the subject very seriously, but there is often dissatisfaction with the quality of the available information systems and the efficiency of the IS/IT function, together with mounting concern regarding IT expenditure and the consistency of hardware and infrastructure policies. It would appear that often this phase is initiated by replacing the DP manager with an external recruit with a good track record and substantial computing experience.

The emphasis in this phase is on the 'delivery' of information systems and, accordingly, the newly appointed IS executive spends most of the time on matters internal to the IS department. The primary role is to restore credibility to the function and/or to create confidence in user/top management that the function really is supporting current needs and is run efficiently. During this phase, IS education is sparse, but where it is provided, it is targetted on DP personnel with a view to improving skills, techniques and project management.

In the 'reorientation' phase, top management (or the Director ultimately responsible for IS) changes the focus of attention from the delivery of basic IS services to the exploitation of IT for competitive advantage. An attempt is made to align IS/IT investment with business strategy. In short, it is in this 'reorientation' phase that 'the business is put into computing'. With this change of direction/emphasis, it is common to appoint an IS executive over the DP Manager. The new post is filled, typically, by an insider: a senior executive who has run a business unit or been active in a corporate role, such as marketing or strategy formulation. They are likely to have only limited experience of DP, but are respected by top management for an ability to bring about change. The focus during this second phase is on the market place; on the external environment of the enterprise; on using IT for competitive advantage, and in extending the value chain through inter-organizational systems (cf. Cash and Konsynski, 1985).

In the 'reorganization' phase, the senior IS executive (by now the IT Director) is concerned with managing the interfaces or relationships between the IS function and the rest of the organization. Some areas will be strategically dependent on IS, others will be looking to IS more in a support role. Some will have significant IT capability, particularly with the advance of end-user computing, and some business executives will be driving IT and IS development. Increasingly IS will be managed along 'federal' lines (Edwards *et al.*, 1989) with IS capability in the centre *and* in business units/functions. These changed and changing relationships require careful management and often 'reorganization', and once again attention is focused on internal (organizational), as opposed to external (market place), concerns.

The concerns and considerations associated with each of the phases of the Hirschheim *et al.* model are summarized in Table 2.3.

Table 2.3 *The Hirschheim et al. model of changing considerations towards information systems management (amended from Hirschheim et al., 1988, p.4.33; Sutherland and Galliers, 1989, p.11)*

Phase/factor	Delivery	Reorientation	Reorganization
IS executive	External IS recruit	Inside business	Same person
Management focus	Within IS/DP	Into the business	The interfaces
Education needs	Credibility	Strategy	Relationship
CEO posture	Concerned	Visionary/champion	Involved
Leadership	The board	The function	Coalition

Towards a revised 'stages of growth' model

The major inadequacies of the early Nolan models relate to their lack of organizational and management focus, and the overly simplistic and subjective assumptions on which they were based. More importantly, they provided little help for the beleaguered DP manager attempting to create a successful IS function within the organization. This, as has been demonstrated, has been remedied in part by the subsequent work of Earl, Bhabuta and Hirschheim *et al.* In all but the latter case, however, the models described how an organization could place itself within a particular stage of IT planning maturity, rather than describing what is needed to be done in order to progress through to the more mature stages of growth.

The models that have been discussed thus far describe elements (technical, managerial and organizational) in the growth of 'computing' within an organization. Were these to be arranged and combined with a structure describing the important elements of an organization generally, then a model depicting the kinds of activities and organizational structures needed for an enterprise to move through IT growth stages (a more comprehensive and useful model) would result.

Such a model, dealing as it would with the growing maturity in the management and use of IT in an organization, would indicate how an organization might develop its use of the technology and its organization of the IS function. However, a means has to be found of bringing together a range of key elements associated with the operation and management of an organization generally in order that the revised model could be developed.

After some considerable literature searching, the so-called Seven 'Ss' used by McKinsey & Company in their management consultancy (Pascale and Athos, 1981) were used to assist in the development of the model. The Seven 'Ss' used in analysis of organizational processes and management are summarized in Table 2.4.

Table 2.4   *The Seven 'Ss' (Pascale and Athos, 1981, p.81)*

Strategy	Plan or course of action leading to the allocation of a firm's scarce resources, over time, to reach identified goals
Structure	Characterization of the organization chart (i.e. functional, decentralized, etc.)
Systems	Procedural reports and routine processes such as meeting formats
Staff	'Demographic' description of important personnel categories within the firm (i.e. engineers, entrepreneurs, MBAs, etc.). 'Staff' is *not* meant in line-staff terms
Style	Characterization of how key managers behave in achieving the organization's goals; also the cultural style of the organization
Skills	Distinctive capabilities of key personnel or the firm as a whole
Superordinate goals	The significant meanings or guiding concepts that an organization imbues in its members. Superordinate goals can be also described as the shared values or culture of the organization

Research method

As a first step, the elements of each of the Seven 'Ss' were considered in the context of each stage in the growth of IT utilization and management, according to the models described. In other words, a description of each of the 'S' elements was attempted in terms of the IT function and the provision of IT services generally, rather than the organization overall. Following a description of each of the 'S' elements in each stage of the model, an indication of what might be done to move into the next stage of the model can be provided. These indicators are based on what constitutes the Seven 'Ss' in the next stage.

Having produced a tentative model, it was then applied to four Perth-based organizations, and amendments made. The approach was to interview four or five senior executives from different areas in each of the organizations studied. These executives were, typically:

(a)   the Chief Executive Officer, or the Deputy
(b)   the Head of a Strategic Business Unit (SBU)
(c)   the IT Director, or Head of the IS function
(d)   the Head of Corporate Planning, or equivalent.

In some instances, for example, where the particular circumstances warranted broader coverage, more than one SBU head was interviewed. The interviews focused on the experiences of each organization in planning, managing and utilizing IT, and on their preparedness to utilize IT strategically. As a result of these interviews, the tentative model was continually refined and each organization eventually assessed in the context of the revised model. As a result of this assessment, conclusions were drawn as to what steps each organization might take (in relation to each of the Seven 'Ss') in order to move on to later growth stages.

Since then, the model has been 'tested' by numerous participants at conferences and short courses, and by clients both in the UK and Australia. As a result it has been further refined.

Revised stages of growth model

The growth in IT maturity in an organization can be represented as six stages, each with its particular set of conditions associated with the Seven 'Ss'. These stages are described in Table 2.5.

The following sections describe each of the stages in the model in detail, using each of the Seven 'Ss' as a basis for the description. Each of the elements constitute an important aspect of how the IT function within the organization might operate at different stages of growth. The stages described are not intended to include any overt (nor covert) negative overtones associated with the early stages of the model. Some of the descriptions may appear to paint an uninviting and somewhat derogatory picture of IT utilization and management within organizations during earlier stages, especially in relation to the DP personnel involved. This is primarily due to the fact that the earlier stages tend to represent a historical perspective of how organizations first began to 'come to grips' with IT. Conversely, the latter stages are essentially a distillation of what are currently considered to be the best features of IS management as organizations begin to utilize IT more strategically.

Table 2.5 *Stages of IT growth in organizations (Sutherland and Galliers, 1989, p.14)*

Stage	Description
One	'Ad Hocracy'
Two	Starting the foundations
Three	Centralized dictatorship
Four	Democratic dialectic and cooperation
Five	Entrepreneurial opportunity
Six	Integrated harmonious relationships

In the past, few in the DP/IT profession paid much attention to the subtle organizational and psychological aspects of implementing and managing IT within organizations. The same could be said of management. Computing was seen as essentially a technical, support function for the most part. The situation is not quite so parlous at the present time, but some DP professionals still exhibit this type of behaviour, despite the increasing concern for IS professionals to exhibit 'hybrid' (i.e. a combination of managerial, organizational and business skills in addition to technical expertise) qualities (BCS, 1990).

Even with very aware DP staff, organizations will still display symptoms of the early stages. Indeed many aspects of the early stages, if implemented correctly, are actually quite important foundations. Correct implementation of IT during the early stages of development may well mean the difference between success or failure during the later stages of an organization's IT development. Indeed, organizations that attempt to move to later stages of the model too soon, without laying the appropriate groundwork of the earlier stages, are more likely to be doomed to IT failure.

Stage 1   'Ad hocracy'

Stage 1 of the model describes the uncontrolled, *ad hoc* approach to the use of IT usually exhibited by organizations initially. All organizations begin in Stage 1. This is not to say that all organizations remain in Stage 1 for any length of time. Some move very quickly to later stages. This may occur through pressure being exerted by a computer vendor, for example, actively attempting to push the client organization into a later stage of maturity.

Strategy

The major (only) strategy in this stage is to acquire hardware and software. Acquisition of IT staff and development of IT skills throughout the organization are for the most part disregarded by management in this initial start-up phase. There is a desire for simple applications to be installed, typically those relating to controlling financial aspects of the business (i.e. accounting systems). The 'strategy' normally employed at this stage is concerned with the acquisition of standard packages and, in many instances, external suppliers may be contracted to develop specific applications, rather than in-house applications being attempted (which would have been the norm prior to the 1980s).

Structure

There is no real organizational structure associated with IT in this stage. IT is simply purchased and installed wherever someone (usually with sufficient purchasing power) requires it to be used. As expenditure on IT represents a relatively large capital outlay for the typically small organizations currently at this stage of development, the CEO/owner is usually actively involved in purchasing. Little thought is given to the organizational impact of the IT, nor to the infrastructure necessary to manage its acquisition and use.

Systems

Any systems development that takes place during this stage tends to be *ad hoc*. Systems are most often unconnected (i.e. developed and operated in isolation). Development and operation of systems is uncoordinated, whether this is across the organization as a whole or within the area requiring the application. Systems tend to be operational in nature, concentrating on the financial aspects of the organization, rather than its core business. The *ad hoc* approach to development and use of information systems results in many being located within, and supporting, just one functional business area. Most of these systems will overlap and are inconsistent in operation and output. Manual systems are typically retained to 'backup' the computerized systems. Systems tend to cover only a limited aspect of the range of work required of the individuals within the area concerned.

Staff

IT staff typically consist of a small number of programmers. A number of programming staff may be employed, but often external contractors are used. Purchase of packaged software means that very few internal IT staff are deemed to be required.

Style

The predominant style associated with the utilization of IT in this stage is that of being unaware and, more significantly, unconcerned with being unaware. IT operates in a virtual vacuum, with almost total disregard as to how it will affect the organization, its processes and human resources. From the IT personnel perspective, the only issues that appear to be of any relevance are technical ones: nothing else is of significance so far as they are concerned. Much of this style can be attributed to the use of external contractors as IT staff. These external contractors will typically show little interest in the organization they are contracted to (they will not be there that long, and their future advancement does not depend on the organization or its management).

Skills

The skills associated with IT use tend to be of a technical nature and rather low level at that. The accent is well and truly on *technology*, as opposed to organizational, business or informational issues. Skills are individually based: while certain staff have or develop particular skills, these are jealously guarded from others. The only IT skills gained by user personnel relate very specifically to particular applications, whether this is a package or a bespoke development. Computers and computer applications tend to be so arcane that non-IT personnel find it extremely difficult to gain the requisite skills to be able to use the few systems that do exist. IT training provided by organizations in Stage 1 is virtually non-existent.

Superordinate goals

Given that very few people working in Stage 1 organizations have a clear conception of what is happening in the IT area (including the IT people themselves), it is difficult to ascribe a set of superordinate goals to this stage of the model. At best, one might describe these as being concerned with obfuscation. IT personnel typically keep whatever they may know and do hidden from those they are supposed to serve, either by design or through ignorance or misguided elitism (mostly the latter). A more unkind evaluation (although possibly a more accurate one!) would suggest that the practitioners in this stage are not capable of formulating well-constructed superordinate goals.

Stage 2   Starting the foundations

Stage 2 of the model marks the beginning of the ascendancy of an IT 'priesthood' in the organization.

Strategy

In this stage, the IT staff (for there is now a permanent cadre of such staff) attempt to find out about user needs and then meet them. This is the era of the IT Audit (cf. Earl, 1989), i.e. simply checking what has and is done, with the future seen simply as being a linear extension of the past. As indicated above, some systems have been installed in Stage 1 (typically packages), and these relate mostly to basic financial processes. Organisations in Stage 2 now concentrate on developing applications associated with other areas of the business. Although the emphasis is still on financial systems, they are now not so narrowly constrained. They are, however, still very much operational systems. No effective planning is performed, even though the IT staff may claim that they do at least plan their own work. What planning is undertaken is usually part of an annual budgetary process. The 'bottom-up' nature of ascertaining computing needs and the lack of adequate planning lead to the perception of a large backlog of systems still to be built, and demands for major increases in DP spending.

Structure

This is the first stage when a separate IT section within the organization is recognized. This section is given various names, but it is typically located under the Finance or Accounting function, as it reflects the main emphasis of IT applications within the organization. The IT section is still quite small, and provides limited services to the broad range of functions in the organization. The growth of internal IT staff usually heralds an era of reducing reliance on outside assistance. The internal IT staff now attempt to gain control of IT matters within the organization and do not usually welcome 'outside' interference.

Systems

Many more applications are developed (or purchased) and installed in the organization during this stage. Whereas Stage 1 may usually be quite short lived, Stage 2 may continue for quite some time. Early on, managers and staff in the organization begin to see computerized applications being installed after what may have been quite a lengthy period of waiting. This early delivery of applications provides an initial boost to the credibility of the IT function, thus lulling them and the rest of the organization into a false sense of security. The self-image of an important and powerful 'priesthood' is reinforced. Even though applications are being installed at a greater rate than previously, there are still substantial gaps in computerization in Stage 2 organizations. At the same time, many of the applications tend to overlap in purpose, function and data storage. Development and operation of applications is invariably centralized, spawning the development of the 'computer centre', and its attendants. Applications remain operational in nature, once again with the concentration being in the financial area, but with some other core business-orientated applications being attempted (although rarely completely implemented to the satisfaction of the end-user). The *ad hoc* and unprepared nature of going about building the first systems (in Stage 1 and early in Stage 2) also leads to a large maintenance load being placed on the IT section. This large maintenance load invariably leads to a growth in the number of IT staff. Usually this occurs in an uncontrolled manner, and leads, as this stage progresses, to a slowing of the pace in which new systems are developed.

Staff

This stage heralds the appearance of a DP Manager, who usually reports to the Financial Controller or equivalent. Apart from the programmers inherited from Stage 1, the DP Manager will be joined by Systems Analysts and Designers: people charged with the responsibility of ensuring that they have adequately understood the requirements of the 'user' and of designing appropriate systems.

Style

The predominant style of the IT staff in this stage is one of 'don't bother me (I'm too busy getting this system up and running at the moment)'. The pressure really is on these staff, and they show it. Their orientation is still technical. They assume that whatever they are doing is what they should be doing to assist the organization. Their job is to go about building the system as quickly as possible, and as technically competently as possible. Involvement with other staff in the organization, especially when these others attempt to be involved in building systems, is not welcomed, since users 'keep changing their minds about what they want'. In other words, the IT staff do not appreciate the changing nature of information needs at this stage (cf. Land, 1982; Oliver and Langford, 1984; Galliers, 1987b).

Skills

Rather than purely technical skills associated with the programming and installation of computing equipment, the IT staff now concentrate on skills associated with building and installing complete systems for the organization. Thus, expertize in systems development methodologies, structured techniques and the like become important at this stage.

Superordinate goals

There is now a cohesive set of superordinate goals shared within the IT function, concerned with the primacy and (in their terms) the inherent appropriateness of technological developments. The predominant situation elsewhere in the organization would be one of confusion, however. Many people are doing many things, but nobody quite knows exactly what is going on, and the whole picture of IT use in the organization is only dimly perceived.

Stage 3   Centralized dictatorship

Strategy

Stage 3 attempts to right the imbalances caused by the *ad hoc* nature of developments in Stage 1 and the 'blind' rush into systems of Stage 2. The need for comprehensive planning is recognized and embraced wholeheartedly by some (usually powerful) members of the management team (including some IT staff). IT is under central control up to this stage, but it is actually *out* of the control of those who are supposedly 'controlling' it. The answer is perceived to be in planning, and typically top-down planning. There is an awareness that many of the systems developed thus far do not actually meet real business needs. There is general recognition that IT should support the organization (rather than the converse) and as such, all IT development must be somehow linked to the corporate/business plans in a fundamentally linear manner. Thus, the overriding strategy is to ensure that a top-down, well-documented IT plan is put into place, from which future IT developments will emanate, and against which further development initiatives will be gauged.

Structure

A comprehensive DP department is incorporated into the organization at this stage. It is centralized, with all 'official' IT power invested in the department and its head (still the DP Manager). The latter may still report to the Financial Controller (Vice President Finance), but their standing in the management team will have grown slightly, although they are still treated as a technical person, and are not usually asked to participate in making 'business' decisions. Senior management have tended to renege on their responsibility to manage and control IT. This may be due to a number of factors, not the least being their almost total lack of understanding of IT, and in many instances, their unwillingness to begin to attempt to understand it. This attitude has then excluded DP staff from the organization's 'business' decision-making process, even though they may have wanted to participate, or may have been capable of making a positive contribution. The attitudes of Stage 2 are further developed in Stage 3, leaving a legacy which causes the DP Manager some discomfort. 'End users' have had some experience with IT for some time now and feel restless under the autocratic centralist regimes of the DP department. Typically, the DP Manager (and others in the department) will tend to ignore 'end users': in some instances letting them run free to do whatever they think fit (cf. Stage 1), but more likely attempting to exercise light control over any end-user developed system, with consequent ill feeling. The DP Manager and the DP department become out of touch with the 'ordinary' user in the organization, and problems in implementation and acceptance of systems developed centrally continue to manifest themselves.

Systems

Most systems are centrally developed, installed, operated and controlled by the DP department. By this stage, DP staff have implemented systems to cover most major operational activities in some form or another (they may not meet all the needs of the users, but they none the less operate in major business areas). At the same time, there are a number of systems which have been put together by end users in an uncontrolled, uncoordinated manner. These systems exhibit all the problems associated with Stage 1 developments, with the further difficulty that they have not been developed using technical expertise, and do not include all the elements that ensure a well-maintained ongoing success for the system in the future. For example, system security is a major problem here. When these systems fail (which they do regularly), the end users typically lay the blame at the feet of the DP Department and demand that they (the DP Department) fix and maintain the system.

Staff

Not only does the DP Department retain (and increase) the previous complement of staff (programmers, analysts, designers), but it grows further, with the addition of Information System Planners, and Database and Data Administration staff. Towards the end of this stage, the DP Manager may have a change in title to that of Information Systems/ Technology Manager or the like. Similarly, the DP Department may be renamed the Information Systems (or Technology) Department.

Style

The predominant style at this stage is one of abrogation (or at least, delegation) of responsibility, from the DP department to other people in the organization, usually the end user. The view taken is that the latter can do whatever they like as regards IT acquisition and IS development – so long as they pay for it. The DP personnel see it as the users' problem if one of *their* systems malfunctions or fails. Similarly, the DP Manager will look to senior management for direction, requiring management commitment and guidance for new developments. Also, senior management of the organization have abrogated their ultimate responsibility for IT within the organization to the DP manager and personnel, despite the fact that they are becoming concerned about control and performance problems with IT.

Skills

Apart from the skills gained through the previous two stages, the major skill demonstrated in Stage 3 is that of project management. Those projects that are centrally instigated are normally well controlled, following strict project management guidelines. The major emphasis is to ensure that the systems that are to be built are built on time and within budget.

Superordinate goals

At this stage, the principal overriding values are those of senior management *concern* with the IT function. Senior management have seen substantial money invested in IT over the period of the first two stages and are now justifiably concerned about whether they will see an adequate return on its investment. As a result, they begin to attempt to ensure that this is achieved. The DP Department becomes defensive about adverse comments regarding how well it is performing, and often expresses how difficult it is to perform well, given the complexities and competing demands.

Stage 4   Democratic dialectic and cooperation

Strategy

The conflicting forces concerned with gaining centralized control and with the move towards end-user computing of the previous stage, has left IT in a state of disarray, with little coordination between the DP department and those using the technology. Thus, the emphasis of Stage 4 is towards integration and coordination. DP thus moves out of its defensive 'ivory tower' posture, into the real world turmoil of the business organization.

Structure

The emphasis in Stage 4 moves towards bringing all users back into the fold. In practice this means that the previously centralized DP department becomes a little more decentralized, with the addition of Information Centres, integration of Records Management, Office Automation (Word Processing) and Library Services to a group now known as the Information Systems or Information Services Department. The Information Systems (or Services) Manager (previously the DP Manager) often moves up a rung in the organizational structure (at the Vice President level or just below), and this often involves a change in title. The new title may be Information Resources Manager or, more commonly in America, the Chief Information Officer (Sobkowich, 1985). In many instances, a new manager is appointed as Information Systems Manager. The incumbent DP manager is overlooked, and is sometimes replaced (cf. Hirschheim *et al.*, 1988). The new IS Manager typically has more widespread business management experience, and may well not hail from the IT area. This new manager may come from another part of the organization, or may be recruited from external sources.

Systems

The organization now adopts a 'federal' approach to information systems management and development (cf. Edwards *et al.*, 1989). Line departments may (and usually do) gain control over the deployment of IT within their department. This results in miniature DP Departments spread throughout the organization. These exhibit characteristics of Stage 2 maturity. In Stage 4, Systems Analysts are now called Business Analysts. They know more about the business of the line department, but they perform much of the same role as the Systems Analyst of old. The Information Services Department now coordinates the use of IT throughout the organization and suggests methods which the separate DP departments should follow. Office Systems are now installed in an integrated and coordinated manner throughout the organization. Previously, they were implemented on a stand-alone basis, with no regard to integration considerations. Some Decision Support Systems (DSS) are attempted, but more often than not in an *ad hoc* manner. The organization is just coming to grips with working together with IT (rather than disparate groups pulling against each other), but a coordinated approach to DSS development through the organization is not as yet a reality.

Staff

As mentioned above, the traditional DP staff of analysts, designers and programmers are joined by Business Analysts. These staff are actually employed by the line departments they serve, but must closely interact with the rest of the DP department personnel. A higher level manager for the Information Services area is installed in the organization, usually at the Vice President level (or just below), as indicated above.

Style

The mood of the previous stage (defensiveness) has now changed to one of cooperation and collaboration. The Head of IT is deliberately chosen as being a person who can ensure that IT works in conjunction with, and to the benefit of, the rest of the organization. One of the major tasks allocated to this manager is to instil this sense of cooperation throughout the IT organization. This task is characterized by skills associated with a democracy. A dialectic is initiated and established throughout the organization for all IT-related issues. The dialectic ensures that proper understanding and cooperation are developed and maintained between IT staff and the rest of the organization. The dialectic can result in some constructive confrontation. Many IT personnel employed during the previous stages may be ill-equipped to handle this type of situation, and thus may be replaced or retrained.

Skills

The skills required of IT personnel in moving from Stage 3 to Stage 4 change dramatically. Although technical capabilities are still required, they are de-emphasized in relation to business skills, and to the overriding need for them to fit in with the rest of the organization (Galliers, 1990). Organizational integration is a major theme, with improved understanding between IT and other organization staff being the result. The IT function gradually gains an understanding of how the business works, and users finally gain a proper insight into IT-related issues. The IT function also gains some business-oriented management for its area, as opposed to the technoprofessional (isolated, defensive) attitude taken in the previous stages.

Supordinate goals

Cooperation is the prevailing attitude throughout Stage 4. All areas in the organization now attempt to gain an understanding of other areas and to work together for the common good and towards a common goal or set of related goals. This is possible only because of the intensive top-down planning work performed in Stage 3 (and carried through into Stage 4). Without the extensive and rigorous planning having been performed earlier, the gains made through the initiation of a dialectic could well be ephemeral.

Stage 5   Entrepreneurial opportunity

At last, the IT function is at the stage of coming out from under the burden of simply providing supporting services to other parts of the organization and can begin to provide a strategic benefit in its own right. The major operational systems are now in place, running relatively smoothly, and providing the opportunity to build strategic systems based on the foundations provided by these operational systems.

Strategy

The predominant strategy at this stage is to actively seek opportunities for the strategic use of IT, to provide a competitive advantage for the organization. This strategy involves substantial environmental scanning. The forces driving IT are predominantly outward looking, with internal operations successfully delegated to other managers.

Structure

Rather than comprising a relatively fixed structure, be it centralized or decentralized, coalitions are now formed between IT and business units in the organization. The 'federal' organization has come of age. Many coalitions are formed, each of them separate, but fitting within the overall plans of the organization, and driven by strategic, corporate (and subsidiary IT) plans. These strategic coalitions flow relatively freely into and out of existence, allowing the organization to respond to changing environmental pressures more readily. The necessary infrastructure (combining elements of both centralization and decentralization) has been put into place in the previous stages to ensure that these fluid coalitions do in fact operate as required, and produce results, both in the short term and the long term (i.e. from a maintenance and an enhancement point of view).

Systems

Systems are now more market-orientated than before. IT is used in an attempt to add value to organizational products and services. This factor, combined with the coalition aspect of the organizational structure in this phase, means most new systems are basically decentralized but with proper central coordination and control. Systems intended to provide a strategic advantage to the organization or to a business unit are developed in this stage. Most of these systems rely heavily on gathering and processing external data in addition to internal data. But in most instances, there is still a distinct lack of real integration between external and internal data. Decision Support Systems (DSS) for senior staff are developed and implemented at this stage. These DSS are possible only because necessary operational systems are in place and integrated appropriately. Most staff have had enough experience associated with IT to be able to specify effectively and use DSS and other Executive Information Systems (EIS).

Staff

The new role at this stage is that of a combined Business and Information Systems Planner. These people are responsible for recognizing and planning for strategic information systems, for the organization as a whole and for individual business units. They have had some years' experience, both in the business (or very similar businesses), and in the IT area (cf. the 'hybrid' concept). They may have come from either area, but are definitely cross-disciplinary.

Style

The predominant style is that of the Product Champion, the rugged individual who conceives of a good idea and pushes it through the necessary approval procedures in order to get it off the ground and working. In this case the idea is for information systems that will lead to a strategic advantage for the organization. Such systems are typically very hard to justify on a standard cost–benefit analysis basis. They require the whole-hearted support of powerful members of the organization to ensure that they are implemented (and even then, they run the risk of being stalled in mid-development).

Skills

This is the stage where IT moves out of the era of being a second string service and support unit, into being an integral part of the successful operation of the organization. The skills required to manage this transition are those of a senior executive. Entrepreneurial and marketing skills within selected IT personnel are also the basic requirements for ensuring success in this stage. Very knowledgeable IT users become quite commonplace. Successful organizations use these people to their full potential, as there is no longer any defensiveness about users acquiring in-depth knowledge about IT use.

Superordinate goals

Opportunity is pre-eminent during this stage. An entrepreneurial (as well as intrapreneurial) attitude is positively encouraged. Everyone is willing to identify and act on opportunities for strategic advantage.

Stage 6 Integrated harmonious relationships

Stage 6 is now reached, the dawning of a new age of sophistication and use of IT. At this stage, one notices harmonious working relationships between IT personnel and other staff in the organization. IT is deeply embedded throughout every aspect of the organization.

Strategy

During this stage, management is concerned with maintaining the comparative strategic advantage that has been hard won in the previous stage(s). This involves a constant reassessment of all uses of IT, both within the organization and in its marketplace(s). Cooperative strategies (strategic alliances) are also in place. Interactive planning, involving monitoring both likely futures as well as present circumstances (cf. Ackoff, 1981), is the focus of strategy formulation.

Structure

The strategic coalitions between IT and business units were somewhat separate and relatively uncontrolled in the previous stage. In this stage, however, they are now centrally coordinated (although not necessarily 'controlled' in any strict sense). An overall corporate view is integrated with the individual business unit views (both the operational and the IT viewpoint).

Systems

Building on the outward-looking strategic of the previous stage, IT now embarks on implementing *inter*-organizational systems (with suppliers, customers, government, etc.). New products and services may now be developed which are IT-based (rather than the technology being first a supporting element).

Staff

During this stage, the IT Head becomes a member of the Board of Directors. This is not a token measure for providing the occasional piece of advice when asked, but rather, as a full member of the Board, the IT Head will play an active part in setting strategic directions. Strategic decisions will then have the required IT element when appropriate from the very beginning, rather than as an afterthought.

Style

The style is now one of interdependence, with IT being but one part of the business team, working together towards making and keeping the organization successful.

Skills

All the skills required of a member of a Board, together with being a senior manager who understands IT and its potentialities, as well as the business, are necessary at this stage. And in keeping with the team approach, IT personnel are very much in tune with the needs and aspirations of the strategic business units with which they work.

Superordinate goals

Interactive planning, harmonious relationships and interdependent team work are the predominant values associated with this stage. The internal focus is on collaborative IT initiatives between groups, brought together to develop strategic information systems products. The external focus is on strategic alliances utilizing shared information systems, and the value chain is extended to include suppliers and customers.

This revised 'stages of growth' model is summarized in Table 2.6.

Application of the revised model

Application of the revised model in the context of the four Perth-based organizations is described in more detail elsewhere (Galliers and Sutherland, 1991). In this context, however, and in subsequent applications, the model has proved useful not only in clarifying the location of each organization in IT maturity terms, but also in providing insights into aspects of IS management and planning which appear to require particular attention. Specific insights into the model's application include the following:

1   Any organization is likely to display characteristics associated with a number of stages for each of the Seven 'S' elements. It is unlikely that any particular organization will find itself entirely within one stage. In addition, it is most likely that different parts of a single organization will be at different stages of growth at any one time. Use of the model in this context provides management with insights into areas/elements requiring particular attention.
2   Elements in early stages of the model must be adequately addressed before related elements in later stages are likely to be successfully undertaken. For instance, Decision Support Systems (DSS) or Executive Information Systems (EIS) are extremely unlikely to be effective without the right kind of basic operational systems/databases in place. Furthermore, an organization simply trying to overcome the large backlog and heavy maintenance load of systems (associated with Stage 2) is unlikely to be able to develop substantial strategic information systems, without further development in, for example, skill levels and planning approaches.

Table 2.6 *A revised 'stages of growth' model (Sutherland and Galliers, 1989, p.23, reproduced in Galliers, 1991, pp.61–62)*

Element	Stage					
	1	*2*	*3*	*4*	*5*	*6*
Strategy	Acquisition of hardware, software, etc.	IT audit Find out and meet user needs (reactive)	Top-down IS planning	Integration, coordination and control	Environmental scanning and opportunity seeking	Maintain comparative strategic advantage Monitor futures Interactive planning
Structure	None	Label of IS Often subordinate to accounting or finance	Data processing department Centralized DP shop End-users running free at Stage 1	Information centres Library records. OA etc. in same unit Information services	SBU coalition(s) (many but separate)	Centrally coordinated coalitions (corporate and SBU views concurrently)
Systems	*Ad hoc* uncconnected Operational Manual and computerized IS Uncoordinated Concentration in financial systems Little maintenance	Many applications Many gaps Overlapping systems Centralized Operational Mainly financial systems Many areas unsatisfied Large backlog Heavy maintenance load	Still mostly centralized Uncontrolled end-user computing Most major business activities covered Database systems	Decentralized approach with some controls, but mostly lack of coordination Some DSS–*ad hoc* Integrated office technology systems	Decentralized systems but central control and coordination Added value systems (more marketing oriented) More DSS–internal, less *ad hoc* Some strategic systems (using external data) Lack of external and internal data integration of communications technologies with computing	Inter-organizational systems (supplier, customer, government links) New IS-based products External–internal data integration

Table 2.6 *(continued)*

Element	Stage					
	1	*2*	*3*	*4*	*5*	*6*
Staff	Programmers/ contractors	Systems analysts DP Manager	IS planners IS Manager Data Base Administrator Data analysts	Business analysts Information Resources Manager (Chief Information Officer)	Corporate/business/ IS planners (one role)	IS Director/ member of board of directors
Style	Unaware	Don't bother me (I'm too busy)	Abrogation/ delegation	Democratic dialectic	Individualistic (product champion)	Business team
Skills	Technical (very low level), individual expertise	Systems development methodology	IS believes it knows what the business needs Project management	Organizational integration IS knows how the business works Users know how IS works (for their area) Business management (for IS staff)	IS Manager – member of senior executive team Knowledgeable users in some IS areas Entrepreneurial marketing skills	All senior management understand IS and its potentialities
Superordinate goals	Obfuscation	Confusion	Senior management concern DP defence	Cooperation	Opportunistic Entrepreneurial Intrapreneurial	Interactive planning

3   Organizations do not need to work slavishly through all the elements of each stage, making the same mistakes as many organizations have done in the past. For example, 'young' organizations can make effective use of top-down information systems planning to circumvent some of the pitfalls associated with this aspect of the first two stages. Typically, however 'skipping' portions of the model can only be successfully accomplished when the senior management of the organization has already experienced the conditions that affect performance in the earlier stages, and thus understand the benefit/advantages of following 'correct' procedures.

4   The positive aspects of earlier stages of the model are not discarded when moving through to the later stages. More 'mature' organizations will incorporate those elements from all proceeding stages to the degree that they are consistent with the later stages. Thus, organization at Stage 5 will still perform Information Systems Planning, they will still have a DP function (of sorts) and will be likely to require Information Centres. The more mature organization will be flexible enough to determine the most appropriate nature of IT use and organization, rather than blindly following the structures and procedures adopted by other organizations.

5   To be effective, organizations should consolidate in most elements up to a particular stage, and then select certain key elements (in accordance with their own planning critiera/priorities), which they should then address in moving to the next stage. Indeed, all elements should be addressed in order to pass more smoothly on to the following stage.

6   It is not necessarily the case that organizations will develop *automatically* towards the more mature stages. Indeed, it has been found that organizations move 'backwards' at times, as a result of a change in personnel or managerial attitudes, see Galliers (1991) for example. Furthermore, it has proved useful at times to chart the development of the organization over a period of time by identifying when (i.e. in what year) each particular stage was reached.

The model has been found to be particularly useful in that it takes a holistic view of information systems management issues, dealing as it does with the development of information systems applications and information systems planning/strategy formulation, the changing nature of required skills, management style/involvement, and organizational structures. While the model cannot pretend to give all the *answers*, it does provide a framework which enables appropriate *questions* to be raised when setting out an appropriate strategy for information systems, giving pointers as to what is feasible as well as desirable in this regard.

Further testing and refinement of the model is taking place, but after two years of application, the authors are confident that the model is sufficiently refined to provide both IT and general management with a usable and useful framework to assist in the task of marshalling their IT resources in line with business imperatives.

While one might argue with the precise detail of the contents of each element at each stage of the model, this does appear not to affect the utility. Its key contribution is in focusing management attention onto a broad range of issues associated with the planning and management of information systems, in surfacing assumptions and attitudes held by key executives about the role IT does and might play in achieving/supporting business objectives and thereby enabling a shared understanding/vision to be achieved, and (most importantly) providing an easily understood means of putting IS/IT management on the senior and middle management agenda.

References

Ackoff, R. L. (1981) *Creating the Corporate Future*, Wiley, New York.

British Computer Society (1990) *From Potential to Reality: 'Hybrids' – A Critical Force in the Application of Information Technology in the 1990s*. A Report by the British Computer Society Task Group on Hybrids, 2 January.

Benbasat, I., Dexter, A., Drury, D. and Goldstein, R. (1984) A critique of the stage hypothesis: theory and empirical evidence. *Communications of the ACM*, **27**(5), 476–485.

Bhabuta, L. (1988) Sustaining productivity and competitiveness by marshalling IT. In *Proceedings: Information Technology Management for Productivity and Strategic Advantage*, IFIP TC-8 Open Conference, Singapore, March.

Cash, J. I. (Jr.) and Konsynski, B. R. (1985) IS Redraws competitive boundaries. *Harvard Business Review*, **63**(2), March–April, 134–142.

Earl, M. J. (1983) Emerging trends in managing new information technologies, Oxford Centre for Management Studies Research Paper 83/4. In *The Management Implications of New Information Technology*. (ed. N. Peircy), 1986, Croom Helm, London.

Earl, M. J. (1986) Information systems strategy formulation. In *Critical Issues in Information Systems Research* (eds R. J. Boland and R. A. Hirschheim) (1987), Wiley, Chichester.

Earl, M. J. (ed.) (1988) *Information Management: The Strategic Dimension*, The Clarendon Press, Oxford.

Earl, M. J. (1989) *Management Strategies for Information Technology*, Prentice Hall, Hemel Hempstead.

Edwards, B., Earl, M. and Feeny, D. (1989) Any way out of the labyrinth of managing IS? RDP89/3, Oxford Institute of Information Management Research and Discussion Paper, Templeton College, Oxford University.

Galliers, R. D. (1987a) Information systems planning in the United Kingdom and Australia: a comparison of current practice. In *Oxford Surveys in*

Information Technology (ed. P. I. Zorkorczy), Vol. 4, Oxford University Press, Oxford, pp.223–255.

Galliers, R. D. (ed.) (1987b) *Information Analysis: Selected Readings*, Addison-Wesley, Wokingham.

Galliers, R. D. (1990) Problems and answers of the IT skills shortage. *The Computer Bulletin*, **2**(4), 25 May.

Galliers, R. D. (1991) Strategic information systems planning: myths, reality and guidelines for successful implementation. *European Journal of Information Systems*, **1**, 55–64.

Galliers, R. D. and Sutherland, A. R. (1991) Organizational learning and IT: steps towards managing and planning strategic information systems. *Warwick Business School Working Paper*, University of Warwick, January.

Gibson, D. and Nolan, R. L. (1974) Managing the four stages of EDP growth. *Harvard Business Review*, **52**(1), January–February.

Gluck, F. W., Kaufman, S. P. and Walleck, A. S. (1980) Strategic management for competitive advantage. *Harvard Business Review*, **58**(4), July–August.

Greiner, L. E. (1972) Evolution and revolution as organisations grow. *Harvard Business Review*, **50**(4), July–August.

Hamilton, S. and Ives, B. (1982) Knowledge utilisation among MIS researchers. *MIS Quarterly*, **6**(12), December.

Hirschheim, R., Earl, M., Feeny, D. and Lockett, M. (1988) An exploration into the management of the information systems function: key issues and an evolutionary model. *Proceedings: Information Technology Management for Productivity and Strategic Advantage*, IFIP TC-8 Open Conference, Singapore, March.

King, J. and Kraemer, K. (1984) Evolution and organizational information systems: an assessment of Nolan's stage model. *Communications of the ACM*, **27**(5), May.

Land, F. F. (1982) Adapting to changing user requirements. *Information and Management*, **5**, Reproduced in Galliers, R. D. (ed.) (1987) *Information Analysis: selected readings*, Addison-Wesley, Wokingham, pp.203–229.

McFarlan, F. W. and McKenney, J. L. (1982) The Information archipelago: gaps and bridges. *Harvard Business Review*, **60**(5), September–October.

McFarlan, F. W., McKenney, J. L. and Pyburn, P. (1983) The information archipelago: plotting a course. *Harvard Business Review*, **61**(1), January–February.

Nolan, R. (1979) Managing the crises in data processing. *Harvard Business Review*, **57**(2), March–April.

Nolan, R. (1984) Managing the advanced stages of computer technology: key research issues. In *The Information Systems Research Challenge* (ed. F. W. McFarlan), Harvard Business School Press, Boston, pp.195–214.

Oliver, I. and Langford, H. (1984) Myths of demons and users. *Proceedings: Australian Computer Conference*, Australian Computer Society Inc., Sydney,

November. Reproduced in Galliers, R. D. (ed.) (1987) *Information Analysis: selected readings*, Addison-Wesley, Wokingham, pp.113–123.

Pascale, R. T. and Athos, A. G. (1981) *The Art of Japanese Management*, Penguin, Harmondsworth.

Sobkowich, R. (1985) When the company picks a CIO, will you be IT? *Computerworld*, 24 June.

Somogyi, E. K. and Galliers, R. D. (1987a) Applied information technology: from data processing to strategic information systems. *Journal of Information Technology*, **2**(1), 30–41, March.

Somogyi, E. K. and Galliers, R. D. (1987b) *Towards Strategic Information Systems*, Abacus Press, Cambridge MA.

Sullivan, C. H. (1985) Systems planning in the information age. *Sloan Management Review*, Winter.

Sutherland, A. R. and Galliers, R. D. (1989) An evolutionary model to assist in the planning of strategic information systems and the management of the information systems function. *School of Information Systems Working Paper*. Curtin University of Technology, Perth. Western Australia, February.

Ward, J., Griffiths, P. and Whitmore, P. (1990) *Strategic Planning for Information Systems*, Wiley, Chichester.

Reproduced from Galliers, R. D. and Sutherland, A. R. (1991) Information systems management and strategy formulation: the 'stages of growth' model revisited. *Journal of Information Systems*, **1**(2), 89–114. Reprinted by permission of the Publishers, Blackwell Scientific Ltd.

Questions for discussion

1   The authors, in describing the Nolan model, state that 'different parts of a single organization may well be at different stages of growth with respect to a single IT'. What implications does this have for the management of IT and for IT strategy?

2   The authors describe several prior models to IT evolution in organizations. What are the relative strengths of the models in (a) their applicability to describe actual situations, and (b) in their usefulness for managers of IT?

3   Do you agree with the underlying assumption that moving through the stages represents a desired advancement in the use of IT in an organization?

4   Can you think of some contextual factors that might predict in which phase an organization would be placed regarding their management of IT and whether they move slowly or quickly through the phases?

5   What implications does the increasing pace of technology advances and the increasingly networked world have for the revised stages of growth model?

3 Information Strategy

Assessment of information strategies in insurance companies

M. T. Smits, K. G. van der Poel and P. M. A. Ribbers

This chapter describes the information strategies of three major insurance companies in the Netherlands. A research model was developed as an aid to describe how managers nowadays deal with information strategy. We report on the linkages between information strategies and business strategies, the roles of the stakeholders involved, and how the results are perceived. We found that in all three companies the executive board, IT management and line management are heavily involved in the information strategy process. The main focus in the three companies is on adjusting IT to business goals and processes, with only some attention directed towards creating a competitive advantage with IT. With respect to the effects of information strategy, we found that none of the three companies systematically evaluate the effects of information strategies on an organizational or a business process level. More case study research is required to look into the evolutionary changes of information strategies within organizations, and the effects of information strategies on the business processes and the use of IT over time.

1 Introduction

The concept of 'strategy' carries several connotations. Its roots in military tradition indicate innovative leadership and bold visions. Anthony (1965) has defined strategic planning as the definition of goals and objectives. Ansoff (1984) sees strategy as a mechanism for coping with a complex and changing environment. Mintzberg (1980) views strategy in five different ways: as a plan (rules leading to a goal); a ploy (a trick to beat competitors); a pattern (a way of behaving); a position (a safe place); and a perspective (a vision, a set of assumptions). Andrews (1980) defines strategy as: 'the pattern of decisions . . . that determines . . . goals, produces principal policies and plans and defines the range of business'.

In general, the concept of strategy relates to corporate strategy, which is the strategy that guides the corporation or enterprise as a whole. Business units within large organizations have business strategies related to their specific product-market situation (Porter, 1987). From corporate or business strategy derives the notion of functional strategies such as marketing strategy, manufacturing strategy, personnel strategy, financial strategy and information strategy. Of interest are the linkages between the functional strategies and the business strategies. Specifically, business strategy and information strategy can be linked in several ways (Parker *et al.*, 1989; Henderson and Venkatraman, 1993).

In this chapter we investigate whether these (theoretical) linkages exist in organizations with a substantial level of sophistication and interest in information management. We describe how managers in these organizations formulate information strategies in practice, which stakeholders are involved, how it links to business strategy, and how the results are perceived. This is done within the context of previous information strategy activities, looking for possible changes in the approach to information strategy. Our purpose is to learn how information intensive organizations make plans with respect to the demand and supply of information, and how this relates to the planning of IT. The research question in this chapter is three-fold: (i) how can the practice of information strategy in an organization be analysed; (ii) what is the actual practice in the insurance industry; and (iii) how does information strategy relate to business strategy?

After scanning the literature we decided to carry out case studies within a small number of organizations, based on interviews with both IS managers as well as general managers, in order to provide a richness in understanding strategy that cannot be obtained via a survey approach (Chan and Huff, 1992). We describe the planning process for information strategies as well as the contents of the plans, as suggested by King (1988) and Walsham and Waema (1994). A framework to analyse an organization's information strategy was derived from the literature and used to gather information from both informants and secondary sources, e.g. company documents. The following section summarizes the information strategy literature, while Section 3 provides an overview of the model used in this research. The final two sections use this model to analyse the information strategy within three major insurance organizations and compare the findings with related research, respectively.

2   Literature on information strategy

Information strategy began to attract interest at the beginning of the 1970s, and many terms have been used since then to address the alignment of information systems and business strategy. Similar terms are, for example, information

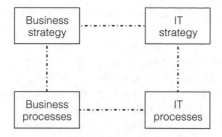

Figure 3.1 *Strategic alignment model (Parker* et al.*, 1989; Henderson and Venkatraman, 1993)*

systems strategy (ISS), information systems strategic planning (ISSP) and strategic information systems planning (SISP). For an extensive review of the literature we refer to Earl (1989), Ward *et al.* (1990), Galliers (1993) and Fitzgerald (1993).

A frequently used term, related to information strategy, is strategic information systems planning (SISP), defined as 'the process of deciding the objectives for organizational computing and identifying potential computer applications which the organization should implement' (Lederer and Sethi, 1988). However, Galliers (1991) views information strategy as only a part of SISP, together with information technology (IT) strategy, information management (IM) strategy, management of change strategy, and human resources strategy. Earl (1989) sees SISP as a combination of information systems strategy (aligning IS with business goals, and exploiting IT for competitive advantage), IM strategy and IT strategy.

In this study we used the term information strategy, and define it as: 'a complex of implicit or explicit visions, goals, guidelines and plans with respect to the supply and the demand of formal information in an organization, sanctioned by management, intended to support the objectives of the organization in the long run, while being able to adjust to the environment'. The definitions might look similar, but strict comparison shows that the SISP definition tends to focus on explicit objectives and on applications and technology. Our definition concentrates on the use and importance of information in an organization, starting with the planning of information (in the end influencing IT, as well as influenced by IT). Therefore we preferred this definition as a starting point to investigate how contemporary organizations deal with their needs for information and the planning of IT. The other three definitions mentioned were subsequently used to complete the research model and to develop the questionnaires, as described in Section 3.

Of particular importance is the linkage between the information strategy and the business strategy in an organization (Parker *et al.*, 1989). Henderson and Venkatraman (1993) propose the strategic alignment model (Figure 3.1) covering the linkages between four domains in an organization: (i) the business strategy domain (BS); (ii) the business processes domain (BP); (iii) the IT strategy domain (ITS); and (iv) the IT processes domain (ITP). They distinguish two main perspectives on how the alignment between the domains can take place. In the first perspective business strategy is the driving force for BP or ITS, ultimately affecting ITP. In the second perspective IT strategy is the driving force for ITP or BS, ultimately affecting BP.

We have analysed the linkages between information strategy and business strategy in several ways: by looking at the attitudes of senior managers (as a part of the information strategy environment), by analysing the information strategy process (with roles, methods and coordination), by analysing the content of the strategy, and by looking at how the effects are evaluated. As a support for these analyses we used the research model, explained in the next section.

3   Research model

The purpose of the model is to provide a framework for case study research into the actual practice of information strategy in contemporary organizations. We wanted to use the model as guideline for structured interviews with managers from various departments and levels, and as a framework to categorize the findings. The model used in this study focuses on four issues: environment, process, form and content, and effects of information strategy. The four components of the model are related to each other in several ways. The main relationship is that the environment influences the process which produces the content (being the output of the strategy process), which yields the effects, which change the environment (the impact or outcome of the strategy) and so close the loop.

There is a fair amount of similarity between this model and the input–process–output (IPO) model of King (1988): the planning process (P) converts several inputs (I) from the environment into a set (O) of mission, objectives, strategies, goals, resource allocations, information architectures and strategic programmes. The main difference is that the IPO model is more prescriptive (specifying components and relationships that should exist in SISP) whereas our model is descriptive and intended to provide structure to the collection of data from interviews and company documents.

The model in Figure 3.2 is based on the ideas of contextualism (Pettigrew, 1987) to consider a strategy in terms of three interrelated components: context, process and content. In contextualism, the main focus of research is to trace the dynamic interlinking between aspects of the components over time. This can be done via longitudinal studies, or, as in the present study, by in-depth retrospect analysis of case material and interviews (Orlikowsky and

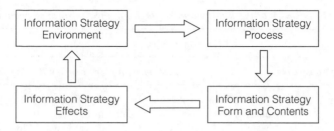

Figure 3.2 *Research model describing four components of information strategy*

Baroudi, 1991; Walsham and Waema, 1994). One important link is how previous strategies affect the actual environment, and how this again influences the strategy process and content. In our model, the context is split into the information strategy environment and the information strategy effects. In this way we could discriminate in our interviews between: (i) 'circumstances influencing the strategy process'; (ii) 'effects and impact of current and previous strategies'; and (iii) 'how (ii) influences the current process'.

In the case of information strategy, contextualism encompasses also the relationships between aspects of information strategy, the IT processes, the business strategy and the business processes (Figure 3.1). A comparison of our model with the model in Figure 3.1 shows that we focus on four components of information strategy, and that business strategy, business processes and IT processes form parts of the two (left side) components. Together these two form the context of information strategy. In Sections 3.1, 3.2, 3.3 and 3.4 the aspects of the four components of the model and the linkages are described in more detail. An overview of the aspects of the four components is given in Table 3.1.

3.1 The information strategy environment

The environment is defined here as all those facts and conditions which are not part of the information strategy itself, nor of the information strategy process, but that can or should influence either of those. There are two distinct views in the literature on factors that are important in the environment. One view categorizes organizations, and describing factors common to all organizations in a category. The second view does not try to group organizations, but just lists environmental factors.

The first view is, for instance, contained in the strategic grid (McFarlan, 1984), namely that conditions in the industry in which a firm operates largely set the scene for its information strategy. The external conditions in the line of industry determine the amount of strategic importance of current and future IT applications for organizations in the industry. Explicit emphasis

Table 3.1   *Summary of the information strategies in three insurance companies*

		Information strategy		
Components/aspects		*In company A*	*In company B*	*In company C*
Environment	Position in the industry	Second tier	Dominant/ niche	Top
	Main distribution channel	Bank	Direct writer	Intermediaries
	Special factor	Recently merged	About to merge	Partner in ADN
	Company revenue	$2000M	$2000M	$3000M
	Employees	2000	2000	4000
	Business strategy	Explicit, known	Explicit, known	Explicit, known
	Internal organization	Product oriented	Market oriented	Product oriented
	Management attitude to IT	Positive	Very positive	Very positive
	IT expenditures/ revenue	< 2%	> 2%	< 2%
	Existing architecture	Central/ decentral	Two tiered	Centralised
Process	Process type	Mech/problem	Political/mech	Mech/political
	Overall methodology	No	No	No
	IT scanning	Yes	Informal	Informal
	SWOT	Informal	Occasionally	Informal
	CSF	No	Occasionally	No
	Role top management	Dominant	Active	Active
	Line management	Active	Active	Present
	IT management	Active	Dominant	Dominant
	Planning specialist	One	–	–
	External consultant	–	–	–
	Alignment	Yes	Yes	Yes
	Impact	Not clear	Yes	Yes
	Organizational learning	No	Some	Some

Table 3.1 *(continued)*

		Information strategy		
Components/aspects		In company A	In company B	In company C
Form and content	Time horizon	Five years	Three years	Three years
	Scope	IS/IT	IS/IT/telecom	IS/IT
	Objectives	Very specific	Explicit	Implicit
	Systems architecture	Evolving	Extensive, clear	Implicit
	Technical architecture	Evolving	Clear	Clear
	Organizational architecture	Clear	Clear	Clear
	Rules, alliances	Implicit, few	Implicit, few	Implicit, strict
	Plans	Projects	Projects, budgets	Projects, budgets
Effects	User satisfaction	Not measured	Not measured	Not measured
	Project results	Evaluated	Evaluated	Evaluated
	Bottom line results	Not measured	Tentative	Not measured

on the environment is also described by Earl (1989), who distinguishes four types of companies with particular traits and preferences for IT, labelled as delayed, drive, dependent and delivery.

The second view in the literature encompasses those authors that search for 'success factors' (or the inverse: 'causes for failure'), to the extent that they attempt to relate the success or failure of information strategies to external factors. Many authors pay attention to specific factors, and several authors give lists and descriptions of factors, such as 'clarity of corporate strategy', 'IT planning resources', 'IT budget', 'future impact of IT', 'present impact of IT' (Premkumar, 1992); 'internal and external political power', 'importance of information', 'experience in planning', 'attitudes to change' (Hopstaken and Kranendonk, 1985); 'uncertainty of IS benefits', 'availability of IT' (Wilson, 1989).

In the context of this study it is not possible to investigate all potential influences, but we provide some structure by dividing the environment of information strategy in four aspects, as shown in Table 3.2:

- *IT opportunities.* These do not indicate only hardware, but also the capabilities of contractors and available services. As IT expands and breaks into sub-specializations, organizations might want to use some form of technology scanning to evaluate the capabilities.

Table 3.2   *Four aspects of the environment of information strategy*

	Technological environment	Organizational environment
External environment	IT opportunities	Position in industry
Internal environment	IT resources	Nature of the organization

- *The position in the industry*, also including competitive and cooperative forces at work in the industry, such as market segmentation and barriers to entry or existing EDI networks.
- *The nature of the organization* includes simple to measure factors such as the size and the financial results of the company, but also factors more difficult to express, such as the organizational structure, the nature and clarity of the corporate strategy and the awareness and attitude of senior management towards IT.
- *The IT resources* reflect past investments in systems, hardware, procedures and people. They are the results of previous information strategies and now determine the competence of the organization to realize the chosen strategy. A specific category is formed by the resources available for the information strategy process, in terms of time, manpower and organizational attention.

3.2   The information strategy process

The information strategy process describes the way in which the information strategy is created or changed. The process dimension of information strategy is borrowed from the step by step methodologies summarized by Theeuwes (1987), King (1988), and others. Added to this are ideas about the importance of the linkage between corporate strategy and information strategy, in the form of 'impact' and 'alignment' (Parker *et al.*, 1989; Henderson and Venkatraman, 1993). This component of the model also distinguishes four main aspects.

An overriding aspect is what is called *process type* (Earl, 1993). Here we employ the typology of Schwenk (1988), who distinguishes three types of strategy process. First, the mechanical type describes a typical mechanistic approach: strategy is the result of a systematic stepwise process, consisting of the right people in the right positions, one group being the engine and another group manipulating the steering wheel. Second, the problem-oriented type describes strategy as the result of the more informal and continuous (learning) process of seeing opportunities and solving problems. Third, the political type describes strategy as the result of personal, political power relations in the organization. A typical statement of a manager in the political model, indicating the personal power and culture, is 'IT strategy? That's me!'.

The core of the information strategy process is defined on the one hand by *methodologies and tools* and on the other hand by *participants and their roles*. These two aspects are closely related, as methodologies often imply certain tools and roles. Methodologies, such as, for example, BSP (Zachman, 1982), typically divide the process in a number of steps and also define the tools or instruments that should be used, such as SWOT analysis (Johnson and Scholes, 1989) or CSF analysis (Rockart, 1979). An important determinant of the information strategy process is the distribution of the responsibility and the roles between the main participants in the process. A distinction is generally made between top management, IS management and line management, but participation by outsiders such as consultants or planning specialists may also be a factor. Two other issues stand out and require attention in this context: the use and functioning of steering committees and the mechanisms used for, and the effectiveness of the linkage between business strategy and information strategy. Both issues have recently been the subject of research (Feeney and Edwards, 1992; Saaksjarvi, 1994).

The final aspect is how and to what extent *organizational learning* is explicitly recognized as part of the strategy process. Presumably, organizations will always learn something from strategic experiences. The question we asked here is whether any mechanisms such as controlled experiments, executive seminars or analysis of the results of previous strategies are part of the information strategy process? The use of such learning activities has been described by Ruohonen (1991) and Lanc (1992).

3.3 The information strategy form and content

Ideas about the form and content of an information strategy were derived from several models from the literature, describing relations between IS, IT and organization. The form of the information strategy defines some formal characteristics, such as the degree of formality, regularity of the documentation, the number of documents and pages used for expressing and communicating the strategy, and the time horizon (Mintzberg, 1991).

The content describes the subject areas or 'issues' for which the strategy is meant to provide solutions or directions. This is likely to be reflected in the contents page of the strategy documentation. The main aspects of the content of the information strategy are scope, objectives, architectures, rules and plans (e.g. Earl, 1989). *Scope* denotes the range of specific types of IT covered in the information strategy (for example, only transaction processing and management information systems, or also telecommunications, office automation or manual information processing) (Blumenthal, 1969; Theeuwes, 1987). *Objectives* are conceived as specific and quantified. They are the targets set for the information function, and the linkages between these targets and the business objectives (Parker *et al.*, 1989; Scott Morton, 1991). The *architectures* can be divided into three parts: systems (or applications), technical and organizational. The applications architecture is sometimes equated to the information strategy and may indeed be the core of it. The technical architecture defines the hardware elements that support the information strategy, notably in the form of an infrastructure. The organizational architecture indicates the distribution of tasks and responsibilities for IT and IS (Theeuwes, 1987). *Rules* include guidelines and standards (or policies) which set a framework for decisions, such as a hurdle rate for investments. It also includes alliances, an increasingly important category of rules concerning make-or-buy decisions (Parker *et al.*, 1989). *Plans* in an information strategy are normally limited to priorities and budgets and do not include detailed designs and project plans (Theeuwes, 1987).

3.4   The information strategy effects

It is important to have effective information strategy planning and effective information strategies, in order to obtain effective IT in organizations (Henderson and Sifonis, 1988; Fitzgerald, 1993; Premkumar and King, 1991). However, measuring the effects of information strategies is very difficult, for several reasons, typically related to the evaluation of strategies in general (King, 1988).

First, there is the time aspect: effects cannot be determined reliably at one moment in time, nor over a fixed period, because the effects can vary significantly over the year(s). Secondly, there is an allocation aspect: it is very difficult to allocate the costs, benefits, people, products, etc. to the specific effects of the information strategy. Thirdly, there is an evolutionary aspect: the information strategy in organizations changes over time, and can only be examined by using 'historical documents' or by 'looking back interviews'. Both are highly subjective sources. Fourthly, there is the scope aspect: the effects of an information strategy can be measured from several scopes of vision, such as:

- the (narrow) scope of one systems development project as result of the information strategy
- the (narrow) scope of changes in the business strategy as results of the information strategy
- the (intermediate) scope of the performance (quality) of the systems development function
- the (intermediate) scope of the performance (quality) of a specific information system, and
- the (broad) scope of (all) information services in the organization (Laudon and Laudon, 1996).

The aspects for which each scope can be measured range from user satisfaction to costs and profits, or market performance of the business unit or the entire organization. We have asked the respondents 'if and how the effects of information strategy are measured'.

3.5 Research method

The model is an aid during the interviews, and structures the description of the information strategy in an organization. It is not a normative model, giving a prescription for the most effective strategy. The model was used to develop two questionnaires to be used in interviews with managers involved with information strategy. The first questionnaire is highly structured (along the aspects of the four components of the model as described in Sections 3.1, 3.2, 3.3 and 3.4), and contains open-ended as well as 'yes–no' questions. It is intended to obtain both factual and attitudinal information from people functionally involved with information strategy (typically IS managers and functional managers). The second questionnaire consists mainly of open-ended questions. It leads from questions about factual decisions taken in the previous years to the discussion of the value and appreciation of information strategy. The second questionnaire is intended to steer interviews with top executives. These relatively open interviews were held after analysis of company documents and the interview results of the first questionnaire. The second questionnaire deals with:

- the key (IS related) decisions taken in the previous years (reasons, effects)
- the information strategy process and the roles of different parties in the organization, and
- the value of the information strategy activities.

The following procedure was followed to investigate the practice of information strategy in each insurance company.

Step 1: Structured interviews (based on the first questionnaire) with the senior IS manager and a senior manager(s) from the business domain.
Step 2: Analysis of written materials (information plans and business plans). The plans were also screened for approximately five specific key decisions.
Step 3: An interview with a member of the executive board (based on the second questionnaire).
Step 4: All collected materials were used to write a detailed case description.

Each interview was taken by two interviewers. The results of each step were returned to the respondents for comments and adjustments. The final result is a validated case description, describing and assessing the information strategy from different perspectives. This procedure resembles the Delphi procedure (Turoff, 1970), whereby several persons are interviewed individually and afterwards confronted anonymously with the variety of responses. Based on the comments, the case descriptions are adjusted several times, until they are acceptable to the parties involved. In the three cases we investigated all respondents gave feedback at least once, participated sincerely, and added notably to the case descriptions. By following these procedures a validated view is obtained from complex subjects such as strategy (Turoff, 1970).

3.6   Three cases in a competitive environment

To select suitable cases for our purpose, we looked for: (i) substantial organizations, with a vested interest in information systems, so that it may be expected that both concepts and practice of information strategy are reasonably familiar; (ii) a branch of industry or commerce where information plays a substantial role; and (iii) an independent organization or business unit with complete or near complete control over its own information strategy. These criteria resulted in the selection of three organizations in the insurance industry, identified as A, B and C. To provide some background about the insurance industry, a sketch of the competitive environment is given below.

Insurance is a sizeable industry in the Netherlands. The total insurance market (excluding pension funds and health insurance) in the Netherlands is nearly $2000 per inhabitant, in total about $30 billion per year. The insurance market in the Netherlands is dominated by about 10 large firms. Insurance companies differentiate themselves through their distribution channels. An insurance company can sell its policies by means of 'direct marketing' (directly to the public and to professional clients), or via 'agents' or independent intermediaries, such as brokers, shops or banks. In particular the bank channel has become very important due to the recent changes in Dutch legislation which has permitted closer cooperation between banks, insurance companies and other financial institutions. As a consequence of the new legislation, several insurance companies have entered into mergers or alliances with banks.

The opening of the Common Market has broadened competition amongst insurance companies in Europe. This has been a factor in the trend towards greater concentration in the industry, as evidenced by takeovers and mergers between insurance companies on a national as well as on a European scale, combining specific (niche) markets and distribution channels.

The primary process of an insurance company relies heavily on information processing. Next to data processing in the back office, recently communication technology has also been used to link the various parties in the value chain. Of importance is the development of the 'assurance data network' (ADN). ADN is a value-added wide area network between insurance companies and their intermediaries. Insurance companies are also known to experiment with and use other advanced information technologies, such as the linking of voice and data processing facilities, and the use of expert systems to support decision making.

4 Findings

In Section 4.1 we give a relatively detailed description of our findings on the information strategy in company A. In Section 4.2 we summarize the findings in the three companies.

4.1 Company A

4.1.1 The information strategy environment

Company A is a large-to-medium sized insurance company, located and active in the Netherlands and dominant in certain niche markets. In 1991 its revenue was over $2000 million and it employed over 2000 people. It has traditionally strong links with one of the large banks in the Netherlands and the offices of that bank form an important distribution channel. In 1991 the company made profits of around $70 million, and it has had a steady development of revenue and profits during the period under investigation.

The corporate position of company A has changed significantly over the last few years. The volume of business has more than doubled, partly by growth, and partly by takeover of specialist and regional competitors. In the wake of the changes in the legal framework for financial and insurance organizations in the Netherlands, the company has entered into a complex merger with a large bank, thus formalizing and intensifying the already existing cooperation. The merger has been reflected in the appointment of some new directors.

The interviewees indicated that they considered the corporate mission and objectives of the company to be clear and well known. Corporate objectives are established annually by the board of directors after an extensive and formal process of consultation. This process was instituted in 1989 and involves a cycle of documentation, conferences and review. Top-management appears to be well aware of the importance of information technology and intend to promote its use, as witnessed by the following statement in the annual report over 1991: 'Information technology is of increasing importance in the financial services industry. An important competitive advantage can be created by making the company distinguish itself from other service providers by means of information technology'.

The main organizational structure of company A consists of a division life insurance and a division short-term (damages) insurance. These divisions have profit responsibility and have their own directors. There is a department of organization and information (O&A) which has a central responsibility for information systems and automation resources. Overall responsibility rests with the Board of Directors. One of the directors holds the portfolio 'automation'. The incumbent has held this position since 1992.

The O&A department consists of around 150 people, including one staff position for strategic planning. A few years ago, when it was last reported, automation expenditure was 2.3 per cent of revenue. Until 1985, the IT infrastructure consisted of large (IBM) mainframes. Since then, separate facilities for office automation have been added and a network of PCs and workstations has been installed. Recently, the data communication facilities with the offices of the partner-bank are being strengthened.

4.1.2   The information strategy process

The first impression of the information strategy process was of a mechanistic process type. The production of the annual 'information plan' is part of the strictly formalized and scheduled corporate planning process. Plans are conceived and written by O&A management and are (after extensive comment by other departments) sanctioned by the board. This was the way in which O&A management saw information strategy. However, subsequent discussions brought to light that during the year many new initiatives with a highly strategic content were taken. This usually happened in response to problems or suggestions from one of the operating divisions and was debated at board level. The portfolio holder in the board of directors played an active role in this. In this sense, the information strategy process was at least partly of the problem-driven type.

Company A did not use a 'commercial' methodology for information strategy, but from time to time used methods such as environmental scanning and SWOT analysis in a more or less formal manner. The O&A department participated in the information strategy process through involvement of the senior manager and of the special staff assistant. Their role was largely to analyse and to make proposals. Line managers from other departments influenced the process directly and indirectly, by making their needs and wishes known, sometimes to the point of insisting on a particular solution. The board had a very significant input and involved itself frequently and emphatically. There were no consultants involved, but there was a beginning of harmonization with the partner-bank. There was some attention to organizational learning, e.g. in the form of an evaluation of the effects of plans, but there was little evidence of conscious development or exploitation of experiences.

4.1.3   The information strategy form and content

There is much emphasis on formal documentation. Four planning documents were studied, covering the period 1986–1997, in total 218 pages. The plans cover information systems and office automation, but not telecommunications. The planning documents cover overlapping periods of 3–5 years. The plans are explicitly anchored in the corporate strategy and make reference to the corporate goals. Increasingly explicit goals and objectives are specified for the IS function, particularly in the most recent planning document. The plans give much prominence to application system development, without demonstrating a clear application architecture. Most attention goes to the production-oriented systems. There is no explicit attention to systems for competitive advantage, but implicitly this is present in attention to cost saving and close cooperation with the partner-bank. The hardware architecture or the organizational structures form implicit parts of the plans, but are not explicitly developed. There is some apparent tension in the jurisdiction over decentralized hardware and systems staff. Over the years the responsibilities slowly shift to the operating divisions, but the manager O&A retains overall responsibility.

Rules and controls are most of the time not a point of discussion in the plans. There is no mention of a steering committee or any other rules or mechanisms to guide IS efforts. However, the last plan specifies quantitative goals that are intended to be evaluated at the end of the planning period. There is a two-vendor hardware policy, but other forms of alliances are not discussed. The increasingly close relationship with the partner-bank is accepted as fact.

To characterize the strategic issues with which the management of company A was most concerned, four key decisions that dominated the information strategy agenda in the past few years were identified. They were:

1 Continuous support for the company-specific client/server model for interaction between corporate offices and intermediaries. Though the real costs had exceeded the original budget by many millions of dollars, the company had stuck to the concept and expected to reap the benefits in terms of competitive position in the next few years.
2 Partial decentralization of control over system development resources, which gave the operating divisions control over priorities for system development, leaving the IS department in a secondary role.
3 Deviation from the in-house development tradition by purchasing a comprehensive application package for the life insurance division.
4 Initiation of discussions with the partner-bank about information strategy issues. This might eventually lead to a decrease in the level of independence of the information strategy.

Finally, the manager O&A indicated his concern about the tension over the distribution of responsibilities for IT by adopting the battle cry 'Divide et impera' ('distribute and control').

4.1.4   The information strategy effects

Company A has developed a substantial IT infrastructure in the course of time. The core of the hardware architecture is formed by the central mainframes with the attached terminal network. More recently some decentralized processing capability has been added. The application architecture is extensive and has been painstakingly developed over the years. However, the application architecture no longer satisfies the requirements, and there is substantial pressure to make rapid enhancements. To this end experiments with software packages have been initiated, started and managed by the operating divisions. These pressures on the application architecture are largely due to new ways of doing business, particularly through the relationship with the partner-bank. Due to these pressures, the O&A organization is also under pressure. The new demands often do not match the available capabilities and the general atmosphere is certainly not relaxed.

Company A carefully screens and justifies all IT projects. However, cost overruns do occur, causing substantial concern at board level. No formal overall evaluation is made and opinions of users are not formally sampled. The board and the management of O&A are both aware of certain misgivings about the IT services in the company, but are convinced that IT is an essential and in the long run a beneficial investment. They are somewhat more dubious about the benefits of the effort spent on the preparation of formal information planning documents.

Management does not consider it possible to relate the investments in IT directly to corporate performance. The ratio of administrative expenses to premium income has decreased a little over the last few years, but it is not considered possible to assign this to automation efforts alone. The net profit margin is currently 3 per cent, but this tends to fluctuate under the influence of developments in damage claims.

4.1.5   Reflection

This case shows the importance of the clarification of terminology. In several interviews time needed to be taken, both at the beginning and during the discussions, to establish a common vocabulary. Without this, the wrong conclusions could easily be drawn. Also, different views on the real issues of the information strategy needed to be reconciled (in our case study research as well as in the company itself). This was inevitable, as various managers contributed to the information strategy from their own interest and expertise. Information strategy also proved to be a sensitive subject and it took some time and mutual trust before true facts and opinions came on the table.

The dominant attitude at company A appeared to be one of concern. The underlying culture was cooperative and collegial, but recent (merger) events had introduced a sense of coming change of which the direction was not yet clear.

Linkage between information strategy and business strategy appears to be assured, because of the diverse group of managers involved in the process, the high amount of time (20 per cent) spent to information strategy by the board of directors, and partial decentralization of system development resources. The impact and importance of IT is acknowledged in the business strategy documents, but no clear examples were found of the translation of IT possibilities into business processes.

4.2 Summary of the findings

It takes considerable time and effort to break through the language and terminology barrier of an information strategy. For example, in one instance it took half the first interview to establish that information strategy can mean more than the annual information plan. The various aspects of the model helped to bring the subject gradually into focus. Without a common terminology, it is easy to obtain misleading responses. It took a period of approximately 10 weeks, and about 50 man hours work, to finish a case study (steps 1–4) for one organization. Answers and explanations given in the interviews in step 1 are clarified and adjusted in the next steps. For example, functional managers indicated that the executive board spent only about 1 day each year on information strategy. The executive board member corrected this to 'more than 20 per cent of my time'. Input from multiple respondents and various levels thus contributes to an accommodated, calibrated view of information strategy.

In the previous section company A was described in detail. An overview of the findings in all three companies is given in Table 3.1. The companies all give IT substantial and high level attention, more than, perhaps, the percentage of total revenue devoted to IT would suggest. The results can be summarized as follows:

- *Environment.* Information strategy awareness is high for all parties in the organizations. Attitudes of general managers and functional managers towards IT were generally positive and deviated little from each other.
- *Process.* Linkage between corporate strategies and information strategies is well established, certainly in the sense of alignment to business goals, but also (though less evident) in the sense of impact of technology on corporate strategies. The use of information technology in the organizations is not an activity that is planned or ruled from one specific department or person. Information strategy is influenced by many parties, partly historically and personally based. Formal methods play a supporting role in the information strategy process. Comprehensive methodologies are not used. SWOT analysis and other techniques tend to be used periodically as building blocks. Technology scanning is seldom done formally. Information strategy typically evolves through a problem-driven process, with both

top-down and bottom-up inputs from IT managers as well as from general managers.

- *Form and contents*. The regularly produced 'information plan' serves as a means of communication within the information systems department and the rest of the organization. The annual planning cycle is a 'staging post' in a continuous information strategy process. Whereas the emphasis is generally on the (application) architectures and plans, reformulation of objectives occasionally received intense attention. Policies and guidelines on aspects such as investment criteria, risk management, security standards and alliances are an essential part of the information strategy, but remain often implicit and are assumed to be known. The strategies of all three organizations are more oriented to information systems and services than to the use of technology or infrastructures.
- *Results*. The companies put increasing emphasis on sophisticated methods to determine and control costs and benefits at the project and implementation level of information strategy. Organizations do not (or only tentatively, in the case of company B) systematically assess the effects and consequences of an information strategy at the business level, nor at the level of a single business process.

5   Comparison with related research

Mantz *et al.* (1991) report on a postal survey among about 350 Dutch organizations (both profit and non-profit). We note the following significant differences between the reported results of this survey and conclusions from our own research:

1   It is stated that in 47 per cent of the cases the IS manager is responsible for the identification of strategic applications. We find in all cases a sharing of this responsibility between top executives, IS managers and line managers, The difference may be due to the fact that we only investigated the insurance industry, or to an underestimation of the involvement of top executives by the single respondents in the Mantz survey, as we encountered.
2   Sixty-one per cent of organizations are reported to use consultants in the information strategy process. We do not encounter this in any significant way. The confusion may have arisen as the process in the Mantz surveys also includes system development and implementation.
3   Sixty-eight per cent claim to require a formal 'control concept', defining the lines and mechanisms as a prerequisite for an information strategy. We found that managers in the insurance industry involved with information strategy are intimately aware of the functioning of their company and do not require such constructs.

Premkumar and King (1991) investigated 245 US business organizations, also by mailing questionnaires. We note the following differences and similarities between our findings and those of Premkumar and King:

1   Low use of standard planning methodologies is reported (22 per cent). We agree. Methodologies such as BSP were previously used, but were abandoned. Companies opt for a continuous and largely informal process, with great personal input from various levels.
2   Low effort spent on information strategy. We find that top executives, as well as senior IS managers in the insurance industry spend a substantial amount of time on information strategy. The survey may come to its conclusion by (implicity) only taking the effort of specialist staff into account, which is indeed a relatively low percentage.
3   A direct link is suggested between observable input to the information strategy and corporate results, such as return on investment. We find that such links are very tenuous and tend to be obscured by other factors. Senior executives do not believe in the possibility of measuring such links and are not inclined to spend serious effort in quantifying them.

Conrath *et al.* (1992) performed a (postal) survey among 67 Canadian top companies. The following differences and similarities are noted between the results of this survey and our findings:

1   Thirty per cent of respondents say that they do not link their information strategy with business strategy. This is contrary to our experience in the insurance industry, where a clear link between the two is established, in the sense of impact as well as of alignment. The explanation may be a preoccupation with formal, written business strategies by the respondents of the survey.
2   Only few companies were found to make a comparison between plan and performance. We agree that explicit evaluation appears to be the exception rather than the rule.
3   Only few companies were found to make a formal analysis of competitors' actions. This is also found in the insurance industry in the Netherlands. However, informally, competing companies tend to know each other very well. Several of the executives we interviewed were personally acquainted with each other. The explanation may be that the need for a formal analysis usually does not arise.

Saaksjarvi (1988) describes the relations between the process of information planning and the success of the planning, judged by IS managers of 100 large industrial and financial organizations in Finland. The planning process and success were measured by using a questionnaire. It was concluded that 44% of the organizations had already integrated IS planning and corporate planning. According to the judgement of the IS managers, successful planning depends on the effective cooperation between general and IS management. In the present study we describe how general and IS management deal with information strategy, the processes and the goals they use in the insurance industry.

Summarizing, this comparison demonstrates that our model-based investigation of information strategy runs parallel to and is flanked by closely related research. However, there are significant differences between the findings in 'postal surveys' and our findings in the cases. Some differences (e.g. on the use of consultants) can be explained because we focus on the insurance industry. Other differences (e.g. 'linkages between information strategy and business goals', and 'effort spent on information strategy') can be explained by the limited power of postal surveys to enlighten complex issues such as information strategy.

6   Conclusions

The research questions were: (i) how can the practice of information strategy in an organization be analysed; (ii) what is the actual practice in the insurance industry; and (iii) how does information strategy relate to business strategy? We also looked for possible changes in the approach to information strategy over a period of about 4 years.

With respect to the research methods employed, we conclude, in line with Earl (1993), Walsham and Waema (1994) and others, that the analysis of information strategy should not be based on the results of only one interview with one (senior) manager, nor should it be based on postal surveys alone. It requires significant effort to obtain an accurate view on information strategy in an organization, due to the complex and often implicit meaning of the concept of information strategy. Our study in a substantial and representative part of the insurance industry in the Netherlands shows significant differences with findings based on surveys reported in the literature: we found more participants involved with, and more effort spent on information strategy, and more efforts to link information strategy to business strategy and processes.

We found that information strategy is a well-known and important concept, with often an implicit meaning to the managers involved. Senior management is heavily involved in information strategy: the members of the executive board in two companies in this study spent up to 20 per cent of their time. This is also reported by Walsham and Waema (1994): the CEO of a building company (500 employees) was involved in information strategy 25 per cent of his time.

We find it peculiar that the organizations spend significant efforts in information strategies but do not evaluate their effects, nor try to learn from previous information strategy planning experiences and effects. The reasons for this might be that managers are not used to evaluating strategies, and, obviously related to this, do not expect to gain useful insights.

Henderson and Venkatraman (1993) described the linkages between business strategy and information strategy in the strategic alignment model (Figure 3.1). In the model they distinguish four (linked) domains in an organization: (i) the business strategy domain; (ii) the business processes domain; (iii) the IT strategy domain; and (iv) the IT processes domain. We have found in the three cases that serious attention to information strategy is paid by various managers from all four domains. The main role can be played by the chief executive from the business strategy domain, or by the senior IT manager, but in each case all domains play an active and important role.

Of importance is how the information strategy and the business strategy are aligned, or linked (Parker *et al.*, 1989; Henderson and Venkatraman, 1993). There are two main perspectives on how alignment can take place. In the first perspective the business strategy is the driving force for the business processes or for the IT strategy, ultimately affecting the IT processes. In the second perspective it is the other way around: the IT strategy is the driving force for the IT processing or the business strategy, ultimately affecting the business processes. In the three cases we encountered mainly the first perspective. More specifically, the business processes and (in a lesser extent) the business strategy are the driving force for the IT processes, which subsequently influence the information strategy. We have not found clear examples indicating a more immediate influence of business strategy on information strategy, or vice versa.

An added dimension to information strategy is offered by the insight in the evolution through the years of the information strategy of the three companies. We found some indications that the roles, responsibilities and influence of the various managers in the three cases change over time, but more case studies are needed to be able to look into the developments of information strategies (Smits and van der Poel, 1996). Additional research, also in other lines of business, is needed to compare and further clarify the relations between the environment, the process, the content, and the effects of information strategy.

References

Andrews, K. R. (1980) *The Concept of Corporate Strategy*, RD Irwin, Boston, MA.

Ansoff, H. I. (1984) *Implanting Strategic Management*, Prentice Hall, London.

Anthony, R. N. (1965) *Planning and Control Systems, a Framework for Analysis*, Harvard University Press, Boston, MA.

Blumenthal, S. C. (1969) *MIS: a Framework for Planning and Development*, McGraw-Hill, New York.

Chan, Y. E. and Huff, S. L. (1992) Strategy, an information systems research perspective. *Journal of Strategic Information Systems*, **1**(4), 191–204.

Conrath, D. W., Ang, J. S. K. and Mattay, S. (1992) Strategic planning for information systems: a survey of Canadian organisations. *Infor*, **30**(4), 364–378.

Earl, M. J. (1989) *Management Strategies for Information Technology*, Prentice Hall, London.

Earl, M. J. (1993) Experiences in strategic information systems planning. *MIS Quarterly*, **17**(1), 1–24.

Feeney, D. F. and Edwards, B. (1992) Understanding the CEO/CIO relationship. Proceedings of the 13th ICIS Conference, pp.119–126.

Fitzgerald, E. P. (1993) Success measures for information systems strategic planning. *Journal of Strategic Information Systems*, **2**(4), 335–350.

Galliers, R. D. (1991) Strategic information systems planning, myths and reality. *European Journal of Information Systems*, **1**(1), 55–64.

Galliers, R. D. (1993) Towards a flexible information architecture: integrating business strategies, information systems strategies and business process redesign. *Journal of Information Systems*, **3**(3), 199–213.

Henderson, J. C. and Sifonis, J. G. (1988) The value of strategic IS planning: understanding consistency, validity, and IS markets. *MIS Quarterly*, **12**(2), 186–200.

Henderson, J. C. and Venkatraman, N. (1993) Strategic alignment: leveraging information technology for transforming organizations. *IBM Systems Journal*, **32**(1), 4–16.

Hopstaken, B. A. A. and Kranendonk, A. (1985) Informatieplanning: een eenvoudige aanpak voor een complex probleem. *Informatie*, **27**(11), 988–998.

Johnson, G. and Scholes, K. (1989) *Exploring Corporate Strategy*, Prentice Hall, New York.

King, W. R. (1988) How effective is your information systems planning? *Long Range Planning*, **21**(5), 103–112.

Lane, D. C. (1992) Modelling as learning: a consultancy approach. *European Journal of Operations Research*, **59**, 64–84 (special issue).

Laudon, K. C. and Laudon, J. P. (1996) *Management Information Systems*, 4th edn, Prentice Hall, New York.

Lederer, A. L. and Sethi, V. (1988) The implementation of strategic ISP methodologies. *MIS Quarterly*, **12**(3), 445–461.

Mantz, E. A., Kleijne, D. and van der Zijden, F. A. P. (1991) Planning en realisatie informatievoorzieningen nog ver uit elkaar. *Informatie*, **33**(12), 847–855.

McFarlan, F. W. (1984) Information technology changes the way you compete. *Harvard Business Review*, **62**(1), 98–103.

Mintzberg, H. (1980) Opening up the definition of strategy. In *The Concept of Corporate Strategy* (ed. R. Andrews), RD Irwin, Boston, MA.

Mintzberg, H. (1991) *Strategy Formulation, Schools of Thought*, Prentice Hall, London.

Orlikowsky, W. and Baroudi, J. (1991) Studying information technology in organizations: research approaches and assumptions. *Information Systems Research*, **2**(1), 1–28.

Parker, M. M., Trainor, H. E. and Benson, R. J. (1989) *Information Strategy and Economics*, Prentice Hall, London.

Pettigrew, A. M. (1987) Context and action in the transformation of the firm. *Journal of Management Studies*, **24**(6), 649–670.

Porter, M. E. (1987) From competitive advantage to corporate strategy. *Harvard Business Review*, **65**(5), 43–59.

Premkumar, G. (1992) An empirical study of IS planning characteristics among industries. *Omega*, **20**(5), 611–629.

Premkumar, G. and King, W. R. (1991) Assessing strategic information systems planning. *Long Range Planning*, **24**, 41–58.

Rockart, J. F. (1979) Chief executives define their own data needs. *Harvard Business Review*, **57**(3), 81–93.

Ruohonen, M. (1991) Information management education in human resource strategy. *International Journal of Information Management*, **11**(2), 126–143.

Saaksjarvi, M. (1988) Information systems planning: what makes it succesful. *Proceedings of the ACC*, pp.524–542.

Saaksjarvi, M. (1994) The roles and success of IS steering committees. *Proceedings of ECIS*, pp.119–130.

Schwenk, C. R. (1988). *The Essence of Strategic Decision Making*, D. C. Heath, Lexington, MA.

Scott Morton, M. S. (1991) *The Corporation of the 1990s: IT and Organizational Performance*, Oxford University Press, New York.

Smits, M. T. and van der Poel, K. G. (1996) The practice of information strategy in six information intensive organizations in the Netherlands. *Journal of Strategic Information Systems*, **5**, 93–110.

Theeuwes, J. A. M. (1987) *Informatieplanning*, Kluwer, Deventer.

Turoff, M. (1970) The design of a policy Delphi. *Technological Forecasting and Social Change*, **2**(2), 149–171.

Walsham, G. and Waema, T. (1994) Information systems strategy and implementation: a case study of a building society. *ACM Transactions on Information Systems*, **12**(2), 150–173.

Ward, J., Griffiths, P. and Whitmore, P. (1990) *Strategic Planning for Information Systems*, Wiley, Chichester.

Wilson, T. D. (1989) The implementation of IS strategies in UK companies. *International Journal of Information Management*, **9**(4), 245–258.

Zachman, J. A. (1982) Business system planning and business information control study: a comparison. *IBM Systems Journal*, **21**, 35–45.

Reproduced from Smits, M. T., van der Poel, V. G. and Ribbers, P. M. A. (1997) Assessment of information strategies in insurance companies in the Netherlands. *Journal of Strategic Information Systems*, **6**(2), June, 129–148. Reprinted by permission of the publishers, Elsevier Science NL.

Questions for discussion

1   Consider the authors' definition of information strategy: 'a complex of implicit or explicit visions, goals, guidelines, and plans with respect to the supply and the demand of formal information in an organization sanctioned by management, intended to support the objectives of the organization in the long run, while being able to adjust to the environment'. How does this differ from the notion of information strategy depicted in Figure 0.1 in the Preface? The authors treat information strategy, IS strategy, IS strategic planning, strategic IS planning as the same thing. How might these be differentiated?

2   The authors examine the link between IS strategy and business strategy by considering the attitudes of senior managers, analysing the information strategy process, analysing the content and forms of the strategies, and looking at how effects are evaluated. What are the limitations of each individually as indicators of the link and what other methods might we use to determine how well IS is linked to business strategy?

3   The authors state that 'attitudes of general managers and functional managers toward IT were generally positive and deviated little from each other'. How generalizable do you think this finding is?

4   The authors state that 'technology scanning is seldom done formally. Information strategy typically evolves through a problem-driven process, with both top-down and bottom-up inputs from IT managers as well as from general managers'. Consider why formal scanning might not be done. What would be the merits of conducting formal scanning?

5   The authors state that organizations do not systematically evaluate the effects and consequences of information strategy, in part because senior managers do not believe in the possibility to measure such links. Suggest an alternative explanation.

6   Consider two perspectives on how alignment can take place: (i) business strategy driving business processes which in turn drive IT strategy which affect IT processes; (ii) IT strategy driving IT processes which ultimately affect business process and business strategy. Discuss the merits of these two approaches.

4 Information Management Strategy (Organizing the Information Systems Function)

Any way out of the labyrinth for managing information systems?

B. R. Edwards, M. J. Earl and D. F. Feeny

Introduction

To judge by the behaviour of many complex organizations, management approaches towards structuring the information systems (IS) function look to be uncertain, diverse and sometimes downright contradictory. Quite different organizational arrangements for IS can be found not only between similar businesses in the same sector, but across different parts of the same business.

'Complex organizations' exist in both the government and private sectors. They are large (over say one billion dollars in annual revenues), diversified and divisionalized into partly autonomous entities, often into strategic business units (SBUs).

Corporations of that sort are common in the Western world, indeed they are commoner than unitary companies at that size. In them the IS organizational issue is very frequently seen to be problematic, commonly demonstrated by controversy and dramatic change. Our experience over many years, and in recent research, shows that the problems exist in patterns, and that there is a small number of general solutions, and that there is a preferred one.

Here are sketches of three frustrated senior executives who could all be from the same corporation. We suggest that they speak for very many of their peers; indeed they are composite portraits made from a number we know.

- An Information Systems (IS) Director in the corporate headquarters of a large multi-divisional group finds that some divisions are simply bypassing corporate IS. They are installing small and not so small systems of various hues. Meanwhile corporate IS is struggling to deliver new applications from a headcount-limited development resource, and the approved application backlog grows. Moreover the heavy costs of running all the services of a corporate data centre make his charge-out rates look extravagant, and the performance of his department suspect.

- A Divisional Chief Executive needs new IS capabilities simply to stay in his present markets, let alone enhance competitive potential. Customers are insisting on electronic exchange of orders and invoices and products support material is being demanded in electronic form. Corporate IS apparently cannot deliver in the needed timeframe, yet would like to veto divisional initiatives to go-it-alone for fear of generating inconsistencies and of duplicating costs. There is controversy about what represents the lowest real total cost.
- The President is being pressed on all sides with the message that IS should be the key strategic enabler for the business, but all he sees is a mess and all he hears are grumbles. His instincts are generally to let divisions behave like true strategic business units (SBUs), having accountability for business performance, and as much autonomy as he can responsibly devolve. Yet he is told that in IS matters, uniquely, there is a need for a corporate approach to 'architectures' and 'infrastructure', in order to achieve corporate coherence and synergy.

It would almost seem as though the complex, multidivisional business stands at a disadvantage compared with simpler businesses in the matter of managing IT. And where does this leave government sector organizations which are almost always complex?

In those caricatures the issues appear to include:

- *Authority for application decisions* – who decides whether a particular application proposal is justified and what priority it should have when there is contention?
- *Technical policy and support structure* – how much need is there for an overall technical structure and for efforts in pursuit of potential corporate synergies?
- *Centralization versus decentralization* – what should be the overall distribution of IS responsibilities and resources between corporate and business unit managements?

None of these are new; but all are becoming more pressing as IS becomes all-pervasive, more demanding of resource and attention and more 'mutual' both within and between businesses. We have been working with business for many years as they have attempted to resolve these conflicts.

We believe from recent research that it is possible to describe quite a small number of approaches to IS arrangements and to comment on the prospects for their success. (A research study was conducted by the authors in fourteen complex organizations headquartered in Europe and North America. A detailed research instrument was applied through interviews with IS Directors, user managers and IS sponsors.)

The first stage of getting control of something is to find words to describe it

It is worth describing the model approaches for IS arrangements. We use 'arrangements' to cover far more than simple organization structure. As will be seen, the models describe where powers reside, how investment and other decisions are made and reviewed, what the missions of various IS groups are, and what management controls are appropriate.

Five types can be described; we have studied all of them. In some very widespread organizations more than one model is present. Three of them are *centralized*, but differ profoundly in their goals and management dynamics. One is decentralized and one is a compromise.

Let's describe the models and illustrate typical arguments in their favour.

Corporate service (centralized)

IS is a unified function reporting to corporate management. There may be distributed equipment, but it is under the operational control of central IS. If business units have people whose focus is systems they are intended to be spokespeople for users, and negotiators with central IS. The service disposes of tens of hundreds of millions of dollars annually and employs hundreds or thousands of people.

The centralized corporate service is justified through features like:

- economies of scale
- critical mass of skills
- opportunity for a corporate systems approach
- priorities adjudicated at corporate level
- 'data is a corporate resource'
- the professionalism possible in a really large IS organization.

Internal bureau (centralized)

This possesses the characteristics of the corporate service but is managed as a profit centre rather than a functional cost centre. It has many of the characteristics of a wholly-owned business subsidiary including targets for profitability, return on investment and cash flow. There will commonly be account managers aligned with nominated business units, and services and applications may be considered as a portfolio of 'products'. Any external business arises accidentally, for example through continuing to service a small business which has been divested.

Justification for the internal bureau has included the following, in addition to those of the central corporate service:

• demonstration of financial probity
• comparability with external data servicers
• motivation for staff in the bureau
• more responsiveness to divisions, owing to a 'market-led' business culture
• prevalence of a profit centre management control system in the corporation at large
• ability to pioneer or prototype new technology through a managed R&D programme which is funded out of operating profits.

Business venture (centralized)

This is like the internal bureau, but it has in addition an explicit mission to seek revenue by offering IS services outside the group. (This could be limited – one unit we know has an objective of 10 per cent external revenue – or unconstrained). Indications that this is the mode would be the existence of published tariffs, marketing literature, dedicated external salesmen, and products which are for external offering only.

Justification beyond the arguments for an internal bureau include:

• enhanced economies of scale, because of even higher capacity becoming justified and further mileage being extracted from assets
• motivational value for professionals and managers in the bureau
• demonstrable competitiveness of costs and services to sceptical group users
• ability to use group businesses to prototype and develop generalized external offerings
• conforming to a corporate direction towards diversification, in this case towards information services
• opportunity to learn 'new tricks' from other external businesses
• enhanced power and business leverage due to greater size.

Decentralized

By contrast to the three above cases, IS is a distributed function. Each business unit contains its own IS capability under its own control, or elects to employ commercial data services. There is no central IS unit or responsibility except for the support of corporate headquarters' functions such as consolidating financial returns. Corporate management review the units' capital and budget submissions for IS only to the extent required for general financial planning and control purposes. A new computer is therefore treated like a new stamping press of similar cost.

Justification for delegating all IS authority and planning includes:

- full consistency with principles of SBU accountability and autonomy
- least impediment to SBU's initiatives for radical IS exploitation
- no impediment to acquisition or divestment of businesses
- no addition to the deadweight of corporate staffs.

Federal

IS is a partly distributed function, with business units containing and controlling some IS capability. There is, in addition, some central IS presence which has responsibility for defined aspects of policy and architecture across the organization. There is often central provision of some common or shared services, which may or may not be coincident with the central IS policy unit. The name of this model deliberately borrows from political vocabulary because the idea of Federal 'powers reserved' is balanced against delegated 'SBU rights'.

The justification for this compromise has included:

- helping to distinguish responsibility for strategy (*what* IS is to contribute) from policy (*how* IS is to be done)
- allowing for fast local decisions on applications and priorities while preserving corporate mediation on selected issues, e.g. security, common systems, vendor selection and procurement practices
- providing a corporate framework for selected corporate provision, e.g. networks, data etc.

Earlier we said that in some complex corporations more than one model might be working. In one case which is worth illustrating, every one is present!

One British-based multinational corporation operated IS at the highest level on a *federal* basis, with a distinct unit having oversight of the worldwide IS policies. There still exists a substantial *internal bureau*, which is the successor to a *corporate service* unit that once served all headquarters functions. That bureau is now accepting business targets which in effect redefine it as an *external bureau*. One major international division within the corporation once operated towards its national business units in a way closest to *decentralized*, but it is now exerting extended control of a truly *federal* nature. There was until recently, one division whose business was to be an *external bureau*.

When we discuss those five models with either IS executives or general business executives, they are able readily to identify their own situation with one or more of them. *There are seldom boundary difficulties.*

It seems extraordinary that as we enter the fourth decade of business computing, there still exists such a diversity of management approaches to IS. Is any one preferred; is there any evidence of differential performance?

But a plague on all your houses!

When we described the five models for the positioning of IS people and powers, we offered a justification for each. There might be said to be little to choose between such well-defined cases, until we look at the downside, or the dangers implicit in each. Here are some criticisms which we have heard of each, sometimes expressed with considerable emotion – particularly by non-IS managers.

Corporate service

This is commonly perceived as:

- inaccessible
- arrogant in its pursuit of technological objectives, and belief that it possessed superior understanding of the dynamics of the business
- unresponsive to SBU needs and priorities
- profligate in its spending, and greedy and unfair in its recharging of costs
- resistant to modern technology's opportunity e.g. distributed systems, user-controlled development.

Internal bureau

Shows possibly all the above, but is in addition:

- biased in its advice, because of its perceived preference to sell its own services even when they might not offer the optimal solution
- reluctant to invest in progressive enhancement of installed systems
- bureaucratic and dominated by administration
- more concerned about its bottom line than about serving the users in the SBUs and therefore shy about investment.

Business venture

Shows the above problems and in addition experiences:

- incompatibility between mission of serving the group's businesses and mission of growing external revenue
- diversion of key, skilled people to development and selling of new services to external customers
- holding 'our' needed solution back while generalizing it to create a marketable common solution or package
- being content to use revenue from group SBUs as cash flow to nourish exciting external ventures
- conflict between the desire to maintain competitive edge through an exclusive application, and the desire to offer it profitably to the industry sector.

Decentralized

Without restraints, it is believed you will get:

- incompatible systems and technology, cutting off emerging potential for common or shared systems
- some SBUs simply doing computing badly
- security exposures
- incompatible IS and IT constraining the business from reorganization
- limited leverage on IT suppliers, owing to diversity; lack of single customer image
- opportunity for 'awakened' SBUs to persist in systems darkness until their industry overtakes them.

Federal

Although this was offered as a constructive compromise, sceptics ask these sorts of questions:

- Who writes the rules and defines the boundaries?
- How can a group-wide IS policy be supported by business line management who don't understand the terminology or appreciate its significance?
- How can it be promulgated by corporate IS people who have no power?
- What happens when the group acquires a new company?
- How do you fund the overheads involved in writing and mediating IS policies?

What that says is that no model is ideal, and that you could screw up just as well with any of them. We saw poor results coming from every one of those models. What, then, are the indicators to nudge a preference one way or another? Basically there are two:

1   Making IS arrangements consistent with the way the business works and is organised.
2   Having regard to the history and traditions of IS in the organisation.

Our shorthand jargon for these is:

'Host organization characteristics', and:
'IS heritage'.

Indicators – or decision rules – in practice

The first indicator says that on a centralized–decentralized spectrum it makes little sense to position IS differently from all the other main business activities. Arrangements for IS should follow the characteristics of the host organization. Applying this decision rule requires a lot of sensitivity and honesty about the real nature of the business, and of how it is changing.

We have seen a number of organizations where a clear move away from one of the three centralized models towards some devolution was in progress. In every case this has been consistent with the degree of decentralization that the rest of the business possessed or was aspiring to. We have also seen one case where a major business in the process of recentralizing had taken he decision to recentralize IS. (We have been struck by the high proportion of businesses in which major refocusing and reorganization at corporate level has been in process, or a feature of recent history. A common concern is to focus better on the 'core business', or as one group put it, 'decluttering the business'.)

The second indicator, IS heritage, or 'where are we coming from?' should, however, be seen as a modifier to the decision rule just stated. In one British metal products corporation it was perceived that the centralized IS organization was a clear misfit with the decentralized management of what were very diverse businesses. The decision was taken to abolish the central IS resource, dispersing part to the larger business units, and instructing smaller units to seek support from local data servicers.

Although the devolution was to be mediated by a newly-created corporate IS consultancy unit, the process was a relative disaster. IS staff declined to move; the businesses were in no way ready to assume responsibility; and there was no tradition of a corporate unit being able to manage a policy across the SBUs. The group's IS remained in frozen immobility, with considerable personal misery, for some time.

A solution which took proper account of 'IS heritage' would have respected the momentum and culture of the existing IS arrangements, sought out where they were really wanting, and ameliorated them. Sudden and sweeping changes in direction of IS arrangement seem rarely to succeed and are costly in terms of organizational disruption and breaks in service.

By contrast, in another British case a food business with dispersed and disparate product divisions was frustrated by a 'business venture' which was its mandated IS supplier. Divisions felt that they were paying too much for systems that did not keep up to date with business needs and were if anything a constraint on their business.

The solution was not to dismantle the bureau, but to remove its mandate, institute a federal policy with a corporate steward of policies, and promote divisional initiatives. One division after another then developed modern networked distribution systems with a new sense of divisional self-help, yet often voluntarily relying on the bureau for technical and development services. This food business began to benefit from a 'best of both worlds' set of IS arrangements.

So, one reason for compromise arrangements is that any abstract ideal based on organizational type needs to be tempered by consideration for the starting position, how remote that is from the ideal, what is politically and personally acceptable, and what really needs fixing. Another quite different reason for compromise is that few host organizations occupy extreme positions of centralization or decentralization anyway, and thus 180° turns in structuring and controlling IS are likely to substitute one misfit IS organization for another.

The problem of organizing IS has often been posed as a question of choosing between decentralization and centralization. The use of such opposites as labels or metaphors may help in understanding the issues to be faced. However, in practice it encourages constrained thinking, suggests inevitable conflict, and does not fit the variety of organizational contexts to which IS functions have to respond. Above all it might suggest that it is impossible to seek a mix of the benefits of centralization and decentralization. We believe such a balance is quite feasible in many circumstances; the federal solution is the key.

The federal solution is of course one of compromise, and for some people 'compromise' is a dirty word. Where compromise consists of sacrificing every point of principle in pursuit of some consensus, that might be valid. But to compromise by combining strengths seems to us responsible.

The federal model offers strengths that suit many variants of the complex business organization, in particular because it is adaptable. IS competence and resource are usually positioned at corporate level *and* in SBUs or divisions. Consequently IS can respond to new demands and imperatives at either level, without a need to create new organizational entities.

There remains a validity for the centralized corporate service for IS where the business organization, however complex, is being managed in a centralized, integrated fashion. It is necessary to be sensitive to the dangers inherent in this style, which were outlined earlier.

Decentralized IS clearly fits where the host organization truly intends to leave its businesses functionally free. In one financial services conglomerate we recently heard it stated that this was to become the model, and that the only value added by corporate was the maintenance of the group logo and the brand image. But the group must be confident that this will remain a stable intention, because the opportunity for SBUs to develop in different directions can make any later attempt to coordinate very difficult.

What businesses are doing

Attracted by the apparent sense behind the federal model, we looked at the proportion of organizations in our research sample which best fitted that model in 1987 compared with four years before that. In 1987 *eight* out of fourteen were federal, compared with *three* out of fourteen earlier. The three centralized models had all declined; corporate from five to two, bureaux from four to three. In many cases major changes had come about because of growing frustration about efficiency and effectiveness. The three caricatures at the beginning of this chapter can lead to explosive tensions. In a number of cases the crisis had only been resolved after escalation to group board level.

Those data appear inconclusive about the bureau models, but in fact we believe that the arguments against the two bureau models are particularly powerful. The business managers to whom we spoke expressed great unease about dependence upon a unit whose mission was to itself. We concluded that of four bureaux which had existed in 1983 *none* would remain as the predominant IS presence in their corporations.

We make these predictions: they will detach themselves and become freestanding data servicers; or they will revert to serving in a federal model as a corporate technical resource; or they will persist as a valued niche provider of specialist services. The driving force for these changes will be the unstoppable demand from SBUs – or corporate management – for truly strategic and business integrated systems that simply cannot be developed on a customer–contractor basis.

The predictions for the other models include further slight increase in federal behaviour, and an increase in decentralized cases followed the adoption – or recognition – of truly decentralized business practices. Table 4.1 summarizes recent change, and our predictions for the future.

Do not imagine, however, that all the federal conditions had come about by conscious decision! In some cases 'federal' is the nearest model to an uneasy *de facto* distribution of power and activity. Some companies have been relieved to discover that their compromise has a name and can be justified, and have used our language to articulate it better.

Table 4.1

IS organization structure	Number in sample		
	4 years ago	*Now*	*Outlook*
Centralized – corporate service	5	2	1
Internal bureau	3	1	0
Business venture	1	2	0
Federal	3	8	9
Decentralized	2	1	4

If there is one message from our work it is that the federal approach to IS arrangements is rational and responsible, and can be made more effective if it is pursued deliberately and rationally. The following section discusses how it can be pursued.

How are they getting on?

We have discussed five approaches to IS arrangements; the businesses in our sample had been selected to represent all of them. We did not know in choosing them how good they were at applying IS in the business, how far they diverged in aspects other than organization, or whether our data gave indications of good practice.

We believe that our research helps in all those questions. We can show why there is, and will remain, diversity; there are different results, and there is a preferred approach. Taking performance first, we found in our study no evidence of striking differences in *efficiency* of provision of IS services, as measured by cost, quality or reliability. (We are not confident that the same would be found if we explored a population of smaller organizations.) The general level of capability in managing the technical service was consistent and high in both centralized and decentralized units. So we suggest that efficient delivery of information services can be provided however the IS function is organized, provided only that the function is adequately resourced.

However, across the organizations we have studied, we found striking differences in *effectiveness*; that is the acknowledged contribution of IS now, and in the future to significant business needs.

This effectiveness aspect relates particularly to one of the issues identified early in this chapter, namely that of 'authority for application decisions'. Now 'authority' sounds like a bureaucratic concept; however, getting application decisions, and getting them rightly resourced, requires a great deal of personal commitment and sense of ownership. What practices foster these characteristics?

Our research has suggested quite strikingly that there are a number of 'preferred' practices. We discovered these by first looking at the effectiveness of IS exploitation in our subject SBUs. This was done by combining views of the actual achievements, the judgements of the business people and the judgements of the IS executives.

The differences were striking and we could rate the cases as high, medium or low on the degree of *integration* between IS and the business which was being achieved: that is, the success at knitting IS applications and services into the fabric of the business. Could we find differences in methods, habits or attitudes between the high integrators and the low? We found seven differences – features which *all* the high integrators showed but *none* of the low integrators did. Here they are:

1   The business executives all declared that future exploitation of IT was going to be of truly strategic significance to business performance. An unremarkable comment, until we reflect that none of the low-integrated group so judged. Now, it is impossible to legislate in favour of this being the required view, but it may well have been affected by the following feature.

2   The highly integrated all had a continuing (rather than a once-off) process for educating business managers in IT capabilities and opportunities. The vehicles varied; the resolution to do it did not.

3   In all the highly-integrated cases there was an IS executive in post in the SBU who operated as a key member of the SBU management team. Titles varied and do not matter; acceptance and involvement do.

4   Coupled with that, each 'highly-integrated' SBU had some IS development resource at its disposal and under its direction. This group did not necessarily undertake all development for the SBU, but it was of sufficient size to enable rapid response to changing business circumstances or priorities. The group did not in all cases line report to the SBU. What mattered was the ability of the SBU to determine the goals and priorities of the development group, and the degree of identification of the group with the culture and personalities of the SBU.

5   All 'high' respondents described a process through which IS opportunity and business plans were reviewed integrally. The IS application and service strategy was developed 'top down' from this, reflecting the relationships described in 3 above. This mode of planning was further confirmed by getting respondents to identify themselves with a number of IS planning caricatures.

6   Initiatives to introduce or pilot new technologies were, in the high integration group, SBU dominated. That is not to say that there was no place for corporate technical support or funding; but that the drive and commitment necessary for an effective pilot project have to emanate from SBU management.

7   In the matter of charging for IS services, all the 'high' respondents operated relatively straightforward cost distribution systems, rather than sophisticated pricing mechanisms. Some organizations had, in fact, reverted
from the sophistication of advanced price-based charging to cost distribution at a high level, e.g. to SBU only. It had been felt that detailed and
subtle pricing had been a distraction and diversion, contributing little.

To summarize that set of evidence, it is clear that SBU ownership of IS
strategy and commitment to it is vital. IS strategy is here defined as those
things which IS is going to do for the business – as opposed to how IS is to
be administered.

Further, it is vital that IS and business management operate in close partnership at SBU level, and feel that jointly they are in control of:

*   the IS application strategy and its delivery resource
*   IS pilot projects.

These will be aided if the SBU management team is continually refreshed
by information about emerging IS opportunity, and the SBU IS executive is
not encumbered by an elaborate financial and charge-out bureaucracy.

Corporate management can set a climate which encourages SBU managements to grasp the initiative in these ways, but it cannot command commitment. In research we found SBUs within the same corporation which lay at
opposite ends of the low-high spectrum in terms of IS integration.

What does the federal authority do?

It is useful to identify and distinguish a number of activities which, in a
federal set-up, take place at corporate level. In relation to the issues raised at ·
the beginning of the chapter, we are now relating to 'technical policy and
support structure'.

1   *Corporate applications.* These may be extensive or minimal in size and
extent, but there must be provision for defining, operating and maintaining them. This is an area where the nature of the complex organization
profoundly affects the approach. For example, some complex organizations operate with a high degree of integration of business operations, and
this integration will be largely enabled through information systems. On
the other hand, a conglomerate group run on a portfolio basis will be
likely to concentrate only on financial reporting and consolidation as
corporate applications. It can be fair to count common systems which

are replicated across a number of congruent business units as corporate systems, because it is through the systems that a consistent business image is presented.

2   *Group policy for information systems and technology.* This is the set of powers reserved through which the corporate executive maintains its desired level of direction of the IS initiatives and resources throughout the group. Broad topic areas from which these may be developed include the following. These topics were found to be the subject of corporate policy in the majority of the researched organizations:

- standards about permissible equipment, suppliers, programs, network services etc.
- standards about how to do things, e.g. defining requirements, implementing solutions, quality and security
- personnel and human resources issues (IS careers, skills, job specifications, trade unions)
- financial arrangements for IS-capital expenditure appraisal, budgeting, chargeout
- relationships and negotiations with IT suppliers
- developing and propagating common systems
- degrees of freedom for SBUs in selecting and using IT, and deciding where to apply it
- use of corporate systems, services or resources.

It is important to note that policies of these sorts are and should be predominantly of an enabling nature, and not seen as straitjackets.

3   *Group provided services in information systems and technology.* The extent of this provision is one of the decisions required from group policy. The management and development of group resources are critical areas. Components of group resources we saw in action in our research included:

- internationally travelling consultants
- systems development groups, both for doing common systems and for commissioned divisional systems
- data centre operations and related technical planning and support services
- industry-specialized R&D pilot, e.g. CADCAM, EDI
- national and international network management
- archiving
- training and education
- support of corporate-wide office automation systems.

The organizational arrangements for these components were varied. Sometimes they co-resided in a single corporate group, sometimes they were separated. Success was related less to structure than to vision, relationships and mutual confidence between SBU and corporate IS entities.

The successful federator

Here we address the third of the issues noted at the beginning – the distribution of responsibilities and resources, or 'centralization versus decentralization'.

What follows is brief, but that does not mean that it is simple in execution. It is folly to imagine that, in a complex corporation, solutions to long-standing problems will be other than complex. Principles, however, can and should be simple and widely understood.

Corporate management, in the name of the Chief Executive, should:

- proceed from an assumption that some form of federalism is both desirable and feasible
- determine not once, but regularly, what topics should lie within the powers reserved to the corporate officers in the IS/IT arena
- create (or adapt) and resource a management system to review and propose IS policies
- understand, negotiate and ultimately promulgate a set of policies and keep them up to date
- articulate and foster the desired extent of SBU ownership of, and accountability for, IS strategies within SBU business plans.
- review and adapt the extent of provision for corporate systems and technology and articulate its mission
- review, and endorse or constructively criticize, both SBU and headquarters plans and performance in respect of IS
- determine the appropriate goals and vehicles for continuing executive enlightenment about IT capability and IS management issues.

Corporate management should not:

- Delegate the definition of either policies or strategies to consultants – although it can be most valuable to consult them.
- Delegate the *determination* of either policies or strategies to IS management at any level – although the IS role in *proposing and negotiating* both cannot be overstated.
- Assume that the appointment of a corporate officer for information at a very high level in the organization absolves general managers from concern about IS; on the contrary, it affords them a peer with whom to argue about it, and a focus for needed staff work, as well as a reporting line for any retained corporate IT resources.
- Relax under an impression that IS/IT is, and will remain, of only peripheral significance in 'our' industry sector; even if this represented a correct assessment in relation to today's IT capability, step advances in IT function or economics over the next decade could transform the opportunity.

- Relax into a feeling that all necessary dispositions for IS policies and strategies have been made, and that corporate management can turn away from those issues to something which addresses 'real' business. The systems which are enabled by information technology are increasingly becoming critical parts of the real business.

Conclusions

We have been surveying the manifold approaches to IS arrangements for years, and we have been amazed at the *diverse* and *contradictory* nature of them. So that we could study them in a systematic way, we defined five model approaches and initially assessed them disinterestedly. The issues that separate them were found to relate to effectiveness in integrating with the business; far less to technical adequacy and efficiency.

So in studying complex organizations we have gained confidence in the stability, and common sense behind the *federal* approach.

The federal approach is not a panacea. Host organization characteristics should be the prime determinant of IS arrangements. So the federal approach will have the best prospects for success in those organizations which plan to maintain certain levels of consistency and planned synergy in the business while devolving much functional management to SBUs. Centralized and decentralized businesses can still sensibly be supported by similarly arranged IS resources, subject to confidence that the business will remain loyal to those extreme styles.

The bureau model is likely to have long-term validity only where the host organization explicitly wishes to make a business of information services, and even then the tendency will be towards separation of group service from outside client service.

We predict, therefore, that the federal solution is the most effective and stable from the complex organizations of today's type.

Finally, creating a federal management is not an overnight event and maintaining it needs continuing effort. It will have the best chances of success where its design is clearly related to the business needs. Above all, the corporate executive must develop a clear vision of why a federal solution is required and how it should work.

The federal solution has the merit that it is best able to cope not only with the typically continuous evolution of host organization design, but also the ongoing experience of IS successes and failures, or 'IS heritage'. The federal approach provides a framework within which complex organizations can work out the most suitable balance of IS arrangements as events unfold – without catastrophic lurches between the extremes of centralization and decentralization.

Reproduced from Edwards, B. R., Earl, M. J. and Feeny, D. F. (1989) Any way out of the labyrinth for managing information systems? Oxford Institute of Information Management, Templeton College, Oxford University, Working paper **RDP89/3**.

Questions for discussion

1 Relate the five structures presented by Edwards *et al.* back to the revised stages of growth model proposed by Galliers and Sutherland in Chapter 2. In which stages would you expect to see these various structures?

2 Debate the various pros and cons of the five structures – is there any clear 'best'? If not, what are the contingencies that influence the effectiveness of any given model?

3 Assume an organization is trying to reposition itself in part by changing its organizational structure: what factors are likely to pose challenges to the ability to change the IS structure also.

4 The authors define IS strategy as 'those things which IS is going to do for the business – as opposed to how IS is to be administered'. Evaluate this definition and suggest an alternative. Compare this with Smits *et al.*'s definition in Chapter 3.

5 Would you agree that the federal model is the model of choice today?

5 Information Technology Strategy

The role of the CEO in the management of change: the case of information technology

E. H. Schein

Introduction

Few people would question the assumption that CEOs have a major impact on the changes that occur in their organizations. Yet there is surprisingly little analysis of just what the nature of this impact is likely to be, whether it will vary by industry, company, or CEO attitude and style, and what empirical data can be gathered to begin to shed some light on these issues (Hambrick, 1988; Thomas, 1988).

The research to be reported in this chapter focuses on a particular area of CEO impact – information technology – but the hypotheses that flow from this research about CEO roles in the management of organization change are more general in nature. In particular, the research reveals that there is a diversity of attitudes and assumptions about the appropriate role of the CEO in the management of change, and we would expect such diversity to apply to areas other than the implementation of information technology.

Analyses of the implementation of information technology (IT) have noted a variety of factors that aid or hinder such implementation. For example, Markus (1984) notes that one can focus on (1) the limitations of the technology itself; (2) the resistance to change on the part of individuals based on personality, cognitive style, or position in the organization; or (3) the interaction between individuals and the technology. Kraemer *et al.* (1989) extend this interactionist perspective by referring to the role of 'state of computing' in given companies reflecting the interaction between the interests of different organizational levels and different functional groups.

One of the limitations of these types of analyses is that they refer to management levels in a general way, referring occasionally to 'top management' or 'senior executives', but it remains unclear what is actually meant and whether any distinctions are drawn between chairmen of boards, chief executive officers (CEOs), chief operating officers (COOs), and division general managers. As Kotter (1982) and others have shown, different general managers do quite different things, so it is important to be precise in specifying whom one is studying.

In their report on the use of 'executive support systems', Rockart and DeLong (1988) do single out CEOs in many of their examples, but their cases are mostly an analysis of successful utilization of IT that illustrates what is possible, not what is normal. The fact that many CEOs have difficulty with IT is acknowledged but not analyzed by them or by other researchers who have focused on CEOs (Gibson and Jackson, 1987; Rockart and DeLong, 1988; Rockart and Treacy, 1982).

Surveys of CEOs, such as those done by Moore (1986), tend to identify CEOs who are successful implementers and analyze their characteristics, but they do little to help us understand the characteristics of the much larger population who are not enthusiastic about IT and who do not wish to use it themselves.

Research focus and method

This study began in 1987 with a decision to interview a broad sample of CEOs in a variety of companies to try to determine in a more general way their assumptions about IT and their attitudes toward the problems of change and implementation. Ten MIT Sloan Fellows, one other graduate student, and I were able to interview ninety-four executives, all of whom were current or past CEOs and, in a few cases, COOs or presidents of divisions in conglomerates or multidivisional companies. Seventy-nine of them clearly fitted the CEO criterion. This sample was arrived at by each Sloan Fellow picking an industry that interested him or her and writing letters to CEOs in a sample of companies in that industry. Sixty percent of the persons contacted in this manner agreed to be interviewed. All were male. Some general characteristics of the sample are listed in Table 5.1.

The interviews, which were focused on personal attitudes and the use of IT, tried to elicit some of the underlying assumptions behind the behavior and attitudes. Common dimensions and variables were chosen for the interview protocol and subsequent analysis but, because we felt it essential to get the CEOs' spontaneous views, we asked our interviewers to allow each CEO to tell his story in his own way. We then combined the protocols in terms of common themes and found that coding reliability was sufficient to pursue our

Table 5.1   *Characteristics of CEO sample**

Average age	56.3 (42–69)
Average years as CEO	7.1 (1–26)
Average number of employees	54 600 (200–800 000)
Industries and range of sales	
Insurance	560×10^6 to 650×10^6
Telecommunications	400×10^6 to 12×10^9
Services	2×10^9 to 3×10^9
Banking	2.5×10^9 to 27×10^9
Aerospace/high-tech	40×10^6 to 50×10^9
Utilities	260×10^6 to 1×10^9
Manufacturing	20×10^6 to 70×10^9

* Data based on 79 CEOs, COOs, and presidents. Sixty per cent of persons contacted agreed to be interviewed.

analysis and to develop constructs, but not high enough to allow us to generalize from this sample to the larger population of CEOs. This study should, therefore, be viewed as exploratory in nature.

Generic CEO roles in the change process

Table 5.2 presents a model of the change process that was originally proposed by Kurt Lewin and elaborated by me to explain changes that had planned, nonvoluntary, and sometimes coercive elements to them (Lewin, 1952; Schein, 1961, 1972, 1987). Lewin correctly foresaw that in living systems any given stable state was a 'quasi-stationary' equilibrium that could be unfrozen, moved, and refrozen, but he did not elaborate in detail how one actually unfreezes a system, moves it, and then refreezes it. Since organizations tend to develop stable routines and cultures, any organization change tends to occur in terms of the stages identified in this model (Schein, 1985). The critical elements in this model are the actual activities implied in each step of the change process, so our analysis focuses on those kinds of CEO activities.

As Table 5.2 shows, one can logically analyze and order the steps necessary in each stage of the change process, though these steps often occur out of sequence or simultaneously. Most of these steps occur through the intervention of some human, to be labeled for this purpose a 'change agent'. All of the activities of the change agent, including diagnostic inquiry, can be thought of as 'interventions' in the sense that they have an effect on the people who are the target of the behavior. It is the pattern of such interventions on the part of CEOs that is the focus of this analysis.

Table 5.2   *A stage model of planned change*

Unfreezing: Creating motivation to change
  Disconfirmation
  Induction of anxiety/guilt
  Creation of psychological safety
Creating change through cognitive redefinition
  Stimulating imitation or identification
  Stimulating scanning
Refreezing: Stabilizing the change
  Integration into personality
  Integration into key relationships and social system

Disconfirmation: the CEO as a disconfirmer

Change will not occur unless there is some motivation to change, and such motivation is most often provided by information that previously held assumptions, attitudes, or behavioral routines are no longer working. The information that things are no longer working, called 'disconfirmation', is typically brought into the organization by those members who are most closely in contact with the external environment, who are most responsible for the performance of the organization, and who have the most internal credibility as sources of information.

CEOs are uniquely suited to be disconfirmers. If things are not going right in their view, they have not only the opportunity but the obligation to start an organizational change process by disconfirming the present state. Normal routines that have become habits in an organization will not change unless someone ceases to respond in the expected manner. Such disconfirming responses will obviously have more weight if they come from the CEO than from someone lower in the hierarchy.

A clear example came from one of our respondents who decided to start the change process toward greater use of IT by announcing that he was personally going to start using a desktop terminal and would henceforth send all critical communications to his subordinates only via electronic mail. In other words, if they sent something by the old system, he would simply not respond, and anyone who did not get a terminal would miss important messages from him.

If there is no disconfirmation from any source, no motivation to change will be aroused. In a complacent organization, therefore, one of the CEO's most critical functions is to generate information or announce decisions that will have a disconfirming effect, thereby initiating the change process.

Induction of anxiety or guilt: the CEO as the 'bad parent'

Disconfirming messages have an impact only if they connect to something we care about. If the CEO ceases to respond to subordinates' behavior in an area irrelevant to their concern, they may simply pay no attention. However, if continuing to behave in the old way makes the subordinates anxious because some important goals may not be met, or makes them feel guilty because some valued ideals will not be met unless a change occurs, then the message will be attended to and discomfort will motivate some activity. It is this step that leads to quips like 'no pain, no gain' or the common assertion among change agents that 'unless the system is hurting somehow, no change will occur'.

CEOs are clearly in a good position to play a key role in anxiety or guilt induction because symbolically and psychologically they occupy a parent role. Probably the best examples from our interviews came from those CEOs who stated outright or subtly implied to their subordinates that the subordinates' failure to learn to use IT meant either that they would fail in their work (anxiety induction) or that they were technologically 'backward' (guilt induction). Whether it is intended or not, a force toward change is induced when the subordinate feels obsolete, out of touch, or in some other way uncomfortable about maintaining his or her old behavior.

Creation of psychological safety: the CEO as the 'good parent'

If too much anxiety or guilt is created, there is the danger that the change targets will react defensively. One of the most likely defenses in this situation is denial, which, in this case, means that the subordinates will cease to 'hear' the disconfirming signals or will rationalize them away. Subordinates will say to themselves, 'The boss doesn't really mean it; he won't persist if I don't go along', and so on.

In the case of the introduction of IT, subordinates may feel that they will be embarrassed by their slow learning ability, or by their inability to type, or by the fact that their poor grammar or spelling will be revealed – all of which they could hide by dictating directly to a secretary. A common error here is to assume that the resistance to change is only the lack of motivation or the unwillingness to put out the effort to learn something new. Much more likely is the defensive avoidance that results from inability to face one's own presumed inadequacies if one does not feel psychologically safe.

CEOs should and do attend to this issue in a variety of ways. One of the commonest is to be totally inflexible on the ultimate goals to be achieved but to be highly flexible and supportive on other issues. For example, the CEO may mandate that desktop workstations will eventually be used by all senior management but allow some leeway in (1) the pace of their introduction; (2) the degree to which selected subordinates would be allowed to continue to use their secretaries to enter data or memos, and, most important; (3) the amount and type of training help that would be available no matter what the cost. Thus subordinates for whom 'going to class' created tension could use individual coaches, perhaps even for long periods of time. CEOs who feel that sending their subordinates to formal classes would threaten them further may consider an individual coach the psychological safety net necessary to support innovation.

How many CEOs played each of these three unfreezing roles cannot be determined because local circumstances varied or data are not available. However, we heard many more stories about the disconfirming and anxiety- or guilt-inducing roles than about the other roles. It was least common to hear stories from CEOs about the necessity to provide psychological safety, even though they were often in the best position to provide it. We have to assume that they are either less sensitive to the need for this role or less willing to talk about it because it appears to be 'soft'. It should be noted, however, that unless all three aspects of the unfreezing process occur to some degree no motivation toward change will be created.

Creating change through cognitive redefinition: the CEO as role model

Ultimately unfreezing creates a motivation and readiness to change. The change target becomes sensitized to the need to learn something new and starts to look around for relevant information. For lasting change to occur, however, the target not only must learn new behaviors but also must cognitively redefine or reframe the issue so that new perceptions, attitudes, and feelings are created as well. Sometimes such cognitive redefinition occurs prior to behavior change, sometimes afterwards in an effort to reduce dissonance (Festinger, 1957). But if it does not occur at all, we are dealing only with temporary change of the sort one sees when people are coerced but not convinced.

The most common source for new information is someone else in the organization who seems to be 'doing it right', in the sense that his or her behavior is getting positively reinforced or 'confirmed'. Such role models not only provide behavioral cues on what to do, but, more important, they permit the target to psychologically identify with the model and thereby absorb some of the new cognitive point of view.

Many CEOs in our interviews discussed how the use of IT made it possible to think in a fundamentally different way about 'managing the business', and part of their problem was to get across these new concepts. For some of their subordinates this meant new assumptions about what a manager does and how a business can and should be managed. They had to reframe the manager's job. If the CEO felt comfortable with his own vision and level of understanding, he became a willing role model, teacher, and object of psychological identification. If he did not, he could deliberately stay away from the situation, conceal his own behavior to a greater degree, disconfirm efforts on the part of sub-ordinates to imitate him or identify with him, or limit his involvement to that of a 'process consultant' (Schein, 1987, 1988). In that role the CEO would help the subordinate redefine his or her own job but would not give advice or solutions.

Some CEOs were outspoken about not wanting to be role models. They sent the message 'Do what I say, not what I do', a situation that arose frequently with entrepreneurs, who often recognized that their own personal style was unusual and not necessarily the correct model for others. Another reason why some CEOs deliberately tried not to be role models was that they wanted to avoid cloning themselves. They believed that an effective organization needs innovative behavior, so they stimulated as much as possible people's efforts to learn in their own way and from their own sources.

If the CEO felt that he personally was the wrong model, but he believed that a correct model existed and that learning from a role model was the best way to learn, he could, of course, manage the change process by bringing into the organization consultants, trainers, or other executives who represented what he wanted to teach.

Stimulating cognitive redefinition through scanning: the CEO as process consultant

Imitation and identification have the virtue that learning can occur rapidly and behavior can be standardized fairly quickly. However, if the goal is for the new behavior to be innovative, then this change mechanism is a disadvantage because it prematurely funnels all changes into the same channels. If the CEO wishes to avoid such premature channeling, he must create circumstances that will 'help the subordinate to learn on his own'. The CEO as a change agent can achieve this result by becoming a process consultant and/or by sending subordinates 'out into the world', to find out what is out there and learn from it (Schein, 1969, 1987, 1988).

The essence of process consultation in this context is for the CEO to become genuinely interested in the subordinate as a learner and to provide whatever help the subordinate appears to need to learn new beliefs, attitudes, values, and behavior, much as a coach elicits from an athlete what that athlete is most capable of. The CEO as process consultant does not advise, teach, or tell. Instead he listens, helps the subordinate identify what the problem is, and helps the subordinate figure out what he or she will do about the problem. Suggesting that the subordinate should 'scan' the environment for ideas is the basic mechanism. The CEO in this role may offer options and alternatives but never recommends any particular course of action as the correct one.

In our interviews we saw many examples of this kind of forced scanning. The CEO would announce that the company had to learn to make better use of IT, would disclaim any special visions or skills in this area, but would expect regular reports on progress. Often, with the help of the IT department, key subordinates would create committees or task forces to scan the environment, inform themselves, and begin to redefine in their own heads what tools and processes they needed. They would then be in a position to educate the CEO.

If this scanning process was to work, however, the steps involved in unfreezing had to have occurred. We found good examples of where CEOs had earlier disconfirmed present practice by strongly asserting that 'something' was not right, without, however, offering a vision or a solution themselves, thus forcing scanning on the part of subordinates.

Refreezing: The CEO as Reinforcer

One of the most frustrating aspects of organizational change is that new behaviors and attitudes do not stick once the initial 'Hawthorne effect' has worn off. The system either reverts to its original state or moves in some brand new direction that may not be desired by the change agent. For new responses to remain stable, they must be 'refrozen', in the sense that they must fit into the personality of the change target and into his or her key relationships. Otherwise a new unfreezing process begins because of personal discomfort or disconfirmation by others in the system.

In order to avoid either of these undesirable outcomes, change agents generally favor projects that involve as much of the total system as possible, and they encourage change mechanisms that draw more on scanning than on identification or imitation. If a person learns through scanning, he or she automatically incorporates only things that fit into the personality, whereas with imitation and identification one often adopts behavior to please the role model, only to drop it later when the role model is no longer an audience.

Similarly, if a person learns something new along with others who are part of his or her work system, the members will reinforce each others' behavior, thus making it more likely that new responses will persist if the whole team or work system has learned them together. In other words, refreezing is most likely to occur when the change occurs through scanning and when the whole work system undergoes change together, and it is least likely to occur when an individual learns alone and through imitation/identification.

The implications for CEO behavior are obvious. If the CEO is the original change agent, he must view as his change target entire groups or subsystems, not isolated individuals, and he must avoid becoming the object of imitation. Furthermore, since he is a prime audience for and reinforcer of change, when change in the right direction occurs, he should strongly confirm and reinforce the new behavior and attitudes.

We infer from our interviews that many CEOs were sensitive to these kinds of issues, but only at an intuitive level. They did not talk as articulately about group norms and the subtleties of change as they did about unfreezing and setting a direction for change. And how they chose to reinforce had much to do with their vision for IT and the longer range goals they saw for it, a topic we will discuss later.

Factors influencing CEO change agent behavior

Having identified the generic change agent roles, we now need to know what, if anything, will determine how a given CEO will actually behave in the process of initiating and managing change. The factors identified in this section can all be thought of as 'partially causal' or influential, and they act in complex combinations rather than as single forces (Figure 5.1). In terms of change theory, each factor can be thought of as either a 'driving' force leading to increased pressure for the system to move in a certain direction or as a 'restraining' force leading to resistance (Schein, 1985, 1987).

Basic assumptions about information technology

We believed that whether they were explicitly aware of it or not, all CEOs had a set of assumptions about IT and a vision of what it could or could not do for them. Table 5.3 and Figure 5.2 present a typology of such assumptions based on (1) basic faith that IT is a good thing for organizations, and (2) the conviction that those things will or will not come about.

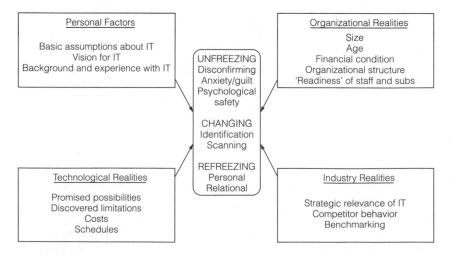

Figure 5.1   *CEO change roles and their determinants*

Table 5.3 *A typology of CEO assumptions about IT*

Utopian idealist: This CEO sees nothing but benefits deriving from the increased use of IT in all areas of *his business and personal life*. He may not see all these benefits in actual use, but he believes firmly that in time all the benefits will be realized.

Realistic utopian: This CEO sees great potential benefits in IT but is not sure that they will all be realized because of hidden costs, resistances in others, and various other sources of difficulty that are not inherent in IT but in its implementation.

Ambivalent: This CEO sees some benefits in some areas but sees potential harm in other areas and/or perceives that the costs may in the end outweigh the benefits; therefore, he is ambivalent in the sense of wanting to push ahead but being cautious and doubtful at the same time.

Realistic skeptic: This CEO is basically doubtful about the benefits of IT, short run or long run, but realizes that the appeal of the technology will bring much of it into organizations anyway; given this reality, the CEO must control carefully what is introduced so as to minimize potential harm or excessive costs.

Utopian skeptic: This CEO believes that IT is primarily harmful in that it undermines other effective managerial processes. It is not merely excessively costly but actually harms organizational effectiveness by encouraging the use of tools, categories of information, and processes of doing work that are less effective than what is currently or potentially possible in terms of other managerial models; he therefore sees his role to be to minimize the harm that IT can do, to undermine its implementation in any way possible, and to control its costs to the utmost degree.

Though the coding was not always totally reliable, we were able to agree enough on the basic types to give a rough approximation of how many of our CEOs fell into each basic category, as shown in Table 5.4 (based on the eighty-four cases analyzed).

In terms of basic assumptions, one can see a degree of realism prevailing. A few CEOs were totally utopian about the potential of IT, but the bulk of them were realistic about the difficulties of changing their organizations. Both of these groups would be expected to exert primarily driving forces in the sense that they would try to unfreeze and change their organizations. The ambivalents and those who saw IT as 'merely a tool' clearly were more cautious in their approach to implementation and would thus be expected to be as much on the restraining as driving force side. There were few real skeptics, so one would not expect strong restraining forces from CEOs except in the form of caution about the potential costs of IT.

To give a flavor of the range of responses from utopianism to skepticism, we quote various comments made during the interviews in Table 5.5.

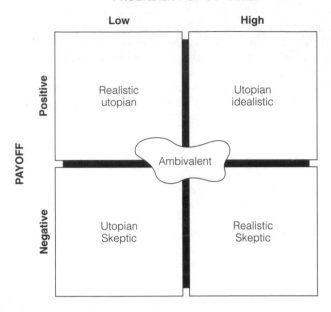

Figure 5.2   *CEO assumptions about IT*

Table 5.4   *Number of CEOs holding different assumptions*

Type	Payoff	Probability of occurrence	Number	%
Utopian idealist	+	+	17	20
Realistic utopian	+	−	46	55
Ambivalent	±	±	19	23
Realistic skeptic	−	+	2	2
Utopian skeptic	−	−	0	0
Total			84	100

Specific visions about information technology

Many CEOs had a positive vision for IT, but there was great diversity in the nature and strength of that vision. Our interviews were not specifically geared to identifying such visions, but they could easily be ordered in terms of a basic typology derived from other research on IT (Rockart, 1979; Zuboff, 1988). For this purpose it is useful to distinguish several levels of 'impact' of IT on organizations, as outlined in Table 5.6.

Table 5.5 *Sample comments from CEOs*

Utopian responses

   'IT enables you to decide where you want to be in the industry and how to get there.'

   'IT makes strategic decisions possible; longer range analysis.'

   'IT will assist in the design of new products and services.'

   'IT helps in generating data and performing complex analyses as input to decision making.'

   'IT is complex and expensive; you can't measure the benefits; it requires more people; but it is the best bargain for the money.'

   'IT permits real-time understanding of the business.'

   'IT is necessary for managing a dynamic business.'

   'IT lets you do things you couldn't otherwise; everything we do in the customer interface area is now done electronically; this is the key to business now and in the future.'

   'We will continue to use IT in the production areas of the business and in the year 2000 we will have no direct manufacturing jobs.'

   'New technologies attract talented people to the organization.'

Skeptical/ambivalent responses

   'Computer-generated data come to be treated as if they represent reality and are not checked for accuracy.'

   'Computer use can become a substitute for thinking.'

   'Computers are causing people to be lazy; the increasing reliance on the computer is reducing the propensity to think.'

   'Business becomes too numbers oriented; people look at the trees, not the forest, and miss the global aspects of the problem.'

   'IT provides too much information.'

   'I saw the last company I worked for get ruined and damn near broken by their MIS group; they are great at creating solutions to nonproblems.'

   'I'm not very impressed with the innovations that have come out of the computer and software industries.'

   'We are able to cost justify equipment, but we really don't know if it makes our people more effective.'

   'Computers may be used unethically; they move lies faster.'

   'IT leads to invasion of privacy.'

Table 5.6 *CEO visions of the potential impact of IT*

The vision to *automate*
The vision to *informate up*
The vision to *informate down*
The vision to *transform*

The vision to automate

Some CEOs in our sample saw the ultimate role of IT to be a way of replacing expensive, unreliable human labor with sophisticated robots, systems, and other IT devices. The promise of IT for them was that it would ultimately save money, improve quality, and thereby make the organization more effective. They tended to look at their organizations from a manufacturing point of view and were preoccupied with cost and/or technological issues.

Such CEOs would tend to be less utopian and more ambivalent or skeptical. The change agent role that they would be most likely to play is either to disconfirm the present cost structure by insisting on automation or to disconfirm the present use of technology by insisting on technological upgrading. In both cases they would focus more on the primary role of IT in the manufacturing process and would be relatively less sensitive either to the possible role of IT in the process of management or to the impact on the management system of the automation they were advocating.

As has also been pointed out, though this vision has long-range implications technologically and may involve major capital expenditures, it often proves to be shortsighted because the human implications are not carefully thought through and the systems in the end do not work as well as they should because they do not take advantage of operator creativity and innovation on the one hand and operator limitations in learning how to run automated systems on the other (Zuboff, 1988). In other words, the deeper assumption that human behavior can be automated in a complex technological environment may not be valid.

The vision to 'informate' up: 'control utopia'

The term 'informate' is taken from Zuboff (1988) and refers to the impact that IT has in making previously concealed parts of a system's processes more visible to people both higher up and lower down in the organization. For the production worker this might mean the ability to manage processes that were previously under the control of management. For managers this usually means the ability to control more precisely all aspects of the process because the information system would provide detailed performance data. For some CEOs, IT could then be the 'ultimate management control tool'. They assume that by installing the right kind of information system they could be completely informed about every aspect of every operation in their organization. Such information would enable them to pinpoint problems rapidly and set into motion remedial measures.

Such a vision appeals to the control-oriented executive and probably is functionally similar to the automation solution, except that what is being automated here is not the production process but the control process. The human hierarchy is being replaced with an information system. Toward this ultimate goal a number of the CEOs who insisted on installing terminals on their own and their subordinates' desks did so in order to facilitate the introduction of a complete communication network and a common information and control system. They could then determine exactly where deviances occurred and act on them immediately.

Some of the resistance encountered from subordinates was probably motivated by their recognition that once such a system was installed, it could easily be abused by a control-oriented CEO. Abuse here would be micromanagement on the part of the CEO, thereby undermining the rest of the organization, and possibly even the validity of the information fed into the system because of the tendency to falsify input data as a counter-reaction to the discomfort and anxiety that the system creates. Unfortunately, the system designers often collude with this type of CEO by reassuring him that they can make the system invulnerable to any kind of falsification.

In terms of our model of change, the type of CEO who is oriented toward control via an upward informating system will be an effective disconfirmer but will have trouble unfreezing the system because he will not be sensitive to the need to provide psychological safety. He may successfully coerce change, but the change will be superficial and unstable because it will not involve any cognitive redefinition on the part of the subordinates who are the change targets.

Such CEOs may be utopian about the potential of IT, but they are expressing an extreme degree of skepticism about human behavior, typical of McGregor's 'Theory X' (McGregor, 1960). As McGregor noted, the very existence of the complete information and control system signals to the rest of the organization that top management does not trust the human organization to inform and control itself adequately.

The vision to informate down

'Informating down' is what Zuboff observed to be the consequences of computerizing production processes and creating automated factories. If the production process was to be automated, it first had to be understood as a total system. To teach operators how to manage the new processes, the whole system had to be made transparent to them. Zuboff observed that not everyone could make the transition from manual work and the use of all the senses to primarily mental work that required a complex diagnosis of what was going on by deciphering what a particular configuration of data on a computer screen or a control panel revealed.

For those who could make the transition, the production process was demystified. One consequence was that supervisors no longer had the power that special knowledge or understanding had previously given them. This 'knowledge power' was now distributed throughout the work force. For many middle managers this loss of power was a direct threat, but for CEOs looking to create the 'factory of the future' this could be an entirely positive vision if they also had a Theory Y set of assumptions about human nature (McGregor, 1960) and were willing to push operational control down in the organization.

In our interviews we could not tell whether the executive advocating this kind of IT solution was genuinely interested in 'informating' his organization, or whether he was secretly hoping for lower costs and more centralized control. But at least in their words these CEOs were advocating a much more radical IT use than what was proposed in either of the previous visions.

In any case, such CEOs would be much more sensitive to the issues of creating psychological safety, both for operators who had to drastically change their concept of what their work would be in the future and for middle managers whose role might disappear altogether. They would also realize that changes of this magnitude would not occur without strong external and internal disconfirmation and induction of guilt or anxiety, and thus be forced to consider all of the stages of getting a change process started.

The vision to transform

A few CEOs saw IT as the basis for a complete transformation of their organization and industry. They could see how IT would change the organization's fundamental relationship to its suppliers and customers, how the introduction of networking, executive support systems, teleconferencing, and other IT innovations would fundamentally alter the nature of the products, markets, and organizational structure, and how these, in combination, would alter organizational boundaries, interorganizational relationships, and even the management process itself.

The role of hierarchy would change in that distributed information would make local problem solving and lateral information sharing much more feasible, and the role of the executive team in the strategy process would change if modeling and various kinds of decision support tools would make it possible to develop alternatives much more rapidly. In a sense IT would make it possible to be simultaneously more centralized around basic strategy and goals and more decentralized around implementation and control.

Power and authority would shift away from position and status toward knowledge and information, and leadership would become less of a role and more of a 'function', that is, more widely distributed as a function of the requirements of the task to be accomplished. More emphasis would fall on groups and teamwork, and boundaries between jobs as well as roles would become more fluid. That, in turn, would require a higher level of professionalization of the work force to deal with higher anxiety levels resulting from role ambiguity (Hirschhorn, 1988).

We encountered a few executives who seemed to be pushing toward this kind of vision, but most of them acknowledged that it would take some time before IT itself would be good enough and cheap enough to make this possible. They correctly foresaw that such transformations would require major cultural change that would take some time and effort to accomplish. Perhaps most troubling to them was the implication that the present work force might not be well enough educated or trained to fulfill the necessary roles in the transformed organization, an issue that is also present in the informated organization.

Such CEOs clearly fell into our utopian idealist category and their behavior in terms of the change model seemed to be oriented toward consistent but careful unfreezing because of their concern that their organizations might not be ready to handle the level of change ultimately required. They were, in this sense, another group who would be sensitive to psychological safety as an issue in the change process.

In summary, the basic assumptions held by the CEO were obviously a critical factor both in terms of how they saw the ultimate potential of IT and how optimistic they felt about the implementation of various IT projects within their organizations. But clearly, their own assumptions were not a sufficient explanation of their behavior. We found in the interview data that a number of other factors operated as powerful driving and restraining forces.

For example, many CEOs felt the technology was not yet good enough or cheap enough to deliver on its potential. These CEOs tended to press their IT community to improve the technology while restraining the organization from 'wasting money' on premature solutions. Other CEOs were greatly influenced by the behavior of their competitors, particularly in industries where IT had already proven its potential to provide strategic advantage. CEOs in larger, more diversified companies tended to let their divisions decide on the use of IT and were often reluctant to impose single systems on diverse subcultures, thereby limiting possibilities for standardization or broader systems integration. In many companies CEOs were very sensitive to the lack of readiness of the employees to utilize IT, or they had other financial priorities that made IT investments undesirable.

The factors identified by our CEOs as major influences on their decisions with regard to IT are, of course, interrelated and interactive. The most striking result, therefore, is the diversity of situations we encountered at the level of the CEO. We were seeking the common elements in how CEOs would structure their own behavior as change agents and found, instead, that the multiplicity of technological, industrial, organizational, and personal forces operating made such generalizations tenuous.

Conclusion

The change agent roles that these different executives take of course differ with their basic orientation and the situation of their organizations. As noted, all of the CEOs were driven by the state of affairs in their industry. Only a small number had utopian transformation visions that went substantially beyond what other companies in their industry were doing. Those few get singled out as heroic change agents by academics and the media, but the reminder from our data is that they are as yet a distinct minority.

The 'bottom line' seems to be that CEOs find themselves in very complex force fields and vary their behavior as change agents accordingly. They feel that the realities of their particular situation in terms of the size, age, structure, and financial condition of their companies, the technological possibilities and limitations, industry benchmarks, employee readiness, and the credibility and skill of their IT management all have to be taken into account in deciding how far and how fast to push the adoption of new IT tools. Many of them believe, therefore, that this complexity calls for the CEO to be an integrative force instead of an IT zealot, though they acknowledge that future generations of CEOs, who will have been educated much more thoroughly in the possibilities of the computer and IT, may be able to take a much more optimistic and proactive stance toward IT.

For the IT skeptic it will be reassuring to realize that there are a good many CEOs out there who are cautious, who have been burned, and who, therefore, are quite realistic about the limitations of today's IT solutions. On the other hand, for the IT utopian it will be very reassuring to know that many of our CEOs do involve themselves actively in IT projects, even if they personally do not use desktop workstations, and many more take IT for granted as a technology and a set of tools that will help their companies in many ways.

Though the focus in this chapter was on IT, it should also be noted in concluding that the CEO change agent roles identified apply to all kinds of organizational change, especially changes of a strategic nature that may require reorganization of work, authority relationships, and management styles. In all organization change and development projects the CEO role should be carefully diagnosed and taken into account, since that role has great power in getting the change process started.

Note

The interviews were conducted and analyzed by Buzzard (1988), Carey (1988), Donaldson (1987), Glassburn (1987), Harman (1987), Homer (1988), Kelly (1987), Kennedy (1987), Lasswell (1987), North (1987), Pilger (1987), Shuff (1988), Stewart (1987), and Sutherland (1988).

References

Buzzard, S. H. (1988) An analysis of factors that influence management of information technology in multidivisional companies. Unpublished master's thesis. Sloan School of Management, MIT.

Carey, D. R. (1988) Information technology: attitudes and implementation. Unpublished master's thesis. Sloan School of Management, MIT.

Dearden, J. (1983) SMR forum: will the computer change the job of top management? *Sloan Management Review*, **25**(1).

Donaldson, H. M. (1987) Executive assumptions about information technology in the service industries. Unpublished master's thesis. Sloan School of Management, MIT.

Festinger, L. (1957) *A Theory of Cognitive Dissonance*, Harper & Row, New York.

Gibson, C. F. and Jackson, B. B. (1987) *The Information Imperative*, D. C. Heath, Lexington, Mass.

Glassburn, A. R. (1987) A study of chief executive officer attitudes toward the use of information technology in executive offices. Unpublished master's thesis. Sloan School of Management, MIT.

Hambrick, D. C. (ed.) (1988) *The Executive Effect: Concepts and Methods for Studying Top Managers*, JAI Press, Greenwich, Conn.

Harman, P. E. (1987) Executive assumptions about information technology in the banking industry. Unpublished master's thesis. Sloan School of Management, MIT.

Hirschhorn, L. (1988) *The Workplace Within*, MIT Press, Cambridge, Mass.

Homer, P. B. (1988) A study of information technology innovation in high technology firms. Unpublished master's thesis. Sloan School of Management, MIT.

Keen, P. G. W. (1983) The on-line CEO: how one executive uses MIS. Unpublished working paper, Microframe, Inc.

Kelly, M. L. (1987) Attitudes and expectations of senior executives about information technology within the consumer electronics industry with emphasis on Japan. Unpublished master's thesis. Sloan School of Management, MIT.

Kennedy, H. E. (1987) CEO Assumptions concerning information technology in high technology firms. Unpublished master's thesis. Sloan School of Management. MIT.

Kotter, J. P. (1982) *The General Managers*, Free Press, New York.

Kraemer, K. L., King, J. L., Dunkle, D. E. and Lane, J. P. (1989) *Managing Information Systems*, Jossey-Bass, San Francisco.

Lasswell, S. W. (1987) Chief executive officer attitudes concerning information technology: a study of high technology and aerospace companies. Unpublished master's thesis. Sloan School of Management, MIT.

Lewin, K. (1952) Group decision and social change. In *Readings in Social Psychology*, rev. ed. (eds G. E. Swanson, T. N. Newcomb and E. L. Hartley), Holt, New York.

Markus, M. L. (1984) *Systems in Organizations*. Pitman, Boston.

McGregor, D. M. (1960) *The Human Side of Enterprise*. McGraw-Hill, New York.

Meyer, N. D. and Boone, M. E. (1987) *The Information Edge*. Gage Educational Publishing, Agincourt, Ontario.

Moore, J. H. (1986) Senior executive computer use. Stanford Graduate Business School. Unpublished working paper.

North, J. B. (1987) Attitudes of telecommunications executives about information technology. Unpublished master's thesis. Sloan School of Management, MIT.

Pilger, D. R. (1987) Chief executive officer attitudes toward information technology in the automotive and manufacturing industries. Unpublished master's thesis. Sloan School of Management, MIT.

Rockart, J. F. (1979) Chief executives define their own data needs. *Harvard Business Review*, March–April, 81–93.

Rockart, J. F. and DeLong, D. W. (1988) *Executive Support Systems*, Dow Jones-Irwin, Homewood, Ill.

Rockart, J. F. and Treacy, M. E. (1982) The CEO goes on-line. *Harvard Business Review*, January–February, 82–88.

Schein, E. H. (1961) *Coercive Persuasion*, Norton, New York.

Schein, E. H. (1969) *Process Consultation*, Addison-Wesley, Reading, Mass.

Schein, E. H. (1972) *Professional Education: Some New Directions*, McGraw-Hill, New York.

Schein, E. H. (1985) *Organizational Culture and Leadership*, Jossey-Bass, San Francisco.

Schein, E. H. (1987) *Process Consultation*, Vol. 2. Addison-Wesley, Reading, Mass.

Schein, E. H. (1988) *Process Consultation*, Vol. I, rev. ed. Addison-Wesley, Reading, Mass.

Shuff, R. F. (1988) A model of the innovation process in information technology. Unpublished master's thesis. Sloan School of Management, MIT.

Stewart, N. S. (1987) Chief executive officers: assumptions about information technology in the insurance industry. Unpublished master's thesis. Sloan School of Management, MIT.

Sutherland, D. J. (1988) The attitudes and management behaviors of senior managers with respect to information technology. Unpublished master's thesis. Sloan School of Management, MIT.

Thomas, A. B. (1988) Does leadership make a difference in organizational performance? *Administrative Science Quarterly*, **33**: 388–400.

Zuboff, S. (1988) *In the Age of the Smart Machine*, Basic Books, New York.

Commentary by Donald Runkle

The one issue that was not discussed in this chapter was the assumption that using information technology (IT) is a very good thing to do. There is very little discussion about whether IT is really worthwhile or not, or if it is really productive. I think that's probably still on the table.

I would say that from GM's (General Motors) standpoint, we have in progress, alive and running, a fascinating test of this chapter. Over the last decade we have had a pretty visionary chairman who fundamentally had the idea of an integrated company from an IT standpoint. But he didn't unfreeze the company before he decided to do the second part of it, which was to move and change it. He bought, as you know, a whole IT company, EDS (Electronic Data Systems). He spent a few billion dollars on EDS. There was little discussion about whether the acquisition was a good idea within the organization as a whole. Subsequent to the purchase he asked the company to begin the move toward an integrated company using a lot more IT, and he did that mostly through praising EDS and urging GM people to change. I would have to say that during that process the sparks flew. It has now settled down substantially, EDS has become much more flexible in the whole operation, and I think we are on our way to an integrated IT company.

I went through Professor Schein's typology, and I would have to say that our CEO is a utopian idealist. I think from the vision standpoint he would be in the category 'automate', replacing expensive, unreliable people with computer technology.

In hindsight, I think that this chapter would have been a good one to read and heed before we tried to integrate EDS into GM. It would have saved us some time and energy. The CEO should have spent a lot more time unfreezing the company and getting it more interested in proceeding. Clearly you still buy a company the size of EDS in a private manner to keep the prices down, but once it was bought it could have been absorbed as a separate subsidiary and then discussed openly with the organization as a whole to let them know that we needed to move toward more IT in the workplace. I also think it would have been very helpful to articulate what is referred to here as a psychological safety net of sorts, but that was not communicated at all and resulted in a great deal of fear as to what exactly was going on. We had a lot of problems in making it all happen. Also, using what is referred to here as 'scanning' would have been helpful.

Roger Smith (the chairman) was not a role model for scanning. He didn't use IT, so the scanning model could have helped us with the unfreezing process. We need to refreeze slowly, too. We are not yet fully unfrozen but are in the process of moving, and I can tell we need to refreeze slowly. My background and experience early in my career have been in this kind of area, and I am very enthusiastic about the capabilities of computers and IT. I would just say that before a company proceeds toward integration too heavily, you first need to simplify and streamline the operations. Do that first, and then document the needs and real requirements as far as what you want for IT, what you want it to do, and then automate what's left. Then book the savings in the beginning of the year, rather than implementing it and seeing what happens, and then booking it later. Put the expected gains in the budget right away.

I thought the model is worthwhile, and I just wish that the chapter had been written in 1983 so we could have read it prior to the EDS acquisition.

Reproduced from *Transforming Organizations*, edited by Thomas A. Kochan and Michael Useem. Copyright © 1992 by Sloan School of Management. Reprinted with permission of the publishers Oxford University Press, Inc.

Questions for discussion

1   Schein proposes various means of introducing change ('unfreezing'). In what circumstances do you think each would work best? Can you think of other approaches that might also create a perceived need for change?
2   What particular issues should a CEO expect to deal with in managing change where information technology is involved? How does this differ to the role played by the CIO?
3   In what circumstances might CEO-led change be particularly important? Or unnecessary?
4   'Unfreezing' is one thing, 'refreezing' is another. What methods would you adopt as a CEO in making the required change 'stick'?
5   Consider CEOs with whom you have come into contact. Utilizing Schein's typology, how would you describe their attitudes towards information technology? How, as an adviser or consultant would you attempt to change those attitudes (if you believe this is necessary)?
6   What particular issues would a CEO face in an informating or transforming change project, in comparison to mere automation?

6 Change Management Strategy

Change agentry – the next information systems frontier

M. L. Markus and R. I. Benjamin

We wrote this chapter to stimulate IS specialists' efforts to become more effective – and more credible – agents of organizational change. It describes what we believe to be a view of the IS specialists' change-agent role that is very commonly held by IS specialists. We believe that this role, while well-intentioned and supported by structural conditions in IS work, often has negative consequences for organizations and for the credibility of IS specialists. Further, it does not fit the emerging structural conditions of IS. We describe two alternative models of what it means to be a change agent, their potential consequences, and the structural conditions that support or inhibit behavior in that role. We conclude that increased behavioral flexibility of IS specialists – the ability to switch roles in different circumstances – would improve organizational effectiveness and IS specialist credibility. Finally, we discuss the implications of our analysis for research, teaching, and practice.

Introduction

We believe that IS specialists generally need to become better agents of organizational change than most are today (Benjamin and Levinson, 1993). In our research and consulting, we have seen many exceptional change agents among the IS ranks. But we have also seen many whose approach to introducing new technology into organizations is ineffective or counterproductive.

Why do IS specialists need to become better agents of organizational change? There are three primary reasons. First, new IT is an organizational intervention (i.e. an attempt to create change). A vast body of research literature shows that how IT is 'implemented' (e.g. how it is specified, designed, or selected; how it is described or 'sold'; how people, facilities, structures, and processes are prepared to accommodate the change) is a major factor in the results organizations achieve from new ITs. Yet, despite our vast knowledge of this dynamic, many organizations continue to fail in IT implementations (Majchrzak, 1992; Markus and Keil, 1994), often at great cost in money, organizational competitiveness, and individual careers.

This same literature also shows that IS specialists *alone* cannot achieve IT implementation success. Executives and managers must do their part, and individual 'users' must do theirs. Why, then, should *IS specialists* improve their change management skills? Shouldn't we just continue to exhort senior business executives to give IT projects better 'top management support'? The answer is that we *do* continue to urge business leaders do their part in IT change management. However, when they do *not*, or when they are not as effective as they should be, IS specialists *who are effective change managers* can often tip the odds of IT projects toward success, whereas those who are technically skilled, but ineffective as change agents, cannot.

Second, IS specialists need to become better organizational change agents because change agentry will most likely become the largest and most important part of intraorganizational IS work in the future. Twenty years ago, almost all IS work was done 'in-house', meaning that IS specialists were employees of the organizations that consumed their products and services. This was the case, in large part, because the software and professional services sectors of the computer world were immature. Today, however, these sectors are strong and growing. Organizations are increasingly outsourcing application development, computer operations, even IS management. Although precise statistics are unavailable, most observers believe that a significant portion of all IS work is now performed by external consultants and vendors.

Transaction cost considerations suggest that IS work that does not require organizational loyalty and/or specialized organizational knowledge and skill will migrate to the marketplace. In essence, this theory predicts that all purely technical IS work will cease to be performed in-house. Conversely, any IS work where organizational loyalty and insider knowledge of the organization – personalities, business process, culture, and politics – are essential or advantageous, will be less vulnerable to outsourcing. IT implementation (introduction, not 'coding') and change management are likely to remain in-house, because this work involves organization-specific knowledge and concern for the best interests of the organization and its members. Further, IT implementation and change management issues are unlikely to diminish in importance or difficulty with time, even if all IS technical work is outsourced and all IT challenges are tamed. And, if change management does indeed become *the* job of IS specialists, then IS specialists need to be able to do this job extremely well – better than most of them are doing it today.

Third, becoming better change agents is bound to improve IS specialists' organizational credibility. Many people think IS specialists have low credibility. CIO, the acronym for chief information officer, is often said to stand for 'career is over'. Outsourcing researchers acknowledge that low credibility of in-house IS specialists is often a factor in the decision to turn the job over to an external specialist. Paul Strassman, former CIO for the Department of Defense and noted IS consultant, says:

> It just happens that the IT community has consistently ranked in surveys as one of the least admired corporate functions. IT therefore becomes an attractive target when there is a quota on how many bodies must leave. (Strassman, 1995a)

We believe there is a strong mutual relationship between credibility and change management skill. First, effective change management *requires* credibility. If managers do not trust IS specialists, they will not let themselves be influenced by their technical competence. On the other hand, effective change management behavior *builds* credibility. When managers see IS specialists behaving in effective ways, they are more likely to trust them and adopt their proposals.

In our experience, ineffective IS specialists often blame their ineffectiveness on their low credibility: 'If only the CEO would tell everyone to listen to us, we could make a difference'. By contrast, effective IS specialists accept the negative stereotypes and quietly work to prove them wrong. By refusing to act within the 'box' created by formal structures and policies and informal expectations about how IS is supposed to do its job, these effective change agents transform not only their interpersonal relationships with their clients, but also the behavior of managers and users in IT projects and decision making. Organizational success and improved IS credibility result.

These are our reasons for believing that IS specialists need to become better change agents. So, what does this really mean? To answer this question, we reread the IS and change management literatures, we interviewed practising IS specialists, we conducted new case studies, and reanalyzed old ones. We learned that there are two basic issues at work.

First, there is substantial disagreement in both theory and practice about what it means to be 'an agent of organizational change'. In fact, we found three completely different definitions of what change agents do and why. The first definition reflects the views of many practising IS specialists, according to our own and others' research. The second model can be identified in various organizational development (OD) texts, such as Schwarz (1994) and Cummings and Huse (1989). The third model comes from the innovation, management, and change politics literatures (e.g. Kanter *et al.*, 1992; Rogers, 1995).

This very lack of consensus about what it means to be a change agent is an impediment to progress because it creates misunderstandings when talked about. Further, given their definitions of what it means to be a change agent, some IS specialists may legitimately see no need for change in their behavior.

Second, we learned that the different change agent roles grow out of, and are maintained by, various structural conditions (cf. Orlikowski, 1992). *Structural conditions* are social and economic arrangements, e.g. reporting relationships and policies, that influence the processes of IS work (e.g. which activities are done by in-house specialists and which by vendors and/or clients) and the outcomes of IS work (e.g. how successful IT projects are and how clients view specialists' credibility and effectiveness). An example is the organizational policy, common 20 years ago but virtually extinct today, requiring all information systems to be built in-house rather than by outside vendors (Friedman, 1989).

Structural conditions help us understand why the IS role is what it is today, and they help us understand why the IS role is difficult (though not impossible) to change. They also tell us where and how we need to intervene to make a difference – for instance, by changing official organizational policies that define the IS function's role and by education and training programs.

This chapter presents three different models of change agentry. The models should be understood as 'ideal types', rather than as empirical categories. Thus, any particular individual or group might exhibit some mix of the models, either at the same time or in different situations. Nevertheless, we believe these models broadly characterize dominant beliefs in each of the three different practice domains explored. In all three models, IS change agentry is understood as a basic orientation toward the goals and means of IS work that shapes what the practitioner does and how she or he does it. Change agentry is not something a specialist might do *instead* of doing IS work. Rather, it is part and parcel of IS work, as it is performed by specialists who are employees of the organizations for which the work is done. Thus, we see change agentry skill as essential to the successful performance of in-house IS work.

For each ideal type, the general role orientation, the probable consequences in terms of client satisfaction and project success, and structural conditions that enable or hinder IS specialists adopting it are described (see Table 6.1 for a summary). The chapter concludes with a discussion of the implications of our analysis for IS research, education, and practice.

The traditional IS change-agent model

In our interviews, IS specialists frequently referred to themselves as change agents. 'I've always thought of myself as an agent of change' is a fairly typical statement. But, when we probed, we found that many IS specialists view information technology as the real cause of change. Despite widespread academic debates on technological determinism – the ability of *technology* (versus people) to cause change – the belief that technology alone can make a big difference is widely held, both in academic and practical circles.

Table 6.1 *Comparison of three models of change agentry*

Agentry model	Traditional IS model	Facilitator model	Advocate model
Role orientation (the change agent's attitudes, beliefs, behaviors)	• Technology causes change • IS specialist has no change responsibilities beyond building technology • Specialist is an agent of change by building technology that causes change; specialist is a technical expert • Specialist is an agent of change by serving the objectives of others; specialist is the manager's pair-of-hands • Specialist does not hold self responsible for achieving change or improvements in organizational performance	• Clients make change using technology; technology alone does not • Facilitator promotes change by helping increase clients' capacity for change • Facilitator avoids exerting expert or other power over clients • Facilitator serves interests of all clients, not just funders and direct participants • Facilitator values clients' informed choice about conditions of facilitator's work; works to reduce client dependence on facilitator • Facilitator does not hold self responsible for change or improvements in organizational performance; clients are	• People, including the change advocate, make change • Advocate influences change targets in direction viewed as desirable by advocate • Advocate increases targets' awareness of the need for change • Advocate champions a particular change direction • Advocate tactics include communication, persuasion, shock, manipulation, power • Advocate and change targets are responsible for change and performance improvements • Advocate shares credit or avoids taking full credit for outcomes
Consequences of model applied to IS work (for professional credibility, project success, etc.)	• Widespread system failures for social reasons • Key systems success factors defined as outside IS role and influence • Technical organizational change blocked by IS • Low IS credibility • IS resistance to role change	• Greater attention to building user capacity might increase project success and IS credibility • Emphasis on client self-sufficiency would reduce client resentment and increase IS credibility • Many new ITs offer more scope to IS specialists who act as facilitators than to those who act as experts/builders	• Role fits a need in situations where IS specialists have or could have better ideas than clients about effective business uses of technology • Role might increase IS credibility; role emphasizes communication, which is a key factor in credibility

Table 6.1 (*continued*)

Agentry model	Traditional IS model	Facilitator model	Advocate model
Structural conditions compatible with role orientation	• IS is sole-source provider of services • Clients have limited technical and sourcing options • Low IS budget pressure exists • IS is centralized, responsible for many clients • IS is 'staff' function – responsible and rewarded for expert/functional performance, not business performance • IS holds 'control' role – with delegated authority over certain processes, decisions, behaviors • IS builds systems	• Facilitator is not a client group member • Facilitator's function lies outside the hierarchical chain-of-command • Facilitator's function is not formally responsible for business results, though some functional responsibility is inevitable	• One type of change advocate has no formal managerial authority and no delegated control, but may have valued resources to dispense • Another type of change advocate has line authority over the change targets and responsibility for achieving business outcomes • A third type of advocate occupies staff positions in the organizations for which change targets work; those who lack delegated control authority have much greater credibility than those who have it
IS Structural conditions incompatible with role orientation	• Decentralized IS • Outsourced IS • Purchased systems • Diversity of client technology and sourcing options • Strong IS budget pressure • New technologies that demand different 'implementation' activities	• Valuable expertise in technical or business subject matters • Formal responsibility for business or technical results • Staff control over clients' processes, decisions, behaviors • Concerns about locus of employment	• Absence of managerial authority over target • Staff control over target's processes, decisions, behavior

For instance, Silver (1990) defines as 'change agents' computer systems with particular characteristics.

IS specialists, it seems, consider themselves change agents because they identify psychologically with the technology they create. Because technology can be relied on to make change, IS specialists don't have to 'do' anything to make change other than build systems or install technology (McWhinney, 1992).

An additional premise of the traditional IS point of view is that the specific goals of technical change should be set by others, usually organizational managers. This allows the specialist to assign responsibility for any un-intended or negative consequences of IT to the people who set the goals. (Managers, however, often blame IS specialists for creating or failing to avert unwanted IT impacts.)

We summarize the role orientation of the IS specialist as follows:

> IT changes people and organizations by enabling them to do things they couldn't previously do and by constraining them to work in different ways than they worked in the past. I am an agent of *change* because I design and build the systems that enable and constrain people and organizations. My role is that of designing and building systems that, when they are used by people and organizations, will produce desirable organizational change. I am also an *agent* of change, because I do not set the goals for organizational change. I do not determine what is a desirable organizational outcome. I act as an agent for the managers of the organization by building systems that, when used, will achieve *their* objectives. I am not responsible for setting the objectives or for achieving them, but only for providing the technological means by which managers and systems users can achieve their objectives. I am an expert in technological matters, not in business matters or in the behavioral issues involving the use of systems.

Consequences

It must be emphasized that an occupational role is not the sole creation of the occupation's members. It is a joint product of what specialists do and what is *done to them* by their clients and others. But obviously, these two things are related. If people feel themselves to have been treated poorly, they often respond in kind.

It is undeniable that many organizations have achieved great results from IT and that much of the success of these undertakings has been due to the efforts of IS specialists. At the same time, we in the IS field owe it to ourselves to analyze dispassionately whether the traditional IS role (as a joint product of IS and clients) has enabled organizations to achieve the maximum possible benefits from their investments in IT. If we have in any way contributed to a shortfall in total benefits, we need to ask if and how we should change. In this context, to identify negative consequences that result from the traditional IS role is not to condemn the role occupants, *but to build a case for changing the IS role.*

Computer historian Andrew Friedman (1989) argues persuasively that in managing their relationships with users over time in various ways (with the obvious collaboration of users and managers), IS specialists have not effectively coped with the human and organizational issues in IT implementation. Building on his work, we see three negative consequences that can be traced, at least in part, to the traditional IS role.

Many IT failures

First, IT failures attributable primarily to 'implementation' problems rather than technical problems abound. Decades of implementation research have confirmed a variety of social success factors for systems (cf. Walton, 1989), but most of them have been defined as outside the traditional IS role (Markus and Keil, 1994). For instance, despite the large and growing literature on end-user training and learning (Compeau *et al.*, 1995), it is our observation that most IS units consider training to be a relatively minor part of their mission (in terms of resources allocated to it). Many IS departments outsource responsibility for systems training to human resources specialists and external vendors. Whatever the economic and practical rationales for these decisions, we believe they reflect deeply-held beliefs (probably shared by managers and human resource specialists, among others) about what is really IS work. By-and-large, those who subscribe to the traditional IS view believe that building systems is IS work, while training users is not.

An excellent example of crucial systems success factors defined as outside the IS job can be seen in a study of groupware implementation. Organizational culture and reward mechanisms inhibited consultants from sharing information in Lotus Notes databases, but IS implementors maintained a deliberate hands-off policy except for technical matters:

> We're [the IS group is] a common carrier – we make no guarantees about data quality. As for the problem of obsolescence, if they [the users] don't know it by now it is not my job to tell them. (Orlikowski and Gash, 1994)

IS inhibiting change

Another consequence of the traditional IS change agentry role is that it can ironically *inhibit* desirable organizational change rather than promote it (Beath, 1991; Markus and Robey, 1995; Nance, 1995). As technical experts, IS specialists are often stereotyped as being in love with technical change. And many of the IS specialists we spoke to described their understandable pleasure in learning new technologies. But this interest does not always mean that new technologies are made available to clients and users, even when the latter *want* them.

IS specialists know that clients always complain about something. A common complaint is that the technical environment is changing too fast for them to keep up. But an equally common complaint is exactly the opposite: that IS isn't moving as fast as clients want in adopting new technologies – for instance, PCs in the 1980s, client-server in the 1990s. And IS specialists often have very good organizational reasons for moving slowly with innovations, such as the benefits that derive from waiting until standards emerge and the desire not to disrupt users' problem-free operating environments.

But IS specialists also have personal/group interests in addition to organizational ones. As is true of all other organizational members, these group and organizational interests occasionally conflict, and IS specialists occasionally place their own goals ahead of organizational ones. Some things they do knowingly. For instance, one specialist told us that he often lied to his clients about the compatibility of technologies they wanted to purchase to limit the range of systems he had to support. But other times, we suspect that IS specialists are unaware of real differences of interests among themselves, clients, and users. They believe that what is in *their* interests is in the organizations' interests, when it is not. For instance, one CIO told us that in his experience most IS managers believe that anything that reduces the IS operating budget is in the interests of the organization. He explained that this is not true. There are numerous ways to reduce the IS budget that shift costs onto user departments and many things that would improve an organization's total performance picture that would require the IS function to change the way it does business. But these changes do not happen because the organization measures only IS functional cost, not total business process cost.

We believe that it is normal and rational behavior for IS specialists to act in line with their own interests and incentives. We also think that doing so is occasionally not in the best interests of the organization in which they work. The most effective practitioners in any occupational group, in our view, are aware of ethical dilemmas posed by conflicts of interest, can discuss them openly as questions of values and ethics (not just as questions of technology and economics), and sometimes, even often, find a win-win solution or subordinate their own needs. By contrast, we found that many IS specialists do not confront these issues directly, relying on organizational standards, persuasion, and manipulation of technical information to get their own way.

The **symptoms** are clients complaining about IS specialists blocking needed technical change, while IS specialists are desiring higher budgets to study new technologies. The **root cause**, in our view, is differences in interests about technical change. Even though technical change is ostensibly what IS specialists are all about, technical change creates problems and vulnerabilities as well as career development for them. Our **interpretation** is that many IS specialists fear that new technologies *in the hands* of users are a threat to their professional credibility and self-esteem. New technology makes them feel vulnerable: Unless they know everything about it, they will look technically incompetent when users inevitably experience problems. Further, even when a new technology's problems are known and tractable, the shakedown period increases their workload and working hours. The **solution**, in our view, is enlargement of IS specialists' roles to encompass change management skill in addition to technical expertise.

Reduced IS credibility

Perhaps *the* major consequence of the traditional IS change management role is credibility erosion. We have already cited Strassmann's (1995a) remark about the IT community as one of the least admired corporate functions. He said this in context of a discussion of IT outsourcing. He found that most of the companies that outsourced IT were poor financial performers – not the result he expected in light of the benefits claimed by IT outsourcing advocates.

In addition to poor organizational financial performance, the poor technical performance of IS departments explains some outsourcing decisions (Earl and Feeny, 1994; Lacity and Hirschheim, 1993). But we have seen numerous instances where IS credibility is low even when technical performance is excellent. Low credibility, despite technical excellence, can be traced to the poor interpersonal relationships that arise between IS specialists and their clients when specialists define their role in the traditional, technology-centered way. We found support for this argument in academic research and the writings of professional consultants.

Several loosely connected streams of research on innovation, impression management, and personal perception suggest that credibility is imperfectly related to technical competence and job skill. Change agents may have low credibility because clients perceive them to be 'heterophilous' (different in background, beliefs systems, interests) (Rogers, 1995) or to lack 'value congruence' (Sitkin and Roth, 1993). Conversely, trust can often be built and maintained through strategies that focus on interpersonal relationships between IS specialists and their clients after some threshold of technical performance has been achieved (Bashein, 1994; Bashein and Markus, 1995).

Similarly, a noted consultant argues that technical specialists can play three different roles in the course of their work for clients: the 'expert' role, the 'pair-of-hands' role, and the 'collaborator' role (Block, 1981). In Block's typology, the essential difference is which party takes the active role and which party takes the inactive role in defining the problem and specifying its solution. In the expert role, the specialist calls the shots, and the client acquiesces. In the pair-of-hands role, the client is in charge, and the specialist does whatever the client tells him or her to do. The collaborator role requires client and specialist to diagnose the problem jointly and to agree on a course for its solution. Although there are times when specialists are required to play the expert and pair-of-hands roles, Block explains that the collaborator role often yields the best results by producing a valid understanding of the problem and greater client willingness to implement the solution.

The other two roles have some advantages from the perspective of the specialist. But these advantages often exact a high price in terms of project success and specialist credibility. Consider the 'expert' role. Experts often have high status, and they feel good when their expertise is used. However, people may distrust and withhold data from those who set themselves up as experts, leading to incorrect diagnoses and solutions. Further, people may lack commitment to implementing solutions proposed by experts. And they may become dependent on experts, which in turn generates resentment and resistance. Dependent clients may fail to acquire routine and simple skills for themselves, thus preventing experts from pursuing opportunities for skill enhancement or promotions. In short, the expert role can reduce specialists' credibility and produce reactions that thwart project success, even when the specialist has great technical skills and professional qualifications. Similarly, Block shows that the pair-of-hands role does not exempt the specialist from client blame when the solution the client wants fails to work.

IS specialists can often be observed to adopt the expert and the pair-of-hands roles in IS development and reengineering projects (Markus and Robey, 1995). The conclusion is that the role behavior of IS specialists is a probable contributor to the high failure rates of projects involving IT. Lawrence (1969) makes a similar point in his classic work: resistance is often people's reaction to the change *agents*, not necessarily to the change itself.

This chapter focuses on the IS specialist's role in IT-enabled organizational change. Thus, our analysis differs somewhat from Block's, which focuses particularly on who (specialist, client, or both collaboratively) should specify what the change should be. Nevertheless, we agree with Block that the roles played by IT specialists while they do their technical work can profoundly affect the quality of the solution, client satisfaction with the solution and willingness to do what it takes to make it a success, and client satisfaction with, and belief in, the competence of the specialist (i.e. the specialists' credibility).

Structural conditions

The traditional IS worldview is highly consistent with the ways in which IS work has historically been structured and managed and is still in many organizations. In the past, the work of internal IS specialists was shaped by three factors (Friedman, 1989):

- policies that established internal IS specialists as sole providers of computer services
- technologies and structures that limited the number of options available to clients and users
- lack of external competition, which protected IS departments from budget cuts

Further, IS specialists typically worked in large centralized IS departments. While many IS managers tend to think of themselves as 'line' managers, because they have huge budgets and run large production facilities, the fact remains that most IS units do not have responsibility for key *organizational* results (e.g. profitability). Instead, they are measured and rewarded for functional unit goals, such as 'delivering usable systems on time, on budget', in the words of the head of a major academic IS department. 'Real' line managers stereotype them as 'staff' – a term with the highly pejorative connotations of 'out of touch with our needs' and 'telling us to do things that don't make business sense'.

These negative perceptions (that is, poor IS credibility) do have a basis in structural conditions. Since IS units were required to support many different organizational groups, they could not be expected to know all their clients' needs well and to serve all their individuals interests equally well. And the functional incentives of IS departments are known to promote goal displacement, such as the cultivation of technical expertise for its own sake and the substitution of functional unit goals for the enterprise goal of performance improvement.

In short, structural conditions make a good explanation for how the IS role evolved to its present form over time. They also make a good prediction of what the IS role is likely to be in the future, under two (unlikely) conditions: (1) that structural conditions stay the same, and (2) that IS specialists do not actively try to change their role. Further, structural conditions tell us a lot about why IS specialists might not want to try to change their role: structural conditions represent the obstacles they face in trying to do so. A former CIO of Dupont recounted how he spent the first five years of his tenure achieving a reliable operation, and the next five unsuccessfully trying to unleash an entrepreneurial, 'help the business', culture. The seeds of his failure lay in his own past success.

On the other hand, we believe there is a very good case for voluntary IS role change. As presented above, the case is that (leaving aside all past blame and all past success) the traditional IS has some consequences *that IS specialists perceive* as negative. An example is 'Career is over'.

Further, the structural conditions that shaped the IS role in the past are changing in ways that demand a proactive change in the IS role. We have already mentioned the trend toward outsourcing. In addition, many organizations that retain IS work in-house have radically decentralized the IS function, giving responsibility for applications development and other IT-related decisions to business unit managers. Finally, many new information technologies – from groupware to the World Wide Web – are acquired as packages, not developed in-house. While they may require customization and content, they don't require the same sorts of development activities that IS specialists have traditionally performed for transaction processing and decision support systems (Farwell *et al.*, 1992).

Where the structural conditions of IS work have changed – for example, where IS is decentralized or outsourced and where systems are bought, not built – the old IS worldview seems distinctly dated. So, when we studied a company that had recently decentralized its IS personnel to the business units, both the CEO and the IS manager told us in no uncertain terms and in almost exactly the same words: 'There are no *systems* projects here, only *business* projects.' We conclude that the IS role *must* change, despite the structural conditions that make it difficult to do so.

In summary, the traditional IS view of change agentry assumes that technology does all the work of organizational change and that 'change agents' only need to change the technology (slowly). This model rationalizes a narrow focus on *building* technology, rather than a broader focus on achieving business results. The next section describes an alternative view of the change agent, coming from the literature and practice of organizational development.

The facilitator model

The OD literature (e.g. Cummings and Huse, 1989; Schwarz, 1994) depicts the change agent's role something like this:

> Organizational change is brought about by people (not technology). In order to make real and lasting change, people in organizations need to be able to make informed choices on the basis of valid information (about others' views, not just about the business issues), and they need to accept responsibility for their own behavior, including the success of the actions they take to create change. I am an agent of change because I help people create the conditions of informed choice, valid information, and personal responsibility. I have an obligation to increase people's capacity to create these conditions so that they do not become or remain dependent on my helping them to do so. I have expertise in various subject matters (such as group dynamics and the effects of rewards on human motivation), but my primary role is one of facilitating the group and organizational processes by which people work on *content* (the particular business issues facing a group, such as the need for an information system). When I act as a process facilitator, I must avoid acting as a content expert and should not express my views about the specific technical or business issues at hand. In

performing my role, it is often, maybe always, the case that different parties have different goals, objectives, and interests in change. Therefore, I must always serve the interests of the 'total client system' (e.g. the organization and its external stakeholders), even when this is in conflict with the interests of the particular managers who 'hired' me as a consultant or with my own personal and professional interests.

This facilitator model of change agentry has several important points of difference from the traditional IS model. The first is belief about what causes change. OD practitioners believe that it is people (clients) who create change, not themselves as change agents or their change 'technology' (e.g. OD interventions). Therefore, OD practitioners intervene in (facilitate) group and organizational processes in ways intended to increase the capacity and skills of the clients to create change. (This is analogous to an IS department defining its role as one of teaching clients and users how to select and build systems for themselves, rather than doing systems building and selection for them.) Further, OD practitioners believe that this increased capacity should extend to the domain of OD work, so that the professional services of OD practitioners are not permanently required by a specific client. OD practitioners do, however, agree with traditional IS specialists in not accepting personal responsibility for whether change actually happens or performance improvement occurs. 'So long as they act effectively, facilitators are not responsible for the group's ineffective behavior or its consequences' (Schwarz, 1994). The client group or organization itself is believed responsible for results (Argyris, 1990).

Second, the facilitator model of change agentry differs from the traditional IS model in how it handles technical or business expertise. OD practitioners view themselves as experts in 'process' (in the sense of behavioral or group process, not in the sense of 'business' process), not as experts in the 'content' of the technical or business issue the client is dealing with. OD practitioners are repeatedly cautioned not to provide factual information, opinions, or recommendations that are unrelated to how the group tackles the problem (Schwarz, 1994). Making the analogy to the IS situation, the *facilitator* (in our change agentry sense) of a JAD session would feel free to describe the next stages of the JAD process or the evidence of an interpersonal conflict in the team, but not to discuss the relative merits of client-server versus mainframe computing or to recommend which software to buy.

A third key difference between the facilitator model and the traditional IS model of change agentry concerns OD practitioners' explicit awareness of their power and the dangers to the client of their using it. (See Markus and Bjørn-Andersen, 1987, for discussion of similar issues in IS.) OD practitioners know that their personal and professional interests do not always coincide with those of a particular client or the 'whole client system' (Schwarz, 1994). And they consider it unethical to use their power in ways that undermine clients' abilities to be informed and responsible. This is why they believe that acting as a content expert (e.g. giving technical advice) is incompatible with the facilitator role: it may exert undue influence on the client's choice.

There is increasing IS interest in, and research on, the facilitation of technology-mediated group meetings and decisions. This is important work, but the parallels between it and our facilitation model of change agentry are imperfect for two reasons: First, our concern is with the facilitation of organizational change, not the facilitation of group meetings *per se* (although much organizational change is, of course, planned in meetings). Second, there is a technical component of GSS facilitation, e.g. running the software, that is irrelevant to our concerns here.

Consequences

Why might IS specialists benefit from moving in the direction of the facilitator model of the change agent role? First, the OD approach to change agentry reduces some of the known points of friction in IS-client relations. For example, clients frequently complain about the imposition and enforcement of IT standards and about slow deployment of new ITs. In the traditional role, IS specialists tend to focus on why such policies are technically correct. This enrages their clients, who see it as self-serving behavior. By adopting more of a facilitator role, IS specialists would do things differently (leaving aside potential future changes in the structures of standards and policy setting). First, the IS specialists would focus on providing full and valid information about the alternatives. This means both pros and cons for each alternative, indicating who benefits and who pays. Second, the IS specialists would disclose their own group interests while encouraging open discussion of differences.

This requires a bit more explanation. One common OD intervention in negotiation situations involves helping people to distinguish between 'positions' (or proposed solutions) and 'interests' (or criteria by which a party judges a solution). When people become emotionally attached to their own positions, they often fail to see that another solution satisfies their interests as well or better, while at the same time meeting others' needs. It is very much easier to satisfy a client who says, 'I want to minimize users' and my relearning costs' than it is for the one who says, 'I want brand X'. Similarly, it's much easier for clients to accommodate IS specialists who say, 'We're afraid that you'll blame us for not meeting budget, schedule, and reliability targets if we go with a client/server architecture where we don't have much experience' than for those who say, 'The mainframe solution is better for this type problem'.

A second advantage of IS adopting more of a facilitator role is that it legitimizes IS responsibility for IT education and training for clients and users. As noted earlier, education, training, and other implementation activities are generally viewed as outside the IS role, in part because formal authority for training usually is assigned elsewhere (e.g. Human Resources). Yet, research and theory suggest that these factors have a profound, if not driving, influence on IS project success (Markus and Keil, 1994; Soh and Markus, 1995). Therefore, the IS function must *take responsibility* to ensure that IT training gets done right, regardless of who is officially in charge of training. Here we are making a distinction between what one CIO called 'an area of responsibility versus an area of active management'. IS specialists may not actively manage (design, deliver, contract for) IT training. Yet, IS units that take responsibility for this critical success factor (by facilitating its effective accomplishment) are much more successful as organizational change agents than those that do not. To do this job effectively, they need to know almost as much about technical learning, training, and communication as they do about IT.

The facilitator model of change agentry also places a value on making clients self-sufficient or independent of practitioner interventions. Dependence breeds resentment, and resentment destroys working relationships and professional credibility. We believe that clients' perceived dependence on IS specialists (whether it reflects a real lack of client skill or is an artifact of organizational IT sourcing policies) is a major factor in the poor credibility of many IS departments and CIOs today. Improved client self-sufficiency might turn this situation around.

A final advantage in movement toward the facilitator model is that many new information technologies provide greater opportunities to IS specialists who act as facilitators than to IS specialists who act as systems builders and technical experts. Interviews with IS specialists suggest that many new information technologies are not viewed as 'part of IS'. Examples include: digital telephony and voice mail, videoconferencing, the World Wide Web, etc. Probing reveals that these technologies are often considered as not part of IS because they are 'boxes'. That is, they provide minimal opportunities for building and development. Yet, many of these pre-programmed new technologies, such as group support systems, require considerable change facilitation skills for their effective deployment and use (in addition to software use facilitation). IS specialists who facilitate their clients' ability to make free, informed, and responsible decisions about IT adoption and use provide a valuable service, even if this work does not display IS technical expertise.

Structural conditions

OD practitioners recognize that certain structural conditions are necessary or at least useful for maintaining their role. They believe that, to be effective, they cannot be members (neither managers nor ordinary members) of the groups they facilitate. Of course, managers and members can successfully practice many facilitation techniques, but membership in the client system prevents them from acting formally as a neutral third-party. In the OD field, much attention is paid to the difficulties of being an internal practitioner. Internal practitioners strive to deal with these difficulties by removing themselves as far as possible from the formal chain-of-command. Ideally, they are organizationally separate from the human resource function and report directly to the chairman or CEO.

These structural conditions can be observed in the methodologies developed for systems development and reengineering projects by people from the OD tradition (cf. Bancroft, 1992; Mumford and Weir, 1979; Walton, 1989). OD-oriented methodologies differ considerably from traditional IS SDLC manuals or reengineering bibles. One striking difference is that IS specialists are never recommended to facilitate the OD-designed processes (although they may in fact do so (cf. Davidson, 1993)). As experts, IS specialists are viewed as ineligible for the facilitator role and consigned to ordinary group membership. By contrast, in the 'user-led design' processes designed by IS specialists, IS specialists often lead the user teams. When they do, they often depart from the prescribed facilitation role in numerous ways (Davidson, 1993). We think this divergence may result in part from the conflict between the IS specialists' role as technical experts and the demands of neutral, third-party facilitation.

In general, the structural conditions that support the facilitator model of change agentry – avoidance of expertise displays, non-member status, lack of line or staff authority over people or performance, etc. – are quite different from the structural conditions under which most internal IS specialists operate. In particular, the following structural conditions present in much IS work create potentially serious obstacles to IS adoption of the facilitator role:

* *Technical expertise.* IS specialists have valuable technical expertise. The facilitator role does not give them a way to use it.
* *Authority for organizational control.* Many IS departments have some organizationally delegated or mandated ability to control the behavior of their clients or to influence clients' decisions on technology issues, such as standards. As setters and enforcers of these rules and policies, IS specialists would be sending mixed messages if they tried, as OD practitioners try, to increase their clients' ability to make their own informed decisions.
* *Authority for technical outcomes.* IS specialists are generally measured, rewarded, and punished for the results they achieve on IS departmental or project budgets, project schedules, and the maintenance of reliable operations. According to the OD worldview, these responsibilities may prevent the practitioner from acting in the best interests of the client system, and thus may inhibit desired change. For instance, IS specialists may occasionally make decisions with the effect of reducing IS departmental budget expenses, while increasing the costs borne by users.

- *Concerns about employment opportunities.* The facilitator model of change agentry places a high value on increasing client self-sufficiency, reducing client dependence, and practitioners working themselves out of a job. If diligently practised, this value would work to promote downsizing and/or outsourcing of IS departments. These potential outcomes conflict with the personal interests many internal IS specialists have in their continuity of employment with a particular company.

In summary, the facilitator model of change agentry has the potential to reduce friction between IS specialists, clients, and users, thereby enabling better systems and IT management and enhanced IS credibility. These advantages make it worthwhile to consider how to move toward the facilitator model, despite obvious structural barriers. A third model of change agentry, drawn from the innovation and business change literature, also has some interesting potential advantages in the context of IS work.

The advocate model

A third model of the change agent role can be seen in the writings of innovation theorists, some line managers and consultants, academics from the organizational change management school, and change champion researchers (cf. Beath, 1991; Kanter *et al.*, 1992; Rogers, 1995; Semler, 1993). The distinguishing feature of this model is that change advocates work to influence people's behavior in particular directions that the *change agents* view as desirable, whether or not the change 'targets' themselves hold similar views. Thus, the advocate model differs sharply both from the traditional IS model, in which the change agent attempts to satisfy users' goals, and from the facilitator model, in which the change agent attempts to help clients realize their goals. By contrast, the advocate attempts to induce change targets – both individuals and groups – to adopt and internalize the change agent's views about what is needed to serve the organization's best interests.

Several recent articles in the trade press provide vivid descriptions of the advocate model. A consultant who has studied organizational change claims that roughly one-third of most companies' middle ranks should be composed of 'change leaders'. Change leaders are not necessarily the people who would be tapped for top management positions; they're 'the funny little fat guys with thick glasses who always get the job done' by operating with more than one leadership style and by doing whatever works (Katzenbach, cited in Sherman, 1995). A recent article by a manager in a software development company provides a window into the advocate model that is interesting because of its IS technical content (Allen, 1995). Similar descriptions of the advocate model of change agentry can be found in the business autobiography of Ricardo Semler (1993), among others.

The advocate model can be summarized as follows:

I cannot make change alone. Change is made through the actions of many people. But people often don't question the way things are done today. I am an agent of change because I see what needs to be done differently and I try to find a way to change people's minds about the need for change in the way we do things today. I often try to change their minds by creating an exciting vision of the future, talking to people about it, and by modeling desired behaviors. But I may also try to shock them with outrageous actions that bring their heads up. Once they see the need for change and adopt my vision of what to change to, they will make the changes themselves. But I'll probably need to remain steadfast in support of my vision of change over long periods of time before they all catch on. And if my position and resources permit, I may need to stabilize and reinforce the change by replacing certain individuals who retard change and by promoting or otherwise rewarding those whose behavior embodies the desired values.

Like the facilitator model of change agentry, the advocate holds that people, not technology, are the causal factors in change. However, the advocate differs from the facilitator in beliefs about the need for participation in identifying the nature and direction of change. Indeed, the advocate thinks of people more as targets of the advocate's interventions than as clients with purposes of their own. In addition, the advocate is much more flexible than the facilitator about the acceptable means of change. The advocate's approach can be summarized as 'whatever works'. The advocate does not insist that the targets make an informed choice based on valid information and does not hesitate to use overt persuasion, covert manipulation, symbolic communication, and even the naked exercise of formal power to achieve a desired change (Buchanan and Boddy, 1992). The most effective advocates pursue changes that serve the organizations' best interests, even when their personal or professional interests conflict.

Consequences

Why might IS specialists benefit from moving in the direction of the advocate model of change agentry? The primary advantage of this model is captured in the old 'programmer's lament': 'Users don't know what they want, and what they want is not what they need.' One of the real sticking points in the line taking leadership over IS (Rockart, 1992) is that many managers remain unaware of how IT can most effectively be deployed in their organizations (although this appears to be changing). So, for example, a CIO of a large, diversified electronics company with 20 years tenure told us that his most successful change strategy was to build small demonstration systems (e.g. client/server prototypes) as vehicles for discussing organizational improvement opportunities with his internal clients. Another sticking point is that many line managers share the traditional IS specialists' belief in the magical power of technology to create organizational change. Thus, IS specialists can add business value by advocating process change and user skill training as key components of IT-enabled organizational performance improvement. While the advocacy of socio-technical change is not the exclusive province of IS specialists (since line executives have an important role here too), there is certainly more room for IS specialists to expand their role in this direction.

Another advantage of the proactive advocate role is its emphasis on communication. In our research and consulting, we have often been struck by the relatively infrequent communications between CIOs and CEOs, between CIOs and the heads of other organizational units, between IS analysts and users, and so forth. We have also heard frequent complaints about the IS function's lack of credibility. We think these two issues are related. One cannot be a successful advocate of major change without many, many interactions and discussions with the change targets. To put it in sports language, change agentry is a contact sport. According to the research literature (Bashein, 1994), credibility is often a side-effect of frequent, pleasurable communication. Therefore, it seems quite likely that IS professional credibility would improve substantially if IS specialists treated good communication with clients as central to their role.

Third, the advocate role may fit the issues of IT infrastructure better than either of the other two models. The major challenge of many in-house IS specialists today is to ensure threshold levels of commonality and interoperability to support internal and external communication and future flexibility. In economists' terms, this is a public goods problem (Markus and Connolly, 1990): because everyone benefits from IT infrastructure, no one wants to pay for it. Therefore, neither rational persuasion based on technical expertise nor a participatory, consensus decision-making approach may result in the optimal organizational result. Most organizations need considerable assistance to negotiate the political shoals of IT infrastructure development (Keen, 1991; Davenport *et al.*, 1992; Strassman, 1995b).

Structural conditions

Various assumptions are made about the structural conditions defining the change advocate's role. Early diffusion of innovation research was largely government funded and focused on change agents who worked for public agencies organizationally independent of the targets (cf. Rogers, 1995). Lacking formal managerial authority over targets, such advocates are structurally unable to mandate or enforce the desired change. (They may, however, have potentially valuable resources to dispense, such as funds, equipment, advice, and positive regard.) For the most part, these advocates are limited to tactics that include: communicating frequently with change targets; empathizing with targets; gaining targets' confidence by stressing their similarity with the targets in social station and attitudes; and working through the targets' 'opinion leaders'.

A second assumption, more common in the management and change literatures, is that the advocate is a line manager with direct authority over the change targets. In this case, the assumption is that the manager theoretically could mandate and enforce the desired change in behavior. However, effective managerial change advocates know this strategy is not likely to be effective, either because the desired change requires people's internalized commitment or because the targets may have good reasons to resist the desired change. (For example, the targets may honestly believe that the change is not in their own best interests or the interests of their firm.) Therefore, these advocates try to create change by behavior modeling and changing organizational symbols, and use displays of power primarily to reinforce and stabilize the change rather than to initiate it.

Later research in the technology and innovation management tradition (cf. Dean, 1987) has focused on internal change champions who occupy staff positions (sometimes in line departments, cf. Beath, 1991) in the organizations where the targets of change are employed. These change agents have some of the same resources that external agents do: access to funds for development, for example, or valuable expertise. And they similarly lack line management authority. Often, however, they have delegated authority from line managers to control certain aspects of their clients' behavior (Block, 1993).

While staff specialists groups often greatly prize their delegated authority, it can seriously undermine their ability to act as effective change agents (Block, 1993). From the targets' point of view, change agents with delegated (versus line) authority to reward and punish targets' behavior lack credibility and legitimacy to a much greater extent than staff advocates without the power to control them (or than line managers with legitimate authority). Staff specialists with control power are universally viewed as people with a particular axe to grind, with interests unaligned with those of the organizations in which they work.

Many internal IS specialists occupy this unenviable position. They lack direct line authority over users and the managers who fund systems projects. But they often have delegated authority to serve as 'guardians of the data resource', 'enforcers of technology standards', and 'approvers of requests for systems, software, and services'. As a result, they may not be able to fill the change advocate role as effectively as external change agents or as staff members (like OD practitioners) who lack or decline to exercise organizational control.

This structural position translates into enormous difficulties when line managers abdicate their essential roles as change advocates and champions in

IT infrastructure projects and business process redesign projects. Almost all projects of this sort are believed to require senior executives to initiate and support the change effort (Hammer and Stanton, 1995). Nevertheless, they often cop out of this role. When they do so, CIOs and IS managers may try to fill the gap. While there is undoubtedly much scope for IS specialists as change advocates, many IS advocates in these big projects are undone by their low credibility (due to their delegated control authority) coupled with their peers' perceptions that senior executives will not back them up. When such projects fail, as they almost invariably do, IS specialists make the perfect fall guys. On the other side of the dilemma, IS specialists may also be blamed for *failing* to step into the breach left by abdicating executives.

Implications

In sorting out the implications of our analysis, we note that our models apply at two levels: the in-house IS function as a whole and the individual IS specialist (e.g. the CIO or a business analyst). We conclude that, for the in-house function as a whole, the traditional IS model is rapidly becoming unviable. (Davenport *et al.*, 1992, have similarly concluded that 'technocracy' is the least effective model of information management.) Our reasons are several: First, the structural conditions that originally shaped the traditional IS role are changing in directions that undercut its effectiveness. Second, the traditional role undermines the credibility of IS specialists. Third, high credibility is needed for in-house IS specialists to contribute to positive organizational change.

On the other hand, neither alternative role clearly dominates. The facilitator role appears to be most useful with respect to black box technologies that don't need user-organization programming (e.g. personal digital assistants and integrated enterprise packages) and for some process reengineering projects; the advocate role appears to be most needed for IT infrastructure and possibly reengineering. The required new IS role may actually be some mix of all three models:

> Our role as the in-house IS function is to help our organization improve, that is, to change in a positive direction relative to the whole organization's best interests. To do this, we must recognize that our view of the organization's best interests does not always coincide with those of others. Therefore, we must sometimes use political advocacy, sometimes employ third-party facilitation skills, and sometimes invoke our technical expertise.

We see several major obstacles to adopting this new role – overreliance on technical expertise, authority to control or influence users' IT decisions, and responsibility for technical outcomes. Technical expertise involves knowing and telling 'the right answer'. But technically right answers can sometimes (often?) be wrong for social or political reasons. Insisting on technically right answers can actually prevent progress by inhibiting a workable organizational consensus around a technically adequate, if somewhat inferior, solution. In order to facilitate consensus, change agents must at least temporarily shelve their expertise and professional interests, because these factors can blind them to technically inferior solutions that are better because they can work (in the social or organizational sense). Similarly, control in the absence of line authority is a weapon that often backfires on those who use it. Control activity makes a staff unit into a political player with a vested interest in the outcome and therefore a prime a target of others' political might, when the unit tries to negotiate an enterprise-wide solution. Finally, responsibility for systems development budgets and schedules can divert IS specialists' attention and interests from bottomline organizational performance (Markus and Keil, 1994).

The first of these obstacles can probably be removed just by a change of mind. If experts can acknowledge that technical excellence is only one of several competing criteria for an effective solution, they will better be able to know when the technical best is not good enough. The second and third obstacles, may, however, require formal change in IT governance policies and structures. To be really effective as an agent of organizational change, the IS unit may have to eschew control authority, e.g. by pushing responsibility for IT standards back to business units or to some consensus organizational decision-making process. At the very least, IS units should probably separate as far as possible those individuals and subunits who perform the control role (e.g. budget approvals) from those whose activities involve IT-related organizational improvement work (e.g. system selection or specification, process reengineering, etc.). Similarly, Markus and Keil (1994) have recommended changes in the way IS units are measured and rewarded to reduce the dysfunctional effects of goal displacement.

Even very small IS departments have some internal job specialization. This suggests that not every IS specialist may have the same degree of client contact or the same involvement in bringing about organizational change. Thus, there is probably some argument for having different individuals specialize in our three change agent roles. And undoubtedly some of this would occur naturally, because of differences in individual skills and temperaments. But our tentative conclusion is that all IS specialists who do or could work with in-house clients need to be intellectually familiar with, and behaviorally skilled in, all three roles in order to be most credible and most able to contribute to organizational success with information technology. In our view, the most effective IS specialists are those who can shift rapidly from one model to another depending on the circumstances. Our following recommendations for research, teaching, and practice reflect this, as yet unconfirmed, hypothesis.

A research agenda

Our analysis suggests the need for new branches of computer personnel and IT management research that builds on work by various researchers such as Farwell *et al.* (1992), Trauth *et al.* (1993) and Todd *et al.* (1995) on IS skills and career paths; Iacono *et al.* (1995) on internal IS relationship managers (also known as internal consultants, client executives, or account managers); Buchanan and Boddy (1992) on project managers; Beath (1991) on IT champions; and Davenport *et al.* (1992) on IT governance.

There are descriptive, explanatory, and prescriptive questions to be answered. Descriptively, we need to know how in-house IS departments and in-house IS specialists in various job types view their roles as agents of change. It would also, of course, be interesting to explore differences between IS specialists who work in-house and those who do similar work as consultants or vendors.

Explanatory research is needed to determine the relationships between the roles IS departments and specialists adopt and (1) organizational or individual differences, (2) structural conditions, and (3) particular types of IT-enabled change situations (e.g. traditional systems development, emerging IT, reengineering projects, infrastructure development). Similarly, we need to determine the relationships between change agent roles and the important outcomes of IS specialist and departmental credibility and organizational success with IT projects. The research in this category would build upon and extend past research in the areas of IS management, particularly the centralization/decentralization/distribution debate. The majority of prior research in that area has emphasized cost and firm financial performance as the key outcome variables of interest (cf. Rockart and Benjamin, 1991; von Simson, 1990) rather than IS credibility and organizational success with IT projects.

Normatively, we also need research on how best to bring about change in IS roles and/or the structural conditions that underpin them. This research lends itself to field quasiexperiments and action research. Academics who partner with IS managers attempting to change practice might make important contributions to theoretical knowledge as well.

Educational reform

One dimension of change agentry is often called interpersonal or 'soft' skills. (Knowledge of organizational behavior and intervention skills is also involved in change agentry.) There is a perennial debate about the place of soft skills training in IS and other technical curricula. We have attended numerous business meetings over the last few years where IS and business executives have complained about the lack of interpersonal skills in their new IS hires. On the other hand, we have heard numerous objections from our academic colleagues, not least of which is that, whatever IS executives say about the need for soft skills, they always *hire* the most technical students. Furthermore, colleagues who have helped develop or teach in IS curricula with a large soft skills component have told us that these programs often collapse over time because of the technical orientations of new faculty members.

Clearly, there are many unanswered questions about the need for, and the efficacy of, interpersonal effectiveness training in IS curricula. We don't know, for example, whether such training would benefit all students or whether it would benefit only those with particular career plans. We also don't know whether IS faculty have the knowledge and skills to teach such courses, even if good educational materials are available.

Despite the unanswered questions, we believe that the IS academic community should engage the soft skills education issue proactively. Some of the answers will undoubtedly emerge from experience. Nevertheless, we have some initial thoughts about the relevant content and program structure.

First, in Table 6.2, we propose an outline of content areas for a 'course' on change agentry. This course has as its objective the development of cognitive, affective, and behavioral knowledge and skill. This means that, in addition to 'content inputs', e.g. lectures and readings on the topics, there should be opportunities for students to practise different role behaviors in circumstances where they can get constructive feedback about the effects of their behavior on others. We find that role plays (with video playback and small group critique) using case scenarios of realistic IS job situations are the best ways to foster affective and behavioral learning. We have seen relatively few published materials that are suitable for this purpose. Boddy and Buchanan's (1992) book on interpersonal skills for project managers is a useful model, but the examples are not tailored specifically to IS situations. We think that IS-tailored materials are essential for students to perceive the course as directly relevant to their career success. We have had some luck developing such scenarios by using excerpts from newspaper and magazine articles, qualitative research reports, and interview transcripts. We call the scenarios 'credibility crunches' because they illustrate how IS specialists can enhance or reduce their own professional credibility by their responses to various situations that occur routinely in IS work. Much simplified examples include:

- The client insists that you acquire/build a system with specific features. You know that the intended hands-on users will find the system too hard to learn or else they will resist using it because of the way it changes familiar tasks or redistributes some important political resources. What do you do?
- You support several different client groups. Your clients have told you their priorities, but your boss in IS has given you a different set of marching orders. What do you do?
- Your client has just discovered that her project is late and seriously over budget. She comes in screaming at you (literally) and threatens to get you fired. What do you say to her?

Table 6.2   *Proposed educational program on change agentry*

Topic	Objectives • to promote cognitive, affective, and behavioral learning about:
Change agentry	• IT as an organizational intervention • What it means to be a change agent regarding IT in organizations • Different types of change agents • Structural conditions that support/hinder IS change agents • Change process and the role of the change agent • Professional credibility and its role in change agent effectiveness • Routine difficulties that derail change processes • How change agents can/should cope with routine change difficulties • Professional, emotional, and ethical dilemmas of change agents • Explicit/implicit change contracts between agents and clients/targets
The Technical Expert	• The history and sociology of professionalism; the role of professional societies legislation, etc. • Why the IS specialist lacks full status as a professional • The pros and cons of professionalism • Recent trends in medicine, law, accounting, and implications for IS • 'Personality' characteristics of technical experts/IS specialists • Technical experts in organizations: the roles and relationships of 'staff'/IS departments • When and how IS technical expertise is appropriately/inappropriately used • How expertise generates defensiveness in both experts and clients • How to cope with defensiveness to avoid derailing change
The Facilitator	• The history of facilitation in psychotherapy and organizational development • IS facilitation examples: JAD, GSS, strategic planning, reengineering • The goals and values of facilitation • The benefits and limitations of IS facilitation • Structural conditions and organizational issues of IS facilitation • The facilitation process and how to facilitate • When IS facilitation is appropriate/inappropriate • The ethical dilemmas of facilitators and how to deal with them

Table 6.2   *(continued)*

Topic	Objectives • *to promote cognitive, affective, and behavioral learning bout:*
The Change Advocate	• The history of change advocacy in grass roots ('radical') politics • The goals, values, and ethics of change advocates • The general manager as change advocate • The IS specialist as change advocate • The tactics of change advocates and how they can be used in IS situations • Credibility/ethical issues in IS change advocacy and how to deal with them

In short, such a course already assumes a level of business experience and personal development that many young IS students may not have. Therefore, we do not recommend that a course in change agentry be offered to beginning IS students. However, a change agentry course would likely have little impact on students if it were offered at the very end of a program with no prior related work. This, we believe, is also the fate of other 'broadening' subjects, like 'computers and society', when they are left to the end of curricula. Therefore we recommend that a change agentry course be the final course in a small track geared to 'professional development'. The first in the track, we believe, should be the 'computers and society' course. We would offer this in the first year of an IS specialist curriculum for two reasons. First, many early IS students are stronger cognitively than behaviorally or affectively, and this course can effectively engage them at the intellectual level, setting the stage for later behavioral and affective growth. Second, this course promotes the development of insight and perspective before the student takes more technical subjects such as systems analysis, and so should precede, rather than follow, those subjects.

The second course in the professional development track would introduce experiential methods to complement cognitive skills development. The focus of this course would be interpersonal skills in the IS context. As with the change agent course, it would make heavy use of IS-specific exercises and role plays. At the content level, it would cover:

- individual differences (cognitive, affective, behavioral) and the student's own personal styles
- active listening skills, interpersonal conflict, interviewing techniques
- recognition of, and intervention in, group and intergroup dynamics.

This course would be a mandatory prerequisite for the course in change agentry, the last in the soft skills track.

Changes in practice

There are two areas of practice in which we see the need for initiatives, in addition to changing the structural conditions governing in-house IS work: (1) in-house training and development for IS specialists, and (2) IS professional ethics.

Recently, one of us had the opportunity to conduct a workshop on professional credibility for a group of high-level staff executives from a variety of disciplines (accounting, HR, IS) in different firms. The participants had many common concerns about their need for credibility to perform change management well and about the structural aspects of their jobs that jeopardized their credibility. The experience led us to believe that these issues should be incorporated into internal development and training programs for IS specialists. Here are our suggestions:

- Partner with internal training staff, organizational development specialists, and/or academics to design and conduct the training. Select trainers who are perceived as neutral (not able to evaluate the participants' job performance) and skilled at giving feedback and dealing with emotional topics.
- Make participation in this type of training voluntary and avoid including bosses and their subordinates in the same training session. (Also avoid large differences in participants' status.) Start experimentally with the most interested participants before trying to craft a large-scale program.
- Don't worry excessively about training materials at first. Experienced professionals can easily generate their own. Before the first workshop, the trainers should interview participants about difficult situations they have faced in the past. These 'critical incidents' can be sanitized and written up to serve as the basis for discussions and role plays of effective and ineffective behaviors. Over time, a much richer set of instructional materials and methods will evolve naturally.
- Document and disseminate some of the key lessons learned from the training sessions. The resulting document can be circulated to people who did not participate directly, sensitizing them to the issues and building their interest in attending the training.

A second area of practice that needs to be revisited in the light of our analysis is IS professional ethics. In-house IS change agentry immediately raises profound ethical dilemmas to a much greater extent than other computer-related work, e.g. hardware development. For instance, when interests differ, as they almost always do, whose interests are to be served: those of the IS specialist or function, those of the user, those of the person or unit paying the bill, those of the organization as a whole? When we examined the ethical guidelines prepared by OD practitioners (cf. Cummings and Huse, 1989), we found that these issues are squarely addressed. But when we examined ethical codes prepared for the computer science community (Anderson *et al.*, 1993; Oz, 1994), we found that they are not. In-house IS specialists clearly must concern themselves with the ethical issues that computer science codes cover well, such as intellectual property rights, privacy, risks, occupational health and safety, etc. But in-house IS specialists face additional ethical dilemmas arising from their change agent role that are not now addressed in relevant ethical codes.

To us, the conclusion is clear. The IS community needs a separate code that specifically addresses the ethical dilemmas faced by *in-house* IS professionals. It can incorporate the ACM and similar codes, but it should also go beyond them to tackle in-house change agentry. We would like to see AIS, SIM, and other leading IS institutions champion this initiative.

Conclusion

We undertook this research to stimulate IS specialists' efforts to become more effective agents of organizational change. We discovered a variety of obstacles. First, we found widely differing views about what it means to be a change agent. Unless these differences are acknowledged directly, miscommunication is likely to arise, inhibiting progress. We found, further, that many IS specialists do not see any need to change, because they already view themselves as effective change agents. However, their definition of the IS change-agent role does not fit the emerging structural conditions of in-house IS work, and this role erodes the credibility of the in-house IS function. In addition, we found several structural barriers to change in the IS change-agentry role, especially overreliance on technical expertise, control authority, and an inappropriate reward system.

Despite these obstacles, we remain optimistic about the prospects for change in the role of the in-house IS specialist. IS managers and executives have the structural ability to act as effective change advocates inside IS departments. Further, IS managers and executives are likely to be effective change advocates with their peers and superiors when the topic is structural change in the IS function. Voluntary efforts on the part of IS departments to relinquish or share the control that their clients so resent could substantially increase IS credibility and influence in major enterprise change efforts.

Acknowledgements

We gratefully acknowledge the assistance of the members of IS366 at the Claremont Graduate School (Spring 1995) in our investigations. This work has benefited greatly from the helpful comments of Bob Zmud and two anonymous reviewers, Chris Sauer, Christina Soh, Ang Soon, Sung Juhn, Carole Agres, Larisa Preiser-Houy, Dan Manson, Jeanne Ross, and Michael Vitale.

References

Allen, C. D. (1995) Succeeding as a clandestine change agent. *Communications of the ACM*, **38**(5), 81–86.

Anderson, R. E., Johnson, D. G., Gotterbarn, D. and Perrolle, J. (1993) Using the new ACM code of ethics in decision making. *Communications of the ACM*, **36**(2), February, 98–107.

Argyris, C. (1990) *Overcoming Organizational Defenses: Facilitating Organizational Learning*, Prentice-Hall, Inc., Englewood Cliffs, NJ.

Bancroft, N. H. (1992) *New Partnerships for Managing Technological Change*, John Wiley & Sons, New York.

Bashein, B. J. (1994) Reengineering the credibility of information systems specialists. Unpublished doctoral dissertation, The Claremont Graduate School, Claremont, CA.

Bashein, B. J. and Markus, M. L. (1995) Reengineering the credibility of information systems specialists. Working paper (available from the first author), California State University, San Marcos, CA.

Beath, C. M. (1991) Supporting the information technology champion. *MIS Quarterly*, **15**(3), September, 355–377.

Benjamin, R. I. and Levinson, E. (1993) A framework for managing IT-enabled change. *Sloan Management Review*, Summer, 23–33.

Block, P. (1981) *Flawless Consulting: A Guide to Getting Your Expertise Used*, Pfeiffer, San Diego, CA.

Block, P. (1993) *Stewardship – Choosing Service Over Self-Interest*, Berrett-Koehler Publishers, San Francisco, CA.

Boddy, D. and Buchanan, D. (1992) *Take the Lead: Interpersonal Skills for Project Managers*, Prentice Hall, New York.

Buchanan, D. and Boddy, D. (1992) *The Expertise of the Change Agent: Public Performance and Backstage Activity*, Prentice Hall, New York.

Compeau, D., Olfman, L., Sein, M. and Webster, J. (1995) End-user training and learning. *Communications of the ACM* **8**(7), July, 24–26.

Cummings, T. G. and Huse, E. F. (1989) *Organization Development and Change*, 4th edn, St. Paul, MN.

Davenport, T. H., Eccles, R. C. and Prusak, L. (1992) Information politics. *Sloan Management Review*, **34**(1), 53–65.

Davidson, E. J. (1993) An exploratory study of joint application design (JAD) in information systems delivery. *Proceedings of the Fourteenth International Conference on Information Systems*, Orlando, FL, pp.271–283.

Dean, J. W., Jr. (1987) Building for the future: the justification process for new technology. In *New Technology as Organizational Innovation* (eds J. M. Pennings and A. Buitendam), Ballinger, Cambridge, MA, pp.35–58.

Earl, M. J. and Feeny, D. F. (1994) Is your CIO adding value? *Sloan Management Review*, Spring, 11–20.

Farwell, D., Kuramoto, L., Lee, D., Trauth, E. and Winslow, C. (1992) A new paradigm for MIS: implications for IS professionals. *Information Systems Management*, **9**(2), 7–14.

Friedman, A. L. (1989) *Computer Systems Development: History, Organization and Implementation*, John Wiley & Sons, Chichester, UK.

Hammer, M. and Stanton, M. A. (1995) *The Reengineering Revolution: A Handbook*, Harper Business, New York.

Iacono, C. S., Subramani, M. and Henderson, J. C. (1995) Entrepreneur or intermediary: the nature of the relationship manager's job. *Proceedings of the Sixteenth International Conference on Information Systems*, Amsterdam, The Netherlands, pp.289–299.

Kanter, R. M., Stein, B. A. and Jick, T. D. (1992) *The Challenge of Organizational Change: How Companies Experience It and Leaders Guide it*, The Free Press, New York.

Keen, P. G. W. (1991) *Shaping the Future: Business Design Through Information Technology*, Harvard Business School Press, Boston, MA.

Lacity, M. C. and Hirschheim, R. (1993) *Information Systems Outsourcing: Myths, Metaphors, and Realities*, John Wiley & Sons, Chichester, UK.

Lawrence, P. R. (1954) How to deal with resistance to change. *Harvard Business Review*, January–February (originally published in 1954), 4–12, 176.

Majchrzak, A. (1992) Management of technological and organizational change. In *Handbook of Industrial Engineering* (ed. G. Salvendy), John Wiley & Sons, New York, pp.767–797.

Markus, M. L. and Bjørn-Anderson, N. (1987) Power over users: its exercise by system professionals. *Communications of the ACM*, **30**(6), June, 498–504.

Markus, M. L. and Connolly, T. (1990) Why CSCW applications fail: problems in the adoption of interdependent work tools. *Proceedings of the Conference on Computer-Supported Cooperative Work*, Los Angeles, CA, pp.371–380.

Markus, M. L. and Keil, M. (1994) If we build it they will come: designing information systems that users want to use. *Sloan Management Review*, Summer, 11–25.

Markus, M. L. and Robey, D. (1995) Business process reengineering and the role of the information systems professional. In *Business Process Reengineering: A Strategic Approach* (eds V. Grover and W. Kettinger), Idea Group Publishing, Middletown, PA, pp.569–589.

McWhinney, W. (1992) *Paths of Change: Strategic Choices for Organizations and Society*, Sage Publications, Newbury Park, CA.

Mumford, E. and Weir, M. (1979) *Computer Systems in Work Design – The ETHICS Method*, John Wiley & Sons, New York.

Nance, W. D. (1995) The roles of information technology and the information systems group in organizational change. Working paper available from author at San Jose State University, San Jose, CA.

Orlikowski, W. J. (1992) The duality of technology: rethinking the concept of technology in organizations. *Organizational Science*, **3**(3), April, 398–427.

Orlikowski, W. J. and Gash, D. C. (1994) Technological frames: making sense of information technology in organizations. *ACM Transactions on Information Systems*, **12**(2), April, 174–207.

Oz, E. (1994) *Ethics for the Information Age*, Wm. C. Brown Communications, Dubuque, IA.

Rockart, J. F. (1992) The line takes the leadership – IS management in a wired society. *Sloan Management Review*, **33**(4), December, 47–54.

Rockart, J. F. and Benjamin, R. I. (1991) The information technology function of the 1990's: a unique hybrid. CISR WP No. 225, Sloan School of Management, Massachusetts Institute of Technology, Cambridge, MA.

Rogers, E. M. (1995) *Diffusion of Innovations*, 4th edn, Free Press, New York.

Schwarz, R. M. (1994) *The Skilled Facilitator: Practical Wisdom for Developing Effective Groups*, Jossey-Bass, San Francisco, CA.

Semler, R. (1993) *Maverick: The Success Story Behind the World's Most Unusual Workplace*, Warner Books, New York.

Sherman, S. (1995) Wanted: company change agents. *Fortune*, 11 December, 197–198.

Silver, M. S. (1990) Decision support systems: directed and nondirected change. *Information Systems Research*, **1**(1), 47–70.

Sitkin, S. B. and Roth, N. L. (1993) Explaining the limited effectiveness of legalistic 'remedies' for trust/distrust. *Organization Science*, **4**(3), August, 367–392.

Soh, C. and Markus, M. L. (1995) How IT creates business value: a process theory synthesis. *Proceedings of the Sixteenth International Conference on Information Systems*, Amsterdam, The Netherlands, pp.29–41.

Strassman, P. A. (1995a) Outsourcing: a game for losers. *Computerworld*, 75, 21 August.

Strassman, P. A. (1995b) *The Politics of Information Management: Policy Guidelines*, The Information Economics Press, New Caanan, CT.

Todd, P. A., McKeen, J. D., and Gallupe, B. R. (1995) The evolution of IS job skills: a content analysis of IS job advertisements from 1970 to 1990. *MIS Quarterly*, **19**(1), March, pp.1–27.

Trauth, E. M., Farwell, D. W. and Lee, D. (1993) The IS expectation gap: industry expectations versus academic preparation. *MIS Quarterly* **17**(3), September, 293–307.

von Simson, E. M. (1990) The 'centrally decentralized' IS organization. *Harvard Business Review*, July–August, 158–162.

Walton, R. E. (1989) *Up and Running: Integrating Information Technology and the Organization*, Harvard Business School Press, Boston, MA, 1989.

Questions for discussion

1 Do you agree or disagree with the proposal that change agentry is a role for the IS specialist? Why?

2 Assess the authors' opinion that 'change agentry will most likely become the largest and most important part of intra-organizational IS work in the future.'

3 Given the authors' claim that low credibility is a problem facing IT in-house, how can IT managers be effective change agents? Keeping in mind the authors' assertion that they have seen 'numerous instances where IS credibility is low even when technology performance is high', what causes low credibility?

4 Give some examples that support the view of technology determinism (the ability of technology, as opposed to people, to cause change). What are some contravening examples?

5 Discuss the three models of the role of IT in change and what each role implies for the IT manager. What do the roles suggest for IS strategy? What might determine which model is most appropriate in a given organization?

6 Can the IT group, as the authors assume, move from one model to another at will? What model might be appropriate at the different stages of growth (see Table 2.6). Discuss the advantages of 'movement toward the facilitator role'. Should IT departments try to move to the facilitator or agent model? Why or why not?

Part Two

Information Systems Planning

Having considered information systems strategy and its various component parts, we now turn to that aspect of strategic information management concerned with information systems planning (cf. the shaded portion of Figure II.1) which, as already noted, we view as the means by which an IS strategy may be developed. We first place IS planning in context and then consider various approaches to, and the process of, IS planning. We conclude Part Two with the vexed question of evaluating the outcomes of the IS planning process. For further reading on IS planning see, for example, Earl (1989) and Ward and Griffiths (1996).

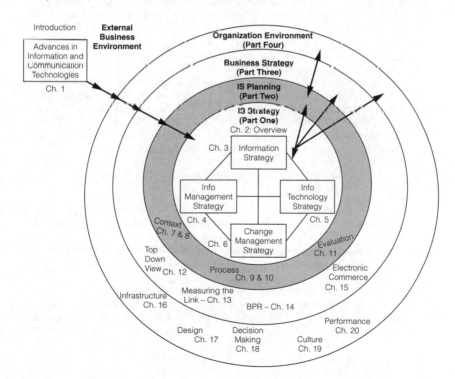

Figure II.1   *The focus of Part Two: information systems planning*

We begin with Chapter 7, By Benjamin and Blunt, which focuses on that aspect of the IS planning environment concerned not only with technological advancements, but something of a vision of what the IT services function of any large organization must become by the year 2000, to enable such advancements to be utilized to their fullest potential. In some ways, this chapter builds on the historical perspective provided by Chapter 1, and on issues for the IS function identified in Chapter 4. The authors paint a picture whereby, by the year 2000, IT provides executives with access to any information, any time, anywhere – presented in any format desired. While technically feasible, the crucial point is that many organizations will not have progressed so far, because of their inability to identify appropriate strategic goals and to manage change (cf. Chapters 5 and 6). In addition to these IT- and IS-related drivers of change, the authors also identify four fundamental business drivers for the twenty-first century organization, namely, restructuring of organizations along business process lines (cf. BPR – considered in greater depth in Chapter 14); the globalization of business (cf. Chapter 8); the changing global labour market; and the increasing volatility of business environments. Their analysis suggests that organizations will continually have to test and refine their IS applications and business processes in response to these business imperatives, and they reflect on these challenges specifically in relation to the role of the IS function within a progressive business organization.

Chapter 8, by Palvia and Palvia, provides another perspective regarding the context in which IS planning takes place as we approach the millennium, i.e. a global perspective. This is particularly important as businesses become increasingly international in their operations. Often, though, we hear trite messages about the global reach and impact of IT. While, of course, the technological reach is there for all to see, as the authors argue, 'it cannot be applied uniformly across the world'. The reasons for this do include some technological barriers, such as the lack of an advanced telecommunications infrastructure in certain countries. More important, however, are some of the different values and concerns that need to be understood when dealing with a variety of cultures. To this end, and in the context of IS management issues, Palvia and Palvia reflect on a range of studies that have been conducted in a variety of countries, on different continents, regarding the key issues identified by those responsible for IT in their organizations. While there are some similarities, as one might expect, among the English-speaking nations of the Western world, there are also some marked differences, certainly as compared to countries in Asia for example. As a result of their analysis, Palvia and Palvia present a model of what they term the global IT environment, which has echoes of the phases of IS development presented in Chapter 1, and the stages of growth framework introduced in Chapter 2. This time though the model relates to the level of IT adoption and the extent to which key issues are infrastructural, operational, managerial or strategic *vis-à-vis* the level of economic growth of a country or region.

We turn next to the different approaches being adopted by organizations in undertaking IS planning. Chapter 9, by Earl, identifies five generic approaches being undertaken by leading firms on both sides of the Atlantic:

- *Technology-driven.* The development of IT architectures as a foundation for expected application needs (equivalent to our interpretation of IT strategy, and sometimes called a 'bottom-up' approach).
- *Method-driven.* The use of techniques – often a consultant's methodology – to identify IS needs by analysing business processes and objectives (see also, business-led, below).
- *Resource-driven.** The establishment of an IT capital and expense budget to satisfy approved projects (essentially a 'wish list' approach).
- *Business-led.* The analysis of business plans to identify how and where IS/IT can most effectively enable these plans to be implemented (often called a 'top-down' approach).
- *Thematic.*† The identification of key themes for IS/IT projects [cf. Rockart's (1979) critical success factor concept].

---

* Earl uses the term 'administrative' for the resource-driven approach.
† Earl uses the term 'organization-led' to describe the thematic approach.

In addition, Earl presents results from field research involving interviews with IS managers, general managers and line managers with a view to identifying their respective opinions regarding for example, the objectives of undertaking, benefits arising from, and factors contributing to, successful – and unsuccessful – IS planning. The results are remarkably similar to earlier empirical field research conducted in the UK and Australia by Galliers (1987), with, for example, top management involvement and support, the existence of a business strategy, and emphasis on business rather than technological imperatives, all being cited.

The chapter that follows, by Lederer and Sethi, appeared in the first edition of *Strategic Information Management*. We have retained this chapter as it remains one of the most recent and comprehensive accounts of the methods actually being used by US companies in their IS planning efforts, and also details some of the problems they are facing. The authors provide, in addition, some guidance regarding ways in which these problems may be overcome. Four popular IS planning methods are also described in some detail. These are: BSP (Business Systems Planning, developed by IBM); PROplanner (Holland Systems Corp.); Information Engineering (IE, by KnowledgeWare), and Method/1 (Andersen Consulting). There are many other methods in use, of course, far too numerous to mention here, but it should be noted that these four are all, almost by definition, of the method-driven variety identified by Earl in Chapter 9. An example of Earl's favoured – thematic – approach (organization-led to use his terminology), might be IBM (UK)'s Executive Information Planning (EIP), whereas IBM's Process Quality Management (PQM) approach combines elements of the method-driven, business-led and thematic approaches. For more detail on EIP and PQM, see Lincoln (1990) and Hardaker and Ward (1987).

One of the issues identified in Chapter 10 as being of considerable concern to information systems planners related to the implementation and assessment of the outcomes of information systems planning efforts – a concern shared by many a senior business executive, as the following quote amply demonstrates: 'I still worry enormously, both about the amount we spend on IT and the increasing difficulty of justifying that expense in terms of the bottom line' (Sir Denys Henderson, Chairman of ICI, quoted in Grindley, 1991). Thus, the topic with which we close Part Two, and the subject of Chapter 11, is concerned with the vexed question of IT evaluation. The author, Leslie Willcocks, has written extensively on this topic (see, e.g., Willcocks and Lester, 1998; Willcocks *et al.*, 1998). In this chapter he focuses attention on the problems associated with IT evaluation, and details and evaluates a number of alternative approaches and techniques. Further reading on this important topic, including the concept of considering investments of a synergistic nature as a 'bundle' rather than individual isolated investments within a 'bundle' (Hendricks *et al.*, 1992; Miller and O'Leary, 1994), can be found in Farbey *et al.* (1995); see also Segars and Grover (1998).

Following Part Two we move on, in Part Three, to a consideration of the information systems strategy–business strategy relationship – the topic of aligning IT with the business in other words, which is, of course, another topic central to strategic information management.

References

Earl, M. J. (1998) *Management Strategies for Information Technology*, Prentice Hall, New York.

Farbey, B., Targett, D. and Land, F. (1995) *Hard Money – Soft Outcomes: Evaluating and Managing IT Investments*, Alfred Waller Ltd., Henley on Thames.

Galliers, R. D. (1987) Information systems planning in the United Kingdom and Australia: a comparison of current practice. In *Oxford Surveys in Information Technology*, 4 (ed. P. I. Zorkoczy), Oxford University Press, Oxford, pp.223–255.

Grindley, K. (ed.) (1991) *Information Technology Review 1991/92*, Price Waterhouse, London.

Hardaker, M. and Ward, B. K. (1987) How to make a team work. *Harvard Business Review*, **65**(6), November/December.

Hendricks, J. A., Bastian, R. C. and Sexton, T. L. (1992) Bundle monitoring of strategic projects. *Management Accounting*, **70**, 31–35.

Lincoln, T. (ed.) (1990) *Managing Information Systems for Profit*, Wiley, Chichester.

Miller, P. and O'Leary, T. (1994) Accounting, 'economic citizenship' and the spatial reordering of manufacture. *Accounting, Organisations and Society*, **19**(1), 15–43.

Rockart, J. F. (1979) Chief executives define their own data needs. *Harvard Business Review*, **27**(4), September–October, 267–289.

Segars, A. H. and Grover, V. (1998) Strategic information systems planning: an investigation of the construct and its measurement. *MIS Quarterly*, **22**(2), June, 139–163.

Ward, J. and Griffiths, P. (1996) *Strategic Planning for Information Systems*, 2nd edn, Wiley, Chichester.

Willcocks, L. P., Graeser, V. and Lester, S. (1998) Cybernomics and IT productivity: not business as usual. *European Management Journal*, **16**(3), September, 272–283.

Willcocks, L. P. and Lester, S. (eds) (1998) *Beyond the IT Productivity Paradox: Assessment Issues*, Wiley, Chichester.

7 Information Systems Plans in Context: The Information Systems Planning Environment

Critical information technology issues in the year 2000

R. I. Benjamin and J. Blunt

Introduction

It's a Monday morning in the year 2000. Executive Joanne Smith gets in her car and voice activates her remote telecommunications access workstation. She requests all voice and mail messages, open and pending, as well as her schedule for the day. Her workstation consolidates the items from home and office databases, and her 'message ordering knowbot', a program she has instructed, delivers the accumulated messages in the order she prefers. By the time Joanne gets to the office she has sent the necessary messages, revised her day's schedule, and completed a to-do list for the week, all of which have been filed in her 'virtual database' by her 'personal organizer knowbot'.

The 'virtual database' has made Joanne's use of information technology (IT) much easier. No longer does she have to be concerned about the physical location of data. She is working on a large proposal for the Acme Corporation today, and although segments of the Acme file physically exist on her home database, her office database, and her company's marketing database, she can access the data from her portable workstation, wherever she is. To help her manage this information resource, Joanne uses an information visualizer that enables her to create and manage dynamic relationships among data collections. This information visualizer has extended the windows metaphor (graphical user interface) of the early 1990s to three-dimensional graphic constructs.

Papers that predict the form of IT in the year 2000 and how it will affect people, organizations, and markets are in plentiful supply. *Scientific American* has devoted a whole issue to this subject, describing how the computing and communications technology of the year 2000 will profoundly change our institutions and the way we work.[1] What is missing is a vision of what the IT function in a large organization must become in order to enable this progress. With some trepidation, we will attempt to fill this gap.

In the early 1980s, one of us published a paper that forecasted the IT environment in 1990.[2] In this chapter, we revisit those predictions and apply the same methodology to a view of the IT environment in the year 2000. We describe the fundamental technology and business assumptions that drive our predictions. Scenarios illustrate how the IT function will evolve in terms of applications, application architectures, application development, management of IT-based change, and economics. Finally, we highlight some key challenges in the next decade for the IT executive and other senior managers.

The 1980 vision of today

Table 7.1 shows to what degree the predictions made in 1980 were realized. The technology predictions tended to be too conservative, and the predictions that required organizational charge tended to be too optimistic. They were as follows:

Table 7.1   *The predictions for the last decade*

		Achieved	*Partly achieved*	*Not achieved*
1	Workstations will be as common as telephones	✓		
2	The distinction between office systems and end-user systems will disappear	✓		
3	Databases and processing power will become more distributed		✓	
4	IT spending as a percent of sales will increase by at least half, relative to sales	✓		
5	The primary value of the centralized IT function will be to provide interconnectability		✓	
6	The 1980s will be a decade of integrating applications across functions			✓
7	All aspects of software will continue to improve steadily		✓	

1 *The rapid spread of workstations.* Everyone who sits at a desk in a corporation will have a workstation by 1990. Workstations will be as common in the office as telephones. The cost of a supported workstation will be about 20 percent of a clerical's salary and less than 10 percent of a professional's salary.

2 *The user interface.* The distinction between office systems and end-user systems will disappear. The terminal will be ubiquitous and multifunctional, able to support end-user, data processing, and office systems tasks.

3 *The distribution of processing.* Databases and processing power within the organization, which are relatively centralized today, will become much more distributed. This distribution will follow some basic rules. Data will be *stored* at a higher organizational level only if it needs to be *integrated* at that level. Application at lower organizational levels will not rely on a staffed data center.

4 *IT spending.* IT spending will increase as a percent of revenue over the decade – by about 50 percent.

5 *Organization of the IT function.* IT management will be concerned with managing the demand for its services rather than rationing its supply. The end user will dominate the use of computing resources. The primary value of the centralized IT function will be to provide interconnectability.

6 *Key application drivers.* The 1980s will be a decade of integrating applications across functions. Organizational frameworks will be developed to encourage application integration across business functions.

7 *Application development.* All aspects of software will continue to improve steadily. However, the demand for software is so great as to appear infinite, and the improvement will be perceived as having little effect on the backlog.

As Table 7.1 shows, not all of these predictions were realized. The developments of the 1980s give us clues to how well we'll progress in the next decade.

IT in the year 2000 – best case scenario

Joanne's computing environment represents a best-case scenario for the year 2000. The essential elements can be described as follows:

- She has a hierarchy of powerful computing capabilities at her disposal; portable computer, home computer, office computer, and various organizational and information service computers.
- All the stationary computers are physically interconnected to very high bandwidth public networks. This means they are linked through a medium – fiber optic cable – that allows large amounts of information to be communicated very quickly.

- Advances in remote telecommunications access technologies allow her to access these resources without a physical connection.
- She uses sophisticated interfaces that incorporate advanced ergonomic design concepts. That is, the computers are extremely user friendly; they have been designed to fit the way people actually work, even to fit the way individuals work.
- Knowbots greatly simplify Joanne's use of information technology. Knowbots are 'programs designed by their users to travel through a network, inspecting and understanding similar kinds of information, regardless of the language or form in which they are expressed'.[3] Among other functions, they provide the data she wants to look at in the order she wants to look at it.[4]

In short, the IT environment gives Joanne access to any information, anytime, anywhere, in any presentation mode she desires.

This scenario is technically feasible. All the elements exist either in commercial products or as prototypes. It is highly likely that a sizeable number of Joannes will exist in ten years, that is, that some key knowledge workers will have access to IT resources of the quality described. However, Joanne's environment is not representative of the typical worker environment we expect for the year 2000. Many organizations will not have progressed so far. How far an organization progresses, and the benefits it obtains from doing so, will depend more upon its ability to identify appropriate strategic goals and to manage change than upon any technical factor. Table 7.2 summarizes our predictions for the year 2000.

The driving assumptions

The year 2000 scenario is based on several assumptions about technology. They are as follows:

Cost performance will improve by two orders of magnitude

Since the 1960s, the core information technologies have shown cost-performance improvements of between 30 percent and 50 percent per year. If this trend continues through the 1990s, the cost-performance ratios of everything – memories, microprocessors, and so forth – will improve by two orders of magnitude, that is, by at least 100 times or 1000 percent. Thus the workstation that can now process 25 million to 100 million instructions per second (MIPS) will be able to process from 500 MIPS to 2000 MIPS. Instead

Table 7.2 *The predictions for the next decade*

Technology
- The cost performance of everything related to IT (e.g. memories, microprocessors, etc.) will improve by two orders of magnitude.
- The billion bit backbone network will be completed; it will be the international highway of business communication.

Architecture and standards
- Client/server will be the predominant technology architecture, and it will evolve into an important application architecture.

Services
- Electronic mail will become ubiquitous, integrating graphics, voice, and text, and it will provide extensive collaborative support capabilities.

Economics
- Major investments will be made to complete and maintain the infrastructure.
- Because technology is increasingly cheaper for all, the advantage will go to those who (a) apply it well and (b) effectively purchase value-added services for implementing it.

Applications
- Applications will be designed and built using high-level business models. Emphasis will be on design of robust applications that adapt to both short-term operational difficulties and evolutionary change.
- The implementation process within and between large businesses is generating larger and more complex applications. Because the design issues are so complex, it is reasonable to expect one or two application disasters.

Change management
- The executives in charge of IT organizations will have to learn change management skills and make sure that these skills are built into the IT organization.

---

of providing 10 million bytes of primary storage in your workstation, it will provide hundreds of millions of bytes of primary storage. And it will have billions of bytes of secondary storage attached, such as disk or optical memory.[5] But this workstation will cost the same $10 000 in real dollars that today's high-performance workstation costs.

These improvements are often indexed to labor costs. If we assume a modest increase in labor costs of 4 percent, the total IT cost-performance improvement relative to labor costs will be 2.5 orders of magnitude per decade.[6] Because the cost performance of IT continues to improve relative to labor and other forms of capital, companies will continue to invest heavily in it. The lesson of the 1970s and 1980s was that IT was a superior investment when it could replace or augment other forms of capital. In addition, as the power of the technology increased, so did the range of its application to new business situations. These trends can only become stronger in the next decade.

All computers will be interconnected via high bandwidth networks

During the mid- to late-1990s, national and international telecommunications backbone networks that operate at a billion bits per second will be implemented. The initial funding for the first of these networks was assured by passage of the Gore bill in December 1991. The prototype is the National Research and Education Network (NREN) in the United States, which today operates at 45 million bits per second.[7] In 1991 NREN for the first time allowed commercial enterprises to access the network.

Within offices, major computing elements will be interconnected with very high-speed local area networks (LAN). Homes will be connected to all of these networks with fiber optic cable, enabling people to work at home and to access a full range of entertainment and educational services. At home and in the office, portable computers will access databases using high-speed remote telecommunications technologies. While traveling, individuals will be connected to backbone networks and the desired databases by remote telecommunications technologies.

To summarize, fixed devices will be connected by fiber, and moving or movable devices will be connected by remote access technologies. Fiber will provide capabilities of up to a billion bits per second, and remote access technologies will provide between 10 million and 100 million bits per second.

Client-server will be the standard architectual model

By the year 2000, hardware configurations will almost universally follow the client-server model. In this model, the 'client' or user operates a workstation that has a certain configuration of hardware and software, and a number of 'servers' – mainframes, minicomputers, communications devices, very powerful workstations, novel printing devices, and servers that provide access to other networks – provide the client with supporting services. This model is already increasing in popularity, and it will dominate because of several key advantages:

* it simplifies the separation of the user interface from the service provided to the user
* it eases functional separation of technology and of applications, thus simplifying growth and maintenance

- within its current range of application capability, installations are reporting savings of 25 percent to 50 percent over mainframe and minicomputer architectures, and
- there is an ever-increasing quantity of software for client-server architectures. Consequently, applications will be distributed across several platforms. That is, programs will be able to share data easily; they will be interconnected and interoperable. Such issues will dominate technology purchase decisions.

Standards for interconnection and interoperability will be developed

The current confusion in standards for interconnection and interoperability of hardware and software will be significantly improved by the year 2000. Vendors are inevitably coming to the conclusion that their markets will be severely constrained unless they make it substantially easier for users to interconnect and interoperate. (The 1982 paper thought that this realization would have occurred long ago.)

Although not ideal, the level of interconnection will be far superior to where it is today. The vast amount of computer power available will make the required conversions and translations as seamless as possible. Consequently, the user 'wizardry' required today to build networks will be much less necessary.

What the final result will be is unclear. Today 'open systems' is almost synonymous with the operating system Unix and the government standard version, Posix.[8] By 2000, open systems solutions will more likely involve the adoption of key standards that enable a mix of environments to cooperate effectively. Perhaps systems will coalesce around Unix, but we think this is unlikely because it is not in the interests of vendors to have one architecture dominant. Traditionally, organizations have sought stability in their technology investment by standardizing to a single family of operating systems. In the next decade, stability will be as or more dependent on standardizing to a single user interface and set of personal support tools.

It is likely that as the necessary standards are developed and accepted, the open solutions will be developed more quickly than proprietary architectures have been. Open solutions change the nature and quality of investment for organizations. Open systems deprive vendors of monopoly profits and create more competition in areas where standards take hold. In order to stay profitable, vendors will have to develop niche products that fit the open systems architecture, and they will have to concentrate on price-performance improvements. The benefit for vendors will be that so many users will be working within the open systems architecture that a much larger potential market will be accessible.

What to expect

IT executives can expect the following in 2000:

A general manager's glossary

Excerpts from P. G. W. Keen, *Every Manager's Guide to Information Techno-logy: A Glossary of Key Terms and Concepts for Today's Business Leader* (Boston: Harvard Business School Press, 1991). © 1991 by Peter G. W. Keen. Reprinted by permission of the publisher.

Bandwidth. Bandwidth is a measure of the carrying capacity of a telecommunications link. It determines the speed at which information can be transmitted and how much information can share the link, and consequently, the practical range of the applications it can support. Fiber optic links currently transmit at rates of from 100 million bits per second (bps) to 2.4 billion bps. At 720 million bps, the entire works of Shakespeare could be transmitted in a quarter of a second!

Computer-Aided Software Engineering (CASE). CASE is the use of computer technology to help improve application systems development. It consists of a set of workstation-based software tools designed to support application developers: data dictionaries to store and validate definitions of items used in programs; diagnostic tools to check for inconsistencies and redundancy; and diagrammatic representations of system designs that can be created quickly and kept up to date and reused in other applications.

Decision Support System (DSS). A decision support system is an information system or analytic model designed to help managers and professionals be more effective in their decision making. The logic of decision support is that the combination of managerial judgement, intuition, and experience and computer analysis, data access, display, and calculation will result in more effective and creative decision making than either a manager or a computer could achieve.

End-User Computing. End-user computing refers to uses of IT that are entirely under the control of business units and do not require traditional IT application systems development and operations expertise.

Millions of Instructions Per Second (MIPS). Millions of instructions per second, or MIPS, is a rough measure of the power of a computer, rather like horsepower is an approximate measure of the performance of an automobile engine.

Open Systems. Users and vendors have a mutual need for vendor- and product-independent standards. 'Open systems' are implicitly vendor-independent and, by extension, interconnectable and 'interoperable.'

Operating System. An operating system is an extensive and complex set of programs that manages the operation of a computer and the applications that run on it. A computer is defined more by its operating system than any other single feature. Major mainframe operating systems include MVS, DOS/VSE, OS/400, and VM for IBM computers and VMS for Digital Equipment Corporation computers.

User Interface. User interface refers to the dialogue between a human being and a computer system. The traditional user interface is the keyboard, from which commands are typed into a computer. Emerging types of user interface include tablets that may be written on with a special pen, light pens that can write directly on the computer screen, and voice commands to the computer.

- The size of computer will not dictate the use of different application programs for the same task (i.e. there will be a high level of 'scalability'). Each major vendor will sell a single computer architecture that spans from the desktop to the largest mainframe. An application programmer will only have to learn and use a single set of tools and standards.
- There will be similar scalability for small- to moderately large-size applications across vendor architectures in the Unix open systems environment.
- The highest performance systems, such as online reservation systems, will continue to operate within the large vendor architecture. Partly this reflects expectations about technology, in particular software robustness and the practicality of distributing massive databases. It also reflects conservatism in systems design and the high risk of making substantial shifts in architectures for core applications.
- The choice of user interface will be independent of the choice of hardware. Next and Sun, for instance, are creating versions of their interfaces to run on IBM PCs.
- Some services will become standardized and available across architectures, such as file transfer, document mail services, and so forth.
- A more sophisticated and extensive market in outsourcing and leasing of resources will develop. Companies will be able not only to buy resources outright from corporations but also to pay on a usage basis for basic processing and telecommunications capacity and for software. A significant advantage of adopting and implementing an open or industry standard architecture will be the flexibility this provides for planning capacity and responding to changing demand, that is, the ability to outsource in demand-driven chunks.

What not to expect

- IT executives cannot expect to distribute certain mission critical applications: the very high-volume, real-time, inventory management systems, such as airline reservation systems. The largest databases will still require proprietary (i.e. nonrelational) solutions to meet performance needs.

Together, these assumptions describe a vast increase in computer power and telecommunications resources, which are made easier to use by wide adoption of client-server architectures and much improved standards for interconnection, display, and data sharing. James Emery, writing in *MIS Quarterly*, suggests that 'these technical advances are rapidly moving us to the position of having a magic genie capable of satisfying almost any logically feasible information need.'[9] The issue is to get the genie focused on critical business concerns.

Fundamental business drivers

Just as there are fundamental technology drivers, there are fundamental business drivers, and we need to understand how they will influence the IT function. Most articles on IT and business strategy provide a list of key business drivers. Although there are many, we have consolidated them into a few basic ones:

- The restructuring of the industrial enterprise. This most important of drivers is referred to in many ways – business reengineering, the lean-production paradigm, the total quality company, and so on. What is consistent is that the traditional, mass-production stovepipe organization is adopting a leaner form of production, and the traditional managerial buffers of inventory, time, and staff are being ruthlessly eliminated.[10]
- The globalization of business. By the year 2000, we will live in a global market society. This is already true of the financial and automotive markets.
- The changing global labor market.
- The increasing volatility of business environments.

Organizations will have to continually test and refine applications and business processes in response to these changes. Companies will need to become tightly interconnected not only internally but also with suppliers and customers. The short supply of labor and skills will force organizations to design better business processes and systems, both within and between organizations, and to make use of extensive expert systems, knowbots, collaborative support, and other capabilities. Malone and Rockart describe how the textile industry, already advanced in integration, could become an electronic marketplace in which databases and consultants are available online, and specialty terms form instantly to solve the problem of the moment.[11]

More organizations will embrace the idea of the 'informated' organization; that is, they will use their internal information to learn how to do their processes better.[12] The informated organization shifts the locus of control from the manager to the worker, who is empowered by accessible information to exercise this control. Thus, organizations will rely to a much greater extent on the accessibility of information at all levels of the hierarchy. This will conflict with more traditional management processes and structures. The design and use of information systems will not be free of organizational politics as each company decides where and how it will compromise on the issues of managerial control and information accessibility.

In summary, these business changes suggest a sustained growth in new applications (for example, to replace the transaction systems of the stovepipe business, to empower workers in information-rich activities, and to help the less skilled) and a continuing high interest by senior managers in where and how the IS budget is spent.

Applications in 2000

It is difficult to predict the specific new applications that will be most important for the IT function. However, we can identify certain classes of applications and how they will change in the coming decade.

Application types

To understand the evolution of applications in the next decade, it is useful to consider applications as falling into three categories:

1 *Business operations systems.* These are the traditional core of the IT function; they have also been described as transaction and control systems. These systems can manage business processes that run in real-time, such as process control, and those that operate on weekly or monthly schedules, such as accounting and settlement systems.
2 *Information repository systems.* These evolved somewhat later in the history of the IT function, as applications were built that isolated data from processing. Unlike transaction systems, the value and function of these systems is largely determined by the content and organization of the database rather than by the structure of the predesigned interactions.
3 *Personal support systems.* These have evolved from the end-user support, timesharing systems of the late 1970s to more advanced support systems today. Their evolution has followed a path from personal task systems (e.g. word processing, spreadsheets, and simple databases) to database access and specialized support systems such as design support and executive managerial support. These higher-level support systems have often incorporated personal task systems and electronic mail capabilities. There is a growing belief that these will become collaborative workgroup support systems.

Application architectures

IT groups charged with developing the information infrastructure have to develop policies and supporting tactical plans to migrate these three categories of applications from the existing base to the level of functionality and integration that we believe will be required in the year 2000.

Business operations systems

IT executives need to understand that business operations systems will get larger and more complex in the coming years in order to respond to pressures to integrate internally and externally, to eliminate wasteful intermediaries, and to speed up business processes. Because of the enormous past investments in these systems, there will be an emphasis in design on building on current capabilities and creating more flexibility.

Organizations may find it advantageous for business operations systems to decompose into two subsets – back office operation and decision support. Consider the order entry process. In the new architecture, the back office component will automatically set up the order in the file, schedule it into production, and assign a delivery date for the customer. The decision support component will give a person the tools to negotiate with the customer regarding the order, terms and conditions, and delivery date. The back office process will change much less frequently than the decision support process, thus providing functional isolation and easier maintenance.

This organization cannot be seen as fixed. What is structured and transactional and what is unstructured and conversational change as we uncover the inherent structure in the process. This has implications for application design and for bringing knowledge-based systems into the application mainstream.

Further, the decision support component can 'surround' the current data structures and transactions and can be built with little or no modification to them. A few companies have successfully implemented surround applications today. The technology to surround existing applications has been developed by small companies operating at the periphery of the major vendors. Some of these technologies are now being acquired by major vendors. They have considerable potential to manage the legacy problem (that is, figuring out how to deal with the legacy of old technology systems that do not fit current business requirements but that seem too expensive to redo) but they cannot be relied upon to make it go away.

We observe three trends in business operations systems:

- IT executives will invest large sums of money in multimedia business operations systems. USAA's image transaction system is an early example.[13] These systems will be able to handle all forms of information used in business processes, from illustrations to voice acknowledgement. Programs that model the human working process, such as voice annotation, will become very important.
- Systems will be designed to adapt more effectively to unforseen changes in the business, the operating environment, and the organization. Traditionally, backup procedures have dealt only with failures, and we have thought of backup as a completely different mode of operation. This is no longer adequate. Given the level of change predicted for the future, backup will evolve into a proactive process that will ensure that systems be available at all times.
- The nature of the legacy systems will have changed, but managing the retirement and replacement of mission critical systems will continue to be near the top of the IT management agenda.

Despite all of these changes, many operational systems developed in the next ten years will be organizational time bombs. Our dependence on information systems is continuing to grow faster than our ability to manage them, and in many organizations responding to immediate needs will divert resources and attention from identifying and implementing quality solutions consistently.

Information repository systems

These will grow rapidly as the concept of the learning organization becomes operationalized. They will (1) be multimedia, (2) provide expert agent assistance (knowbots), (3) come in many levels of aggregation, including very fine line-item detail, and (4) be distributed to where the need for data access is highest. People will be able to define their own virtual repository in terms of other repositories and look to knowbots to find the data that interests them. As Zuboff suggested, much effort will be expended in deciding who has access rights to what data, a critical design and implementation issue.

Personal and collaborative support systems

We currently see several contradictory trends that must mutually coexist:

- Support systems will become more segmented by specialty. That is, software will include more of the intellectual content of tasks, in some cases as components are added to basic packages and in others as specialized applications are developed. For example, a will-writing program is more that just another word processor, but it can be created using one. Similar niche products will appear that are targeted at specific occupations and tasks.
- Basic support capabilities will become standardized as standard user interfaces and modules become accepted. For example, electronic mail that integrates graphics, voice, and text will become ubiquitous.
- The distinction between some types of support systems will blur over time. For example, managerial support systems are currently encompassing elements of executive support and decision support systems.
- Desktop tools, which have lost their 'virginal' simplicity and, in the race for product differentiation, have become an almost unmanageable menagerie, will have to be rethought to provide users with the truly flexible capabilities needed to do their work. Mark Weiser describes research at Xerox PARC that is trying to develop what he calls 'ubiquitous computing ... where you are unaware of it.'[14]
- Collaborative work tools will become more important. The first generation of PCs led to development of significant new applications such as spreadsheets. Now that the norm is networked terminals, we should expect new applications that support teamwork to evolve. Already electronic

mail, bulletin boards, and conferencing software provide a basic infrastructure for communication. Increasingly we will see software that allows people to work together collaboratively and interactively. Tools that allow two users to display and amend the same document simultaneously will be commonly available. More sophisticated applications may use technology related to 'artificial reality' to enable groups to create, share, and manage very large amounts of information.

Integrating systems with the business

Currently we are in the third stage of a four-stage evolution of conceptual thinking in the IT function. Each stage is defined by what the IT function has to deliver in order to support the organization effectively. They are as follows:

1   *Automation*. Initially, application design was directed at automating existing manual systems. Progress could easily be measured by monitoring the systems portfolio. Masses of information were made available, but access was, and largely still is, exceedingly difficult. Much of the data was locked up in files accessed only by particular programs. Information could not be shared across applications or platforms. The dominant method of giving out information to its users was as line printer reports that found their most productive use as children's drawing paper.

2   *Access to information*. Before automation could be completed, it became clear that we were better at collecting information than disseminating it. Since about 1970, the dominant concern of IT groups has been to reverse this trend. On-line systems replaced batch systems. PCs and workstations are no longer stand-alone devices. Data modeling and database management systems are enabling the integration of information at appropriate levels in order to support the organization's information needs. The problem of providing secure information access is a dominant driver of IT investment today and will continue to be a major consideration.

3   *Filtering information*. Today, instead of being starved of information, managers and workers are in danger of dying from a surfeit of communication. The average information content of 'information' is rapidly falling. When the number of electronic mail messages per day exceeds two hundred, they cease to attract attention. To stay productive, organizations are going to have to invest in the development of knowbots and other forms of active information filtering. If information access is a key driver for current investment, providing the right information filtering capabilities emerges as a major challenge.

4   *Modeling information*. When information is accessible and filtered, then the question must be asked, 'What do I do with it?' Expert systems, modeling systems, and executive and managerial support systems all

have a role to play in modeling information to make it more useful. The application of information models will require a proactive effort far beyond that required to order and filter data, but it will be necessary to ensure a good fit with business processes.

Information modeling cannot be managed without bringing together all three application segments – business operations, information repositories, and personal support systems. In addition, information modeling will require development of new models that integrate business process and systems design. Examples of these are Jay Forrester's systems dynamics and Stafford Beer's work on cybernetic models. These have been around for several decades, but they have not been brought into the IT mainstream. IT has developed mostly static models focused on describing system function and content, even though information systems are only one element in the total system of the organization. The implementation of large-scale applications and new technologies is not only technically complex, it can change the social and political structure of organizations. Yet often companies commit large sums to fund applications without understanding the full implications of their decision. We do not expect managers to continue to tolerate this level of risk, and what is accepted today as best practice will in the next few years come to be viewed as naive and unprofessional.

Managers need models that include a description of both structure and policy, thus enabling them to explore the implications of change. These models should be integrated with the organization's operational systems. It will be a challenge for many IT organizations to service this need as it requires mastery of disciplines outside the compass of most IT professionals.

Client-server application model

This model, shown in Figure 7.1, integrates the three classes of applications described above. The support systems are in the workstations, and the business operations systems and information repositories are in the servers. The various clients and servers can communicate with each other through standard EDI-like transactions or object references.

This model represents a dramatic break from design concepts that were developed when the mainframe was the dominant information processing technology. IT has long advocated systems and information integration. Consequently it has searched for ever larger, more complex applications that will integrate everything into a single solution. The alternative – designing many smaller applications that can communicate and cooperate – has been considered too difficult, unstable, and probably inferior to a single solution. Client-server architecture is going to force a revaluation of that trade-off. To give an example: a company and supplier may integrate their complementary processes

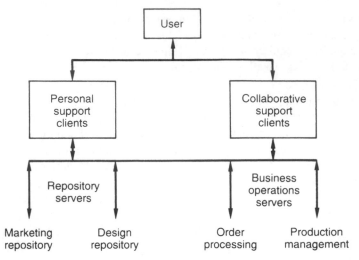

Figure 7.1   *Client-server application model*

by communicating via EDI and electronic mail. Today, if the same two functions were within a single company, there would be a tendency to develop a
single application with one integrated database. In the future we will reverse
this process. Instead of trying to build as much logic as possible into large
applications, we are going to break up applications into smaller distributable
modules. Defined interfaces will be seen as opportunities, not as barriers.
Distributed systems, when well designed, will be reliable and will allow
system components to operate asynchronously. Methods of application design
that are common in factory and process automation will become common for
providing support to traditional business and management processes. Increasingly we will conceptualize information systems as communicating cells,
each dependent upon the whole but capable of providing independent support
for local tasks and operations.

The more advanced companies will achieve integration of the three types
of applications through a client-server application model. However, at best
this implementation will be only partially achieved by large organizations in
the next ten years.

Distribution of processing

Computer processing will increasingly be distributed to where the work is
done, subject to seveal constraints:

• Systems will need to operate at relatively high-performance levels even
  when segments are down, including the center of the system. For example,
  when an airline computer reservation system is down at a major airport,
  the rest of the system must be protected.

- Recovery will need to be nearly automatic after a breakdown. This is the concept of the self-healing process.
- Recovery will need to restore high-value information first. Take a system monitoring a multinational portfolio of bank loans. Following a break-down, the system will recapture information in order of importance, using criteria such as loan size, the risk of breaching the credit limit, and the borrower's credit worthiness. Transactions will be posted in a sequence that updates the data most critical for decision making first. This implies that the recovery system 'understands' the business's needs.
- The operational aspects of managing a data center, such as backup pro-cedures, mounting of tapes, and so on, must be automated. Distributed computing on the scale we are discussing is viable only if operational costs are reduced through automation.

To summarize, the distribution of processing will be driven by the economics of computation and telecommunications and by the need to fit processing into organizational work patterns – none of which favor centralized processing. Integrity in large multilocation applications will still demand that master data and updating process be stored at one or at most a few locations.

Application development

Our systems today are like London's phone system. When British Telecom (BT) considered replacing the existing analog exchanges in London with modern digital switches, it found the task almost impossible. During the bombing in World War II, engineers had gone out each day to repair the damage done the previous night. Working against time, they did whatever was needed to get service back. After the war, BT had no plans of the real network, only a map of how it was originally designed. Our current systems have the same relationship to their documentation. Usually, on the day sys-tems are computerized, the documentation is already in error. From then on, through upgrades, maintenance, and emergency patches, we increasingly lose track of how the system operates. The result: critical systems that are expens-ive to maintain and impossible to replace.

Many companies are working intensively on modular design, reusable code, and client-server architectures, and these contributions are helping us to move away from this trap. Yet these depend upon a revolution in systems develop-ment practices.

Application models will contribute to this revolution. Unlike applications, which have the services and data structures embedded in them, application models can be used to generate the services and data infrastructure specific to an organization's needs. Each 'application' will have to conform to the same standards used by the applications with which it shares data. It will not be acceptable to make applications conform by modifying the source code.

PC applications running under common user interfaces such as Windows are already using this concept. They have a special installation routine that identifies other packages and builds appropriate links with them. With the development of multimedia application and program-to-program protocols such as Dynamic Data Exchange (DDE) and Object Linking and Embedding (OLE) in Windows, and Publish and Subscribe in the Macintosh, these tools are going to become even more complex.

Generally these install routines work bottom up; each application tries to understand its environment and build what it needs. For enterprise-wide, distributed applications, top-down models will be needed that understand how the applications are to work together. The key building blocks for these models are the information repositories and object request brokers that the major vendors are just beginning to deliver.[15] This is a technology in its infancy, but these models will become key organizational resources for managing a diverse distributed resource.

Another important influence on systems development is computer-aided software engineering (CASE). CASE tools automate many of the necessary tasks that used to involve tinkering with the programs code, such as linking data to process requirements. In the future, designers will develop systems using high-level modeling tools, from which code will be generated in one clean step. Systems will have self-documenting tools that automatically keep track of all changes. More important, *all* maintenance will be done by changing the design model, not the code. Even a failure of a critical production system will have to be rectified with fully auditable tools, without any loss of service. To reach these goals, we will need to adopt such technologies as tight modularization and dynamic linking so that changes can be made incrementally and almost immediately to the system as it operates. The ultimate test of success will be the retirement of all systems programmers' tools that give direct access to physical memory or disk sectors and that act outside the normal security system.

CASE tools have been developed and marketed largely as productivity tools and mostly for systems professionals. Organizations often have not reaped the promised benefits because they have not understood the need to develop new processes for developing systems. Computer-aided engineering (CAE) has had a similar history. The real pay-off from CAE became available only when organizations began to see its possibility for changing the relationship between design and manufacturing engineering. Implementing CASE, like implementing CAE, is a severe organizational change problem, and it can be successful only when senior executives are willing to pay the price that complex culture change entails. In a recent meeting of senior IT executives, nearly all conceded that there was little understanding among themselves, their management, their users, and their senior staff that CASE was an essential to their organizations' success as was CAE.

Given where we are, the best we can expect is that the 1990s will be the decade of CASE the way the 1980s was the decade of CAE. If this is so, we can expect only moderate success in implementing CASE within very large organizations. However, there are examples of small to medium companies using the available tools to develop fairly complete portfolios of systems.[16] These companies are the forerunners. They succeed because (1) they make a serious organizational commitment; (2) they either start with a clean slate, or they clearly identify ways to work around legacy systems; and (3) they understand that this is an iterative learning process that will challenge basic assumptions.

Despite the trends toward modular design, reusable code, and client-server architectures, larger systems will continue to be built, and they will be built faster and more accurately. As this happens, it will become abundantly clear that accelerating the rate of technical implementation will only be possible if priority is given to managing the consequent changes in work and organization.

Managing technology-based change

Research from the Massachusetts Institute of Technology Management in the 1990s Program suggests that the major reason that the benefits of IT implementation have been so slow in coming is that organizational change is not adequately managed.[17] This thesis seems unarguable to most observers, but there is considerable skepticism that anything can be done about the problem. The reality is that progress *must* be made on this front if the IT executive is to succeed in this decade.

Successful implementation of systems has never been easy. Laudon comments, 'Building an information system, . . . an on-line, distributed, integrated customer service system, . . . is generally not an exercise in 'rationality'. It is a statement of war or at the very least a threat to all interests that are currently involved in any way with customer service.[18] However, the problem will become more severe in this decade: the technology is allowing us to build ever larger and more complex systems, and supporting interdependent business processes will require those larger and more complex systems. Thus IT will continue to be involved in a change process that, at the same time, it makes more complex. IT complicates the change process in a number of ways; it moves the locus of knowledge and hence power in the organization, it changes the time dimension of processes and decisions, and it enables new organizational constructs to be implemented.

Consequently, organizational issues, resistance, and other change management problems become more pronounced. IT executives need to be aware that there is a body of literature and practice in organizational change that has been and can be applied to their problems and that they need to be the champion for technology-enabled change.[19]

Even with a commitment to change management, companies are likely to find that people's inability to change, not technology, is the limiting factor in transforming organizations.

Economic considerations

The IT executive will need to be aware of some important long-term economic considerations in devising strategies:

1   Technology will be increasingly cheaper and equally available for all companies. More software will be available through retail and mail-order supplies. Even Unix software will be available ready to install on most platforms using vendor-supplied install routines. The same economies in software development and merchandising currently enjoyed for the IBM PC and Apple Macintosh platforms will spread to the other major platforms. Thus, advantage will accrue to those companies that develop improved business processes and decision processes more effectively (cheaper, faster, and of higher quality) than their competitors. In the year 2000, the cost differential in the acquisition of computer technology will be smaller than today. There will be fewer economies of scale available to larger companies. Also, in the race to increase the power of systems, the cost difference between competing platforms will tend to decrease. All workstations are getting cheaper at roughly the same pace. The absolute cost differential for any size machine will decrease. In addition, chips – the raw material – are likely to become more standardized and shared across product lines. In a commodity business there will be less advantage to selecting one vendor or another. There will continue to be significant differences in how well companies implement technology and therefore in the benefits they achieve. How well a technology is used is a function of organizational learning. In this sense the choice of vendor will continue to remain crucial – not the hardware vendor, but the systems integrator consultant.

2   Companies will have to make major investments to complete their IT infrastructures and to keep them current. For example, the workstation population can be expected to turn over at least twice in the coming ten-year period owing to technology cost-performance improvements and the availability of new software. Consider a company that is roughly at maximum penetration of 1 workstation per employee with a total of 10 000 workstations. It would then have a minimum capital cost of 20 000 times at least $5000 per workstation, or $100 million over the decade, irrespective of other infrastructure items. Facing up to the implications of infrastructure completion and reinvestment will not be easy.

IT function in the year 2000

There are an ample number of future predictions for the IT function.[20] The IT function in the year 2000 will most probably continue its evolution as a hybrid – manager of infrastructure and staff advisor to senior executives and user organizations. As Dixon and John note, 'IT manages the technology, and line executives manage the application of the technology through partnerships with IT'.[21] Learning how to work effectively with all the stakeholders, including vendors, to accomplish the necessary changes will be a major task of the decade.

IT will retain a strategic role because it is the gatekeeper for introducing and integrating new technology and processes. The IT function's critical knowledge, which is knowing how to navigate a course to technical integration, will evolve to become a mix of technical, business, organizational, and consulting skills.

Key challenges for the decade

The initial vision of the future in this chapter was deliberately high tech. Most organizations will not be operating at that level, and the major challenge for IT executives will be helping their organizations exploit the technology opportunities.

Although the list could be quite long, we highlight a few key challenges for the IT executive in these interesting years to come:

- Managing the evolving infrastructure – overseeing the movement to scalable client-server architectures, introducing exciting new enabling technologies, preserving current investments, generating capital to complete the infrastructure and revitalize it as it becomes obsolete, and learning how to operate a worldwide utility that ranks in complexity with moderate-sized telephone companies of today.
- Managing infrastructure financing – deciding when to take advantage of outsourcing, resource leasing, and other techniques that give the organization access to scalable power on demand without compromising the organization's development of competitive advantage technology.
- Moving toward the new application architectures necessary to transform organizational business and decision processes – continuing to distribute function to where work is done, segmenting application logic along client and server lines, and so forth. Some solutions will come from vendors as they upgrade their systems planning and integration methodologies. The most important of these technologies will require the organization to develop its own models that describe its business process and to link them to its technology systems. This information architecture will be the road

map for the systems development process and the anchor for justifying IT investment. Without an understandable information architecture, IT will be unable to bridge the gulf between the new technologies and the business's strategic directions.

- Addressing the implications of managed organizational change both for CASE and for reengineered business process. CASE is moving rapidly from a future goal to a current critical success factor. The technology will continue to change rapidly. This is going to put the IT organization under considerable stress. Current skills will become obsolete, and the cost structure of IT will be transformed. The senior IT executive has to manage a complete transformation of the function while ensuring quality support for customers. This will not happen through benign neglect. Active strategies for managing the institutionalization of CASE, prototyping the developing technology, and moving up the learning curve until the technology is absorbed by the IT and user organizations will require energy and new skills. Reengineered business processes are technologies that must be transferred into the organization, with similar implications for changes in skills and learning. Largely missing in organizations today is a person to take responsibility for managing technology-driven organizational change, for learning what can be done and how to apply it, and for acting as a change champion. It may be that the success or viability of the IT organization will depend on how well it fills this vacuum.
- Managing the new buy-versus-make paradigm. Each company has a history and a culture that make it more or less successful at using packages and at building applications from scratch. The quantity of technology now available and the increasing level of integration mean that most major applications will be hybrids. Successful companies will be those that manage integration most effectively and apply in-house resources to the tasks with the highest payoff.

Overarching all these issues is the fact that no company is an island. As a web of networks develops and people begin to focus on linkages across and outside organizations, key standards will be developed that will come to define 'open systems'. Successful IT managers will understand the standard development process and position their organization to benefit from others' investments.

Surprises

This chapter started with the hypothesis that it was possible to make reasonable predictions of the future of IT based upon a few long-term trends. But prospective futurologists are advised to consider the track record of their profession. In many ways the future is bound to surprise us. Yet we can guess where some of the surprises will come from. They are those areas where there is no useful track record or analog from the past.

Mobile MIPS

With powerful portable workstations becoming commonplace, how will they be transformed? Will we see special purpose systems targeted to the needs of particular professions or modular designs with plug-in hardware for particular tasks? The ergonomics and economics of personal tools are still maturing.

We do not even pretend to guess the full consequences of the next generation of cellular laptops. Currently, the extra power is being devoted to better interfaces, pen and voice. Yet the cost-performance trend of the technology is such that there will be resources to do significant work. What will that be? Does this enable a new class of independent or franchised professionals who take industry-specific solutions to clients? How will schools integrate the use of portable knowledge bases in classes?

Data – available, accessible and interconnected

The amount of data – text, numbers, pictures, voice, and video – in databases and accessible is going to explode. The universal data highways will bring a vast array of information to anyone who wishes to tap it. Yet access to information has always been a source of power and influence, and access to megadatabases will change relationships among individuals, organizations, and the state. As a society we are only beginning to understand the practices and ethics of data collection and management. The outcry over Lotus's Marketplace™ system and current concerns about credit reporting systems are examples of the issues to be addressed and the stakes involved. At another level there are likely to be new classes of services and products. In a glut of data there will be a market for editors to sift, choose, compare, validate, and present information, whether those editors are knowbots or people.

Integration

In combination, the mobility of computing and the availability of vast amounts of data will produce combinations and applications that are truly unpredictable today.

New systems development

What effect will the new systems development tools have on the design of business processes? If we can build systems using flexible, adaptable, and innovative technology, what does that say for the way we change business processes? Are we going to see the end of the big application? Will it be replaced by iterative, evolutionary development of improved processes? Indeed, will the technology of systems development at last put business managers back in control of creating and managing the systems they use?

References

1   *Scientific American*. September 1991. The issue is devoted to a series of articles on how computers and telecommunications are changing the way we live and work.
2   R. I. Benjamin, 'Information Technology in the 1990s: A Long-Range Planning Scenario.' *MIS Quarterly*. June 1982. pp.11–31.
3   M. L. Dertouzos. 'Communications. Computers and Networks.' *Scientific American*. September 1991, pp.30–37.
4   T. W. Malone, J. Yates, and R. Benjamin. 'The Logic of Electronic Markets.' *Harvard Business Review*. May–June 1989, pp.166–172.
5   'A Talk with INTEL.' *Byte*. April 1990, pp.131–140.
6   J. Yates and R. I. Benjamin. *'The Past and Present as a Window on the Future.'* in *The Corporation of the 1990s*, M. S. Scott Morton, ed. (New York: Oxford University Press, 1991) pp.61–92.
7   V. G. Gerf, 'Networks,' *Scientific American*, September 1991, pp.42–51.
8   Unix, developed by Bell Labs in the early 1970s, is an 'operating system, a religion, a political movement, and a mass of committees', according to Peter Keen. 'It has been a favourite operating system of technical experts . . . owing to its "portability" across different operating environments and hardware, its support of "multitasking" (running a number of different programs at the same time), and its building-block philosophy of systems development (building libraries of small "blocks" from which complex systems can be built).' See: P. G. W. Keen, *Every Manager's Guide to Information Technology* (Boston: Harvard Business School Press. 1991), pp.156–157.
9   J. C. Emery, 'Editor's Comments,' *MIS Quarterly*, December 1991, pp.xxi–xxiii.
10   M. J. Piore and C. F. Sabel, *The Second Industrial Divide. Possibilities for Prosperity* (New York Basic Books, 1984); and J. P. Womack, D. T. Jones and D. Roos, *The Machine That Changed the World* (New York: Rawson Associates, 1990).
11   T. W. Malone and J. F. Rockart, 'Computers, Networks, and the Corporation,' *Scientific American*. September 1991, pp.92–99.
12   S. Zuboff, *In the Age of the Smart Machine: The Future of Work and Power* (New York: Basic Books, 1988).

13 'Billing Systems Improve Accuracy, Billing Cycle,' *Modern Office Technology*, February 1990; and C. A. Plesums and R. W. Bartels, 'Large-Scale Image Systems: USA A Case Study,' *IBM Systems Journal 23* (1990): 343–355.

14 M. Weiser, 'The Computer for the Twenty-First Century,' *Scientific American*, September 1991, pp.66–75.

15 Object request brokers are technologies that allow the user to access programs developed by other companies or groups much as the telephone directory allows a user to speak with someone. These tools give more people access to pre-existing solutions. See: H. M. Osher, 'Object Request Brokers,' *Byte*, January 1991, p.172.

16 K. Swanson, D. McComb, J. Smith, and D. McCubbrey, 'The Application Software Factory: Applying Total Quality Techniques to Systems Development,' *MIS Quarterly*, December 1991, pp.567–579.

17 M. S. Scott Morton, ed., *The Corporation of the 1990s* (New York: Oxford University Press, 1991), pp.13–23.

18 K. Laudon. *A General Model for Understanding the Relationship between Information Technology and Organizations* (New York: New York University, Center for Research on Information Systems. January 1989).

19 See E. H. Schein. *Innovative Cultures and Organizations* (Cambridge, Massachusetts: MIT Sloan School of Management, Working Paper No. 88–064, November 1988); and E. H. Schein, *Planning and Managing Change* (Cambridge, Massachusetts; MIT Sloan School of Management. Working Paper No. 88–056, October 1988).

20 J. F. Rockart and R. Benjamin, *The Information Technology Function of the 1990s: A Unique Hybrid* (Cambridge, Massachusetts; MIT Sloan School of Management, Center for Information Systems Research, Working Paper No. 225, June 1991); and E. M. Von Simson, 'The "Centrally Decentralized" IS Organization,' *Harvard Business Review*, July–August 1990, pp.158–162.

21 P. J. Dixon and D. A. John, 'Technology Issues Facing Corporate Management in the 1990s,' *MIS Quarterly*, September 1989, pp.247–255.

Questions for discussion

1 Revisit the predictions from 1980 summarized in Table 7.1: would the realization look different by today's standards?

2   The authors state 'Joanne's computing represents a best case scenario for the year 2000'. Compare this scenario to the reality of today. What has been achieved and what is still lacking?

3   This best case scenario is based on an information strategy of 'any information, anytime, anywhere, in any presentation modes'. What are the downsides to an information strategy based upon such a philosophy?

4   Table 7.2 gives predictions for the year 2000. How well do the authors' predictions for 2000 reflect the situation today? What does this suggest about how fast IT really does, or does not, change? What does this suggest about the ability of the IT function to adapt? What are the implications for IT strategy? (In answering this question, students may wish also to revisit question 4 in Chapter 3.)

5   The authors present some fundamental technology and fundamental business drivers of changes. Which among these appear to have been the most significant?

6   Do you agree with the authors' assessment that we are at the 'third stage of four stage evolution of conceptual thinking in the IT function'?

8 Information Systems Plans in Context: A Global Perspective

Understanding the global information technology environment: representative world issues

P. C. Palvia and S. C. Palvia

As an increasing number of businesses expand their operations into international markets, in order to succeed they need to understand the considerable cultural, economic, and political diversity that exists in different parts of the world. For these reasons, while information technology is a critical enabler and many times driver of global business expansion, it cannot be applied uniformly across the world. This chapter is aimed at analyzing the key information systems/technology (IS/IT) issues identified during the last decade in different regions of the world. Spurred by periodic key IS issues studies in the USA, several researchers have attempted to do the same for many other countries. We summarize many of their findings, and provide insights into the various differences and similarities among countries. A precursory model is developed to help understand the underlying causes into the nature of the issues. Elements of a more detailed model, worthy of further exploration, are also presented.

Introduction

During the past few years, the world has witnessed an unprecedented expansion of business into global markets. The idea of a 'global village', envisioned by McLuhan (1964), has finally come true. At the same time there is realization that information technology (IT) has played a crucial role in the race towards globalization. IT has been a critical enabler of globalization in most cases and a driver in some cases. Today, multinational corporations and governments increasingly rely on information technology (IT) for conducting international business. Therefore, in order to exploit fully the vast potential of IT, it is extremely important for corporate executives and chief information officers to understand the nature of the global information technology environment. In this chapter, we aim to provide not only this understanding, but also provide insights into the nature of world IT issues.

Reports of key management information systems (MIS or IS) and IT* management issues have continually appeared in the United States. For example, a stream of articles on MIS issues in the USA has appeared in the *MIS Quarterly* (Ball and Harris, 1992; Brancheau *et al.*, 1987; Dickson *et al.*, 1984; Niederman *et al.*, 1991). A study by Deans *et al.* (1991) identified and prioritized international IS issues in US – based multinational corporations. As technology is assimilated into other countries, researchers have begun to identify IS/IT issues in these countries. Several such studies have appeared recently: representative examples include: North American and European issues (CSC Index, 1995), Canada issues (Carey, 1992), Australia issues (Watson, 1989), Hong Kong issues (Burn *et al.*, 1993), India issues (Palvia and Palvia, 1992), and Singapore issues (Rao *et al.*, 1987). Such studies are perceived to be of value as they not only identify issues critical to determining strategies for organizations, but also provide direction for future MIS education, practice, and research.

A comparison of the cited studies reveals that the key IS issues in different countries vary to a considerable degree. In order to exploit fully IT for global business, it is imperative that the key IS issues of different countries are identified and dealt with appropriately in the conduct of international business. While an examination of IS issues of the entire word is impractical and infeasible, and even the data are not readily available, we summarize issues from a few countries selectcd on the basis of their level of economic development. Four categories of economic development are defined: advanced, newly industrialized, developing (operational), and under-developed. This classification is somewhat parallel to that used by many international agencies (e.g. the United Nations). Countries discussed in this chapter loosely fit this classification.

While some level of generalization is possible based on the countries discussed herein and is intended, we need to clearly point out the limitations. The chapter does not cover the entire world. Only a few countries are surveyed and while they may represent many other countries, they do not represent all. Second, the classification of a country into one of the above four classes may be disputable, and furthermore, there is certainly a range within each class.

---

* The terms: management information systems (MIS), information systems (IS), and to some degree information technology (IT) are used interchangeably.

Lastly, some countries may simply defy our classification scheme (e.g. Russia and the former socialist nations).

Key MIS issues in advanced nations

Advanced and industrialized nations include the United States, Western European countries, Japan, and Australia among others. Key IS issues have been systematically and periodically researched in the United States over the past fifteen years (Ball and Harris, 1992; Brancheau *et al.*, 1987; Dickson *et al.*, 1984; Hartog and Herbert, 1986; Niederman *et al.*, 1991). As of this writing, an effort is underway at the MIS Research Center at the University of Minnesota to compile a contemporary list of key IS issues in USA based on a Delphi study to obtain opinions from IS executives (Janz *et al.*, 1994). Preliminary rankings from an intermediate step of this study are shown in Table 8.1. While a few new issues have appeared in the new list (e.g. business process re-engineering), there is not a substantial departure from the 1991 list of issues reported by Niederman *et al.* (1991). Also, as reported by CSC Index (1995), the IS issues in Western Europe are very similar to the North American issues (Tables 8.2 and 8.3). This similarity is also seen in Australian issues (Table 8.4) and West Europe issues that were reported by Watson and Brancheau (1991). As the 1991 issues study by Niederman *et al.* is well-known, meets methodological rigor, and is widely distributed, it will be discussed below as representative of IS issues of advanced nations.

Key issue ranks

A ranked list of IS management issues as reported by Niederman *et al.* (1991) is shown in Table 8.5. These issues were captured by a three-round Delphi survey of senior IS executives in the US. It should be noted these ranks represent the opinions of the members of the Society for Information Management (SIM). Typically, the SIM membership comprises large private organizations. The top ten issues are reviewed below. The review draws heavily from the Niederman *et al.* article.

- *Rank 1. Information architecture.* An information architecture is a high level map of the information requirements of an organization. Also called the enterprise model, it provides the overall framework to guide application development and database development. It includes the major classes of information (i.e. entities), and their relationships to the various functions and processes in the organization. The steps included in enterprise modeling include functional decomposition, entity-relationship diagrams, and planning matrices (McFadden and Hoffer, 1994).

Table 8.1   *Key issues in information systems management – USA (1994)*

Rank	Description of the issue
#1	Building a responsive IT infrastructure
#2	Facilitating and managing business process redesign
#3	Developing and managing distributed systems
#4	Developing and implementing an information architecture
#5	Planning and managing communication networks
#6	Improving and effectiveness of software development
#7	Making effective use of the data resource
#8	Aligning the IS organization within the enterprise
#9	Recruiting and developing IS human resources
#10	Improving IS strategic planning
#11	Managing the existing portfolio of legacy applications
#12	Measuring IS effectiveness and productivity

Source: Janz, B. D., Brancheau, J. C. and Wetherbe, J. C. Key information systems management issues. MISRC Working Paper, University of Minnesota, 1994.

Table 8.2   *Key issues in information systems management – North America (1995)*

Rank	Description of the issue
#1	Aligning I/S and corporate goals
#2	Instituting cross-functional information systems
#3	Organizing and utilizing data
#4	Re-engineering business processes through I/T
#5	Improving the I/S human resource
#6	Enabling change and nimbleness
#7	Connecting to customers/suppliers
#8	Creating an information architecture
#9	Updating obsolete systems
#10	Improving the systems-development process
#11	Educating management on I/T
#12	Changing technology platforms
#13	Using I/S for competitive advantage
#14	Developing an I/S strategic plan
#15	Capitalizing on advances in I/T
#16	Integrating systems
#17	Cutting I/S costs
#18	Providing help-desk services
#19	Moving to open systems
#20	Improving leadership skills of I/S management

Source: The Eighth Annual Survey of I/S Management Issues, 1995. CSC Index Group.

Table 8.3   *Key issues in information systems management – Europe (1995)*

Rank	Description of the issue
#1	Instituting cross-functional information systems
#2	Improving the I/S human resource
#3	Re-engineering business processes through I/T
Tie	Cutting I/S costs (tie)
#5	Creating an information architecture
#6	Aligning I/S and corporate goals
#7	Improving the systems-development process
#8	Educating management on I/T
#9	Organizing and utilizing data
Tie	Changing technology platforms (tie)
#11	Integrating systems
#12	Using I/S for competitive advantage
Tie	Enabling change and nimbleness (tie)
#14	Developing an I/S strategic plan
#15	Connecting to customers/suppliers
Tie	Providing help-desk services (tie)
#17	Moving to open systems
#18	Updating obsolete systems
#19	Determining the value of information systems
#20	Capitalizing on advances in I/T

Source: The Eighth Annual Survey of I/S Management Issues, 1995. CSC Index Group.

Table 8.4   *Key issues in information systems management – Australia (1993)*

Rank	Description of the issue
#1	Improving IS strategic planning
#2	Building a responsive IT infrastructure
#3	Aligning the IS organization with that of the enterprise
#4	Promoting effectiveness of the data resource
#5	Using IS for competitive advantage
#6	Developing an information architecture
#7	Improving data integrity and quality assurance
#8	Improving the quality of software development
#9	Increasing the understanding of the role and contribution of IS
#10	Planning for disaster recovery

Source: Pervan, G. P. Results from a study of Key Issues in Australian IS Management.
4th Australian Conference on Information Systems. September 28, 1993. University of
Queensland, St. Lucia. Brisbane, Queensland.

Table 8.5   *Key issues in information systems management (1991)*

Rank	Description of the issue
#1	Developing an information architecture
#2	Making effective use of the data resource
#3	Improving IS strategic planning
#4	Specifying, recruiting, and developing IS human resources
#5	Facilitating organizational learning and use of IS technologies
#6	Building a responsive IT infrastructure
#7	Aligning the IS organization with that of the enterprise
#8	Using information systems for competitive advantage
#9	Improving the quality of software development
#10	Planning and implementing a telecommunications system
#11	Increasing understanding of role and contribution of IS
#12	Enabling multi-vendor data interchange and integration
#13	Developing and managing distributed systems
#14	Planning and using CASE technology
#15	Planning and managing the applications portfolio
#16	Measuring IS effectiveness and productivity
#17	Facilitating and managing decision and executive support systems
#18	Facilitating and managing end-user computing
#19	Improving information security and control
#20	Establishing effective disaster recovery capabilities

Source: Niederman, F., Brancheau, J. C. and Wetherbe, J. C. Information systems management issues for the 1990's. *MIS Quarterly*, December 1991.

- *Rank 2. Data resource*. Data should be regarded as a vital resource for an organization, especially for the information systems function and application development. Data and information are corporate resources, and not in the domain of an individual or a subgroup, but for the benefit of the entire organization. Firms collect massive amounts of not only internal data but also vast amounts of data from external sources, such as customers, suppliers, government and other firms. These data should be properly harnessed and leveraged for optimizing the benefit to the organization. The establishment of large corporate databases, as well as the emergence of firms specializing in specific types of databases (e.g. Dow Jones, Compuserve, Compustat, Data Resources, etc.) underscores the value of the data resource.
- *Rank 3. Strategic planning*. Strategic IT planning refers to IT planning that supports business goals, missions, and strategy. With the role of IT elevated to a strategic tool for obtaining competitive advantage and achieving superior performance, the need for strategic IT planning is of paramount importance. Yet, strategic planning remains a thorny issue for both

senior IS and non-IS executives. The rate of technological change requires the ability to develop quick courses of action at economical costs, before they become obsolete. Further exacerbating the situation is rapid organizational change as well as environmental change outside the organization. Perhaps because of the difficulties, this issue has remained one of the top issues in all previous key issue studies.

* *Rank 4. IS Human resources.* Human resources for IS include technical as well as managerial personnel. This issue reappeared in the top ten list, after an absence in the previous study of 1986. This factor includes such concerns as planning for human resources, hiring, retaining, and developing human resources. While there is no acute shortage of IS talent, the rapid technological change creates shortage of specialized skills. For example, object oriented programmers are in short supply and in great demand at the present time. Another phenomenon of the last decade which has serious implications for human resources is IS downsizing and outsourcing. Organizations need to decide which IS functions can be outsourced to external vendors and which need to be retained in-house. These decisions have strategic implications for the company.

* *Rank 5. Organizational learning.* This issue calls for continued organizational learning about the applications of information technology, and productive use of information systems. Historically, information systems have been initiated by IS managers, and they have been the purveyors of information technology. However, the organizations that prosper will have to make proper use of information technologies and will have to use IT in the whole organization. As recent examples will indicate, line managers are taking initiatives for the development of IT applications, and end user computing is becoming pervasive. These trends bode well for organizational IT learning; however, such applications need to expand to a broader range of companies.

* *Rank 6. Technology infrastructure.* Infrastructure includes such components as organization's diverse computers, telecommunication networks (both LANs and WANs), databases, operating systems, system software, and business applications. A new issue that emerged in the 1991 study, it refers to the development of a sound technology infrastructure that will support business strategy and organizational goals. The appearance of this issue may have again been driven by strategic concerns. A lack of a coordinated strategy for technology infrastructure may have prevented companies from taking timely advantage of business opportunities as they emerged.

* *Rank 7. IS organization alignment.* The organizational positioning of the IS department within the company has a direct impact on its effectiveness. In early days of computing, IS was relegated to Accounting or Personnel departments, and had the image of a service/overhead function. While that image has been mostly erased, there are still issues relating to its proper

alignment. For those who view IS as a strategic function, the IS department has moved up in the organizational hierarchy. Large companies today have positions such as Chief Information Officer (CIO) and vice-president of information technology. Another issue relating to alignment is the question of centralized, decentralized, or distributed IS organization. Technology can effectively support any option; the key issue is that the IS organization should be consistent with the company organization and philosophy.

* *Rank 8. Competitive advantage.* Information technology and information systems in a firm can be used in ways that provide a decided advantage over its competitors. Early examples of firms using IT in such manner include American Airlines, United Airlines, American Hospital Supply Co., and Merrill Lynch. The 1980s provided a major thrust for using information technology as a source of competitive advantage. This issue still ranks among senior IS executives as one of the top issues. Information systems dubbed as 'strategic information systems' are targeted towards customers, suppliers, or competitors, and are an essential part of a company's competitive strategy. While targeting information systems at external entities is one source of competitive advantage, other sources include using IT for organizational redesign, improving organizational effectiveness, streamlining of business processes, and integration of business activities.

* *Rank 9. Software development.* The development of software represents a major expenditure for the IS organization, yet it remains fraught with problems of poor quality, unmet needs, constant delays, and exceeded budgets. At the same time, the organization is presented with more options: in-house development, software packages, and outsourcing. Newer developments, e.g. software engineering methodologies, prototyping and CASE tools, promise to provide some much-needed help. However, organizations are further challenged as they have to constantly evaluate new technologies and development paradigms, such as distributed processing, visual languages and object oriented programming. For example, much of the new development is being done using the C++ or similar programming languages.

* *Rank 10. Telecommunication systems.* Telecommunication systems provide the backbone for an organization to do business anywhere anytime, without being constrained by time or distance. While the earlier focus in telecommunication systems was on connecting users to a centralized mainframe computer, the renewed emphasis is on providing connectivity between different computing centers and users, who are widely dispersed geographically, and many times globally. Telecommunication networks also need to substantially multiply their bandwidth in order to carry all types of signals: data, graphics, voice, and video. Challenges that face the

implementation of telecommunication systems include huge financial investments and lack of common industry standards. Yet, for those who have implemented backbone networks, the rewards have been tremendous.

Other issues

Issues ranked just below the top ten include understanding the role of IS, multi-vendor data interchange and integration, managing distributed systems, and planning and using CASE technology. It is apparent that these issues have a strategic orientation, and relate to planning and successful use of emerging technologies in the organization.

Key MIS issues in newly industrialized nations

Several countries have made rapid economic growth in just over a decade. These countries have emerged as the 'newly industrialized countries' (NICs) and are now beginning to prosper. While the precise categorization of any country into any class is somewhat contentious, and is also subject to movement over time, countries like Taiwan, Hong Kong, Ireland, South Korea, and Singapore fall into this group. The latest key issue results that are available from some of these countries are included in the chapter. Singapore issues were reported by Rao *et al.* (1987), Hong Kong issues by Burn *et al.* (1993), and Taiwan issues by Wang (1994) and Palvia and Wang (1995). The Singapore results are shown in Table 8.6, and Hong Kong results in

Table 8.6 *Key issues in information systems management – Singapore (1987)*

Rank	Description of the issue
#1	Measuring and improving IS effectiveness
#2	Facilitating and managing end-user computing
#3	Keeping current with new technology and systems
#4	Integrating OA, DP, and telecommunications
#5	Training and educating DP personnel
#6	Security and control
#7	Disaster recovery program
#8	Translating IT into competitive advantage
#9	Having top management understand the needs and perspectives of MIS department (IS role and contribution)
#10	Impact of new technology on people and their role in the company

Source: Rao, K. V., Huff, F. P. and Davis, G. B. Critical issues in the management of information systems: a comparison of Singapore and the USA. *Information Technology*, 1:3, 1987, pp.11–19.

Table 8.7   *Key issues in information systems management – Hong Kong (1989)*

Rank	Description of the issue
#1	Retaining, recruiting and training MIS/IT/DP personnel
#2	Information systems/technology planning
#3	Aligning MIS/DP organization
#4	Systems reliability and availability
#5	Utilization of data resources
#6	Managing end-user/personal computing
#7	Application software development
#8	Information systems for competitive advantage
#9	Telecommunications technology
#10	Integrating of data processing, office automation, and telecommunications
Tie	Software quality assurance standards

Source: Burn, J., Saxena, K. B. C., Ma, Louis and Cheung, Hin Keung. Critical issues of IS management in Hong Kong: a cultural comparison. *Journal of Global Information Management*, Vol. I, No.4, Fall 1993, pp.28–37.

Table 8.7. Once again, there is a certain degree of similarity between these country issues. We discuss only the Taiwan issues as representative of issues of newly industrialized countries, as it is the most recent study of all and one of the authors was directly involved with it.

Key issue ranks

The key IS issues in Taiwan were obtained by conducting a survey of senior managers in Taiwan, who were well-versed in technology (Wang, 1994; Palvia and Wang, 1995). Responses were obtained from 297 managers on a 7-point Likert scale on 30 issues. The majority of the respondents were IS executives. A wide range of organizations, both in terms of size and type of business, were represented in the study. The ranked list is provided in Table 8.8. Once again, we focus on the top ten issues.

*   *Rank 1. Communication between IS department and end users*. Communication between these two groups of people is necessary as one group is the user and the other builder. End users in Taiwan seem to be not able to specify their information needs accurately to the IS group. They also have an unrealistic expectation of the computer's capabilities and expect the IS staff to quickly automate all of their operations. At the same time, IS employees may lack a good understanding of the organization's business processes, and use terminology that end users do not understand. The communication problem between the users and the IS community is

Table 8.8 *Key issues in information systems management – Taiwan (1994)*

Rank	Description of the issue
#1	Communication between the IS department and end users
#2	Top management support
#3	IS strategic planning
#4	Competitive advantage
#5	Goal alignment
#6	Computerization of routine work
#7	IT infrastructure
#8	System integration
#9	Software development productivity
#10	System friendliness
#11	Security and control
#12	Software development quality
Tie	IS standards (tie)
#14	Data resource
#15	IS funding level
#16	IS role and contribution
#17	User participation
#18	Recruit, train, and promote IS staff
#19	Information architecture
#20	Placement of IS department

Source: Palvia, P. and Wang, Pien. An expanded global information technology issue model: an addition of newly industrialized countries. *Journal of Information Technology Management*, Vol. VI, No.2, 1995, pp.29–39.

further aggravated due to the low level of communication skills among IS graduates.

• *Rank 2. Top management support.* Top management support is required as IS projects require major financial and human resources. They also may take long periods of time to complete. As such, the call for top management support is pervasive in the MIS literature. Taiwan is no exception. Top management support was found to be especially important in encouraging the use of microcomputers in Taiwan (Igbaria, 1992). Senior management is expected to demonstrate its support by both allocating a suitable budget for the IS department, and by showing leadership and involvement. At the same time, top management support will strengthen the IS department by helping acquire the support of other functional departments. Without strong top management endorsement and support, the IS department would have little chance to achieve its mission.

• *Rank 3. IS strategic planning.* IS strategic planning in Taiwan is difficult due to rapid changes in technology, lack of familiarity with IS planning methodologies, inadequate understanding of business processes, short term orientation of firms, absence of successful domestic planning models, top management's unwillingness to provide adequate funding to implement strategy, and lack of top management support for the planning process. Lack of appropriate strategic planning in other countries has had the effect of producing system failures and creating uncoordinated 'islands of automation'.

- *Rank 4. Competitive advantage.* In the private sector, several retail, whole-sale, transportation, and media firms have begun to build information systems that can be utilized to make new inroads, create business oppor-tunities, and enable an organization to differentiate itself in the market place. Even public organizations have made progress. Stories of how pub-lic organizations (e.g. a government-run hospital and the administrative office of a village) use IT to improve their administrative effectiveness and reduce the waiting time of clients, have been reported. The aggressive promotion of IT by the government has helped to raise further the IS practitioner's consciousness of the competitive impacts of information technology.

- *Rank 5. Goal alignment.* The needs and goals of the IS department can often be at odds with the organizational goals. A major incongruence results in potential conflicts and sub-optimization of IS resources. IS staff are often interested in developing large scale and technically advanced systems which may not meet the needs of the business and the end users. In order to assure goal alignment, senior management needs to clearly communicate the organization's goals, policies, and strategies to the IS staff. In fact, a carefully crafted IS strategic planning process (issue #3) would facilitate goal alignment.

- *Rank 6. Computerization of routine work.* In the USA, computerization of routine work (such as accounting functions and transaction processing) was the first priority and was done in the 1960s and 1970s. Even though Taiwan is classified as a newly industrialized country, the extent of computer usage in business is far behind that in USA. As a paradox, the production of IT products has had a striking growth in Taiwan, while the businesses themselves have been slow in adopting the technology. In a sense, the IS evolution in many organizations is still in Nolan's initial stages (Nolan, 1979). For these organizations, automation of routine work (i.e. transaction processing systems) is evolving, yet critical.

- *Rank 7. IT infrastructure.* In vibrant economies, a responsive IT infra-structure is vital to the flexibility and changing needs of a business organ-ization. The technology infrastructure issue is exacerbated by a combination of evolving technology platforms, integration of custom-engineered and packaged application software, and the rigidity of existing applications. Many Taiwanese organizations are gradually realizing that building an infrastructure, which will support existing business applications while remaining responsive to changes, is a key to long-term enterprise productivity.

- *Rank 8. System integration.* Integration of various system components into a unified whole provide benefits of synergy, effectiveness, and added value to the user. Many IS managers in Taiwan are recognizing the need to integrate the 'islands of automation' (e.g. data processing, office automation, factory automation) into an integrated single entity. In the past, the execution of systems integration had encountered great difficulty due to lack of IS standards, insufficient technical ability, and inadequate coordination among functional departments. However, open systems, networks, client/server architecture, and standardization of IT products (promoted by the government) are expected to make systems integration easier in the future.

- *Rank 9. Software development productivity.* Productivity is measured simply by the ratio of outputs to inputs. On both outputs, e.g. the quality and magnitude of software produced, and inputs, e.g. total time to complete a project and total person-hours, IS has had a dismal record. In interviews conducted during the research process, both IS professionals and end users complained that it takes excessively long to build and modify applications. The speed of development is not able to keep pace with changing business needs. Possible explanations and reasons that were stated include: insufficient technical skills, high IS staff turnover, lack of use of software productivity tools, and inadequate user participation. However, new software technology seems to offer hope, e.g. CASE tools, object oriented languages and visual programming languages.

- *Rank 10. System friendliness.* Ease of use and user-oriented features are essential to the success and continued use of a software product, as the popularity of graphical user interface (GUI) will testify. Unfriendly and difficult-to-use systems encounter strong resistance from end users at all managerial levels in Taiwan. The development of a friendlier interface is critical not only for the success of the software and hardware vendors, but also for the ultimate acceptance by the end user. Two reasons can be given for the significance of this issue in a non-advanced country. First, the users may be comparatively unfamiliar and untrained in the use of information technology. Second, a lot of software is imported from the advanced nations of the West and may not necessarily meet the human factor requirements of the host nation.

Other issues

Issues rated just below the top ten included: information security and control, and software development quality. As organizations in Taiwan increase the use of IT for business operations, there is a greater risk of disclosure, destruction, and contamination of data. The high turnover of IS professionals causes great concern for managers that proprietary information may be disclosed to competitors. Probable reasons associated with software quality problems include: lack of business process understanding and technical skills of the IS staff, high turnover among IS staff, and inadequate user participation. Issues rated at the bottom include: open systems, distributed systems, telecommunications, CASE, and expert systems. While these technologies have been introduced in Taiwan, their implementation is in a primitive stage. Also, end-user computing was rated low as it is not prevalent in the country. However, as employees and the general population acquire greater computer literacy, due partly to government efforts, this issue is expected to become more prominent.

Key MIS issues in developing nations

Countries which can be loosely described as developing countries include: Argentina, Brazil, India, and Mexico. These countries have been using information technology for a number of years, yet their level of IT sophistication and types of applications may be wanting in several respects. For example, La Rovere *et al*. (1996) report that Brazil faces several difficulties in network diffusion. Much of this is caused by lack of integrated policy towards informatics and telecommunication industries, and paucity of quality training programs. Similar obstacles are faced by many of the other Latin American countries. In Pakistan, Hassan (1994) describes environmental and cultural constraints in utilizing information technologies. With the emergence of many eastern block countries out of closed and guarded environments, and the general trend towards globalization, information is now available about the IT readiness of these countries. Much of this information is derived from individual experiences, general observations, and case studies (e.g. Chepaitis, 1994; Goodman, 1991). Yet, many of them seem to face similar problems.

Russia and other former Soviet Union countries defy a natural classification into any of our four classes. In fact, the World Bank places the former socialist countries in a distinctly separate category. In their commentary, Goodman and McHenry (1991) described two sectors of Soviet computing: the state sector which included development and deployment of a full range of highly sophisticated computers, and the mixed sector of private, state, foreign and black-market activities which were struggling in the sustained use of information technology. Roche (1992) and Roche *et al*. (1992) made similar observations. While giant centrally planned enterprises were created that emulated technological developments of the West, little computer equipment was either designed for or used by management and consumers. Thus, while Russia and former Soviet Union countries have made great strides in selected technological areas (e.g. the space program and aerospace industry), the general consumer sector and management have lagged behind significantly in IT utilization. As many reports would indicate, Russian IT issues are therefore characteristic of issues in developing countries. According to Chepaitis (1994), lack of adequate supply of quality information and poor information culture are IS issues reflective of Russia.

A prioritized list of ranked issues based on a systematic study is available for India. We present these results as an example of issues from a developed country.

Key issue ranks

The key IS issues in India were obtained by Palvia and Palvia (1992) and were based on data collection from top-level and middle-level Indian managers. These managers either worked directly with computers and information systems, or had been exposed to them by other means. The issues were first generated using the nominal grouping technique and brainstorming, and were then ranked by participant managers in two seminars in India. A fully ranked list is provided in Table 8.9; the top issues are discussed below. The discussion draws primarily from Palvia and Palvia (1992) and Palvia *et al.* (1992).

- *Rank 1. Understanding and awareness of MIS contribution.* An appreciation of the benefits and potential applications of MIS is absolutely necessary for successful IT deployment. There is a general lack of knowledge among Indian managers as to what management information systems can do for their business. The need for computer-based systems is neither a high priority nor widely recognized. Unless the potential contribution of MIS is clearly understood, advances in technological resources are not likely to be of much help. The lack of understanding is partly due to the traditional reliance on manual systems. The ready availability of a large number of semi-skilled and skilled personnel makes the operation of manual systems satisfactory, and prevents management from looking at superior alternatives.
- *Rank 2. Human resources and personnel for MIS.* Higher national priorities and lower priorities assigned to IS development have caused the neglect of IS human resource development. India is somewhat of an enigma in this regard. In the last several years, India has become a primary location for international outsourcing contracts; yet there is a great demand and shortage within the country for those trained in developing business information systems. While many universities and educational institutes are attempting to meet the burgeoning demand, some of these efforts may be misdirected from an IS point of view. The current emphasis on education seems to be on technological aspects rather than on the application of IS concepts to business needs.

Table 8.9   *Key issues in information systems management – India (1992)*

Rank	Description of the issue
#1	Understanding/awareness of MIS contribution
#2	Human resources/personnel for MIS
#3	Quality of input data
#4	Educating senior managers about MIS
#5	User friendliness of systems
#6	Continuing training and education of MIS staff
#7	Maintenance of software
Tie	Standards in hardware and software (tie)
#9	Data security
#10	Packaged applications software availability
Tie	Cultural and style barriers (tie)
#12	Maintenance of hardware
#13	Aligning MIS with organization
#14	Need for external/environmental data
#15	MIS productivity/effectiveness
#16	Applications portfolio
#17	Computer hardware
#18	MIS strategic planning
#19	Effect of political climate of country
#20	Telecommunications

Source: Palvia, P. and Palvia, S. MIS issues in India and a comparison with the United States: Technical Note. *International Information Systems*, Vol. I, No.2, April 1992, pp.100–110.

- *Rank 3. Quality of input data*. Information systems rely on accurate and reliable data. The age-old adage of GIGO (Garbage In Garbage Out) is well known in MIS, and directly impacts the quality of IS. This issue has also been seen in Russia (Chepaitis, 1994) and other developing countries. While not reported as a key issue in US studies, it appears that developing countries have inferior input data due to several reasons: lack of information literacy and information culture among workers as well as a less-than-adequate infrastructure for collecting data. Some managers reported experiences of excessive errors in data transcription as well as deliberate corruption of data. The underlying causes may be mistrust of and intimidation caused by computer processing, resulting in carelessness, apathy and sabotage.
- *Rank 4. Educating senior managers about MIS*. This issue suggests a possible response to the top-ranked issue dealing with the lack of understanding and awareness of the role of MIS in organizations. It appears that senior managers do not truly understand the full potential of information technology. They need to be educated not so much about the technology

per se, but more so about its many applications in business. For example, besides transaction processing, IT can be used for building executive information systems and strategic systems. Exposure to such possibilities by way of education and training can provide new and innovative ideas to managers to utilize IT fruitfully. In the authors' opinion, any education must be supplemented with business cases and some hands-on training.

- *Rank 5. User friendliness of systems.* The appearance of this issue in a developing nation may be attributed to several factors. First, the users in a developing nation are generally novices and untrained in the use of information technology; thus they may not be at ease with computer interfaces. Second, much of the software and systems are imported from Western and advanced nations. This software is geared to the needs of their people and may not be user-friendly in regard to the needs and cultural backgrounds of users in the importing nation. A hypothesis can be made that the ergonomic characteristics of an information system are at least partially dependent on the cultural and educational background of the people using them.

- *Rank 6. Continuing training and education of the MIS staff.* The education issue comes up once again, this time in the context of MIS personnel. Rapid advances in technology and a lower level of IT preparedness in developing countries put further pressure on MIS personnel to keep pace with the technology. Another challenge here is to not only provide training on the technology but to be able to do that from a business perspective. Specifically, two of the problems reported were: many current training plans attempt to train a large number of people simultaneously at the expense of quality, and there is a lack of proper training available for MIS professionals in business functions.

- *Rank 7 (tie). Maintenance of software, and standards in hardware and software.* These two related issues were tied in rank. Maintenance refers to fixing and updating production software when there are bugs or new requirements. Maintenance is a problem because of inadequate resources and competition for resources from new applications. Compared to developed nations, developing nations suffer from an inadequate supply of trained programmers. The problem is compounded if the majority of the software is purchased as packaged software. The maintenance effort is likely to be high if the quality and applicability of the purchased system is low. The quality of a system depends, in part, on the existence and enforcement of hardware and software standards, which brings us to the next issue.

The issue of standards in hardware and software is an important one in developing countries as much software and hardware (especially hardware) is imported from other countries. The problems of hardware/software standards are compounded significantly when buying hardware and software produced by different vendors in different nations, each with its own proprietary systems. While some international standards exist (e.g. in programming languages and telecommunications); the ultimate challenge will be to develop an exhaustive set of standards, and then to be able to enforce them.

- *Rank 9. Data security.* An organization's data is a valuable corporate resource, and needs to be protected else it may be abused to the organization's detriment. Data contained in manual systems was not very vulnerable to breach of security due to either unavailability of ready access or inordinately long access times. As a result, many information workers have developed poor practices and habits in data handling. With computerized systems, this attitude can cause severe data security and integrity problems. Newer controls and security provisions, which were unheard of in manual systems, may need to be built which may themselves cause resistance in adoption.

- *Rank 10 (tie). Packaged Applications Software Availability, and Cultural Barriers.* These two issues were tied in rank. Off-the-shelf packaged application software provides an inexpensive alternative to in-house development. All around the world, a lot of software is purchased off-the-shelf. An inadequate supply of MIS personnel (an issue discussed earlier) further necessitates an increased reliance on packaged software. While much packaged software is now being made available, there is need to develop more that meets the specific business requirements unique to developing nations.

  Culture plays a role in the application of information technology (Ein-Dor *et al.*, 1993), albeit sometimes in subtle ways. For example, in one governmental office, secretaries and clerical people were mandated to use word-processing equipment. But as soon as the mandate was removed, they went back to typewriters and manual procedures. Apparently, they trusted the familiar equipment more, and it gave them a greater sense of control. Chepaitis (1994) provides the example of Russia, where people have never gathered, shared, and managed bountiful information. As a result, information is often hoarded for personal gain rather than freely shared or invested.

Other issues

Issues ranked just after the ones discussed above included maintenance of hardware and alignment of MIS with the organization. Many organizations are buying personal computers, and their maintenance sometimes becomes a problem due to limited vendor presence and delays in procuring parts. Aligning of MIS with the organization is an issue of moderate importance. According to an Indian manager, beyond alignment, the organizational culture and philosophy itself has to change to accept the role of MIS. Applications portfolio is not a major issue as most businesses are in the initial stages of information systems growth and are in the process of computerizing basic operations. For the same reasons, MIS strategic planning was not rated high, and telecommunications was considered not of immediate interest but more a concern of the future.

Key MIS issues in underdeveloped nations

Underdeveloped or basic countries are characterized by low or stagnant economic growth, low GNP, high levels of poverty, low literacy rates, high unemployment, agriculture as the dominant sector, and poor national infrastructure. While precise categorization is difficult, subjective and arguable, countries like Bangladesh, Cuba, Haiti, Jordan, Kenya, Nigeria, Iran, Iraq, and Zimbabwe may be included in this group. Note that countries may move in and out of a particular class over time. In this chapter, we use two African countries: Kenya and Zimbabwe as examples of underdeveloped nations.

Key issue ranks

The key MIS issues of Kenya and Zimbabwe were reported by Palvia *et al.* (1992), and were based on a study completed by Zigli in 1990. The methodology used in Zigli's study was based on the India study by Palvia and Palvia (1992). The same questionnaire, with minor modifications, was used to collect the data. A number of in-depth personal interviews with senior information systems executives were conducted utilizing the questionnaire for data collection and as the basis for discussions. Information was also gathered from local trade publications and other secondary sources.

The computing industry in both countries at the time appeared to be competing in an environment that was strongly influenced by government and a lack of 'hard foreign currency'. The hard currency situation was exacerbated by the virtual absence of indigenous hardware and software production, resulting in an inventory of outdated hardware and software. In addition, IT was accorded a very low priority by the government. As a result, purchases of equipment were being made from wherever possible, leading to mixed vendor shops and associated problems. Given the basic nature of IT adoption in these countries, only seven issues emerged with any degree of consensus. These are shown in Table 8.10 and are discussed in line with the 1990 study reported in Palvia *et al.* (1992).

• *Rank 1. Obsolescence of computing equipment.* Of greatest concern was the state of obsolescence of most computer equipment. The need for state of the art equipment is urgent and was a critical concern for the IS executives.

Table 8.10   *Key issues in information systems management – underdeveloped nations of Africa (1992)*

Rank	Description of the issue
#1	Obsolescence of computing equipment (hardware)
Tie	Obsolescence of operating and applications computer programs (software) (tie)
#3	Proliferation of mixed vendor shops (hardware and software)
#4	Availability of skilled MIS personnel and opportunities for professional development for MIS managers and non-managers
#5	Possible government intervention/influence in computer market
#6	Establishment of professional standards
#7	Improvement of IS productivity

Source: Palvia, P., Palvia, S. and Zigli, R. M. Global information technology environment: key MIS issues in advanced and less developed nations. In *The Global Issues of Information Technology Management*, edited by S. Palvia, P. Palvia and R. M. Zigli, Idea Group Publishing, 1992.

The current inventory is aging fast and simply does not meet the requirements of most businesses. A major contributing factor is the balance of trade and more specifically, the shortage of 'hard' foreign currency. These computers were state of the art twenty years ago but no longer. Not much progress has been made in 20 years. In fact, some regression may have occurred. These computers have now gone through two or three iterations of emulations, and both efficiency and effectiveness have suffered. The short-fall of computer equipment not only affects the private sector but the public sector as well. Overall, national infrastructures of both countries appear ill-prepared to advance information technology to bring them on a par with the rest of the world.

- *Rank. Obsolescence of software.* The inventory of software (including operating systems and application programs) is also quite dated. Most of the packages are of the word processor and spreadsheet variety, or their emulations. Only recently have relational databases been introduced into both countries. The acute shortage of 'hard' foreign currency precludes firms from purchasing software from overseas vendors, and further leads to exceptionally high rates of software piracy (especially for microcomputers). Major systems development is a rare occurrence. There seems to be simply no concept of integrated business systems, e.g. in manufacturing or accounting. However, some contemporary software is being introduced on a limited scale. For example, the relational database package Oracle is now being distributed in both countries by local software firms.
- *Rank 3. Proliferation of mixed vendor shops.* There are many vendors to choose from within one country, let alone the number of vendors in the entire world. While competition among vendors should raise the quality

and reduce the cost of technology acquisition, it may also cause severe problems if vendor selection is not done carefully. Due to lack of coherent policies on part of the government and the firms, many purchases of hardware and software are made on an opportunistic and ad-hoc basis from whatever source and vendor that happens to be available at the time. This has led to the proliferation of mixed vendor shops. Of course, mixed vendor shops have added to the problems of IS management, operation, and maintenance. Mixed vendor shops were seen as a major detriment to efficiency and productivity by a number of firms in the interview sample.

- *Rank 4. Availability of skilled MIS personnel and professional development.* There is a shortage of people with computing and systems skills. Finding trained personnel and keeping existing information systems people current with the latest advances in IT are vital concerns of information systems managers in these less developed nations. There are too few qualified people and they are being spread too thin. This issue has implications for the educational system of underdeveloped nations: they must incorporate education and training in high technology areas, do it fast, and keep their programs constantly updated lest they become obsolete again.

- *Rank 5. Possible government intervention in the computer industry.* In economics dominated by government control, there is always the risk of government intervention in the computer industry, thereby threatening to reduce competition and increasing the probability of a monopoly. While a selected few may benefit from government actions, the larger business community tends to suffer. Such intervention may occur in the form of issuance of import licenses to new, local businesses in an effort to encourage their growth. Unfortunately, these new firms sell their licenses to existing, larger vendors. Both the sellers and the buyers realize substantial profits. Another example of government action is the mandated markups on imported parts and equipment. As a result of these markups (equaling or exceeding 100%), virtual cartels have emerged, and the cost of computers, computer peripherals and computer software has become one of the highest in the world.

- *Rank 6. Establishment of professional standards.* The lack of professional standards threatens the entry of non-professionals and untrained people into the MIS field, thereby further aggravating the IS quality issue. Therefore, the professional data processing societies in these two countries are very anxious to gain 'official' approval authorizing them to establish or participate in the establishment of standards of behavior and expertise for MIS professionals. The establishment of such standards will go a long way towards the development of better quality IS products. It should also improve productivity, the subject of the next issue.

- *Rank 7. Improvement of IS productivity.* Productivity is a concern in these two nations as a result of lack of professionalism, lack of access to state of the art productivity tools, and deteriorating hardware and software. In general, the productivity concern seems to extend to all aspects and areas of information systems. Over the last decade, there has been considerable emphasis on productivity in the advanced nations, and serious efforts have been made to enhance productivity (e.g. in the use of fourth generation languages, and CASE tools). However, in the less-developed countries, while being recognized as a problem, productivity appears to take a back seat to often more pressing problems.

Other issues

The existence of archaic hardware and software and the inability to acquire modern resources have caused an ever-widening technological gap and thereby a loss of competitiveness of the domestic businesses that depend upon such equipment. Erosion of the competitive position of firms was an issue expressed by several local executives. Another issue cited by some executives is the question of the local manufacture of hardware and software. This appears to be a polarizing issue. The foreign based vendors, as one would expect, oppose local manufacture, while users and the government favor it. However, software development may be a prime determinant in the evolution of information technology in less-developed nations, as in the case of India and Philippines.

What was perhaps surprising were the issues not mentioned by the participants. For example, understanding of MIS by senior executives did not emerge as an issue of significant concern. Using IS for competitive advantage is another issue that did not surface in the interview process. In general, the strategic dimensions of information technology do not seem to be as important as the operational issues.

A model of global information technology environment

In summary, we have presented key IS management issues for representative countries in each of the four classes, and made comments about several other countries. Space considerations prevent us from discussing results from other countries that might be available. For example, key issues not discussed in this chapter, but investigated and available in the literature, include the following countries: United Kingdom (Galliers *et al.*, 1994), Gulf countries (Badrii, 1992), Estonia (Dexter *et al.*, 1993), and Slovenia (Dekeleva and Zupancic, 1993).

In any case, our discussion shows that there can be major differences between issues of different countries, and few commonalties. There are more common issues between USA and Taiwan, and fewer between other countries. As an overall impression, it seems that advanced countries are driven by strategic needs, developing countries by operational needs, and underdeveloped countries by infrastructural needs. Based on this observation, Palvia *et al*. (1992) posited an initial model of country specific MIS issues based on economic development of the country. This model classified countries into three categories based on the level of economic growth. These categories are: advanced countries (e.g. United States, Canada, Japan), developing/operational countries (e.g. India, Russia, Argentina, Brazil), and underdeveloped/basic countries (e.g. Kenya, Chile, Iran, Nigeria). They acknowledged that the placement of a country into a particular category is subject to some debate, and that countries may change categories over time. Nevertheless, they were able to make some broad generalizations on the nature of IS issues based on economic growth of a nation. According to the model, the level of information technology adoption increases from one stage to next, i.e. from underdeveloped to developing to advanced nations. Quite striking are the types of MIS issues at each stage of economic development. In the underdeveloped countries, the infrastructural issues dominate (e.g. the very availability of computer hardware, operating and applications software, and human resources for MIS). In the developing countries, operational issues are paramount (e.g. management's awareness of MIS capabilities, human resource development for MIS, quality of data, standards). Advanced country issues are characterized by strategic needs (e.g. information architecture, data resource management, strategic planning for MIS, organizational learning).

While the Palvia *et al*. (1992) model appears to be generally sound, the Taiwan study included in this chapter and experience from other countries has led us to refine the model (Figure 8.1). Another class of countries has been added to the original three-way classification. Several countries have emerged as the newly industrialized countries (NICs) in the last decade and are now prospering. Examples of such countries include Taiwan, South Korea, Hong Kong and Singapore. If we extrapolate the Taiwan issues to NICs in general, then the majority of NIC issues are somewhat unique and different from other classes. To reiterate, representative NIC issues include: communication between IS department and end users, top management support, software development productivity, goal alignment, and security and control. Clearly, most of these issues are above the routine operational and infrastructural issues faced by organizations in underdeveloped and developing nations. Yet, they are lower in their strategic orientation as compared to the advanced nations. These issues then can most appropriately labeled as 'management and control' issues reflective of growing technology adoption. In a sense, the refined 'global information technology environment' model is similar to the Nolan stage model (1979), which posited the need for a control stage to contain and manage the proliferation of IS activities in an organization. The main difference is that our model explains the nature of IT conditions and practices based on economic conditions in different countries.

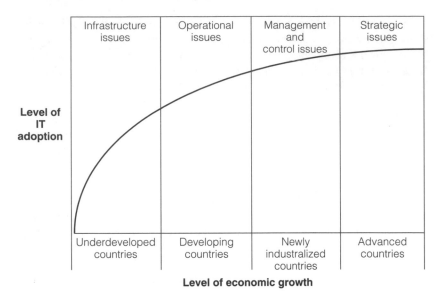

Figure 8.1   *A model of global information technology environment*

The addition of NICs into the model is also supported by the 'management and control' oriented policies being exercised in these countries. For example, Taiwan, Singapore, and South Korea have one or two government agencies which have coordinated and implemented explicit national IT plans since the 1980s. These three country governments explicitly promote and manage the production and use of IT products. Computerization is a national goal and essential to maintaining the competitiveness of the national economy in the global environment.

The model depicted in Figure 8.1 provides a first attempt in understanding the complex global IT environment. We recognize that there are limitations and other elements may be necessary for a deeper understanding of the global IT environment, or the environment of any particular country. For example, the inclusion of Russia and socialist countries under the 'developing/operational' country class may be an object of concern for some. Singapore might also be a special case, as it is not really a country, but a city-state, and has a benevolent ruler form of government. Nevertheless, the above model may be a starting point for an organization considering expansion into other world markets, and attempting to evaluate the role and use of information technology in its pursuit.

Basic elements of a more complete model for global IT environment are offered in Figure 8.2. Some summary comments are made about this model here; more elaboration and expansion are subjects of further investigation. Besides level of economic growth, other factors critical to information

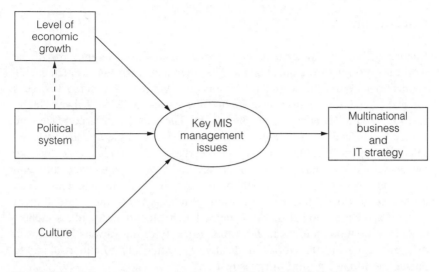

Figure 8.2 *A proposed comprehensive model for global IT environment*

technology adoption by firms in a country include its culture and political system. National culture comprises the values, beliefs, and behavior patterns dominant in a country, and has a strong influence on institutional and organizational patterns of behavior. Ein-Dor *et al.* (1993) presented a framework for the role of culture in IS, and presented some culturally sensitive findings. Shore and Venkatachalam (1995) explored the impact of culture on systems analysis and design issues. Based on the emerging literature on international and cross-cultural IS, it is a reasonable argument to make that national culture would have an impact on IS priorities.

The political system and government policies also have an impact on the IT readiness of a nation, as can be seen in the startling differences found among western countries, Russia, Eastern European countries, and Pacific Rim countries. Government, inspired by its political beliefs, may take a hands-off (yet supportive) approach towards IT developments (as in the USA and other free economies). At the other extreme, in spite of all good intentions, the government may impose a wide array of overly restrictive policies (as in some communist countries). As another alternative, government may pursue an aggressive policy of rapid technology growth, and provide necessary incentives and infrastructure to firms (as in Taiwan, Singapore, and South Korea). The dotted line shown in Figure 8.2 indicates that the political system of a nation also has an influence on its economic growth. Finally, as shown in the model, a good understanding of the global IT environment will be a key factor in the development of a suitable business and IT strategy of the multinational firm.

Conclusions

Reports of information systems management issues in different parts of the world are useful to organizations as they begin to plan and implement IT applications across the world. In this chapter, we have presented IS issues for many countries, and have examined the issues in USA, Taiwan, India, and Kenya and Zimbabwe in greater depth. The world is a large place, and attempting to understand the critical issues in every single country, or even selected countries, would be an arduous, perhaps an imprudent task. Instead, we have divided countries into four classes, and have provided an example in each class. An elementary model for the global IT environment has been postulated based on this categorization. While generalizations are fraught with risks, the provision of such a model will help practitioners and researchers alike in a preliminary assessment of the criticality of the various IT issues in different regions of the world. In closing, we would like to exhort others to pursue the following lines of investigation:

1   Develop and validate sound models that seek to explain the country issues. A simple model was presented in Figure 8.1. Elements of a more comprehensive model may include economic growth, national culture, and political system as causal factors, among others (as in Figure 8.2).
2   Evaluate the predictive capability of such models as well as report on the use of the models for prediction. While descriptive studies are helpful in identifying the key issues of individual countries at a point in time, this can be an enormous and time-consuming proposition given the number of countries in the world and the temporal nature of the issues. However, if the determinants of the key issues are known, then a preliminary estimation of the issues will be easier to make.
3   Use the model for focused research. For example, if culture is identified as one of the factors influencing IT needs, then it can be explored in more detail both in terms of culture components and IT components that are influenced by it.
4   Develop a comprehensive universal instrument and methodology that can be applied globally to identify the key IS issues. This instrument should then be administered simultaneously (or approximately in the same time frame) by a group of researchers in different countries. One of the limitations of previous 'key issue' studies is that they have used different questionnaires, different time frames, and different methods to assess the issues. While difficult, this undertaking will be very helpful in obtaining reliable results.
5   Develop specific practical implications and uses of the 'key issues' results. How can they be incorporated into the formulation of national policy, corporate policy or IS policies within an organization?

References

Badri, M. A. (1992) Critical issues in information systems management: an international perspective. *International Journal of Information Management*, **12**, 179–191.

Ball, L. and Harris, R. (1982) SMIS members: a membership analysis. *MIS Quarterly*, **6**(1), March, 19–38.

Brancheau, J. C. and Wetherbe, J. C. (1987) Key issues in information systems management. *MIS Quarterly*, March, 23–46.

Burn, J., Saxena, K. B. C., Ma, L. and Cheung, H. K. (1993) Critical issues of IS management in Hong Kong: a cultural comparison. *Journal of Global Information Management*, **1**(4), Fall, pp.28–37.

Carey, D. (1992) Rating the top MIS issues in Canada. *Canadian Datasystems*, June, 23–26.

Chepaitis, E. V. (1994) After the command economy: Russia's information culture and its impact on information resource management. *Journal of Global Information Management*, **2**(1), Winter, pp.5–11.

CSC Index (1995) *Critical Issues Information Systems Management for 1995*, Cambridge, Massachusetts.

Deans, P. C., Karawan, K. R., Goslar, M. D., Ricks, D. A. and Toyne, B. (1991) Identification of key international information systems issues: U.S.-based multinational corporations. *Journal of Management Information Systems*, **27**(4), Spring, 27–50.

Dekeleva, S. and Zupancic, J. (1993) Key issues in information systems management: a Delphi study in Slovenia. In DeGross J. I., Bostrom, R. P. and Robey, D., Eds. *Proceedings of the Fourteenth International Conference on Information Systems*, Orlando, Fl.

Dexter, A. S., Janson, M. A., Kiudorf, E. and Laast-Laas, J. (1993) Key information technology issues in Estonia. *Journal of Strategic Information Systems*, June, **2**(2), 139–152.

Dickson, G. W., Leitheiser, R. L., Nechis, M. and Wetherbe, J. C. (1984) Key information systems issues for the 1980's. *MIS Quarterly*, **8**(3), September, 135–148.

Ein-Dor, P., Segev, E. and Orgad, M. (1993) The effect of national culture on IS: implication for international information systems. *Journal of Global Information Management*, Winter, 33–44.

Galliers, R. D., Merali, Y. and Spearing, L. (1994) Coping with information technology? How British executives perceive the key information systems management issues in the mid-1990s. *Journal of Information Technology*, **9**(3), 223–238.

Goodman, S. E. (1991) Computing and the resuscitation of Romania. *Communications of the ACM*, **34**(9), September, 19–22.

Goodman, S. E. and McHenry, W. K. (1991) The Soviet computer industry: A tale of two sectors. *Communications of the ACM*, **34**(6), June, pp.25–29.

Hartog, C. and Martin H. (1986) 1985 opinion survey of MIS managers: key issues. *MIS Quarterly*, December, 351–361.

Hassan, S. Z. (1994) Environmental constraints in utilizing information technologies in Pakistan. *Journal of Global Information Management*, **2**(4), Fall, 30–39.

Igbaria, M. (1992) An examination of microcomputer usage in Taiwan. *Information & Management*, **22**, 19–28.

Janz, B., Brancheau, J. and Wetherbe, J. (1994) Key issues in IS management. Working Paper, *MIS Research Center*, University of Minnesota.

La Rovere, R. L., Tigre, P. B. and Fagundes, J. (1996) Information networks diffusion in Brazil: global and local factors. In *Global Information Technology and Systems Management: Key Issues and Trends*, ed. P. Palvia, S. Palvia and E. Roche, Ivy League Publishing, New Hampshire.

McFadden, F. R. and Hoffer, J. A. (1994) *Modern Database Management*, 4th edn, Benjamin Cummings Pub. Co., California.

McLuhan, M. (1964) *Understanding Media: The Extensions of Man*, McGraw-Hill, New York.

Niederman, F., Brancheau, J. C. and Wetherbe, J. C. (1991) Information systems management issues for the 1990s. *MIS Quarterly*, December, 475–495.

Nolan, R. L. (1979) Managing the crises in data processing. *Harvard Business Review*, **57**(2), March-April, 115–126.

Palvia, P. and Palvia, S. (1992) MIS issues in India, and a comparison with the United States. *International Information Systems*, April, 100–110.

Palvia, P., Palvia, S. and Zigli, R. M. (1992) Global information technology environment: key MIS issues in advanced and less developed nations. In *The Global Issues of Information Technology Management* (eds S. Palvia, P. Palvia and R. M. Zigli), Idea Group Publishing, Harrisburg, PA.

Palvia, P. and Wang, P. (1995) An expanded global information technology issues model: an addition of newly industrialized countries. *Journal of Information Technology Management*, **VI**(2), 29–39.

Rao, K. V., Huff, F. P. and Davis, G. B. (1987) Critical issues in the management of information systems: a comparison of Singapore and the USA. *Information Technology*, **1**(3), 11–19.

Roche, E. M. (1992) *Managing Information Technology in Multinational Corporations*, Macmillan Pub. Co., New York.

Roche, E. M., Goodman, S. E. and Chen, H. (1992) The landscape of international computing. *Advances in Computers*, **35**, Spring.

Shore, B. and Venkatachalam, A. R. (1995) The role of national culture in systems analysis and design. *Journal of Global Information Management*, **3**(3), Summer, 5–14.

Wang, P. (1994) Information management systems issues in the Republic of China for the 1990s. *Information and Management*, **26**, 341–352.

Watson, R. T. (1989) Key issues in information systems management: an Australian perspective – 1988. *Australian Computer Journal*, **21**(3), 118–129.
Watson, R. T. and Brancheau, J. C. (1991) Key issues in information systems management: an international perspective. *Information and Management*, **20**, 213–223.

Questions for discussion

1 For each of the four groups (industrialized, newly industrialized, developing, underdeveloped),
   – were you surprised by any of the issues included or by any issues not included?
   – what changes would you expect to see now (given that the chapter first appeared in 1996)?
   – over which issues does an IT manager have control, or not have control?
2 What are the implications of the different key issues for IT management in a multinational firm?
3 What are the implications for the so-called networked world?
4 Why would you expect different key issues in different major economic segments?
5 What are the implications of these key issues for small-medium sized local firms?
6 Consider similarities of Figure 8.1 with the 'stages of growth' model, discussed in Chapter 2. Is it basically the same conceptualization but just at a different level of analysis?

Further background reading

Watson, R. T., Kelly, G. G., Galliers, R. D., and Brancheau, J. C. (1997). Key issues in Information Systems Management: An international comparison, *Journal of Management Information Systems*, **13**(4), Spring, 91–115.

9 Approaches to Information Systems Planning

Experiences in strategic information systems planning*

M. J. Earl

Strategic information systems planning (SISP) remains a top concern of many organizations. Accordingly, researchers have investigated SISP practice and proposed both formal methods and principles of good practice. SISP cannot be understood by considering formal methods alone. The processes of planning and the implementation of plans are equally important. However, there have been very few field investigations of these phenomena. This study examines SISP experience in 27 companies and, unusually, relies on interviews not only with IS managers but also with general managers and line managers. By adopting this broader perspective, the investigation reveals companies were using five different SISP approaches: Business-Led, Method-Driven, Administrative, Technological, and Organizational. Each approach has different characteristics and, therefore, a different likelihood of success. The results show that the Organizational Approach appears to be most effective. The taxonomy of the five approaches potentially provides a diagnostic tool for analyzing and evaluating an organization's experience with SISP.

Introduction

For many IS executives, strategic information systems planning (SISP) continues to be a critical issue.[1] It is also reportedly the top IS concern of chief executives (Moynihan, 1990). At the same time, it is almost axiomatic that information systems management be based on SISP (Synott and Gruber, 1982). Furthermore, as investment in information technology has been promoted to both support business strategy or create strategic options (Earl, 1988;

---

* An earlier version of this chapter was published in *Proceedings of the International Conference on Information Systems*, Copenhagen, Denmark, December 1990.

Henderson and Venkatraman, 1989), an 'industry' of SISP has grown as IT manufacturers and management consultants have developed methodologies and techniques. Thus, SISP appears to be a rich and important activity for researchers. So far, researchers have provided surveys of practice and problems, models and frameworks for theory-building, and propositions and methods to put into action.[2]

The literature recommends that SISP target the following areas:

- aligning investment in IS with business goals
- exploiting IT for competitive advantage
- directing efficient and effective management of IS resources
- developing technology policies and architectures

It has been suggested (Earl, 1989) that the first two areas are concerned with information systems strategy, the third with information management strategy, and the fourth with information technology strategy. In survey-based research to date, it is usually the first two areas that dominate. Indeed, SISP has been defined in this light (Lederer and Sethi, 1988) as 'the process of deciding the objectives for organizational computing and identifying potential computer applications which the organization should implement' (p.445). This definition was used in our investigation of SISP activity in 27 United Kingdom-based companies.

Calls have been made recently for better understanding of strategic planning in general, including SISP, and especially for studies of actual planning behavior in organizations (Boynton and Zmud, 1987; Henderson and Sifonis, 1988). As doubts continue to be raised about the pay-off of IT, it does seem important to examine the reality of generally accepted IS management practices such as SISP. Thus, in this investigation we used field studies to capture the *experiences* of large companies that had attempted some degree of formal IS planning.[3]

We were also interested as to whether any particular SISP techniques were more effective than others. This question proved difficult to answer, as discussed below, and is perhaps even irrelevant. Techniques were found to be only one element of SISP, with process and implementation being equally important. Therefore, a more descriptive construct embodying these three elements – the SISP *approach* – was examined. Five different approaches were identified; the experience of the organizations studied suggests that one approach may be more effective than the others.

Methodology

In 1988–89, a two-stage survey was conducted to discover the intents, outcomes, and experiences of SISP efforts. First, case studies captured the history of six companies previously studied by the author. These retrospective case histories were based on accounts of the IS director and/or IS strategic planner and on internal documentation of these companies. The cases suggested or confirmed questions to ask in the second stage. Undoubtedly, these cases influenced the perspective of the researcher.

In the second stage, 21 different UK companies were investigated through field studies. All were large companies that were among the leaders in the banking, insurance, transport, retailing, electronics, IT, automobile, aerospace, oil, chemical, services, and food and drink industries. Annual revenues averaged £4.5 billion. They were all headquartered in the UK or had significant national or regional IS functions within multi-national companies headquartered elsewhere. Their experience with formal SISP activities ranged from one to 20 years.[4] The scope of SISP could be either at the business unit level, the corporate level, or both. The results from this second stage are reported in this chapter.

Within each firm, the author carried out in-depth interviews, typically lasting two to four hours, with three 'stakeholders'. A total of 63 executives were interviewed. The IS director or IS strategic planner was interviewed first, followed by the CEO or a general manager, and finally a senior line or user manager. Management prescriptions often state that SISP requires a combination or coalition of line managers contributing application ideas or making system requests, general managers setting direction and priorities, and IS professionals suggesting what can be achieved technically. Additionally, interviewing these three stakeholders provides some triangulation, both as a check on the views of the IS function and as a useful, but not perfect, cross-section of corporate memory.

Because the IS director selected the interviewees, there could have been some sample bias. However, parameters were laid down on how to select interviewees, and the responses did not indicate any prior collusion in aligning opinions. Respondents were supposed to be the IS executives most involved with SISP (which may or may not be the CIO), the CEO or general manager most involved in strategic decisions on IS, and a 'typical' user line manager who had contributed to SISP activities.

Interviews were conducted using questionnaires to ensure completeness and replicability, but a mix of unstructured, semi-structured, and structured interrogation was employed.[5] Typically, a simple question was posed in an open manner (often requiring enlargement to overcome differences in organizational language), and raw responses were recorded. The same question was then asked in a closed manner, requesting quantitative responses using scores, ranking, and Likert-type scales. Particular attention was paid to anecdotes, tangents, and 'asides'. In this way, it was hoped to collect data sets for both qualitative and quantitative analysis. Interviews focused on intents, outcomes, and experiences of SISP.

It was also attempted to record experiences with particular SISP methodologies and relate their use to success, benefits and problems. However, this aim proved to be inappropriate (because firms often had employed a variety of techniques and procedures over time), and later was jettisoned in favor of recording the variety and richness of planning behavior the respondents recalled. This study is therefore exploratory, with a focus on theory development.[6]

Interests, methods, and outcomes

Data were collected on the stimuli, aims, benefits, success factors, problems, procedures, and methods of SISP. These data have been statistically examined, but only a minimum of results is presented here as a necessary context to the principal findings of the study.[7]

Respondents were asked to state their firms' current *objectives* for SISP. The dominant objective was alignment of IS with business needs, with 69.8 percent of respondents ranking it as most important and 93.7 percent ranking it in their top five objectives (Table 9.1). Interview comments reinforced the importance of this objective. The search for competitive advantage applications was ranked second, reflecting the increased strategic awareness of IT in the late 1980s. Gaining top management commitment was third. The only difference among the stakeholders was that IS directors placed top management commitment above the competitive advantage goal, perhaps reflecting a desire for functional sponsorship and a clear mandate.

Table 9.1 suggests that companies have more than one objective for SISP; narrative responses usually identified two or three objectives spontaneously.

Table 9.1 *Objectives of SISP*

Rank order	Objective	Respondents selecting (n = 63)	Primary frequency	Sum of ranks	Mean rank
1	Aligning IS with business needs	59	44	276	4.38
2	Seek competitive advantage from IT	45	8	161	2.55
3	Gain top management commitment	36	6	115	1.83
4	Forecast IS resource requirements	35	1	80	1.27
5	Establish technology path and policies	30	2	77	1.22

Table 9.2   *SISP benefits*

Rank order	Benefit	Respondents selecting (n = 63)	Primary frequency	Sum of ranks	Mean rank
1	Aligning IS with business needs	49	31	208	3.30
2	Top management support	27	7	94	1.49
3	Better priority setting	35	3	75	1.19
4	Competitive advantage applications	21	4	67	1.06
5	Top management involvement	19	3	60	0.95
6	User/line management involvement	21	2	58	0.92

Not surprisingly, the respondents' views on *benefits* were similar and also indicated a multidimensional picture (Table 9.2). All respondents were able to select confidently from a structured list. Alignment of IS again stood out, with 49 percent ranking it first and 78 percent ranking it in the top five benefits. Top management support, better priority setting, competitive advantage applications, top management involvement, and user-management involvement were the other prime benefits reported.

Respondents also evaluated their firm's *success* with SISP. Success measures have been discussed elsewhere (Raghunathan and King, 1988). Most have relied upon satisfaction scores (Galliers, 1987), absence of problems (Lederer and Sethi, 1988), or audit checklists (King, 1988). Respondents were given no criterion of success but were given scale anchors to help them record a score from 1 (low) to 5 (high), as shown in Appendix B.

Ten percent of all respondents claimed their SISP had been 'highly successful', 59 percent reported it had been 'successful but there was room for improvement', and 69 percent rated SISP as worthwhile or better. Thirty-one percent were dissatisfied with their firm's SISP. There were differences between stakeholders; whereas 76 percent of IS directors gave a score above 3, only 67 percent of general managers and 57 percent of user mangers were as content. Because the mean score by company was 3.73, and the modal company score was 4, the typical experience can be described as worthwhile but in need of some improvement.

A complementary question revealed a somewhat different picture. Interviewees were asked in what ways SISP had been *unsuccessful*. Sixty-five different types of disappointment were recorded. In such a long list none was dominant. Nevertheless, Table 9.3 summarizes the five most commonly

Table 9.3 *Unsuccessful features of SISP*

Rank order	Unsuccessful features
1	Resource constraints
2	Not fully implemented
3	Lack of top management acceptance
4	Length of time involved
5	Poor user-IS relationships

Table 9.4 *SISP concerns by stakeholder*

	Total citations	%	IS directors (n = 21)		General managers (n = 21)		User managers (n = 21)	
			Citations	%	Citations	%	Citations	%
Method	45	36	14	36	18	44	13	28
Process	39	31	9	23	11	27	19	41
Implementation	42	33	16	41	12	29	14	31
	126	100	39	100	41	100	46	100

mentioned features contributing to dissatisfaction. We will henceforth refer to these as 'concerns'.

It is apparent that concerns extend beyond technique or methodology, the focus of several researchers, and the horizon of most suppliers. Accordingly we examined the 65 different concerns looking for a pattern. This inductive and subjective clustering produced an interesting classification. The cited concerns could be grouped almost equally into three distinct categories (assuming equal weighting to each concern): method, process, and implementation, as shown in Table 9.4. The full list of concerns is reproduced in Appendix C.

Method concerns centered on the SISP technique, procedure, or methodology employed. Firms commonly had used proprietary methods, such as Method 1, BSP, or Information Engineering, or applied generally available techniques, such as critical success factors or value chain analysis. Others had invented their own methods, often customizing well-known techniques. Among the stated concerns were lack of strategic thinking, excessive internal focus, too much or too little attention to architecture, excessive time and resource requirements, and ineffective resource allocation mechanisms. General managers especially emphasized these concerns, perhaps because they have high expectations but find IS strategy making difficult.

Implementation was a common concern. Even where SISP was judged to have been successful, the resultant strategies or plans were not always followed up or fully implemented. Even though clear directions might be set and commitments made to develop new applications, projects often were not initiated and systems development did not proceed. This discovery supports the findings of earlier work (Lederer and Sethi, 1988). Evidence from the interviews suggests that typically resources were not made available, management was hesitant, technological constraints arose, or organizational resistance emerged. Where plans were implemented, other concerns arose, including technical quality, the time and cost involved, or the lack of benefits realized. Implementation concerns were raised most by IS directors, perhaps because they are charged with delivery or because they hoped SISP would provide hitherto elusive strategic direction of their function. Of course, it can be claimed that a strategy that is not implemented or poorly implemented is no strategy at all – a tendency not unknown in business strategy making (Mintzberg, 1987). Indeed, implementation has been proposed as a measure of success in SISP (Lederer and Sethi, 1988).

Process concerns included lack of line management participation, poor IS-user relationships, inadequate user awareness and education, and low management ownership of the philosophy and practice of SISP. Line managers were particularly vocal about the management and enactment of SISP methods and procedures and whether they fit the organizational context.

Analysis of the reported concerns therefore suggests that method, process, and implementation are all necessary conditions for successful SISP (Figure 9.1). Indeed, when respondents volunteered success factors for SISP based on their organizations' experience, they conveyed this multiple perspective (see Table 9.5). The highest ranked factors of 'top management involvement', and 'top management support' can be seen as process factors, while 'business strategy available' and 'study the business before technology' have more to do with method. 'Good IS management' partly relates to implementation. Past research has identified similar concerns (Lederer and Mendelow, 1987), and the more prescriptive literature has suggested some of these success factors (Synott and Gruber, 1982). However, the experience of organizations in this study indicates that no single factor is likely to lead to universal success in SISP. Instead, successful SISP is more probable when organizations realize that method, process, and implementation are all necessary issue sets to be managed.

In particular, consultants, managers, and researchers would seem well advised to look beyond method alone in practising SISP. Furthermore, researchers cannot assume that SISP requires selection and use of just one method or one special planning exercise. Typically, it seems that firms use several methods over time. An average of 2.3 methods (both proprietary and in-house) had been employed by the 21 companies studied. Nine of them had tried three or

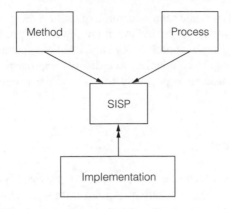

Figure 9.1 *Necessary conditions for successful SISP*

Table 9.5 *Success factors in SISP*

Rank order	Success factor	Respondents selecting	Primary frequency	Sum of ranks	Mean rank
1	Top management involvement	42	15	160	2.55
2	Top management support	34	17	140	2.22
3	Business strategy available	26	9	99	1.57
4	Study business before technology	23	9	87	1.38
5	Good IS management	17	1	41	0.65

more. Retrospectively isolating and identifying the effect of a method there-fore becomes difficult for researchers. It may also be misleading because, as discovered in these interviews, firms engage in a variety of strategic planning activities and behavior. This became apparent when respondents were asked the open-ended question, 'Please summarize the approach you have adopted in developing your IS strategy (or identifying which IT applications to develop in the long run)'. In reply they usually recounted a rich history of initiatives, events, crises, techniques, organizational changes, successes, and failures all interwoven in a context of how IS resources had been managed.

Prompted both by the list of concerns and narrative histories of planning-related events, the focus of this study therefore shifted. The object of analysis became the SISP *approach*. This we viewed as the interaction of method, process, and implementation, as well as the variety of activities and behaviors upon which the respondents had reflected. The accounts of interviewees, the 'untutored' responses to the semi-structured questions, the documents supplied, and the 'asides' followed up by the interviewer all produced descriptive data on each company's approach. Once the salient features of SISP were compared across the 21 companies, five distinct approaches were identified. These were then used retrospectively to classify the experiences of the six case study firms.

SISP approaches

An approach is not a technique *per se*. Nor is it necessarily an explicit study or formal, codified routine so often implied in past accounts and studies of SISP. As in most forms of business planning, it cannot often be captured by one event, a single procedure, or a particular technique. An approach may comprise a mix of procedures, techniques, user-IS interactions, special ana-lyses, and random discoveries. There are likely to be some formal activities and some informal behavior. Sometimes IS planning is a special endeavor and sometimes it is part of business planning at large. However, when members of the organization describe how decisions on IS strategy are initiated and made, a coherent picture is gradually painted where the underpinning philosophy, emphasis, and influences stand out. These are the principal distinguishing features of an approach. The *elements* of an approach can be seen as the nature and place of method, the attention to and style of process, and the focus on and probability of implementation.

The five approaches are labelled as Business-Led, Method-Driven, Administrative, Technological, and Organizational. They are delineated as ideal types in Table 9.6. Several distinctors are apparent in each approach. Each represents a particular philosophy (either explicit or implicit), displays its own dynamics, and has different strengths and weaknesses. Whereas some factors for success are suggested by each approach, not all approaches seem to be equally effective.

Business-led approach

The *Business-Led Approach* was adopted by four companies and two of the case study firms. The underpinning 'assumption' of this approach is that current business direction or plans are the only basis upon which IS plans can be built and that, therefore, business planning should drive SISP. The emphasis is on the business leading IS and not the other way around. Business plans or strategies are analyzed to identify where information systems are most required. Often this linkage is an annual endeavor and is the responsibility of the IS director or IS strategic planner (or team). The IS strategic plan is later presented to the board for questioning, approval, and priority-setting.

Table 9.6   *SISP approaches*

	Business-Led	Method-Driven	Administrative	Technological	Organizational
Emphasis	Business	Technique	Resources	Model	Learning
Basis	Business plans	Best method	Procedure	Rigor	Partnership
Ends	Plan	Strategy	Portfolio	Architecture	Themes
Methods	Ours	Best	None	Engineering	Any way
Nature	Business	Top-down	Bottom-up	Blueprints	Interactive
Influencer	IS planner	Consultants	Committees	Method	Teams
Relation to business strategy	Fix points	Derive	Criteria	Objectives	Look at business
Priority setting	The board	Method recommends	Central committee	Compromise	Emerge
IS role	Driver	Initiator	Bureaucrat	Architect	Team member
Metaphor	It's common sense	It's good for you	Survival of the fittest	We nearly aborted it	Thinking IS all the time

General managers see this approach as simple, 'business-like', and a matter of common sense. IS executives often see this form of SISP as their most critical task and welcome the long overdue mandate from senior management. However, they soon discover that business strategies are neither clear nor detailed enough to specify IS needs. Thus, interpretation and further analysis become necessary. Documents have to be studied, managers interviewed, meetings convened, working papers written, and tentative proposals on the IS implications of business plans put forward. 'Home-spun' procedures are developed on a trial and error basis to discover and propose the IT implications of business plans. It may be especially difficult to promote the notion that IT itself may offer some new strategic options. The IS planners often feel that they have to 'take the lead' to make any progress or indeed to engage the business in the exercise. They also discover that some top executives may be more forceful in their views and expectations than others.

Users and line managers are likely to be involved very little. The emphasis on top-level input and business plans reduces the potential contribution of users and the visibility of local requirements. Users, perceiving SISP as remote, complain of inadequate involvement. Because the IS strategy becomes the product of the IS function, user support is not guaranteed. Top management, having substantially delegated SISP to the specialists, may be unsure of the recommendations and be hesitant to commit resources, thus impairing implementation.

Nevertheless, some advantages can accrue. Information systems are seen as a strategic resource, and the IS function receives greater legitimacy. Important strategic thrusts that require IT support can be identified, and if the business strategy is clearly and fully presented, the IS strategy can be well-aligned. Indeed, in one of the prior case study companies that adopted this approach, a clear business plan for survival led to IT applications that were admired by many industry watchers. However, despite this achievement, the IS function is still perceived by all three sets of stakeholders as poorly integrated into the business as a whole.

Method-driven approach

The *Method-Driven Approach* was present in two companies and two of the case study firms. Adherents of this approach appear to assume that SISP is enhanced by, or depends on, use of a formal technique or method. The IS director may believe that management will not think about IS needs and opportunities without the use of a formal method or the intervention of consultants. Indeed, recognition or anticipation of some of the frustrations typical of the Business-Led Approach may prompt the desire for method. However, any method will not do. There is typically a search for the 'best method', or at least one better than the last method adopted.

Once again, business strategies may be found to be deficient for the purpose of SISP. The introduction of a formal method rarely provides a remedy, however, because it is unlikely to be a strong enough business strategy technique. Also, the method's practitioners are unlikely to be skilled or credible at such work. Furthermore, as formal methods are usually sponsored by the IS department, they may fail to win the support or involvement of the business at large. Thus, a second or third method may be attempted while the IS department tries to elicit or verify the business strategy and to encourage a wider set of stakeholders to participate. Often, a vendor or consultant plays a significant role. As the challenges unfold, stakeholders determine the 'best' method, often as a result of the qualities of the consultants as much as the techniques themselves. The consultants often become the drivers of the SISP exercise and therefore have substantial influence on the recommendations.

Users may judge Method-Driven exercises as 'unreal' and 'high level' and as having excluded the managers who matter, namely themselves. General managers can see the studies as 'business strategy making in disguise' and thus become somewhat resistant and not easily persuaded of the priorities or options suggested by the application of the method. IS strategic plans may then lose their credibility and never be fully initiated. The exercises and recommendations may be forgotten. Often they are labelled the 'xyz' strategy, where 'xyz' is the name of the consulting firm employed; in other words, these strategies are rarely 'owned' by the business.

Formal methods do not always fail completely. Although a succession of methods achieved little in the companies studied, managers judged that each method had been good in some unanticipated way for the business or the IS department.[8] For example, in one firm it showed the need for business strategies, and in another it informed IS management about business imperatives. In the former firm, IS directors were heard to say the experience had been 'good for the company, showing up the gaps in strategic thinking!' Nevertheless, formal strategy studies could leave behind embryonic strategic thrusts, ideas waiting for the right time, or new thinking that could be exploited or built upon later in unforeseen ways.

Administrative approach

The *Administrative Approach* was found in five companies. The emphasis here is on resource planning. The wider management planning and control procedures were expected to achieve the aims of SISP through formal procedures for allocating IS resources. Typically, IS development proposals were submitted by business units or departments to committees who examined project viability, common system possibilities, and resource consequences. In some cases, resource planners did the staff work as proposals ascended the annual hierarchical approval procedure. The Administrative Approach was the parallel of, or could be attached to, the firm's normal financial planning or capital budgeting routine. The outcome of the approach was a one-year or multi-year development portfolio of approved projects. Typically no application is developed until it is on the plan. A planning investment or steering committee makes all decisions and agrees on any changes.

Respondents identified significant down sides to the Administrative Approach. It was seen as not strategic, as being 'bottom-up' rather than 'top-down'. Ideas for radical change were not identified, strategic thinking was absent, inertia and 'business as usual' dominated, and enterprise-level applications remained in the background. More emotional were the claims about conflicts, dramas, and game playing – all perhaps inevitable in an essentially resource allocation procedure. The emphasis on resource planning sometimes led to a resource-constrained outcome. For example, spending limits were often applied, and boards and CEOs were accused of applying cuts to the IS budget, assuming that in doing so no damage was being done to the business as a whole.

Some benefits of this approach were identified. Everybody knew about the procedure; it was visible, and all users and units had the opportunity to submit proposals. Indeed, an SISP procedure and timetable for SISP were commonly published as part of the company policy and procedures manual. Users, who were encouraged to make application development requests, did produce some ideas for building competitive advantage. Also, it seemed that radical, transformational IT applications could arise in these companies despite the apparently bottom-up, cautious procedure. The most radical applications emerged when the CEO or finance director broke the administrative rules and informally proposed and sanctioned an IS investment.

By emphasizing viability, project approval, and resource planning, the administrative approach produced application development portfolios that were eventually implemented. Not only financial criteria guided these choices. New strategic guidelines, such as customer service or quality improvement, were also influential. Finally, the Administrative Approach often fitted the planning and control style of the company. IS was managed in congruence with other activities, which permitted complemetary resources to be allocated in parallel. Indeed, unless the IS function complied with procedures, no resources were forthcoming.

Technological approach

The *Technological Approach* was adopted by four companies and two of the case study firms. This approach is based on the assumption that an information systems-oriented model of the business is a necessary outcome of SISP and, therefore, that analytical modelling methods are appropriate. This approach is different from the Method-Driven Approach in two principal characteristics. First, the end product is a business model (or series of models). Second, a formal method is applied based on mapping the activities, processes, and data flows of the business. The emphasis is on deriving architectures or blueprints for IT and IS, and often Information Engineering terminology is used. Architectures for data, computing, communications, and applications might be produced, and computer-aided software engineering (CASE) might be among the tools employed. A proprietary technology-oriented method might be used or adapted in-house. Both IS directors and general mangers tend to emphasize the objectives of rigorous analysis and of building a robust infrastructure.

This approach is demanding in terms of both effort and resource requirements. These also tend to be high-profile activities. Stakeholders commented on the length of time involved in the analysis and/or the implementation. User managers reacted negatively to the complexity of the analysis and the outputs and reported a tendency for technical dependencies to displace business priorities. In one case, management was unsure of the validity and meaning of the blueprints generated and could not determine what proposals mattered most. A second study of the same type, but using a different technological method, was commissioned. This produced a different but equally unconvincing set of blueprints.

These characteristics could lead to declining top management support or even user rebellion. In one firm, the users called for an enterprise modelling exercise to be aborted. In one of the case study firms, development of the blueprint applications was axed by top management three and a half years after initiation. In another, two generations of IS management departed after organizational conflict concerning the validity of the technological model proposed.

Some success was claimed for the Technological Approach. Benefits were salvaged by factoring down the approach into smaller exercises. In one case this produced a database definition, and in another it led to an IT architecture for the finance function. Some IS directors claimed these outcomes were valuable in building better IT infrastructures.

Organizational approach

The *Organizational Approach* was used in six companies and one of the case study firms. The underpinning assumption here is quite different. It is that SISP is not a special or neat and tidy endeavor but is based on IS decisions being made through continuous integration between the IS function and the organization. The way IT applications are identified and selected is described in much more multi-dimensional and subtle language. The approach is not without method, but methods are employed as required and to fit a particular purpose. For example, value analysis may be used, workshops arranged, business investigation projects set up, and vendor visits organized. The emphasis, however, is on process, especially management understanding and involvement. For some of these companies, a major SISP method had been applied in the past, but in retrospect it was seen to have been as much a process enabler as an analytical investigation. Executive teamwork and an understanding of how IT might contribute to the business were often left behind by the method rather than specific recommendations for IS investment. Organizational learning was important and evident in at least three ways.

First, IS development concentrated on only one or two themes growing in scope over several years as the organization began to appreciate the potential benefits. Examples of such themes included a food company concentrating on providing high service levels to customers, an insurance company conentrating on low-cost administration, and a chemical company concentrating on product development performance. Second, special studies were important. Often multidisciplinary senior executive project teams or full-time task forces were assigned to tackle a business problem from which a major IS initiative would later emerge. The presence of an IS executive in the multidisciplinary team was felt to be important to the emergence of a strategic theme because this person could suggest why, where, and how IT could help. Teamwork was the principal influence in IS strategy making. Third, there was a focus on implementation. Themes were broken down into identifiable and frequent deliverables. Conversely, occasional project cost and time overruns were acceptable if they allowed evolving ideas to be incorporated. In some ways, IS strategies were discovered through implementation. These three learning characteristics can be seen collectively as a preference for incremental strategy making.

The approach is therefore *organizational* because:

1   Collective learning across the organization is evident.
2   Organizational devices or instruments (teams, task forces, workshops, etc.) are used to tackle business problems or pursue initiatives.
3   The IS function works in close partnership with the rest of the organization, especially through having IS managers on management teams or placing IS executives on task forces.
4   Devolution of some IS capability is common, not only to divisions, but also to functions, factories, and departments.
5   In some companies SISP is neither special nor abnormal. It is part of the normal business planning of the organization.
6   IS strategies often emerge from ongoing organizational activities, such as trial and error changes to business practices, continuous and incremental enhancement of existing applications, and occasional system initiatives and experiments within the business.

In one of the companies, planning was 'counter-cultural'. Nevertheless, in the character described above, planning still happened. In another company there were no IS plans, just business plans. In another, IS was enjoying a year or more of low profile until the company discovered the next theme. In most of these firms, IS decisions were being made all the time and at any time.

Respondents reported some disadvantages of this approach. Some IS directors worried about how the next theme would be generated. Also, because the approach is somewhat fuzzy or soft, they were not always confident that it could be transplanted to another part of the business. Indeed, a new CEO, management team, or management style could erode the process without the effect being apparent for some time. One IS director believed the incrementalism of the Organizational Approach led to creation of inferior infrastructures.

The five approaches appear to be different in scope, character, and outcome. Table 9.7 differentiates them using the three characteristics that seem to help other organizations position themselves. Also, slogans are offered to capture the essence of each approach. Strengths and weaknesses of each approach are contained in Table 9.8.

Table 9.7 *Five approaches summarized*

	Business-Led	Method-Driven	Administrative	Technological	Organizational
Underpinning assumption	Business plans and needs should drive IS plans	IS strategies will be enhanced by use of a formal SISP method	SISP should follow and conform with the firm's management planning and control procedures	SISP is an exercise in business and information modelling	SISP is a continuous decision-making activity shared by the business and IS
Emphasis of approach	Business leads IS and not vice versa	Selection of the best method	Identification and allocation of IS resources to meet agreed needs	Production of models and blueprints	Organizational learning about business problems and opportunities and the IT contribution
Major influence of outcomes	IS planners	Practitioners of the method	Resource planning and steering committees	Modelling method employed	Permanent and *ad hoc* teams of key managers, including IS
Slogan	Business drives IS	Strategy needs method	Follow the rules	IS needs blueprints	Themes with teams

It is also possible to indicate the apparent differences of each approach in terms of the three factors suggested in Figure 9.1 as necessary for success: method, process, and implementation. Table 9.9 attempts a summary.

In the Business-Led Approach, method scores low because no formal technique is used; process is rated low because the exercise is commonly IS dominated; but implementation is medium because the boards tend to at least approve some projects. In the Method-Driven Approach, method is high by definition, but process is largely ignored and implementation barely or rarely initiated. In the Administrative Approach, only a procedure exists as method. However, its dependence on user inputs suggests a medium rating on process. Because of its resource allocation emphasis, approved projects are generally implemented. The Technological Approach is generally method-intensive and insensitive to process. It can, however, lead to some specific implementation of an infrastructure. The Organizational Approach uses any method or devices that fit the need; it explicitly invests in process and emphasizes implementation.

Table 9.8 *Strengths and weaknesses of SISP approaches*

	Business-Led	Method-Driven	Administrative	Technological	Organizational
Strengths	Simple	Provides a methodology	System viability	Rigor	Becomes normal
	Business first	Plugs strategy gaps	System synergies	Focus on infrastructure	Emphasis on implementation
	Raises IS status	Raises strategy profile	Encourages user input	Favors integrated tools	Promotes IS-user partnership
Weaknesses	*Ad hoc* method	User involvement	Non-strategic	Lacks management support	Generation of new themes
	Lacks management commitment	Too influenced by method	Bureaucratic	Only partial implementation	Soft methodology
	Depends on quality of business strategy	Implementation unlikely	Resource-constrained	Complexity	Architecture becomes difficult

Table 9.9 *SISP approaches vs. three conditions for success*

	Business-Led	Method-Driven	Administrative	Technological	Organizational
Method	Low	High	Low	High	Medium
Process	Low	Low	Medium	Low	High
Implementation	Medium	Low	High	Medium	High

Preliminary evaluations

The five approaches were identified by comparing the events, experiences, and lessons described by the interviewees. As the investigation proved to be exploratory, the classification of approaches is descriptive and was derived by inductive interpretation of organizational experiences. Table 9.6, therefore, should be seen as an ideal model that caricatures the approaches in order to aid theory development. One way of 'validating' the model is to compare it with prior research in both IS and general management to assess whether the approaches 'ring true'.

Related theories

Difficulties encountered in the Business-Led Approach have been noted by others. The availability of formal business strategies for SISP cannot be assumed (Bowman *et al.*, 1983; Lederer and Mendelow, 1986). Nor can we assume that business strategies are communicated to the organization at large, are clear and stable, or are valuable in identifying IS needs (Earl, 1989; Lederer and Mendelow, 1989). Indeed, the quality of the process of business planning itself may often be suspect (Lederer and Sethi, 1988). In other words, while the Business-Led Approach may be especially appealing to general managers, the challenges are likely to be significant.

There is considerable literature on the top-down, more business-strategy–oriented SISP methods implied by the Method-Driven Approach, but most of it is conjectural or normative. Vendors can be very persuasive about the need for a methodology that explicitly connects IS to business thinking (Bowman *et al.*, 1983). Other researchers have argued that sometimes the business strategy must be explicated first (King, 1978; Lederer and Mendelow, 1987). This was a belief of the IS directors in the Method-Driven companies, but one general manager complained that this was 'business strategy making in disguise'.

The Administrative Approach reflects the prescriptions and practices of bureaucratic models of planning and control. We must turn to the general management literature for insights into this approach. Quinn (1977) has pointed out the strategy-making limitations of bottom-up planning procedures. He argues that big change rarely originates in this way and that, furthermore, annual planning processes rarely foster innovation. Both the political behavior stimulated by hierarchical resource allocation mechanisms and the business-as-usual inertia of budgetary planning have been well-documented elsewhere (Bowers, 1970; Danziger, 1978).

The Technological Approach may be the extreme case of how the IT industry and its professionals tend to apply computer science thinking to planning. The deficiencies of these methods have been noted in accounts of the more extensive IS planning methods and, in particular, of Information Engineering techniques. For instance, managers are often unhappy with the time and cost involved (Goodhue *et al.*, 1988; Moynihan, 1990). Others note that IS priorities are by definition dependent on the sequence required for architecture building (Hackathorn and Karimi, 1988; Inmon, 1986). The voluminous data generated by this class of method has also been reported (Bowman *et al.*, 1983; Inmon, 1986).

The Organizational Approach does not fit easily with the technical and prescriptive IS literature, but similar patterns have been observed by the more behavioral studies of business strategy making. It is now known that organizations rarely use the rational-analytical approaches touted in the planning literature when they make significant changes in strategy (Quinn, 1978). Rather, strategies often evolve from fragmented, incremental, and largely intuitive processes. Quinn believed this was the quite natural, proper way to cope with the unknowable – proceeding flexibly and experimentally from broad concepts to specific commitments.

Mintzberg's (1983) view of strategy making is similar. It emphasizes small project-based multiskilled teams, cross-functional liaison devices, and selective decentralization. Indeed, Mintzberg's view succinctly summarizes the Organizational Approach. He argues that often strategy is formed, rather than formulated, as actions converge into patterns and as analysis and implementation merge into a fluid process of learning. Furthermore, Mintzberg sees strategy making in reality as a mixture of the formal and informal and the analytical and emergent. Top managers, he argues, should create a context in which strategic thinking and discovery mingle, and then they should intervene where necessary to shape and support new ways forward.

In IS research, Henderson (1989) may have implicitly argued for the Organizational Approach when he called for an iterative, ongoing IS planning process to build and sustain partnership. He suggested partnership mechanisms such as task forces, cross-functional teams, multi-tiered and cross-functional networks, and collaborative planning without planners. Henderson and Sifonis (1988) identify the importance of learning in SISP, and de Geus (1988) sees all planning as learning and teamwork as central to organizational learning. Goodhue *et al.* (1988) and Moynihan (1990) argue that SISP needs

Table 9.10 *Mean success scores by approach*

	Business-Led	Method-Driven	Administrative	Technological	Organizational
Total means	3.25	3.83	3.60	4.00	3.94
IS directors	3.50	4.50	3.60	4.25	4.00
General managers	3.00	4.00	3.40	4.00	4.17
Line managers	3.25	3.00	3.80	3.75	3.66
Number of firms	4	2	5	4	6

Note: 5 = high; 1 = low.

to deliver good enough applications rather than optimal models. These propositions could be seen as recognition of the need to learn by doing and to deliver benefits. There is therefore a literature to support the Organizational Approach.

Data assessment

The field data itself can be used to assess the suggested taxonomy of approaches. Questions that arise are: do the approaches actually exist, and is it possible to clearly differentiate between them? Analysis of variance tests on reported success scores indicated that differences between approaches are significant, but differences between stakeholder sets are not.[9] This is one indication that *approach* is a distinct and meaningful way of analyzing SISP in action.

A second obvious question is whether any approaches are more effective than others. It is perhaps premature to ask this question of a taxonomy suggested by the data. Caution would advise further validation of the framework first, followed by carefully designed measurement tests. However, this study provides an opportunity for an early, if tentative, evaluation of this sort.

For example, as shown in Table 9.10, success scores can be correlated with SISP approach. Overall mean scores are shown, as well as scores for each stakeholder set. No approach differed widely from the mean score (3.73) across all companies. However, the most intensive approach in terms of technique (Technological) earned the highest score, perhaps because it represents what respondents thought an IS planning methodology should look like. Conversely, the Business-Led Approach, which lacks formal methodologies, earned the lowest scores. There are, of course, legitimate doubts about the

Table 9.11   *SISP concerns per firm*

	Business-Led	Method-Driven	Administrative	Technological	Organizational
Method	2.75	2.50	2.80	1.75	1.33
Process	0.75	3.00	1.60	2.50	2.16
Implementation	2.75	1.00	1.60	3.00	1.83
Total	6.25	6.50	6.00	7.25	5.32
Number of Firms	4	2	5	4	6

Table 9.12   *Competitive advantage propensity*

Approach	Competitive advantage application frequency
Business-Led	4.0 applications per firm
Method-Driven	1.5 applications per firm
Administrative	3.6 applications per firm
Technological	2.5 applications per firm
Organizational	4.8 applications per firm

meaning or reliability of these success scores because respondents were so keen to discuss the unsuccessful features.

Accordingly, another available measure is to analyze the frequency of concerns reported by firm, assuming each carries equal weight. Table 9.11 breaks out these data by method, process, and implementation concerns. The Organizational Approach has the least concerns attributed to it in total. The Business-Led Approach was characterized by high dissatisfaction with method and implementation. The Method-Driven Approach was perceived to be unsuccessful on process and, ironically, on method, while opinion was less harsh on implementation, perhaps because implementation experience itself is low. The Administrative Approach, as might be predicted, is not well-regarded on method. These data are not widely divergent from the qualitative analysis in Table 9.9.

Another measure is the potential of each approach for generating competitive advantage applications. Respondents were asked to identify and describe such applications and trace their histories. No attempt was made by the researcher to check the competitive advantage claimed or to assess whether the applications deserved the label. Although only 14 percent of all such applications were reported to have been generated by a formal SISP study, it is interesting to compare achievement rates of the firms in each approach (Table 9.12). Method-Driven and Technological Approaches do not appear

Table 9.13 *Multidimensional ranking of SISP approaches*

	Business-Led	Method-Driven	Administrative	Technological	Organizational
Success score ranking	5	3	4	1	2
Least concerns ranking	2	3	4	5	1
Competitive advantage potential ranking	2	5	3	4	1
Sum of ranks	9	11	11	10	4
Overall ranking	2	4	4	3	1

promising. Little is ever initiated in the Method-Driven Approach, while competitiveness is rarely the focus of the Technological Approach. The Administrative Approach appears to be more conducive, perhaps because user ideas receive a hearing. Forty-two percent of competitive advantage applications discovered in all the firms originated from user requests. In the Business-Led Approach, some obviously necessary applications are actioned. In the Organizational Approach, most of the themes pursued were perceived to have produced a competitive advantage.

These three qualitative measures can be combined to produce a multidimensional score. Other scholars have suggested that a number of performance measures are required to measure the effectiveness of SISP (Raghunathan and King, 1988). Table 9.13 ranks each approach according to the three measures discussed above (where 1 = top and 5 = bottom). In summing the ranks, the Organizational Approach appears to be substantially superior. Furthermore, all the other approaches score relatively low on this basis.

Thus, both qualitative and quantitative evidence suggest that the Organizational Approach is likely to be the best SISP approach to use and, thus, a candidate for further study. The Organizational Approach is perhaps the least formal and structured. It also differs significantly from conventional prescriptions in the literature and practice.

Implications for research

Many prior studies of SISP have been based on the views of IS managers alone. A novel aspect of this study was that the attitudes and experiences of general managers and users were also examined. In reporting back the results to the respondents in the survey companies, an interesting reaction occurred. The stakeholders were asked to select which approach best described their experience with SISP. If only IS professionals were present, their conclusions often differed from the final interpretative results. However, when all three stakeholders were present, a lively discussion ensued and, eventually, unprompted, the group's views moved toward an interpretation consistent with both the data presented and the approach attributed to the firm. This is another soft form of validation. More important, it indicates that *approach* is not only a multi-dimensional construct but also captures a multi-stakeholder perspective. This suggests that studies of IS management practice can be enriched if they look beyond the boundaries of the IS department.

Another characteristic of prior work on SISP is the assumption that formal methods are used and in principle are appropriate (Lederer and Sethi, 1988; 1991). A systematic linkage to the organization's business planning procedures is also commonly assumed (Boynton and Zmud, 1987; Karimi, 1988). The findings of this study suggest that these may be false assumptions and that, besides studying formal methods, researchers should continue to investigate matters of process while also paying attention to implementation. Indeed, in the field of business strategy, it was studies of the *process* of strategy making that led to the 'alternative' theories of the strategic management of the firm developed by Quinn (1978) and Mintzberg (1987).

The Organizational Approach to SISP suggested by this study might also be seen as an 'alternative' school of thought. This particular approach, therefore, should be investigated further to understand it in more detail, to assess its effectiveness more rigorously, and to discover how to make it work.

Finally, additional studies are required to further validate and then perhaps develop these findings. Some of the parameters suggested here to distinguish the approaches could be taken as variables and investigated on larger samples to verify the classification. Researchers could also explore whether different approaches fit, or work better in, different contexts. Candidate situational factors include information intensity of the sector, environmental uncertainty, the organization's management planning and control style, and the maturity of the organization's IS management experience.

Implications for practice

For practitioners, this study provides two general lessons. First, SISP requires a holistic or interdependent view. Methods may be necessary, but they could fail if the process factors receive no attention. It is also important to explicitly and positively incorporate implementation plans and decisions in the strategic planning cycle.

Second, successful SISP seems to require users and line managers working in partnership with the IS function. This may not only generate relevant application ideas, but it will tend to create ownership of both process and outcomes.

The taxonomy of SISP approaches emerging from this study might be interpreted for practice in at leat four different ways. First, it can be used as a diagnostic tool to position a firm's current SISP efforts. The strengths and weaknesses identified in the research then could suggest how the current approach could be improved. We have found that frameworks used in this way are likely to be more helpful if users and general managers as well as IS professionals join together in the diagnosis.

Second, the taxonomy can be used to design a situation-specific (customized) approach on a 'mix-and-match' basis. It may be possible to design a potentially more effective hybrid. The author is aware of one company experimenting at building a combination of the Organizational and Technological Approaches. One of the study companies that had adopted the Organizational Approach to derive its IS strategy also sought some of the espoused benefits of the Technological Approach by continuously formulating a shadow blueprint for IT architecture. This may be one way of reconciling the apparent contradictions of the Organizaitonal and Technological Approaches.

Third, based on our current understanding it appears that the Organizational Approach is more effective than others. Therefore, firms might seriously consider adopting it. This could involve setting up mechanisms and responsibility structures to encourage IS-user partnerships, devolving IS planning and development capability, ensuring IS managers are members of all permanent and *ad hoc* teams, recognizing IS strategic thinking as a continuous and periodic activity, identifying and pursuing business themes, and accepting 'good enough' solutions and building on them. Above all, firms might encourage any mechanisms that promote organizational learning about the scope of IT.

Another interpretation is that the Organizational Approach describes how most IS strategies actually are developed, despite the more formal and rational endeavors of IS managers or management at large. The reality may be a continuous interaction of formal methods and informal behavior and of intended and unintended strategies. If so, SISP in practice should be eclectic, selecting and trying methods and process initiatives to fit the needs of the time. One consequence of this view might be recognition and acceptance that planning need not always generate plans and that plans may arise without a formal planning process.

Finally, it can be revealing for an organization to recall the period when IS appeared to be contributing most effectively to the business and to describe the SISP approach in use (whether by design or not) at the time. This may then indicate which approach is most likely to succeed for that organization. Often when a particularly successful IS project is recalled, its history is seen to resemble the Organizational Approach.

Conclusions

This study evolved into a broad, behavioral exploration of experiences in large organizations. The breadth of perspective led to the proposition that SISP is more than method or technique alone. In addition, process issues and the question of implementation appear to be important. These interdependent elements combine to form an approach. Five different SISP approaches were identified, and one, the Organizational Approach, appears superior.

For practitioners, the taxonomy of SISP approaches provides a diagnostic tool to use in evaluating the effectiveness of their SISP efforts and in learning from their own experiences. Whether rethinking SISP or introducing it for the first time, firms may want to consider adopting the Organizational Approach. Two reasons led to this recommendation. First, among the companies explored, it seemed the most effective approach. Second, this study casts doubt on several of the by now 'traditional' SISP practices that have been advocated and developed in recent years.

The 'approach' construct presented in this chapter, the taxonomy of SISP approaches derived, and the indication that the least formal and least analytical approach seems to be most effective all offer new directions for SISP research and theory development.

Notes

1 See, for example, surveys by Dickson *et al.* (1984), Hartog and Herbert (1986), Brancheau and Wetherbe (1987), and Niederman *et al.* (1991).

2 Propositions and methods include Zani's (1970) early top-down proposal, King's (1978) more sophisticated linkage of the organization's IS strategy set to the business strategy set, and focused techniques such as critical success factors (Bullen and Rockart, 1981) and value chain analysis (Porter and Millar, 1985). These are supplemented by product literature such as Andersen's (1983) Method 1 or IBM's (1975) Business System Planning. The models and frameworks for developing a theory of SISP include Boynton and Zmud (1987), Henderson and Sifonis (1988), and Henderson and Venkatraman (1989). Empirical works include a survey of practice by Galliers (1987), analysis of methods by Sullivan (1985), investigation of problems by Lederer and Sethi (1988), assessment of success by Lederer and Mendelow (1987) and Raghunathan and King

(1988), and evaluation of particular techniques such as strategic data planning (Goodhue *et al.*, 1992).

3 Prior work has tended to use mail questionnaires targeted at IS executives. However, researchers have called for broader studies and for surveys of the experiences and perspectives of top managers, corporate planners, and users (Lederer and Mendelow, 1989; Lederer and Sethi, 1988; Raghunathan and King, 1988).

4 Characteristics of the sample companies are summarized in Appendix A.

5 Extracts from the interview questionnaires are shown in Appendix B.

6 This exploration through field studies was in the spirit of 'grounded theory' (Glaser and Strauss, 1967).

7 Fuller descriptive statistics can be seen in an early research report (Earl, 1990).

8 Methods employed included proprietary, generic, and customized techniques.

9 Differences between approaches are significant at the 10 percent level (f = 0.056). Differences between stakeholder sets are not significant (f = 0.126). No interaction was discovered between the two classifications.

References

Arthur Andersen & Co. (1983) *Method/1: Information Systems Methodology: An Introduction*, The Company, Chicago, IL.

Bowers, J. L. (1970) *Managing the Resource Allocation Process: A Study of Corporate Planning and Investment*, Division of Research, Graduate School of Business Administration, Harvard University, Boston, MA.

Bowman B., Davis, G., and Wetherbe, J. (1983) Three stage model of MIS planning. *Information and Management*, **6**(1), August, 11–25.

Boynton, A. C. and Zmud, R. W. (1987) Information technology planning in the 1990's: directions for practice and research. *MIS Quarterly* **11**(1), March, 59–71.

Brancheau, J. C. and Wetherbe, J. C. (1987) Key issues in Information systems management. *MIS Quarterly*, **11**(1), March, 23–45.

Bullen, C. V. and Rockart, J. F. (1981) A primer on critical success factors. CISR Working Paper No. 69, Center for Information Systems Research, Massachusetts Institute of Technology, Cambridge, MA, June.

Danziger, J. N. (1978) *Making Budgets: Public Resource Allocation*, Sage Publications, Beverly Hills, CA.

de Geus, A. P. (1988) Planning as learning. *Harvard Business Review*, **66**(2), March–April, 70–74.

Dickson, G. W., Leitheiser, R. L., Wetherbe, J. C. and Nechis, M. (1984) Key information systems issues for the 1980's. *MIS Quarterly*, **10**(3), September, 135–159.

Earl, M. J. (ed.) (1988) *Information Management: The Strategic Dimension*, Oxford University Press, Oxford.

Earl, M. J. (1990) *Management Strategies for Information Technology*, Prentice Hall, London.

Earl, M. J. (1990) Strategic information systems planning in UK Companies: early results of a field study. Oxford Institute of Information Management Research and Discussion Paper 90/1, Templeton College, Oxford.

Galliers, R. D. (1987) *Information Systems Planning in Britain and Australia in the Mid-1980's: Key Success Factors*, unpublished doctoral dissertation, University of London.

Glaser, B. G. and Strauss, A. L. (1967) *The Discovery of Grounded Theory: Strategies for Qualitative Research*, Aldine Publishing Company, Chicago, IL.

Goodhue, D. L., Quillard. J. A. and Rockart, J. F. (1988) Managing the data resource: a contingency perspective. *MIS Quarterly*, **12**(3), September, 373–391.

Goodhue, D. L., Kirsch, L. J., Quillard, J. A. and Wybo, M. D. (1992) Strategic data planning: lessons from the field. *MIS Quarterly*, **16**(1), March, 11–34.

Hackathorn, R. D. and Karimi, J. (1988) A framework for comparing information engineering methods. *MIS Quarterly*, **12**(2), June, 203–220.

Hartog, C. and Herbert, M. (1986) 1985 opinion survey of MIS managers: key issues. *MIS Quarterly*, **10**(4), December, 351–361.

Henderson, J. C. (1989) Building and sustaining partnership between line and I/S managers. CISR Working Paper No. 195. Center for Information Systems Research, Massachusetts Institute of Technology, Cambridge, MA, September.

Henderson, J. C. and Sifonis, J. G. (1988) The value of strategic IS planning: understanding consistency, validity, and IS markets. *MIS Quarterly*, **12**(2), June, 187–200.

Henderson, J. C. and Venkatraman, N. (1989) Strategic alignment: a framework for strategic information technology management. CISR Working Paper No. 190, Center for Information Systems Research, Massachusetts Institute of Technology, Cambridge, MA, August.

IBM Corporation (1975) *Business Systems Planning – Information Systems Planning Guide*, Publication #GE20-0527-4, White Plains, NY.

Inmon, W. H. (1986) *Information Systems Architecture*, Prentice Hall, Englewood Cliffs, NJ.

Karimi, J. (1988) Strategic planning for information systems: requirements and information engineering methods. *Journal of Management Information Systems*, **4**(4), Spring, 5–24.

King, W. R. (1978) Strategic planning for management information systems. *MIS Quarterly*, **2**(1), March, 22–37.

King, W. R. (1988) How effective is your information systems planning? *Long Range Planning*, **1**(1), October, 7–12.

Lederer, A. L. and Mendelow, A. L. (1986) Issues in information systems planning. *Information and Management*, **10**(5), May, 245–254.

Lederer, A. L. and Mendelow, A. L. (1987) Information resource planning: overcoming difficulties in identifying top management's objectives. *MIS Quarterly*, **11**(3), September, 389–399.

Lederer, A. L. and Mendelow, A. L. (1989) Co-ordination of information systems plans with business plans. *Journal of Management Information Systems*, **6**(2), Fall, 5–19.

Lederer, A. L. and Sethi, V. (1988) The implementation of strategic information systems planning methodologies. *MIS Quarterly*, **12**(3), September, 445–461.

Lederer, A. L. and Sethi, V. (1991) Critical dimensions of strategic information systems planning. *Decision Sciences*, **22**(1), Winter, 104–119.

Mintzberg, H. (1983) *Structure in Fives: Designing Effective Organizations*, Prentice Hall, Englewood Cliffs, NJ.

Mintzberg, H. (1987) Crafting strategy. *Harvard Business Review*, **66**(4), July–August, 66–75.

Moynihan, T. (1990) What chief executives and senior managers want from their IT departments. *MIS Quarterly*, **14**(1), March, 15–26.

Niederman, F., Brancheau, J. C. and Wetherbe, J. C. (1991) Information systems management issues for the 1990s. *MIS Quarterly*, **15**(4), December, 475–500.

Porter, M. E. and Millar, V. E. (1985) How information gives you competitive advantage. *Harvard Business Review*, **66**(4), July–August, 149–160.

Quinn, J. B. (1977) Strategic goals, plans and politics. *Sloan Management Review*, **19**(1), Fall, 21–37.

Quinn, J. B. (1978) Strategic change: logical incrementalism. *Sloan Management Review*, **20**(1), Fall, 7–21.

Raghunathan, T. S. and King. W. R. (1988) The impact of information systems planning on the organization. *OMEGA*, **16**(2), 85–93.

Sullivan, C. H., Jr. (1985) Systems planning in the information age. *Sloan Management Review*, **26**(2), Winter, 3–11.

Synott, W. R. and Gruber, W. H. (1982) *Information Resource Management: Opportunities and Strategies for the 1980's*, J. Wiley and Sons, New York.

Zani, W. M. (1970) Blueprint for MIS. *Harvard Business Review*, **48**(6), November–December, 95–100.

Appendix A: Field study companies

Descriptive statistics for field study companies

	Company	Annual revenue (£B)	Annual IS expenditure (£M)	Years of SISP experience
1	Banking	1.7*	450	4
2	Banking	1.9*	275	2
3	Retailing	4.2	80	4
4	Retailing	0.56	8	4
5	Insurance	2.8†	30	11
6	Insurance	0.9†	15	15
7	Travel	0.75	8	4
8	Electronics	1.35	25	3
9	Aerospace	4.1	120	17
10	Aerospace	2.1	54	20
11	IT	3.9	77	21
12	IT	0.6	18	11
13	Telecommunications	0.9	50	6
14	Automobile	0.5	14	9
15	Food	4.5	40	1
16	Oil	55.0	1000	6
17	Chemicals	2.18	5	10
18	Food	1.4	20	8
19	Accountancy/Consultancy	0.55	1	5
20	Brewing	1.7	23	9
21	Food/Consumer	2.5	27	1

* Operating costs.
† premium income.

Appendix B: Interview questionnaire

Structured (closed) questions

1	What prompted you to develop an IS/IT strategy?	(RO)
3	What were the objectives in developing an IS/IT strategy?	(RO)
4a	What are the outputs of your IS/IT strategy development?	(MC)
4b	What are the content headings of your IS strategic plan or strategy?	(MC)
5	What methods have you used in developing your IS strategy; when; why?	(MC)

7   What have been the benefits of strategic information systems
    planning?   (RO)
8   How successful has SISP been?   (LS)
9   What have you found to be key success factors in SISP?   (RO)
10 How is your SISP connected to other business planning
    processes?   (MC)
11 How do you review your IS strategies?   (MC)
12 What are the major problems you have encountered in SISP?   (RO)

All these questions were asked using multiple-choice lists (MC), Likert-type
scale (LS), or rank-order lists (RO).

Example rank-order questions

3   What were the objectives in developing an IS/IT strategy?
    Tick   *Rank*
    ....   Align IS development with business needs   ......
    ....   Revamp the IS/IT function   ......
    ....   Seek competitive advantage from IT   ......
    ....   Establish technology path and policies   ......
    ....   Forecast IS requirements   ......
    ....   Gain top management commitment   ......
    ....   Other (specify)   ......

Example multiple choice questions

5   What methods have you used in developing your IS strategy; when, why?
    When   *Method*   *Why*
    ....   Critical success factors   ....
    ....   Stages of growth   ....
    ....   Business systems planning   ....
    ....   Enterprise modelling   ....
    ....   Information engineering   ....
    ....   Method 1   ....
    ....   Other proprietary (specify)   ....
    ....   In-house IS strategy   ....
    ....   In-house business strategy   ....
    ....   In-house application search techniques   ....
    ....   Informal   ....
    ....   Other (specify)   ....

Example Likert-type scale question

8a How successful has SISP been on the following scale?

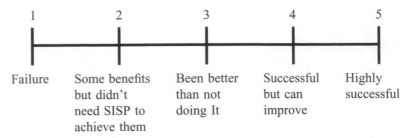

Semi-structured (open) questions

2a   Please summarize the approach you have adopted in developing your IS strategy (or in identifying and deciding which IT applications to develop in the long run).

2b   What are the key elements of your IS strategy?

6a   Have you developed any applications that have given competitive advantage in recent years? If so, what?

6b   How was each of these applications identified and developed?

8b   In what ways has SISP been unsuccessful?

13   Can you describe any key turning points in your SISP experience, such as changes in aims, approach, method, benefits, success factors or problems?

Appendix C: Concerns or unsuccessful features of SISP

Method concerns

1   It did not lead to management identifying applications supportable at a cost
2   No regeneration or review
3   Failed to discover our competitors' moves or understand their improvements
4   Not enough planning; too much emphasis on development and projects
5   It was not connected to business planning
6   It was too internally focused
7   Sensibly allocating resources to needs was a problem
8   Business needs were ignored or not identified
9   Not flexible or reactive enough
10   Not coordinated
11   Not enough consideration of architecture
12   Priority-setting and resource allocation were questionable
13   The plans were soon out of date
14   Business direction and plans were inadequate
15   Not enough strategic thinking
16   The thinking was too functional and applications-oriented and not process-based

17   It was too technical and not business-based
18   It was overtheoretical and too complicated
19   It could have been done quicker; it took too long
20   It developed a bureaucracy of its own
21   We have not solved identification of corporate-wide needs
22   The architecture was questionable; people were not convinced by it
23   We still don't know how to incorporate and meet short-term needs
24   We did not complete the company-entity model
25   We found it difficult justifying the benefits
26   It was too much about automating today's operations
27   It was too *ad hoc*; insufficient method
28   Many of the recommendations did not meet user aspirations

Process concerns

1   Some businesses were less good at, and less committed to, planning than others
2   The exercise was abrogated to the IS department
3   Inadequate understanding across all management
4   Line management involvement was unsatisfactory
5   Lack of senior management involvement
6   No top management buy-in
7   The strategy was not sold or communicated enough
8   We still have poor user-IS relationships
9   Too many IS people have not worked outside of IS
10   Poor IT understanding of customer and business needs
11   Line management buy-in was low
12   Little cross-divisional learning
13   IS management quality was below par
14   Senior executives were not made aware of the scale of change required
15   Users lacked understanding of IT and its methods
16   It was too user-driven in one period
17   We are still learning how to do planning studies
18   Planning almost never works; there are too many 'dramas'
19   The culture has not changed enough
20   We oversold the plan
21   Too much conflict between organizational units

Implementation concerns

1   We have not broken the resource constraints
2   We have not implemented as much as we should
3   It was not carried through into resource planning
4   The necessary technology planning was not done

5   We have not achieved the system benefits
6   We made technical mistakes
7   Some of the needs are still unsatisfied
8   Appropriate hardware or software was not available
9   Cost and time budget returns
10   We were not good at specifying the detailed requirements
11   Defining staffing needs was a problem
12   We have not gotten anything off the ground yet
13   We had insufficient skilled development resources
14   Regulatory impediments
15   We were overambitious and tried to change too much
16   We still have to catch up technically

Reprinted by special permission from *MIS Quarterly*, **17**(1), March 1993, 1–24. Copyright 1993 by the Society for Information Management and the Management Information Systems Research Center at the University of Minnesota.

Questions for discussion

1   Consider the success factors listed in Table 9.5 – is it worth undertaking SISP without top management involvement?
2   Compare the author's concept of SISP to that of information strategy from Smits *et al.* (in Chapter 3).
3   Debate the strengths and weaknesses of the approaches to SISP. Assuming time constraints prevent an 'everything goes' approach, which approach:
    – might help improve IS credibility?
    – might do the most to align IT with business strategy?
    – might do the most to enable the competitive uses of IT?
    – might do the most to achieve organization-wide vision?
    – might be more appropriate at the different stages of growth?
    – might best deal with management of change issues?
4   The author states that 'successful SISP seems to require users and line managers working in partnership with the IS function'. Who should be involved in SISP and how should those involved be determined?
5   Think of a possible hybrid approach (keeping in mind time, resource and people constraints).

10 The Information Systems Planning Process

Meeting the challenges of information systems planning

A. L. Lederer and V. Sethi

Introduction

Strategic information systems planning (SISP) is a critical issue facing today's businesses. Because SISP can identify the most appropriate targets for computerization, it can make a huge contribution to businesses and to other organizations. Effective SISP can help organizations use information systems to implement business strategies and reach business goals. It can also enable organizations to use information systems to create new business strategies. Recent research has shown that the quality of the planning process significantly influences the contribution which information systems can make to an organization's performance.[1] Moreover, the failure to carry out SISP carefully can result in lost opportunities and wasted resources.[2]

To perform effective SISP, organizations conventionally apply one of several methodologies. However, carrying out such a process is a key problem facing management.[3]

SISP also presents many complex technical questions. These deal with computer hardware, software, databases, and telecommunications technologies. In many organizations, as a result of this complexity, there is a tendency to let the computer experts handle SISP.

However, SISP is too important to delegate to technicians. Business planners are increasingly recognizing the potential impact of information technology, learning more about it, and participating in SISP studies despite their lack of technical experience.

This chapter defines and explains SISP. It illustrates four popular SISP methodologies. Then, based on a survey of 80 organizations, we discuss the problems of carrying out SISP. We also suggest some potential actions which business planners can take to deal with the problems.

What is SISP?

Information systems planning has evolved over the last 15 years. In the late 1970s, its primary objectives were to improve communication between computer users and MIS departments, increase top management support for computing, better forecast and allocate information system resource requirements, determine opportunities for improving the MIS department and identify new and higher payback computer applications.[4]

More recently, two new objectives have emerged. They are the identification of strategic information systems applications[5] – those that can give the organization a competitive edge – and the development of an organization-wide information architecture.[6]

While the importance of identifying strategic information systems applications is obvious, the importance of the organization-wide information architecture of information systems that share common data and communicate easily with each other is highly desirable. Just as new business ventures must mesh with the organization's existing endeavours, new systems applications must fit with the existing information architecture.

Unfortunately, an organization's commitment to construct an organization-wide information architecture vastly complicates SISP. Thus organizations have often failed to build such an architecture. Instead, their piecemeal approach has resulted in disjointed systems that temporarily solved minor problems in isolated areas of the organization. This has caused redundant efforts and exorbitant costs.

Thus, this chapter embraces two distinct yet usually simultaneously performed approaches to SISP. On one hand, SISP entails the search for high-impact applications with the ability to create an advantage over competitors.[7] Thus, SISP helps organizations use information systems in innovative ways to build barricrs against new entrants, change the basis of competition, generate new products, build in switching costs, or change the balance of power in supplier relationships.[8] As such, SISP promotes innovation and creativity. It might employ idea generating techniques such as brainstorming,[9] value chain analysis,[10] or the customer resource life cycle.

On the other hand SISP is the process of identifying a portfolio of computer-based applications to assist an organization in executing its current business plans and thus realizing its existing business goals. SISP may mean the selection of rather prosaic applications, almost as if from a predefined list, that would best fit the current and projected needs of the organization. These applications would guide the creation of the organization-wide information architecture of large databases and systems of computer programs. The distinction between the two approaches results in the former being referred to as attempting to *impact* organizational strategies and the latter as attempting to *align* MIS objectives with organizational goals.

Carrying out SISP

To carry out SISP, an organization usually selects an existing methodology and then embarks on a major, intensive study. The organization forms teams of business planners and computer users with MIS specialists as members or as advisors. It is likely to use the SISP vendor's educational support to train the teams and consulting support to guide and audit the study. It carries out a multi-step procedure over several weeks or months. The duration depends on the scope of the study. In addition to identifying the portfolio of applications, it prioritizes them. It defines databases, data elements, and a network of computers and communications equipment to support the applications. It also prepares a schedule for developing and installing them.

Organizations usually apply one of several methodologies to carry out this process. Four popular ones are Business Systems Planning[11] PROplanner,[12] Information Engineering,[13] and Method/1.[14] These will be described briefly as contemporary, illustrative methodologies although the four undergo continuous change and improvement. They were selected because, together, they accounted for over half the responses to the survey described later.

Business Systems Planning (BSP), developed by IBM, involves *top-down* planning with *bottom-up* implementation. From the top-down, the study team first recognizes its firm's business mission, objectives and functions, and how these determine the business processes. It analyses the processes for their data needs. From the bottom-up, it then identifies the data currently required to perform the processes. The final BSP plan describes an overall information systems architecture comprised of databases and applications as well as the installation schedule of individual systems. Table 10.1 details the steps in a BSP study.

BSP places heavy emphasis on top management commitment and involvement. Top executive sponsorship is seen as critical. MIS analysts might serve primarily in an advisory capacity.

PROplanner, by Holland Systems Corp. in Ann Arbor, Michigan, helps planners analyse major functional areas within the organization. They then define a Business Function Model. They derive a Data Architecture from the Business Function Model by combining the organization's information requirements into generic data entities and broad databases. They then identify an Information Systems Architecture of specific new applications and an implementation schedule.

PROplanner offers automated storage, manipulation, and presentation of the data collected during SISP. PROplanner software produces reports in various formats and levels of detail. *Affinity* reports show the frequencies of accesses to data. *Clustering* reports guide database design. Menus direct the planner through on-line data collection during the process. A data dictionary (a computerized list of all data on the database) permits planners to share

Table 10.1   *Description of BSP study steps*

Enterprise Analysis   The team documents the strategic business planning process and how the organization carries it out. It presents this information in a matrix for the executive sponsor to validate.

Enterprise Modelling   The team identifies the organization's business processes, using a technique known as value chain analysis, and then presents them in a matrix showing each's relationship to each business strategy (from the Enterprise Analysis). The team identifies the organization's entities (such as product, customer, vendor, order, part) and presents them in a matrix showing how each is tied to each process.

Executive Interviews   The team asks key executives about potential information opportunities needed to support their enterprise strategy (from the Enterprise Analysis), the processes (from the Enterprise Modelling) they are responsible for, and the entities (from the Enterprise Modelling) they manage. Each executive identifies a value and priority ranking for each information opportunity.

Information Opportunity Analysis   The team groups the opportunities by processes and entitles to separate 'quick fix' opportunities. It then analyses the remaining information opportunities, develops support recommendations, and prioritizes them.

I/S Strategies and Recommendations   The team assesses the organization's information management in terms of its information systems/enterprise alignment, ongoing information planning, tactical information planning, data management, and application development. It then defines new strategies and recommends them to executive management.

Data Architecture Design   The team prepares a high level design of proposed databases by diagramming how the organization uses its entities in support of its processes (entities and processes were defined during Enterprise Modelling) and identifying critical pieces of information describing the entities.

Process Architecture Design   The team prepares a plan for developing high priority applications and for integrating all proposed applications. It does this by tying business processes to their proposed applications.

Existing Systems Review   The team reviews existing applications to evaluate their technical and functional quality by interviewing users and information systems specialists.

Implementation Planning   The team considers the quality of existing systems (from the Existing Systems Review) and the proposed applications (from the Process Architecture Design) and develops a plan identifying those to discard, keep, enhance, or re-develop.

Information Management Recommendations   The team develops and presents a series of recommendations to help it carry out the plans that it prepared in Implementation Planning.

PRO planner data with an existing data dictionary or other automated design tools.

Information Engineering (IE), by Knowledge Ware in Atlanta, provides techniques for building Enterprise Models, Data Models, and Process Models. These make up a comprehensive knowledge base that developers later use to create and maintain information systems.

In conjunction with IE, every general manager may participate in a critical success factors (CSF) inquiry, the popular technique for identifying issues that business executives view as the most vital for their organization's success. The resulting factors will then guide the strategic information planning endeavour by helping identify future management control systems.

IE provides several software packages for facilitating the strategic information planning effort. However, IE differs from some other methodologies by providing automated tools to link its output to subsequent systems development efforts. For example, integrated with IE is an application generator to produce computer programs written in the COBOL programming language without handcoding.

Method/1, the methodology of Andersen Consulting (a division of Arthur Andersen & Co.), consists of 10 phases of work segments that an organization completes to create its strategic plan. The first five formulate information strategy. The final five further formulate the information strategy but also develop action plans. A break between the first and final five provides a top management checkpoint and an opportunity to adjust and revise. By design, however, a typical organization using Method/1 need not complete all the work segments at the same level of detail. Instead, planners evaluate each work segment in terms of the organization's objectives.

Method/1 focuses heavily on the assessment of the current business organization, its objectives, and its competitive environment. It also stresses the tactics required for changing the organization when it implements the plan.

Method/1 follows a layered approach. The top layer is the methodology itself. A middle layer of techniques supports the methodology and a bottom layer of tools supports the techniques. Examples of the many techniques are focus groups, Delphi studies, matrix analysis, dataflow diagramming and functional decomposition. FOUNDATION, Andersen Consulting's computer-aided software engineering tool set, includes computer programs that support Method/1.

Besides BSP, PRO planner, IE and Method/1, firms might choose Information Quality Analysis,[15] Business Information Analysis and Integration Technique,[16] Business Information Characterization Study,[17] CSF, Ends/Means Analysis,[18] Nolan Norton Methodology,[19] Portfolio Management,[20] Strategy Set Transformation,[21] Value Chain Analysis, or the Customer Resource Life Cycle. Also, firms often select features of these methodologies and then, possibly with outside assistance, tailor their own in-house approach.[22]

Problems with the methodologies

Planners have long recognized that SISP is an intricate and complex activity fraught with problems.[23] Several authors have described these problems based on field surveys, cases, and conceptual studies. An exhaustive review of their most significant articles served as the basis of a comprehensive list of the problems for our research.

To organize the problems, we classified them as tied to resources, process, or output. Resource-related problems address issues of time, money, personnel, and top management support for the initiation of the study. Process-related problems involve the limitations of the analysis. Output-related problems deal with the comprehensive and appropriateness of the final plan. We derived these categories from a similar scheme used to define the components of IS planning. (Research Appendix 1 lists the problems studied in the surveys, cases and conceptual studies. The problems have been paraphrased, simplified, and classified.)

A survey of strategic information systems planners

To understand better the problems of SISP, we developed a questionnaire with two main parts. In the first part, respondents identified the methodology they had used during an SISP study. They also rated the extent to which they had encountered each of the aforementioned problems as 'not a problem', 'an insignificant problem', 'a minor problem', 'a major problem', or 'an extreme problem'. Similar studies have used this scale.

The second part asked about the implementation of plans. Planners indicated the extent to which different outputs of the plan had been affected. This conforms to the recommendation that a criterion for evaluating a planning system is the extent to which the final plan actually guides the strategic direction of an organization. In this part, the subjects also answered questions about their satisfaction with various aspects of the SISP experience.

We mailed the questionnaire to 251 organizations in two groups. The first included systems planners who were members of the Strategic Data Planning Institute, a Rockville, Maryland group under the auspices of Barnett Data Systems. The second was another group of systems planners.[24]

While 163 firms returned completed surveys, 80 (or 32 per cent) had carried out an SISP study and they provided usable data. Considering the length and complexity of the questionnaire, this is a high response rate.

Evidence of SISP problems: carrying out plans

In general, the respondents were fairly satisfied with their SISP experience. Their average rating for overall satisfaction with the SISP methodology was 3.55 where a neutral score would have been 3.00 (on the scale of zero to six

Table 10.2 *Overall satisfaction with SISP*

	Average	Satisfied	Neutral	Dissatisfied
The methodology	3.55	54%	23%	23%
The resources	3.02	38%	24%	38%
The process	3.68	48%	17%	25%
The output	3.38	55%	17%	28%
Carrying out the plan	2.53	32%	15%	53%

in which zero was 'extremely dissatisfied' and six was 'extremely satisfied'). Satisfaction scores for the different dimensions of SISP were also only slightly favourable. Satisfaction was 3.68 with the SISP process, 3.38 with the SISP output, and 3.02 with the SISP resource requirements.

However, satisfaction with the carrying out of final SISP plans was lower (2.53). In fact, only 32 per cent of respondents were satisfied with the extent of carrying them out while 53 per cent were dissatisfied. Table 10.2 summarizes the respondents' satisfaction with these aspects of the SISP.

Further evidence focusing on the plan implementation problem stems from the contrast between the elapsed planning horizon and the degree of completion of SISP recommended projects. The average planning horizon of the SISP studies was 3.73 years while an average of 2.1 years had passed since the studies' completion. Thus, 56 per cent of the planning horizons had elapsed. However, out of an average of 23.4 projects recommended in the SISP studies, only 5.7 (24 per cent) had been started. Hence, it appears that firms were failing to start projects as rapidly as necessary in order to complete them during the planning horizon. There may have been insufficient project start-ups in order to realize the plan.

In addition to *not* starting projects in the plan, organizations instead had begun projects that were *not* part of their SISP plan. These latter projects were about 38 per cent of all projects started during the 2.1 years after the study.

Actions for planners

Below are the 18 most severe problems – which at least 25 per cent of the respondents described as an 'extreme' or 'major' problem. Because each can be seen as closely tied to Leadership, Implementation, or Resource issues, they are categorized into those three groups. They are then ordered within the groups by their severity. (Research Appendix 2 ranks all of the reported problems. The 'Extreme or Major Problem' column in the table shows the percentage of subjects rating the problem as such. The 'Minor Problem' displays the similar percentage. Subjects could also rate each as 'Insignificant' or 'Not a Problem'.)

We offer an interpretation of each problem and suggestions to both top management and other business planners considering an SISP study. Many of the suggestions are based on the successful SISP experiences of Raychem Corp., a world-wide materials sciences company based in Menlo Park, California with over 10 000 employees in 41 countries. Raychem conducted SISP studies in 1978 and 1990.[25] The company thus had the chance to carry out and implement an SISP study, and to learn from the experience.

The interpretations and suggestions provide a checklist for debate and discussion, and eventually, for improved SISP.

Leadership issues

It is Difficult to Secure Top Management Commitment for Implementing the Plan (No. 1 – the Most Serious – of the 18)

Over half the respondents called this an extreme or major problem. It means that once their study was completed and in writing, they struggled to convince top management to authorize the development of the recommended applications. This is consistent with the percentages in the previous section.

Such a finding suggests that top management might not understand the plan or might lack confidence in the MIS department's ability to carry it out. It thus suggests that top management carefully consider its commitment to implementing a plan even before authorizing the time and money needed to prepare the plan.

Likewise, planners proposing an SISP study should assess in advance the likelihood that their top management will refuse to fund the newly recommended projects. They may also want to determine tactics to improve the likelihood of funding. In Raychem's 1978 study, the CEO served as sponsor and hence the likelihood of implementing its findings was substantially improved.

The Success of the Methodology is Greatly Dependent on the Team Leader (No. 3)

If the team leader cannot convince top management to support the study or cannot obtain a top management mandate to convince functional area management and MIS management to participate, the study is probably doomed. The team leader motivates team members and pulls the project along. The team leader must be a respected veteran in the organization's business and a dynamic leader comfortable with current technology.

Organizations should reduce their dependency on their team leader. One way to do so is by using a well-structured and well-defined methodology to simplify the team leader's job. Likewise, by obtaining as much visible, top management support as possible, the organization will depend less on the team leader's personal ties to top management. In Raychem's case, dependency on the team leader was reduced because the team consisted of members with broad, corporate rather than parochial, departmental views. Such members can enable the team leader to serve as a project manager rather than force the individual to be a project champion.

It is Difficult to Find a Team Leader who Meets the Criteria Specified by the Methodology (No. 4)

As with the previous item, management will have to look hard to find a business-wise and technology-savvy leader. Such people are scarce. Management must choose that person carefully.

It is Difficult to Convince Top Management to Approve the Methodology (No. 8)

It is not only difficult to convince top management to implement the final plan (as in the first item above) but also difficult to convince top management to even fund the initial SISP study. SISP is slow and costly. Meanwhile, many top managers want working systems immediately, not plans for an uncertain future. Thus, advocates of SISP should prepare convincing arguments to authorize the funding of the study.

In Raychem's case, four executives – including two vice presidents – from different areas of the firm met several times with the CEO in 1978. Because he felt that information technology was expensive but was not sufficiently providing him with the information required to run the company, the executives were able to convince him to approve the SISP study and be its sponsor.

Implementation issues

Implementing the Projects and the Data Architecture Identified in the Plan Requires Substantial Further Analysis (No. 2)

Nearly half the respondents found this an extreme or major problem. SISP often fell short of providing the analysis needed to start the design and programming of the individual computer applications. The methodology did not provide the specifications necessary to begin the design of the recommended projects. This meant duplicating the investigation initially needed to make the recommendations.

This result suggests that prospective strategic information systems planners should seek a methodology that provides features to guide them into implementation. Some vendors offer such methodologies. Otherwise, planners should be prepared for the frustrations of delays and duplicated effort before seeing their plans reach fruition.

In Raychem's case, the planners drew up a matrix showing business processes and classes of data. The matrix reduced the need for further analysis somewhat by helping the firm decide the applications to standardize on a corporate basis and those to implement in regional offices. As another means of reducing the need for more analysis, Raychem set up model databases for all corporate applications to access.

The Methodology Fails to Take into Account Issues Related to Plan Implementation (No. 7)

The exercise may produce an excellent plan. It may produce a list of significant, high-impact applications.

However, as in earlier items, the planning study may fail to include the actions that will bring the plan to fruition. For example, the study might ignore the development of a strategy to ensure the final decisions to proceed with specific applications. It might fail to address the resistance of those managers who oppose the plan.

Again, planners need to pay careful attention to ensure that the plan is actually followed and not prematurely discarded.

The Documentation does not Adequately Describe the Steps that Should be Followed for Implementing the Methodology (No. 12)

The documentation describing some proprietary SISP methodologies is inadequate. It gives insufficient guidance to planners. Some of it may be erroneous, ambiguous, or contradictory.

Planners who purchase a proprietary methodology should read its documentation carefully before signing the contract. Planners who develop their own methodology should be prepared to devote significant energy to its documentation.

In Raychem's case, it chose BSP in 1978 simply because there were no other methodologies at the time. For its 1990 study, Raychem planners interviewed a number of consulting companies with proprietory methodologies before choosing the Index Group from Boston. Raychem then used extensive training to compensate for any potential deficiencies in the documentation.

The Strategic Information Systems Plan Fails to Provide Priorities for Developing Specific Databases (No. 13)

Both top management and functional area management must agree with the plan's priorities. For example, they must concur on whether the organization builds a marketing database, a financial database, or a production database. They must agree on what to do first and what to delay.

Without top management agreement on the priorities of the targeted databases, the plan will never be executed. Without functional area management concurrence, battles to change the priorities will rage. Such changes can result in temporarily halting ongoing projects while starting others. One risk is pre-eminent: Everything is started but nothing is finished.

Planners should be certain that the plan stipulates priorities and that top management and functional area management sincerely accept them.

Raychem approached this problem by culling 10 agreed upon, broad initiatives from 35 proposals in the 1990 study. Instead of choosing to establish database priorities during the study, it later established priorities for the numerous projects spawned by the initiatives.

The Strategic Information Systems Plan Fails to Determine an Overall Data Architecture for the Organization (No. 14)

Although the major objective of many SISP methodologies is to determine an overall data architecture, many respondents were disappointed with their success in doing so. They were disappointed with the identification of the architecture's specific databases and with the linkages between them. To many respondents, despite the huge effort, the portfolio of applications may appear piecemeal and disjointed.

Although these may appear to be technical issues, planners should still understand major data architecture issues and should check to be sure that their SISP will provide such an overall, integrated architecture, and not just a list of applications.

The Strategic Information Systems Plan Fails to Sufficiently Address the Need for Data Administration in the Organization (No. 18)

Because long-range plans usually call for the expansion of databases, the need for more data administration personnel – people whose sole role is ensuring that databases are up and working – is often necessary. In many organizations, the data administration function has grown dramatically in recent years. It may continue to expand and the implications of this necessary growth can be easy to ignore. Planners should thus be sure that their long-range plan includes the role of data administration in the organization's future. In Raychem's case, a data administration function was established as a result of its 1978 study.

Resource issues

The Methodology Lacks Sufficient Computer Support (No. 5)

SISP can produce reams of reports, charts, matrices and diagrams. Planners cannot manage that volume of data efficiently and effectively without automated support.

When planners buy an existing methodology, they should carefully scrutinize the vendor's computer support. They should examine the screens and
reports. On the other hand, if they customize their own methodology, they
must be certain not to underestimate the need for such support. In some
organizations, the expense of developing computer support in-house might
compel the organization to then buy an existing methodology rather than
tailor its own.

The Planning Exercise Takes Very Long (No. 6)

The study takes weeks or even months. This may be well beyond the span of
attention of many organizations. Too many business managers expect results
almost immediately and lose interest if the study drags on. Moreover, many
organizations undergo major changes even during the planning period.

Most importantly, an overrun during the planning exercise may reduce top
management's confidence in the organization's ability to carry out the final
plan. Hence planners should strive to keep the duration of the planning study
as short as possible.

Raychem's 1978 study required 3 months but its 1990 study required 9. In
1990, planners chose to risk the consequences of a longer study because it
enabled them to involve more senior level executives albeit on a part-time
basis. Planners could have completed a briefer study with lower level executives on a full-time basis. However, the planners felt the study under such
circumstances would have been less credible. They clearly felt that the potential problem of insufficient top management commitment described above
was more serious than the problem of a lengthy study!

The Strategic Information Plan Fails to Include an Overall Personnel and Training Plan for the MIS Department (No. 8)

Many MIS departments lack the necessary skills to carry out the innovative
and complex projects recommended by an SISP study. A strategic information systems plan thus needs to consider new personnel to add to the MIS
Department. The SISP study will probably recommend additions to existing
positions, permanent information systems planners, and a variety of such new
positions as expert systems specialists, local area and wide area network
specialists, desktop-publishers, and many others. An SISP study also often
recommends training current MIS staff in today's personal computer, network,
and database technologies.

Planners will need to be certain that their study accurately assesses current
MIS department skills and staffing. They will also need to allocate the time
and resources to ensure the presence of critical new personnel and the training of existing personnel. Raychem included a statement supporting such
training in its 1990 study.

It is Difficult to Find Team Members who Meet the Criteria Specified by the Methodology (No. 10)

Qualified team members, in addition to team leaders (as in an earlier item above), are scarce. Team members from functional area departments must feel comfortable with information technology while computer specialists need to understand the business. Both need excellent communication skills and must have the time to participate. Hence, management should check the credentials of their team members carefully and be certain that their schedules allow them to participate fully in the planning process.

To find qualified team members, Raychem's planners in its 1990 study first drew up lists of business unit functions and geographical locations. They used it to identify a mix of team members from a variety of units in various locations. World-wide, senior managers helped identify team members who would be seen as leaders with objective views and diverse backgrounds. Such team members made the final study more credible.

The Strategic Information Systems Plan Fails to Include an Overall Financial Plan for the MIS Department (No. 11)

Responsible top management frequently demands financial justification for new projects. Because computer projects appear different from other capital projects, planners might treat them differently. Because top management will scrutinize and probably challenge costs and benefits in the long-range plan, planners must be sure that any costs and benefits are defensible.

In 1990, Raychem did not provide specific cost and benefit figures because of its concern that technological change would render them inaccurate later on. However, the firm did use various financial tests to reduce its initially suggested initiatives from 35 to 10. Moreover, planners did cost justify individual projects as they were spawned from the initiatives.

The Planning Exercise is Very Expensive (No. 15)

The planning exercise demands an exorbitant number of hours from top management, functional area management, and the MIS department. These are often the organization's busiest, most productive, and highest paid managers, precisely the people who lack the time to devote to the study.

Hence, management must be convinced that the planning study is both essential and well worth the time demanded of its top people.

The Strategic Information Systems Plan Fails to Sufficiently Address the Role of a Permanent MIS Planning Group (No. 16)

Like general business planning, strategic systems planning is not a one-time endeavour. It is an ongoing process where planners periodically review the plan and the issues behind it. Many information systems planners feel that a permanent planning group devoted solely to the information systems is essential, but that their planning endeavours failed to establish one.

As with many other planning efforts, planners should view the SISP exercise as an initial effort in an ongoing process. They should also consider the need for a permanent planning function devoted to SISP. In Raychem's 1978 study, the company formed a planning committee of executives from around the company. In their 1990 study, the management refined their procedures to ensure that planning committee members would serve as sponsors of each of the 10 initiatives and that they also report progress on them to the CEO.

Many Support Personnel are Required for Data Gathering and Analysis During the Study (No. 17)

To understand the current business processes and information systems support, many staff members must collect and collate data about the organization. Planners are concerned about their time and expense.

Planners should be sceptical if the vendor of a methodology suggests that staff support will be negligible. Moreover, planners may want to budget for some surplus staff support. Raychem controlled the cost of data gathering and analysis by having team members gather and analyse the data in the business units with which they were familiar.

Implications

There are two broad approaches to SISP. The *impact* approach entails the identification of a small number of information systems applications that can give the organization a competitive edge. It involves innovation and creativity in using information systems to create new business strategies by building barriers against new entrants, changing the basis of competition, generating new products, building in switching costs, or changing the balance of power in supplier relationships.

The *align* approach entails the development of an organization-wide information architecture of applications to guide the creation of large databases and computer systems to support current business strategies. It typically involves identifying a larger number of carefully integrated conventional applications that support these strategies.

Some organizations may attempt to follow both approaches equally while others may follow one more so than the other. Thus the two approaches suggest that perhaps the different groups of problems may carry different weights during the SISP process. The matrix in Figure 10.1 shows the approaches, categories with summarized problem statements, and weights in each cell.

Approaches

Issues	'Impact'	'Align'
LEADERSHIP Difficult to Secure Top Management Commitment for Implementation Success Dependent on Team Leader Difficult to Find Team Leader Meeting Criteria Difficult to Obtain Top Management Approval	Critical	Important
IMPLEMENTATION Requires Further Analysis Ignores Plan Implementation Issues Documentation is Inadequate for Implementation No Priorities for Developing Databases No Overall Data Architecture is Determined No Data Administration Need Addressed	Very important	Very important
RESOURCES Methodology Lacks Sufficient Computer Support Planning Exercise Takes Long Time No Training Plan for IS Department Difficult to Find Team Members Meeting Criteria No Financial Plan for IS Department Very Expensive No Permanent IS Planning Group Many Support Personnel Required	Important	Critical

Figure 10.1   *Where information systems planning fails*

For example, when seeking new and unconventional applications under the impact, leadership may play a more critical role. Without experienced, articulate and technology savvy leadership in the SISP study, it may be difficult to convince top management to gamble on radical innovation. This does not suggest that leadership is unimportant when attempting to plan applications for alignment but rather that it may be more critical under the impact approach.

Because the align approach typically affects larger numbers of lower-level employees, the potential for resource problems is perhaps greater. The possible widespread effects increase the complexity of the align approach. Thus resource issues are probably of more critical concern in this approach.

Finally, regardless of whether the approach is 'impact' or 'alignment', implementation is still often perceived as the key to successful SISP. Thus whether an organization is attempting to identify a few high-impact applications or many integrated and conventional ones, implementation issues remain equally important.

Conclusion

Effective SISP is a major challenge facing business executives today. It is an essential activity for unlocking the significant potential that information technology offers to organizations. This chapter has examined the challenges of SISP.

In summary, strategic information systems planners are not particularly satisfied with SISP. After all, it requires extensive resources. Top management commitment is often difficult to obtain. When the SISP study is complete, further analysis may be required before the plan can be executed. The execution of the plan might not be very extensive. Thus, while SISP offers a great deal – the potential to use information technology to realize current business strategies and to create new ones – too often it is not satisfactorily done.

In fact, despite its complex information technology ingredient, SISP is very similar to many other business planning endeavours. For this reason alone, the involvement of top management and business planners has become increasingly indispensable.

References

1   G. Premkumar and W. R. King. Assessing strategic information systems planning. *Long Range Planning*. October (1991).
2   W. R. King. How effective is your information systems planning? *Long Range Planning*. **21**(5), 103–112 (1988).
3   A. L. Lederer and A. L. Mendelow. Issues in information systems planning. *Information and Management*. pp.245–254. May (1986); A. L. Lederer and V. Sethi. The implementation of strategic information systems planning methodologies. *MIS Quarterly*. **12**(3), 445–461. September (1988); and S. W. Sinclair. The three domains of information systems planning. *Journal of Information Systems Management*. **3**(2), 8–16. Spring (1986).
4   E. R. McLean and J. V. Soden. *Strategic Planning for MIS*. John Wiley and Sons. Inc. (1977).

5   PRISM. Information systems planning in the contemporary environment final report. December (1986). Index Systems. Inc. Cambridge, MA and M. R. Vitale, B. Ives and C. M. Beath. Linking information technology and corporate strategy an organizational view. *Proceedings of the Seventh International Conference on Information Systems.* pp.265–276. San Diego. CA. 15–17 December (1986).

6   R. Moskowitz. Strategic systems planning shifts to data-oriented approach. *Computerworld.* pp.109–119, 12 May (1986).

7   E. K. Clemons. Information systems for sustainable competitive advantage. *Information and Management.* **1**(3), 131–136. October (1986). B. Ives and G. Learmonth. The information system as a competitive weapon. *Communications of the ACM.* **27**(12), 1193–1201. December (1985). F. W. McFarlan. Information technology changes the way you compete. *Harvard Business Review.* **62**(3), 98–103. May–June (1984). G. L. Parsons. Information technology: a new competitive weapon. *Sloan Management Review.* **25**(1), 3–14. Fall (1983): and C. Wiseman. *Strategy and Computers Information Systems as Competitive Weapons.* Dow Jones-Irwin, Homewood. IL (1985).

8   M. E. Porter. *Competitive Advantage Creating and Sustaining Superior Performance.* New York, Free Press (1985).

9   N. Rackoff. C. Wiseman and W. A. Ulrich. Information systems for competitive advantage and implementation of planning process. *MIS Quarterly.* **9**(4), 285–294. December (1985).

10 M. E. Porter. *Competitive Advantage Creating and Sustaining Superior Performance.* Free Press, New York (1985).

11 IBM Corporation. *Business Systems Planning – Information Systems Planning Guide* Publication No GE20 0527–4 (1975).

12 Holland Systems Coporation. *4FRONT strategy Method Guide.* Ann Arbor. MI (1989).

13 J. Martin. *STRATEGIC Information Planning Methodologies.* Prentice-Hall Inc. Englewood Cliffs. NJ (1989).

14 Andersen Consulting. *Foundation Method/1 Information Planning.* Version 8.0. Chicago. IL (1987).

15 J. R. Vacca. IBM's information quality analysis. *Computerworld.* 10 December (1984).

16 W. M. Carlson. Business information analysis and integration technique (BIAIT) a new horizon. *Data Base.* pp.3–9. Spring (1979).

17 D. V. Kerner. Business information characterization study. *Data Base.* 10–17, Spring (1979).

18 J. C. Wetherbe and G. B. Davis. Strategic Planning through Ends/ Means Analysis. MISRC Working Paper. 1982. University of Minnesota.

19 R. Moskowitz. Strategic systems planning shifts to data-oriented approach. *Computerworld.* pp.109–119, 12 May (1986).

20   F. W. McFarlan. Portfolio approach to information systems. *Harvard Business Review.* **59**(5), 142–150, September–October (1981).
21   W. R. King. Strategic planning for management information systems. *MIS Quarterly.* pp.27–37, March (1978).
22   C. H. Sullivan Jr. An evolutionary new logic redefines strategic systems planning. *Information Strategy. The Executive's Journal.* **3**(2), 13–19. Winter (1986).
23   F. W. McFarlan. Problems in planning the information system. *Harvard Business Review.* **49**(2), 75–89, March–April (1971).
24   J. R. Vacca. BSP How is it working. *Computerworld.* March (1983).
25   Interviews with Paul Osborn, an executive at Raychem, who provided details about the firm's SISP experiences.

Related reading

M. Hosoda, CIM at Nippon Seiko Co. *Long Range Planning.* **23**(5), 10–21 (1990).
G. K. Janssens and L. Cuyvers. EDI – A strategic weapon in international trade. *Long Range Planning.* **24**(2), 46–53 (1991).

Research Appendix 1: SISP survey items: resources, processes and output

Resources
1   The size of the planning team is very large.
2   It is difficult to find a team leader who meets the criteria specified by the methodology.
3   It is difficult to find team members who meet the criteria specified by the methodology.
4   The success of the methodology is greatly dependent on the team leader.
5   Many support personnel are required for data gathering and analysis during the study.
6   The planning exercise takes very long.
7   The planning exercise is very expensive.
8   The documentation does not adequately describe the steps that should be followed for implementing the methodology.
9   The methodology lacks sufficient computer support.
10   Adequate external consultant support is not available for implementing the methodology.
11   The methodology is not based on any theoretical framework.
12   The planning horizon considered by the methodology is inappropriate.
13   It is difficult to convince top management to approve the methodology.

14 The methodology makes inappropriate assumptions about organization structure.
15 The methodology makes inappropriate assumptions about organization size.

Process
The Methodology
1 fails to take into account organizational goals and strategies;
2 fails to assess the current information systems applications portfolio;
3 fails to analyse the current strengths and weaknesses of the IS department;
4 fails to take into account legal and environmental issues;
5 fails to assess the external technological environment;
6 fails to assess the organization's competitive environment;
7 fails to take into account issues related to plan implementation;
8 fails to take into account changes in the organization during SISP;
9 does not sufficiently involve users;
10 managers find it difficult to answer questions specified by the methodology;
11 requires too much top management involvement;
12 requires too much user involvement;
13 the planning procedure is rigid; and
14 does not sufficiently involve top management.

SISP Output:
1 fails to provide a statement of organizational objectives for the IS department;
2 fails to designate specific new steering committees;
3 fails to identify specific new products;
4 fails to determine a uniform basis for priorities projects;
5 fails to determine an overall data architecture for the organization;
6 fails to provide priorities for developing specific databases;
7 fails to sufficiently address the need for Data Administration in the organization;
8 fails to include an overall organizational hardware plan;
9 fails to include an overall organizational data communications plan;
10 fails to outline changes in the reporting relationships in the IS department;
11 fails to include an overall personnel and training plan for the IS department;
12 fails to include an overall financial plan for the IS department;
13 fails to sufficiently address the role of a permanent IS planning group;
14 plans are not flexible enough to take into account unanticipated changes in the organization and its environment;
15 is not in accordance with the expectations of top management;
16 Implementing the projects and the data architecture identified in the SISP output requires substantial further analysis;
17 It is difficult to secure top management commitment for implementing the plan;

18   The experiences from implementing the methodology are not sufficiently transferable across divisions;
19   The final output document is not very useful; and
20   The SISP output does not capture all the information that was developed during the study.

Research Appendix 2: Extent of SISP problems

Abbreviated problem statement

Item No		Extreme or major problem	Minor problem
017	Difficult to secure top management commitment	52%	16%
016	Requires further analysis	46%	31%
R4	Success dependent on team leader	41%	30%
R2	Difficult to find team leader meeting criteria	37%	17%
R9	Methodology lacks sufficient computer support	36%	27%
R6	Planning exercise takes long time	33%	30%
P7	Ignores plan implementation issues	33%	18%
R13	Difficult to obtain top management approval	32%	36%
O11	No training plan for IS department	30%	29%
R3	Difficult to find team members meeting criteria	30%	24%
O12	No financial plan for IS department	29%	28%
R8	Documentation is inadequate	28%	33%
O6	No priorities for developing databases	27%	26%
O5	No overall data architecture is determined	27%	22%
R7	Very expensive	26%	29%
O13	No permanent IS planning group	26%	24%
R5	Many support personnel required	26%	23%
O7	No data administration need addressed	26%	16%
O18	Experiences not sufficiently transferable	24%	19%
O9	No organizational data communications plan	22%	38%
O10	No changes in IS reporting relationships	22%	31%

Item No		Extreme or major problem	Minor problem
O4	No prioritization scheme provided	22%	19%
O15	Output belies top management expectations	22%	15%
P3	No analysis of IS department strengths/weaknesses	21%	32%
O8	No hardware plan	20%	36%
P11	Heavy top management involvement	20%	21%
O14	Resulting plans are inflexible	20%	18%
P5	No analysis of technological environment	19%	20%
P12	Too much user involvement	18%	28%
O19	Final output document not very useful	18%	20%
P10	Questions difficult for managers to answer	17%	39%
O20	Information during study not captured	17%	25%
P4	Methodology ignores legal/ environmental issues	14%	16%
R14	Bad assumptions about organization structure	14%	14%
P8	Ignores organization changes during SISP	13%	25%
O1	No objectives for IS department are provided	13%	21%
P9	Insufficient user involvement	13%	5%
R1	Very large planning team required	12%	21%
P6	Methodology ignores competitive environment	12%	19%
O3	No new projects identified in final plans	12%	13%
O2	Output fails to designate new steering committees	11%	18%
P13	Rigidity of planning procedure	9%	17%
P2	No assessment of current applications portfolio	9%	16%
P14	Lack of top management involvement	9%	13%
P1	Ignores organizational goals and strategies	8%	10%
R12	Inappropriate planning horizon	6%	7%
R10	Inadequate consultant support	5%	11%
R15	Inappropriate size assumptions	4%	8%
R11	No theoretical framework	3%	5%

Questions for discussion

1   How might the appropriate planning process vary according to the context of IT and to the stage of growth?
2   Do you agree that the 'quality of the planning process significantly influences the contribution which IS can make to an organization's performance'?
3   The authors state that 'an organization's commitment to construct an organization-wide information architecture vastly complicates SISP. Thus, organizations have often failed to build such an architecture'. What are other factors, aside from commitment, that affect whether an organization has constructed an organization-wide information architecture?
4   Of the two major goals of SISP – impact (the search for high-impact applications and the creation of competitive advantage) and alignment (the identification of a portfolio of computer-based applications to assist and organization in executing business plans) – which do you recommend? Should the SISP also vary according to the stage of growth? Is it possible consciously to plan for strategic IS (i.e. the 'impact' goal)?
5   The authors state that 'advocates of SISP should prepare convincing arguments to authorize the funding of the study'. What are some convincing arguments for why SISP should be carried out?
6   What would be the role of a permanent planning group? How might such a group overcome some of the major problems of SISP raised by the authors?

11 Evaluating the Outcomes of Information Systems Plans

Managing information technology evaluation – techniques and processes*

L. P. Willcocks

As far as I am concerned we could write off our IT expenditure over the last five years to the training budget. (Senior executive, quoted by Earl, 1990)

. . . the area of measurement is the biggest single failure of information systems while it is the single biggest issue in front of our board of directors. I am frustrated by our inability to measure cost and benefit. (Head of IT: AT and T quoted in Coleman and Jamieson, 1991)

Introduction

Information Technology (IT) now represents substantial financial investment. By 1993, UK company expenditure on IT was exceeding £12 billion per year, equivalent to an average of over 1.5% of annual turnover. Public sector IT spend, excluding Ministry of Defence operational equipment, was over £2 billion per year, or 1% of total public expenditure. The size and continuing growth in IT investments, coupled with a recessionary climate and concerns over cost containment from early 1990, have served to place IT issues above the parapet in most organizations, perhaps irretrievably. Understandably, senior managers need to question the returns from such investments and whether the IT route has been and can be, a wise decision.

This is reinforced in those organizations where IT investment has been a high risk, hidden cost process, often producing disappointed expectations. This is a difficult area about which to generalize, but research studies suggest

* An earlier version of this chapter appeared in the *European Management Journal*, Vol. 10, No. 2. June, pp.220–229.

that at least 20% of expenditure is wasted and between 30% and 40% of IT projects realize no net benefits, however measured (for reviews of research see Willcocks, 1993). The reasons for failure to deliver on IT potential can be complex. However major barriers, identified by a range of studies, occur in how the IT investment is evaluated and controlled (see for example Grindley, 1991; Kearney, 1990; Wilson, 1991). These barriers are not insurmountable. The purpose of this chapter is to report on recent research and indicate ways forward.

Evaluation: emerging problems

Taking a management perspective, evaluation is about establishing by quantitative and/or qualitative means the worth of IT to the organization. Evaluation brings into play notions of costs, benefits, risk and value. It also implies an organizational process by which these factors are assessed, whether formally or informally.

There are major problems in evaluation. Many organizations find themselves in a Catch 22. For competitive reasons they cannot afford not to invest in IT, but economically they cannot find sufficient justification, and evaluation practice cannot provide enough underpinning, for making the investment. One thing all informed commentators agree on: there are no reliable measures for assessing the impact of IT. At the same time there are a number of common problem areas that can be addressed. Our own research shows the following to be the most common:

- inappropriate measures
- budgeting practice conceals full costs
- understating human and organizational costs
- understating knock-on costs
- overstating costs
- neglecting 'intangible' benefits
- not fully investigating risk
- failure to devote evaluation time and effort to a major capital asset
- failure to take into account time-scale of likely benefits.

This list is by no means exhaustive of the problems faced (a full discussion of these problems and others appears in Willcocks, 1992a). Most occur through neglect, and once identified are relatively easy to rectify. A more fundamental and all too common failure is in not relating IT needs to the information needs of the organization. This relates to the broader issue of strategic alignment.

Strategy and information systems

The *organizational investment climate* has a key bearing on how investment is organized and conducted, and what priorities are assigned to different IT investment proposals. This is affected by:

- the financial health and market position of the organization
- industry sector pressures
- the organizational business strategy and direction
- the management and decision-making culture.

As an example of the second, 1989–90 research by Datasolve showed IT investment priorities in the retail sector focusing mainly on achieving more timely information, in financial services around better quality service to customers, and in manufacturing on more complete information for decision-making. As to decision-making culture, senior management attitude to risk can range from conservative to innovative, their decision-making styles from directive to consensus-driven (Butler Cox, 1990). As one example, conservative consensus-driven management would tend to take a relatively slow, incremental approach, with large-scale IT investment being unlikely. The third factor will be focused on here, that is creating a strategic climate in which IT investments can be related to organizational direction. Shaping the context in which IT evaluation is conducted is a necessary, frequently neglected prelude to then applying appropriate evaluation techniques and approaches. This section focuses on a few valuable pointers and approaches that work in practice to facilitate IT investment decisions that add value to the organization.

Alignment

A fundamental starting point is the need for alignment of business/organizational needs, what is done with IT, and plans for human resources, organizational structures and processes. The highly publicized 1990 Landmark Study tends to conflate these into alignment of business, organization and IT strategies (Scott Morton, 1991; Walton, 1989). A simpler approach is to suggest that the word 'strategy' should be used only when these different plans are aligned. There is much evidence to suggest that such alignment rarely exists. In a study of 86 UK companies Ernst and Young (1990) found only two aligned. Detailed research also shows lack of alignment to be a common problem in public sector informatization (Willcocks, 1992b). The case of an advertising agency (cited by Willcocks and Mason, 1994) provides a useful illustrative example:

Case: An advertising agency
In the mid-1980s this agency installed accounting and market forecasting systems at a cost of nearly £100 000. There was no real evaluation of the

worth of the IT to the business. It was installed largely because one director had seen similar systems running at a competitor. Its existing systems
had been perfectly adequate and the market forecasting system ended up
being used just to impress clients. At the same time as the system was
being installed the agency sacked over 36 staff and asked its managers not
to spend more than £200 a week on expenses. The company was taken
over in 1986. Clearly there had been no integrated plan on the business,
human resource, organizational and IT fronts. This passed on into its IT
evaluation practice. In the end the IT amplifier effect may well have operated. IT was not used to address the core, or indeed any, of the needs of the
business. A bad management was made correspondingly worse by the
application of IT.

One result of such lack of alignment is that IT evaluation practice tends to
become separated from business needs and plans on the one hand, and from
organizational realities that can influence IT implementation and subsequent
effectiveness on the other. Both need to be included in IT evaluation, and
indeed are in the more comprehensive evaluation methods, notably the information economics approach (see below).

Another critical alignment is that between what is done with IT and how
that fits with the information needs of the organization. Most management
attention has tended to fall on the 'technology' rather than the 'information'
element in what is called IT. Hochstrasser and Griffiths (1991) found in their
sample no single company with a fully developed and comprehensive strategy on information. Yet it would seem to be difficult to perform a meaningful
evaluation of IT investment without some corporate control framework establishing information requirements in relationship to business/organizational
goals and purpose, prioritization of information needs and, for example, how
cross-corporate information flows need to be managed. An information strategy directs IT investment, and establishes policies and priorities against which
investment can be assessed. It may also help to establish that some information needs can be met without the IT vehicle.

IT Strategic grid

The McFarlan and McKenney (1983) grid is a much-travelled, but useful
framework for focusing management attention on the IT evaluation question:
where does and will IT give us added value? A variant is shown below in
Figure 11.1.

Cases: Two manufacturing companies

Used by the author with a group of senior managers in a pharmaceutical
company, it was found that too much investment had been allowed on

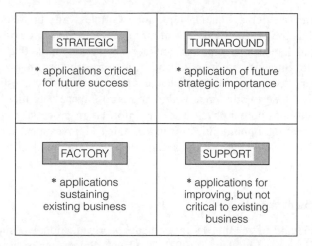

Figure 11.1 *Strategic grid analysis*

turnaround projects. In a period of downturn in business it was recognized that the investment in the previous three years should have been in strategic systems. It was resolved to tighten and refocus IT evaluation practice. In a highly decentralized multinational mainly in the printing/publishing industry, it was found that most of the twenty businesses were investing in factory and support systems. In a recessionary climate competitors were not forcing the issue on other types of system, the company was not strong on IT know-how, and it was decided that the risk-averse policy on IT evaluation, with strong emphasis on cost justification should continue.

The strategic grid is useful for classifying systems then demonstrating, through discussion, where IT investment has been made and where it should be applied. It can help to demonstrate that IT investments are not being made into core systems, or into business growth or competitiveness. It can also help to indicate that there is room for IT investment in more speculative ventures, given the spread of investment risk across different systems. It may also provoke management into spending more, or less, on IT. One frequent outcome is a demand to reassess which evaluation techniques are more appropriate to different types of system.

Value chain

Porter and Millar (1991) have also been useful in establishing the need for value chain analysis. This looks at where value is generated inside the organization, but also in its external relationships, for example with suppliers and cus-tomers. Thus the primary activities of a typical manufacturing company may be: inbound logistics, operations, outbound logistics, marketing and sales, and service. Support activities will be: firm infrastructure, human resource management, technology development and procurement. The question here is what can be done to add value within and across these activities? As every value activity has both a physical and an information-processing component, it is clear that the opportunities for value-added IT investment may well be considerable. Value chain analysis helps to focus attention on where these will be.

IT investment mapping

Another method of relating IT investment to organizational/business needs has been developed by Peters (1993). The basic dimensions of the map were arrived at after reviewing the main investment concerns arising in over 50 IT projects. The benefits to the organization appeared as one of the most frequent attributes of the IT investment (see Figure 11.2).

Thus one dimension of the map is benefits ranging from the more tangible arising from productivity enhancing applications to the less tangible from business expansion applications. Peters also found that the orientation of the investment toward the business was also frequently used in evaluation. He classifies these as *infrastructure*, e.g. telecommunications, software/hardware environment; *business operations*, e.g. finance and accounts, purchasing, pro-cessing orders; and *market influencing*, e.g. increasing repeat sales, improving distribution channels. Figure 11.3 shows the map being used in a hypothetical example to compare current and planned business strategy in terms of invest-ment orientation and benefits required, against current and planned IT invest-ment strategy.

Mapping can reveal gaps and overlaps in these two areas and help senior management to get them more closely aligned. As a further example:

> a company with a clearly defined, product-differentiated strategy of innova-tion would do well to reconsider IT investments which appeared to show undue bias towards a price-differentiated strategy of cost reduction and enhancing productivity.

Multiple methodology

Finally, Earl (1989) wisely opts for a multiple methodology approach to IS strategy formulation. This again helps us in the aim of relating IT investment more closely with the strategic aims and direction of the organization and its key needs. One element here is a *top-down approach*. Thus a critical success

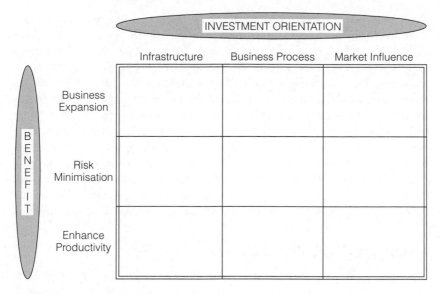

Figure 11.2   *Investment mapping*

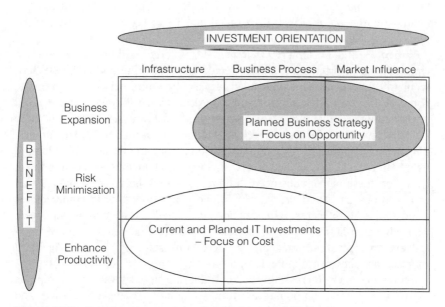

Figure 11.3   *Investment map comparing business and IT plans*

factors analysis might be used to establish key business objectives, decompose these into critical success factors, then establish the IS needs that will drive these CSFs. A *bottom-up evaluation* would start with an evaluation of current systems. This may reveal gaps in the coverage by systems, for example in the marketing function or in terms of degree of integration of systems across functions. Evaluation may also find gaps in the technical quality of systems and in their business value. This permits decisions on renewing, removing, maintaining or enhancing current sysems. The final leg of Earl's multiple methodology is '*inside-out innovation*'. The purpose here is to 'identify opportunities afforded by IT which may yield competitive advantage or create new strategic options'. The purpose of the whole threefold methodology is, through an internal and external analysis of needs and opportunities, to relate the development of IS applications to business/organizational need and strategy.

Evaluating feasibility: findings

The right 'strategic climate' is a vital prerequisite for evaluating IT projects at their feasibility stage. Here, we find out how organizations go about IT feasibility evaluation and what pointers for improved practice can be gained from the accumulated evidence. The picture is not an encouraging one. Organizations have found it increasingly difficult to justify the costs surrounding the purchase, development and use of IT. The value of IT/IS investments are more often justified by faith alone, or perhaps what adds up to the same thing, by understating costs and using mainly notional figures for benefit realization (see Farbey *et al.*, 1992; PA Consulting, 1990; Price Waterhouse, 1989; Strassman, 1990; Willcocks and Lester, 1993).

Willcocks and Lester (1993) looked at 50 organizations drawn from a cross-section of private and public sector manufacturing and services. Subsequently this research was extended into a follow-up interview programme. Some of the consolidated results are recorded in what follows. We found all organizations completing evaluation at the feasibility stage, though there was a fall off in the extent to which evaluation was carried out at later stages. This means that considerable weight falls on getting the feasibility evaluation right. High levels of satisfaction with evaluation methods were recorded. However, these perceptions need to be qualified by the fact that only 8% of organizations measured the impact of the evaluation, that is could tell us whether the IT investment subsequently achieved a higher or lower return than other non-IT investments. Additionally there emerged a range of inadequacies in evaluation practice at the feasibility stage of projects. The most common are shown in Figure 11.4.

Senior managers increasingly talk of, and are urged toward, the strategic use of IT. This means doing new things, gaining a competitive edge, and becoming more effective, rather than using IT merely to automate routine

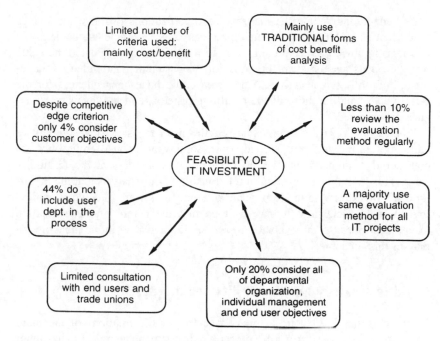

Figure 11.4   *IT evaluation: feasibility findings*

operations, do existing things better, and perhaps reduce the headcount. However only 16% of organizations used over four criteria on which to base their
evaluation. Cost/benefit was used by 62% as their predominant criterion in
the evaluation process. *The survey evidence here suggests that organizations
may be missing IS opportunities, but also taking on large risks, through
utilizing narrow evaluation approaches that do not clarify and assess less
tangible inputs and benefits.* There was also little evidence of a concern for
assessing risk in any formal manner. However the need to see and evaluate
risks and 'soft' hidden costs would seem to be essential, given the history of
IT investment as a 'high risk, hidden cost' process.

A sizable minority of organizations (44%) did not include the user department in the evaluation process at the feasibility stage. This cuts off a vital
source of information and critique on the degree to which an IT proposal is
organizationally feasible and will deliver on user requirements. Only a small
minority of organizations accepted IT proposals from a wide variety of groups
and individuals. In this respect most ignored the third element in Earl's
multiple methodology (see above). Despite the large literature emphasizing
consultation with the workforce as a source of ideas, know-how and as part
of the process of reducing resistance to change, only 36% of organizations
consulted users about evaluation at the feasibility stage, while only 18%

consulted unions. While the majority of organizations (80%) evaluated IT investments against organizational objectives, only 22% acted strategically in considering objectives from the bottom to the top, that is evaluated the value of IT projects against all of organization, departmental individual management, and end-user objectives. This again could have consequences for the effectiveness and usability of the resulting systems, and the levels of resistance experienced.

Finally, most organizations endorsed the need to assess the competitive edge implied by an IT project. However, somewhat inconsistently, only 4% considered customer objectives in the evaluation process at the feasibility stage. This finding is interesting in relationship to our analysis that the majority of IT investment in the respondent organizations were directed at achieving internal efficiencies. It may well be that the nature of the evaluation techniques, but also the evaluation *process* adopted, had influential roles to play in this outcome.

Linking strategy and feasibility techniques

Much work has been done to break free from the limitations of the more traditional, finance-based forms of capital investment appraisal. The major concerns seem to be to relate evaluation techniques to the type of IT project, and to develop techniques that relate the IT investment to business/organization value. A further development is in more sophisticated ways of including risk assessment in the evaluation procedures for IT investment. *A method of evaluation needs to be reliable, that is consistent in its measurement over time, able to discriminate between good and indifferent investments, able to measure what it purports to measure, and be administratively/organizationally feasible in its application.*

Return on management

Strassman (1990) has done much iconoclastic work in the attempt to modernize IT investment evaluation. He concludes that:

> Many methods for giving advice about computers have one thing in common. They serve as a vehicle to facilitate proposals for additional funding . . . the current techniques ultimately reflect their origins in a technology push from the experts, vendors, consultants, instead of a 'strategy' pull from the profit centre managers.

He has produced the very interesting concept of Return on Management (ROM). ROM is a measure of performance based on the added value to an organization provided by management. Strassman's assumption here is that in the modern organization information costs *are* the costs of managing the enterprise. If ROM is calculated before then after IT is applied to an organization then the IT contribution to the business, so difficult to isolate using more traditional measures, can be assessed. ROM is calculated in several stages. First, using the organization's financial results, the total value-added is established. This is the difference between net revenues and payments to external suppliers. The contribution of capital is then separated from that of labour. Operating costs are then deducted from labour value-added to leave management value-added. ROM is management value-added divided by the costs of management. There are some problems with how this figure is arrived at, and whether it really represents what IT has contributed to business performance. For example, there are difficulties in distinguishing between operational and management information. Perhaps ROM is merely a measure in some cases, and a fairly indirect one, of how effectively management information is used. A more serious criticism lies with the usability of the approach and its attractiveness to practising managers. This may be reflected in its lack of use, at least in the UK, as identified in different surveys (see Butler Cox, 1990; Coleman and Jamieson, 1991; Willcocks and Lester, 1993).

Matching objectives, projects and techniques

A major way forward on IT evaluation is to match techniques to objectives and types of projects. A starting point is to allow business strategy and purpose to define the category of IT investment. Butler Cox (1990) suggests five main purposes:

1   surviving and functioning as a business;
2   improving business performance by cost reduction/increasing sales;
3   achieving a competitive leap;
4   enabling the benefits of other IT investments to be realized;
5   being prepared to compete effectively in the future.

The matching IT investments can then be categorised, respectively, as:

1   *Mandatory investments*, for example accounting systems to permit reporting within the organization, regulatory requirements demanding VAT recording systems; competitive pressure making a system obligatory, e.g. EPOS amongst large retail outlets.
2   *Investments to improve performance*, for example Allied Dunbar and several UK insurance companies have introduced laptop computers for sales people, partly with the aim of increasing sales.
3   *Competitive edge investments*, for example SABRE at American Airlines, and Merrill Lynch's cash management account system in the mid-1980s.

4   *Infrastructure investments*. These are important to make because they give organizations several more degrees of freedom to manoeuvre in the future.
5   *Research investments*. In our sample we found a bank and three companies in the computer industry waiving normal capital investment criteria on some IT projects, citing their research and learning value. The amounts were small and referred to case tools in one case, and expert systems in the others.

There seems to be no shortage of such classifications now available. One of the more simple but useful is the sixfold classification shown in Figure 11.5.

Once assessed against, and accepted as aligned with required business purpose, a specific IT investment can be classified, then fitted on to the cost-benefit map (Figure 11.5 is meant to be suggestive only). This will assist in identifying where the evaluation emphasis should fall. For example, an 'efficiency' project could be adequately assessed utilizing traditional financial investment appraisal approaches; a different emphasis will be required in the method chosen to assess a 'competitive edge' project. Figure 11.6 is one view of the possible spread of appropriateness of some of the evaluation methods now available.

From cost-benefit to value

A particularly ambitious attempt to deal with many of the problems in IT evaluation – both at the level of methodology and of process – is represented in the information economics approach (Parker *et al*. 1988). This builds on the critique of traditional approaches, without jettisoning where the latter may be useful.

Information economics looks beyond benefit to value. Benefit is a 'discrete economic effect'. Value is seen as a broader concept based on the effect IT investment has on the business performance of the enterprise. How value is arrived at is shown in Figure 11.7. The first stage is building on traditional cost benefit analysis with four highly relevant techniques to establish an enhanced return on investment calculation. These are:

(a)   *Value linking*. This assesses IT costs which create additional benefits to other departments through ripple, knock-on effects.
(b)   *Value acceleration*. This assesses additional benefits in the form of reduced time-scales for operations.
(c)   *Value restructuring*. Techniques are used to measure the benefit of restructuring a department, jobs or personnel usage as a result of introducing IT. This technique is particularly helpful where the relationship to performance is obscure or not established. R&D, legal and personnel are examples of departments where this may be usefully applied.

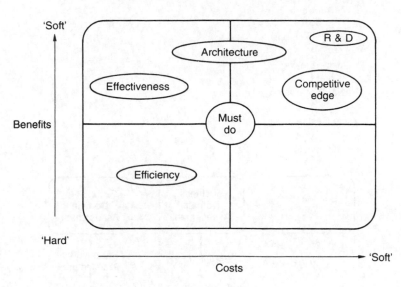

Figure 11.5 *Classifying IT projects*

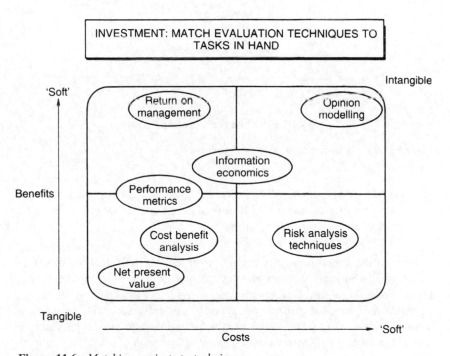

Figure 11.6 *Matching projects to techniques*

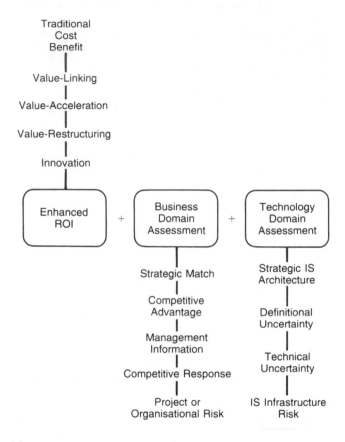

Figure 11.7   *The information economics approach*

(d)   *Innovation valuation*. This considers the value of gaining and sustaining a competitive advantage, while calculating the risks or cost of being a pioneer and of the project failing.

Information economics then enhances the cost-benefit analysis still further through business domain and technology domain assessments. These are shown in Figure 11.7. Here *strategic match* refers to assessing the degree to which the proposed project corresponds to established goals; *competitive advantage* to assessing the degree to which the proposed project provides an advantage in the marketplace; *management information* to assessing the contribution toward the management need for information on core activities;

competitive response to assessing the degree of corporate risk associated with not undertaking the project; and *strategic architecture* to measuring the degree to which the proposed project fits into the overall information systems direction.

Case: Truck leasing company

As an example of what happens when such factors and business domain assessment are neglected in the evaluation, Parker *et al.* (1988) point to the case of a large US truck leasing company. Here they found that on a 'hard' ROI analysis IT projects on preventative maintenance, route scheduling and despatching went top of the list. When a business domain assessment was carried out by line managers customer/sales profile system was evaluated as having the largest potential effect on business performance. An important infrastructure project – a Database 2 conversion/installation – also scored highly where previously it was scored bottom of eight project options. Clearly the evaluation technique and process can have a significant business impact where economic resources are finite and prioritization and drop decisions become inevitable.

The other categories in Figure 11.7 can be briefly described:

- *Organizational risk* – looking at how equipped the organization is to implement the project in terms of personnel, skills and experience.
- *IS infrastructure risk* – assessing how far the entire IS organization needs, and is prepared to support, the project.
- *Definitional uncertainty* – assessing the degree to which the requirements and/or the specifications of the project are known. Incidentally, research into more than 130 organizations shows this to be a primary barrier to the effective delivery of IT (Willcocks, 1993). Also assessed are the complexity of the area and the probability of non-routine changes.
- *Technical uncertainty* – evaluating a project's dependence on new or untried technologies.

Information economics provides an impressive array of concepts and techniques for assessing the business value of proposed IT investments. The concern for fitting IT evaluation into a corporate planning process and for bringing both business managers and IS professionals into the assessment process is also very welcome.

Some of the critics of information economics suggest that it may be over-mechanistic if applied to all projects. It can be time-consuming and may lack credibility with senior management, particularly given the subjective basis of much of the scoring. The latter problem is also inherent in the process of arriving at the weighting of the importance to assign to the different factors before scoring begins. Additionally there are statistical problems with the suggested scoring methods. For example, a scoring range of 1/5 may do little to differentiate between the ROI of two different projects. Moreover, even if a project scores nil on one risk, e.g. organizational risk, and in practice this risk may sink the project, the overall assessment by information economics may cancel out the impact of this score and show the IT investment to be a reasonable one. Clearly much depends on careful interpretation of the results, and much of the value for decision-makers and stakeholders may well come from the raised awareness of issues from undergoing the process of evaluation rather that from its statistical outcome. Another problem are may lie in the truncated assessment of organizational risk. Here, for example, there is no explicit assessment of the likelihood of a project to engender resistance to change because of, say, its job reduction or work restructuring implications. This may be compounded by the focus on bringing user managers, but one suspects not lower level users, into the assessment process.

Much of the criticism, however, ignores how adaptable the basic information economics framework can be to particular organizational circumstances and needs. Certainly this has been a finding in trials in organizations as varied as British Airports Authority, a Central Government Department and a major food retailer.

Case: Retail food company

In the final case Ong (1991) investigated a three-phase branch stock management system. Some of the findings are instructive. Managers suggested including the measurement of risk associated with interfacing systems and the difficulties in gaining user acceptance of the project. In practice few of the managers could calculate the enhanced ROI because of the large amount of data required and, in a large organization, its spread across different locations. Some felt the evaluation was time-independent; different results could be expected at different times. The assessment of risk needed to be expanded to include not only technical and project risk but also the risk/impact of failure to an organization of its size. In its highly competitive industry any unfavourable venture can have serious knock-on impacts and most firms tend to be risk-conscious, even risk-averse.

Such findings tend to reinforce the view that information economics provides one of the more comprehensive approaches to assessing the potential value to the organization of its IT investments, but that it needs to be tailored, developed, in some cases extended, to meet evaluation needs in different organizations. Even so, information economics remains a major contribution to advancing modern evaluation practice.

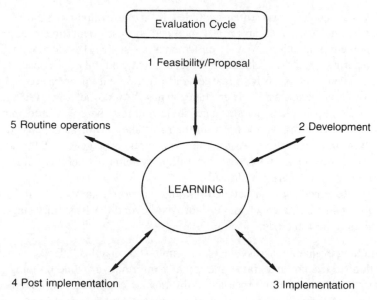

Figure 11.8 *The evaluation cycle*

CODA: From development to routine operations

This chapter has focused primarily on the front-end of evaluation practice and how it can be improved. In research on evaluation beyond the feasibility stage of projects, we have found evaluation variously carried on through four main additional stages. Respondent organizations supported the notion of an evaluation learning cycle, with evaluation at each stage feeding into the next to establish a learning spiral across time – useful for controlling a specific project, but also for building organizational know-how on IT and its management (see Figure 11.8). The full research findings are detailed elsewhere (see Willcocks and Lester, 1993). However, some of the limitations in evaluation techniques and processes discovered are worth commenting on here.

We found only weak linkage between evaluations carried out at different stages. As one example, 80% of organizations had experienced abandoning projects at the development stage due to negative evaluation. The major reasons given were changing organizational or user needs and/or 'gone over budget'. When we reassembled data, abandonment clearly related to under-playing these objectives at the feasibility stage. Furthermore, all organizations abandoning projects because 'over budget' depended heavily on cost-benefit in their earlier feasibility evaluation, thus probably understating development and second-order costs. We found only weak evidence of organizations applying their development stage evaluation, and indeed their experiences at subsequent stages, to improving feasibility evaluation techniques and processes.

Key stakeholders were often excluded from the evaluation process. For example, only 9% of organizations included the user departments/users in development evaluation. At the implementation stage 31% do not include user departments, 52% exclude the IT department, and only 6% consult trade unions. There seemed to be a marked fall-off in attention given to, and the results of, evaluation across later stages. Thus 20% do not carry out evaluation at the post-implementation stage, some claiming there was little point in doing so. Of the 56% who learn from their mistakes at this stage, 25% do so from 'informal evaluation'. At the routine operations stage, only 20% use in their evaluation criteria systems capability, systems availability, organizational needs and departmental needs.

These, together with our detailed findings, suggest a number of guidelines on how evaluation practice can be improved beyond the feasibility stage. At a minimum these include:

1   Linking evaluation across stages and time – this enables 'islands of evaluation' to become integrated and mutually informative, while building into the overall evaluation process possibilities for continuous improvement.
2   Many organizations can usefully reconsider the degree to which key stakeholders are participants in evaluation at all stages.
3   The relative neglect given to assessing the actual against the posited impact of IT, and the fall-off in interest in evaluation at later stages, mean that the effectiveness of feasibility evaluation becomes difficult to assess and difficult to improve. The concept of learning would seem central to evaluation practice but tends to be applied in a fragmented way.
4   The increasing clamour for adequate evaluation techniques is necessary, but may reveal a quick-fix orientation to the problem. It can shift attention from what may be a more difficult, but in the long term more value-added area, which is getting the process right.

Conclusions

The high expenditure on IT, growing usage that goes to the core of organizational functioning, together with disappointed expectations about its impact have all served to raise the profile of how IT investment can be evaluated. It is not only an underdeveloped, but also an undermanaged area which organizations can increasingly ill-afford to neglect. There are well-established traps that can now be avoided. *Organizations need to shape the context in which effective evaluation practice can be conducted. Traditional techniques cannot be relied upon in themselves to assess the types of technologies and how they are increasingly being applied in organizational settings. A range of modern techniques can be tailored and applied. However, techniques can only complement, not substitute for developing evaluation as a process, and the deeper organizational learning about IT that entails.* Past evaluation practice has been geared to asking questions about the price of IT. Increasingly it produces less than useful answers. The future challenge is to move to the problem of value of IT to the organization, and build techniques and processes that can go some way to answering the resulting questions.

References

Butler Cox Foundation (1990) Getting value from information technology. Research Report 75, June, Butler Cox, London.

Coleman T. and Jamieson, M. (1991) Information systems: evaluating intangible benefits at the feasibility stage of project appraisal. Unpublished MBA thesis, City University Business School, London.

Earl, M. (1989) *Management Strategies for Information Technology*, Prentice Hall, London.

Earl, M. (1990) Education: The foundation for effective IT strategies. IT and the new manager conference. *Computer Weekly/Business Intelligence*, June, London.

Ernst and Young, (1990) Strategic Alignment Report· UK Survey, Ernst and Young, London.

Farbey, B., Land, F. and Targett, D. (1992) Evaluating investments in IT. *Journal of Information Technology*, 7(2), 100–112.

Grindley, K. (1991) *Managing IT at Board Level*, Pitman, London.

Hochstrasser, B. and Griffiths, C. (1991) *Controlling IT Investments: Strategy and Management*, Chapman and Hall, London.

Kearney, A. T. (1990) *Breaking the Barriers: IT Effectiveness in Great Britain and Ireland*, A. T. Kearney/CIMA, London .

McFarlan, F. and McKenney, J. (1983) *Corporate Information Systems Management: The Issues Facing Senior Executives*, Dow Jones Irwin, New York.

Ong, D. (1991) Evaluating IS investments: a case study in applying the information economics approach. Unpublished thesis, City University, London.

PA Consulting Group, (1990) *The Impact of the Current Climate on IT – The Survey Report*, PA Consulting Group, London.

Parker, M., Benson, R., and Trainor, H. (1988) *Information Economics*, Prentice Hall, London.

Peters, G. (1993) Evaluating your computer investment strategy. In *Information Management: Evaluation of Information Systems Investments* (ed. L. Willcocks), Chapman and Hall, London, pp.99–112.

Porter, M. and Millar, V. (1991) How information gives you competitive advantage. In *Revolution in Real Time: Managing Information Technology in the 1990s* (ed. W. McGowan), Harvard Business School Press, Boston, pp.59–82.

Price Waterhouse (1989) *Information Technology Review 1989/90*, Price Waterhouse, London.

Scott Morton, M. (ed.) (1991) *The Corporation of the 1990s*, Oxford University Press, Oxford.

Strassman, P. A. (1990) *The Business Value of Computers*, The Information Economics Press, New Canaan, CT.

Walton, R. (1989) *Up and Running*, Harvard Business School Press, Boston.

Willcocks, L. (1992a) Evaluating information technology investments: research findings and reappraisal. *Journal of Information Systems*, **2**(3), 242–268.

Willcocks, L. (1992b) The manager as technologist? In *Rediscovering Public Services Management* (eds L. Willcocks and J. Harrow), McGraw-Hill, London.

Willcocks, L. (ed.) (1993) *Information Management: Evaluation of Informations Systems Investments*, Chapman and Hall, London.

Willcocks, L. and Lester, S. (1993) Evaluation and control of IS investments. OXIIM Research and Discussion Paper 93/5, Templeton College, Oxford.

Willcocks, L. and Mason, D. (1994) *Computerising Work: People, Systems Design and Workplace Relations*, 2nd edn, Alfred Waller Publications, Henley-on-Thames.

Wilson, T. (1991) Overcoming the barriers to implementation of information systems strategies. *Journal of Information Technology*, **6**(1), 39–44.

Adapted from Willcocks, L. (1992) IT evaluation: managing the catch 22. *The European Management Journal*, **10**(2), 220–229. Reprinted by permission of the author and Elsevier Science.

Questions for discussion

1   The value of IT/IS investments is more often justified by faith alone, or perhaps what adds up to the same thing, by understanding costs and using mainly notional figures for benefit realization. Discuss the reasons for which IT evaluation is rendered so difficult.

2   Evaluate the three major evaluation techniques the author discusses – ROM; Matching objectives, projects and techniques; and information economics.

3   Again refer back to the revised stages of growth model introduced in Chapter 2: might different evaluation techniques be appropriate at different phases?

4   Who should be involved in the IT evaluation process?

5   Given the two approaches to SISP (impact and alignment) proposed by Lederer and Sethi in Chapter 10, what evaluation approach might be appropriate for the two SISP approaches?

Part Three

The Information Systems Strategy–Business Strategy Relationship

We now turn, in Parts Three and Four, to the contexts within which both information systems planning and information systems strategy take place. First, in Part Three, we consider the information systems strategy–business strategy relationship, while in Part Four we consider information systems strategy in the wider organizational environment. As can be seen from Figure III.1 (cf. the shaded portion of the diagram), our focus in Part Three is on aspects of the relationship itself (Chapters 12 and 13), and on key strategic issues that have exercised minds in recent years, namely business process reengineering and electronic commerce (Chapters 14 and 15).

In the first edition of *Strategic Information Management* we included an article by Clemons and Row (1991), which reflected the then state-of-the-art thinking on the attainment of competit ive advantage from the astute utilization of information technology. This article was representative of many on this topic that appeared in the period from the mid-1980s through to the 1990s. The earlier articles focused on the issue of *obtaining* competitive advantage from IT (see, e.g. Ives and Learmonth, 1984, McFarlan, 1984; Cash and Konsynski, 1985; Porter and Millar, 1985; Copeland and McKenney, 1988), while concerns in the latter part of the period were directed more towards *sustaining* that advantage (see, e.g. Feeny and Ives, 1990; 1997; Mata *et al.*, 1995).

In reviewing the information systems strategy–business strategy relationship in this the second edition of *Strategic Information Management*, we change the focus somewhat by reflecting more of the thinking of the 1990s on this important topic. As we saw in Chapter 9, key objectives of IS strategy include, in rank order: aligning IS with business needs, seeking competitive advantage from IT, and gaining top management commitment to key IT projects. In Chapter 12, Jarvenpaa and Ives reflect on the question of aligning IT and the business by providing a chief executive officer (CEO) perspective on the topic. They set out to explore CEO perceptions of (i) the role of IT as a tool of business strategy; (ii) how instrumental it is to their business plans; (iii) the problems and opportunities presented by IT, and (iv) the importance of IT over time, across industry, and between firms that are doing well as against those that are doing poorly. This chapter is important in that it tends to confirm Rosmanelli and Tushman's (1988) view that top executives, by their perceptions and decisions, 'can and do systematically influence the content and character of organizational activity'. This is illustrated, *inter alia*, by a letter to the shareholders of the UK's Midland Bank by the chairman of the Group, Sir Kit McMahon, 'to reorient the organization during low organizational performance and drastic environmental changes'. In it, he describes how he perceives IT as a catalyst for change. As the authors suggest: 'The letter symbolizes McMahon's vision for IT by legitimizing, explaining, and rationalizing

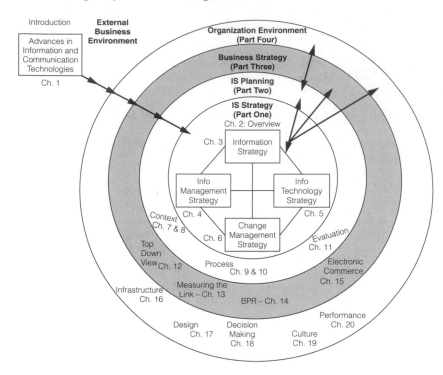

Figure III.1   *The focus of Part-Three: the information systems strategy–business strategy relationship*

the organization's recent investments in IT – investments which he clearly hoped could restore Midland to a state of satisfactory performance.'

From this 'view from the top', we turn, in Chapter 13, to issues associated with *measuring* the linkage between business and IT objectives. Written by Reich and Benbasat, this chapter is based on empirical field research conducted in ten business units of three large Canadian life insurance companies. The authors identified two useful dimensions to the measurement of the linkage, namely: (i) intellectual (i.e. the internal consistency and external validity of the content of business and IS plans), and (ii) social (i.e. the extent of understanding between business and IS executives regarding one another's objectives and plans). In addition they provide a scheme showing 'different ways of conceptualizing and identifying short- and long-term aspects of the [latter]. One represents a state in which the goals and strategies of the next one–two years of business and IT activity are understood by all managers. The other represents a state in which all managers share a common vision of how IT will shape the business in the more distant future'. The scheme is in some ways complementary to that posed in Chapter 2, which aims to provide a shared understanding of the *current* position with respect to the alignment or 'fit' of IT with the business. For further reading on the relationship between IS and business strategy, and on the chief executive officer–chief information officer relationship, see, for example, Zviran (1990), Baets (1992), Henderson and Venkatraman (1992), and Feeny *et al.* (1992; 1997).

The final two chapters of Part Three focus on two topics that have been the subject of much attention, and not a little hyperbole, during the 1990s, namely business process reengineering (BPR) and electronic commerce. Chapter 14, by Huizing, Koster and Bouman, develops the theme of alignment, or fit, by focusing attention on BPR and organizational performance. Based on survey research, this chapter suggests that 'consistent reengineering endeavors generally result in greater benefits than do inconsistent change efforts'. Very few, though, 'have succeeded in creating a "magical mix" between the level of ambition and the design and change management measures actually taken'. Implications of their findings to managers include: (i) an appropriate level of ambition for BPR projects should be identified, otherwise the risks may be too great (cf. Galliers, 1997), and (ii) the level of ambition should be translated into a consistent package of design and change management measures, in order to bring about an appropriate 'mindset' among key players in the change process. In setting the scene for their research, the authors also provide a useful review of the literature on the concept of fit. For further reading on BPR, and the dangers of focusing solely on IT and business processes, at the expense of the human dimension, see Davenport (1996); and for a balanced treatment of the topic, based on a review of earlier BPR endeavours, see Sauer *et al.* (1997).

The final chapter in Part Three deals with the topic of strategies in response to the potential of electronic commerce. By Lee and Clark, Chapter 15 provides us with an intriguing view of four cases where electronic market systems have been adopted: two successful, and two failed. Noting the potential of IT in reducing transaction costs and increasing market efficiency, the authors demonstrate how economic benefits from such adoptions can be achieved. Conversely, adoption barriers are also identified 'by analyzing transaction risks and resistance resulting from reengineering' (cf. Chapter 14). As a result of this analysis, the authors claim that successful deployment of electronic markets and redesign of market processes using electronic commerce solutions is less about information technology *per se*, but much more about understanding and managing the barriers and the projected economic benefits.* For further reading on aspects of electronic commerce, see, e.g. Rayport and Sviokla (1995), Benjamin and Wigand (1995), and Holland (1998).

Having introduced aspects of the requirement for a strong linkage between business and information systems strategy here, we turn in Part Four to considerations of the linkage with the wider organizational environment.

References

Baets, W. (1992) Aligning information systems with business strategy. *Journal of Strategic Information Systems*, **1**(4), December, 205–213.

Benjamin, R. I. and Wigand, R. (1995) Electronic markets and the virtual value chains on the Information Superhighway. *Sloan Management Review*, Winter, 62–72.

Cash, Jr., J. I. and Konsynski, B. R. (1985) IS redraws competitive boundaries. *Harvard Business Review*, **63**(2), March/April, 134–142.

Clemons, E. K. and Row, M. C. (1991) Sustaining information technology advantage: the role of structural differences. *MIS Quarterly*, **15**(3), September, 275–292. Reproduced in Galliers, R. D. and Baker, B. S. H. (1994), *op cit.*, 167–192.

Copeland, D. G. and McKenney, J. L. (1988) Airline reservation systems: lessons from history. *MIS Quarterly*, **12**(3), September, 353–370.

Davenport, T. H. (1996) Why reengineering failed. The fad that forgot people. *Fast Company*, Premier Issue, 70–74.

---

* This point can and should be extended still further. The whole question of communication and trust between individuals working in virtual teams, often in widely dispersed locations, and also separated by time, is of critical importance to organizations as they increasingly develop, market and sell their goods and services utilizing the Internet. For more on this fascinating and most crucial of topics, see, for example: Fritz *et al.* (1998); Jarvenpaa *et al.* (1998) and Jarvenpaa and Leidner (1998).

Feeny, D. F., Edwards, B. and Simpson, K. (1992) Understanding the CEO/CIO relationship. *MIS Quarterly*, **16**(4), 435–448.

Feeny, D. F., Edwards, B. and Simpson, K. (1997) Understanding the CEO–CIO relationship. In Willcocks, L. *et al.* (1997), *op cit.*, 22–42.

Feeny, D. F. and Ives, B. (1990) In search of sustainability: reaping long-term advantage from investments in information technology. *Journal of Management Information Systems*, **7**(1), Summer.

Feeny, D. F. and Ives, B. (1997) IT as a basis for sustainable competitive advantage. In Willcocks, L. *et al.* (1997), *op cit.*, 43–63.

Fritz, M. B., Narasimhan, S. and Rhee, H. S. (1998) Communication and coordination in the virtual office. *Journal of Management Information Systems*, **14**(4), 7–28.

Galliers, R. D. (1997) Against obliteration: reducing the risk in business process change. In Sauer *et al.* (1997), *op cit.*, 169–186.

Galliers, R. D. and Baker, B. S. H. (ed.) (1994) *Strategic Information Management: Challenges and Strategies in Managing Information Systems*, Butterworth-Heinemann, Oxford.

Henderson, J. C. and Venkatramam, N. (1992) Strategic alignment: a model for organizational transformation through information technology. In *Transforming Organizations* (eds T. A. Kocham and M. Useem), Oxford University Press, New York.

Holland, C. (ed.) (1998) Special Issue of the *Journal of Strategic Information Systems* on Electronic Commerce, **7**(3), September.

Ives, B. and Learmonth, G. P. (1984) Information systems as a competitive weapon. *Communications of the ACM*, **27**(12), December, 1193–1201.

Jarvenpaa, S., Knoll, K. and Leidner, D. E. (1998) Is anybody out there? Trust in global virtual teams. *Journal of Management Information Systems*, **14**(4), 29–64.

Jarvenpaa, S. and Leidner, D. E. (1998) Trust and communication in global virtual teams. *Organization Science* (forthcoming). Also in *Journal of Computer Mediated Communication*: (http://www.ascuse.org/jcmc/vo13/issue4/jarvenpaa.html).

McFarlan, F. W. (1984) Information technology changes the way you compete. *Harvard Business Review*, **62**(3), May/June, 98–102.

Mata, F. J. Fuerst, W. L. and Barney, J. B. (1995) Information technology and sustained competitive advantage: a resource-based analysis. *MIS Quarterly*, **19**(4), December, 487–505.

Porter, M. and Millar, V. E. (1985) How information gives you competitive advantage. *Harvard Business Review*, **63**(4), July/August, 149–160.

Rayport, J. F. and Sviokla, J. J. (1995) Exploiting the virtual value chain. *Harvard Business Review*, **73**(6), November/December, 75–85.

Rosmanelli, E. and Tushman, M. L. (1988) Executive leadership and organizational outcomes: an evolutionary perspective. In *The Executive Effect: Concepts and Methods for Studying Top Managers* (ed. D. C. Hambrick), JAI Press, Inc., Greenwich, Connecticut.

Sauer, C., Yetton, P. *et al.* (1997) *Steps to the Future: Fresh Thinking on the Management of IT-Based Organizational Tranformation*, Jossey-Bass, San Francisco, California.

Willcocks, L. Feeny, D. and Islei, G. (1997) *Managing IT as a Strategic Resource*, McGraw-Hill, London.

Zviran, M. (1990) Relationship between organizational and information systems objectives: some empirical evidence, *Journal of Management Information Systems*, **7**(1), Summer, 65–84.

12 Information Systems and Business Strategy: An Overview

Information technology and corporate strategy: a view from the top

S. L. Jarvenpaa and B. Ives

Letters to shareholders in 649 annual reports published between 1972 and 1987 were analyzed for CEOs' views about information technology. Significant differences were found across industries – banking, publishing, petroleum, and retailing – in the number of times information technology was mentioned, the types of applications discussed, and the content of the discussion. The results of the industry analysis were in keeping with expectations based on the relative information intensity of the various industries. An analysis of the letters over time suggests that the position of IT in the firm, at least as seen by the CEO, was not much different in 1987 than it had been in 1982, but has expanded considerably from its position in 1972 and 1973. Reassuringly, we also found that the number of IT related phrases in the CEOs' letters to the shareholders was positively correlated with the firm's yearly net profits as a percentage of sales. A lagged analysis on profitability data could not, however, resolve the competing explanations for the correlation between profits and the number of IT-related phrases. These findings contribute new insights concerning strategic information systems and support the use of annual report data in analyzing organizational information technology phenomena.

Introduction

I am convinced that one of the key factors for success for any bank in the future will be its ability to marshal the resources of computing and telecommunications

in direct support of its business objectives. . . . The Group has begun to consolidate and standardize its various data centres . . . much has been done to achieve
a proper partnership and mutual understanding between the business sectors
and specialist IT managers to allow the Group to extract a full return from
its investment in IT . . . IT has helped the Bank to maintain its competitive
edge; in the development of completely new corporate banking systems . . . a
major programme of IT education at all levels of management has begun . . . we
were fortunate to obtain the services of Gene Lockhart as our first IT director.
(Chairman's Letter, 1987 Annual Report, The Midland Group)

The Chairman's letter of the annual report: a status report to the shareholders,
but also an opportunity to impress financial analysts, reassure suppliers, cajole
customers, signal competitors, or revitalize employees – a few pages to capture
the highlights of the year while summarizing the firm's plans and aspirations
for the future. For publicly traded companies the letter to the shareholders
provides a consistent set of windows from which an observer can watch as
strategy evolves or comes unglued.

If information technology plays a significant role in corporate strategy,
then the letter to the shareholders may reflect that role. For example, in his
1987 letter to the shareholders, abstracted above, Sir Kit McMahon, Chairman
of the United Kingdom's Midland Group, proclaims that Information Technology (IT)[1] will play a significant role in the Bank's corporate strategy for
1988 and beyond. Twelve sentences of McMahon's letter discuss issues
related to IT reorganization and IT strategy, while only three are devoted to
the Bank's dramatic decision to write off £916 million in bad loans.

The Chairman's letter to the shareholders presents a unique observation
deck for the researcher interested in examining strategy (Ginsberg, 1988).
Bowman (1984) demonstrates that, 'content analysis of annual reports can be
of real usefulness for understanding some issues of corporate strategy' (p.70).
Bettman and Weitz (1983) contend that the chairman's letter, which is a
standardized component of the report,[2] provides comparable, and more objective data on organizations than interviews. Although public relations departments may assist in writing the letters, Bettman and Weitz (1983) point out
that the letters 'are subject to a great deal of public scrutiny', thus leading
to 'severe consequences if obvious biases are shown in the causal reasoning
presented' (p.171). Salancik and Meindl (1984) argue convincingly that the
'president of a firm could not easily disclaim the contents of a letter he signed
and published' (p.243). Pfeffer (1981), recognizing the utility of the chairman's

---

[1] Information technology refers to computer, communications, or office technology.
[2] The letter reviews (1) the financial position of the company and provides explanation for the
results, briefly discusses (2) the major events such as acquisitions, divestitures, new product
introductions, changes in senior management, etc., and puts forth (3) the outlook and the short-
and long-term strategies and how to reach them.

letter as a source of 'objective' data on organizations, has called for increased research use of annual report data.

The chairman's letter of the annual report hence provides a well established research window into the highest levels of publicly traded corporations. Within this chapter we use that window to observe CEOs' perspectives on IT and strategy.

IT and corporate strategy: the status of current research

Since the early 1980's the terms 'information technology' and 'corporate strategy' have been coupled with recurring regularity in the information systems literature. IT, we are told, can provide new forms of customer service, new distribution channels, new information based products, or can even rearrange industry boundaries (Cash *et al.*, 1988; Cash and Konsynski, 1985; Porter and Millar, 1985). Examples of such strategic IT[3] applications are frequently cited (Wiseman, 1985; Keen, 1981) and frameworks are proposed to help understand (e.g. Benjamin *et al.*, 1984), identify, and categorize similar opportunities (e.g. Johnston and Vitale, 1988; Porter and Millar, 1985; Ives and Learmonth, 1984; Gerstein and Reisman, 1982).

But, as an area of academic research, IT and corporate strategy has been soundly criticized. With some exceptions (e.g. Runge, 1985; Reich and Benbasat, 1988), the work in the area has been anecdotal or conceptual rather than empirical or theoretical. The studies have used convenience samples – companies which have already achieved public acclaim for successful strategic uses of information technology. Bakos and Treacy (1986) state 'Much of the current work on the strategic impacts of information technology . . . makes little or no use of bodies of theory related to either strategy or competition' (p.117). Similarly, Clemons and Kimbrough (1986) find,

> This literature largely relies on a common and perhaps overworked collection of examples. . . . Unhappily, neither the literature nor the oral tradition goes into much depth; both are largely anecdotal. Little is understood by way of general principles or theory about why certain moves work or are likely to work, or why others fail. (p.99)

The lack of rigor is not surprising. Empiricism is hampered by the immaturity of the research area, the necessity of treating the organization as the unit of analysis, the lack of measures to assess the effects of strategic IT, and the understandable reluctance of management to let researchers get too close to the formulation and communication of strategy. Capturing the Chief

---

[3] A strategic IT implies that IT 'changes a firm's product or the way a firm competes in the industry'.

Executives' perspective presents further challenges due to scheduling and availability constraints and, occasionally, a reluctance to expose their ignorance of the phenomena in question. A single exception is the work of Brancheau and Wetherbe (1987) in which they included 12 'general managers' in addition to 68 information systems executives in a Delphi study designed to ascertain the key issues in information management.[4]

The current study is a small step toward empiricism. Using eight years of CEO-level data drawn from 88 companies, the study evaluates the state of strategic IT from the viewpoint of the firm's Chief Executive.

IT and corporate strategy: the CEO's perspective

In an earlier era, when IT expenditures were considered to be back office investments, the Chief Executive Officer's view of IT, though interesting, was not usually seen as vital to success. Back office investments in IT tended to be based on expense reductions; an IT steering committee backed up by an accountant with a return on investment calculator assured senior management that investments in IT were well founded. The chief executive's only role was to ensure that expense controls were in place and to referee resource disputes among the business units or functional areas. But as the IT portfolio moved out of the back office and into new products, product delivery systems, and customer service applications, the benefits have tended to move from the expense to the revenue category. Justifications here are often driven by intuition and gut feel, with a push from the top often required to lubricate or circumvent approval processes best suited for justifying applications solely on the basis of hard savings (Runge, 1985; Ives and Vitale, 1988).

It is now widely believed that to exploit strategic opportunities from IT, the Chief Executive must view IT as a component of corporate strategy. As applications of IT become a necessary element of organizational strategy, the Chief Executive Officer's views and leadership about investments in IT are anticipated to become considerably more relevant and, presumably, more instrumental in corporate success or failure (Clemons and Row, 1988). Parsons (1984), among others (Benjamin *et al.*, 1984; Dooley and Kanter, 1985; Bakos and Treacy, 1986), argues that 'in order for IT to become a viable competitive weapon, senior management must understand how IT may impact the competitive environment and strategy of the business' (p.4). The importance of senior management commitment to IT initiatives has been echoed by many others (Cash *et al.*, 1988; Izzo, 1987; Keen, 1988). Rockart (1988), for example, claims that 'information technology is far too important, in 1988, to

---

[4] A general manager was the president, vice-president, or corporate general manager to whom the firm's chief IT executive reported.

be left to information technologists' (p.59). IT may also provide opportunities to engender economies of scope across diverse business units or functional areas – opportunities that may only be obvious or implementable from corporate offices. Porter and Millar (1985) argue that 'general managers must be involved to ensure that cross-functional linkages [made possible by IT] are exploited' (p.159).

Some empirical evidence supports these assertions. King's (1986) survey of 51 IT executives found that the lack of top management support was seen as the strongest inhibitors of a company's efforts to create strategic applications. In a study of eleven strategic IT applications in nine Canadian companies, Reich and Benbasat (1988) found that 50% of respondents reported the support of the Chief Executive officer as being very important in developing strategic applications; eighty percent of the systems had been given a high profile by senior management during the development process. Johnston and Carrico (1988) cite an instance where a CEO took it upon himself to promote IT as a competitive weapon; the CEO persistently challenged both his line executive cadre and IT people to 'find ways to change the rules in our business so that we can use our IS resources to win' (p.41). A strong positive orientation toward IT from the CEO's office seems essential for the corporation to have an IT vision and a conducive environment for developing strategic applications.

The research questions

But, what are the Chief Executives' perceptions about the role of IT as a tool of corporate strategy? How instrumental do business leaders view IT to be to their plans? What problems and opportunities do they perceive that IT presents? And how do the Chief Executives' perceptions of the importance of IT vary over time in a firm, across industry, and between firms that are doing well and firms that are doing poorly? We will study these perceptions by analyzing the reasoning expressed in CEOs' letters to shareholders.

Industry differences

The strategic role of IT and the CEO's perceptions of the importance of IT are believed to vary across industry boundaries. Such differences, if they exist, should be reflected by CEOs' comments about IT in their letters. Cash *et al.* (1988) argue via their Strategic Grid framework that IT is more strategic in some industries than in others. Porter and Millar (1985) propose that industries characterized by high 'information intensity' in their products and processes will have greater opportunities to exploit IT than those that do not. Johnston and Carrico (1988) also hypothesize differences in the utility of IT across industry boundaries, providing some tentative support for this claim based on interviews with IT executives and senior line management. By contrast, Reich and Benbasat (1988) did not find support for the notion that competitive advantage is more likely when organizations' products have high versus low information content. However, the study by Reich and Benbasat had a 'preponderance of financial institutions in it' (p.35), thus decreasing the likelihood of detecting industry differences.

Changes over time

Information technologies' hypothesized strategic role is frequently postulated to have grown over time. If so, we might expect to find a corresponding increase over time in the extent to which IT was mentioned in the Chairman's letter to Stockholders. Gibson and Nolan (1974) first predicted IT's maturation in the organization through stages. Although the Gibson and Nolan stage model has proven difficult to validate (Drury, 1983; Benbasat *et al.*, 1984; King and Kraemer, 1984), some modest evidence supports the elevation of the IT's role in the organization over time. Rockart (1988) envisions that IT has moved through a series of 'eras', and has most recently entered an era which he describes as the 'wired society'. In the wired society, systems 'almost always require major, sometimes radical, alternations in an organization's structure, personnel, roles, and business processes' (p.60), and therefore require 'change processes effectively managed by those responsible for the management of the business itself' (p.60). Cash *et al.* (1988) also postulate that the strategic role of IT changes over time in industries and firms within industries.

There is some empirical evidence demonstrating an escalation of IT's role in organizations. A Delphi study conducted by Brancheau and Wetherbe (1987) found that respondents viewed the use of information for competitive advantage as a critical issue of information systems management in 1986, though the issue had not arisen in a similar study done three years earlier (Dickson *et al.*, 1984). There is also evidence that over time more senior 'technology officers' report to the highest level in the organization. Benjamin *et al.* (1985) found that in 1983, sixty percent of the chief IT executives surveyed were positioned within two levels of the CEO and 20% reported directly to the CEO. A 1968 survey by Davis (1974) reported that only 32% were within two levels from the CEO and 12% reported directly to the CEO.

The nature of services and applications provided by the information systems group is also believed to have changed over time. The production and installation of home grown systems has to some extent given way in priority to the provision of services such as education, consultancy, and package evaluation (Benjamin *et al.*, 1985). The new, strategic applications also tend to be targeted at the customer or the distribution channel rather than on systems for internal efficiency. For industries where information is itself a product, we would expect to see an increasing number of IT applications that pertain directly to the product. Such differences, if in fact true, should be reflected in the events discussed by the CEO in the annual report.

Winners versus losers

The view that industry leaders, or 'winners', will make more aggressive use of IT than 'losers' is at the heart of the argument promoting IT for competitive advantage. We hoped to verify this assumption by relating the firm's performance with the extent to which IT was mentioned in the CEO's letter to shareholders. Although some studies (e.g. PIMS, 1984) have found that high performing companies allocate a significantly greater proportion of their revenues to IT expenditures than companies with lower performance, there is little empirical evidence to conclude that the existence of IT vision or the extensive use of IT increases organizational performance. The lack of evidence is largely due to the nonexistence of measures to assess IT impact. Even within a single industry, e.g. airlines, it is very difficult to directly link changes in a competitive position to particular investments in IT (Copeland and McKenney, 1988). The CEO's views might, however, be considered as one possible surrogate measure for IT impact on the organizational and industry level. If events related to IT have been noticed by the CEO, and discussed and tied to strategy in the Chairman's letter, strategic IT may have had some positive impact on organizational performance and position in the market. Hence, we expected that in those firms where strategic IT has had a notable impact on performance, the Chairman's letter was likely to focus on IT issues.

Methodology

The annual report's letter to the shareholders presents a modest opportunity to examine the CEO's views about IT, and to cast some light on the above research questions. Whether the letters actually represent the true beliefs of the CEO, or complete and accurate statements of past corporate behaviors or future intentions, is unknown and somewhat irrelevant given that the letters are largely undeniable by the CEO. For this exploratory research then, the letters can effectively serve as rough surrogates for CEOs' views and the status of IT in the organization. In this section we describe how the Chairman's letters were used in the study.[5]

---

[5] Recently, several papers have been published in the *Administrative Science Quarterly* that have used CEO's letters as the primary source of data on corporate strategy and reasoning (see Bettman and Weitz, 1983; Salancik and Meindl, 1984).

Preliminary methodology check

The first step was a simple validation of the methodology. If the Chairman's letter to the stockholders was to serve as a surrogate measure of the Chairman's actual views about IT, then we required reassurance that annual reports were a reasonable source of such statements. To test this assumption, we identified 10 firms that had developed systems which had become popular success stories as strategic applications of IT, and whose CEOs were known to have made public statements about applications. The firms and the applications are listed in Appendix A. For each firm we examined annual reports from 1982–1987, looking for some mention of the application in the Chairman's letter.

As Appendix A shows, the results were reassuring. CEOs' letters from all of the ten organizations examined included statements of the application and its organizational implications in one or more annual reports during the years examined. The Chairman's letter seemed to be a reasonable source of information on CEOs' views about IT, at least for the success stories.

Sample selection

A total of eighty-eight firms were included in the main study – the firms were selected from four industries including banking, publishing, petroleum, and retailing. Industries were selected so as to provide a wide diversity of IT potential. We contend that banking is an industry whose product, like publishing, is information; they are long time users of IT, invest a large percentage of their operating budgets on IT, and are generally considered to be strategic users of IT (Cash *et al.*, 1988). Retailers are increasingly dependent on cost-effective, reliable IT operations. Nonetheless, retailers generally do not use information within their products and have only recently begun to aggressively use the massive point-of-purchase data at their disposal, to fine tune their operations. Publishing has long been a user of IT in support of the production and delivery process (e.g. electronic editing and composition systems, satellite transmission), but recently has begun to move toward platforms based on emerging information technologies (e.g. videotext, CD-Rom) as vehicles for packaging information products. Petroleum, with the exception of oil exploration, seems to rely little on strategic IT, using it instead primarily as a back office, support tool. Johnston and Carrico (1988), for instance, note that, 'the executives in the oil . . . companies do not perceive as much information content in the key relationships, have products whose value is not as strictly time dependent, and do not perceive competitive pressures that dictate an all-out effort to build IT advantages' (p.41).

In each industry 'winners' and 'losers' were initially selected based on growth in revenues over the years from 1982 to 1987. The choice of sales growth as an indicator of a firm's success is a debatable one. Bettman and Weitz (1983), however, felt that revenue growth 'was the most visible and easily interpretable indicator', and 'depends on accounting conventions to a lesser extent that other potential indicators' (p.176). Revenue figures, and total assets in case of banks, were obtained from the Fortune 500 lists appearing in special issues of *Fortune* in 1983 through 1988.[6,7] Firms selected were among Fortune 500 firms for the last six years.[8] The twelve firms with the greatest average annual growth in a given industry over the six years were selected as the 'winners' while the thirteen with the least growth were the 'losers'. The firms in each industry are shown in Appendix B.

Content analysis of letters

Annual reports were obtained for each of the firms for the years 1982 through 1987, resulting in 528 reports.[9] The 1982–1987 period was selected because it includes the years in which 'information for competitive advantage' was discovered and enshrined by the business and academic press. The Chairman's letter was copied, read, and all words related to IT were underlined. The analysis proceeded following the general principles put forth by Krippendorff (1980) for the content analysis method. An IT-related phrase was a unit of analysis and was defined as an instance of a word or a set of words that, 'Discusses the management, application, investment, organization of computer, communications, or office technology for improving or modifying operations, establishing linkages with customers, supplies, competitors, channel partners, or the development of new products.' Each IT-related phrase referred to only one instance of an IT-related event, opportunity, or problem. An initial test with a subset of reports found that two readers were in near 97% agreement concerning the identification of IT related phrases. Therefore this task was subsequently carried out by a single reader.

46.9 percent of the 1982–1987 annual reports were found to have one or more IT-related phrases. For these 243 reports a rater counted up the total number of IT-related phrases. Two raters, who were unfamiliar with the purpose of the study, independently coded each of the IT-related phrases using the coding scheme shown in Appendix C.

[6] Caution must be used in cross-industry comparisons because of the different criterion (assets versus revenue) used to select banks versus the firms in the other three industries.

[7] *Fortune* lists the company only if more than 50% of their operating revenues come from industry-related activities; the companies are listed in Fortune 500 on the basis of their revenues; only public firms are ranked.

[8] In petroleum annual reports for only 22 out of the 25 companies were available. The eleven highest growth petroleum companies that issued annual reports constituted the winners; the eleven lowest growth firms that issued annual reports were treated as the losers. Publishing had only sixteen Fortune 500 companies in total. The eight with the highest growth were declared as the winners; the eight with the lowest growth were the losers.

[9] We were unable to obtain 10 of the 528 letters to shareholders. Thus the actual sample was 518 letters.

Given the exploratory and descriptive nature of the study, we sought a coding scheme that captured the main IT issues discussed by CEOs in annual reports while providing evidence to examine the questions and propositions put forth in the previous section. The coding scheme was empirically derived based on a set of recent annual reports from banks and retailers in the UK. The coding scheme had two levels, each capturing a different aspect of the IT-related phrase: (1) the context in which IT was discussed in the letter (financial performance, major event of the year, or future outlook), and (2) the nature of IT investment/problem/opportunity expressed (increase in general IT expenses, investment in IT to offer new products, investment in IT to change a production or service process, IT executive change, consolidation of systems, etc.). The context of each IT-related investment/problem/opportunity discussed by the CEO was coded, in keeping with Salancik and Meindl's (1984) warning that views are context dependent. Three sets of pilot data were used to test and refine the coding scheme.

Two raters were trained using the above mentioned sample of UK annual reports. Disagreements between the raters on the training sample were discussed and resolved before the raters moved on to the study sample. To assess the degree of agreement in the study sample, the raters' responses were statistically compared and found to be acceptable.[10] The ratings of the rater who was more knowledgeable in corporate management and strategy were used in the subsequent analysis.

Final methodology check

We also conducted a field validation of the methodology to assure that there is indeed a relationship between the CEO letter content and both the CEO's views of IT and the strategic use of IT within the organization. We sent a questionnaire to the senior IT executive in each of the 88 companies. The questionnaire asked them to evaluate their CEO's views about IT and to rate the state of IT in the organization. Each company in the sample was contacted via telephone to obtain the name of the most senior IT executive in the firm. Fifty-six IT executives contacted responded.

Encouraging support was found for the use of CEO letters to study the information technology phenomenon. Table 12.1 shows that IT executives' responses to the question of 'How important does your CEO perceive IT to be for your firm?' significantly correlated with the number of IT-related phrases

[10] The phrases were compiled into an agreement matrix, and the proportion of agreement and the Kappa Coefficient were calculated. The raw proportion of agreement was 0.92 for Level 1 codes and 0.90 for Level 2 codes. The Kappa Coefficient, which measures the proportion of agreement between raters after agreement which can be attributed to chance has been removed (Cohen, 1960), was 0.84 and 0.86, respectively. These reliabilities are very comparable to those reported in Bettman and Weitz (1983) and Salancik and Meindl (1984).

Table 12.1 *Correlation between the field questionnaire responses and the IT-related phrases in CEO letters*

Field questionnaire	IT-related phrases	
	1987 CEO letter	1986 CEO letter
CEO perceived importance of IT for the firm	0.35	0.33
	($p < 0.01$)	($p < 0.05$)
Company's current strategic use of IT	0.40	0.39
	($p < 0.01$)	($p < 0.01$)

All statistics are Pearson Product Moment Correlation Coefficients.

in the company's 1987 and 1986 Chairman's letters. The 6-point Likert-like scale for the question ranged from 'no concern for IT' to 'IT is single most critical factor for firm'. A significant correlation was also found between the IT-related phrases and the responses to the question of 'How would you describe your firm's use of information technology?'. The latter question had a 5-point scale that ranged from 'laggard' to 'industry leader'. The results of the methodology check were reassuring given that independent responses on the CEO views were obtained from the IT executive rather than the CEO's office (for more details on the survey, see Jarvenpaa and Ives, 1989).

Results

Table 12.2 shows a breakdown, by industry, of the percentage of companies and the percentage of 1982–1987 letters in which the chief executive mentioned information technology to the stockholders. Over 90% of the companies in banking, publishing, and retailing had included IT-related phrases in the Chairman's letter at least once during the 1982–1987 timeframe. However, in keeping with the expectations of Johnston and Carrico (1988), IT was rarely mentioned in the petroleum industry. Table 12.3 shows the average number of phrases per chairman's letter for those letters that had references to IT. As a basis for comparison, in his Chairman's letter to the 1987 annual report for the Midland Group, Sir Kit McMahon used 16 phrases to discuss information technology, far more than the three phrase average for his U.S. banking peers who chose to discuss IT. Publishing led the four industries, although petroleum, lagging far behind, was the only industry to statistically differ from the other three.

Content analysis of the IT-related phrases demonstrated that CEOs are far more likely to discuss IT in the context of the past year's events rather than

Table 12.2   *Percentage of companies and letters with IT-related phrases during 1982–1987*

Industry	Companies with IT-related phrases	Letters with IT-related phrases
Banking	92%	53%
Publishing	94%	64%
Petroleum	50%	16%
Retailing	92%	57%

Table 12.3   *Mean number of IT-related phrases in letters with IT phrases during 1982–1987*

	(*No. of companies*)	*Letters with IT phrases* ($n = 243$)	
		Mean	*Std*
Total	(88)	3.1	2.5
Banking	(25)	3.3	2.8
Publishing	(16)	3.9	2.7
Petroleum	(22)	1.3	0.9
Retailing	(25)	2.8	1.9

they are to link IT to either financial performance or future events. From Table 12.4 we see that 70% of the IT-related phrases focused on IT activities over the previous year ('we equipped 305 stores with checkstand scanning systems' [Safeway, 1983]) while a relatively small, 8%, placed IT statements within a financial context ('The information systems arm ... bringing in more than $30 million in annual revenues' [Norwest, 1986]). Where financial performance was linked to statements about IT, as at Norwest, it was generally done in a favorable way. Of the eighteen phrases that included unfavorable statements about IT investments, many represented major strategic failures that shareholders would have already learned about from other sources ('The 1982 loss was due mainly to costs associated with *The New York Times* Information System' [*The New York Times*, 1982]). Less costly failures, including some such as home banking or videodisk that had been enthusiastically endorsed in previous annual reports, were generally allowed to slide into obscurity with no further notice in the report.

The phrases reporting the major IT events of the year dealt mostly with new IT-related products ('NCNB became the first bank to offer home banking

Table 12.4   *Context and nature of IT-related phrases and attributions to strategy*

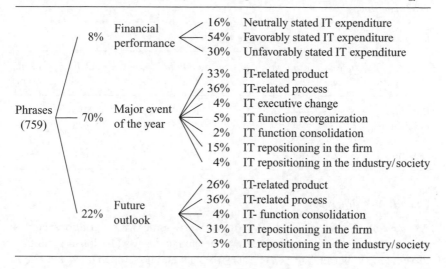

	16%	Neutrally stated IT expenditure
8% Financial performance	54%	Favorably stated IT expenditure
	30%	Unfavorably stated IT expenditure
	33%	IT-related product
	36%	IT-related process
	4%	IT executive change
Phrases (759) 70% Major event of the year	5%	IT function reorganization
	2%	IT function consolidation
	15%	IT repositioning in the firm
	4%	IT repositioning in the industry/society
	26%	IT-related product
	36%	IT-related process
22% Future outlook	4%	IT- function consolidation
	31%	IT repositioning in the firm
	3%	IT repositioning in the industry/society

in North Carolina' [1985]), production processes ('Our electronic pre-press system was expanded with the installation of satellite receiving earth stations . . .' [Donnelly, 1983]), or umbrella statements about the increasing importance of IT (i.e. repositioning) in the firm ('. . . We view technology as the key to our delivery of both wholesale and retail banking products and services' [First Interstate, 1985]). A few announcements of executive changes were included in the letters, and announcements of corporate reorganizations and consolidations were occasionally found ('We continue to improve our efficiency and productivity through the consolidation of backroom processing activities in centralized locations . . .' [Bank of America, 1985]). Industry- or society-wide implications of technology were discussed in some letters ('How can we invest in a proven technology that I am certain can fill the void in classrooms left by the miserable failure of computers as teaching instruments?' [Harcourt, 1985]).

The research questions described previously predicted that the CEO's perspective on information technology, as reflected in the letters to the shareholders, would vary from industry to industry, over time, and between successful and less successful firms. The following sections describe the results in each of these three areas.

Industry differences

There were significant industry differences in the quantity of IT phrases as well as in the nature of those phrases.

Table 12.5 *Consistency with which IT was mentioned by companies during 1982–1987 timeframe*

Industry	Percentage of companies with IT phrases						
	None in 6 years	*Only in 1 yr*	*Only in 2 yrs*	*Only in 3 yrs*	*Only in 4 yrs*	*Only in 5 yrs*	*In all 6 yrs*
Banking	8%	8%	20%	16%	24%	24%	0%
Publishing	6%	19%	6%	13%	13%	6%	37%
Petroleum	50%	27%	9%	9%	0%	5%	0%
Retailing	8%	20%	4%	16%	16%	20%	16%

Quantitative differences

As was evident from Table 12.2, there were some wide variations across industry in the number of chairmen who elected to discuss IT. Not surprisingly, there were similar industry differences in what and how much they said about IT, if they elected to say anything at all. Table 12.5 shows, by industry, the number of companies who never mentioned IT from 1982–1987, the number who mentioned it only one year, the number who mentioned it twice during 1982–1987, and so on. Over 60% of the companies in retailing, banking, and publishing discussed IT in at least half of their annual reports. In petroleum only one of 22 firms mentioned IT in more than half of their 1982–1987 annual reports, and that consisted of a set of very similar short statements concerning credit card processing that appeared in five successive letters to shareholders (e.g. 'Automating credit transactions is a major part of our effort to minimize costs and serve customers more effficietly' [Shell Oil, 1983]).

Notably, industry differences also existed in terms of the length of the letter. On average, the letter in retailing was 17 paragraphs long, 21 in publishing, 25 in banking, and 26 in petroleum. But what percentage of the letters was actually devoted to IT rather than other topics? IT-related phrases accounted for 2% of the letter (of those which discussed IT) in petroleum, 6 percent in retailing, 8 percent in banking, and 11 percent in publishing. Reassuringly, a comparison of the percentage of the chairmen's letters devoted to IT and the total phrases devoted to IT (from Table 12.3) produced similar results, with petroleum at the bottom and publishing at the top of both lists.

Content differences

Perhaps more interesting, however, are the industry differences in the topics addressed. The results of the analysis of phrases regarding financial performance, displayed in Table 12.6, are interesting though they do not reach

Table 12.6   *Total number of phrases in content categories during 1982–1987*

Content categories	Industry			
	Banking	Publishing	Petroleum	Retailing
Financial performance	15	28	0	18
Neutrally stated IT expenditure	1	4	0	5
Favorably stated IT expenditure	5	18	0	10
Unfavorably stated IT expenditure	9	6	0	3
Major event of the year	203	153	21	153
IT related product	83	70	3	13
IT related process	40	43	10	96
IT executive change	3	3	2	14
IT function reorganization	12	7	2	6
IT function consolidation	9	0	0	0
IT repositioning in the firm	45	20	1	20
IT repositioning in the industry or society	7	9	1	4
Other	4	1	2	0
Future outlook	43	55	7	64
IT related product	13	24	0	9
IT related process	10	10	4	39
IT executive change	0	0	0	0
IT function reorganization	0	0	0	0
IT function consolidation	3	0	1	0
IT repositioning in the firm	17	18	1	15
IT repositioning in the industry or society	0	3	1	1

statistical significance.[11] Here we see that banks had proportionally more IT expenditures being described as a burden to the company ('non interest expenses rose 24% during 1984, this was primarily due to increases in . . . systems investments' [First Chicago, 1984]), while retailers and publishers were more inclined to describe IT investments as contributing to profitability.

Generally, the results in Table 12.6 were in keeping with the expectations put forth in the strategic IT literature. Banks and publishers during 1982–1987 had more IT phrases pertaining to the firm's products rather than to the production processes, both in describing the past year's activities and future outlook. Retailers focused IT-related phrases on operations rather than on

[11] The raw data for all dependent variables were transformed to a square root scale to achieve the homogeneity of the variances for the variables across industries and years, a necessary precondition for the use of analysis of variance (ANOVA).

products (exceptions included Toy's-'R-Us's interest in computer-based toys). This pattern held for the past year's events and future outlook. Retailers were more likely than other industries to use the shareholders' letter as a vehicle for announcing IT executive changes. But the retailers were joined by the publishers and bankers in using the chairman's letter to make announcements about the repositioning of IT within the firm. Such repositioning phrases were usually stated either in terms of past or present events rather than future outlook. Bankers were significantly more likely to discuss the reorganization or consolidation of IT functions that had occurred within the year. Publishing had more overall statements on the implications of IT in industry and society than the other three industries.

The industry differences must be viewed with caution, however, as the shareholders' letter seems to be used in different ways by different industries. For instance, a retailing executive explained to us that retailers have long used their shareholders' letter to confer star status on their managing executives. He, therefore, found it unsurprising that retailing mentioned the promotion of an executive more often than other industries, but he noted that it has only been in recent years that IT executives had begun to be so honored.

In a subsequent analysis we also looked at the specific types of technology and applications mentioned by chief executives to understand the types of IT investments that capture the CEO's attention and are considered significant enough to report to shareholders. Industry differences here were strong. Table 12.7 presents the technologies and applications that were mentioned by the chief executives for at least three firms in a given industry. It is noteworthy that, except in petroleum, corporate networks and satellites were among the four most frequently mentioned technologies in letters to the shareholders. In comparison, the recently much ballyhooed applications of 'expert systems' did not appear a single time in the letters of any of the industries, although applications have been reported in other pubic sources for all four industries. *Business data processing systems* was the only entry to appear on all four lists, and was number one in both the petroleum and retailing industries. Bread and butter applications such as inventory control (retailing), credit card processing (petroleum), and advertising and circulation (publishing) continue to attract senior management attention.

Time differences

As Figure 12.1 demonstrates, we did not find the increase we had expected in the number of phrases devoted to IT as we moved from 1982 to 1987. In fact, if the average phrases from the years of 1982 and 1983 are compared with those from 1986 and 1987, we see a decline. The decrease is mainly attributable to the banking industry, where the average for 1986–1987 is 37% lower than that for 1982–1983. The other industries held essentially the same over

Table 12.7 *Types of IT-technologies and applications mentioned in letters*

Industry	Technology/Application	Letters mentioning technology	Companies mentioning technology
Banking	ATM	29	13
(25 firms)	Integrated retail banking system	12	10
	Corporate networks and satellite	11	8
	Home banking	10	8
	Data processing services	9	7
	Treasury management system	9	7
	Point-of-sale	9	5
	Management info system	5	5
	Business DP system	5	4
	Electronic funds transfer	5	4
Publishing	Online information and database services	26	9
(16 firms)	Corporate networks and satellite	22	11
	Electronic production systems	14	12
	Videotext	11	6
	CD-ROM	5	3
	Business DP systems	3	3
Petroleum	Business DP systems	9	3
(22 firms)	Production automation	4	4
Retailing	Business DP systems	28	12
(25 firms)	Optical scanning	24	9
	Point-of-sale	15	10
	Corporate networks and satellite	14	6
	Management info systems	12	8
	Instore computers	8	4

time, except that in 1982 publishing had considerably more IT-related phrases than in any subsequent year (primarily due to that industry's fascination with videotext, which peaked in 1982). Comparisons of phrase content over the 1982 to 1987 timeframe revealed no significant differences.

These results ran counter to our expectations and certainly flew in the face of the literature boasting both the successes and value of strategic information systems. Our initial analysis suggested that the position of IT in the organizations as reflected in the chief executives' letters to the shareholders had not changed, or perhaps had deteriorated somewhat, during the 1982–1987 timeframe. Perhaps the time frame we examined had been too short to adequately capture the changes that had occurred in CEOs' perceptions concerning IT.

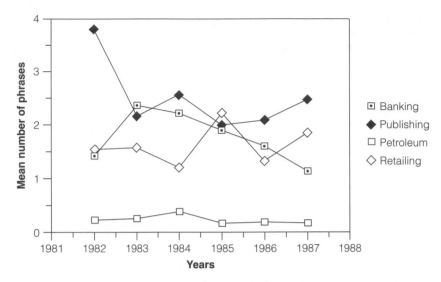

Figure 12.1   *Mean number of IT-related phrases over 1982–1987 timeframe*

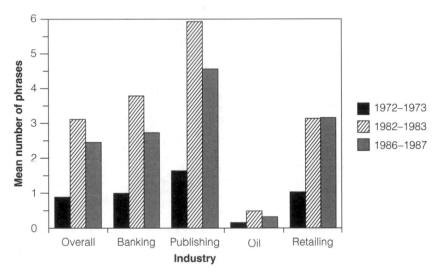

Figure 12.2   *Mean number of IT-related phrases in 1972–1973, 1982–1983, and 1986–1987*

Consequently we decided to also examine the letters from 1972 and 1973 and to compare those with the later set.

Figure 12.2 compares, by industry, the average number of phrases in which the Chief Executive discussed IT for the years of 1972–1973, 1982–1983, and 1986–1987. From Figure 12.2 it is apparent that there have been dramatic

Table 12.8 *Correlation between a firm's yearly profits as a percentage of sales and CEO letter phrases**

	CEOs' letters for 88 companies during 1982–1987			
	Total no. of phrases	No. on financial performance	No. on major event of the year	No. on future outlook
Firm yearly net profits as a percentage of sales	0.20[†]	0.15[†]	0.15[†]	16[†]

* All statistics are Pearson Product Moment Correlation Coefficients.
[†] Significance level 0.01.

increases in the number of phrases that CEOs have devoted to IT in the last 15 years. The most recent data suggests, however, that this attention to IT may have peaked or even begun to decline in the industries examined.

Winners versus losers

We initially selected the industry 'winners' and 'losers' on the basis of average annual growth in revenues over the years from 1982–1987. This selection was done on the basis of previous research (Bettman and Weitz, 1983) which argued that the choice of sales growth as an indicator of a firm's success is the most visible and interpretable indicator, and is less influenced by accounting conventions than other potential indicators. An analysis of total IT-related phrases and the content of IT-related phrases in the four industries found no relationship with the average annual growth of the firms over the 1982–1987 timeframe.

Our original approach to categorizing winners and losers was questionable, given the six-year time horizon. As the time horizon lengthens, the sensitivity of profits to accounting conventions tends to dissipate, while the bias introduced by firms electing to grow through acquisition increases. Hence, we decided to examine whether the firm's yearly profits as a percentage of revenues (or total assets, in the case of banks) were related to the number of IT-related phrases and the content of the IT-related phrases in letters to shareholders. The results for our sample of 88 companies, shown in Table 12.8, were encouraging. Total phrases within the CEO's letter were significantly related to profitability – the more the CEO talked about IT the better the firms's profitability. An analysis within industries showed that the significance of the relationship was strong ($p < 0.01$), except in retailing ($p < 0.1$). The correlation coefficients for banking, publishing, petroleum, and retailing were 0.21, 0.22, 0.26, and 0.14 respectively. However, caution is necessary in making comparisons across industries, because of the use of assets rather than sales in determining the profitability of banks. Numerous differences were evident among the content of the phrases – again, with the direction of the relationship favoring the more profitable firms. Moreover, the results are probably somewhat conservative given that the firms selected for inclusion in the study were chosen on the basis of strong or weak revenue growth rather than profits.

Still, the correlational analysis depicted in Table 12.8 permits no inferences about causality. Some critics may convincingly argue that profitable firms have more money to spend and therefore elect to invest more on, and talk more about, fashionable information technology initiatives. Therefore, we conducted two lagged analyses on the profitability data. In the first we compared profits in one year (ranging from 1982 to 1985) with total IT-related phrases for two subsequent years (ranging in from 1983–1987). In the second we reversed the procedure, comparing number of phrases for a given year with profits in two subsequent years. The results show a positive correlation between profits and IT-related phrases on both lagged analyses. A slightly stronger relationship between the IT-related phrases and two subsequent years' profits was found (correlation coefficient = 0.23) than between a particular year's profit and two subsequent years' phrases on IT (correlation coefficient = 0.17). The data hence suggests that the more the CEOs talked about IT, the higher the company's profits in the future years; but the competing hypothesis – higher profits will cause CEOs to talk more about, and perhaps invest more in, IT during subsequent years – cannot be refuted.

Discussion

Information for strategic advantage has received considerable attention in the general business and information systems literature over the last five years. But what do the leaders of large US business organizations perceive the impact of IT to be, and how do those perceptions vary over time, from industry to industry, and across successful and less successful firms? The current study casts some empirical light on those questions. First, there are clearly a number of senior managers who do not see information technology as a critical issue to present to the shareholders. Eighty-four percent of CEOs' letters in the petroleum industry never mentioned IT over the 1982–1987 timeframe; even in banking, long a bastion of information technology, 8% of the firms and 47% of the letters never refer to IT. Where IT is mentioned, the discussion is often brief – such a letter on average contains three phrases about IT. Still, there are CEOs that enthusiastically discuss IT in their annual reports, and the amount of such discussion has increased since 1972.

The notions of information intensity put forth by Porter and Millar (1985) received limited empirical support. Petroleum, an industry that we characterized as having relatively low information intensity within the product and within the production process, proved to rarely contain references to IT within the CEO's letter to the shareholders. Retailing, where information plays an important role in the production process but a minor one in the product, produced results reflecting the CEOs' focus on information intensity in the production process. Likewise, the letters in banking and publishing mirrored the information intensity predicted for their industry on both the product and the production process.

As we expected, there was an increase in the attention the shareholders' letters devoted to information technology through the 1970's and early 80's. We were surprised, however, to find fewer mentions in the most recent years surveyed. One might hypothesize that IT has recently become a less important agent of change to the CEO. Alternatively, it may have become less necessary to educate an increasingly more sophisticated shareholder concerning the potential of IT initiatives.

The analysis of phrase content also revealed some interesting findings reflecting both changes over time and within particular industries. Both publishing and banking discussed the repositioning of IT within the firm, perhaps highlighting the need within those two industries to increasingly retarget IT initiatives from a focus on the production process to a focus on products. For publishing, in particular, this may reflect a new understanding of the role IT can play in producing new 'knowledge dissemination platforms'. Retailers' increasing use of the prestigious shareholders' letter to note a change in the staffing of the IT function may underscore a new understanding of the potential, strategic role of IT within retailing. This is further supported in that retailing was the single industry in which mentions of IT actually increased in 1986–1987. CEOs of banks, on the other hand, have become less inclined to talk about IT, perhaps reflecting their attention on the recent spate of bank mergers and acquisitions. When bankers do talk about IT, they have become more likely than their colleagues in other industries to view expenditures on IT in an unfavorable light. This may reflect the current drive towards systems-derived economies of scale that are usually expected to result from bank mergers.

Caution is advised in interpreting these results, as there are numerous competing explanations for these findings. For instance, increases in an organization's performance might make IT investments more feasible, or, as noted by Bowman (1978), Bettman and Weitz (1983), and Salancik and Meindl (1984), CEOs of firms that are in trouble have been found to focus their letters on external, uncontrollable or environmental, rather than internal, controllable, events. The letters also tend to be positive, and probably intentionally avoid negative issues whenever possible. Negative statements concerning IT performance probably already have been brought to the attention of the shareholders via the business press. The reader should also note that this sample included large Fortune 500 companies. The size of the organization might influence the CEO's views of IT, IT usage, and the relationship of

IT use and organizational performance. Finally, the uses and length of annual reports vary by industry.

In general the results, characterized by infrequent, brief, and recently decreasing mentions of IT, might give cause to question the strategic information systems concept. But one result, the profitability analysis, can be viewed with some cautious optimism. Organizations in which the CEO talks to the shareholders about IT initiatives appear to do better than those organizations of our sample in which the CEO does not share such information. The results are also tentatively confirming on an industry level. The relationship between profitablity and the number of IT-related phrases was highly significant for the industries except for retailing, where only a weak relationship was found. Perhaps the poor showing for retailing may reflect the industry's position as a relative newcomer to the strategic application of information technology.

A number of previous studies (e.g. Bender, 1987; Cron and Sobol, 1983), as suggested by Weill and Olson (1988), have investigated the relationship between IT investments and corporate performance. None has demonstrated the direction of causality. The current study makes a modest attempt to examine the alternative explanations for the profit/IT investment relationship and finds evidence for a reciprocal relationship. That is, investment in IT may lead to greater profits, and greater profits may, in turn, increase the company's willingness to invest in IT. More work needs to be done in this area, however.

It is notable that technologies and applications that CEOs chose to discuss in their letters to shareholders focused on a firm's life blood (i.e. primary products and production processes), customer linkages, and platforms – not on administrative systems, decision support applications, or facilitative (e.g. 4th generation language, data base, expert systems) technologies. The technologies and applications mentioned might suggest what types of IT investments attract the CEO's attention. The investments discussed appeared to meet one of the following three criteria: (1) an industry fad such as videotext in 1982 or homebanking in 1984, (2) a major cost of doing business such as optical scanners and point-of-sale systems, or (3) new infrastructure or platform that made *new* products or production processes possible (e.g. satellite networks). Interestingly, the letters suggested a disappearance of some industry boundaries that are commonly associated with technologies and applications. For example, a publisher was investing in home banking (Knight Ridder); a retailer (Southland) discussed major investments in ATM networks, while another (JCPenney) was providing a credit checking network for gasoline retailers.

Our findings also suggest that a broad, industry-wide survey of the Chairman's letter to shareholders can provide a number of useful insights for a firm's IT management, such as: (1) strategic IT developments in rival firms, (2) technology developments among lead users of IT, and (3) readiness of suppliers and customers for IT linked vertical partnerships. An analysis of the type of technologies mentioned in the letters of lead users might provide some valuable information for a firm's technology audit as well as the basis for design of educational programs. The chairman's letter also provides IT management with another window with which to observe the CEO's perspective on information technology. Further understanding this perspective may be of some help in framing justifications for investments in technological infrastructure. An executive who has made the transition from IT management to executive management demonstrated to us how an understanding of the senior executive's perspective would have helped him in his IT management position:

> When I was managing IT, I was concerned with such issues as selling my boss on the latest release of IMS. When I got to be the boss, I wanted my IT manager to come to me with ways to turn this organization around – upgrading IMS was the last thing on my mind unless someone could show me how such an upgrade could get us new customers, and then I was all ears.

For the academic reader, this study demonstrates that the CEO's letter to the shareholders presents a useful research tool for analyzing the relationship between strategy and information technology, and also perhaps the relationship between strategy, IT, and organizational performance. Unlike many methodologies used for information systems research, the methodology is replicable and can readily be applied to other industries and other research questions. Moreover, it provides the means to tap the perspectives of executive-level management in a format that is readily available, longitudinal, and somewhat consistent across publicly held firms.

Other sources of secondary data may prove useful for research relating IT and an organization's strategy. Future investigations might use the Profit Impact of Market Strategic (PIMS) program and database (see Buzzell and Gale, 1987) to better understand how information technology impacts corporate strategy and performance. As of mid-1986, the database contained financial, strategic, and market data (for at least 4 years) for more than 2,600 business units. In the field of strategic planning, Wills and Beasly (1982) contend that 'the PIMS program has produced the most comprehensive set of research findings' (p.437). Computerized indices of newspaper and magazine articles can also provide powerful tools for tracking technological innovations through time.

Conclusion

The chapter examined executive managers' views of IT across industries, and the state of IT in those firms. An analysis of CEOs' views of IT is important. The recent literature on executive leadership, and specifically the metamorphosis model by Romanelli and Tushman (1988), maintains that senior executives, via their perceptions and decisions, can and do systematically influence the content and character of organizational activity. The letter to the shareholders by Midland's Sir Kit McMahon, abstracted at the start of this chapter, provides an apt illustration of McMahon's use of IT interventions, both substantive and symbolic, to reorient the organization during low organizational performance and drastic environmental changes. After recognizing earlier in his 1987 Letter that the Midland Group was writing off £916 million in bad loans, McMahon went on to describe with some enthusiasm his hopes for IT and his appointment of a new IT head to the Group's board of directors. The Letter symbolizes McMahon's vision for IT by legitimizing, explaining, and rationalizing the organization's recent investments in IT – investments which he clearly hoped could restore Midland to a state of satisfactory performance.

Finally, transitions in information technology seem to hit industries in waves. Publishing appears to be in the midst of one (electronic publishing), retailing is harvesting the benefits of others (POS, scanning, corporate networks), while banking (ATMs, corporate networks) and petroleum (the operations research models of the late 60's and early 70's) are waiting for a new set of technologies to break around them. Our research tentatively suggests that it is no longer worthwhile to discuss the generic notion of information for competitive advantage. Each technology, and the information transformations which that technology engenders, should be considered on an industry by industry basis.

Appendix A

Company/strategic application	Sample quotes from CEOs' letters
Federal Express/COSMOS	The company's new package tracing system, COSMOS, has set a new standard for the industry. Optical scanners track packages . . . making it possible to provide customers with prompt and accurate information as to the status of their shipments. Cosmos IIB tracking system was phased into operation during 1987. Virtually instantaneous package-status information will be available to all of our customers. This is part of our strategy to give our customers the kind of complete service none of our competitors can match

Company/strategic application	Sample quotes from CEOs' letters
Federal Express/ZapMail	ZapMail is an important new communications service . . . electronic transmission of high-quality duplicates of documents almost anywhere in the country
	The decision to phase out ZapMail was a difficult one
Bergen Brunswig OMNIPhase/Compuphase/ AIM	Our company leads the industry in distribution technology . . . automated systems for order entry and inventory control
	We completed development of Compuphase, a pharmacy computer that will greatly increase the efficiency of the pharmacist by automating numerous tasks
	Due to electronic order entry and other computerized services, our prices are sufficiently competitive
	The latest upgrading of CompuPhase supports prescription processing in pharmacies. Omniphase, the first point-of-sale system marketed by a drug wholesaler, improves management of the pharmacy's non-prescription business. AIM, a third new program, will provide a wide range of management reports and analysis for pharmacies
	The future will belong to strong national companies that use advancing technology to control distribution costs and offer customers continually improving services
Baxter Travenoll/ASAP (developed by AHS)	Within the company and at customer locations, our computerized systems assist in ordering, tracking and managing supplies
	American also offers added value through services such as computer software packages that help hospitals and

Company/strategic application	Sample quotes from CEOs' letters

	laboratories know their true costs. . . . Our network of highly modern distribution centers is linked by the computerized network that has been developed over many years by American
CitiBank/Electronic Banking/Home Banking	. . . 7000 of them [terminals] in our customers' offices or homes-to keep us at the forefront of the industry
	Citicorp's ability to deliver prompt, accurate information electronically to the corporate treasurer's desk, to the consumer's home, or to our account officers in 95 countries . . . is vital part of our ongoing business
	In the emerging financial world, technology and telecommunications are eliminating barriers of time and distance that once isolated national markets . . . symbolic of leadership [in technology] was the last June's launching of Western Union's Westar satellite, which made Citicorp the first financial institution to own its own satellite transponders. . . . To build productivity and service, we continue our support of new systems and electronic banking efforts
Merrill Lynch/Cash Management Account	We believe in backing our staff with the best possible technology . . . such technology simply enhances the value of personalized financial service which requires highly professional account executives
	Our pioneering Cash Management Account . . . we expanded its scope, created a version for business
	Our landmark Cash Management Account, adding a series of new features designed to respond to changing client needs

Company/strategic application	Sample quotes from CEOs' letters
McKesson/Economost	As part of a major program to improve productivity and continually upgrade the quality of our customer services, we are making major expenditures for the expansion of our advanced automated order-entry and other computer-based systems
	Perhaps the single greatest advantage that the McKesson distribution companies enjoy has been – and will continue to be – in computer technology
	Our ability to adapt the Drug Group's 'Econo' computer services and materials handling expertise to office products demonstrates that our systems and skills are clearly applicable to a wide range of distribution businesses
General Electric/Business Information Center	GE began a major business-to-business marketing campaign in 1984 that included the opening of the Business Information Center. Staffed by company experts, the Center helps make GE more accessible and responsive to businesses looking for commercial or industrial products and services
	To be competitive, our service businesses must use the latest technology
American Airlines/SABRE Reservation System	The highlights of 1982 . . . the success of our travel agency automation program
	Our SABRE computer reservation system continues as a principal source of other revenue
	Our great frustration in 1987 was our inability to market SABRE, the finest computer reservations system in the world, to travel agents in Europe
United Airlines/APOLLO Reservation System	Covia markets our Apollo Travel Services computerized travel reservations system and our business-management systems to travel agents and others

Company/strategic application	Sample quotes from CEOs' letters
	United, British Airways, KLM Royal Dutch Airlines and Swissair announce a new venture to provide a computer information and reservations systems for the travel industry in Europe
American Express/Corporate Travel Card, Gold Card Report Credit authorizer's assistant	To remain as a leader in the application of new technologies, ensuring quality service and further advancing productivity

Appendix B: Companies included in the study sample by industry

Banking

BancOne
BankAmerica
Bank of Boston
Barnett Banks of Florida
Chase Manhattan
Citizens and South
Continental Illinois
First Interstate
First Chicago
First City BancCorp
First Union
Irving Bank

J. P. Morgan
Manufacturer's Hanover
Marine Midland
National City BanCorporation
National City Corporation
NBD
NCNB
Norwest
PNC Financial Corp.
Republic of N. Y.
Security Pacific
Sovran
Texas Commerce

Publishing

American Greetings
Deluxe Checks
Donnelly
Dow Jones
Gannett
Harcourt Brace Jovanovich
Knight Ridder
Macmillan

McGraw-Hill
Media General
Meredith
N. Y. Times
Time Inc
Times Mirror
Tribune
Washington Post

Petroleum

Agway	Mobil
Amerada Hess	Murphy Oil
American Petrofina	Pennzoil
Ashland Oil	Phillips
Atlantic Richfield	Shell Oil
Coastal Corp.	Sun
Crown Central	Tenneco
Diamond Shamrock	Texaco
Exxon	Tosco
Kerr McGee	USX
Mapco	Witco

Retailing

Allied	May Department Stores
American Stores	Melville
Best Products	Safeway Stores
Carter-Hawley	Service Merchandise
Dayton-Hudson	Southland
Federated Department Stores	Stop and Shop
F. W. Woolworth	Toys 'R' Us
Great Atlantic & Pacific Tea	Waldbaum
JCPenney	Walgreen
KMart	WalMart Stores
Kroeger	Winn-Dixie Stores
Lucky Stores	Zayre
Marriotts	

Appendix C: Coding scheme (and examples)

A. Overall Quantitative Measures
  # of reports with IT-related phrases.
  # of companies with IT-related phrases.
  # of IT-related phrases.
B. Content Analysis Measures (All examples, where appropriate, are from the Midland Group's 1987 letter to shareholders)

Context of IT phrase (Level 1 codes)	Nature of IT phrase (Level 2 codes)
Financial performance (Definition: review of the financial position of the company and provide explanation for results)	– *Neutrally stated IT expenditure* – *Favorably stated IT expenditure* – *Unfavorably stated IT expenditure*
Major event of the year (Definition: discusses the year's major happenings in the firm and in the industry)	– *Investment in IT to offer products* ('the launch of Telepath a sophisticated treasury workstation') – *Investment in IT to change production or production economics* ('branch cashiers are equipped with automated counter terminals') – *IT executive change* ('we were fortunate to obtain the services of Gene Lockhart as our first director') – *IT reorganization* ('we had an opportunity to reorganize a number of support functions, notably information technology') – *IT consolidation* ('the Group has begun to consolidate and standardize its various data centres') – *IT repositioning in the firm* ('Last year was a landmark year for IT in Midland Group') – *IT repositioning in the industry* or society ('IT is one factor which will progressively determine the basis for competitive success in the banking industry')
Future Outlook (Definition: puts forth future short and long-term activities of the company)	[Same as for 'Major event of the year']

References

Bakos, J. Y. and Treacy, M. E. (1986) Information technology and corporate strategy: a research perspective. *MIS Quart.*, June, 107–119.

Benbasat, I., Dexter, A. S., Drury, D. H. and Goldstein, R. C. (1984) A critique of the stage hypothesis: theory and empirical evidence. *Comm. ACM*, **27**(5), May, 476–485.

Bender, D. (1986) Financial impact of information processing, *J. MIS*, **3**(2), 232–238.

Benjamin, R. I., Dickinson, C. Jr. and Rockart, J. F. (1985) Changing role of the corporate information systems officer. *MIS Quart.*, September, 177–188.

Benjamin, R. I., Rockart, J. F., Scott Morton, M. C. and Wyman, J. (1984) Information technology: a strategic opportunity. *Sloan Management Rev.*, Spring, 3–9.

Bettman, R. J. and Weitz, B. A. (1983) Attributions in the board room: causal reasoning in corporate annual reports. *Administrative Science Quart.*, **28**, 165–183.

Bowman, E. H. (1978) Strategy, annual reports, and alchemy. *California Management Rev.*, **20**(3), Spring, 64–71.

Bowman, E. H. (1984) Content analysis of annual reports for corporate strategy and risk. *Interfaces*, **14**(1), January–February, 61–71.

Brancheau, J. C. and Wetherbe, J. C. (1987) Key issues in information systems management. *MIS Quart.*, **11**(1), March, 23–45.

Buzzell, R. D. and Gale, B. T. (1987) *The PIMS Principles: Linking Strategy to Performance*, The Free Press, New York.

Cash, J. I. Jr. and Konsynski, B. R. (1985) IS redraws competitive boundaries. *Harvard Bus. Rev.*, March–April, 134–142.

Cash, J. I., McFarlan, F. W. and McKenney, J. L. (1988) *Corporate Information Systems Management: The Issues Facing Senior Executives*, Irwin, Homewood, Illinois.

Clemons, E. K. and Kimbrough, S. O. (1996) Information systems, telecommunications, and their effects on industrial organization, *Proc. Seventh Internat. Conf. Information Systems*, San Diego, CA, pp.99–108.

Clemons, E. K. and Row, M. (1988) McKesson Drug Company: a case study of Economost – a strategic information system. *J. Management Information Systems*, **5**(1), Summer, 36–50.

Cohen, J. (1960) A coefficient of agreement for nominal scales. *Educational and Psychological Measurement*, **20**(1), 37–46.

Copeland, D. G. and McKenney, J. L. (1988) Airline reservations systems: lessons from history. *MIS Quart.*, September, 353–370.

Cron, W. and Sobol, M. (1983) The relationship between computerization and performance: a strategy for maximizing economic benefits of computerization. *Information and Management*, **6**, 171–181.

Davis, G. B. (1974) *Management Information Systems*, McGraw-Hill, New York.

Dickson, G. W., Leitheiser, R. L., R. L., Nechis, R. L. and Wetherbe, J. C. (1984) Key information systems issues for the 1980's. *MIS Quart.*, **8**(3), September, 135–148.

Dooley, R. E. and Kanter, J. (1985) Conflict at the top: its impact on the organization. *MIS Quart.*, **9**(1), March, 5–6.

Drury, D. H. (1983) An empirical assessment of the stages of DP growth. *MIS Quart.*, June, 59–70.

Gerstein, M. and Reisman, H. (1982) Creating competitive advantage with computer technology. *J. Business Strategy*, **3**(1), Summer, 53–60.

Gibson, C. F. and Nolan, R. L. (1974) Managing the four stages of EDP growth. *Harvard Bus. Rev.*, January–February, 76–88.

Ginsberg, A. (1988) Measuring and modelling changes in strategy: theoretical foundations and empirical directions. *Strategic Management J.*, **9**, 559–575.

Ives, B. and Learmonth G. P., (1984) The information system as a competitive weapon. *Comm. ACM*, **27**(12), December, 1193–1201.

Ives, B. and Vitale, M. R. (1988) After the sale: leveraging maintenance with information technology. *MIS Quart.*, March, 7–21.

Izzo, J. (1987) A view of tomorrow's systems architecture. *In Embattled Fortress*, Jossey-Bass, San Francisco, CA.

Jarvenpaa, S. L. and Ives, B. (1989) Executive involvement and participation in managing information technology: a model and a field survey. Working Paper, MSIS Department, University of Texas at Austin, March.

Johnston, H. R. and Carrico, S. R. (1988) Developing capabilities to use information strategically. *MIS Quart.*, **12**(1), March, 37–50.

Johnston, H. R. and Vitale, M. R. (1988) Creating competitive advantage with interorganizational information systems. *MIS Quart.*, June, 153–165.

Keen, P. G. W. (1981) Telecommunications and business policy: the coming impacts of communication on management. CISR Working Paper 81, Center for Information Systems Research, Massachusetts Institute of Technology, Cambridge, MA, September.

Keen, P. G. W. (1988) *Competing in Time: Using Telecommunications for Competitive Advantage*, Ballinger Publishing Company, Cambridge, MA.

King, W. R. (1986) Seeking competitive advantage using information-intensive strategies. *Proc. New York University Symposium on Strategic Uses of Information Technology*, May, 11–27.

King, J. L. and Kraemer, K. L. (1984) Evolution and organizational information systems: an assessment of Nolan's stage model. *Comm. ACM*, **27**(5), 466–475.

Krippendorff, K. (1980) *Content Analysis: An Introduction to Its Methodology*, Sage Publications, Beverly Hills, CA.

Parsons, G. L. (1984) Information technology: a new competitive advantage. *Sloan Management Rev.*, Fall, 3–26.

Pfeffer, J. (1981) Management as symbolic action: the creation and maintenance of organizational paradigms. *In Research in Organizational Behavior*, Vol. 3 (eds Cummings L. L. and Staw B. M.), JAI Press Inc., Greenwich Connecticut, 1–52.

PIMS Program (1984) *Management Productivity and Information Techno-logy*, The Strategic Planning Institute, Cambridge, Mass.

Porter, M. E. and Millar, V. E. (1985) How information gives you competit-ive advantage. *Harvard Bus. Rev.*, July–August, 149–160.

Reich, B. H. and Benbasat, I. (1988) An empirical investigation of factors influ-encing the success of customer-oriented strategic systems. Working paper 88-MIS-010, Faculty of Commerce and Business Administration, The University of British Columbia, Vancouver, Canada, May.

Rockart, J. F. (1988) The line takes the leadership – IS management in a wired society. *Sloan Management Rev.*, Summer, 57–64.

Romanelli, E. and Tushman, M. L. (1988) Executive leadership and organiza-tional outcomes: an evolutionary perspective. *In The Executive Effect: Concepts and Methods for Studying Top Managers* (ed. Hambrick D. C.), JAI Press, Inc., Greenwich, Connecticut.

Runge, D. A. (1985) Using telecommunications for competitive advantage. Unpublished doctoral dissertation, Oxford University.

Salancik, G. R. and Meindl, J. R. (1984) Corporate attributions as strategic illusions of management control. *Administrative Science Quart.*, **29**, 238–254.

Weill, P. and Olson, M. H. (1988) Managing investment in information technology: mini-case examples and implications. Working Paper, Graduate School of Business Administration, New York University, July.

Wills, L. A. and Beasly, J. E. (1982) The use of strategic planning techniques in the United Kingdom. *OMEGA*, **10**, 433–440.

Wiseman, C. (1985) Competitive advantage and information technology. *Bankers Magazine*, **168**(5), September–October, 55–59.

Questions for discussion

1 Why is the CEO's perspective of IT important? At what stages is it most important?

2 The authors suggest that IT may be more important in some industries than others. Give examples of industries where IT is critical and of indus-tries where IT appears less critical. Try to classify the industries in a meaningful way.

3 Distinguish between the concepts of strategic information systems and IT as a tool for corporate strategy.

4   The authors assume that 'those firms where strategic IT has had a notable impact on performance, the chairman's letter was likely to focus on IT issues.' Do you agree with this assumption?

5   As an exercise, analyze an organisation's annual report of your choice for references to IT. What are the gaps? To what extent do you believe (on this evidence) that the organisation's business and IT strategies are aligned?

6   Consider the authors' assumption of industries likely to be advanced users of IT: would you agree today with the assessment that the financial sector is ahead of retailing, which in turn leads publishing and petroleum in use of IT?

7   Look at Table 12.7. Consider how this might be different today.

8   Consider the statement: 'this attention to IT may have peaked or even begun to decline in the industries examined'. Do you agree or disagree with this conclusion?

13 Measuring the Information Systems–Business Strategy Relationship

Measuring the linkage between business and information technology objectives

B. H. Reich and I. Benbasat

The establishment of linkage between business and information technology objectives has consistently been reported as one of the key concerns of information systems (IS) managers. The two objectives of this chapter are: (1) to clarify the nature of the linkage construct, and (2) to report on a project that developed and tested measures of the social dimension of linkage. According to our research, the linkage construct has two dimensions:

1 *Intellectual*. The content of information technology and business plans are internally consistent and externally valid.
2 *Social*. The IS and business executives understand each others' objectives and plans.

We conducted a study of measurement issues associated with the *social* dimension of linkage. The following candidate measures of linkage were examined:

1 Cross references between written business and information technology plans.
2 IS and business executives' mutual understanding of each others' current objectives.
3 Congruence between IS and business executives' long-term visions for information technology deployment.
4 Executives' self-reported rating of linkage.

Data were collected from 10 business units in three large Canadian life insurance companies. In addition to examining written documents such as strategic plans and minutes of steering committee meetings, extensive interviews were conducted with information systems and business unit executives. Based on this data, understanding of current objectives and shared vision for the utilization of information technology are proposed as the most promising potential measures for short- and long-term aspects of the social dimension of linkage, respectively. With some precautions, self-reports may also be used as a surrogate measure for short-term linkage.

Introduction

In recent surveys of information systems and business managers (Galliers *et al.*, 1994; Index Group, 1988; Niederman *et al.*, 1991), information technology (IT) planning has consistently been rated as one of their most important concerns. A review of the empirical literature reveals that one issue, **the linkage of IS plans with organizational objectives**, has been among the top problems reported by information systems (IS) managers and business executives (*Computerworld*, 1994; Galliers, 1987; Lederer and Mendelow, 1986).

In a broader sense, information technology management can be conceptualized as a problem of coordinating the relationship between the business domain and the IT domain (Sambamurthy and Zmud, 1992). In this context, IS planning is only one of several mechanisms that can be utilized to accomplish this task. To date, the literature has lacked a comprehensive treatment of this issue, which we have labelled 'linkage'.*

Although the need for linkage has been well recognized (Parker *et al.*, 1989) and companies report low success rates in attaining it (Conrath *et al.*, 1992; Earl, 1987; Galliers, 1987), there are few studies of how companies perceive the linkage issue or how they actually organize and act to achieve it. Consequently, we conducted research to understand the meaning and dimensions of the linkage construct.†

The two objectives of this chapter are: (1) to clarify the nature of the **linkage construct**, and (2) to report on a project that developed and tested measures of the **social dimension** of the linkage construct. Our long-term goal is to develop a clear understanding of linkage and how it is achieved in order to aid organizations whose ability to harness the power of IT is critical to their

---

* In addition to 'linkage', several other terms are used in the literature – *alignment* (Galliers, 1987; Henderson and Venkatraman, 1992; Parker *et al.*, 1989), *fit* (Das *et al.*, 1991; Venkatraman, 1989), and *coordination* (Lederer and Mendelow, 1989). Because the underlying concepts are very similar, we do not distinguish between them and use 'linkage' exclusively.
† A related study of the factors influencing the achievement of linkage is described in Reich and Benbasat (1994) and Reich (1993).

success. Development of valid and reliable instruments to be used in large-scale surveys is an important step toward this goal.

The next section of this chapter defines and discusses the linkage construct. The following sections describe the research design and discuss the candidate measures used to evaluate the level of linkage in an organization, respectively. The subsequent section presents the results, and the final section discusses the implications of our findings for researchers and practitioners.

The linkage construct: definitions and dimensions

In order to develop a comprehensive view of linkage, we: (1) defined a broad band of connections between IT and business, from short-term plans to long-term vision, (2) differentiated between the *cause* and *outcome* views of linkage, and (3) distinguished between the *intellectual* and *social* dimensions of linkage. The result of each of these activities is described below.

In the IT literature, the concept of linkage emanates from an IT planning perspective. Several authors have suggested that IT plans should be linked to other artifacts in business, such as business plans (Conrath *et al.*, 1992; Lederer and Mendelow, 1986), business strategies (Pyburn, 1983) or business objectives (Galliers, 1987; Zviran, 1990).

Because the IT literature is not consistent in describing what the IT plans should be linked to, this study includes the broadest possible set of linkages between the IS function and the business. Our preliminary definition of link age is '**the degree to which the IT mission, objectives, and plans support and are supported by the business mission, objectives, and plans.**' In this definition, 'objectives' refers to the goals and the strategies of an organizational unit. This definition is further developed in the next two sections.

Distinguishing causes from effects in linkage

In the IT literature, there has been little distinction between linkage as an organizational *process* or as an *outcome* of these processes. In our view, certain organizational processes (e.g. communication, planning) lead to the state of 'being linked'. We therefore consider the organizational processes as potential *causes* of linkage and linkage as the *effect*.

The first attempt to dimensionalize linkage is found in the accounting literature. Shank *et al.* (1973) suggest that business plans and budgets could be tightly or loosely linked, depending on three characteristics: (1) *content* linkage between the plans and budgets, (2) *timing* linkage between the planning and budgeting systems, and (3) *organizational* linkage between the people doing the planning and budgeting. These three dimensions were adopted by IT researchers (Lederer and Mendelow, 1989), who stated that 'coordination . . . can be achieved in three dimensions – content, timing and personnel'. Using the cause/effect distinction, the content dimension is the effect (i.e. linkage), and the timing and organizational dimensions are potential causes of linkage.

The multiple items used to measure linkage in a large US study (Cresap, McCormick, and Paget Co., 1983) can also be partitioned into causes and effects. These items are:

1   The business plan states information systems needs.
2   The IS plan makes reference to items in the business plans.
3   IS plans are closely checked against business plans.
4   Line and staff managers participate actively in IS planning.
5   Business and IS planning calendars are carefully synchronized.

Using our definition, the first two items measure linkage, and the last three are among the causes of linkage.

Intellectual and social dimensions of linkage

Horovitz (1984) made an important distinction between the intellectual and social dimensions of the process of strategic business planning. In the Horovitz model, the intellectual dimension refers to the particular methodologies, techniques, and data used in the formulation of strategy. The social dimension refers to factors such as the choice of actors, their degree of involvement, and the methods of communication and decision making. By applying this distinction to linkage and focusing on linkage as a resultant state, two separate dimensions of linkage are identified. The intellectual dimension of linkage is the state in which IT and business objectives are consistent and valid. The social dimension is the state in which business and IS executives in an organizational unit understand and are committed to each other's mission, objectives, and plans.

Potentially promising strategies and plans may be poorly executed or even subverted because organizational actors are not aware of or are not committed to them (i.e. a low level of the social dimension of linkage). On the other hand, perfect implementation of a flawed plan (e.g. a low level of the intellectual dimension of linkage) may create suboptimal results. It seems that both dimensions, intellectual and social, are necessary for an organization to make full use of IT in support of, or as a catalyst for, business strategy.

By placing the dimensions of linkage on one axis and the cause and effect distinction on another, the result is a framework (Table 13.1) to guide the study of linkage.

The intellectual dimension of linkage

Factors and processes in Quadrant 1 of Table 13.1 (the influences on the intellectual dimension of linkage) have been studied extensively since the

Table 13.1   *A research framework for studying linkage*

Dimension of linkage		Potential FACTORS influencing linkage (causes)		LINKAGE (effect)
Intellectual dimension	I	The methodologies for formulation of IT and business mission, objectives and plans, and the comprehensiveness of the planning activities	II	The degree to which the set of IT and business mission, objectives, and plans are internally consistent and externally valid
Social dimension	III	Choice of actors, timing, decision making, and communication used in the formulation of mission, objectives, and plans for IT and the business	IV	The levels of understanding to the business and IT mission, objectives, and plans by IS and business executives

inception of strategic business planning in the mid seventies (e.g. Henderson and Venkatraman, 1992; Raghunathan and Raghunathan, 1990; Sullivan, 1985).

Until recently, less attention had been paid to describing and measuring the result of these activities (the intellectual dimension of linkage, i.e. Quadrant II). Henderson and Sifonis (1988) provided a framework for this dimension by suggesting that strategic plans need internal consistency and external validity. In the context of linkage, this idea would result in two aspects of the intellectual dimension of linkage:

1   Business and IT planning outputs are internally consistent, i.e. the IT mission, objectives, and plans chosen are consistent with the stated business mission and objectives.
2   Business and IT planning outputs are externally valid, i.e. they are comprehensive and balanced with respect to external business and IT environments. For example, if new technology exists that could impact the business strategy, it has been included in the IT strategy.

There are three empirical studies that have operationalized the 'internal consistency' aspect. Zviran (1990) used data from 131 companies to identify 16 separate IT objectives (e.g. incorporate IS in service systems, provide information on finished goods inventory). Jarvenpaa and Ives (1993) created a typology of global business and IT strategies that 'matched'. Chan and Huff (1992) created and validated and instrument to measure the degree of IT support for certain business strategies (e.g. aggressiveness, defensiveness, analysis). They reported positive correlations between a high level of 'fit' (between business and IT objectives) and perceived business performance.

These studies have begun the research process of defining and measuring internal consistency between IT and business strategies and plans. There is no research yet in the IS field that attempts to measure the 'external validity' aspect of linkage or to evaluate the appropriateness of an organization's IT strategy.

The social dimension of linkage

Several studies have focused on Quadrant III factors and processes such as top management support (Lederer and Mendelow, 1989; Raghunathan and Raghunathan, 1990), communication of business plans (Calhoun and Lederer, 1990), IS steering committees (Doll and Torkzadeh, 1987) and planning styles (Pyburn, 1983). One problem with this research has been that the dependent variable (Quadrant IV), whether it was linkage or IS planning success, has been less carefully defined and measured. *Providing a better understanding of this dimension of linkage is the objective of our study.*

The social dimension of linkage is defined as '**the level of mutual understanding of and commitment to the business and IT mission, objectives, and plans** by organizational members. Specifically, IS executives understand and are committed to the business mission, objectives, and plans; and business executives understand and are committed to the IT mission, objectives, and plans.

The remainder of this chapter reports on a study that created and tested measures to operationalize the 'mutual understanding' aspect of the social dimension of linkage. The 'commitment' aspect was not empirically investigated, since it was added to our definition subsequent to the completion of this study. However, the commitment construct is discussed further in the 'Recommendations for Researchers' section.

Research design

Sample and informants

The sample for this study of the social dimension of linkage involved 10 business units within three large Canadian life insurance companies. Of the 10, three business units sold individual insurance products, three sold group insurance, two sold retirement assets, one sold reinsurance, and one was responsible for investments. Each business unit had responsibility for setting its own strategic goals and plans, and each had an IS unit contained within it to design and build its information systems. To ensure confidentiality, the specific business units are not identified.

Informants having the following roles were interviewed: senior business executives, senior IS executives, members (if any) of the IT Steering Committees, and any technological 'gatekeepers'. In total, 57 interviews with 45 informants were conducted; the senior IS executives were interviewed several times. With the exception of Business Unit 4, in which we interviewed only two people, at least three informants from each business unit were interviewed.

A wealth of written material was collected from each site, including a copy of the most recently produced one- and five-year business and IT plans, strategy papers, and project proposals. A list of the interviewees and the written documents is provided in Appendix A.

Data collection, analysis, and reliability issues

The data collection and analysis process **for each business unit** proceeded in two major phases – preparation of the site report and verification of the site report. The first phase, executed by the first author, consisted of the following steps: perusal of written documents to familiarize the researcher with the local 'jargon'; customization of interview guides; interviews and creation of field notes; and analysis of transcribed interview tapes, field notes, and written documents to prepare a site report. The second phase consisted of: analysis of the site report by the second author; amending the site report (if necessary); removing from the site report direct quotes and other data that would breach the anonymity of individual informants; obtaining written or verbal feedback on the amended site report from the senior IS executive at the site; correcting the site report (if necessary); presentation of findings to the business and IS executives at the site; and again amending the site report (if necessary).

Included in the steps noted above were two precautions taken to reduce researcher bias in the site reports. Each site report contained extensive quotes from interviewees, quotes from written documents, and interpretive comments so that the second author was exposed to as much raw data as was practical (Sviokla, 1986; Yin, 1989). Transcripts of the audiotaped interviews were also made available. Based on this data, the second author was asked to assess the degree of linkage. Based on the second author's comments, the data were reinterpreted if necessary, and the site report was modified.

This modified site report was sent to the chief informant, who in all cases was the IS executive. This person was asked to comment on the veracity of the data and the linkage ratings. All eight informants (two of the 10 sites were debriefed verbally) annotated and returned their write-ups, and one requested significant changes based on missing information. A follow-up phone interview and meeting were held to correct this situation, and the site report was changed.

The next phase was the analysis **across all of the business units**. There were two phases: a re-examination of the candidate measures, and a comparative data analysis of them. First, each linkage measure was examined across all sites to ensure that the scales had been applied consistently. Approximately three months was spent in re-examining the raw data and rerating the sites on linkage measures. This effort resulted in a few adjustments in the ratings and greatly increased the reliability of the interpretive analysis. Second, as discussed in the 'Results' section, each measure was examined to test its validity and usefulness for later survey studies.

The data displays used the scatterplot format suggested by Miles and Huberman (1994, p.199) in their authoritative text on qualitative data analysis. The displays are designed and intended to be visually interpreted by the reader. While this study relies mainly on qualitative data and interpretative analysis, our study provides, for interested readers, statistical analysis in addition to the graphical displays to show the relationship between various measures of linkage. It should be noted, however, that because of the small sample size of 10 business units, the power of the test is low, especially since the Spearman correlation used is highly sensitive to sample size.

For the purposes of correlation analysis, the data shown later in Table 13.7 was converted to three ordinal categories of low, medium, and high. In cases of split ratings, e.g. high–moderate (e.g. column 5 of Table 13.7), it was entered as the *higher* level; in cases of 'no vision' or 'no plans' (e.g. columns 3 and 4 of Table 13.7), it was entered as *low*. With the Spearman correlations, both one- and two-tailed significance levels are reported. The one-tailed significance level would apply if one expects the various linkage measures to be positively correlated, which is in line with our expectations. The two-tailed test is more conservative and does not *a priori* assume such a relationship.

Measuring the social dimension of linkage

Two sources of evidence were identified to assess the level of mutual understanding between business and IS executives in a business unit. One was the 'minds' of the executives, the other was their written documents. Accordingly, senior executives were interviewed and the strategic plans and documents of the business units were examined. Although it would have been expedient to concentrate solely on written plans, several studies (Calhoun and Lederer, 1990; Lederer and Mendelow, 1986; 1989) had warned that detailed, written business plans are often not produced. Since there seemed to be no theoretical reason why the absence of written business plans would necessarily indicate a low level of linkage, we decided to explore the knowledge and opinions of IS and business executives.

Table 13.2 *Sources of evidence for the social dimension of linkage*

Source/time	Written documents	Minds of executives
Short-term linkage	Written one-year business plans outline the IT projects that are needed to support organizational strategies and programs Written one-year IT plans mention the organizational reasons for their projects and activities	Business executives understand current IT objectives IS executives understand current business objectives *Executives' self-rating of linkage*
Long-term linkage	Written five-year business plans outline a vision for IT and relate it to the organizational mission Written five-year IT plans outline an IT vision that reflects the mission and long-term goals of the organization.	IS and business executives share a common vision of the role and contribution of IT to the organization's mission *Executives' self-rating of linkage*

Two potential timeframes of linkage were also identified: short term (i.e. understanding of current plans) and long term (i.e. shared vision for the future of IT within the business unit). This allowed us to identify situations in which: (1) business and IS executives understood each other's short-term plans and objectives, but did not have a vision for IT in the future, and (2) executives had an agreed-upon mission and goals for IT, but had not yet formulated the short-term plans that would achieve them. Although the ideal would be to have both short- and long-term linkages in place, it seemed pragmatic to look for evidence of both and not to bias the study one way or another at the outset.

Putting these two ideas together, we conceptualized the social dimension of linkage along two axes (source and timeframe) and created some preliminary definitions of high levels of linkage for each quadrant. These are shown in Table 13.2.*

Although the goal of this project was to find objective ways to measure linkage, we realized that researcher-imposed measures (e.g. examining written documents and measuring congruence in understanding and vision) may not reflect reality as perceived by individuals and groups within an organization. As a validity check, executives were asked to assess their own level of

* We use 'five-year' as the timeframe for long-term linkage since this was the planning horizon of the business units in our sample. With increasingly frequent changes in the business environment, this timeframe might be shortened in future studies.

linkage and to discuss their rating with us. This source of linkage evidence is shown in italics in Table 13.2.*

The development of scales for each of the four aspects of linkage depicted in Table 13.2 is discussed in the following sections.

Written documents

Written plans can be used as evidence of both the intellectual and the social dimensions of linkage. For the intellectual dimension, one would make judgments about the quality of 'fit' that exists between the business and IT plans and also judge their ability to deal effectively with the external environment of the organization. To measure the social dimension, we looked for the explicit, surface-level connections between plans as *evidence of the fact that IS and business executives understood and supported what each other was doing*.

Cresap, McCormick and Paget Co. (1983) measured linkage by asking respondents to identify the extent to which 'the business plan states information system needs' and 'the IS plan makes reference to items in the business plan'. Instead of asking executives how much cross referencing there was between their business and IT plans, this study examined the current IT and business plans (both the one- and the five-year plans) for actual evidence of cross referencing in them.

We discussed and discarded the idea of counting the number of cross references in each document, recognizing, for example, that three references in one plan may be a higher level of linkage than five in another, because of differences in levels of reporting detail and requirements for IT support. Our solution, to avoid biases in coding, was to create a simple binary coding scheme – either there were references to IT projects in the business plans (and business strategies in the IT plans) or there were not. Examples of direction given to IT in the business plan could include general strategies, e.g. 'our systems must be upgraded to improve the customer service function', or specific ones, such as 'the new XXX product will require significant changes to the administrative systems'.

Cross references in short-term (one-year) plans

The scale used to rate the short-term linkage is shown in Table 13.3. An example of a high level of linkage from the sample data is also shown.

---

* This study also systematically investigated another potential measure for linkage – *the time that IS people are involved in new product development*. It was suggested to us by executives in several business units that early involvement was an indicator of high levels of linkage. We concluded that this measure was more useful as a factor influencing linkage than as a measure of the linkage construct. Further details are in Reich (1993).

Table 13.3 *Scale used to measure linkage in written one-year plans*

Linkage rating	
High	Two plans are in existence: the short-term business plan references the current IT objectives **and** the IT plan references the current business objectives, **or** One integrated business and IT plan: The plan is formatted such that either: (1) the IT objectives are placed under business unit goals, or (2) the IT objectives are contained in a separate section in the business plan but are articulated in terms of business unit objectives Example of high linkage within a business plan: *'implement an electronic application that will (a) reduce unit costs in support of the new business process, (b) make it easier for the agent to sell the product, (c) provide the client with enhanced services including . . .'*
Moderate	Two plans in existence: **Either** the short-term business plan references the IT projects **or** the IT plan references the business objectives. One of the plans may be missing **or** One integrated IT and business plan: The IT objectives are contained in a separate section of the plan but are not articulated in terms of business goals
Low	The short-term business plan does not reference the IT projects **and** the IT plan does not reference the business objectives
No plans	There is no short-term plan for the business unit **and** no short-term plan for the IT function within the business unit

Cross references in long-term (five-year) plans

Table 13.4 contains the scale used to rate long-term linkage and an example of a moderate rating.

Minds of executives

In addition to gathering self-reports on linkage (described in the 'Self-reports about linkage' section), we tried to identify more precisely the nature of the executives' understanding of business and IT mission, objectives, and plans. Short-term linkage was assessed by asking about current business strategies and IT projects; longer-term linkage was assessed by asking about the role and vision for IT in the organization in the next five years.

Table 13.4   *Scale used to measure linkage in written five-year plans*

Linkage rating	
High	The long-term business plan identifies general ways that IT will be used in support of business goals, **and** the IT plan places its objectives into the context of business objectives or performance
Moderate	**Either** the long-term business plan gives IT some direction, **or** the long-term IT plan exhibits knowledge of and support for the long-term business plan. One of the plans may be missing
	Example of a high level of cross referencing in a business strategy document: *'efficiency will have to be combined with more timely and responsive transaction activity. The introduction of the system to allow agents to instantly issue contracts will be a real enhancement to compete at lower unit costs . . . the use of software to help agents plan clients' portfolios will be important . . .'* There was no five-year IT plan and so the overall linkage rating was moderate
Low	The long-term business plan does not reference IT **and** the long-term IT plan does not mention business objectives
No plans	There is no five-year business plan **and** no five-year IT plan that is operative within the business unit

Understanding of current objectives

Understanding of current objectives, defined as the goals and strategies for business and IT for the next one–two years, was measured by assessing: (1) the level of understanding that IS executives had about current business objectives, and (2) the level of understanding that business executives had about current IT objectives and then creating an overall score for the business unit.

Several problems were expected and influenced the scale formation. First, people in different roles might use different terms to describe the same strategy. The solution was to use the written plans and follow-up questions to clarify the meanings of the terminology used. Second, IS and business executives might exhibit different levels of understanding. The solution was to rate each group separately and to average the scores of the two groups of executives. Third, obtaining a single score for several executives required measurement theory about weighting responses. Options included averaging, using the lowest or highest score of the group, or favoring the views of a specific role. Our solution, admittedly imperfect, was to keep the scale very simple and to favor the score of the operational head of the business unit

Table 13.5 *Scale used to measure understanding of current objectives*

Linkage rating	
High: IS execs	The IS executives can identify the current objectives of the business unit. These objectives were the ones written in the business plan or articulated by senior business executives Example: Head of BU: *'We are going to concentrate on expense control . . . we are going to change our regional offices to profit centers . . . we will be designing a product. . . . our idea is to hook up agents as part of a partnership strategy'* Head of IS: *'Our business objectives are expense control through automation, improving service to the "good" agents, specific new products and improving our professional image'*
Business execs	The business executives can identify most or all of the current high-priority projects of the IS group
Moderate (IS or business)	The IS and business executives have only a general understanding of each others' current objectives but cannot identify specific, high-priority ones
Low (IS or business)	Neither the IS nor the business executives can identify each others' major current objectives Example: Head of BU: *'The IS head probably has his own strategies. I probably haven't gotten around to reading them yet and I would think that they are in support of the ones we are looking at'* Head of IS: *'I want to move to a broader technical platform, to get more effective use of PCs and to get into local area networks'*
Unknown	No business or IS current objectives have been formulated

(BU) or IS group over his/her subordinates or superiors. For example, in one of the business units, we interviewed the senior VP, who was in charge of two BUs, and the VP, who was in charge of the BU in question. We assigned more weight to the response of the VP, since he was most directly involved in creating and implementing short-term plans.

The process of creating a score for the BU on understanding of current objectives was as follows: (1) create a score for each individual, (2) determine two representative scores – one for the business executives and one for the IS executives, and (3) average these two scores.

The result was ratings of high, high–moderate, moderate, etc. The scale used is shown in Table 13.5, along with selected examples of high and low ratings.

Shared vision for IT (long term)

Vision was defined as a clear expectation of the role IT would play in contributing to the long-term success of the organizational unit. Issues such as what business processes would benefit the most from the application of IT, how the benefits would be realized, and what other changes would occur in the business environment were considered to be part of vision. It was measured by comparing the open-ended vision statements obtained in interviews from IS and business executives and assessing their congruence using the scale shown in Table 13.6. Examples of high and low levels of congruence in vision are provided in the table.

Self-reports about linkage

To ensure that the respondents were given an opportunity to explain their views, a self-report of linkage was obtained by asking each executive interviewed (1) to rate linkage for the business unit as high, moderate, or low, and (2) to give rationale and evidence supporting their rating. Each executive interviewed was asked the following questions:

1   If we define linkage as the congruence between the business unit goals/ strategies and the IS strategies/plans, how would you rate linkage within your business unit?
2   Why did you rate linkage as . . . ?

From these questions, a subjective rating of linkage (question 1), and the executive's ideas on what constitutes linkage (question 2) were derived. Ratings given by interviewees were averaged to create the BU rating. A detailed presentation of the answers to question 2 are provided in Appendix B and discussed in the 'Self-reports of linkage' section under 'Results'.

Results

Within each business unit, short-term linkage was evaluated by assessing: (1) cross references in written one-year business and IT plans, and (2) understanding of current objectives and plans. Long-term linkage was measured by assessing: (1) cross references in written five-year business and IT plans, and (2) shared vision about the future role of IT in the business unit.

Some congruence was expected between the two measures of long-term linkage and the two measures of shorter-term linkage, but there were no predictions about self-reports.

Table 13.6 *Scale used to measure congruence in shared vision for IT*

Linkage rating	
High	Business executives and the IS executives agree on the overall ways in which IT will contribute to the future of the business unit
	Example of a congruent IT vision, focused on the client-company interface:
	Head of BU: *'In the long run, IT will allow us to provide higher quality service to our customers at lower unit costs . . . to get electronic hooks into our customers and make it hard for them to leave us'*
	VP, Finance: *'Use of IT in the economies of scale focus . . . to keep costs down. That will be defensive. There is much more benefit in the front-end use of technology – in the field and underwriting. Single source of data entry by the user'*
	VP, Marketing: *'Lots of new ways to use IT – selling through terminals, POS . . .'*
Moderate	There is some agreement on how IT will contribute to the future of the business unit. Some executives might have conflicting or no visions for IT
Low	The visions expressed for IT by the executives do not show any congruence. Several visions might be expressed, but they differ on the overall value of IT or on the business processes to which IT can be most effectively applied
	Example 1: no congruence in vision for IT:
	Head of BU: *'You sort of have to be as good as your competitor but you don't gain anything extra. Management information will help us analyze our business better and we'll get to see whether we are actually getting the target loss rations. . . .'*
	Head of IS: *'I believe that technology is a thing to support decentralization. . . . you can use technology to restructure the way we do business and achieve efficiencies'*
	Example 2: lots of conflicting visions, no congruence:
	Head of Administration: *'Our vision is to have a paperless office'*
	Head of Marketing: *'Two IT strategies are important: paying the agent early and issuing the policy on site'*
	Head of IS: *'IS goals are flexibility, managed data redundancy, cooperative processing . . .'*
No vision	None of the executives have any clear vision for the role of IT within the business unit

Table 13.7   *A summary of the linkage findings in the business units*

BU	Understanding of current objectives	Cross references in written plans	Shared vision for IT	Self-reports
1	Execs – low IS – high	5 yr – low 1 yr – high	High	High
2	Execs – high IS – moderate	5 yr – moderate 1 yr – high	High	High–moderate
3	Execs – moderate IS – low	5 yr – moderate 1 yr – high	High	High
4	Execs – low IS – low	No 5 yr plans 1 yr – high	No vision	Low
5	Execs – high IS – high	No 5 yr plans 1 yr – moderate	High	Moderate
6	Execs – moderate IS – moderate	No 5 yr plans 1 yr – moderate	No vision	High
7	Execs – moderate IS – high	5 yr – moderate 1 yr – high	Low	High
8	Execs – low IS – low	5 yr – moderate 1 yr – moderate	Low	Moderate
9	Execs – high IS – high	5 yr – moderate 1 yr – high	Moderate	High–moderate
10	Execs – high IS – high	5 yr – moderate 1 yr – high	No vision	High

Table 13.7 reports the summary of the linkage findings. The ratings for business and IS executives on understanding of current objectives are shown separately. Very few business units achieved uniformly high or low ratings on all measures.

After determining the ratings for each BU on each scale, the value of each candidate measure was assessed using the following criteria: (1) representation of the underlying meaning of the social dimension of linkage (i.e. construct validity), (2) ability to identify the variance in linkage within a sample of business units, (3) potential ease of application in large-scale surveys, and (4) congruence with other measures of the same aspect of linkage (i.e. convergent validity). Analysis of the measures is reported in the next sections.

Short-term linkage

Understanding of current objectives

At the outset, some differences were anticipated between IS and business executives' understanding of each others' current objectives. This occurred in four business units, but only one (BU 1) showed an extreme difference. According to our informants, the IS executive had not shared his internal objectives (i.e. platforms, IS productivity) with the business executives. The IS executive was in charge of the business planning process and so clearly identified all business goals. In all units, the ratings were averaged and carried forward into the across-sites analysis.

Using our criteria, we assess this candidate measure as follows:

1 *Construct validity*. This measure, although it was subject to recall and recency problems, captured the understanding of each executive at the time the data collection was done. Averaged over a group of executives within the unit and measured with a simple ordinal scale, it showed promise as a representation of the state of understanding in a BU.

2 *Variance*. Executives were not reluctant to reveal their lack of knowledge or to disclose their strategies. Answers to these questions varied from 'I don't know' to a detailed listing of objectives (*There are eight major goals for the unit this year. We discuss them at our management meetings biweekly. They are: to alter the product mix, to improve the sales productivity . . .*). The resulting data exhibited wide variance within our sample.

3 *Ease of application*. The main problem found with this measure is the amount of interpretation necessary to rate congruence (e.g. is 'lowering expense gaps' the same objective as 'reducing unit costs'?). This problem would be exacerbated in large-scale survey studies unless a more structured question format could be devised.

Cross references in written one-year plans

In six of the business units, there were two one-year plans – one for business and one for IT objectives. In the other four units there was one integrated business plan referring to projects from all departments, including IS.

Using these criteria, we assess this candidate measure as follows:

1 *Construct validity*. Our analysis revealed a number of problems with this measure. The business units varied widely in the degree of importance they attached to the creation and communication of written plans. In one business unit, the short-term plans were created by senior executives, circulated to all supervisors and managers, and the BU head conducted a meeting with each of the 40 managers to discuss them. In another unit, each department head contributed a section, then the document was edited for style conformity and sent out to senior managers. In a third unit, the BU head wrote the prose, and each unit contributed budget numbers. Without knowing how the report was prepared, it is difficult to argue that it represents the collective understanding of the executives in a business

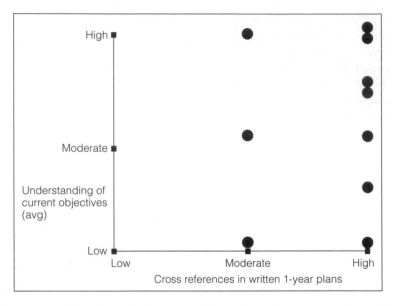

Figure 13.1   *The relationship between understanding of current objectives and cross references in one-year plans (• = business unit)*

unit. A single manager could have created a plan with high levels of cross referencing but not have shared his/her insights with other executives. A second problem is that as a historical document, created up to a year ago, it may not represent current levels of understanding. Some respondents noted that their written plans had not been updated recently, although their strategies had changed.

2   *Variance.* There was not much variance on this measure, with seven business units rated as high and three as moderate. The measure did not seem to represent the true variance that existed in our sample, e.g. in BU 4 and 8, most measures rated low, but this measure rated high or moderate.

3   *Ease of application.* This measure is difficult to apply in a large sample situation since most organizations are reluctant to release their written plans to researchers unknown to them. However, executives could be asked for their opinion about cross references, as other researchers have done.

Congruence between the two measures of short-term linkage

The 'cross references in written plans' measure did not exhibit much congruence with 'understanding of current objectives', the other potential measure for short-term linkage. Figure 13.1 displays the relationship between these two measures, showing that for both high and moderate linkage in written plans, there is a wide range of linkage exhibited in the 'understanding of current objectives'. The Spearman correlation coefficient between these two measures is 0.25 (one-tailed significance = 0.25, two-tailed = 0.49).

This lack of congruence might be attributed to a number of reasons. First, written plans may have been prepared by few people and not widely shared within the business unit. Second, the lag between the time the plan was written and the time the research interview took place could have affected the congruence. Third, the interview format may not have been conducive to a correct recollection of current objectives.

However, since there were several units in which a high level of cross referencing in written plans was exhibited but business and IS executives could not identify each other's objectives, we concluded that written plans are often outdated documents without the construct validity necessary to represent the mutual understanding dimension of linkage. Because 'understanding of current objectives' captured linkage at the time of the interview, exhibited higher variance in the sample than cross references in written plans, and exhibited congruence with the self-reports of linkage (discussed later), it seemed to be the better candidate measure for short-term linkage.

Long-term linkage

Cross references in written five-year plans

Ratings for this measure of long-term linkage, the level of cross referencing in five-year business and IT plans, were influenced heavily by the absence of long-term plans. Of the 10 business units, seven had written, long-term business plans, but only one had a written, long-term IT strategic plan. All business units had a list of IT projects that would require more than a year to complete, but they lacked a written description of the IT strategy and objectives adopted for the business unit. It is quite possible that IT strategies had been formulated within the business units and existed in the minds of executives, but they had never been formalized. Only one IS group had created and published a strategic plan. Another IS group was in the process of creating a strategic plan, but the draft of the plan that was provided to the researchers was very technology oriented and would not have rated highly on the linkage measure.

Of the seven business units with written, long-term business plans, six made reference to IT directions, and one plan did not contain any IT references. Ironically, this last plan belonged to the business unit in which the lone IT strategy had been formulated. Examples from business plans that referenced IT activities are:

- The introduction of the Marketing Support System to allow agents to. . . . will be a real enhancement to compete at lower cost.

- Technology will continue to improve . . . there will be a greater contact between the client and the insurance company and less between the client and the distributor.

Resulting ratings, as shown in Table 13.7, were six moderate, one low, and three no plans. Except for BU 7, none of the other units had written, long-term (three-, four-, or five-year) strategic plans. In essence, they had no written IT strategy at all, regardless of the timeframe. We considered recalibrating the scale to reflect this reality in the sample, but this action would have been contrary to the intent of the measure, which was to determine if written plans referenced each other.

In this study we were not able to delve into the reasons as to why a business unit would not develop written IT plans. Perhaps a few references to IT directions in the business plan was deemed to be an IT strategy. Perhaps the turbulence in the Canadian insurance industry and in the IT sector led these units to focus on shorter-term goals. For example, many of the IS areas were in the early stages of considering a move to smaller distributed platforms, and no consensus had developed. We understand this reluctance to commit to a longer-term strategy, but we adhere to the prescriptive view that written documents, whether they are one-page vision statements or 50-page detailed plans, are necessary to communicate current thinking, stimulate debate, and develop consensus.

Using our criteria, we assess this candidate measure as follows:

1 *Construct validity.* This measure has the same problems as the written short-term plan measure, i.e. one cannot tell from looking at the plans who prepared them or how widely they are understood. They are documents that can be several months or years old and may not reflect current understanding.
2 *Variance.* Because there were so few business units with both IT and business plans in written form, this measure may not be able to reflect the real variance in long-term linkage among the business units. We do not believe that the existence of long-term written IT plans is a necessary precondition for linkage.
3 *Ease of application.* This measure is limited to small studies, since companies are not likely to send in copies of their business or IT plans in a survey study. Also, this measure is ideally suited to business units that do create written long-term plans, but according to our data and observations of other researchers, many do not.

Shared vision for IT

On the 'congruence in shared vision for IT' measure, four business units rated high, one moderate, two low, and three exhibited no vision. Usually, within a business unit which exhibited high shared vision for IT, a single theme was present; for example, the use of IT by agents in underwriting, or the use of IT to streamline and lower the cost of specific administrative activities. Using our criteria, we assess this candidate measure as follows:

1 *Construct validity.* In a long interview setting, respondents were quite forthcoming about their vision, or lack of it, for IT in the future. Some managers had a specific end state in mind, e.g. 'we need programs to support our agents and allow us to write more policies on the spot'. Some executives admitted that they had no idea what IT could do for the BU and they were relying on the IS professionals to create the plans. When several executives mentioned the same end state or revealed a lack of vision, a simple nominal scale was quite easy to apply. Overall, this measure seemed to reflect the underlying meaning of the long-term aspect of linkage, i.e. shared vision of the potential for IT within the business unit, captured at the time of the interview.

2 *Variance.* Interview questions about vision for IT elicited a wide range of responses. Examples are 'the IS department should be smaller', 'we can get electronic hooks into the customers', 'we don't have any IT direction', 'have user analysts report to the divisions', and 'a paperless office'. The result was a wide variance in the linkage ratings and a recognition by us that more structure needed to be applied in the questioning.

3 *Ease of application.* This measure, as implemented in our study, requires significant interpretation by the researchers, and this would limit its application to small sample studies. However, with a generic list of IT strategies provided to the respondent, it may be suitable for surveys.

Congruence between the measures of long-term linkage

We had expected the written five-year plan measure to correlate highly with the measure of the shared vision for IT because they were different sources and manifestations of long-term thinking. Figure 13.2 shows that there was a very low association between these two measures. The Spearman correlation coefficient is -0.08 (one-tailed significance $= 0.42$, two-tailed $= 0.83$). The lack of a written plan did not preclude the possibility that both IS and business executives had shared long-term visions for IT (see BU 5 in Table 13.7). Also, a moderate level of cross references in the plans did not indicate that the business unit would have a shared vision.

The shared vision measure, as applied, did allow us to separate the 10 business units into those that exhibited no shared vision, low congruence in shared vision, and high congruence in shared vision. Therefore, we concluded that 'shared vision for IT', subject to some refinements in the way it is investigated (discussed in the concluding comments), was a good potential

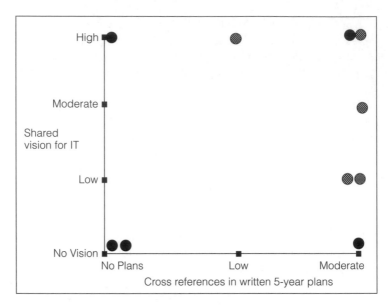

Figure 13.2 *The relationship between shared vision for IT and cross references in five-year plans*

measure for long-term linkage. Also, it was always available, unlike written long-term plans that were either not available or not accessible.

Self-reports of linkage

Each executive was asked to rate the linkage within his/her business unit (as high, moderate, or low), and to explain the reasons for assigning a particular rating. After averaging the subjective ratings over all executives in each business unit, seven units were rated as high or moderate–high, two as moderate, and one as low.

Overall, self-reports of linkage within the business units were higher than ratings of linkage based on the other two measures that showed promise: understanding of current objectives and shared vision. Figure 13.3 shows the ratings on understanding of current objectives plotted against the self reports. Figure 13.4 shows the rankings on shared vision plotted against the self-reports.

There is a much stronger association between self-reports and current objectives (Spearman correlation of 0.50; one-tailed significance = 0.07, two-tailed = 0.14) than there is between self-reports and shared vision (Spearman correlation of 0.21; one-tailed significance = 0.28, two-tailed = 0.56). In fact, the correlation between self-reports and current objectives (0.50) is the highest

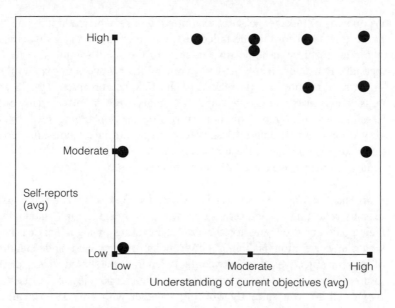

Figure 13.3 *The relationship between understanding of current objectives and self-reports*

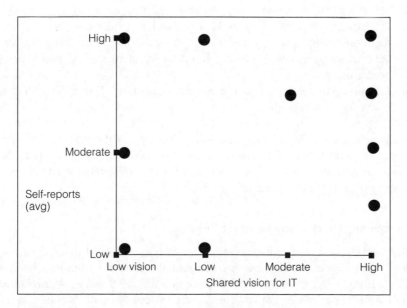

Figure 13.4 *The relationship between shared vision for IT and self-reports*

among all pairs of linkage measures examined in this chapter, and it is significant at the 0.10 level for the one-tailed test, which is based on the hypothesis that the relationship will be positive in spite of the small sample size.

Appendix B lists the many reasons given by interviewees to explain their self-reports. Some are directly related to the linkage construct, e.g. 'IS and business plans are synonymous', and 'no goals were in place'. However, 'process' issues (e.g. good communication, business planning process, IT delivery times) and 'structural' issues (e.g. IS reporting relationships, committee make-up) dominated these assessments.

Using our criteria, we assess this candidate measure as follows:

1 *Construct validity*. As shown in Appendix B, executives often used reasons reflecting the **current** situation in the business unit, rather than their goals and strategies for the future, in rating linkage. This explains why the correlation is higher between self-reports and understanding of current objectives than between self-reports and shared vision of the future. It appears that the executives were often responding to the question 'how well are you currently working together with your IS executives' rather than 'how closely are your business and IT objectives linked' when providing self-reports of linkage. Few of the executives related their measurement to 'objective' evidence such as shared goals or realized benefits from IT.

2 *Variance*. It seems that when asked in interview format, both business and IS executives tend to skew the self-report measure upwards and give their IS departments or themselves the benefit of the doubt or else rate them on 'trying' rather than delivering. As a result, there was little variance in this measure, with the 'high' or 'moderate–high' rating being predominant.

3 *Ease of application*. This is the easiest measure of all to apply, either in interview or survey format.

We concluded that the self-reported linkage measure, although it tended to be higher in ratings than other measures due to reporting bias, was a potential surrogate measure for short-term linkage if it is administered properly, as is discussed in the final section of the chapter.

Comparing short- and long-term linkage

Our next step was to test the assumption that two aspects of linkage, namely short- and long-term, exist and are substantially different from one another. The self-report measure had exhibited (see Figures 13.3 and 13.4) a relationship with 'understanding of current objectives' but not with 'shared vision'. Figure 13.5 contains a graph of the data from the two most promising 'objective'

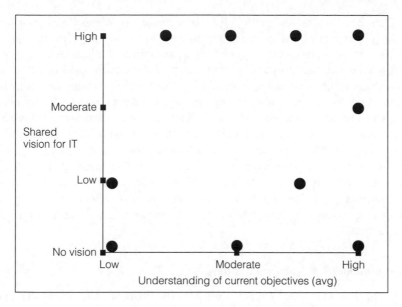

Figure 13.5   *The relationship between measures of short- and long-term linkage: understanding of current objectives and shared vision for IT*

measures – 'understanding of current objectives' and 'shared vision for IT'. They exhibit low correlation with one another (Spearman correlation of 0.27; one-tailed significance = 0.23, two-tailed = 0.45), indicating that they represent two distinct aspects of the linkage construct, namely short- and long-term linkage.

Concluding comments

This study identified two dimensions of linkage and investigated several ways to measure one of them, namely the social dimension, in an effort to provide measures that might be valid and reliable in *large sample* studies.

From the investigation of four potential measures, we ended up with two viable possibilities, namely, 'understanding of current objectives' and 'congruence in IT vision', plus a third, 'self-reports', if administered appropriately. We discarded the 'written reports' measure since it was impractical to obtain current plans in large sample studies, and long-term IT plans were often not available. We also felt that asking people to comment on their written plans in a survey instrument would be stretching their ability to answer correctly. Many people interviewed had not looked at the written plans in the last few months.

Our investigation also verified the existence of two distinct aspects of the social dimension of linkage based on time – short- and long-term linkage.

The next sections discuss ways in which to proceed, both in advancing our measurement capabilities and in application of the current findings. Prior to providing recommendations, it should be noted that the insurance industry, from which the business units in our sample were drawn, was under financial pressure during the time of the data collection. Many units were rethinking their strategies, and this uncertainty provided us with interviewees who were willing to discuss their IT situations in very open and frank terms. This environmental pressure may have provided us with lower ratings for linkage than in a profitable, stable industry. To the extent that the profit erosion and uncertainty in the Canadian insurance industry reflects the reality of many other industries, these findings may have more, or less, validity outside the sample.

Recommendations for practitioners

This study has provided a scheme to show the different ways of conceptualizing and identifying short- and long-term aspects of the social dimension of linkage. One represents a state in which the goals and strategies of the next one–two years of business and IT activity are understood by all managers. The other represents a state in which all managers share a common vision of how IT will shape the business in the more distant future. The proposed measures provide a means to conduct a linkage 'audit' in order to assess the level and types of linkage within an organizational subunit. A sample set of questions is included in Appendix C. These questions could be used as part of a questionnaire or could be asked in interviews. Once this information is available, practitioners can evaluate their own business units and better understand any sources of differences, confusion, or conflict if the proper level of linkage does not exist. Action to remedy these differences through improved communication could then be taken. Long-term vision for IT is more difficult to create and would require deliberate actions on the part of IS executives. Vision 'scenarios' can be created, couched in business rather than technology language, and discussed at planning events. Examples from other business units, companies, or industries can be used to expand the executives' concept of what is possible.

The proposed measures could also be used to identify the extent to which linkage, as stated and intended in written short- and long-term IT or business plans, is in fact understood correctly by different executives by comparing planned linkage to current mutual understanding and visions, obtained through alternative means as discussed in this chapter. If a discrepancy between written plans and executives' understanding exists, then an investigation should be conducted to determine why and how it has occurred – e.g. was it due to unrevised plans not keeping up with changing business conditions, or was it due to a lack of proper communication of the outcomes of a formal planning process? By identifying the nature of the problem, the appropriate courses of action to alleviate them could be determined.

We have also observed that executives mistakenly believe that linkage exists, when only the factors that might lead to linkage are present. In other words, self-reports are sometimes incorrect. Again, a linkage 'audit' would assist in showing executives which types of linkage, and at what levels, really exist and whether other conditions are preventing the influence factors that could lead to linkage from taking effect, for example, while a steering committee is in place, the topics discussed are narrowly focused on technology issues only (Reich and Benbasat, 1994).

Some of our observations indicate that, contrary to the prescriptions of the normative literature, which suggest that both short- and long-term linkage is required, some organizations can operate quite satisfactorily without high levels of both long- and short-term linkage. For example, BU 3 had no agreed-upon short-term plans for the business (i.e. product mix) or for IT, but they had built a shared vision of the target environment, including the contribution of IT. Because of this shared vision, they were not concerned about the temporary lack of direction and ranked themselves as having high levels of linkage. On the other hand, BU 10 had clear plans for the next one–two years for IT but had not formulated a long-term vision. They were discussing several alternatives and were confident that, in time, one would emerge.

The above findings about the lack of long-term linkage notwithstanding, IT can often create strategic opportunities for business units, especially in industries that are information intensive and where some vision of the future of IT exists. Organizations with high levels of long-term linkage could leverage this asset by regularly scanning the IT environment. Technology that is a good fit for long-term objectives can be readily identified and brought in for evaluation. Organizations without a clear vision may find the technological choices bewildering and may waste organizational resources evaluating hardware and software without any definite basis upon which to select among alternatives. The measures provided in this chapter are therefore helpful to figure out what the current level of linkage is, and they would be a catalyst to take corrective action if it does not exist.

Recommendations for researchers

Based on the findings of this study, our recommended approach to measure the two aspects of the social dimension of linkage is to interview or survey respondents to collect data about 'understanding of current objectives' and 'shared IT vision'.

For short-term linkage, asking respondents to rate their business units on linkage may also be an acceptable alternative. However, any self-report measures should be used with caution since respondents derive it by anchoring to the factors they believe influence linkage, rather than to linkage itself. It is therefore important to ask the respondent the reasons for providing a particular linkage rating to differentiate outcome-based ratings from process-based ratings. It is also important to specify the time-frame being investigated in order to have the respondent focus on the shorter- as well as longer-term strategic issues.

At the beginning of this project, we had not identified a typology of 'visions' to be used in measuring the 'congruence in IT vision'. Because our questions were open-ended and the responses were unstructured and unfocused, our ability to precisely assess the degree of congruence was hampered. For example, several of our respondents produced vision statements that were tied closely to their domain of responsibility, rather than representing a vision of IT for the organization. Based on this observation, when one is collecting data via interviews or surveys, we suggest that questions eliciting vision statements should be carefully structured. Closed questions (e.g. based on Feeny *et al.*, 1992; Zviran, 1990) plus open-ended questions could be used to elicit several aspects of vision: a list of benefits expected from IT, a set of areas of the organization where IT might impact success, or a range of effects that might result from the application of IT. In this way, it would be possible to capture a more complete picture of the respondents' expectations for IT than open, unstructured questions could do. A sample of these questions is shown in Appendix C.

Previous studies have used single respondents, usually the IS manager. This work has shown that the perceptions and understanding of the IS and business executives are not necessarily in agreement. We therefore recommend that both groups be sampled.

As was seen in this research, business units within a single organization can exhibit different levels of linkage, making an overall single measure inappropriate in a complex organization. Another complication uncovered in previous work (Reich, 1993) is that corporate business and IT strategies will probably exhibit a different level of linkage than their counterparts within the business units. Researchers should keep the linkage measures centered around a single dyad of business and IT strategies, i.e. at the corporate or the business unit level.

Linkage ratings based on written plans are suspect in terms of their validity. We observed that short-term linkage, as reflected in executives' responses, was often not congruent with what was stated in the written plans. It is likely that written plans are, by definition, always out of date depending on how often they are revised.

It can be seen from these recommendations and from the suggested questions in Appendix C that precisely measuring linkage within a business site is difficult, since it requires multiple respondents and a questionnaire that makes sense within the industry and the life cycle of the site. In our current state of knowledge, a simple 'high, medium, low' scale, measured reliably and validly, would be a step forward and would provide enough data to allow researchers and practitioners to investigate the effects of linkage and to diagnose and prescribe for situations in which linkage was low. These are the ultimate goals of the research.

As mentioned in the second section, the social dimension of linkage is conceptualized as 'mutual understanding of and commitment to the objectives . . .' The concept of 'commitment' was not measured in this research because it was added to the model after the research was underway. We believe that the concept of commitment is important, however, since mutual understanding alone is not sufficient to ascertain or predict successful implementation of IT or business objectives.

There is recent research that suggests one possible way in which commitment might be conceptualized and measured. Hartwick and Barki (1994) discuss the relationship between user involvement and attitudes. User involvement affects user attitude, which is a predictor of system usage. Fishbein and Ajzen (1975) define attitude as the amount of affect one feels for or against some object (e.g. the IT plans and strategies). User involvement is a belief that refers to the extent to which a person believes an object is important and of personal relevance (Hartwick and Barki, 1994).

Using these concepts for the research on linkage, we could conceptualize commitment along the same lines as user involvement. Therefore, a high level of 'commitment' on the part of business executives would mean they felt that the IT objectives were important and relevant to them. A high level of social dimension of linkage would mean that IS executives (business executives) both understood business (IT) objectives and felt that they were important and relevant to them. Scales for measurement of commitment could be created from adapting, refining, and testing the instruments developed by Hartwick and Barki (1994).

In closing, we hope that this study has moved our understanding of the linkage construct forward and laid the foundations for further empirical work to refine the measures.

Appendix A

Interviewees and archival data from each of the Business Units (BU)

BU	Business executives	IS executives	Written business plans	Written IT plans	Other IT strategy documents
BU 1	– SVP, BU – VP, Marketing	– VP, Admin, and IS – Director, Admin. Systems	– 5 yr Strategy 1991–1995 – 5 yr Operating Plan 1991–1995 – 1991 Plan	– No separate 5 or 1 yr IT plan produced – Projects embedded in 1991 Plan – Unpublished 5 yr technology strategies	– Minutes from 2 representative monthly planning meetings of the BU executives
BU 2	– SVP, BU – VP, Marketing and Administration – VP, Finance	– VP, Admin. and IS – Director, IS	– Strategic plan 1990–1995 – 1990 business plan	– 1991 IT plan	– Various reports on systems strategy (1984, 1987, 1989, 1991)
BU 3	– VP, Finance – Director, Administration – Director, Marketing	– Director, IS – Manager, Systems Development	– Background sections, business strategy, 1991–1995 – 1991 plans	– No 5 yr or 1 yr IT plan compiled – IT projects embedded in the 1991 Plan	– 2 memos re: systems priorities
BU 4	– VP, Operations	– Director, IS	– excerpts from 1991 strategic plan (not finished) – 1990 business plan	– IT planning documents, 1989, 1990 – no 1991 IT Plan – no 5 yr IT plan	– Mission, goals, objectives for IS, 1989 – Strategic planning output, 1990
BU 5	– SVP, BU – Manager, Marketing Administration	– Manager, Systems Development	– Strategic marketing plan 1991	– no unitied IT strategy – 1991 Projects	

BU 6	– SVP, BU – Director, Finance	– Manager, Admin. and IS	– Administration plan, 1991	– 1991 IT plan	
BU 7	– VP, Administration – AVP, Marketing	– AVP, IS	– Strategic plan 1991–1995 – 1991 Business plan	– IT strategy 1990–1995 – 1991 IT plans – 1991 projects	– Minutes from 6 months Steering Committee meetings – 'Impact of IT on Insurance 1991–1995' document
BU 8	– SVP, 2 BU's – VP, BU	– AVP, IS	– Strategic plan 1991–1995 – Operating plan 1991	– 1991 planning summary – 1991 key programs	– Minutes from 5 months of Steering Committee meetings – 1991 IS staff review
BU 9	– SVP, 2 BU's – VP, BU – AVP and Controller	– AVP, IS	– Strategic plans 1990–1995, 1991–1996 – 1991 plan	– 1991 IT plan	– Minutes from 3 months of Steering Committee meetings – Technology directions, 1990
BU 10	– SVP, 2 BU's – VP, BU	– AVP, IS – Manager, IS	– Strategic plan 1991–1995 – Business plan, 1991	– No 1991 IT Plan – IT projects imbedded in 1991 business plan	– Minutes from 2 months of Steering Committee meetings – Systems strategy report, 1988

Appendix B

Reasons given by respondents for their subjective ratings of linkage

BU	Reasons used by BU executives	Reasons used by IS executives
BU 1	1 IS visits sales offices.(+) 2 IS understands the business.(+) Rating: **high** 1 IS people interested in business.(+) 2 Business planning meetings.(+) 3 Lack of business targets for a major IT initiative.(−) Rating: **high**	1 Business planning process.(+) 2 IS reporting to the BU.(+) Rating: **high** 1 IS and business plans are synonymous.(+) 2 Liaison devices for communication.(+) 3 IS reporting to the BU.(+) Rating: **high**
BU 2	1 Prioritizing process.(+) 2 Early participation in new product development.(+) 3 IS is learning the business.(+) Rating: **high** 1 IS understands business objectives.(+) 2 Deliverables take too long.(−) 3 IS has weakened their position against competition.(−) Rating: **high** 1 IS doesn't understand the business well enough.(−) 2 IS doesn't show leadership.(−) Rating: **moderate**	1 IS is too reactive, doesn't show leadership.(−) 2 Business areas are not excited by IS projects, not supportive.(−) Rating: **moderate**
BU 3	1 IS interested in the business.(+) 2 IS understands business.(+) 3 IS reports to the BU, no conflict of interest.(+) 4 Regular management meetings.(+) Rating: **high** 1 No goals in place.(−) 2 Slow getting IS systems delivered.(−) Rating: **moderate** 1 IS Director understands priorities.(+) Rating: **high**	1 IS is part of senior management.(+) 2 IS coordinates business planning process.(+) Rating: **high** 1 Close working arrangements between IS and senior executives.(+) 2 Early participation in new product development.(+) 3 No clear long-term goals.(−) Rating: **high**
BU 4	1 IS has no input into business planning.(−) 2 Line management does not accept responsibility for IS.(−) 3 IS operates in a vacuum.(−) Rating: **low**	1 IS has too much discretion within the BU.(−) 2 No business direction for IS.(−) Rating: **low**
BU 5	1 Strong IS/line individual in the BU.(+) 2 Stronger relationships between programmers and BU analysts.(+) 3 Programmers report to central IS, not to the BU.(−)	1 IS needs to be involved earlier in new product development.(−) Rating: **moderate**

4 Programmers do not understand business, are not connected to it.(−)

5 Business plan gives direction to IS.(+)   Rating: **moderate**

BU 6
1 IS history is very positive.(+)
2 Good communication within the BU.(+)
3 System directly supports business strategy.(+)   Rating: **high**

BU 7
1 The key business executive understands IT well.(+)
2 IS reports to the BU.(+)
3 Steering Committee format isolates IS issues.(−)   Rating: **high**

1 IS presence on cross functional committees helps to understand business.(+)
2 IS does not report to the SVP. (−)
3 Not enough trust at the first line manager level.(−)   Rating: **moderate**

1 Management meetings include IS, both routine and off-site.(+)
2 IS is on new product development teams.(+)
3 Close ties between operating plan and strategy.(+)   Rating: **high**

BU 8
1 Main areas of strategy are supported by systems projects.(+)
2 IS not delivering on schedule.(−)
3 IS needs a better understanding of business priorities.(−)
4 Incentive system rewards linkage and compliance.(+)   Rating: **moderate**

1 Good communication between IS and business. (+)
2 Weak strategic business planning processes. (−)   Rating: **moderate**

BU 9
1 BU was starved for technology historically (−)
2 IS needs to understand the business better.(−)   Rating: **moderate**

1 Reporting relationship not clear.(−)
2 No agreed upon business strategy.(−)
3 IS people need a better understanding of the business.(−)   Rating: **moderate**

1 Good prioritization process.(+)
2 IS people are located close to the business people.(+)
3 Need for some quick deliverables.(−)
4 IS people need some business experience.(−)   Rating: **high**

BU 10 1 Meetings deal with IS and other issues simultaneously.(+)   Rating: **high**

1 Good support from executives.(+)   Rating: **high**

1 BU is simple to operate, the IT problems are not too complicated.(+)
2 Less strategic dependence on IT.(+)   Rating: **high**

Note: Reasons given by each respondent are shown separately. A (+) sign means that the respondent felt the reason positively influenced link-age. A(−) sign means the opposite.

Appendix C

Sample interview/survey questions to measure linkage

1   Short-Term Linkage

    a   Self-Reports
        see 'Self-Reports About Linkage' section of the chapter
    b   Understanding of Current Objectives

For each executive:

1   Are you aware of the ourrent (1–2 year) business goals and strategies for your business unit (BU)?
2   If, NO, why not . . . e.g.
    a   They have not been formulated.
    b   I was not involved in creating them.
    c   I recently joined the unit.
    d   I am not a member of the senior management team.
    e   They have not been communicated to me.
3   If YES, please state the three most important business goals.
4   From the following list, identify the three business goals that most closely match those in your BU e.g.
    a   expand the market for existing products/services
    b   obtain more market share for existing products/services
    c   create new products/services
    d   improve the profitability of existing products/services
    etc. . . .
5   From the following list, identify the three business strategies that most closely match those of your BU, e.g.
    a   improve customcr satisfaction
    b   improve the features of the products/services
    c   lower the production costs of the products/services
    d   lower the distribution costs of the products/services
    e   lower the after sales costs of the products/services
    f   improve financial management
6   Are you aware of the current IT goals and strategies for your business unit?
7   If NO, why not?
    same as number 2
8   If YES, please state the three most important IT goals:
9   From the following list, identify the short-term IT goals that most closely match those of your unit. e.g.
    a   complete projects already identified
    b   create an IT plan

    c   improve productivity of IT people

    d   improve understanding and usage of IT in the business unit

    e   change the hardware/software infrastructure

2 Long-Term Linkage

1   Are you aware of the long-term business plans of your unit?
etc. . . . as in short-term linkage for questions 2, 3, 4 . . .

5   Please identify the long-term IT vision that most closely matches that of your business unit:

    a   provide IT to help the salespeople improve productivity

    b   provide IT to link different sites in support of a global strategy

    c   provide IT to make the production and distribution process more efficient

    d   provide common databases for decision making and planning
etc. . . . taken from Zviran (1990)

References

Calhoun, K. J. and Lederer, A. L. (1990) From strategic business planning to strategic information systems planning: the missing Link. *Journal of Information Technology Management,* **1**(1), 1–6.

Chan, Y. F. and Huff, S. L. (1992) The development of instruments to assess information systems and company strategy and performance. Working Paper 92–06, University of Western Ontario.

Computerworld (1994), May 19, p.84.

Conrath, D. W., Ang, J. S. K. and Mattey, S. (1992) Strategic planning for information systems: a survey of Canadian organizations. *INFOR, The Canadian Journal of Information Processing and Operations Research,* **30**(4), November, 364–378.

Cresap, McCormick, and Paget Company (1983) *Information Systems Planning to Support Business Objectives: A Survey of Practices,* Cresap, McCormick, and Paget Co., New York.

Das, S., Zahra, S. A. and Warketin, M. E. (1991) Integrating the content and process of strategic MIS planning with competitive strategy. *Decision Sciences,* **22**(5), November–December, 953–985.

Doll, W. J. and Torkzadeh, G. (1987) The relationship of MIS steering committees to the size of firm and formalization of MIS planning. *Comunications of the ACM,* **30**(11), November, 972–978.

Earl, M. J. (1987) Information strategy formulation. In *Critical Issues in Information Systems Research* (eds R. J. Boland and R. A. Hirschheim), Wiley, Chichester, pp.157–178.

Feeny, D. F., Edwards, B. and Simpson, K. (1992) Understanding the CEO/ CIO relationship. *Proceedings of the Thirteenth International Conference on Information Systems*, Dallas, TX, December, pp.119–126.

Fishbein, M. and Ajzen, I. (1975) *Belief, Attitude, Intention, and Behavior: An Introduction to Theory and Research*, Addison-Wesley, Reading, MA.

Galliers, R. D. (1987) *Information System Planning in Britain and Australia in the mid-1980s: Key Success Factors*. Ph.D. dissertation, University of London.

Galliers, R. D., Merali, Y. and Spearing, L. (1994) Coping with information technology? How British executives perceive the key issues in the mid-1990's. *Journal of Information Technology*, **9**(4), 223–238.

Hartwick, J. and Barki, H. (1994) Explaining the role of user participation in information systems use. *Management Science*, **40**(4), April, 440–465.

Henderson, J. and Sifonis, J. (1988) Understanding the value of IS planning: understanding consistency, validity and IS markets. *MIS Quarterly*, **12**(2), June, 187–200.

Henderson, J. C. and Venkatraman, N. (1992) Strategic alignment: a model for organizational transformation through information technology. In *Transforming Organizations* (eds T. A. Kocham and M. Useem), Oxford University Press, New York.

Horovitz, J. (1984) New perspectives on strategic management. *Journal of Business Strategy*, **4**(3), Winter, 19–33.

Index Group (1988) *Critical Issues of Information Systems Management in 1988*, CSC Index, Boston, MA, January.

Jarvenpaa, S. L. and Ives, B. (1993) Organizing for global competition: the fit of information technology. *Decision Sciences*, **24**(3), May–June, 547–580.

Lederer, A. and Mendelow, A. (1986) Issues in information systems planning. *Information and Management*, **10**(5), May, 245–254.

Lederer, A. and Mendelow, A. (1989) The coordination of information systems plans with business plans. *Journal of Management Information Systems*, **6**(2), Fall, 5–19.

Miles, M. B. and Huberman, A. M. (1994) *Qualitative Data Analysis*, Sage Publications, Newbury Park, CA.

Niederman, F., Brancheau, J. and Wetherbe, J. (1991) Information systems management issues in the 1990s. *MIS Quarterly*, **15**(4), December, 474–500.

Parker, M. M., Trainor, E. H. and Benson, R. J. (1989) *Information Strategy and Economics*, Prentice Hall Inc., Englewood Cliffs, NJ.

Pyburn, P. (1983) Linking the MIS plan with corporate strategy: an exploratory study. *MIS Quarterly*, **7**(2), June, 1–14.

Raghunathan, B. and Raghunathan, T. S. (1990) Planning system success: replication and extension to the information systems context. Working Paper, University of Toledo, Toledo, OH.

Reich, B. H. (1993) *Investigating the Linkage between Business and Information Technology Objectives: A Multiple Case Study in the Insurance Industry*, unpublished Ph.D. dissertation, University of British Columbia, Vancouver, BC.

Reich, B. H. and Benbasat, I. (1994) Understanding the factors influencing linkage between business and IT objectives. Working Paper, Simon Fraser University, Burnaby, B. C., Canada.

Sambamurthy, V. and Zmud, R. W. (1992) *Managing IT for Success: The Empowering Business Partnership*, Financial Executives Research Foundation, NJ.

Shank, R., Niblock, E. G. and Sandalls, W. T., Jr. (1973) Balance creativity and practicality in formal planning. *Harvard Business Review*, **51**(1), January–February, 87–95.

Sullivan, C., Jr. (1985) Systems planning in the information age. *Sloan Management Review*, **26**(2), Winter, 3–12.

Sviokla, J. J. (1986) *Planpower, XCON, and Mudman: An In-depth Analysis into 3 Commercial Expert Systems in Use*, Ph.D. dissertation, Harvard University, Cambridge, MA.

Venkatraman, N. (1989) The concept of fit in strategy research: toward verbal and statistical correspondence. *Academy of Management Review*, **14**(3), 423–444.

Yin, R. K. (1989) *Case Study Research: Design and Methods*, 2nd edn, Sage Publications, Newbury Park, CA.

Zviran, M. (1990) Relationship between organizational and information systems objectives: some empirical evidence. *Journal of Management Information Systems*, **7**(1), Summer, 65–84.

Questions for discussion

1 The authors state that the IT literature is not consistent in describing what the IT plans should be linked to. What should be the focus of an IT plan?
2 Assume you are an IT manager and wish to assess how well IT is aligned with your organization, how might you go about this? What do you think of the authors' method of determining alignment?
   – compare with that of Jarvenpaa and Ives (Chapter 12) for determining the CEO's perspective of the importance of IT.
   – compare with that of Smits *et al.* (Chapter 3) for determining the link between IS and business strategy.

3   There is much talk of the importance of senior management's IS vision of IT in SISP planning success – how is an IT manager to know what the vision of senior management is as regards IT? Can the IT manager shape the vision of senior managers, and how?

4   The authors define vision as 'a clear expectation of the role IT would play in contributing to the long-term success of the organizational unit'. Critique this definition. In comparison to other functions (finance, marketing, for example), is it more or less important for IT to have a shared vision with business executives?

5   The authors found that all business units had a list of IT projects that would require more than a year to complete, but they lacked a written description of the IT strategy and objectives adopted for the business unit. Furthermore, 'only one IS group had created and published a strategy plan'. What might be the reason for this? What purpose would a formal plan serve? Do you think such a plan might be an important means of improving IS credibility or of spreading a shared vision of IT in the organization?

14 Information Systems Strategy and Business Process Reengineering

Balance in business reengineering: fit and performance

A. Huizing, E. Koster and W. Bouman

This chapter addresses the complex relationship between fit and organizational performance in business reengineering. First, a framework for analysis based on the concept of fit is proposed. Three generic archetypes for three levels of ambitions are defined. Archetypes or ideal-type patterns of change are consistent packages of design and change management measures. It is hypothesized that organizations that change according to an ideal-type pattern outperform organizations that follow a different, inconsistent pattern. On the basis of a questionnaire sent to organizations involved in reengineering, this chapter shows that consistent reengineering endeavors generally result in greater benefits than do inconsistent change efforts. It also demonstrates that only a minority of organizations have succeeded in creating a 'magical mix' between the level of ambition and the design and change management measures actually taken. Finally, the managerial implications and future research challenges are described.

Introduction

The management and organization literature is imbued with the notion of 'fit', 'match', or 'balance'. Organizations are urged to align their strategy to their environment, to bring internal factors like structure, systems, style, and culture in line with their strategy, and to maintain a balance during the process of organizational change.[9,28,29,37,43,50,51,54] The business reengineering literature is no exception to this trend.[15,27,34,39,69] While these theories vary widely in subject matter, they share the common proposition that an organizational outcome is the consequence of a fit between two or more factors or dimensions.[65] Conversely, misfits or mismatches between such dimensions are held to reduce organizational performance.

The notion of fit is not just a theoretical stance lacking any practical relevance. On the contrary, in our study, to which we will refer later, 90 percent of the respondents affirm that 'management by matching'[9] is *the* critical success factor in reengineering. Moreover, many cases presented in the reengineering literature implicitly or explicitly provide anecdotal evidence supporting the idea of fit.[11,26,62]

With so much theoretical attention and practical relevance, the notion of fit would seem to be common sense rather than a matter for vehement debate; however, there are three factors that contradict this: First, achieving fit is a fragile process.[50,51] Mismatches easily occur. Therefore, fit should be a matter of central concern to both academics and practitioners. Second, most empirical studies on reengineering lack a multidimensional view.[10,14,21] They are directed toward the identification of single critical success factors, such as the commitment of top management or intensive communications, whose mutual interactions are not investigated at all. Neglecting the notion of fit, they leave the process of achieving fit to the intuition of the manager. Third, in the search for explanations for organizational performance, there is a continuous debate over which dimensions need to be balanced.[12,36,37,49] For instance, in the reengineering literature, the relationship between organizational performance and the breadth and depth of change processes has been studied.[31] Many of these studies can be criticized, however, for focusing on organizational design and ignoring change management issues. Only recently is change management beginning to receive the attention it deserves.[30,35]

With this chapter we hope to contribute to the debate on fit and its relationship to organizational performance. Our goal is to synthesize findings from previous literature on organizational design, change management, performance, and business reengineering into a coherent framework that will help managers achieve fit in complex change processes. We also conducted an empirical study to validate the framework. The framework was operationalized into a questionnaire that was sent to change managers who had experience leading business reengineering projects or programs. The following questions have guided us:

1   Do organizations that achieve fit in a business reengineering change process outperform organizations that change in an unbalanced way?
2   Is there evidence that reengineering success depends on the number of misfits that emerge during the change process?

Fit and organizational performance

Is fit in reengineering an essential factor to explain organizational performance? To study this relationship, we first have to choose which dimensions
of organizational change to include in the concept of fit. Our framework distinguishes five dimensions: level of ambition, breadth, depth, planning, and
coordination of the change process (see Figure 14.1 for the complete framework). As will be explained subsequently, level of ambition is the contingency factor in our study, while the other four dimensions are the independent
factors. Breadth and depth relate to organizational design; planning and coordination concern change management issues. Each of these dimensions can
contribute to reengineering success. However, treating an organization or a
change process as being decomposable into discrete dimensions that can be
examined separately does no justice to the complex interactions between
these dimensions. How these dimensions interact can also be a vital factor in
explaining organizational performance.[50,65]

To gain an explicit understanding of the interactions between the distinguished dimensions, a measure of synthesis is needed.[29,47,51] Archetypes or
ideal-type patterns of change can serve this purpose.[65] By archetypes or ideal-
type patterns we mean consistent packages of design and change management measures that correspond with the level of ambition set. To account for
the fact that organizations differ in their level of ambition, our framework
consists of three archetypes. It seems logical to assume that an appropriate set
of design and change management measures varies with the level of ambition.[3,62] Metaphorically speaking, climbing Mount Everest simply demands a
more powerful arsenal of measures than climbing a sand dune. We therefore
distinguish between organizations with relatively low, medium, and high
ambitions. As can be seen from Figure 14.1, the matching archetypes are
labeled the 'local project', the 'cross-functional project', and the 'companywide
program'. These labels reflect that an ever larger part of the entire business
system is affected by the reengineering effort.

The first archetype stands for an incremental, bottom-up, narrow change
of an existing process within an operational function that requires relatively simple change management measures. From the perspective of the total
business system, a local project leads to minor adjustments such as locally improved customer contacts. These minor adjustments, however, should
be sufficient to realize the relatively low ambitions of the organization.
The second archetype reflects a middle-out, average change focused on the
interdependence of activities across distinct functional lines that demands
extended planning and coordination measures. It leads to a radical change
in a substantial yet distinct part of the organization. The last archetype
describes a top-down, large-scale reengineering effort. To achieve the relatively high level of ambition, the focus is on transforming the whole business

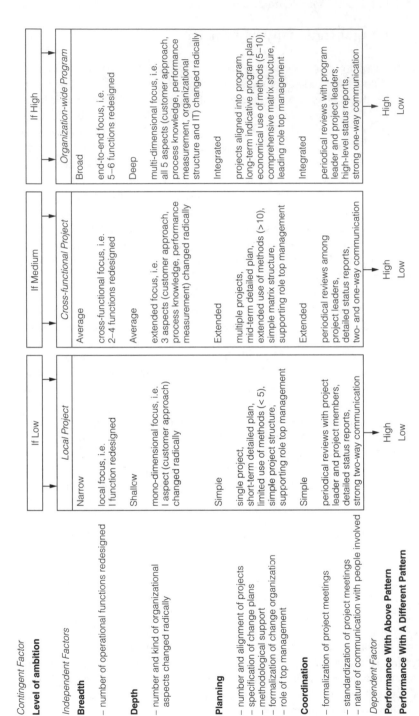

Figure 14.1 *Hypothesis in level of ambition contingent model*

Contingent Factor
Level of ambition

	If Low	If Medium	If High
	Local Project	*Cross-functional Project*	*Organization-wide Program*
Independent Factors			
Breadth	Narrow	Average	Broad
– number of operational functions redesigned	local focus, i.e. 1 function redesigned	cross-functional focus, i.e. 2–4 functions redesigned	end-to-end focus, i.e. 5–6 functions redesigned
Depth	Shallow	Average	Deep
– number and kind of organizational aspects changed radically	mono-dimensional focus, i.e. 1 aspect (customer approach) changed radically	extended focus, i.e. 3 aspects (customer approach, process knowledge, performance measurement) changed radically	multi-dimensional focus, i.e. all 5 aspects (customer approach, process knowledge, performance measurement, organizational structure and IT) changed radically
Planning	Simple	Extended	Integrated
– number and alignment of projects – specification of change plans – methodological support – formalization of change organization – role of top management	single project, short-term detailed plan, limited use of methods (< 5), simple project structure, supporting role top management	multiple projects, mid-term detailed plan, extended use of methods (>10), simple matrix structure, supporting role top management	projects aligned into program, long-term indicative program plan, economical use of methods (5–10), comprehensive matrix structure, leading role top management
Coordination	Simple	Extended	Integrated
– formalization of project meetings – standardization of project meetings – nature of communication with people involved	periodical reviews with project leader and project members, detailed status reports, strong two-way communication	periodical reviews among project leaders, detailed status reports, two- and one-way communication	periodical reviews with program leader and project leaders, high-level status reports, strong one-way communication
Dependent Factor			
Performance With Above Pattern	High	High	High
Performance With A Different Pattern	Low	Low	Low

system, which places great demands on organizational design and change management.

The three archetypes reflect how the notion of fit has been conceptualized. If organizations succeed in combining the distinguished dimensions into an ideal-type pattern of change, they achieve fit. If they deviate from such a pattern, our framework suggests that they will suffer from one to four misfits. In that case, the breadth, depth, planning, and/or coordination dimensions are not properly synchronized with the organization's aspirations. Such misfits or deviations are hypothesized to lead to reduced performance.

Hypothesis: The three ideal-type patterns of change are models of success that will outperform any other pattern.

The archetypes enable us to make a distinction between organizations that change according to an ideal-type pattern and organizations that follow a different pattern – that is, organizations that face at least one misfit. To test the hypothesis, the resulting groups of (what we have called) consistent and inconsistent organizations have to be compared with each other on the basis of a measure for reengineering success. Reengineering success, the dependent factor in our framework, is defined later. The organizations studied can also be grouped according to the number of misfits they faced. These groups can be correlated with the success measure to show the effect of a growing number of deviations on reengineering success.

In the next three sections the archetypes are further illustrated and underpinned. Each archetype consists of four 'minipatterns' that relate to the breadth, depth, planning, and coordination dimensions. These dimensions are defined, and the minipatterns are specified. The definition of a measure for reengineering success concludes our framework.

Level of ambition: the contingency factor

The process of achieving fit begins, conceptually at least, by aligning the organization to its environment.[50] If a strategic gap is perceived, organizations normally reflect on current performance and the improvements needed. By stating their ambitions, organizations try to bridge the gap with the environment. At the same time, a gap is revealed between the organization's ambitions and its resources.[32] This second gap has to be closed by taking appropriate design and change management measures.[27,31,33] Therefore, achieving fit not only means that the strategic gap has to be bridged, but also implies that the package of reengineering measures is properly attuned to the level of ambition. The level of ambition is therefore the pivot or contingency factor in our framework. This chapter discusses only the relationships between ambitions and the set of measures with which organizations hope to achieve the improvements needed. Whether organizations actually succeed in closing the gap with the environment as a result of reengineering remains outside the scope of this chapter.

In this study, the level of ambition is determined by the number and size of the *intended* performance improvements and whether or not a sustainable competitive advantage or breakpoint is pursued (Figure 14.2). This definition is based on three general considerations found in the reengineering literature. First, with regard to the kind of performance improvements to be pursued, managers are stimulated to listen to customers to hear the value they put on products and services.[15,37,39,64] Since value to the customer cannot be assessed in purely financial terms,[39] the level of ambition will typically express a multitude of financial and nonfinancial value metrics, such as reduction of cost and improvement of customer satisfaction. Second, in order to motivate and mobilize the organization and to enhance the tangibility of an organization's strategy, it is emphasized that managers quantify their aspirations.[7,16,34] Finally, to gain market dominance, organizations are urged to strive for a breakpoint – that is, to pursue excellence in one or more of the relevant value metrics.[39,63]

In other words, the reengineering literature stimulates organizations to pursue a high level of ambition, leading to a radical change that places high demands on the design and change management measures to be taken. However, not every organization wants to change radically, is able to do so, or has the courage to do so. In practice, organizations trade off among the need to change, the ability to change, and the risks involved in changing the organization,[4] and this process leads to different levels of ambition. As we have said, we account for these differences by dividing the organizations studied into three groups: those striving for relatively low, medium, and high ambitions.

Breadth, depth, planning, coordination: the independent factors

Regardless of which level of ambition organizations choose, aspirations have to be translated into an appropriate package of reengineering measures. In this section, we argue that these measures can be arranged into four dimensions of organizational change: breadth, depth, planning, and coordination of the change process. Breadth and depth apply to organizational design; planning and coordination relate to change management issues. These four dimensions and level of ambition, together with their constituent elements, are included in Figure 14.2.

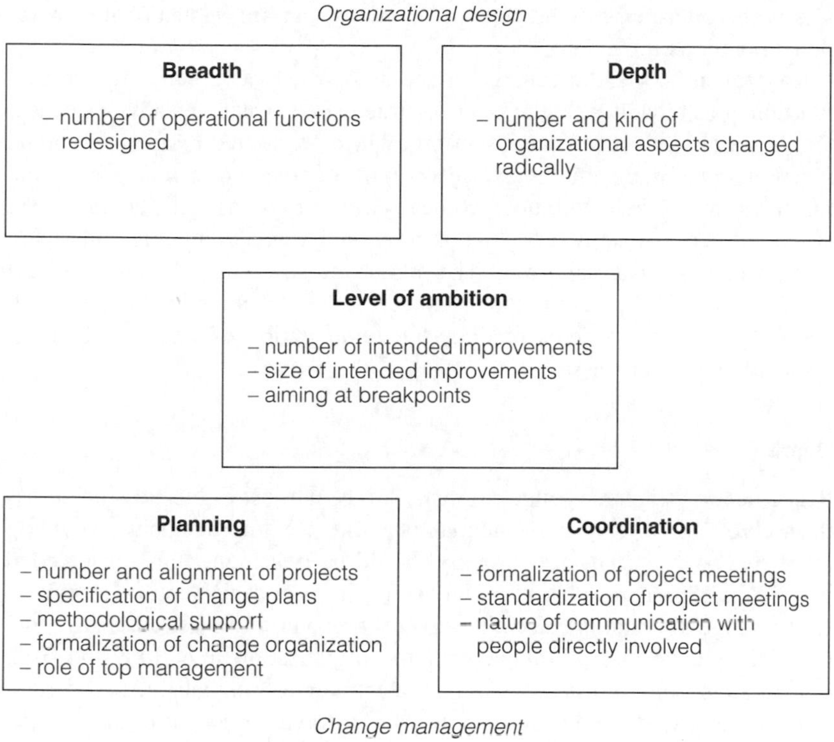

Organizational design

Breadth	Depth
– number of operational functions redesigned	– number and kind of organizational aspects changed radically

Level of ambition

– number of intended improvements
– size of intended improvements
– aiming at breakpoints

Planning	Coordination
– number and alignment of projects – specification of change plans – methodological support – formalization of change organization – role of top management	– formalization of project meetings – standardization of project meetings – nature of communication with people directly involved

Change management

Figure 14.2   *Dimensions of organizational change*

Breadth

Delivering value to the customer seems to be the strategic imperative of the 1990s. Consequently, reengineering has to result in performance improvements that are clearly recognizable to customers. This requirement puts business processes at the center of theoretical and practical attention, for it is at the operational level that products and services are delivered to the customer.[39] Before embarking on reengineering, the activities that are critical for value creation first have to be identified. Then which critical activities will be included in the change process have to be decided.

We describe breadth as the number of critical activities or operational functions tackled in the reengineering effort (Figure 14.2). Inspired by Porter's value chain,[58] six critical activities are distinguished: procurement, inbound logistics, production, marketing and sales, outbound logistics, and service. A business process is one sequence of functional activities.[15,39,41] Such business processes are central to business functioning and have a direct relationship with the external customer. Changing a business process or parts of it inherently affects the management and support functions that are related to the operational functions involved.

Consequently, breadth can be defined as narrowly as a single operational function or as broadly as entire business processes.[31] Archetypically, we expect that *less* ambitious reengineering efforts will be restricted to one operational function, *moderately* ambitious projects will involve two to four operational functions, and *highly* ambitious companywide programs will include most, if not all, critical activities. In this way, a basic assumption underlying reengineering is made concrete: The higher the ambitions, the more critical activities should be taken into account.[18,31,34,39,41] Achieving breakthrough performance improvements requires the reintegration of traditionally fragmented business processes.

Depth

Reengineering triggers changes of many kinds, not just of business processes themselves.[33] To achieve substantial performance improvements, anything associated with the business process should be refashioned in an integrated way.[31,39] In this regard, all kinds of innovative ideas or design options stemming from a range of academic disciplines might prove useful: mass customization, self-managing teams, the division of the organization into front and back offices, supporting processes with new technologies, the balanced scorecard, activity-based costing, and so on.[25,42,56,60,61] However, a danger of such single options is that they will live a life on their own in separate corners of the organization. It is the challenging task of the redesign team to combine such options fruitfully into a logical and consistent new organizational design. The redesign team also has to decide on the radicalness with which the design options have to be applied.

By depth we mean the number and kind of organizational aspects or levers that change profoundly as a result of reengineering (see Figure 14.2). To analyze this dimension, we have combined fifty design options described in the aforementioned literature into five organizational aspects: the customer approach, process knowledge, organizational structure, information technology, and performance measurement (for examples of the design options used, see the Appendix).

Changing the organizational aspects has to contribute to the behavioral change needed to achieve the ambitions set for the change process. It is generally assumed that the higher the ambitions, the more organizational aspects should be changed radically.[3,31,34,39] It is also suggested that customer and process-oriented change levers have more impact on organizational performance than do investments in other levers.[5,13,30,52,60] In fact, the reengineering literature warns against traditional restructuring or information systems improvement.[15,34] We therefore hold that every kind of reengineering, including *less* ambitious change efforts, should focus first on the customer. For *medium* ambitions, radical changes should also be sought in building up process knowledge and new performance measures to reinforce the reassessed relationship with the customer and the business process perspective. Creating supporting performance measures can strongly affect organizational behavior in a desired direction.[42] On top of this, *highly* ambitious reengineering initiatives should embed these changes in radically new organizational structures and information systems by applying design options such as delayering, decentralization, shared databases, and systems integration.

Planning

Reengineering efforts have to be prepared and structured to force implementation of the new organizational design.[3,30,35,66] In this regard, many planning decisions have to be made. It has to be decided whether change activities can be grouped into one or more autonomous projects or whether they need to be aligned into a formal change program.[41,57,67] Other planning issues involve the phasing of change activities into short-, middle-, or long-term change plans,[3,38] and the number and kind of methods and techniques that will be applied to specify these plans.[14,31,34] Change can also be achieved within the existing hierarchy or through the establishment of temporary governance structures, which can vary from simple project structures to comprehensive matrix structures.[45,46] Finally, it has to be decided at what hierarchical level the change leader role should be fullfilled and, consequently, what the most appropriate role is for top management.[38,66]

With respect to the planning dimension, we refer to five change management measures: the number and alignment of projects, the specification of change plans, the methodological support of change managers, the formalization of the change organization, and the role of top management (see Figure 14.2). In view of the level of ambition, managers have to decide upon these planning measures in order to guarantee a firm and effective grip on the change process. It is assumed that the higher the ambitions, the higher the demands on the preparation and structuring of the change effort.[48] Naturally, the larger the number of change activities and people involved, the greater the emphasis should be on aligning the change activities and formalizing the change organization to keep the change effort manageable. These considerations underpin the following 'minipatterns'.

In the achievement of *low* ambitions, we hold that effective planning takes place by defining a single project and a detailed, short-term project plan, for which a limited number of supporting methods and techniques are used. The small project domain suggests that existing governance structures or simple project structures are effective means of uniting those involved in the change effort. Lower management leadership is assumed to be most fruitful in this kind of reengineering,[5,20] for leadership should be fulfilled at a management level that just oversees that project domain.[67,68] In fact, active, ongoing involvement of top management suggests a waste of management capacity.

In *moderately* ambitious change efforts, it is expected that multiple projects are defined that are underpinned by detailed, solid project plans for which methods and techniques are extensively used. An extended yet simple matrix structure, uniting people from different disciplines and management levels, indicates adequate structuring of the reengineering effort. In fact, comprehensive matrix structures comprising numerous steering committees and task forces should be avoided, for they can easily add to the complexity of the change process.[20,22,46] Moreover, in view of the enlarged project domain, middle management's proactive leadership is assumed to be most effective in this kind of reengineering.[5,45,67,68]

Highly ambitious change efforts need tight alignment of projects into a formal change program[6,17,22,38] underpinned by a compelling vision, that is, by an indicative, long-term program plan with one or more quantified goals rather than highly detailed specifications.[5,18,30,34] Otherwise, the change effort can easily dissolve into a list of confusing and incompatible projects that can take the organization in the wrong direction or nowhere at all.[45] Considering the complexity of highly ambitious change efforts, the economic use of methods and techniques to examine market and competitive realities is required to prevent 'analysis paralysis'.[34,38] In addition, comprehensive matrix structures need to be established to ensure broad participation throughout the organization.[38,45,66] Finally, top management's active leadership is required, for this kind of reengineering should be directed by a 'tough-minded' program leader with a high degree of formal authority.[6,13,14,31,34,45]

Coordination

Facilitating communication among change managers and with 'change targets' – that is, those people directly affected by the changes – is crucial in the realization of change. Since reengineering often fails because project and program leaders lose focus on the scope and goals of the change effort, keeping track of change effort progress is a key issue for management.[7,14,30] It therefore has to be decided whether or not formal periodical reviews of the change process have to take place and who needs to participate in these meetings: team members, project leaders, and/or program leaders?[66] Decisions also have to be made with respect to the standardization of these meetings – whether detailed or high-level status reports can be used to ensure efficient information exchange and documentation. Besides, communication with those directly affected by the changes is required to overcome resistance to change.[14,34,35] In general, all existing formal and informal communication

channels should be used to broadcast plans for change.[1,22,31,45] More specifically, it has to be decided how those directly affected by the changes should
be informed about the change process: by two-way communication that offers
'change targets' explicit opportunities to influence the course of the change
process, or by one-way communication, for instance through large-scale pres-
entations, videos, and bulletins?[38,66]

By coordination we mean three change management measures used to
gather and convey information needed to attune the change activities during
the reengineering effort: the formalization of project meetings, the standardization of project meetings, and the nature of communication with those
directly affected by the changes (see Figure 14.2). With respect to the level
of ambition set, managers have to decide upon these coordination measures
in order to help sustain a greater focus on and commitment to the goals
set for the change process. We expect that the higher the ambitions are, the
more pressing the demands on coordination will be.[6,48,66] Evidently, tailored
measures must be taken to prevent communications from becoming either
insufficient or too exhaustive.

We hold that, in the pursuit of *low* ambitions, formal project meetings
between the project leader and project members, based on detailed progress
reports, are sufficient to keep track of the change effort's progress. Communication with those directly affected by the changes is assumed to entail two-
way communication, for higher commitment to the change process can be
obtained in this way.[30] When *medium* ambitions are the goal, formal periodical reviews among the various project leaders, informing each other by
written status reports, are assumed to be an effective way of attuning change
activities. Coordination with the rest of the organization suggests a mixture of
two-way and one-way communication, for the larger the number of people
involved in the change process, the less feasible it becomes to consider all
individual interests. In *highly* ambitious reengineering, the change activities
need to be coordinated at the highest level in the change organization's hierarchy. Formal periodical change reviews among the program coordinator and
project leaders therefore have to be built into the change management process
to monitor the attainment of milestones at critical junctures.[6,30,57] In addition,
these program meetings should be standardized using high-level milestone
reports, for a strong emphasis on project documentation can easily draw too
much attention to highly detailed matters, especially in major reengineering
endeavors.[38] Such reports help to keep efforts focused on the main issues and
prevent 'micro-management'. Furthermore, extensive and reinforcing top-
down communication with those directly affected by the changes is needed
in order to resolve the conflicts of interests that inevitably arise.[13,24,38] Consequently, rather coercive, one-way communications are required in addition
to two-way communications, to prevent communications from becoming too
exhaustive and compromising.

Reengineering success: the dependent factor

We have described three archetypal patterns of change. Each archetype consists of four minipatterns relating to the breadth, depth, planning, and coordination dimensions. Deviations from these minipatterns on any or all dimensions are hypothesized to lead to reduced performance. To recapitulate, our hypothesis states that the three archetypes are models of success that will outperform any other pattern. To test this hypothesis, a measure for reengineering success is needed.

Reengineering success is defined as the number and size of the *achieved* performance improvements. We will discuss this measure in more detail in the next section. For now it suffices to say that the respondents were explicitly asked to show the effect of reengineering on the overall performance of the organization or business unit. The success measure not only shows how successful each organization has been in its reengineering endeavor, but it also provides us with a standardized measure to compare organizations with each other. This can be done in two ways. First, consistent organizations can be compared with inconsistent organizations, that is, organizations that faced at least one misfit. Second, we can correlate the number of misfits that emerged in the change efforts to reengineering success. The hypothesis cannot be rejected if organizations deviating from the ideal-type pattern of change, as well as the number of misfits, are significantly and negatively correlated with reengineering success.

Research methodology

Many previous studies on business reengineering are casuistic,[11,26,62] and there are few empirical studies with generalizable results.[30] To promote generalizability, to achieve greater contextual richness, and in search of a stronger theoretical foundation for business reengineering, the framework we have just described was operationalized into a questionnaire. This data-collection method allows for replicability and permits some degree of statistical power.[40] Figure 14.3 outlines the steps taken in our research design.

The sixteen-page questionnaire was pretested among several methodologists as well as in a pilot project. The revised questionnaire consisted of a mixture of closed and open questions covering the distinguished dimensions of our framework and background details of the organization and respondent. The questionnaire was constructed using five-point scales and discrete categories. Since the study draws on relevant theories, perspectives, and literature, the content validity of the questionnaire is claimed on theoretical grounds. An outline of the questionnaire is included in the Appendix.

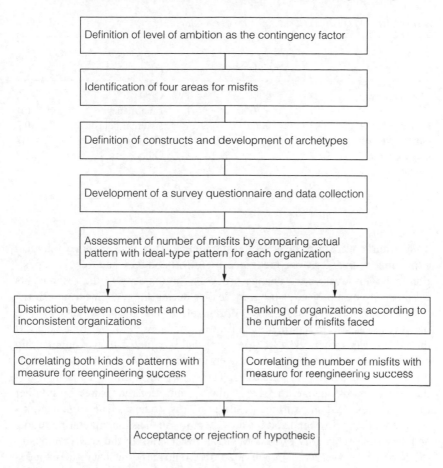

Figure 14.3   *Steps in the research design*

Research Base

The unit of analysis in our study was the change process or reengineering effort, defined as a period in the development of an organization or a business unit in which several related goal-oriented change activities are undertaken to realize a more or less radical change in the form or functioning of an organization. Data were collected from Dutch organizations and business units. These organizations stem from the networks of the Department of Information Management at the University of Amsterdam and the Dutch Association of Business Engineers (ABE). The ABE is a leading forum for reengineering professionals in the Netherlands. Organizations were contacted beforehand to find out whether or not they were interested in participating in the project.

Table 14.1 *Profile of organizations and respondents*

Branch	%	Size (no. employees)	%	Respondent's current position	%
Manufacturing	12.1	< 200	36.4	CEO	21.2
Trade	9.1	200–1000	36.4	Line manager	6.1
Banking/finance	24.2	> 1000	27.3	External consultant	30.3
Other services	27.3			IT manager	21.2
Government	21.2			Other staff	21.2
Nonprofit	3.0				
Other	3.0				

Two criteria were used to select respondents: They had to have practical experience with at least one reengineering effort and they had to be in a position to largely oversee the change process. The majority of the respondents fulfilled a role as project or program leader during the reengineering effort.

Questionnaires were sent to 160 organizations and business units. A total of 90 responses were returned, resulting in a response rate of 56 percent. Of these 90 organizations, 33 (36.7 percent) had completed their reengineering effort and were able to respond to the entire questionnaire. This study reports on these 33 reengineering initiatives. Table 14.1 shows the sectors in which the organizations operate, the size of the organizations measured by number of employees, and the current position of respondents. The organizations represent all governmental and business sectors, such as manufacturing, trade, and services. A majority of the organizations operate in the service industry (51.5 percent). Measured by number of employees, the data set includes small, medium-size, and large organizations.

Operationalization of the dimensions

The contingency factor (level of ambition), the four independent factors (breadth, depth, planning, and coordination), and the dependent factor (reengineering success) in our framework have been operationalized into constructs. In this way, the complexity of analyzing the innumerable interactions between the constituent elements of these factors (see Figure 14.2) has been reduced to four areas in which misfits can arise.

The *level of ambition* was determined by asking respondents to indicate the number and size of the *intended* performance improvements and whether or not a sustainable competitive advantage was pursued. They could choose from a generic set of ten indicators or benefit categories: reduction of cost, cycle time, lead time and time to market, and improvement of customer satisfaction, delivery reliability, price/performance ratio, productivity, market share and information services (note 1). Each of these indicators could be marked or quantified by a percentage. To assess the level of ambition, the number of marked indicators was multiplied by a standardized size score of the quantified indicators and divided by the maximum number of indicators. The resulting score was multiplied by a constant factor if a breakpoint was targeted. Next, based on the ambition scores, the thirty-three organizations were divided into three equal groups: low, medium, and high (note 2). *Reengineering success* was assessed by using the same generic set of benefit categories that was applied in determining the level of ambition. However, now the number and size of the *achieved* performance improvements were taken into account. As a result, the success scores could vary between the values 0 and 1.

With respect to the four independent factors, the following procedure was applied. In order to determine whether or not a misfit occurred on the *breadth* dimension, the indicated number of critical activities redesigned was compared with the number defined in the ideal-type pattern. With regard to the *depth* dimension, respondents were asked to indicate on a Likert scale to what degree fifty design options were changed (1 = strongly decreased and 5 = strongly increased). To decide how radically each of the five organizational aspects was changed, the number of design options was multiplied by points given on the Likert scale. A depth score of more than 60 percent of the maximum score was held to distinguish between radically and nonradically changed aspects. This means that many design options had to be applied intensively before the changes related to any one organizational aspect were labeled 'radical'. The questions concerning the *planning* and *coordination* dimensions were closed questions with discrete answer alternatives. The answers could be directly compared with the appropriate minipatterns. As for methodological support, depending on the number of methods and techniques applied, organizations were allocated to one of the three distinguished categories: limited (<5), extended (>10), and economical use (5 < x < 10). Thus, for each dimension, a deviation of the specified minipattern produced a misfit (note 3).

Findings on fit and performance

We started by posing two questions: 'Do organizations that achieve fit in a reengineering process outperform organizations that change in an unbalanced way?' and 'Is there evidence that reengineering success depends on the number of misfits that emerge during the change process?' To answer these questions, first, we correlate consistent and inconsistent organizations to reengineering success, then we provide details on how ambitious and successful the

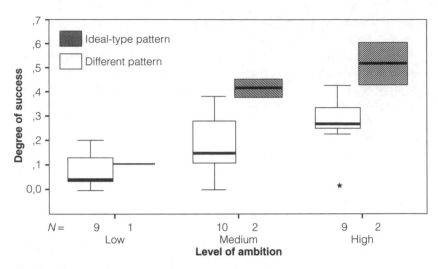

Figure 14.4   *Patterns of change and success*
Note: Boxplots provide a simple graphical means of visualizing the distribution
of scores in each of the distinguished groups. The upper and lower boundaries
of the boxes are the upper and lower quartiles. The box length is the interquartile
distance, and the box contains the middle 50% of values in a group. The horizontal
line inside the box identifies the group median. The larger the box, the greater the
spread of the observations. Any points between 1.5 and 3 interquartile ranges from
the end of the box (outliers) are marked with circles. The lines emanating from
each box (the whiskers) extend to the smallest and largest observations in a group
that are not outliers. Points more than 3 interquartile distances away from the box
(extreme values) are marked with asterisks.[53]

thirty-three reengineering efforts studied have been. We then examine breadth,
depth, planning, and coordination in greater detail. Finally, we demonstrate the
effect of a growing number of misfits on reengineering success.

Ideal types versus different patterns

In order to appreciate the balance or fit of the reengineering initiatives
studied, we compared the actual change patterns followed with the ideal-
type patterns that suited the chosen level of ambition. We hold that organizations are in balance if, and only if, no mismatches emerged in the process
of change. Figure 14.4 shows that only 15 percent of the investigated organizations actually succeeded in achieving fit to its fullest extent. Of thirty-three
cases, one organization with low ambitions, two with medium ambitions,
and two with high ambitions followed the ideal-type pattern. Others suffered
from all kinds of mismatches resulting in substantially lower reengineering
outcomes. In general, higher performance gains accrued when the level of

Table 14.2 *Ambitions and reengineering success*

Operational improvements	Low ambitions		Medium ambitions		High ambitions	
	Intended	Achieved	Intended	Achieved	Intended	Achieved
Average number of improvements	2.7	2.1	5.7	5.0	7.5	6.7
Average height of improvements (%):						
(a) reduction of cost	21.67	18.75	13.00	12.40	31.25	22.75
(b) cycle time	48.75	63.33	10.00	10.00	51.38	57.50
(c) lead time	–	–	–	10.00	36.00	53.00
(d) delivery reliability	–	–	10.33	7.00	50.00	42.20
(e) price/performance ratio	25.00	–	15.00	8.00	105.00	40.33
(f) productivity	15.00	30.00	10.00	7.00	78.75	123.00
(g) time to market	–	–	20.00	18.00	35.00	38.00
(h) market share	–	–	6.00	6.00	11.67	9.67
(i) customer satisfaction	–	–	21.67	19.50	26.25	23.60
(j) information services	–	–	33.33	25.00	61.25	58.75

ambition was accompanied by corresponding measures along the other four dimensions. The correlation between fit and reengineering success is strong and highly significant (Spearman correlation coefficient of 0.4352 with $p < 0.01$). This finding, although it is based on a limited set of thirty-three observations, answers our first research question. Organizations that achieve fit in a reengineering undertaking generally outperform organizations that change in an unbalanced way.

Ambitions and success

Most reengineering initiatives aim at and achieve simultaneous gains in a number of performance measures. There are, however, considerable differences between the three ambition categories. Table 14.2 summarizes some of these differences. Through these numbers and percentages, more insight can be gained into which performance gains were intended and achieved, and to what degree.

With respect to the average number of intended improvements, organizations with low, medium, and high ambitions reported 2.7, 5.7, and 7.5 improvements, respectively. On average, they realized 2.1, 5.0, and 6.7 performance gains. Most organizations pursued and achieved a mixture of financial and nonfinancial improvements. The most popular intended improvements were reduction of cycle time, improvement of customer satisfaction, and reduction of costs: respectively 75 percent, 70 percent, and 69 percent of the change efforts included these intentions (whether quantified or not quantified). The relatively high number of improvements reported on customer satisfaction reflects the fact that the majority of organizations initiated reengineering with an outward focus. To be more specific, the higher the ambitions, the more customer satisfaction improvement was intended and achieved. Breakpoints were pursued by sixteen organizations (two in the low ambition group, and seven in the medium and high ambition groups). As for the realized performance gains, the same three indicators were mentioned in the top three: reduction of cycle time, reduction of costs, and improvement of customer satisfaction were reported respectively by 66 percent, 66 percent, and 54 percent of the respondents (whether quantified or not quantified). The figures indicate that improving customer satisfaction is a more difficult task for organizations than cutting costs or reducing cycle times, since there is a relatively large gap between ambition and achievement (70 percent versus 54 percent).

Furthermore, only about 50 percent of the realized performance improvements were quantified. The same applies to the intended performance gains. It would seem that the message stressed in the reengineering literature,[7,15,33,38] that organizations should quantify aspirations and benefits, has not reached many organizations. Since explicit expectations and goals can support the realization of benefits, it can be stated that these organizations have not made the most of their opportunities. Finally, in agreement with past studies,[14,31] reengineering success increases with the level of ambition. In general, the highest performance gains were achieved by the most ambitious organizations (see Table 14.2). However, only a minority of the organizations studied matched the achievements made in the spectacular cases mentioned in the literature.[15,37,39] This calls into question the relationship between reengineering and dramatic performance improvements.

Breadth, depth, planning, coordination, and success

To add insight to the foregoing general conclusion derived from Figure 14.4, we must analyze the four dimensions underlying the concept of fit to find out if and how breadth, depth, planning, and coordination are correlated to reengineering success. First, *breadth* appears to be neither strongly nor significantly related to reengineering success (Spearman correlation coefficient of 0.2526 with $p > 0.05$). Thus, we were not able to prove that reengineering success depends on the number of operational functions tackled in the change effort. This finding contradicts past studies.[31] Further research is needed to examine the impact of process definition and delineation on reengineering success.[30] Second, a strong and significant relationship between *depth* and reengineering success is found (Spearman correlation coefficient of 0.5789 with $p < 0.01$). Clearly, this finding reveals and reaffirms the fundamental nature of highly ambitious reengineering initiatives that typically entail multidimensional and radical changes. It also supports the assumption that less ambitious reengineering should preferably be focused on the customer approach (if relatively low ambitions are pursued), as well as on process knowledge and performance measurement (if medium ambitions are the aim).

If we reflect on these findings relating to breadth and depth, we find that many reengineering initiatives are internally focused. Many change efforts are not directed toward critical activities at the customer interface, but are targeted at operational functions such as procurement and inbound logistics. Moreover, with regard to the five change levers distinguished in our study, many organizations are inclined toward structural and technological changes, while they neglect other organizational aspects. These observations place the outward focus shown in the ambitions set in a different light: The aspiration to achieve a higher level of customer satisfaction is often not translated into matching design measures.

Third, our study reaffirms that the way the change effort is prepared and structured directly influences reengineering outcomes. The *planning* dimension is strongly and significantly related to reengineering success (Spearman correlation coefficient of 0.4986 with $p < 0.01$). Therefore, greater benefits accrue if sufficient and appropriate planning measures are taken to guide the change effort. For example, with respect to leadership, the findings support previous research in that active senior management leadership is crucial in major reengineering initiatives.[14,30,31] However, this study also demonstrates that top management's ongoing involvement is misplaced in less ambitious reengineering efforts as it increases senior management's tendency to micromanage the change process instead of focusing on strategic objectives. Likewise, carefully aligning projects into a program and formally assigning people to project teams and steering committees is critical to success if large-scale change processes have to be managed. On the other hand, such measures are rather overdone or even harmful in less ambitious change efforts.

Fourth, the way the change effort is *coordinated* strongly and significantly affects reengineering success (Spearman correlation coefficient of 0.4620 with $p < 0.01$). This finding demonstrates that the extent and nature of coordination activities are related to reengineering outcomes. For instance, in highly ambitious change efforts there is a pressing need for periodic reviews between project and program leaders. Not addressing this need will be detrimental to the process of change. In less ambitious efforts, there is no need for such extensive coordination since relatively autonomous projects are defined.

Hence, decisions with regard to planning and coordination of the change process need to be balanced; otherwise they can easily undermine the reengineering effort. In fact, many organizations actually do undermine their own change endeavors by either underestimating or overestimating the change management measures required. Necessary decisions, such as reducing the number of projects to leverage on the existing change resources and assigning line managers with appropriate authority to direct the changes, often fail to take place or are postponed until the change process stagnates.

The Number of misfits

Finally, we ranked the thirty-three organizations according to the number of misfits they faced in their reengineering initiatives. This number reflects the distance between the actual pattern followed and the ideal-type pattern that corresponds to the level of ambition set. If no mismatches emerged in the change process, the organization changed according to an ideal-type pattern. If four misfits are shown, the distance between the actual pattern and the archetype is maximal.

As indicated in Figure 14.5, an increasing number of misfits results in decreasing reengineering success. The magnitude of this correlation is the highest of all relationships discussed in this chapter (Spearman correlation coefficient of -0.6819 with $p < 0.01$). Clearly, the more the actual pattern deviates from the ideal-type pattern – that is, the larger the distance between both patterns – the more the synergistic benefits of designing and implementing balanced change will be lost. This finding answers our second research question. Reengineering outcomes generally depend on the distance between the actual pattern and the ideal-type pattern of change.

To conclude, given the strong and significant relationships revealed by our study (summarized in Table 14.3), we cannot reject the hypothesis. Although the number of organizations matching the three archetypes is small, which limits the generalizability of our findings, in this study fit nevertheless seems to be an essential factor explaining reengineering success and, therefore, organizational performance.

Managerial implications and conclusion

A number of practical implications can be derived from our study to support managers in balancing and rebalancing their change efforts. Explicitly managing fit implies that:

1   An appropriate level of ambition is determined. The necessity to change, that is, the need for performance improvements, increases with the extent of the strategic gap with the environment. Subsequently, this need has to be balanced with the organization's ability to change and the risks

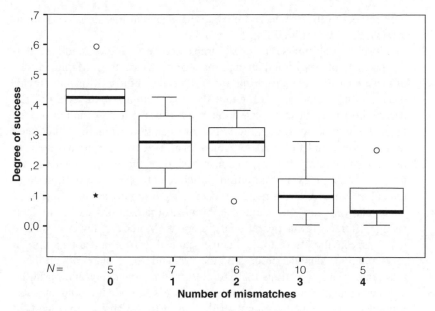

Figure 14.5 *Distance from ideal-type patterns and success*

Table 14.3 *Findings*

Relationship with re-engineering success	Spearman correlation coefficient	Significance level (p value)
1 Fit	0.4352	< 0.01
2 Breadth	0.2526	> 0.05
3 Depth	0.5789	< 0.01
4 Planning	0.4986	< 0.01
5 Coordination	0.4620	< 0.01
6 Number of misfits	−0.6819	< 0.01

involved in changing the organization.[4] Because it is the purpose of reengineering to achieve improvements that are clearly recognizable in the market or the environment in which the organization operates, the objectives set should have an outward focus.[34,39] Delivering value to the customer should be the focus of attention for managers. Besides selecting financial and nonfinancial indicators, managers must quantify perform-ance indicators in order to motivate and mobilize the organization.[7,16,42] The resulting set of clear, competitive metrics will focus the organization on the highlighted areas of expected gains and will guide the decisions with respect to the design and change management measures required to achieve the level of ambition.

2   The level of ambition set is ideally translated into a logical and harmonious package of design and change management measures. Manipulations of these measures have to bring about the right 'mindset' for implementing the desired changes throughout the organization. With regard to the design measures, it can be stated that the higher the level of ambition, the larger the number of critical activities or operational functions that need to be tackled, and the more organizational aspects have to be changed radically, ultimately leading to the redesign of the entire business system.[19,31,34] A high level of ambition should lead to the incorporation of all critical activities and to a radical redesign of all organizational aspects.[8,31] With relatively low or medium ambitions, organizations can limit their change effort to fewer operational functions. Moreover, fewer organizational aspects then have to be changed radically. If organizations opt for less ambitious change processes, they should focus their attention on those operational functions that are closest to the customer and on radically changing the customer approach, process knowledge, and the performance measurement system. With respect to the change management measures, it is important formally to assign change managers with enough authority to direct the changes, to define a manageable set of clearly specified projects, and to facilitate effective communication among change managers and with those directly affected by the changes. The higher the level of ambition, the more pressing the need for senior management involvement and the alignment of projects into an integrated change program in order to keep the change effort focused and to leverage the ever-scarce change resources available.[6,35,45]

To conclude, this chapter demonstrates that fit is indeed a vital factor in explaining organizational performance. The notion of fit was also acknowledged by 90 percent of our respondents, who stated that management by matching was *the* critical success factor in business reengineering. However, the majority of the organizations (85 percent) showed a non–ideal-type pattern of change, implying that fit is not easily achieved in reengineering practice. Fit should therefore be managed explicitly. 'Management by matching' means that decisions with respect to level of ambition, breadth, depth, planning, and coordination of the change process are made in conjunction with one another so that the whole package assumes, and maintains, a logical integrity. The distinguished dimensions of organizational change have to be balanced and, if mismatches emerge, rebalanced. Since such mismatches readily occur, achieving fit is a fragile process that needs constant care. In this regard, the three archetypes presented in this chapter may prove to be helpful concepts for change managers.

Directions for future research

This chapter represents a step toward improved understanding of the complex interactions between fit and organizational performance. It should be noted, however, that the archetypes in the framework employed are in need of both theoretical and empirical elaboration. By incorporating more reengineering initiatives into our data set of thirty-three organizations, results with more generalizability can be generated. Besides, other researchers are encouraged to further develop theory and research on reengineering within the archetype approach, to explore general patterns of change rather than strive to identify individual success factors. To elaborate on this line of enquiry, a variety of quantitative and qualitative assessments of reengineering initiatives will prove useful. Clearly, much work remains to be done in order to improve the robustness of the dimensions of organizational change and reengineering success and their operationalization into measureable constructs. Finally, future research on reengineering may include other dimensions. It would be particularly interesting to examine whether the chosen level of ambitions actually fits the requirements imposed by the environment of the organization, since organizations should pursue not only internal consistency but also external congruence in order reach a higher level of performance.

Notes

1   If they saw fit to do so, respondents were invited to add other indicators to this set of benefit categories. At their specification, quality improvement, culture change, and 'others' were added.

2   This procedure resulted in three groups consisting of ten, twelve, and eleven organizations, respectively. The reason for this 'skewedness' was that, at the line of demarcation between the low and medium level of ambition, two organizations had exactly the same ambition score. Both organizations were arbitrarily allocated to the medium level of ambition group.

3   The definitions mentioned in Figure 14.1 were slightly relaxed because the differences in the ambition scores of the organizations located near the lines that demarcate the ambition groups were small. In other words, the highest ambition scores in a lower ambition group do not differ greatly from the lowest ambition scores in the higher ambition group. For breadth, this means that organizations falling into the low and high ambition groups were allowed to redesign, respectively, two (instead of only one) and four (instead of at least five) critical activities. For depth, a match of four out of five organizational aspects still yielded a consistent minipattern. With regard to planning and coordination, one misfit in the constituent elements of the minipatterns was overlooked, i.e. four out of five and two out of three elements (respectively) had to match the ideal-type pattern.

References

1   Argyris, C. Good communication that blocks learning. *Harvard Business Review, 72*, 4 (July–August 1994), 77–85.
2   Arthur D. Little. *Results of the European Survey: The Arthur D. Little Survey on the High Performance Business*. London: Arthur D. Little, 1993.
3   Batelaan, M. V. *Implementing Business Redesign from Plateau to Plateau*. Utrecht: Nolan, Norton & Co., 1995.
4   Batelaan, M. V., and Wildschut, E. Bestaat business process redesign? *Holland Management Review, 40* (1994), 40–46.
5   Beer, M.; Eisenstat, R. A.; and Spector, B. Waarom veranderingprogramma's geen verandering teweegbrengen. *Holland Management Review, 31* (1992), 7–16.
6   Benjamin, R. I., and Levinson, E. A framework for managing IT-enabled change. *Sloan Management Review* (Summer 1993), 23–33.
7   Bertsch, B., and Williams, R. How multinational CEOs make change programmes stick. *Longe Range Planning, 27*, 5 (1994), 12–24.
8   Bouman, W.; Huizing, A.; Koster, E.; Mink, J.; Oliehoek, M.; Pels Rijcken, L.; and de Vries, E. *Business Reengineering – Het Regisseren van Complexe Organisatieverandering*. Amsterdam: Associatie Business Engineers/Universiteit van Amsterdam, 1995.
9   Broekstra, G. *Het Creëren van Intelligente Organisaties*. Delft: Eburon, 1989.
10   Bushoff, R.; Eijckelhoff, M.; and Nijziel, R. *Business Process Redesign in de verzekeringsbranche*. Amersfoort: Twijnstra Gudde, 1995.
11   Caron, J. R.; Jarvenpaa, S. L.; and Stoddard, D. B. Business reengineering at CIGNA Corporation: experiences and lessons learned from the first five years. *MIS Quarterly, 18*, 3 (1994), 233–250.
12   Chan, Y. E., and Huff, S. L. Strategy: an information systems research perspective. *Journal of Strategic Information Systems, 1*, 4 (September 1992), 191–204.
13   Cooper, R., and Markus, M. L. Human reengineering. *Sloan Management Review* (Summer 1995), 39–50.
14   CSC Index. *State of Reengineering Report*. Cambridge, MA: CSC Index, 1994.
15   Davenport, T. H. *Process Innovation – Reengineering Work through Information Technology*. Boston: Harvard Business School Press, 1993.
16   Davenport, T. H., and Beers, M. C. Managing information about processes. *Journal of Management Information Systems, 12*, 1 (Summer 1995), 57–80.
17   Davenport, T. H., and Short, J. E. The new industrial engineering: information technology and business process redesign. *Sloan Management Review, 31*, 4 (Summer 1990), 11–27.

18 Davenport, T. H., and Stoddard, D. B. Reengineering: business change of mythic proportions? *MIS Quarterly, 18*, 2 (June 1994), 121–127.

19 Davidson, W. H. Beyond re-engineering: the three phases of business transformation. *IBM Systems Journal, 32*, 1 (1993), 65–79.

20 Dixon, J. R. Arnold, P. Heineke, J. Kim, J. S. and Mulligan, P. Business process reengineering: improving in new directions. *California Management Review, 36*, 4 (Summer 1994), 93–108.

21 Drew, S. BPR in financial services: factors for success. *Longe Range Planning, 27*, 5 (1994), 25–41.

22 Duck, J. D. Managing change: the art of balancing. *Harvard Business Review, 71*, 6 (November–December 1993), 109–118.

23 Dunphy, D., and Stace, D. Transformational and coercive strategies for planned organizational change: beyond the O. D. model. *Organization Studies, 9*, 3 (1988), 317–334.

24 Dunphy, D., and Stace, D. The strategic management of corporate change. *Human Relations, 46*, 8 (1993), 905–920.

25 Earl, M. J. The new and the old of business process redesign. *Journal of Strategic Information Systems, 3*, 1 (1994), 5–22.

26 Earl, M. J.; Sampler, J. L.; and Short, J. E. Strategies for business process reengineering: evidence from field studies. *Journal of Management Information Systems, 12*, 1 (Summer 1995), 31–56.

27 Edwards, C., and Peppard, J. W. Forging a link between business strategy and business reengineering. *European Management Journal, 12*, 4 (December 1994), 62–75.

28 French, W. L., and Bell, C. H. *Organization Development: Behavioral Science Interventions for Organization Improvement*. Englewood Cliffs, NJ: Prentice-Hall, 1990.

29 Greenwood, R., and Hinings, C. R. Organizational design types, tracks and the dynamics of strategic change. *Organization Studies, 9*, 3 (1988), 293–316.

30 Grover, V.; Jeong, S. R.; Kettinger, W. J.; and Teng, J. T. C. The implementation of business process reengineering. *Journal of Management Information Systems, 12*, 1 (Summer 1995), 109–144.

31 Hall, G.; Rosenthal, J.; and Wade, J. How to make reengineering really work. *Harvard Business Review, 71*, 6 (November–December 1993), 119–131.

32 Hamel, G., and Prahalad, C. K. Strategy as stretch and leverage. *Harvard Business Review, 71*, 2 (March–April 1993), 75–84.

33 Hammer, M. Reengineering work: don't automate, obliterate. *Harvard Business Review, 68*, 4 (July–August 1990), 104–112.

34 Hammer, M., and Champy, J. *Reengineering the Corporation – A Manifesto for Business Revolution*. London: Nicholas Brealey, 1993.

35 Hammer, M., and Stanton, M. A. *The Reengineering Revolution: A Handbook*. New York: HarperCollins, 1995.

36   Hannan, M., and Freeman, J. Population ecology of organization. *American Journal of Sociology, 82*, (1977), 929–964.

37   Henderson, J. C., and Venkatraman, N. Strategic alignment: a model for organizational transformation through information technology. *IBM Systems Journal, 32*, 1 (1993), 4–16.

38   Heygate, R. Accelerating front-line change. *McKinsey Quarterly*, 1 (1992), 134–147.

39   Johansson, H. J.; McHugh, P.; Pendlebury, A. J.; and Wheeler, W. A. *Business Process Reengineering – Breakpoint Strategies for Market Dominance*. Chichester, UK: John Wiley, 1993.

40   Judd, C. M.; Smith, E. R.; and Kidder, L. H. *Research Methods in Social Relations*. Fort Worth, TX: Holt, Rinehart and Winston, 1991.

41   Kaplan, R. B., and Murdock, L. Core process redesign: rethinking the corporation. *McKinsey Quarterly, 2* (1991), 27–43.

42   Kaplan, R. S., and Norton, D. P. The balanced scorecard: measures that drive performance. *Harvard Business Review, 70*, 1 (January–February 1992), 71–79.

43   Khandwalla, P. N. *The Design of Organizations*. New York: Harcourt Brace Jovanovich, 1977.

44   Kochan, T. A., and Useem, M. *Transforming Organizations*. New York: Oxford University Press, 1992.

45   Kotter, J. P. Leading change: why transformation efforts fail. *Harvard Business Review, 73*, 2 (March–April 1995), 59–67.

46   de Laat, P. B. Matrisering van projectorganisaties: overwegingen van congruentie en consistentie. *Management & Organisatie, 4* (1993), 259–284.

47   Laughlin, R. C. Environmental disturbances and organizational transitions and transformations: some alternative models. *Organization Studies, 12*, 2 (1991), 209–232.

48   de Leeuw, A. C. J. *Besturen van veranderingsprocessen: fundamenteel en praktijkgericht management van organisatieveranderingen*. Assen, Netherlands: Van Gorcum, 1994.

49   MacDonald, H. The strategic alignment process. In M. S. Scott Morton (ed.), *The Corporation of the 1990s*. New York: Oxford University Press, 1991.

50   Miles, R. E., and Snow, C. C. *Fit, Failure, and the Hall of Fame – How Companies Succeed or Fail*. New York: Free Press, 1994.

51   Mintzberg, H. *The Structuring of Organizations: The Synthesis of the Research*. Englewood Cliffs, NJ: Prentice-Hall, 1979.

52   Nievelt, M. C. A. Managing with information technology, a decade of wasted money? *Compact* (Summer 1992), 15–24.

53   Norusis, M. J. *SPSS Advanced Statistics 6.1*. Chicago: SPSS Inc., 1994.

54   Pascale, R. T., and Athos, A. G. *The Art of Japanese Management*. New York: Warner Books, 1981.

55 Peters, T. J., and Waterman, R. W. *In Search of Excellence*. New York: Harper and Row, 1982.

56 Pine, B. J., II. *Mass Customization – The New Frontier in Business Competition*. Boston: Harvard Business School Press, 1993.

57 Pinto, J. K., and Slevin, D. P. Critical success factors in effective project implementation. In D. I. Cleland and W. R. King (eds.), *Project Management Handbook*. New York: Van Nostrand Reinhold, 1988.

58 Porter, M. E. *Competitive Advantage: Creating and Sustaining Superior Performance*. New York: Free Press, 1985.

59 Quinn, J. B. *Intelligent Enterprise – A Knowledge and Service Based Paradigm for Industry*. New York: Free Press, 1992.

60 Schlesinger, L. A., and Heskett, J. A. The service-driven service company. *Harvard Business Review* (September–October 1991), 71–81.

61 Shonk, J. H. *Team-Based Organizations: Developing a Successful Team Environment*. Homewood, IL: Irwin, 1992.

62 Stoddard, D. B., and Jarvenpaa, S. L. Business process redesign: tactics for managing radical change. *Journal of Management Information Systems, 12*, 1 (Summer 1995), 81–107.

63 Treacy, M. E., and Wiersema, F. *The Discipline of Market Leaders*. Boston: Harvard Business School Press, 1994.

64 Vantrappen, H. Creating customer value by streamlining business processes. *Long Range Planning, 25*, 1 (1992) 53–62.

65 Van de Ven, A. H., and Drazin, R. The concept of fit in contingency theory. *Research in Organizational Behavior, 7* (1985), 333–365.

66 Vrakking, W. J., ed. *Management van Organisatieverandering: Ontwikkelingen en Ideeen*. Lelystad, Netherlands: Koniklijke Vermande, 1992.

67 Wijnen, G. *Programma-management. Doelgerichte Aanpak van Complexe Vraagstukken*. Deventer, Netherlands: Kluwer, 1994.

68 Wijnen, G.; Weggeman, M.; and Kor, R. *Verbeteren en Vernieuwen van Organisaties: Essentiële Managementtaken*. Deventer, Netherlands: Kluwer Bedrijfswetenschappen, 1993.

69 Zairi, M., and Sinclair, D. Business process re-engineering and process management: a survey of current practice and future trends in integrated management. *Management Decision, 33*, 3 (1995), 3–6.

Appendix: Questionnaire – selected items

The original questionnaire consisted of sixteen pages in Dutch. The complete list of questions can be found in Reference 8. An outline indicating the main clusters of questions is given below.

A. Level of ambition

1.1   Indicate on the following set of indicators which performance improvements were *intended*. If possible, quantify these intended improvements with a percentage.

	Intended	Quantified (%)
Cost	–	–
Cycle time (etc.)	–	–

1.2   Did your business unit strive for a 'breakpoint', i.e. a competitive advantage?

B. Reengineering success

2.1   Indicate on the following set of indicators which performance improvements were *achieved*. If possible, quantify these achieved improvements with a percentage.

	Achieved	Quantified (%)
Cost	–	–
Cycle time (etc.)	–	–

C. Breadth

3.1   Indicate which operational functions have been redesigned during the reengineering effort.

• Inbound logistics • Procurement • Production • Outbound logistics • Marketing and Sales • Service

D. Depth

4.1   To what extent were the following design options applied?

	Strongly decreased	Decreased	Not used	Increased	Strongly increased
Organizational structure					
Number of hierarchical layers					
Decentralization (etc.)					
Process knowledge					
Use of activity-based costing					
Knowledge of cycle time (etc.)					
Information technology					
Number of shared databases					

Workflow management
systems (etc.)
Customer approach
  Frequency of
  customer needs
  research
  Segmentation into
  customer groups (etc.)
Performance measurement
  Use of nonfinancial
  indicators
  by management
  Use of financial
  indicators by
  work force (etc.)

E. Planning

5.1   How was the reengineering initiative structured?

   • One project • Multiple projects • One integrated change program

5.2   To what degree was the reengineering initiative specified?

   We used a • detailed, short-term project plan • several midrange project
   plans • an indicative program plan • Other

5.3   What methods and tools were used during the reengineering effort?

   • SWOT analysis • Customer research • Competitive analysis • Process
   modeling • Risk analysis • Prototyping • Process analysis • Simulation
   • Feasibility study • Repositories • Benchmarking • Project management
   tools • Pilot studies • Analysis of core competences • Milestone planning • Other

5.4   Was the reengineering initiative carried out using a temporary governance structure?

   • No, we used the existing governance structure • Yes, we used a formalized project organization stucture
   The formally assigned key roles were: • Project members • Project
   leader(s) • Program leader • Steering committee

5.5   What was the role of senior management?

   • Not involved in the initiative • Supported the initiative • Active ongoing
   leadership

F. Coordination

6.1 Did periodical change reviews of the reengineering initiative take place? If so, indicate who participated in these periodical reviews.

• No • Project members and project leader • Various project leaders • Program leader and project leaders • Other

6.2 Were these meetings standardized by written progress reports?

• No • Yes, we used high-level progress reports • Yes, we used detailed progress reports • Yes, we used both • Other

6.3 How was the initiative communicated to those directly affected by the changes?

• People directly involved participated • Several information meetings were held to introduce and discuss the initiative • Formal information bulletins and memos were used to announce the news about the initiative • Other

Reproduced from Huizing, A., Koster, E. and Bouman, W. (1997) Balance in reengineering: an empirical study of fit and performance, *Journal of Management Information Systems*, **14**(1), Summer, 93–118. Reprinted with permission of the publishers, M. E. Sharpe Inc.

Questions for discussion

1 There has been some debate as to whether reengineering was a fad or a successful application of IT to improve business performance. Which perspective do you hold and why?
2 Examine Figure 14.1. Do you have any preconceived notions that one model is better than the others? For breakthrough improvements in performance, must ambition be high?
3 The authors state that 'we therefore hold that every kind of reengineering, including less ambitious change efforts, should focus first on the customer'. The findings also indicated that 'improving customer satisfaction is a more difficult task than cutting costs of reducing cycle time'. What are ways IT improves relationships, with the customer, both within the context of reengineering and outside it?
4 Are there other models that might be effective in achieving breakthrough performance, such as a series of low-ambition projects?
5 What conclusions do you draw from the fact that only 15% of the investigated organizations actually succeeded in achieving fit?
6 Explain the result that the reengineering success depends on the number of operational functions tackled in the change effort.

15 Strategies in Response to the Potential of Electronic Commerce

Market process reengineering through electronic market systems: opportunities and challenges

H. G. Lee and T. H. Clark

Over the past few years, various electronic market systems have been introduced by market-making firms to improve transaction effectiveness and efficiency within their markets. Although successful implementation of electronic marketplaces may be found in several industries, some systems have failed or their penetration pace is slower than was projected, indicating that significant barriers remain. This chapter analyzes the economic forces and barriers behind the electronic market adoptions from the perspective of market process reengineering. Four cases of electronic market adoptions – two successful and two failed – are used for this analysis. Economic benefits are examined by investigating how the market process innovation enabled by information technology (IT) reduces transaction costs and increases market efficiency. Adoption barriers are identified by analyzing transaction risks and resistance resulting from the reengineering. Successful deployment of electronic market systems requires taking into account these barriers along with the economic benefits of adoption. The chapter presents suggestions based on these case studies, which are relevant to the analysis, design, and implementation of electronic market systems by market-making firms.

Introduction

Electronic markets have become increasingly popular alternatives to traditional forms of commerce as the costs of electronic communications decline and as the ability to convey complex information through networks increases. The role of market-making firms, such as commodity exchanges or livestock auctions, is to reduce the cost of carrying out transactions. These organizations have emerged to facilitate their member traders' transactions and to establish trade rules governing the rights and duties of those carrying out transactions in their facilities.[11,21] Over the past decade, many market-making firms have adopted electronic market systems to increase transaction effectiveness and efficiency within their markets. One characteristic shared by these systems is the decoupling of the logistics (product flows) from the market transactions through on-line trading.

This chapter examines market-making firms' adoptions of electronic commerce by investigating the fundamental economic and social attributes that influence market efficiency and transaction risks. Although electronic marketplaces have been adopted successfully in several industries, the translation of technical possibilities into institutional realities is often slow or ends in failure. There are clearly barriers as well as opportunities. The key questions driving this research are: What are the major economic forces driving electronic market adoptions by market-making firms? What risks or barriers behind electronic market adoptions limit successful implementation? Why do electronic markets often fail, despite economic benefits that are well documented at the time of adoption? What strategies can market-making firms employ to reduce barriers and to avoid adoption failure?

Much has been written in recent years about changes in cooperative strategies and industry structures associated with electronic hierarchies and electronic markets. Malone, Yates, and Benjamin suggested that the introduction of electronic commerce would lead to greater use of markets rather than hierarchies as IT reduced transaction costs.[27] Hess and Kemerer tested this electronic market hypothesis using a case study of computerized loan organization systems.[20] Gurbaxani and Whang integrated the transaction-cost argument with an internal agency cost to examine firm boundaries.[16] Many authors have pointed out that firms using electronic commerce often produced new forms of organization, such as networks[35] and value-adding partnerships,[22] instead of simply increasing firms' reliance on markets. Clemons, Reddi, and Row argued that, when firms increased outsourcing, they do so with a limited number of long-term trading partners due to increased opportunistic and operational risks.[7,8] Bakos and Brynjolfsson included the concept of noncontractible investments in coordination costs to explain why buying firms limited the number of suppliers.[4,5]

The study of electronic commerce for market-making firms requires a different approach from these previous works. Neither the question of the economic coordination mechanism (hierarchies, networks, or markets) nor the question of firm boundaries (produce or outsource) is relevant. The analysis needs to begin with an understanding of traditional market processes and to investigate how conventional transaction methods are changed as a result of electronic market adoption. This chapter examines the evolution of electronic market systems from a reengineering perspective, which we call market process reengineering (MPR). That is, we view the introduction of the on-line trading system as a strategic move by market-making firms to innovate the transaction process within institutional markets.

The advantage of MPR is that it allows us to analyze both opportunities and barriers associated with electronic market adoptions. On the one hand, economic incentives can be examined by studying how the new transaction process, enabled by IT, improves market efficiency. On the other hand, analysis of resistance to the change can explain failed adoptions. This chapter investigates four cases of electronic market adoptions from various industries: CALM for livestock trading, AUCNET for used-car trading, Information Auctioning for potted plants trading, and CATS for meat trading. All of these systems have been introduced by existing or new market-making firms to bring innovation to traditional market processes. CALM and AUCNET have been successful since the beginning of their services. The other two systems ceased operations after only one or two years. By analyzing both successful and failed cases, we examine the barriers as well as the economic forces behind the adoption of electronic market systems, and develop suggestions and strategies for market-making firms to limit the risks of failure in adopting electronic commerce applications.

Market-making firms and electronic markets

Why organized markets emerge

We consider market-making firms as social institutions in which a large number of commodity exchanges of a specific type regularly take place, facilitated and structured by institutional rules governing the exchange. Market transactions involve contractual agreement and the exchange of property rights; market-making firms provide mechanisms to structure, organize, and legitimate these activities. An example of a market-making firm is an auction market, which involves the use of a specified method, custom, or routine for reaching agreement on a price (note 1). The auction organization offers trading rules that structure the bidding process and trade settlement, in addition to publicity, clerical work, bidding place, storage space, and so on. Thus, market-making firms provide not only places for exchanges but also institutional rules to standardize and legitimate exchanges made within their facilities.[21]

Transaction costs are the costs of obtaining relevant information, of bargaining and making decisions, and of policing and enforcing contracts.[10] They can be reduced if traders complete transactions in markets organized by market-making firms, rather than in fragmented, nonmarket exchange[21] (note 2). The costs of obtaining relevant information are reduced dramatically through creation of an organized market since market-making firms help publicize prices as well as other relevant information. Regularized access to contacts within the market itself reduces costs by making it easier to find preferable trading counterparts. Bargaining costs can be reduced too as market-making firms help establish procedures and conventions for reaching a bargain, and traders more easily formulate their expectations about what kind of deal they may strike. Furthermore, deals are likely to be carried out more rapidly since the options for transacting with alternative buyers and sellers present in the market are clear to both parties. Policing and enforcement costs can be reduced because market-making firms bring norms of conduct and codes of practice for buyers or sellers. The individual is not alone in ensuring that the contract is carried out because market-making firms regulate all the transaction activities in great detail, such as the responsibilities of parties and the terms of settlements.

Electronic market systems for market-making firms

We differentiate electronic market adoptions by market-making firms from consumer electronic shopping systems over the Internet. The tremendous growth of the Internet, and particularly of the World Wide Web, has dramatically increased the number of new intermediaries such as Web Shop, Internet Mall, IndustryNet, and Internet Shopping Network, which interpose themselves between producers and customers in the industry value chain to take advantage of new types of economies of scale, scope, and knowledge enabled by the Internet.[31] These intermediaries allow vendors to advertise their products to millions of prospective consumers, while allowing customers to place orders electronically.[19]

These new electronic intermediaries in cyberspace, however, do not include discovering the market price of goods,[25] although they have potential to influence retail prices by increasing competition among suppliers.[3] They usually employ posted-off pricing,[32] where producers list ask prices and consumers decide how many items to buy at the posted price. In these systems, suppliers are price makers and on-line trading systems help determine quantities traded at relatively fixed prices. This contrasts with market-making firms' electronic market systems, one of whose major functions is to determine the market price of goods. Sellers who join the market institutions (such as farmers in livestock auction) have fixed quantities for supply without price tags: Sellers are price takers, not price makers, although they have a certain level of reserve prices. Electronic market systems play an important role in determining the market price of goods through either electronic auctions or electronic negotiations.[25]

In addition, buyers who purchase goods in market institutions are not end consumers but typically wholesalers who resell their purchased items to retailers. Since the quality of offered products varies widely (even products from the same producer differ in quality time to time, as in the case of agricultural products such as livestock or cut flowers), descriptions of the product quality are essential to buyers who regularly join the institutions to purchase goods at the wholesale level. In contrast, products sold in electronic shopping systems over the Internet are mostly standardized and mass-produced (products from one supplier are identical). These systems typically target retail consumers who purchase goods based on price tags and brand names.

Finally, traders completing transactions through market-making firms are subject to institutional rules established to reduce transaction uncertainties and to protect member traders against transaction conflicts. Agreement over the governing rules can be facilitated because the members meet frequently and deal in a restricted range of goods. It is possible to enforce the rules because the opportunity to trade on the exchange itself is of great value: withholding permission to trade is a sanction sufficiently severe to ensure compliance for most member traders. When the transaction facilities are scattered and owned by a vast number of people, as in the case of various on-line shopping systems over the Internet, the establishment and administration of a private legal system would be very difficult. Those who operate in these markets therefore have to depend on the legal system at the state level.

It is nevertheless possible for existing or new market-making firms to use the Internet to build electronic market systems. In the past, for example, the Federal Communications Commission (FCC) allocated radio spectra either by lottery or by comparative hearings (note 3). In an attempt to revamp the method of allocating public resources, the FCC implemented an Auction Bidding System (ABS) to sell broadband Personal Communications Service (PCS) licenses to public bidders.[40] Through a high-tech auction designed to maximize revenues quickly, the FCC sold 99 broadband PCS licenses for 51 market regions in 1995 and raised $7.7 billion for the U.S. Treasury. Although the auction was held in Washington, DC, firms throughout the country used the on-line electronic messages to place their bids.[2] Unlike on-line shoppers for retail goods in the Internet, however, participants had to sign the agreement for trading rules that specify every detail of the bidding processes and responsibilities of bidders; anyone who violated the agreement was left out of the market.

Market process reengineering

Decoupling product flow from market transactions

Business process redesign (BPR), also known as reengineering, enables organizational transformation.[13,14,18] Firms embrace a BPR approach when a radical improvement can be achieved by realigning business process with information technology (IT) change. BPR requires a firm to step back from current business processes to consider its overall business objective; only then can it create radical change to realize improvements of any magnitude.[17] Information technology is usually a necessary but insufficient factor in achieving BPR. Successful reengineering is not an IT initiative but, rather, a business initiative, although IT has been described as both a strategic catalyst and an enabler of BPR.[15,34]

Market-making firms in various industries have used the BPR approach to redesign existing processes inside their firms. When goods arrive at the market for sale, a clerk enters information regarding the producer, product type, and quantity into the control computer. Once transactions occur, either by face-to-face auction or negotiation, the computer consolidates all purchase information for settlement of accounts and generates transaction reports for buyers and sellers. Thus, IT is already being used to speed up existing transaction processes while reducing labor costs. However, the use of computers for BPR inside market-making firms does not necessarily require changing the market transaction process and associated institutional rules governing these market processes.

Market-making firms have come to understand that the market process can be redesigned using telecommunications as well as computers. In traditional transactions, suppliers had to bring their products to the marketplace and buyers wishing to purchase goods also had to be present at the market in order to inspect the goods and to participate in the bidding process. Goods sold by either auctions or negotiations were handed over to buyers who transported them back to the buyer's location. In the new approach, product flow is separated from the market transactions by connecting the central computer with terminals at member traders' locations using communication networks (Figure 15.1). In this new virtual marketplace, transactions are based on information and products move from sellers directly to buyers only after on-line transactions are completed.

On-line trading is not automation of traditional market processes, but market process reengineering which brings innovation to the transaction process and to the role of market makers. Suppliers offer their products in electronic forms instead of transporting them to the markets. Buyers place electronic bids in their offices rather than coming to the market. Transactions are executed based upon information seen on computer terminals, with no need for

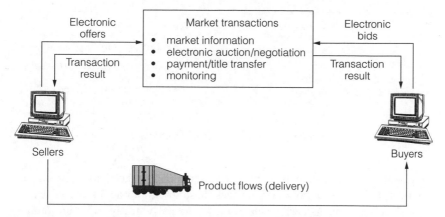

Figure 15.1 *Decoupling of product flows from market transactions*

products to be present physically. Goods remain at suppliers' locations and are not shipped until the transaction is completed.

Research framework and methodology

Our research model presumes that market makers adopting electronic market systems would encounter barriers to realizing the expected improvements in market efficiency (Figure 15.2). To implement electronic market systems successfully, adoption barriers must be identified and properly managed, along with implementing systems to improve transaction efficiency and effectiveness. The success of the adoption depends on creating and sustaining the identified economic gains while reducing potential barriers. This chapter identifies economic gains and barriers resulting from electronic market adoptions and examines how firms can manage risks and barriers in the course of market process reengineering.

Increased transaction effectiveness and efficiency

Every market transaction consists of *information gathering*, *contract formation*, and *trade settlement*.[25] Information gathering reflects the process by which traders obtain information on potential trading counterparts that best fit their preferences. Once trading opportunities are discovered, traders move on to contract formation, such as reaching an agreement on transaction prices. If potential trading parties fail to agree on transaction terms, negotiations may have to be repeated with many firms before a contract is finally formulated. Many market-making firms adopt auction mechanisms to expedite this bargaining procedure and to find the market value of goods promptly. The trade settlement process clears transactions through physical exchange of goods and

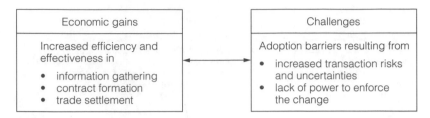

Economic gains	Challenges
Increased efficiency and effectiveness in • information gathering • contract formation • trade settlement	Adoption barriers resulting from • increased transaction risks and uncertainties • lack of power to enforce the change

Figure 15.2   *Opportunities and challenges of electronic market adoptions*

payment. The economic benefits from electronic-market adoptions can be investigated to reveal how IT improves these three transaction processes.

For information gathering, electronic markets typically offer pre-trading and post-trading information that can be accessed by market participants at any time. Traders who could get information regarding available trading partners upon their arrival at the market are now better informed in advance about the prospective trading partners. Furthermore, most electronic market systems provide an electronic bulletin board that displays information on recent transactions, including quantities of products recently sold, product quality characteristics, and prices paid by buyers. This post-trading information keeps traders well informed on the market price of goods with specific characteristics of interest to buyers or sellers, thereby facilitating selling and buying decisions. Since traders can obtain this information and execute transactions without coming to markets, they save both time and money.

For contract formation, sellers in open markets often establish reservation prices for exchanges because they do not have perfect information about the consequences of their actions in markets. The reservation price plays a role as sequentially rational rules under incomplete market information.[33] Suppliers who brought their products to traditional markets often had to accept prices lower than their reservation prices. This is common with perishable products or when the transportation costs of bringing the products back home are high. If product flows are separated from the market transactions, sellers can keep their reservation prices relatively firm unless they urgently need cash for their products. Thus, electronic markets can strengthen supplier power in some market environments, resulting in increased average prices for their goods.

Electronic markets can become a national marketplace by eliminating geographical constraints and can broaden the range of choices for buyers. Traditional markets (such as auctions for agricultural products) typically consist of several regional markets scattered around the country. Regional markets are limited in transaction volume since they need to hold inventory until the moment of sale. The transaction depends on the pool of products held or stored in the regional market. Electronic markets allow the pool of product offers to be enlarged without expanding physical infrastructure, such as storage capacity. The establishment of national, as opposed to regional, markets increases the buyers' chances of finding preferred trading parties in terms of prices and product quality.

Electronic markets can also benefit the trade settlement process. Since goods are delivered directly from suppliers to buyers after an on-line transaction, the transportation logistics from suppliers to the markets are eliminated. Often, direct shipping reduces product damage during packaging, loading, and unloading. Furthermore, the use of electronic markets facilitate electronic auditing, which helps firms monitor transactions.

Barriers of electronic market adoptions

For traders used to coming to a market for exchange of goods, the idea of separating logistics from the market transaction through on-line trading is revolutionary. Anything associated with the new transaction method – institutional rules, market structures, management systems, relationships with member traders, and technical complexity – must be redesigned to accommodate the change. Many member traders' longstanding policies and traditions may be affected, and innovation leaders often encounter resistance from those who prefer the status quo. Market-making firms that initiate electronic market systems are thus likely to face two types of adoption barriers: (1) *transaction risks* created by the new alternative market form, and (2) *lack of the market power* necessary to enforce the change.

Two important assumptions of human behaviors in transaction-cost analysis are bounded rationality and opportunism, which result in the risks and uncertainties of transactions in open markets[37,38] (note 4). As discussed earlier, one of the primary functions of market-making firms is to reduce transaction risks through institutional rules. However, the adoption of electronic markets is likely to increase transaction risks or uncertainties. For instance, buyers have to make purchasing decisions based on information without physically inspecting products, thus facing the risk of incomplete and distorted information. Sellers may doubt that their goods would be appropriately valued in the unproved market system, particularly when there is a strong possibility that they would suffer from lower prices due to inactive trading at the newly created electronic markets. When market participants perceive these risks or uncertainties involved with the change exceed the benefits expected using the new approach, they will be reluctant to adopt the new transaction process (note 5).

BPR generally requires a top-down approach.[14,18] The inertia of old processes and structures often makes it extremely difficult to introduce radical changes. BPR therefore needs to be initiated by top management, who has the authority to lead the reengineering through the organization. Market process reengineering is also likely to encounter resistance from market participants.

The resistance may be nothing more than inertia, but it also stems from a healthy suspicion of new and unproven market systems. Furthermore, parties affected adversely by the change are expected to fight reengineering efforts. Unlike BPR within a firm, however, market-making firms can hardly impose a top-down style of reengineering. Although they can initiate the reengineering process, market-making firms generally lack sufficient power to force adoption. Without the active participation of member traders, the reengineering effort is doomed. The only way for market-making firms to achieve their reengineering objective is to convince their member traders of benefits of the new process.

The next two sections discuss four cases of electronic market adoptions – their economic incentives and adoption barriers, respectively – within our research framework. The data are gathered from interviews as well as secondary sources. Two cases (CALM and AUCNET) were published as successful adoptions in the early 1990s.[6,36] Although our analysis refers to these publications, further data have been gathered by interviews, in particular from the market process reengineering perspective. The analysis for the two failed cases is based on interviews and internal documents from the companies involved in these efforts.

Economic forces of electronic market adoptions

This discussion of four cases focuses on market process reengineering (how electronic markets have brought innovation to traditional market transaction processes) and its resulting economic gains (increased market efficiency). The improvement of transaction effectiveness and efficiency, enabled by electronic market systems, is investigated along the three transaction process dimensions discussed above: information gathering, contract formation, and trade settlement. Table 15.1 compares the four cases in terms of trading items, traditional transaction methods, initiating market-making firms, operation period, system throughout, new price discovery methods, and their evaluations. The observed values of the electronic market adoptions are summarized in Table 15.2.

CALM for livestock trading in Australia

The pastoral industry remains important to Australia, which is the largest beef exporter in the world and has the largest sheep population of any country. Australia currently has a population of about 26 million cattle, 121 million sheep/lambs, and 2.7 million pigs. In 1995, about 10 million cattle, 34 million sheep/lambs, and 5 million pigs were traded at US$4.1 billion. The profitability of the pastoral industry depends on effective and efficient trading

Table 15.1 *Four cases*

	CALM	AUCNET	IA	CATS
Traded items	Livestock (cattle, sheep/lambs, pigs)	Used cars	Potted plants	Fresh meat
Traditional trading method	Saleyard auction (on-site auction)	Auto auction (on-site auction)	Flower auction (on-site auction)	Negotiations/ formula pricing
Market-making firms	Australian Meat and Livestock Corporation	AUCNET Inc.	VBA (the largest flower auction in Holland)	American Meat Exchange
Operation period	July 1987–present	June 1985– present	January 1994– October 1995	June 1981– June 1982
Throughput	2.1 million livestock heads in 1995	232 000 cars listed in 1995	10 percent of transaction for potted plants within VBA	109 transactions during the service
Pricing in electronic markets	Electronic auction	Electronic auction	Dutch auction	Electronic negotiation
Evaluation	Success with growth rate of 20 percent in throughput	Success with growth rate of 26 success in throughput	Failed adoption (ceased operation)	Failed adoption (ceased operation)

in livestock. The need to sell many animals several times during their lives increases the importance of effective livestock trading within the pastoral value chain (note 6).

Livestock is traded among local producers; there is also farmgate trading where traveling buyers negotiate contracts with producers on-site. This offers the producer convenience but does not necessarily result in a competitive price. Thus, for many years, the dominant mechanism for livestock sales has been saleyard trading where farmers can market their products through face-to-face auctions. There are over 100 saleyard auctions throughout Australia. Suppliers are typically local farmers who bring their products to auctions for sale. Buyers are usually meat exporters/processors, wholesalers, meat retailers (supermarket chains), and agencies that purchase the store stock for their client farmers.

In the early 1980s, Australian Meat and Livestock Corporation (AMLC), an industry statutory authority responsible for marketing livestock in Australia and overseas, initiated a reengineering project for the livestock trading

Table 15.2   *Observed economic gains (increased market efficiency)*

	Information gathering	Contract formation	Trade settlement
CALM	Market intelligence service (post-trading information) facilitates traders' selling and buying decisions	Farmers are no longer forced to sell their products at prices lower than reserve prices Buyers have more choices than in regional saleyard auctions	Direct shipping from farmers to buyers reduces transportation costs and damages to products
AUCNET	Auction schedule distributed in advance saves dealers' time involved with bidding Dealers can download the images/data and talk with clients about offered products	Trading volume can be increased without parking spaces at auction sites Buyers enjoy more vehicle choices not available in traditional auto auctions	Unsold vehicles do not have to be brought back to sellers' locations
IA	Pre-trading information enables wholesalers to consult with retailers and to establish a bidding strategy in advance	Growers can keep reserve prices firm Buyers can specify packaging requirements before delivery	Growers' direct delivery to buyers relieves auction of storage and traffic problems
CATS	Traders can browse listed bids/offers to select trading counterparts Summarized information on transaction history helps traders negotiate prices	Nationwide database of bids and offers induces more competitive market prices than formula-based pricing Small firms can bypass brokers for transactions	

process.[6] The objective was to establish a network for electronic sale of cattle, sheep/lambs, and pigs in order to improve market efficiency and the match between product characteristics and market demands. After a trial system in 1983 in the New England region, AMLC formed a new division in 1985, Computer Aided Livestock Marketing (CALM), to lead the industry toward electronic market systems. CALM service was commercially launched in July 1987.

CALM is an electronic auction system for buying and selling cattle, sheep/ lambs, and pigs on the basis of product descriptions, while the stock remain on the farmers' property or feedlot. Buyers can bid electronically from anywhere in Australia. Traders link their workstations to the central computer using Telecom Australia's X.25 packet-switching network. To list a lot on a CALM auction, a vendor arranges for a CALM-accredited assessor to prepare an assessment of his or her lot. The information about products that will be auctioned off is normally released one clear working day ahead of the auction. The electronic auction takes the format of either sequential auction or simultaneous auction.[6] Once sold by CALM, the products are shipped directly to buyers.

CALM has significantly reduced the cost of obtaining market information on livestock trading. CALM market intelligence service, available since mid-1991, comprises a number of components, including statistical reports on CALM transactions, historical trends in CALM sale prices, and market commentaries on domestic and overseas market details. During the contract formation, CALM has decreased the pressure on the producer to sell at whatever price is being offered at the saleyard because failure to sell does incur effort or cost for returning the stock to their feedlot. CALM listed over 2.1 million livestock in 1995, far more than were offered in any single regional market, thus enabling buyers to purchase products that better fit their preferences. Finally, the livestock does not have to travel to a saleyard in CALM; thus, there is no transportion cost of bringing the stock to the saleyard. This lowers the stress on the animals and reduces handling and the resultant bruising, and so brings higher-quality product to the buyer.

Since CALM service was launched, the number of livestock traded through CALM has increased at a compound annual growth rate of 20 percent. In 1995, CALM sold 234 000 cattle,1 840 000 sheep/lambs, and 82 500 pigs through the electronic auction, with just 252 employees. This transaction accounts for US$109 million (60 percent for cattle, 32 percent for sheep/ lambs, and 8 percent for pigs). The CALM throughput is expected to grow at over 15 percent per year during the next decade, further penetrating the traditional saleyard auction trading.

AUCNET for used-car trading in Japan

Japanese consumers generally purchase second-hand cars from licensed dealers. A complex web of title registration and regulation makes direct trading of used cars between individuals difficult. Avoiding the risks of hidden defects and securing financial loan also lead Japanese consumers to prefer dealing with reliable and substantial used-car dealers. If a vehicle desired by a consumer is not in his inventory, a used-car dealer typically goes to the auctions, rather than rely on his competitors' inventory. In 1995, over 3.6 million used cars worth ¥1482 billion (US$15 billion) were sold through 144 auto auctions in Japan.

In a traditional auto auction, vehicles, buyers, and sellers are assembled at auction sites. Traders are typically used-car dealers who either seek vehicles for their clients or wish to sell trade-ins. Cars are brought onto the auction floor one at a time, and buyers bid by holding up their hand. Although cars are inspected prior to the auction by auto mechanics, an estimated 80 to 90 percent of the buyers personally inspect the cars prior to the auction. Thus, the product flow is coupled with the auction process.

AUCNET was introduced in 1986 by an entrepreneurial used-car dealer who realized that computers and advanced communication technology could eliminate an immense amount of time wasted in the search for cars. The AUCNET system is a centralized on-line wholesale market in which cars are sold using video images, character-based data, and a standardized inspector rating.[36] Sellers must have their vehicles inspected by AUCNET mechanics, who assess damage and summarize the quality rank in a single number (from 1 to 10). A car sold through AUCNET remains at the seller's location until the transaction is completed. Then a transport company typically delivers it directly to the buyer. During the electronic auction, sellers and buyers are linked to AUCNET's central host computer via satellite.

AUCNET's advantage over traditional auto auctions is its ability to help dealers gather information. Attending conventional auto auctions is time-consuming. Because there is no precise schedule for when certain cars will be sold, a dealer might spend an entire day at a traditional auction to bid on one or two cars. Since used-car dealers usually are salespeople themselves, they lose sales opportunities while attending traditional auctions. Since the AUCNET auction schedule is distributed in advance, used-car dealers can download the data and images of offered cars through the satellite network and can limit their time spent in the auction process to only the cars they are interested in buying. Dealers can also show the information to customers and include these cars in their bidding list based on clients' requests.

Most traditional auto auctions in Japan are held in metropolitan areas where parking spaces for used-car sales is becoming increasingly sparse and expensive. Traditional auctions therefore are limited in the number of used cars they can accommodate for sales. AUCNET created the largest auto auction without using a single parking space; in 1995, it listed over 230 000 used cars. AUCNET can easily accommodate increasing sales volume, with an expected annual growth rate of 15 percent projected over the next five years. As a result, buyers in AUCNET enjoy greater vehicle choices than are available in regional auto auctions and for this reason are willing to pay higher average prices. Furthermore, used-car sellers in the past had to carry significant transportation costs to move a car to the auction site and back again if it was not sold. About 45 percent of cars brought to the auto auction sites remained unsold. AUCNET eliminated such costs by decoupling the logistics from the market transactions.

With these advantages over traditional auto auctions, AUCNET's through-put has increased at an annual compound growth rate of 26 percent since its initial operation. In 1995, when AUCNET listed over 230 000 used cars, the company recorded an operating profit of ¥1.8 billion (US$18 million) on sales of ¥6.1 billion (US$61 million) with just 136 employees. The member-ship network among dealers has continued to expand at a rate of about 100 per quarter, reaching 4150 at the end of 1995.

Information auctioning for potted plant trading in Holland

The florist industry, associated with the cultivation and trading of cut flowers and potted plants, is a major economic sector in the Netherlands. The Dutch flower industry, which has almost an 80 percent share of the world export market, produced over US$3.5 billion transactions in 1995. Auction organ-izations, which are typically cooperatives of growers and are obliged to sell all their member farmers' products through their auction processes, are key institutions for coordinating global supplies and demands. For example, Bloemenveiling Aalsmeer (VBA), the largest auction market with 43 percent of market share of eleven flower auctions, is a cooperative of about 5000 growers. Buyers are typically large organizations, such as exporters, whole-salers, and retail chains.

Because cut flowers are perishable goods, fast market transaction and delivery are vital in the supply chain. In traditional flower auctions, cut flowers and potted plants are brought to the market the night before the auction. Upon arrival, products are inspected by the auction's own inspectors (the flower master) and kept in large cooling areas until the moment of auction. The flower master's inspection remarks are recorded in computers so that they can be displayed during the auction. The auction normally starts early in the morning and continues until all the products are sold by Dutch auction rules, where an auctioneer begins by asking a high price and gradually lowers the price until some bidder takes the offer. Cut flowers and potted plants are carried through the auction hall during the auction so that buyers can make purchasing deci-sions based on what they see. After sale, the lots are driven out and loaded into vans or trucks arranged by buyers. In this way, products auctioned in the morning can be sold the same evening or the next morning at florists and retailers in Europe, North America, and practically any other part of the world.

In January 1994, VBA launched Information Auctioning to reengineer the traditional auction process of potted plants.[23] The sheer scale of individual transactions required large storage spaces and generated substantial traffic to and from the VBA auction house. VBA realized that this traffic would be unmanageable within the decade, given a 10 percent annual growth rate, since the available space for expansion was already nearly exhausted. The objective of Information Auctioning was to separate the logistics of potted plants from the auction process. In Information Auctioning, growers send a sample, rather than the entire quantity available, along with information about the main supply to VBA. Buyers bid for the main supply based on the product sample in auction halls. The main supply remains at growers' locations to be packaged and shipped to the buyer after transactions are completed. Growers, buyers, and auctions use electronic communications to coordinate all the information exchanged in this process.

Information Auctioning does not completely separate product flow from the market transactions. A sample lot of the offered product must still be sent to the market and buyers still personally attended the bidding at the auction halls. VBA decided to adopt this approach in order to work as practically as possible within existing transaction conventions. Because it is difficult to describe florist products electronically, VBA feared that buyers might balk at a radical transition to completely on-line trading. VBA assumed that Information Auctioning would serve as a milestone for its long-term reengineering goal of completely separating logistics from market transactions.

Information Auctioning enables buyers to browse the entire database of offered products the day before the auction. This contrasts with traditional auctions, where buyers could get the information of available products only on the day of auction. This pre-trading information is a significant benefit to wholesalers (buyers). The prices of cut flowers and potted plants change significantly day by day depending on supply and demand, often varying up to 20 or 30 percent in sequential trading days. Wholesalers (buyers) can communicate with retailers based upon this information to come up with bidding strategies, such as what to buy, how many lots to buy, and how much to pay.

In traditional auction markets, growers have to sell out their perishable products regardless of the market price received. Since Information Auctioning decouples the product flows of the main supply from the market process, a grower can keep his reservation price relatively firm. If no buyer is willing to pay higher than the grower's reserve price, the grower may withdraw the products from the market and offer them again later on, since products are not harvested until sold. In return, buyers benefit because they can specify the packaging requirement for delivery (note 7). Information Auctioning also expected to resolve storage and traffic problems for VBA. Direct delivery of goods from growers to buyers would allow VBA to increase its transaction volume without expanding its physical storage capacity.

Despite all these expected benefits, however, the penetration rate of Information Auctioning was disappointing for the first several months of operation.

VBA undertook various rule changes to induce traders to switch to the new transaction method. Even so, Information Auctioning executed only 10 percent of the product sales – much less than the planned goal of 45 percent. VBA officially stopped the Information Auctioning service in September 1995. VBA encountered unexpected resistance and failed to deal with the barriers it faced; these are discussed later.

CATS for meat trading in the United States

Wholesaling is a vital link in the marketing process of the US meat industry. Wholesale trading of fresh meat takes place for a variety of reasons. Because of the perishability of the meat products, the market transactions rely heavily on cooler and holding capacity, which is more easily available in wholesalers. Regulations, such as the late 1920s Consent Decree, prohibit some meat packers from retailing, thus necessitating wholesaling for market transactions. In 1995, over 135 million slaughtered cattle, hogs, and sheep were distributed by wholesalers for domestic consumption and export to foreign markets. In 1981, when CATS was introduced, the US meat industry produced more than 39 billion pounds of meat.

In wholesale markets, fresh meat is generally traded either on a negotiated basis or on a formula basis. A negotiated trade is a transaction where delivery, quality, quantity, and price are agreed on at one time by a seller and a buyer. A formula-priced transaction differs in that the transaction price is based on prices published by a market reporting service on the day prior to shipping.

Formula pricing, which accounts for 80 percent of all meat trading, has been questioned on the grounds of market price manipulation and adequacy of market information. Formula prices are based on prices that are reported voluntarily, and the reporting mechanism involves personal discretion on the part of the market information services. Thus, large firms could use market reporting services to affect prices in a self-serving manner that may be detrimental to other market participants, including consumers and farm producers. Another problem was the adequacy of market information. A large percentage of negotiated transactions is not reported to market reporting services. It is estimated that sales data on less than 2 percent of U.S. federally inspected slaughter is reported to market reporting services.[30] A considerable portion of the market is insulated from use as a source of price information, further increasing the potential of market price manipulation by large firms.

The Computer Assisted Trading System (CATS), an electronic meat trading system at the wholesale level, was introduced in 1981 by American Meat Exchange (AME) to address concerns about the accuracy and adequacy of market information.[30] AME, one of the three market reporting service companies at that time, thought that the redesign of the meat market process using electronic networks would create desirable conditions for a competitive market and greater pricing efficiency. In CATS, a trader could place bids and offers using terminals connected to the central computer through local telephone or toll-free WATS lines. This order information was then made available to all other eligible traders. Unlike the other three cases discussed here, however, all of which employ auction mechanisms for discovering value of goods, the transaction price in CATS was determined by several rounds of electronic negotiations. The electronic communications between trading parties continued until either a transaction was consummated or a party withdrew from the negotiation.

CATS enabled traders to review selected bids and offers and helped them obtain pre-trading information. It also supplied traders with daily transaction information, a chronological (or otherwise sorted) listing of transactions for each region, and a summary of price and quantity information for each item. Price and quantity information was summarized for product and transaction type to facilitate the traders' market analysis.

CATS was expected to resolve the *thin* market problem of formula-based trading by increasing competition among buyers and sellers. Since CATS was capable of connecting many buyers and sellers, and reporting market information to traders regardless of their geographical location or market power, it was expected to *thicken* the market and to provide competitive pricing. In addition, CATS was intended to allow traders to bypass brokers to locate potential trading partners. AME thought that this would encourage relatively small farmers and buyers, who relied on brokerage agencies, to join the system and that it would result in more fair and competitive pricing than formula-pricing, which was dominated by a few large firms.

The AME's electronic market adoption, however, failed. AME launched the CATS service in June 1981 and suspended its operation in November of the same year. During this period, 981 bids and 1693 offers were placed and 109 transactions were executed through the CATS. The disappointed AME officially terminated the CATS operation in June 1982. Like Information Auctioning, AME failed to foresee and prepare for certain barriers and resistance to new electronic market adoptions.

Analysis of adoption barriers

Market-making firms initiated the electronic market systems with clear visions of their potential economic benefits. Why, then, did Information Auctioning and CATS fail, despite tangible benefits comparable to those of CALM and AUCNET? The difference between successful and failed adoptions lies in the management of barriers introduced by the change. We identify three types of adoption barriers that prevent market-making firms from implementing

Table 15.3 *Adoption barriers and tactics to overcome them*

	Observed barriers	*Tactics to overcome them*
CALM	Transaction disputes over misinformation of products Thin market may result in transaction penalties for both farmers and buyers	Establishment of AUS-MEAT for standard product descriptions and on-site product inspection Industrywide commitment and promotions
AUCNET	Buyers may mistrust electronic description of used cars Retaliation from JUCDA	Standardization of car inspection and rigorous inspection process Antitrust complaints and publicity
IA	Quality uncertainty of offered products Inactive trading may hurt both growers and buyers	Use of sample lots to represent the main supply Various auction rule changes
CATS	Quality uncertainty of offered products Resistance from big wholesalers due to their loss of market price control	Use of NAMP's Meat Buyer Guide without on-site inspection Resolution of trade disputes through bilateral negotiations between buyer and seller

successful electronic market systems. Table 15.3 summarizes observed barriers or uncertainties that result from the establishment of electronic marketplaces in these four cases, together with tactics employed to reduce these barriers by the initiating market-making firms.

Electronic product description

Market process reengineering requires that buyers purchase products from descriptions (information) without physically inspecting them. This creates new uncertainties for buyers since it can magnify information asymmetry (note 8). If the market-making firms fail to ensure that product information properly reflects the original products or if they are not equipped to protect buyers from misinformation, buyers will resist the new system. Product evaluation (inspection) becomes a challenging task when product flows are separated from market transactions. Unlike traditional markets, where all products are brought to a central site and can be easily inspected, initiating market institutions need to decentralize their inspection structures for market process reengineering.

The major concern of CALM developers was that product misinformation in the system might discourage buyers from purchasing livestock based on the information provided. To address this issue, AMLC established the Authority for Uniform Specification of Meat and Livestock (AUS-MEAT) in 1985 to focus on quality standards and provide accurate and consistent descriptions of livestock. CALM requires that all supply lots be inspected by CALM-accredited assessors who describe the quality of livestock using four-level standard measures. CALM's institutional rules also include arbitration procedures that can be used to resolve disputes arising from product misinformation.

Standard car ratings and rigorous inspection processes have been fundamental to the success of AUCNET. Used-car sellers must have their vehicles inspected by AUCNET mechanics. The inspection results are summarized in a single number, between 1 and 10 (10 indicates a new car; 5 or 6 could be resold to the consumer without additional work). For most buyers, this number is the key decision variable when buying a car, even though they may have access to more detailed inspection results. In addition, AUCNET targets relatively high-quality cars in an attempt to further reduce buyers' risks. A car rated lower than 4 cannot be sold on AUCNET. The average price of a car sold on AUCNET is ¥1 280 000 (US$13 000), compared with ¥670 000 (US$7000) for traditional auctions; these numbers indicate that the vehicles sold in AUCNET are relatively late models.

When VBA launched Information Auctioning, it hoped that the use of samples could solve the problem of product description. Most buyers, however, did not trust the samples to represent the entire product supply adequately: samples were always assumed to be the best slots out of the main supply. Without well-standardized product rating and inspection for the main supply, the use of samples increased the risk of information asymmetry.

CATS adopted the National Association of Meat Purveyors (NAMP) Meat Buyer Guide to represent meat products whose qualities vary widely depending on cutting methods and specifications. However, CATS had no instruments to check the reliability of data entered by sellers. Buyers had to assume that the description, entered by suppliers, was a proper representation of the offered products. Furthermore, CATS failed to provide the clearinghouse function, leaving responsibility for resolving trade disputes to individual traders.

Thin market

Traders who take their orders to a new, less active, and less liquid market face uncertain execution and liquidity penalty.[9] In the absence of significant order flow, when their orders will be executed is uncertain. In addition, attempts to buy and sell in a thin market may create an imbalance of demand and supply, which may hurt prospective buyers or sellers. If the new system fails to provide a critical mass large enough to induce traders to switch to a new market form, traders will not join the system because of economic penalties of inferior execution (note 9).

CALM was introduced by AMLC, a statutory authority with the power to lead the livestock industry into electronic trading. AMLC started the CALM operation using funds from the industry levy that applied to all animals slaughtered or exported live in Australia. CALM enjoyed industrywide commitment to its service from the beginning, as well as strong support from the minister and the Department of Primary Industry and Energy. Its active promotions, such as free insurance for products traded over the CALM, also helped CALM promptly achieve the initial critical mass necessary for the impacts of electronic markets to be felt.

Information Auctioning lagged behind its intended market penetration rate because of the lack of significant order flows. Despite its advantages over traditional auctions, the benefits of shifting trading into this new market form were not strongly felt by participants, partly because there were not enough market counterparts. The thin market resulted in lower prices than those of traditional auctions. As a result, growers had to bear costs to modify packaging to suit the buyers but received no extra compensation for their services. In response, VBA established a price floor (minimum price) to reduce price volatility and auctioned the main supply prior to the sample lots in an attempt to make the new market more active. The change of rules, however, did not make the new market active enough to overcome the thin-market problem.

Resistance to change

The inertia resulting from large investments in existing infrastructures and the reluctance of traders to embark on a new round of organizational learning may serve as barriers to successful implementation of electronic marketplaces. The change of the transaction process using computer and communications technology can generate confusion and discomfort to traders if they have limited IT knowledge. Opponents often argue that traditional markets serve as an important socialization venue and thus cannot be replaced by electronic marketplaces. Moreover, firms affected adversely by an electronic market are expected to resist and oppose the system.

As a new market institution, AUCNET faced retaliation from traditional auction markets which felt threatened by the new system. In the beginning of its service, AUCNET secured about 1000 reservations from used-car dealers. Then, the Japanese Used Car Dealer Association (JUCDA), which ran most traditional auto auctions, announced it was against AUCNET and threatened that members who joined AUCNET would be stripped of their membership in JUCDA. When more than half of the reservations were withdrawn,

AUCNET used antitrust complaints and publicity in the press to get the government to prevent JUCDA from blocking AUCNET.

CATS was introduced by AME, a private company that lacked the market power to enforce the change in the meat industry. It began its services without industrywide commitment. The objective of CATS was to make the market more competitive by reducing the large firms' influence on meat pricing (formula pricing). Large wholesalers, whose participation was critical to its success, were not enthusiastic about the new process. CATS both lacked regulatory power to overcome the large firms' resistance and failed to offer them strong enough incentives to join the system.

Implications for management

The central claim of this chapter is that successful deployment of electronic markets requires consideration of the barriers resulting from market process reengineering along with the projected economic benefits. To blame immature technologies in the early 1980s for the failure of CATS is unreasonable since the IT used by CATS had already been used successfully by the cotton industry in the TELCOT system, which began operation in 1978.[26] Likewise, IT was not a major impediment to Information Auctioning, which was launched more recently and used well-proven technologies. Most risks, uncertainties, and barriers stem from social and economic factors, rather than IT-related obstacles. This finding is consistent with many BPR research results:[15,34] IT is a necessary but insufficient factor for reengineering. The success of electronic market adoptions is as dependent on the management of barriers as it is on the economic benefits enabled by the IT. Some cautious suggestions can be made on the basis of the four case studies to assist market-making firms in the analysis, design, and implementation of electronic market systems.

Standard product quality rating and inspection

Recent advances in multimedia technology allow more product groups to be traded electronically. Although the use of multimedia representation may help buyers make purchasing decisions, by itself it will not eliminate the product uncertainty encountered by buyers in electronic markets. Before Information Auctioning, another flower auction market in the Netherlands introduced Video Auctioning, where the physical presence of cut flowers was replaced by pictures displayed on a big screen during the auction process.[23] That system also failed. Similarly, Slide Auction was implemented before the advent of AUCNET by traditional Japanese used-car auctions.[36] The Slide Auction, designed to hold auctions by using 35mm color slides, also ended in failure. None of these failed systems provided adequate product quality specifications and assurances.

There are two features that are crucial for reducing the uncertainties involved in product descriptions in electronic markets: (1) certain standards for product ratings, and (2) a trusted party to carry out product inspection. The failures of Information Auctioning, Video Auctioning, and Slide Auction were due to the lack of standardized quality ratings. CATS used an industrywide standard for meat product descriptions but did not employ an inspection procedure to verify the sellers' descriptions. The emphasis on building standard product ratings and rigorous inspection process accounts for much of the success of CALM and AUCNET (note 10).

Quick achievement of critical mass

Participation externality affects the dynamics of the introduction and adoption of electronic market systems.[24,25] The benefits realized by individual participants in an electronic market system increase as more organizations join the system. Without a critical mass of users, an electronic market system is unlikely to spread its usage and may be extinguished. The quick achievement of initial critical mass accounts for much of the success in CALM and AUCNET. Within two years of its operation, CALM listed over 110 000 cattle and 517 000 sheep/lambs, and secured more than 5000 registered users. AUCNET focused on the participation externality and managed to list over 44 000 vehicles in two years.

CALM was able to accomplish critical mass partly thanks to industrywide commitment and government support. In the case of AUCNET, the new market institution induced a large number of traders to switch to the electronic marketplace by providing strong incentives to join the system without any support from a third party. With or without government support, the planning of strategies to obtain a critical mass of early adopters is crucial so that participation externalities can make the impact of the new process felt.

Preparation for resistance and retaliation

In view of the inertia of old transaction processes and structures, the strain of implementing a market process reengineering plan can hardly be overestimated. Since traders need to be aware of the advantages of the new transaction process, education and promotion of the concept, including IT-related technical supports, must be a prominent part of the plan. Opponents of electronic markets often proclaim the disadvantages of electronic marketplaces compared with traditional markets, since traders cannot capture all the market information on traditional transaction methods.[28] In financial trading, for instance, it is important to know who is bidding, who is offering, and who is trading with whom. This information gives a trader some guidance regarding the nature of trading activity and price movements. Thus, initiating firms need to design the electronic market system carefully so that traders can use their terminals to garner as much information as is available (or more) on the traditional trading floor.

Firms that are affected adversely by an electronic market can be expected to fight the system. For instance, AUCNET had to rely on government authority to overcome JUCDA's retaliatory efforts (note 11). Retaliation is more likely when there are many firms whose power is relatively equal or when the affected parties are able to unite against the initiating firm. Without a strategy to deal with potential retaliations, the initiating firm may be caught without an appropriate response and therefore jeopardize its investments.

Conclusion

We expect the adoption of electronic commerce applications by existing or new market makers to grow rapidly as the cost of communicating information between firms decreases. We have investigated here the evolution of electronic market adoption by such market-making firms. The implementation of electronic markets is viewed as market process reengineering aimed at decoupling product flow from market transactions through on-line trading. We have taken a close look at how IT-enabled reengineering increases market efficiency as well as barriers.

Firms interested in redesigning market processes using electronic commerce solutions need to plan carefully to overcome adoption barriers that could cast a shadow over the benefits of the proposed new market processes. By examining the barriers and facilitators of success in the case studies presented, market makers can be better prepared to design electronic markets that increase market efficiency and overcome barriers to adoptions.

Notes

1   Market-making firms can also be established in formats other than the auction. In NASDAQ and the London Stock Exchange, for instance, investors trade with financial intermediaries (dealers) based on dealers' quoted prices. Both NASDAQ and the London Stock Exchange are governed by detailed trading rules, including responsibility of intermediary roles such as affirmative obligations.[12]

2   In transaction cost economics, first suggested by Coase[10] and expanded by Williamson,[37,38,39] transaction costs are used to explain why firms (or hierarchies) emerge. The transaction cost economics suggests that the costs and difficulties associated with market transactions sometimes favor hierarchies (or in-house production) over markets as an economic

governance structure. Hodgson[21] employs the transaction cost theory to address the question of why organized markets, or market institutions, are favored against fragmented, less-organized markets, without institutional rules.

3 With open lotteries, nearly 400 000 applications for cellular licenses were received, and the FCC had to bear significant processing costs. Moreover, it required lengthy delays to introduce services since many licenses were resold to other cellular providers. After this lottery fiasco, the FCC used comparative hearings to award cellular licenses in thirty markets, but this took almost two years and millions of dollars spent on lobbying by firms attempting to influence the outcome.

4 In addition to these two behavioral assumptions, Williamson presented three characteristics of transactions – uncertainty, frequency of transactions, and asset specificity – to explain the economic governing mechanisms between markets and hierarchies.

5 Our use of the term 'transaction risks' has a narrower, system-oriented focus compared with its use in References 7 and 8, which study transaction risks extensively in the context of interorganizational information systems. In these previous works, transaction risks are those risks accruing from firms' reliance on coordination with independent partners. In contrast, we address the transaction risks that are newly created as a result of the electronic market adoption within market institutions.

6 Livestock is sold either for slaughter or for breeding stock. Products traded in breeding purposes include store stocks for medium-term resale and feedlotting stocks for short-term resale. These stocks may be resold later in the market by different traders.

7 There are three methods for potted plant packaging. In traditional auctions, purchased products may not be packaged in a way preferred by the buyer. Since products are not packaged yet at the moment of the transaction, buyers in Information Auctioning can specify their packaging preferences before delivery.

8 Akerlof[1] presents transactions in second-hand cars as an example of markets with asymmetric information. It would be very costly for a buyer of a second-hand car to determine accurately its true quality. There is certainly no guarantee that the owner of the car would disclose his or her knowledge about its history and quality during the transaction, particularly if the vehicle is a 'lemon' that the seller is eager to unload.

9 In the financial-market literature, this phenomenon is called the 'liquidity trap' or 'central market defense', and represents a crucial economic dynamic for new market designs, including electronic trading systems, because of the importance of the liquidity in financial exchanges.[9,12]

10 Another example is TELCOT, an electronic market system introduced by the Plain Cotton Cooperative Association (PCCA) for cotton trading.[26]

In TELCOT, cotton farmers send six-ounce samples of each bale (500-pound cotton package) to the Department of Agriculture, which determines the grades of cotton based on well-standardized measures. The standard attributes assessed by the government enable buyers to purchase cotton before seeing it.

11 The experience of HAM (the Hog Auction Market), an electronic market system for pig trading in Singapore, offers another example of retaliation from affected parties. When HAM was introduced, pig importers, who were afraid of being squeezed out of the pig market process by HAM, understandably protested the system by boycott and legal injunction.[29] The government, convinced that HAM would ultimately benefit local consumers, had to resort to regulatory powers to overcome the brokers' court injunction, which would have killed the HAM system.

References

1 Akerlof, G. A. The market for 'lemons': qualitative uncertainty and the market mechanism. *Quarterly Journal of Economics*, *84* (August 1970), 488–500.

2 Anthes, G. H. FCC auction built on client/server: software enables simultaneous bidding. *Computerworld* (April 3 1995), 58.

3 Bakos, J. A strategic analysis of electronic marketplaces. *MIS Quarterly*, *15*, 3 (September 1991), 295–310.

4 Bakos, J., and Brynjolfsson, E. From vendors to partners: information technology and incomplete contracts in buyer-seller relationships. *Journal of Organizational Computing*, *3*, 3 (1993), 301–328.

5 Bakos, J., and Brynjolfsson, E. Information technology, incentives, and the optimal number of suppliers. *Journal of Management Information Systems*, *10*, 2 (Fall 1993), 37–53.

6 Clarke, R., and Jenkins, M. The strategic intent of on-line trading systems: a case study in national livestock marketing. *Journal of Strategic Information Systems*, *2*, 1 (March 1993), 57–76.

7 Clemons, E.; Reddi, S. P.; and Row, M. The impact of information technology on the organization of economic activities: the 'move to the middle' hypothesis. *Journal of Management Information Systems*, *10*, 2 (Fall 1993), 9–35.

8 Clemons, E., and Row, M. Information technology and industrial cooperation: the changing economics of coordination and ownership. *Journal of Management Information Systems*, *9*, 2 (Fall 1992), 9–28.

9 Clemons, E., and Weber, B. Evaluating the prospects for alternative electronic securities market. *Proceedings of the 12th International Conference on Information Systems*. New York: 1991, pp. 53–61.

10   Coase, R. H. The nature of the firm. *Economica N. S.*, *4* (1937), 386–405.

11   Coase, R. H. *The Firm, the Market and the Law*. Chicago: University of Chicago Press, 1988.

12   Cohen, K. J.; Maier, S. F.; Schwartz, R. A.; and Whitcomb, D. K. *The Microstructure of Securities Markets*. Englewood Cliffs, NJ: Prentice-Hall, 1986.

13   Davenport, T. H. *Process Innovation*. Boston: Harvard Business School Press, 1993.

14   Davenport, T. H., and Short, J. E. The new industrial engineering: information technology and business process redesign. *Sloan Management Review*, *31*, 4, (Summer 1990), 11–27.

15   Davenport, T. H., and Stoddard, D. B. Reengineering: business change of mythic propositions? *MIS Quarterly*, *18*, 2 (June 1994), 121–127.

16   Gurbaxani, V., and Whang, S. The impacts of information systems on organizations and markets. *Communications of the ACM*, *34*, 1 (January 1991), 59–73.

17   Hammer, M. Reengineering work: don't automate, obliterate. *Harvard Business Review*, *68*, 4 (July–August 1990), 104–112.

18   Hammer, M., and Champy, J. *Reengineering the Corporation*. New York: Harper Business, 1993.

19   Hayes, C. Cashing in the home shopping boom. *Black Enterprise*, *25*, 7 (July 1995), 120–133.

20   Hess, C. M., and Kemerer, C. F. Computerized loan organization system: an industry case study of the electronic markets hypothesis. *MIS Quarterly*, *18*, 3 (September 1994), 251–274.

21   Hodgson, G. M. *Economics and Institutions*. Philadelphia: University of Pennsylvania Press, 1988.

22   Johnston, R., and Lawrence, P. Beyond vertical integration: the rise of the value-adding partnership. *Harvard Business Review*, *66*, 4 (July–August 1988), 94–101.

23   Kambil, A., and van Heck, E. Information technology, competition and market transformations: re-engineering the Dutch flower auctions. Working Paper (Stern no. IS-95–1), Center for Research on Information Systems, New York University, January 1995.

24   Katz, M. L., and Shapiro, C. Network externalities, competition and compatibility. *American Economic Review*, *75* (Spring 1985), 70–83.

25   Lee, H. G., and Clark, T. Impacts of electronic marketplace on transaction cost and market structure. *International Journal of Electronic Commerce*, *1*, 1 (1996), 127–149.

26   Lindsey, D.; Cheney, P.; Kasper, G.; and Ives, B. TELCOT: an application of information technology for competitive advantage in the cotton industry. *MIS Quarterly*, *14*, 4 (December 1990), 347–357.

27   Malone, T.; Yates, J.; and Benjamin, R. Electronic markets and electronic hierarchies. *Communication of the ACM, 30,* 6 (June 1987), 484–497.

28   Massimb, M. N., and Phelps, B. D. Electronic trading, market structure and liquidity. *Financial Analysis Journal* (January–February 1994), 39–50.

29   Neo, B. S. The implementation of an electronic market for pig trading in Singapore. *Journal of Strategic Information Systems, 1,* 5 (December 1992), 278–288.

30   Sarhan, M. E., and Nelson, K. E. Evaluation of the pilot test of the computer assisted trading system, CATS, for wholesale meat in the U.S. Project report of Department of Agricultural Economics, University of Illinois at Urbana-Champaign, 1983.

31   Sarkar, M. B.; Bulter, B.; and Steinfield, C. Intermediaries and cybermediaries: a continuing role for mediating players in the electronic marketplace. *Journal of Computer-Mediated Communication, 1,* 3 (1996), http://www.usc.edu/dept/annenberg/journal.html.

32   Smith, V. L., and Williams, A. W. Experimental market economics. *Scientific American, 267* (December 1992), 116–121.

33   Stigler, G. J. Public regulation of the securities markets. *Journal of Business, 37* (April 1964), 117–134.

34   Stoddard, D. B., and Jarvenpaa, S. L. Business process redesign: tactics for managing radical change. *Journal of Management Information Systems, 12,* 1 (Summer 1995), 81–107.

35   Thorelli, H. B. Networks: between markets and hierarchies. *Strategic Management Journal, 7* (1986), 37–51.

36   Warbelow, A., and Kokuryo, J. AUCNET: TV Auction Network System. *Harvard Business School Case Study,* 9–190-001, July 1989.

37   Williamson, O. Transaction-cost economics: the governance of contractual relations. *Journal of Law and Economics, 22,* 2 (October 1979), 233–261.

38   Williamson, O. The economics of organization: the transaction cost approach. *American Journal of Sociology, 87,* 3 (November 1981), 548–577.

39   Williamson, O. *The Economic Institutions of Capitalism.* New York: Free Press, 1985.

40   Young, D. The PCS auction: a post-game wrap-up. *Telecommunications* (July 1995), 21–24.

Reproduced from, Lee, H. G. and Clark, T. H. (1996–97) Market process reengineering through electronic market systems: opportunities and challenges *Journal of Management Information Systems,* **13**(3), Winter, 113–136. Reprinted with permission of the publishers. M. E. Sharpe, Inc.

Questions for discussion

1 Identify other electronics markets that have been successful or unsuccessful and explain why.

2 Figure 15.2 lists two challenges to electronic markets: (a) increased transaction risks and uncertainties, and (b) lack of power to enforce the change. Think of some others. In the case of electronic shopping, what are the major challenges? What are the risks from both the buyer and seller perspective?

3 How can some of the barriers be overcome (such as lack of trust in information, thin markets, and resistance to change), both in the context of electronic markets and electronic shopping?

4 The authors state that 'most risks, uncertainties, and barriers stem from social and economic rather than IT-related obstacles'. What are some of the IT-related obstacles?

5 For organizations considering electronic commerce, what are some of the implications from these cases?

Part Four

Information Systems Strategy and the Organizational Environment

The focus of this final part of the book is the outer shaded portion of our conceptualization of strategic information management, reproduced below as Figure IV.1. It is concerned with

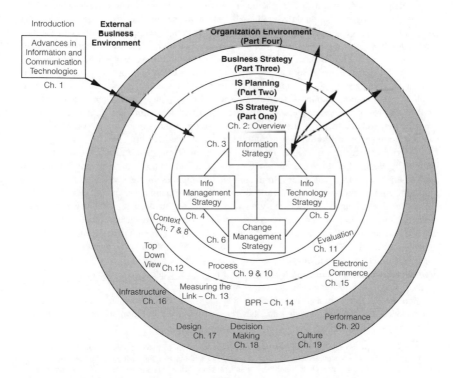

Figure IV.1   *The focus of Part Four: Information systems strategy and the organization environment*

the wider context within which information systems strategy takes place: the organizational environment. As such, it reflects on such issues as information technology and the globalization of business; alternative organizational arrangements; decision making in organizations, and organizational culture and knowledge management. We conclude with a further consideration of IT's impact on organizational performance (cf. Chapter 11).

Part Four commences, in Chapter 16, with a consideration of what we term the information technology strategy, and the issues confronting global firms in coordinating their business on a worldwide basis.* We saw, in Chapter 8, that IS management issues are likely to differ according to the extent of economic development in, and the cultural values exhibited by, different countries. In Chapter 16, Karimi and Konsynski focus attention on alternative organizational forms associated with different global strategies and consider the need to align the information technology infrastructure with these alternatives in mind. Useful illustrations are given from various, very different, parts of the world including, for example, Finland and Singapore, as well as North America. Key issues associated with, for example, different regulatory environments and transborder data flows, are highlighted. A key point that this chapter makes, graphically – as does Chapter 17 – relates to the kind of relationship that should exist between considerations of organizational form and IT infrastructure, highlighted by the innermost circle of our conceptualization of strategic information management in Figure IV.1. For further reading on transnational organizations and associated strategic management issues see, for example, Ohmae (1988) and Porter (1990).

Chapter 17, by Lambert and Peppard, complements the preceding chapter by also looking at IT and new organizational forms. By the latter they mean structure, systems, management style, cultures, roles, responsibilities, skills and the like. The authors remind us that 'Organizations must adopt a form that is appropriate to their strategy and the competitive position within which they find themselves', bearing in mind the opportunities afforded by IT. A range of alternative organizational forms are presented, as is a framework which should prove useful when dealing with the myriad complex issues associated with migrating towards an appropriate new form. Their framework pays considerable attention to change management issues (cf., once again, the innermost circle of our conceptualization of strategic information management, and Chapters 5 and 6). For further reading on the general topic of organizational transformation, see Kochan and Useem (1992), from which Chapter 5 is extracted. For more on IT and organizational transformation, see, for example, Scott Morton (1991), and Galliers and Baets (1998).

We turn our attention, in Chapter 18, to the effects of IT on organizational decision making. Written by Huber, this chapter is not alone in this collection in being of particular relevance to MBA audiences, drawing, as it does, from a range of disciplines, in this instance from the worlds of organization science and communications, as well as information systems. As Gibbons (1995) has argued, it is through transdisciplinary research of this kind that new knowledge is more likely to be obtained. Huber's intent is to reinvestigate components of organization theory, given that much of this had been formulated 'when the nature and mix of communication technologies were relatively constant, both across time and across organizations of the same general type'. Citing the advent of electronic mail, image transmission, computer conferencing, expert systems, external information retrieval systems, and the like, Huber sets out to explore how such new technologies as these might impact organizational forms, intelligence and decision making. A series of propositions are set forth, connected with constructs and concepts, from which a conceptual theory is developed. He concludes, *inter alia*, that researchers in organization science 'should study

---

* We pointed out previously the various interpretations put on commonly used expressions in the general field of strategic information management. In this chapter, the authors use the term information management strategy to describe an approach to establish an information technology architecture. We use information technology strategy to describe this concept. Aspects that the authors touch on concerned with organizing the information systems function, and ensuring the requisite expertise is in place, for example, do fall within our conception of information management strategy, however.

advanced information technology as . . . an intervention or jolt in the life of an organization that may have unanticipated consequences with respect to evolved organizational design'. The collective experiences of our readers are likely to conclude that he is right on this score! More positively, he also concludes that IT is likely to improve decision making and enable new organizational forms. Reasons for possible impediments to the former, however, are uncovered in Chapter 19 that then follows. For further reading on IT and organizational structure and decision making, see, for example, Fiedler *et al.* (1996); Leidner and Elam (1993, 1995); Molloy and Schwenk (1995); Orlikowski and Robey (1991) and Tavakolian (1989).

In Chapter 19, Leidner reflects on the issues associated with current attempts to implement Knowledge Management Systems (KMS) in organizations and their, at times, limited impact, due to clashes with corporate culture. The author introduces the chapter with an insightful account of developments over the years in information systems designed to support managerial and operational activity in organizations, preceding the more recent developments in KMS. Providing a complementary account to that presented in Chapter 1, Leidner focuses attention on the implementation effects and requirements of various types of information system, from Management Information Systems (MIS), to Decision Support Systems (DSS), to Executive Information Systems (EIS), to KMS. She notes a trend from a 'one system for all users', to a 'one system for one user', to an 'anyone, anywhere, anytime' information provision strategy in line with these developments. Reflecting on organizational culture issues, Leidner illustrates how the necessity for user participation in the information systems development and design process has progressed, in the light of these developments, from involvement during earlier stages of analysis and design, to active contribution of user knowledge with KMS. This is where her concept of information culture comes in, with a series of propositions that help illustrate, among other things, the circumstances in which knowledge is more or less likely to be shared by actors in organizations, dependent on their view as to whether this information is an individual or corporate asset.

We conclude, in Chapter 20, with a further look at what has been termed the IT productivity paradox – the problem that many organizations face in obtaining business advantage from their IT, despite the dramatic developments in the technology that we have witnessed over recent years, and despite the considerable investment made in this technology by many companies.* Written by Willcocks and Lester, it proposes a means of linking business and information systems IS strategy by prioritizing IT investments, setting interlinking performance measures and considering external IT services as well as internally developed solutions. In many ways, then, the holistic stance taken by the authors makes Chapter 20 an appropriate place to bring our consideration of strategic information management to a close, since it tries to integrate many – although by no means all – of the issues raised in the book. The overall intention of the chapter, as well as *Strategic Information Management* as a whole, has been to enable organizations to obtain greater business value from their investments in IT. This can only be achieved by executives understanding the issues, getting involved and taking responsibility in this key area. We hope we have gone some way in assisting in this process.

References

Brynjolfsson, E. (1996) The contribution of Information Technology to consumer welfare. *Information Systems Research*, 7(3), September, 281–300.

Brynjolfsson, E. and Hitt, L. M. (1993) Paradox lost? Firm-level evidence on the returns to Information Systems spending. *Management Science*, April.

* For further reading on the IT Productivity Paradox and the general topic of the business contribution of IT, and its measurement, see, for example, Brynjolfsson (1996); Brynjolfsson and Hitt (1993), and Hitt *et al.* (1996). See also additional references given in relation to Chapter 11.

Fiedler, K. D., Grover, V. and Teng, J. T. C. (1996) An empirically derived taxonomy of Information Technology structure and its relationship to organizational structure. *Journal of Management Information Systems*, **13**(1), Summer, 9–34.

Galliers, R. D. and Baets, W. R. J. (1998) *Information Technology and Organizational Transformation: Innovation for the 21st Century Organization*, Wiley, Chichester.

Gibbons, M. (1995) *The New Production of Knowledge: The Dynamics of Science and Research in Contemporary Societies*, Sage, London.

Hitt, L. M. and Brynjolffson, E. (1996) Productivity, business profitability and consumer surplus: three measures of Information Technology value. *MIS Quarterly*, **20**(2), 121–142.

Kochan, T. A. and Useem, M. (eds) (1992) *Transforming Organizations*, Oxford University Press, New York.

Leidner, D. E. and Elam, J. J. (1993) Executive information systems; their impact on executive decision making. *Journal of Management Information Systems*, **10**(3), 139–156.

Leidner, D. E. and Elam, J. J. (1995) The impact of executive information systems on organizational design, intelligence and decision making. *Organization Science*, **6**(6), 645–665.

Molloy, S. and Schwenk, C. R. (1995) The effects of Information Technology on strategic decision making. *Journal of Management Studies*, **32**(5), 283–311.

Ohmae, K. (1989) The global logic of strategic alliances. *Harvard Business Review*, **70**(2), March–April, 143–154.

Orlikowski, W. and Robey, D. (1991) Information Technology and the structuring of organizations. *Information Systems Research*, **2**(2), 143–169.

Porter, M. E. (1990) *The Competitive Advantage of Nations*, Macmillan, Basingstoke.

Scott Morton, M. S. (ed.) (1991) *The Corporation of the 1990s: Information Technology and Organizational Transformation*, Oxford University Press, New York.

Tavakolian, H. (1989) Linking the Information Technology structure with organizational competitive strategy: a survey. *MIS Quarterly*, **13**(3), September, 309–319.

16 The Information Technology Infrastructure–Organizational Structure Relationship

Globalization and information management strategies

J. Karimi and B. R. Konsynski

1 Introduction

Recently, the globalization of competition has become the rule rather than the exception for a number of industries.[39] To compete effectively, at home or globally, firms often must coordinate their activities on a worldwide basis. Although many global firms have an explicit global business strategy, few have a corresponding strategy for managing information technology internationally. Many firms have information interchange protocols across their multinational organizational structures, but few have global information technology architectures. A global information management strategy is needed as a result of (1) *industry globalization*: the growing globalization trend in many industries and the associated reliance on information technologies for coordination and operation, and (2) *national competitive posture*: the aggregation of separate domestic strategies in individual countries that may contend with coordination. While Procter and Gamble contends with the need to address more effectively its global market in the branded packaged goods industry, Singapore requires improved coordination and control of trade documentation in order to compete more effectively in the cross-industry trade environment that is vital to the economic health of that nation. Each approach recognizes the growing information intensity in their expanding markets. Each in turn must meet the challenges brought about by the need for cross-cultural and cross-industry cooperation.

Globalization trends demand an evaluation of the skills portfolio that organizations require in order to participate effectively in their changing markets. Porter[41] suggests that coordination among increasingly complex networks of activities dispersed worldwide is becoming a prime source of competitive advantage: global strategies frequently involve coordination with coalition partners as well as among a firm's own subsidiaries. The benefits associated with globalization of industries are not tied to countries' policies and practice. Rather, they are associated with how the activities in the industry value chain are performed by the firm's worldwide systems. These systems involve partnerships[31] with independent entities that involve information and management process interchange across legal organization boundaries, as well as across national boundaries.

For a global firm, the coordination concerns involve an analysis of how similar or linked activities are performed in different countries. Coordination[31] involves the management of the exchange of information, goods, expertise, technology, and finances. Many business functions play a role in such coordination – logistics, order fulfillment, financial, etc. Coordination involves sharing and use, by different facilities, of information about the activities within the firm's value chain.[30] In global industries, these skills permit a firm to (1) be flexible in responding to competitors in different countries and markets, (2) respond in one country (or region) to a change in another, (3) scan markets around the world, (4) transfer knowledge between units in different countries, (5) reduce costs, (6) enhance effectiveness, and (7) preserve diversity in final products and in production location. The innovations in information technology (IT) in the past two decades have greatly reduced coordination costs by reducing both the time and cost of communicating information. Market and product innovation often involves coordination and partnership across a diverse set of organizational and geographically dispersed entities. Several studies[26,27,38,42] suggest ways in which companies/nations achieve competitive advantage through innovation.

Organizations must begin to manage the evolution of a global IT architecture that forms an infrastructure for the coordination needs of a global management team. The country-centered, multinational firm will give way to truly global organizations that will carry little national identity.[49,50] It is a major challenge to general management to build and manage the technical infrastructure that supports a unique global enterprise culture. This chapter deals with issues that arise in the evolution of a global business strategy and its alignment with the evolving global IT strategy.

Below we present issues related to the radical changes taking place in both the global business environment and the IT environment, with changes in one area driving changes in the other. Section 2 describes changes taking place in the global business environment as a result of globalization. It highlights elements from previous research findings on the effects of globalization on the organizational strategies/structures and coordination/control strategies. Section 3 deals with the information technology dimension and addresses the issue of development of a global information systems (GIS) management strategy.

The section emphasizes the need for 'alignment' of business and techno-logical evolution as a result of the radical changes in the global business environment and technology. Section 4 summarizes and presents other chal-lenges to senior managers that are emerging in the global business environment.

2 Globalization and changes in the business environment

Since World War II, a number of factors have changed the manner of competi-tion in the global business community. The particular catalyst for globalization and for evolving patterns of international competition varies among indus-tries. Among the causative factors are increased similarity in available infra-structure, distribution channels, and marketing approaches among countries, as well as a fluid global capital market that allows large flows of funds between countries. Additional causes include falling political and tariff barriers, a growing number of regional economic pacts that facilitate trade relations, and the increasing impact of the technological revolution in restructuring and integrating industries. Manufacturing issues associated with flexibility, labor cost differentials, and other factors also play a role in these market trends.

Widespread globalization is also evident in a number of industries that were once largely separate domestic industries, such as software, telecom-munications, and services.[9,32,40] In the decade of the 1990s, the political changes in the Soviet Union and the Eastern European countries, plus the evolution of the European Common Market toward a single European market without national borders or barriers,[13] also have led to growing international competi-tion. Other factors are changing the economic dynamics in the Pacific Rim area, with changes in Hong Kong, Japan, China and Taiwan, Korea, Singa-pore, and the reentry of certain nations to the global economic community (e.g. Vietnam).

Previous research indicates that significant changes have taken place in organizational strategies/structure during the 1980s because of ever-increasing global competition and growth in the communications and information-processing industry. Researchers in international business have pointed out that the struc-ture of a global firm's value chain is the key to its strategy: its fit with the environmental requirements that determine economic performance.[3,15,37,40] Another study found that, in successful global firms, organization structure and strategy are matched by selecting the most efficient or lowest cost struc-ture that satisfies the information-processing requirements inherent in the strategy.[12] That is, the firm's strategy and its information-processing re-quirements must be in alignment with the firm's organizational structure and information-processing capabilities. To understand changes in organizational designs for global forms, these changes are highlighted in relation to the changes in strategies.

2.1   Evolution of the global firm's strategy/structure

Global strategy is defined by Porter[40] as strategy from which 'a firm seeks to gain competitive advantage from its international presence through either a concentrated configuration of activities, or coordinating among dispersed activities, or both'. Configuration involves the location(s) in the world where each activity in the value chain is performed, it characterizes the organizational structure of a global firm. A global firm faces a number of options in both configuration and coordination for each activity in the value chain. As implied by these definitions, there is no one pattern of international competition, neither is there one type of global strategy.

Bartlett[3,4] suggests that for a global firm value-chain activities are pulled together by two environmental forces: (1) national differentiation, i.e. diversity in individual country-markets; and (2) global integration, i.e. coordination among activities in various countries. For global firms, forces for integration and national differentiation can vary depending on their global strategies. Table 16.1 shows the evolution of the global firms' strategy/structure and their coordination/control strategies as a result of globalization of competition. The vocabulary of Bartlett[4] and Porter[40] will be further used in our framework.

Under a *multinational* strategy, a firm might differentiate its products to meet local needs to respond to diverse interests. In such an approach, the firm might delegate considerable operating independence and strategic freedom to its foreign subsidiaries. Under this *decentralized* organizational structure, highly autonomous national companies are often managed as a portfolio of offshore investments rather than as a single international business. A subsidiary is focused on its local market. Coordination and control are achieved primarily through personal relationships between top corporate management and subsidiary managers than by written rules, procedures, or a formal organizational structure. Strategic decisions are decentralized and top management is involved mainly in monitoring the results of foreign operations. Figure 16.1 presents this organizational strategy/structure.

This model was the classic strategy/structure adopted by most European-based companies expanding before World War II. Examples include Unilever in branded packaged products, Philips in consumer electronics, and ITT in telecommunications switching. However, much changed for European companies in the 1970s with the reduction of certain tariff barriers by the EEC and with the entrance of both American and Japanese firms into local markets.

In the machine lubricant industry, automotive motor oil tends toward a multinational competitive environment. Countries have different driving standards and regulations and regional weather conditions. Domestic firms tend to emerge as leaders (for example, Quaker State and Pennzoil in the United States). At the same time, multinationals with country subsidies (such as

Table 16.1 *Global business environment – strategy/structure and coordination control*

Business strategy/ structure	Strategic management processes	Tactical business processes	Coordination and control processes
Multinational/ decentralized – federation	Informal HQ– subsidiary relationships; strategic decisions are decentralized	Mainly financial flows; capital out and dividends back	Socialization; careful recruitment, development, and acculturation of key decision makers
Global/centralized federation	Tight central control of decisions, resources and information	One-way flows of goods, resources and information	Centralization; substantive decision making by senior management
International/ coordinated – federation	Formal management planning and control systems allow tighter HQ–subsidiary linkages	Assets, resources, responsibilities decentralized but controlled from HQ	Formalization; formal systems, policies and standards to guide choice
Transnational/ integrated – network	Complex process of coordination and cooperation in an environment of shared decision making	Large flows of technology, finances, people, and information among interdependent units	Co-opting; the entire portfolio of coordinating and control mechanisms
Interorganizational/ coordinated federation of business groups	Share activities and gain competitive advantage by lowering costs and raising differentiation	Vertical disaggregation of functions	Formalization; multiple and flexible coordination and control functions

Castrol, UK) become leaders in regional markets. In the lodging industry, many segments are multinational as a result of the fact that a majority of activities in the value chain are strongly tied to buyer location. Further, differences associated with national and regional preferences and lifestyle lead to few benefits from global coordination.

Under a pure *global* strategy, a firm may seek competitive advantage by capitalizing on the economies associated with standardized product design, global-scale manufacturing, and a centralized control of world-wide operation. The key parts of a firm's value-chain activities (typically product design or manufacturing) are geographically concentrated. They are either retained

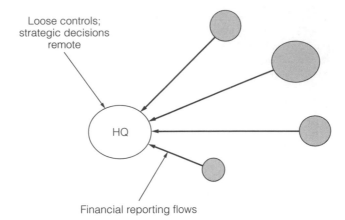

Figure 16.1 *Multinational strategy with decentralized organizational structure*

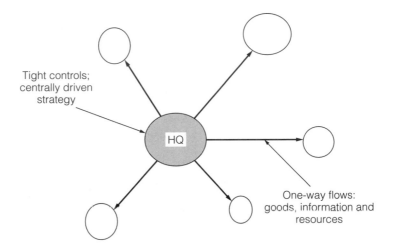

Figure 16.2 *Global strategy with centralized organizational structure*

at the center, or they are centrally controlled. Under this *centralized* organizational structure, there are primarily one-way flows of goods, information, and resources from headquarters to subsidiaries; key strategic decisions for worldwide operations are made centrally by senior management. Figure 16.2 depicts this organizational strategy/structure.

This export-based strategy was/is typical in Japanese-based companies in the postwar years. They typically require highly coordinated activities among subsidiaries. Examples include KAO in branded packaged products, Matsushita in consumer electronics, NEC in telecommunications switching, and Toyota

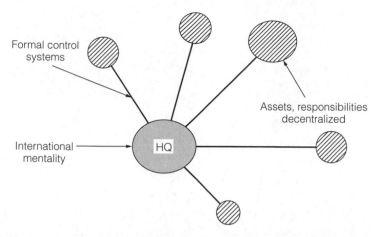

Figure 16.3   *International strategy with coordinated federation organizational structure*

in the automobile industry. Toyota started by capitalizing on a tightly controlled operation that emphasized worldwide export of fairly standardized automobile models from global-scale plants in Toyota City, Japan. Lately, because of growing protectionist sentiments and lower factory costs in less-developed countries, Toyota (among others) has found it necessary to establish production sites in less-developed countries in order to sustain its competitive edge. The marine engine lubricant industry is a global industry that requires a global strategy. Ships move freely around the world and require that brand oil be available wherever they put into port. Brand reputations thus become global issues. Successful marine engine lubricant competitors (such as Shell, Exxon, and British Petroleum) are good examples of global enterprises.

In the area of business-oriented luxury hotels, competitors differ from the majority of hotel accommodations and the competition is more global. Global competitors such as Hilton, Marriott, and Sheraton have a wide range of dispersed properties that employ common brand names, common format, common service standards, and worldwide reservation systems to gain marketing advantage in serving the highly mobile business travelers. Expectations of global standards for service and quality are high.

Under an *international strategy*, a firm transfers knowledge and expertise to overseas environments that are less advanced in technology and market development. Local subsidiaries are often free to adapt new strategies, products, processes, and/or ideas. Under this *coordinated federation* organizational structure, the subsidiaries' dependence on the parent company for new processes and ideas requires a great deal more coordination and control by headquarters than under a classic multinational strategy. Figure 16.3 depicts this organizational strategy/structure.

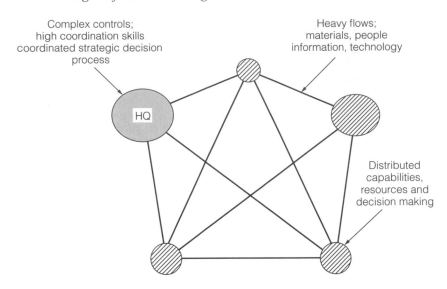

Figure 16.4   *Transnational strategy with integrated-network organizational structure*

This strategy/structure defines the managerial culture of many US-based companies. Examples include Procter and Gamble in branded packaged products, General Electric in consumer electronics, and Ericsson in telecommunications switching. These companies have a reputation for professional management that implies a willingness to delegate responsibility while retaining overall control through sophisticated systems and specialist corporate staffs. But, under this structure, international subsidiaries are more dependent on the transfer of knowledge and information than are subsidiaries under a multinational strategy; the parent company makes a greater use of formal systems and controls in its relations with subsidiaries.

Under a *transnational* strategy, a firm coordinates a number of national operations while retaining the ability to respond to national interests and preferences. National subsidiaries are no longer viewed as the implementors of centrally-developed strategies. Each, however, is viewed as a source of ideas, capabilities, and knowledge that can be beneficial to the company as a whole. It is not unusual for companies to coordinate product development, marketing approaches, and overall competitive strategy across interdependent national units. Under this *integrated network* organizational structure, top managers are responsible for: (1) coordinating the development of strategic objectives and operating policies, (2) coordinating logistics among operating divisions, and (3) coordinating the flow of information among divisions.[3] Figure 16.4 presents this organizational strategy/structure.

During the 1980s, forces of global competition required global firms to be more responsive nationally. As a result, the transnational strategies are being adopted by increasing numbers of global firms.[3] This adoption is becoming necessary because of the need for worldwide coordination and integration of activities upstream in the value chain (e.g. inbound logistics, operations) and because of the need for a greater degree of national differentiation and responsiveness at the downstream end (e.g. marketing, sales, and services). For example, adoption of a transnational mode allowed companies such as Procter and Gamble, NEC, and Unilever to respond effectively to the new and complex demands of their international business environments. They were able to replace exports with local manufacture and to develop more locally differentiated products.[3,9] In contrast, the inability to develop a similar organizational capability is seen by some to be a factor contributing to the strategic and competitive difficulties faced by companies such as ITT, GE, and KAO.

Special situations relate to another form of the *coordinated federation* organizational structure, *interorganizational* design, which is a particular form of the organizational framework represented in Figure 16.4. An interorganizational design consists of two or more organizations that have chosen to cooperate by combining their strengths to overcome individual weaknesses.[51] There are two modes of interorganizational design: equity and non-equity collaboration. *Equity collaborations* are seen in joint ventures, minority equity investments, and franchises. *Non-equity collaborations* are seen in forms of licensing arrangements, marketing and distribution agreements, and interorganizational systems.[2,21,30,31] For example, in the airline industry, achieving the economies of scale in developing and managing a large-scale reservation system are now beyond the capacities of the medium-sized airlines. In Europe, two major coalitions have been created, the Amadeus Coalition and the Galileo Coalition. Software for Amadeus is built around System One, the computer reservation system for Continental and Eastern. Galileo makes use of United's software. Even the largest carriers have acknowledged their inability to manage a large-scale reservation system by themselves; they have joined coalitions.[31]

Another highly visible example that demonstrates the notion of regional or national coordination in order to compete in a global market is the paper industry of Finland. The 19 Finnish paper companies comprise a $3 billion industry that is heavily dependent on exports. Recently they determined that, to compete effectively in that service-oriented business, they must provide online electronic data interchange (EDI) interfaces with key customers and their sales offices. The Finnpap organization combined the efforts of the mill owners to develop an information system that reaches around the globe. The initial budget estimate of $40 million for five years has grown to an annual commitment of $10 million for the foreseeable future. None of the individual companies in the Finnish paper industry had the size, skills, and/or financial strength to create and deliver the world-class services necessary to compete against the large American, Canadian, and other global competitors. A regional cooperation was needed among the competitors in order to compete in the global market.

There has been a virtual explosion in the use of interorganizational designs for both global and domestic firms as a result of increased global competition during the 1980s. In 1983 alone, the number of domestic joint ventures announced in communications and information systems products and services industries exceeded the sum of all previously announced joint ventures in those sectors.[17] Research suggests that interorganizational designs can lead to (1) 'vertical disaggregation' of functions (e.g. marketing, distribution) typically conducted within the boundaries of a single organization performed independently by the organizations within the network, (2) the use of 'brokers,' or structure-independent organizations, to link together the different organizational units into 'business groups' for performance of specific tasks, and (3) the substitution of 'full disclosure information systems' in traditional organization for lengthy trust-building processes based on experience.[36]

2.2   Evolution of the global firm's coordination control strategies

Strategic control is considered to be the key element for the 'integration' of a firm's value-chain activities; it is defined as 'the extent of influence that a head office has over a subsidiary concerning decisions that affect subsidiary strategy'.[10] Previous research found that, as resources such as capital, technology, and management become vested in the subsidiaries, head offices cannot continue to rely on control over these resources as means of influencing subsidiary strategy.[1,10,44] The nature of strategic control by the head office over its subsidiaries shifts with time; there is a need for new forms of administrative control mechanisms such as those offered through improved information management strategies.

In a study of nine large worldwide companies and by interviewing 236 managers both in corporate headquarters and in a number of different national subsidiaries, Bartlett and Ghoshal[4] found that many companies had reached a coordination crisis by 1980. New competitive pressures were requiring the global firms to develop multiple strategic capabilities, even as other environment forces led them to reconfigure their historical organization structures. Many familiar means of coordination (e.g. socialization, centralization, and formalization – shown in Table 16.1) characteristically proved inadequate to this new challenge.

The study further reports that European companies began to see the power and simplicity of more centralized coordination of subsidiaries. The Japanese increasingly adopted more formal systems, routines, and policies to supplement their traditional time-consuming, case-by-case negotiations. American managers took new interest in shaping and managing the previously ignored informal processes and value systems in their firms. The study also found that the challenge for many global firms was not to find the organizational structure that provided the best fit with their global strategies, but to build and manage the appropriate decision-making processes that can respond to multiple changing environmental demands. Furthermore, because of evolving global strategies from multinational to transnational, decision making is no longer concentrated at corporate headquarters. Today's global firm must be able to carry a great deal of complex information to diverse locations in its integrated network of operations.

As we have seen, research on international business suggests that globalization has caused a change in the coordination/control needs of global firms. As a result, new organizational designs are created to meet new organizational coordination needs and to deal with increased organizational complexity and size. The traditional organizational designs[18,29] such as functional, multidivisional, and matrix forms, are largely inappropriate for today's global firms.

Research further suggests that different organizational strategies/structures are necessary across products or businesses with diverse (global) environment demands. In response, there have been two relatively new trends in organizational strategies: (1) a shift from a multinational strategy with decentralized organizational structures to a transnational strategy and globally integrated networks of operations, and (2) a rapid proliferation of interorganizational designs and structurally independent organizational units and business groups.

In short, the success in global competition depends largely on (1) a proper fit between an organization's business strategy and its structure, (2) an organization's ability to adapt its structure in order to balance the environmental forces of national differentiation and global integration for its value-chain activities, and (3) the manner of coordination/control of the organization's value-chain activities. As presented above, the globalization of competition and the evolving business environment suggest that the success of today's global firms' business and its coordination/control strategies may be linked to a global information management strategy. In the following section, the roles and characteristics of global information systems (GIS) and their differences with traditional distributed data-processing systems are discussed. A global information system management strategy is proposed. The need for 'alignment' of the organization's business strategy/structure with its information system management strategy is emphasized as part of this strategy.

3 Global information systems

Due to the dramatic changes in IT, and the increased skills in organizations to deploy and exploit those advances, there are an increasing number of applications of IT by global firms in both service and manufacturing industries. The earliest were in international banking, airline, and credit authorization. However, during the 1980s, due to rapid improvements in communication and IT, more and more activities of global firms were coordinated using information systems. At the same time, patterns in the economies of IT development are changing.[19,22,38] The existence or near completion of public national data networks and of public or quasi-public regional and international networks in virtually all developed (and a few developing) countries has resulted in rapid growth in data-service industries, e.g. data processing, software, information storage and retrieval, and telecommunications services.[26,46]

Today global firms not only rely on data-service industries and IT to speed up message transmission (e.g. for ordering, marketing, distribution, and invoicing), but also to improve the management of corporate systems by: (1) improving corporate functions such as financial control, strategic planning, and inventory control, and (2) changing the manner in which global firms actually engage in production (e.g. in manufacturing, R&D, design and engineering, CAD/CAM/CAE).[46] Therefore, more and more of global firms' mechanisms for planning, control and coordination, and reporting depend on information technology. According to the head of information systems at the $35 billion chemical giant, information systems will either be a facilitator or an inhibitor of globalization during the 1990s.[35]

A *global information system* (GIS) is a distributed data-processing system that crosses national boundaries.[7] There are a number of differences between domestic distributed systems[25] and GISs. Because GISs cross national boundaries, unlike domestic distributed systems, they are exposed to wide variations in business environments, availability of resources, and technological and regulatory environments. These are explained briefly below.

Business Environment. From the perspective of the home-base country, there are differences in language, culture, nationality, and professional management disciplines among subsidiary organizations. Due to differences in local management philosophy, business/technology planning responsibilities are often fragmented rather than focused in one budgetary area. Business/technology planning, monitoring, and control and coordination functions are often difficult and require unique management skills.[24]

Infrastructure. The predictability and stability of available infrastructure in a given country are major issues when making the country a hub for a global firm: 'It is a fact of life that some countries are tougher to do business in than others.'[8] Regional economic dependence on particular industry and cross-industry infrastructure may be informative. Singapore[26] has provided, through TradeNet, a platform for fast, efficient trade document processing. Hong Kong,[27] on the other hand, is still dealing with its unique position as the gateway to the People's Republic of China, and its historic 'free port' policies in developing its TradeLink platform. Lufthansa, Japan Airlines, Cathay Pacific, and other airlines are trying to pool their global IT infrastructure in order to deliver a global logistics system. At the same time, global banks are exploring the influence their IT architectures have on the portfolio of instruments they can offer on a global basis.[37]

Resource availability can vary due to import restrictions or to lack of local vendor support. Since few vendors provide worldwide service, many firms are limited in choice of vendors in a single project, because of operational risk. Finally, availability of telecommunications equipment/technology (e.g. LAN, private microwave, fiber optic, satellite earth stations, switching devices, and other technologies) varies among countries and geographic regions.

Regulatory Environments. Changes in government, economy, and social policy can lead to critical changes in the telecommunications regulations that pose serious constraints on the operation of GLSs. The price and availability of service, and cross-border data-flow restrictions vary widely from one country to another.

The PTT (post, telephone, and telegraph) in most countries sets prices based on volume of traffic rather than based on fixed-cost leased facilities. By doing so, the PTT increases its own revenues and, at the same time, prevents global firms from exploiting economies of scale. The nature of the internal infrastucture systems may also influence the interest and ability to leverage regulation.[38,49,50]

There are regulations restricting usage of leased lines or import of hardware/software for GISs. These affect the GIS options possible in different countries: restrictions on connections between leased lines and public telephone networks, the use of dial-up data transmission, and the use of electronic mail systems for communications. It is not unusual for some companies to build their own 'phone company' in order to reduce dependence on government-run organizations.[8] Hardware/software import policies also make local information processing uneconomical in some countries. For example, both Canada and Brazil have high duties on imported hardware, and there are software import valuation policies in France, Saudi Arabia, and Israel.[6]

Transborder Data Flow (TBDF) regulations, in part, govern the content of international data flows.[5] Examples are requirements to process certain kinds of data and to maintain certain business records locally, and the fact that some countries don't mind data being 'transmitted in' but oppose interactive applications in which data are 'transmitted out'. Although the major reasons for regulating the content of TBDF are privacy protection and economic and national security concerns, these regulations can adversely affect the economies of GSs by forcing global firms to decentralize their operations, increase operating costs, and/or prohibit certain applications.

Standards. International, national, and industry standards play a key role in permitting global firms to 'leverage' their systems development investment as much as possible. Telecommunication standards vary widely from one country to another concerning the technical details of connecting equipment and agreements on formats and procedures. However, the conversion of the world's telecommunications facilities into an integrated digital network (IDN) is well underway, and most observers agree that a worldwide integrated digital network and the integrated services digital network (ISDN) will soon become a reality.[34,48] The challenge is not a problem of technology – the necessary technology already exists. Integration depends on creating the necessary standards and getting all countries to agree.

Telecommunications standards are set by various domestic governments or international agencies, and by major equipment vendors (e.g. IBM's System Network Architecture (SNA), Wang's Wangnet, Digital Equipment's DecNet, etc). There are also standards set by groups of firms within the same industry, such as SWIFT (Society for Worldwide International Funds Transfer) for international funds transfers and cash management, EDI (Electronic Data Interchange) for formatted business transactions such as purchase orders between companies (ANSI, EDIFACT, etc.),[16] and SQL (Structured Query Language) as a common form of interface for coordinating data across many databases.

3.1   Global information management strategy

Table 16.2 shows the alternative information systems management strategy/ structure as a result of the evolution in global business environment and technology. New information technologies are allowing closer integration of adjacent steps on the value-added chain through the development of electronic markets and electronic hierarchies.[33] As that study reports, the overall effect of technology is the change of coordination mechanisms. This will result in an increase in the proportion of economic activities coordinated by markets rather than by hierarchies. This also supports and explains change in the global firm's strategies from multinational, global strategies to international (interorganizational), transnational strategies.

The task of managing across corporate boundaries has much in common with that of managing across national borders. Managing strategic partnership, coalitions, and alliances has forced managers to shift their thinking from the traditional task of controlling a hierarchy to managing a network.[11,31,43] As discussed earlier, managers in transnational organizations must gather, exchange, and process large volumes of information; formal strategies/structure cannot support such huge information-processing needs. Because of the widespread distribution of organizational units and the relative infrequency of direct contacts among those in disparate units in a transnational firm, top management has a better opportunity to shape relationships among managers simply by being able to influence the nature and frequency of contacts by using a proper information system management strategy.

The strategy should contain the senior management policy on corporate information systems architecture (ISA). Corporate ISA (1) provides a guide

Table 16.2 *Alignment of global and information management strategies*

Business strategy/ structure	Coordination control strategy	Coordination control mechanisms	IS strategy structure
Multinational decentralized – federation	Socialization	*Hierarchies*; managerial decisions determine the flow of materials and services	Decentralization/ standalone databases and processes
Global/centralized – federation	Centralization		Centralization/ centralized databases and processes
International and interorganizational/ coordinated federation	Formalization	*Markets*; market forces determine the flow of materials and services	IOS/linked databases and processes
Transnational integrated network	Co-opting		Integrated architecture/shared databases and processes

for systems development, (2) facilitates the integration and data sharing among applications, and (3) supports development of integrated, corporate systems that are based on a data resource with corporate-wide accessibility.[19] Corporate ISA for a global firm is a high-level map of the information and technology requirements of a firm as a whole; it is composed of network, data, and application and technology architectures. In the international environment, the network and data architectures are generally considered to be the key enabling technologies because they are the highway systems for a wide range of traffic.[24]

A new GIS management strategy needs to address organizational structural issues related to coordination and configuration of value-chain activities, by proper ISA design. The key components of a GIS management strategy are (1) a centralized and/or coordinated business/technology strategy on establishing data communications architecture and standards, (2) a centralized and/ or coordinated data management strategy for creation of corporate databases, and (3) alignment of global business and GIS management strategy. These are explained below.

3.1.1 Network management strategy and architecture

Network architecure describes where applications are executed, where databases are located, and what communications links are needed among locations.

It also sets standards ensuring that all other ISA components are interrelated and working together. The architecture is important in providing standards for interconnecting very different systems instead of requiring commonality of systems. At present, the potential for network architecture is determined more often by vendors than by general industry or organizational standards.[24]

Architecture. Research on international business points out that the structure of a global firm's value chain is the key to its strategy; its fit with environmental requirements derives economic performance. However, the environments of GISs are external to their global firms and thus cannot be controlled. Services provided by GISs must be globally coordinated, integrated, standardized, and tailored to accommodate national differences and individual national markets.

Deciding on appropriate network architecture is a leading management and technology issue. Research in the global banking industry found that an international bank providing a wide range of global electronic wholesale banking services has some automated systems that need to be globally standardized (e.g. global balance reporting system), while others (e.g. global letter of credit system) need to be tailored to individual countries' markets.[37] The research also suggests that appropriate structure for GISs may vary for different product and service portfolios: uniform centralization/decentralization of strategy/ structure may not be appropriate for all GIS applications. Further, the research found that international banks cannot expect to optimize the structure of environmentally diverse information systems with a symmetrical approach to GIS architecture, since any such approach may set limits on the product and service portfolios called for by the bank's global business strategy. An asymmetrical approach, structuring each system to suit the environmental needs of the service delivered, although more complex, can significantly improve international banks' operational performance. Such an approach may, however, significantly increase coordination costs.

Standards. Use of standards is an important strategic move for most companies, since many of today's companies limit the number of intercompany formats they support. With the success in the development and adoption of global standards, in particular in narrow areas (e.g. EDIFACT), it is much harder to make standards mistakes than was possible several years ago. By using standards, companies can broaden their choice of trading partners in the future. Absence of uniform data and communications standards in international, national, and industry environments means that no single product can address more than a fraction of the hardware and communications protocols scattered throughout a firm.

Standards are often set by government rules and regulations, major computers and communications vendors, and/or cooperative arrangements within an industry. Regardless of how the standards are set, they are critical to the operations of GISs. Because standards are the key to connectivity of a set of heterogeneous systems, explicit senior management policy on standards is important to promote adoption and compliance. There should be one central policy regarding key technologies/standards (e.g. EDI, SQL). This policy should include a management agenda for understanding both standards and the standard-setting process within industry, national, and international environments.[23] Such a central policy accomplishes several objectives, reducing cost, avoiding vendor viability, achieving economies of scale, reducing potential interface problems, and facilitiating transborder data flow. Therefore, decisions about the components of network architectures and standards require a move toward centralized, corporate management coordination and control. However, decisions regarding adding traffic need decentralized planning; they require conformity by IS managers to data communications standards.

3.1.2 Data management strategy and architecture

Data architecture concerns the arrangement of databases within an organization. Although every organization that keeps data has a data architecture, in most organizations it is the result of evolution of application databases in its various departments and not the result of a well-planned data management strategy.[14,45] Data management problems are amplified for large global firms with diverse product families. For a global firm with congested data highways, the problems of getting the right data in the right amount to the right people at the right time multiply as global markets emerge.[8]

Lack of a centralized information management strategy often causes corporate entities (e.g. customers and products) to have multiple attributes, coding schemes, and values across databases.[14] This makes linkages or data sharing among value activities difficult at best; establishing linkages requires excessive time and human resources; costs and performance of other data-related activities within the value chain are affected. These factors make important performance and correlation data unavailable to top management for decision making, thereby creating important obstacles to the firm's competitive position and its future competitive advantage.

Strategy/Architecture. To increase coordination among a global firm's value-chain activites, its data architecture should be designed based on an integrated data management strategy. This strategy should mandate creation of a set of *corporate databases* derived from the firm's value-chain activities. A recent study has pointed out the significance of a firm's value-chain activities in deploying IT strategically;[20] however, no specific information management strategy is proposed.

Corporate data is used by more than one functional area within the value-chain activities. In contrast, department data is often used mainly by departments within the functional area that comprises a value-chain activity. Corporate data is used by departments across functions.

Corporate databases should be based on business entities involved in value-chain activities rather than around individual applications. A firm must define (1) appropriate measures of performance for each value activity (e.g. sales volume by market by period), (2) corporate entities by which the performance is measured (e.g. product, package type), (3) relationships among the entities defined, (4) entities' value sets, coding schemes, and attributes, (5) corporate databases derived from the entities, and (6) relationships among the corporate databases. For example, for a direct value-adding activity such as marketing and sales within a firm's value chain, the corporate databases may include: advertisement, brand, market, promotion, sales.

Given this data management strategy, corporate databases are defined independent of applications; they are accessible by all potential users. This data management strategy allows a firm's senior management to (1) integrate and coordinate information with the value-adding and support activities within the value chain, (2) identify significant trends in performance data, and (3) compare local activities to activities in other comparable locations.

This data management strategy creates an important advantage for a global firm, because activities used for the firm's strategic business planning are used to define the corporate databases. The critical establishment of linkage between strategic business planning and strategic information systems planning is possible when this strategy is used, because the activities that create value for the firm customers also create data the firm needs to operate. However, the strategy does not imply that all application databases should be replaced by corporate databases. Application databases should remain (directly or indirectly) as long as the applications exist; but there should be a disciplined flow of data among corporate, functional, and application databases.

3.1.3   Alignment of global business and GIS management strategy: a plan for action

One challenge facing management today is the necessity for the organization to align its business strategy/structure to its information systems management/development strategy. A proper design of critical linkages among a firm's value-chain activities results in an effective business design involving information technology and an improved coordination with coalition partners, as well as among a firm's own subsidiaries. Previous research has emphasized the benefits of establishing proper linkages between business-strategic planning and technology-strategic planning for an organization.[22,28] Among these are proper strategic positioning of an organization, improvements in organizational effectiveness, efficiency and performance, and full exploitation of information technology investment.

Establishing the necessary alignment requires the involvement of and co-operation with both the senior business planner and the senior IS technology manager. This results in a new set of responsibilities and skills for both. For the senior business planner, new sets of responsibilities include (1) formal integration of the strategic business plan with the strategic IS plan, (2) examination of the business needs associated with a centralized and/or coordinated network, technology, and data management strategy, (3) review of the network architecture as a key enabling technology for the firm's competitive strategy and assessment of the impact of network alternatives on business strategy, (4) awareness of key technologies/standards and standard-setting processes at the industry, national, and international levels, (5) championing the rapidly expanding use of industry, national, and international standards.

For the senior information technology manager, new and critical responsibilities include (1) awareness of the firm's business challenges in the changing global environment and involvement in shaping the firm's leverage of information technology in its global business strategy, (2) preparing a systems development environment that recognizes the long-term company-wide perspective in a multi-regional and multi-cultural environment, (3) planning the development of the application portfolio on the basis of the firm's current business and its global strategic posture in the future, (4) making the 'business purpose' of the strategic systems development projects clear in a global business context, (5) selecting and recommending key technologies/standards for linking systems across geographic and cultural boundaries, (6) setting automation of linkages among the internal/external activities within the firm's value chain as goals and selling them to others, (7) designing corporate databases derived from the firm's value-chain activities, accounting for business cultural differences, and (8) facilitating corporate restructuring through the provision of flexibility in business services.

4 Summary and conclusions

Changes in technologies and market structures have shifted competition from national to a global scope. This has resulted in the need for new organizational strategies/structures. Traditional organizational designs are not appropriate for the new strategies, because they evolved in response to different competitive pressures. New organizational structures need to achieve both flexibility and coordination among the firm's diverse activities in the new international markets.

Globalization trends have resulted in a variety of organizational designs that have created both business and information management challenges. A global information systems (GIS) management strategy is required.

The key components of a GIS management strategy should include: (1) a centralized and/or coordinated business/technology strategy on establishing data communications infrastructure, architecture, and standards, (2) a centralized and/or coordinated data management strategy for design of corporate databases, and (3) alignment of global business and GIS management strategy. Such a GIS management strategy is appropriate today because it facilitates coordination among a firm's value-chain activities and among business units, and because it provides the firm with the flexibility and coordination necessary to deal effectively with changes in technologies and market structures. It also aligns information systems management strategy with corporate business strategy as it provides a foundation for designing information systems architecture (ISA).

In addition to the global enterprise's competitive posture, globalization also refers to the competitive posture of nations and city-states.[26,27] The issues related to coordination and control in the global enterprise also invest the nation/state to review the alignment of its cross-industry competitive posture.[31,42] It is incumbent on governments to seek appropriate levels of intervention in the business practices of the state that influence the state's competitive position in the global business community.

The challenges to general managers in the emerging global economic environment extend beyond the IT infrastructure. At the same time, with the information intensity in the markets (products, services, and channel systems) and the information intensity associated with coordination across geographic, cultural, and organizational barriers, global general managers will rely increasingly on information technologies to support their management processes. The proper alignment of the evolving global information management strategy and the global organizational strategy will be important to the positioning of the global firm in the global economic community.

References

1   Baliga, B. R., and Jaeger, A. M. Multinational corporations, control systems and delegation issues. *Journal of International Business Studies*, 15, 2 (Fall 1984), 25–40.

2   Barrett, S., and Konsynski, B. Interorganizational information sharing systems. *MIS Quarterly*, special issue (1982), 93–105.

3   Bartlett, C. A., and Ghoshal, S. Organizing for worldwide effectiveness: the transnational solution. *California Management Review*, 31, 1 (1988), 1–21.

4   Bartlett, C. A., and Ghoshal, S. *Managing across Borders: The Transnational Solution*. Boston: Harvard Business School Press, 1989.

5   Basche, J. Regulating international data transmission: the impact on managing international business. Research report no. 852 from the Conference Board. New York, 1983.

6   *Business Week*. Special report on telecommunications: the global battle (October 1983).

7 Buss, M. Managing international information systems. *Harvard Business Review*, special series (1980).

8 Carlyle, R. E. Managing IS at multinationals. *Datamation* (March 1, 1988), 54–66.

9 Chandler, A. D. The evolution of modern global competition. In [39], 405–488.

10 Doz, Y. L., and Prahalad, C. K. Headquarters influence and strategic control in MNCs. *Sloan Management Review* (Fall 1981), 15–29.

11 Eccles, R. G., and Crane, D. B. Managing through networks in investment banking. *California Management Review*, 30 (Fall 1987), 176–195.

12 Engelhoff. W. Strategy and structure in multinational corporations: an information processing approach. *Administrative Science Quarterly*, 27, 3 (1982), 435–458.

13 Frenke, K. A. The European community and information technology. *Communications of the ACM* (special section the EC '92), 33, 4 (1990), 404–412.

14 Goodhue, D. L.; Quillard, J. A. and Rockart, J. F. Managing the data resource: a contingency perspective. *MIS Quarterly*, 12, 3 (September 1988), 372–391.

15 Ghoshal, S., and Noria, N. International differentiation within multinational corporations. *Strategic Management Journal*, 10, 4 (July/August 1989), 323–337.

16 Hansen, J. V., and Hill, N. C. Control and audit of electronic data interchange. *MIS Quarterly*, 13, 4 (December 1989), 403–413.

17 Harrigan K. R. *Strategies for Joint Ventures*. Lexington, MA: 1985.

18 Huber, G. P. The nature and design of post industrial organization. *Management Science*, 30 (1984), 928–951.

19 Iramon, W. H. *Information Systems Architecture*. Englewood Cliffs, NJ: Prentice-Hall, 1986.

20 Johnston, H. R., and Carrico, S. R. Developing capabilities to use information strategically. *MIS Quarterly*, 12, 1 (March 1988), 36–48.

21 Johnston, H. R., and Vitale, M. Creating competitive advantage with interorganizational information systems. *MIS Quarterly*, 12, 2 (June 1988), 152–165.

22 Karimi, J. Strategic planning for information systems: requirements and information engineering methods. *Journal of Management Information Systems*, 4, 4 (Spring 1988), 5–24.

23 Keen, P. G. An international perspective on managing information technologies. ICIT Briefing Paper no. 4101, 1987.

24 Keen, P. G. *Competing in Time: Using Telecommunications for Competitive Advantage*. Cambridge, MA: Ballinger Publishing Co., 1988.

25 King, J. Centralized vs. decentralized options. *Computing Surveys* (December 1983).

26   King, J., and Konsynski, B. Singapore TradeNet: a tale of one city. N1-191-009, Harvard Business School, 1990.

27   King, J., and Konsynski, B. Hong Kong TradeLink: news from the second city. N1-191-026. Harvard Business School, 1990.

28   King, W. R. Strategic planning for IS: the state of practice and research. *MIS Quarterly*, 9, 2 (June 1985), Editor's comment, vi–vii.

29   Knight, K. Matrix organization: a review. *Journal of Management Studies*, 13 (1976), 111–130.

30   Konsynski, B., and Warbelow, A. Cooperating to compete: modeling interorganizational interchange, Harvard Business School working paper 90-002, 1989.

31   Konsynski, B., and McFarlan, W. Information partnerships – shared data, shared scale. *Harvard Business Review* (September/October 1990), 114–120.

32   Lu, M., and Farrell, C. Software development: an international perspective. *The Journal of Systems and Software*, 9 (1989), 305–309.

33   Malone, T. W.; Yates, J. and Benjamin, R. I. Electronic markets and electronic hierarchies. *Communications of the AGM*, 30, 6 (June 1987), 484–497.

34   Martin, J., and Leben, J. *Principles of Data Communications*. Englewood Cliffs, NJ: Prentice-Hall, 1988.

35   Mead, T. The IS innovator at DuPont. *Datamation* (April 15, 1990), 61–68.

36   Miles, R. E., and Snow, C. C. Organizations: new concepts for new forms. *California Management Review*, 28 (1986), 62–73.

37   Mookerjee, A. S. Global Electronic Wholesale Banking Delivery System Structure. PhD thesis, Harvard University, 1988.

38   O'Callaghan, R., and Konsynski, B. Banco Santander: el banco en casa, 9-189-185, Harvard Business School, 1989.

39   Porter, M. E. *Competition in Global Industries*. Cambridge, MA: Harvard Business School Press, 1986.

40   Porter, M. E. Competition in global industries: a conceptual framework. In [39], 15–59.

41   Porter, M. E. From competitive advantage to corporate strategy. *Harvard Business Review* (May/June 1987), 43–59.

42   Porter, M. E. The competitive advantage of nations. *Harvard Business Review* (March/April 1990), 73–92.

43   Powell, W. Hybrid organizational arrangements. *California Management Review*, 30 (Fall 1987), 67–87.

44   Prahalad, C. K., and Doz, Y. L. An approach to strategic control in MNCs. *Sloan Management Review* (Summer 1981), 5–13.

45   Romero, V. Data Architecture: The Newsletter for Corporate Data Planners and Designers, 1, 1 (September/October 1988).

46 Sauvant, K. International transactions in services: the politics of transborder data flows. *The Atwater Series on World Information Economy*, 1. Boulder: Westview Press, 1986.
47 Selig, G. J. A framework for multinational information systems planning. *Information and Management*, 5 (June 1982), 95–115.
48 Stallings, W. *ISDN: An Introduction*. New York: Macmillan, 1989.
49 Warbelow, A.; Kokuryo, J. and Konsynski, B. Aucnet: TV auction network system. 9-190-001, Harvard Business School, 1989, p.19.
50 Warbelow, A.; Fjeldstad, O. and Konsynski, B. Bankenes Betalings-Sentral A/S: the Norwegian bank giro. N9-191-037, Harvard Business School, 1990, p.17.
51 Zammuto, R. *Organization Design: Structure, Strategy, and Environment*. The Dryden Press, forthcoming.

Reproduced from Karimi, J. and Konsynski, B. R. (1991) Globalization and information management strategies. *Journal of Management Information Systems*, Spring, **7**(4), 7–26. Reprinted with permission. Copyright 1991 by M. E. Sharpe, Inc.

Questions for discussion

1 Evaluate the organizational strategies the authors present. What are the implications for IT architecture?
2 Do you agree with the major premise that 'the globalization of competition and the evolving business environment suggest that the success of [a] global firms' business and its coordination/control strategies may be linked to a global information management strategy'?
3 Will changes taking place in Europe (e.g. pan-European legislation, the introduction of the Euro) reduce the impact of some of the factors complicating international IS, such as the business environment, infrastructure, regulations, transborder dataflow, and standards?
4 The authors present a one-on-one alignment of IT strategy and organizational strategy. Is this realistic? Are there other effective alignments? How might effective alignment be achieved?
5 Assuming different stages of growth in different countries, what might be the appropriate role of the central IT group in a large multinational organization?

17 The Information Technology–Organizational Design Relationship

Information technology and new organizational forms

Rob Lambert and Joe Peppard

Throughout the 1980s there was a tremendous emphasis on business strategy. Many organizations developed sophisticated strategies with scant attention given to their ability and capability to deliver these strategies. Over the past few years a tremendous amount written about the organization of the 1990s, its characteristics and the key enabling role of information technology. While this presents us with a destination in general terms, little attention is given in how to get there. This chapter addresses this concern, beginning by reviewing six perspectives which best represent current thinking on new ways of organizing and outlines their characteristics. Having identified their key characteristics, three key issues which now dominate the management agenda are proposed. The vision: where do we want to be in terms of our organizational form? Gap analysis and planning: how do we get there? and Managing the migration: how do we manage this process of reaching our destination? Extending the traditional information systems/information technology strategic planning model, a framework is presented which addresses these concerns. This framework is structured around the triumvirate of vision, planning and delivery with considerable iteration between planning and delivery to ensure the required form is met.

Introduction

Academics, consultants and managers continually debate the most effective organizational form. [Organizational form includes structure, systems, management style, cultures, roles, responsibilities, skills, etc.] If there is agreement it is that there is no one best way to develop organizations to achieve the best mix of structure, systems, management style, culture, roles, responsibilities and skills. One lesson is clear and it is that organizations must adopt a form that is appropriate to their strategy and the competitive position within which they find themselves. Recently there has been a spate of papers challenging traditional ways of organizing and their underlying assumptions and proposing alternative approaches. Many of these approaches are dependent on opportunities provided by information technology (IT).

Clearly the situation within which organizations find themselves today is radically different than from earlier times. As we saw in the previous chapter, the 1990s has been characterized by globalization of markets, intensification of competition, acceleration of product life cycles, and growing complexity with suppliers, buyers, governments and other stakeholder organizations. Rapidly changing and more powerful technology provides new opportunities. To be competitive in these conditions requires different organizational forms than in more stable times. It is well recognized that responsiveness, flexibility and innovation will be key corporate attributes for successful organizations. Information plays a critical role in improving these within today's organization. However, traditional organizational forms have significant limitations in supporting the information-based organization.

Information technology must share responsibility for much of the rigidity and inflexibility in organizations. By automating tasks IT cemented hierarchy with reporting systems, and rigidified behaviour through standardization. Indeed, often technology has not resulted in fundamental changes in how work is performed: rather it has allowed it to be done more efficiently. The irony is that IT can also help us break out of traditional modes of organizing and facilitate new organizational forms which previously would have been impossible. The challenge therefore is not only to consider new organizational forms but also to identify the critical issues that must be managed to allow this transformation to begin.

It is our intention to map out some of the themes relating to new ways of organizing which have been emerging over the past decade. We also want to clear up the confusion which is often encountered when reading such literature where similar ideas are often shrouded with new names. In particular, we explore the role of IT in facilitating new ways of organizing.

In order to place this chapter in perspective, we begin by briefly tracing developments in organization theory. This review is not intended to be exhaustive, but to give a flavour of just some of the main themes which have emerged over the years. We then explore some of the perspectives that have been proposed in the recent management literature, identify the main themes of each, the critical management issues and combine these into a framework which we believe is useful in giving direction to managing the transformation process.

Historical viewpoint

Whenever people have come together to accomplish some task, organizations have existed. The family, the church, the military are examples of early organizations. Each had their own structure, hierarchy, tasks, role and authority. The modern business organization, however, is a relatively recent phenomenon whose evolution can be traced to two important historical inferences: the industrial revolution and changes in the law.

The industrial revolution, which occurred largely in England during the 1770s, saw the substitution of machine power for human work and marked the beginning of the factory system of work. It spawned a new way of producing goods and offered opportunities which saw business increase to a scale never previously possible. The early Company Acts provided limited liability for individuals who came together for business purposes. Both these events led to the emergence of the professional manager, i.e. someone who managed the business but who did not own it. The increase in scale of organizations required a management structure and organizational form.

Early attempts to formulate appropriate organization form focused on determining the anatomy of formal organization. This so-called classical approach was built around four key pillars: division of labour, functional processes, structure, and span of control (Scott, 1961). Included here is the scientific management approach pioneered by Frederick Taylor (1911) which proposed one best way of accomplishing tasks. The objective was to increase productivity by standardizing and structuring jobs performed by humans. It spawned mass production with its emphasis on economies of scale. Although initially the concept applied to factory-floor workers, its application spread progressively in most organizational activity. Harrington Emerson took Taylor's ideas and applied them to the organizational structure with an emphasis on the organization's objectives. He emphasized, in a set of organizational 'principles' he developed, the use of experts in organizations to improve organizational efficiency (Emerson, 1917).

This mechanistic view was subsequently challenged by an emerging view stressing the human and social factors in work. Drawing on industrial psychology and social theory, the behavioural school argued that the human element was just as important. Themes such as motivation and leadership dominated the writings of subscribers to this view (e.g. Maslow, 1943, 1954; Mayo, 1971; McClelland, 1976).

Over the past 40 years organizational theorists have been concerned with the formal structure of organization and the implications these structures have on decision-making and performance. Weber (1947), for example, argued that hierarchy, formal rules, formal procedures, and professional managerial authority would increase efficiency.

Ever since Adam Smith (1910) articulated the importance of division of labour in a developing economy this notion has become ingrained in the design of organizations. Functionalism due to specialization is a salient feature of most organizations. Too often, however, this had led to an ineffective organization with each functional unit pursuing its own objectives. To overcome inherent weaknesses in this view, both the systems approach and the strategy thesis seek to integrate diverse functional unit objectives.

The systems movement originated from attempts to develop a general theory of systems that would be common to all disciplines (Bertalanfy, 1956). Challenging the reductionist approach of physics and chemistry the focus was on the whole being greater than the sum of the parts. Organizations were conceptualized as systems composed of subsystems which were linked and related to each other. Indeed, the systems approach is the dominant philosophy in designing organizational information systems. Systems theory also made the distinction between closed systems, i.e. those that focus primarily on their internal operations, and open systems which are affected by their interaction with their external environment. Early organizational theories tended to adopt a closed systems view. However, by adopting a more open approach it was clear that environmental issues were equally important.

The strategy movement which originated from Harvard Business School in the 1950s highlighted the importance of having an overall corporate strategy to integrate these various functional areas and how the organization can best impact its environment. The argument was that without an overall corporate strategy, each functional unit would pursue its own goals very often to the detriment of the organization as a whole. The decade of the 1970s saw many formalized, analytical approaches to strategic planning being proposed such as the Boston Consulting Group's planning portfolio (Henderson, 1979) and Ansoff's product portfolio matrix (Ansoff, 1979). Competitor analysis and the search for competitive advantage was the dominant theme of the 1980s, greatly influenced by the work of Porter (1980, 1985).

Chandler (1962), in his seminal study of US industries, saw structure following strategy. His thesis was that different strategies required different organizational structures to support them. Organizations that seek innovation demand flexible structures. Organizations that attempt to be low cost operators must maximize efficiency and the mechanistic structure helps achieve this. However, theorists such as Mintzberg (1979) and Thompson (1961) have emphasized the systemic aspect of structure, showing how structure can influence strategy and decision-making while hindering adaptation to the external environment.

The contingency theorists argued that the form an organization took is a function of the environment (Lawrence and Lorsch, 1970). Mintzberg, Miller and others talk about organizational configurations that bring strategy, structure, and context into natural co-alignment (Miller, 1986, 1987; Miller and Mintzberg, 1984). They argue that key forces or imperatives explain and give rise to many common configurations. The form an organization would take would reflect its dominant imperative.

We are not arguing that these forms or perspectives were inappropriate. In their time they represented the best forms that supported contemporary management thinking. For instance, despite its neglect of human aspects, scientific management yielded vast increases in productivity. However, the dynamic element which precipitated many of these approaches has also rendered them ineffective. Where are many of the *excellent* companies which Peters and Waterman (1982) wrote about 10 years ago? Perhaps they stuck to the knitting and ran out of wool. Perhaps the competition started using knitting machines or, indeed, the market now no longer has the need for wool products.

Recently Mintzberg (1991) has refined his thinking on organizational form and considered another view of organizational effectiveness, in which organizations do not slot themselves into established images so much as continually to build their own unique solutions to problems.

Given today's competitive conditions it is clear that one of the challenges facing management in the 1990s is to develop more dynamic organizations harnessing the power and capability of IT. What form such organizations will take is yet unclear. However, a picture of what this form will look like and how to initiate its development is beginning to emerge.

New perspectives

Over the past few years there have been a number of papers calling for the reappraisal of the form taken by organizations and for the widely accepted assumptions governing organizations to be re-evaluated. *Fortune, International Management* and *Business Week* have recently run articles looking at the organization of the 21st century indicating clearly that this topic is on the general management agenda as well as a focus of academic studies. In our research we have identified six perspectives which we feel represent current thinking on new ways of organizing. These are: network organizations; task focused teams; networked group; horizontal organizations; learning organizations; and matrix management.

In the sections that follow, we examine these perspectives briefly, with reference to key articles and research findings, and we identify salient themes. We then synthesize these themes into a framework which presents the key issues to be considered in the transformation process to a new organizational form.

Network organization

In their early work Miles and Snow (1978) discuss how market forces could be injected into traditional organizational structures to make them more efficient and responsive. In so doing they exhibit characteristics of delayering, downsizing, and operating through a network of market-sensitive business

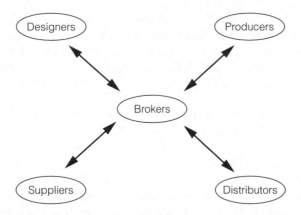

Figure 17.1 *Illustration of a network structure*

units. The driving force towards such an organization form are competitive pressures demanding both efficiency and effectiveness and the increasing speed necessary to adopt to market pressures and competitors' innovations. In essence, the network organization is in response to market forces. Included in this perspective are outsourcing, value adding partnerships, strategic alliances and business network design.

With a network structure, one firm may research and design a product, another may engineer and manufacture it, distribution may be handled by another, and so on. A firm focuses on what it does well, outsourcing to other firms for resources that are required in addition (Figure 17.1). However, care must be exercised in outsourcing: Bettis *et al.* (1992) report that improper use of outsourcing can destroy the future of a business.

Three specific types of network organization are discussed by Snow *et al.* (1992):

*   *Internal network*, typically arises to capture entrepreneurial and market benefits without having the company engage in much outsourcing. The basis logic is that internal units have to operate with prices set by the market instead of artificial transfer prices. They will constantly seek to innovate and increase performance.
*   *Stable network*, typically employs partial outsourcing and is a way of injecting flexibility into the overall value chain.
*   *Dynamic network*, provides both specialization and flexibility, with outsourcing expected.

Recent changes in the UK National Health Service (NHS) have seen the development of an internal market for health care as shown by General

Practitioner Fund holders and the competitive role of NHS Trusts. The distinction between purchaser and provider organization represents the emergence of the networked organization. District Health Authorities now purchase health services based on the health needs assessment of the community from a variety of sources. Provider organizations need to be more cost and quality conscious.

In order for networks to exist, close relationships must be built with both suppliers and buyers along what Porter (1985) refers to as the value system. Johnson and Lawrence (1988) have coined the term value-adding partnerships (VAPs) to describe such relationships, which are more than just conventional electronic data interchange (EDI) links. They depend largely on the attitudes and practices of the participating managers. Asda Superstores and Procter and Gamble (P&G) now cooperate with each other beyond sending just orders and invoices via EDI. For instance Asda now provide forecasting information to P&G in an open way that was not previously management practice. In return, P&G are more responsive in meeting replenishment requirements. General Motors has renamed its purchasing department the 'supplier development' department.

For a network organization to exist it requires the capability of IT to facilitate communication and co-ordination among the various units. This is especially so when firms are operating in global markets. Further, IT facilitates VAPs; it does not create them.

Strategic alliances

Strategic alliances with both competitors and others in the industry value system are key strategies adopted by many organizations in the late 1980s (Hamel *et al.*, 1989; Nakomoto, 1992; Ohmae, 1989). McKinsey's estimate that the rate of joint venture formation between US companies and international partners has been growing by 27 per cent since 1985 (Ernst and Bleeke, 1993).

Collaboration may be considered a low cost route for new companies to gain technology and market access (Hamel *et al.*, 1989). Many European companies have developed pan-European alliances to help rationalize operations and share costs. Banks and other financial institutions use each others' communication networks for ATM transactions. Corning, the $3 billion-a-year glass and ceramics maker, is renowned for making partnerships. Among Corning's bedfellows are Dow Chemicals, Siemens (Germany's electronics conglomerate) and Vitro (Mexico's biggest glass maker). Alliances are so central to Corning's strategy that the corporation now defines itself as a 'network of organizations'. The multi-layered structure of today's computer industry and the large number of firms it now contains, means that any single firm, no matter how powerful, must work closely with many others. Often, this is in order to obtain access to technology or management expertise. A

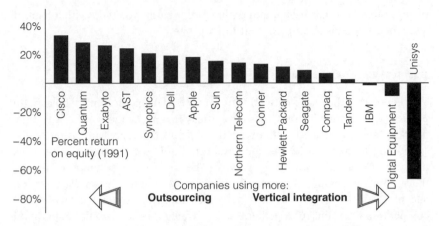

Figure 17.2   *Outsourcing versus integration in electronics companies*
(*Source*: *Fortune*, 8 February 1993)

web of many joint ventures, cross-equity holdings and marketing pacts now
entangles every firm in the industry.

Outsourcing

There is an argument that organizations should focus on core competencies and outsource all other activities. This has been a successful strategy
followed by many companies. For excmple, Nike and Reebok have both
prospered by concentrating on their strengths in designing and marketing
high-tech fashionable sports footwear. Nike owns one small factory. Virtually
all footwear production is contracted to suppliers in Taiwan, South Korea
and other Asian countries. Dell Computers prospers by concentrating on two
aspects of the computer business where the virtually integrated companies are
vulnerable: marketing and service. Dell owns no plants and leases two small
factories to assemble computers from outsourced parts. Figure 17.2 illustrates
the relative success of electronics companies who outsource as against the
vertically integrated companies.

   Japanese financial-industrial groups are an advanced manifestation of a
dynamic network. Called *keiretsu*, they are able to make long-term investments in technology and manufacturing, command the supply chain from
components and capital equipment to end products and coordinate their strategic approaches to block foreign competition and penetrate world markets.
There are also close relations between the banks and group companies, often
cemented by banks holding company shares. It is interesting to note that
many German companies have similar relations with their banks and very
often bankers sit on the board of directors. *Business Week* (1992) recently

reported that Ford has been making plans for what it would do with a bank if and when US legislation permits it to own one.

Business network redesign

The concept of business network redesign (BNR) has become increasingly popular where organizations seek to address major changes in the way they interface and do business with external entities. BNR represents using IT for 'designing the nature of exchange among multiple participants in a business network' (Venkatraman, 1991, p.140). The underlying assumption is that the sources of competitive advantage lie partly within a given organization and partly in the larger business network. Using IT, suppliers, buyers and competitors, are linked together via a strategy of electronic integration (Venkatraman, 1991).

BNR needs to be distinguished from EDI, which refers to the technical features, and inter-organizational systems (IOS), which refers to the characteristics of a specific system.

Redesigning an industry network is something akin to the dynamic structure of Snow *et al.* (1992) where an active relationship is cultivated between members of the network. Terms such as strategic alliance and value-adding partnerships are equally relevant here as they are with dynamic networks. Extending the industry network by introducing outsourcing is also feasible.

Task focused teams

Reich (1987) argues that a 'collective entrepreneurship' with few middle-level managers and only modest differences between senior management and junior staff is developing in some organizations. Drucker (1988) concurs and contends the organization of the future will be more information-based, flatter, more task oriented, driven more by professional specialists, and more dependent upon clearly focused issues. He proposes that such an organization will resemble a hospital or symphony orchestra rather than a typical manufacturing firm. For example, in a hospital much of the work is done in teams as required by an individual patient's diagnosis and condition. Drucker argues that these *ad hoc* decision-making structures will provide the basis for a permanent organizational form.

The emphasis on the team is a common theme which is emerging from the other perspectives on organizations. The team is seen as being the building block of the new organization and not the individual as has traditionally been the case. Katzenbach and Smith (1992) define a team as a 'small number of people with complementary skills who are committed to a common purpose,

Table 17.1 *Mechanistic versus organic organizations*

Element	Mechanistic organization	Organic organization
Channels of communication	Highly structured Controlled information flow	Open; free flow of information
Operating style	Must be uniform and restricted	Allowed to vary freely
Authority for decisions	Based on formal line-management position	Based on expertise of the individual
Adaptability	Reluctant, with the insistence holding fast to tried and tested principles in spite of changes in circumstances	Free, in response to changing circumstances
Work emphasis	On formal, laid down procedures	On getting things done unconstrained by formality
Control	Tight, through sophisticated control sytems	Loose and informal, with emphasis on cooperation
Behaviour	Constrained, and required to conform to job description	Flexible and shaped the individual to meet the needs of the situation and personality
Participation	Superiors make decisions with minimum consultation and minimum involvement of subordinates	Participation and group consensus frequently used

Source: D. P. Slevin and J. G. Colvin (1990).

performance goals and approach for which they hold themselves mutually accountable'. They suggest that there is a common link between teams, individual behaviour change and high performance.

High performance teams play a crucial role within Asea Brown Boveri (ABB), the Swedish–Swiss conglomerate. Here, their T50 programme is seeking to reduce cycle time by 50 per cent. These teams were as a result of a major change of attitude in the organization. Management by directives was replaced by management by goals and trust; individual piece-rate payment changed to group bonuses; controlling staffs moved to support teams; and there was one union agreement for all employees.

Drucker's notion of teams echoes Burns and Stalker's (1961) organic organization as opposed to the more mechanistic type of organization. Table 17.1 contrasts these views and presents their distinguishing organizational characteristics.

Increasingly, firms are using teams to coordinate development across functional areas and thus reduce product development times (Krachenberg *et al.*, 1988; Lyons *et al.*, 1990). For example, if we look at pharmaceuticals and telecommunications, the traditional sequential flow of research, development, manufacturing and marketing is being replaced by synchrony: specialists from all these functions working together as a team. Terms such as 'concurrent engineering', 'design for manufacturability', 'simultaneous engineering', 'design-integrated manufacturing' and 'design-to-process' are being used increasingly in organizations to incorporate cross-functional teams and methodologies to integrate engineering and design with manufacturing process (Kumpe and Bolwijn, 1988; Dean and Susman, 1989; Griffin *et al.*, 1991).

Since 1990 British Aerospace (BAe) has been actively promoting simultaneous engineering in its engineering division, having examined a number of initiatives. They saw the total quality management (TQM) message being difficult to get across and not very relevant to engineering. While process review was appealing it was limited in scope if only done inside engineering. For BAe, multifunctional teams are key to the success of their programmes. There is a clear focus on goals, the top level plan is robust to change, dependencies are less critical as they are dealt with by the team, members develop mutual role acknowledgement generating an achievement culture.

However, the notion of teams is nothing new. Value analysis and value engineering have been popular in many manufacturing firms since the 1950s. Although employees from various disciplines were brought together, the focus was on products; the new conceptualization is much broader. What is new about Drucker's vision is the role that IT will play. IT greatly facilitates task-based teams especially in enabling geographically dispersed groups to improve the coordination of their activities through enhanced electronic communication. Rockart and Short (1989) see self-governing units as being one of the impacts of IT.

The networked group

According to Charan (1991) a network is a recognized group of managers assembled by the CEO and the senior executive team. The membership is drawn from across company functional areas, business units, from different levels in the hierachy and from different locations. Such a network brings together a mix of managers whose business skills, personal motivations, and functional expertise allow them to drive a large company like a small company. The foundation of a network is its social architecture, which differs in important ways from structure. As such, it differs from Miles and Snow's (1987) concept of network in that it is internally focused.

- networks differ from teams, cross-functional task forces or other assemblages designed to break hierarchy
- networks are not temporary; teams generally disband when the reason they were assembled is accomplished
- networks are dynamic; they do not merely solve problems that have been defined for them
- networks make demands on senior management.

In most organizations, information flows upwards and is thus prone to distortion and manipulation. In a network, especially a global network that extends across borders, information must be visible and simultaneous. Members of the network receive the same information at the same time. Not only must hard information be presented, but also more qualitative information, not just external information but members' experiences, successes, views and problems.

The single most important level for reinforcing behaviour in networks is evaluation. Every manager, regardless of position or seniority, responds to the criteria by which he or she is evaluated, who conducts the review, and how it is conducted. For a network to survive top management must focus on behaviour and horizontal leadership: Does a manager share information willingly and openly? Does he or she ask for and offer help? Is he or she emotionally committed to the business? Docs the manager exercise informal leadership to energize the work of sub-networks?

Horizontal organizations

Questioning the validity of the vertical orientation of organizations a number of writers have proposed what they call the horizontal organization. Such organizations have clearly defined customer facing divisions and processes to improve performance.

Ostrof and Smith (1992) contend that performance improvements will be difficult to achieve for companies organized in a traditional vertical fashion. While the advantage of vertical organizations may be functional excellence it suffers from the problem of coordination. With many of today's competitive demands requiring coordination rather than functional specialization, traditional vertical organizations have a hard time responding to the challenges of the 1990s.

In the horizontal organization, work is primarily structured around a small number of business processes or work flows which link the activities of employees to the needs and capabilities of suppliers and customers in a way that improves the performance of all three.

Table 17.2   *Blueprint for a horizontal organization*

- Organize around process not task
- Flatten hierarchy by minimizing the subdivision of work flows and non-value-added activities
- Assign ownership of processes and process performance
- Link performance objectives and evaluation to customer satisfaction
- Make teams, not individuals, the principal building blocks or organization performance and design
- Combine managerial and non-managerial activities as often as possible
- Treat multiple competencies as the rule, not the exception
- Inform and train people on a 'just-in-time to perform' basis not on a 'need to know' basis
- Maximize supplier and customer contact
- Reward individual skill development and team performance, not individual performance

---

Source: Ostrof and Smith (1992).

Ostrof and Smith (1992) list 10 principles at the heart of horizontal organizations which are listed in Table 17.2. Although not arguing for the replacement of vertical organizations they recommend that each company must seek its own unique balance between the horizontal and vertical features needed to deliver performance.

BT was one of the early companies to recognize the ineffectiveness of the traditional vertical organization. Through project Sovereign and its process management initiatives, BT has reorganized itself into customer facing divisions and has embarked on significant performance improvement activity. Senior managers are now process owners with responsibility for service delivery as opposed to being functional heads. In a recent interview, BT's chairman revealed that AT&T, MCI and Deutsche Telecom have all restructured themselves following the BT model, setting up distinct business and personal communication divisions and separating network management from customer facing elements (Lorenz, 1993).

The horizontal design is seen as a key enabler to organizational flexibility and responsiveness. Time is critical in today's fast changing business environment (Stalk, 1988). Organizations need to be able to respond to customer demands with little delay and just-in-time (JIT) is just one manifestation of this. Kotler and Stonich (1991) have coined the term 'turbo marketing' to describe this requirement to make and deliver goods and services faster than competitors.

Multinational corporations face additional challenges making horizontal organizations work. As a result of their research Poynter and White (1990) have identified five activities needed to create and maintain a horizontal organization spanning a number of countries:

1   *Create shared values.* Collaborative decision making is not possible unless an organization has shared decision premises, a common culture or set of business values.
2   *Enabling the horizontal network.* To counteract the tendency for an organization to (re)assert vertical relationships, initiatives, such as giving headquarters' executives dual responsibilities, should be put in place.
3   *Redefine managers' roles.* The skills, abilities and approaches required for the horizontal organization are different than those from conventional vertical organizations. Fundamentally, senior managers must create, maintain and define an organization context that promotes lateral decision making oriented towards the achievement of competitive advantage world-wide.
4   *Assessing results.* Assignment of performance responsibility and availability for results within horizontal organizations is problematic. The people involved in horizontal collaborative efforts change over time and their individual contributions are difficult to measure.
5   *Evaluating people.* Evaluating executives in terms of their acceptance and application of a common set of beliefs is particularly appropriate for international management because of the shortcomings of orthodox vertical measures of evaluating people.

Business process redesign

This focus on process has become an important management focus over the past few years, with business process redesign (BPR) figuring highly on many corporate agendas (Dumaine, 1989; Butler Cox Foundation, 1991; Heygate and Breback, 1991; Kaplan and Murdock, 1991). BPR first entered the management nomenclature as a result of research conducted at MIT (Davenport and Short, 1990; Scott Morton, 1991). In their 'Management in the 1990s' research project they identified BPR as an evolutionary way of exploiting the capabilities of IT for more than just efficiency gains (Scott Morton, 1991).

Consider how IT is currently implemented in organizations: localized exploitation – typically to improve the efficiency of a particular task; and internal integration – integration of key internal applications to establish a common IT platform for the business.

With an internal focus, both of the above overlay on the existing tasks and activities thus retaining existing organization structures. This is what Hammer (1990) has referred to as 'paving the cow path'. Most IT systems design methodologies reinforce this view. BPR, however, questions the validity of existing ways of organizing work and is concerned with redesigning the organization around fundamental business processes.

BPR is the analysis and design of work flows and processes within organizations. It has also been called business re-engineering, process re-engineering, process innovation and core process redesign. The crucial element is the concentration on process rather than events or activities. A business process can be defined as a set of related activities that cuts across functional boundaries or specializations in order to realize a business objective. A set of processes is a business system.* Processes are seen to have two important characteristics: (i) they have customers, that is, processes have defined business outcomes and there are recipients of outcomes (customers can be either internal or external); (ii) they cross functional boundaries, i.e. they normally occur across or between organizational functional units. Examples include research and development, mortgage application appraisal, developing a budget, ordering from suppliers, creating a marketing plan, new product development, customer order fulfilment, flow of materials (purchasing, receiving, manufacturing).

Most companies still operate with thousands of specialists who are judged and rewarded by how well they perform their separate functions – with little knowledge or concern about how these fit into the complex process of turning raw material, capital and labour into a product or service. Activities and events are thus snap shots of a larger process. The Japanese realized that focusing on individual activities in the value chain was not sufficient. Superior performance was gained by focusing on the total process. So while Western managers focused on managing inventories, the Japanese saw that eliminating delays in the production process was the key to reducing instability, decreased cost, increased productivity and service.

However, BPR is not a new concept: its origins can be found in work study organization and methods (O&M) of the 1960s. It also has its roots in the quality revolution where the stress is on improving quality by identifying, studying, and improving the processes that make and deliver a product or service. The scope of quality management is often narrow, however, with responsibility lying in functional areas and thus not as rigorous as process redesign. The emphasis of BPR is on how different processes are carried out. The objective is to re-evaluate these processes and to redesign them so that they are aligned more closely to business objectives.

The philosophy of BPR is fundamentally different from the systems approach with which it might be confused. The systems approach is a theoretical framework which recognizes the interdependence of functional units and seeks to integrate them by integrating information flows. With BPR the emphasis is on processes which transcend functional units. It seeks to challenge existing assumptions relating to how the organization operates. It emphasizes a top down customer focused approach often using IT as the mechanism for coordination and control.

---

* For a discussion on the 'process' notion see Chris Edwards and Joe Peppard *Business Process Redesign: Hype, Hope or Hypocrisy?* Cranfield School of Management, Cranfield, Bedford, 1993.

The benefits of taking a process approach is to reduce costs, increase quality, while increasing responsiveness and flexibility. IT is often the essential ingredient by which the process concept can be turned into a practical proposition. Processes can also be redesigned to take account of the latest developments in technology.

Learning organizations

There has been renewed interest over the past few years in the learning organization (Garvin, 1993; Hayes *et al.*, 1988; Kochan and Useem, 1992; Stata, 1989; Senge, 1990a, 1990b, 1991; Quinn Mills and Friesen, 1992). The argument is that current patterns of behaviour in large organizations are typically 'hard wired' in structure, in information systems, incentive schemes, hiring and promotion practice, working practices, and so on. To break down such behaviour, organizations need the capability to harness the learning capabilities of their members. The learning organization is able to sustain consistent internal innovation or 'learning' with the immediate goals of improving quality, enhancing customer or supplier relationships, or more effectively executing business strategy (Quinn Mills and Friesen, 1992). This notion has similarities to the work of Argyris (1976, 1982).

Argyris identified two types of learning that can occur in organizations: adaptive learning and generative learning. Typically, organizations engage in adaptive or 'single-loop' learning and thus cope with situations within which they find themselves. For example, comparing budgeted against actual figures and taking appropriate action. Generative or double-loop learning, however, requires new ways of looking at the world, challenging assumptions, goals, and norms.

Implementing executive information systems (EIS) typically requires users to first adapt to using technology to obtain their required information, i.e. adaptive learning. However, to exploit the potential of EIS fully, systems users must proactively develop and test models of the use of EIS in the management process, i.e. double-loop learning. Zuboff's (1988) work refers to the criticality of line managers developing spatial models to exploit fully the potential of information systems available to them.

Mintzberg (1973) claims that the way executives use information that they collect is to develop mental images – models of how the organization and its environment function. Hedberg and Jonsson (1978) assert that to be able to operate at all, managers look at the world and intuitively create a myth or theory of what is happening in the world. With this in mind, they create a strategy to react to this myth so that they can form defence networks against information overflows from other myths and map information into definitions of their situations. They then test the strategy out on the world and evaluate its success.

Mason and Mitroff (1981) suggest that assumptions are the basic elements of a strategist's frame of reference or world view. Since assumptions form the basis of strategies, it is important that they be consistent with the information available to strategists (Schwenk, 1988). However, most decision-makers are unaware of the particular set of assumptions they hold and of methods that can help them in examining and assessing the strength of their assumptions (Mason and Mitroff, 1981; Mitroff and Linstone, 1993). The accuracy of these assumptions may be affected by their cognitive heuristics and biases. DeGeus (1988) suggests that planning is learning. However, planning is based on assumptions that should be constantly challenged.

Organization learning theory suggests that learning often cannot begin until unlearning has taken place (Burgelman, 1983). This requires a realization of the current position. Senge (1990a) talks about creative tension where a vision (picture of what might be) of the future pulls the organization from its current reality position. This is more than adaptation and is very much proactive.

Quinn Mills and Friesen (1992) list three key characteristics of a learning organization: (i) *It must make a commitment to knowledge.* This includes promoting mechanisms to encourage the collection and dissemination of knowledge and ideas throughout the organization. This may include research, discussion groups, seminars, hiring practices. (ii) *It must have a mechanism for renewal.* A learning organization must promote an environment where knowledge is incorporated into practices, processes and procedures. (iii) *It must possess an openness to the outside world.* The organization must be responsive to what is occurring outside of it.

Many organizations have implemented information systems in an attempt to improve organizational learning. For example, groupware products such as Lotus Notes or IBM's TeamFocus facilitate the sharing of ideas and expertise within an organization.

At Price Waterhouse they have 9000 employees linked together using Lotus Notes. Auditors in offices all over the world can keep up to date on relevant topics; anyone with an interest in a subject can read information and add their own contribution. By using groupware, Boeing has cut the time needed to complete a wide range of products by an average of 90 per cent or to one-tenth of what similar work took in the past.

Over the long run, superior performance depends on superior learning. The key message is that the learning organization requires new leadership skills and capabilities. The essence of the learning organization is that it is not just the top that does the thinking; rather it must occur at every level. Hayes *et al.* (1988) argue that in effect the organization of the 1990s will be a learning organization, one in which workers teach themselves how to analyse and solve problems.

Matrix management

Bartlett and Ghoshal (1990) argue that strategic thinking has far outdistanced organizational capabilities which are incapable of carrying out sophisticated strategies. In their search for a more effective form they argue that companies that have been most successful at developing multi-dimensional organizations first attend to the culture of the organization; then change the systems and relationships which facilitate the flow of information. Finally, they realign the organizational structure towards the new focus.

They call this matrix management although it is different from the 1970s concept of matrix management. They argue that while the notion of matrix management had appeal, it proved unmanageable – especially in an international context. Matrix management tended to pull people in several directions at once. Management needs to manage complexity rather than minimize it.

They contend that the most successful companies are those where top executives recognize the need to manage the new environmental and competitive demands by focusing less on the quest for an ideal structure and more on developing the abilities, behaviour and performance of individual managers. This has echoes of Peters and Waterman's (1982) bias for action.

People are the key to managing complex strategies and organizations. The 'organizational psychology' needs to be changed in order to reshape the understanding, identification, and commitment of its employees. Three principal characteristics common to those that managed the task most effectively are identified:

- *Build a shared vision.* Break down traditional mindsets by developing and communicating a clear sense of corporate purpose that extends into every corner of the company and gives context and meaning to each manager's particular roles and responsibilities.
- *Develop human resources.* Turn individual manager's perceptions, capabilities, and relationships into the building blocks of the organization.
- *Co-opting management efforts.* Get individuals and organizational groups into the broader vision by inviting them to contribute to the corporate agenda and then giving them direct responsibility for implementation.

While matrix management as a structural objective (the 1970s conceptualization) may not be possible, the essence can still be achieved. Management needs to develop a matrix of flexible perspectives and relationships in their mind.

A framework

Each of the perspectives presented above challenges traditional views of organizations. The arguments are based around a total re-evaluation of the assumptions which underlie organizational form, i.e. the best mix of structure, systems, management style, culture, roles, responsibilities and skills. From the different viewpoints presented we can get a glimpse of the characteristics of the 21st century organization. Key characteristics of these organizations are:

- constantly challenging traditional organizational assumptions
- evolution through learning at all levels
- multi-disciplinary self-managing teams with mutual role acknowledgement
- a reward structure based on team performance
- increased flexibility and responsiveness
- an achievement rather than blame culture
- an organizational wide and industry wide vision
- a vision of what kind of organizational form is required
- process driven with a customer focus
- fast response with time compression
- information based
- IT enabled.

This list of characteristics is perhaps not surprising. They have been advocated in both the academic and general management literature over recent years. Of course we cannot categorically say that organizations structured in a traditional way will not survive, although it is hard to see them thriving. We do suggest, however, that an organization critically reviews its form to determine whether it should incorporate some of these characteristics and the extent to which these should be adopted.

While we do have a destination in general terms there are three key issues which we feel need to be addressed in practice:

- *The vision.* The precise destination for a particular organization, i.e. where do we need to be? This is very much the visioning process where organizational requirements are determined. The precise final form will be unique to each organization depending on the organization itself and the context within which it exists. While form will depend on the strategy of the business many organizations fail to consider the organization's ability to deliver this strategy. This must go beyond defining structure and incorporate culture, reward systems, human resource requirements, etc. These in some sense could be seen as representing the organization form's critical success factors (CSFs).

- *Gap analysis.* A critical understanding of where the organization is now in relation to this organization vision should be established. The role which IT will play in the new organization should also be assessed. In short, we are attempting to describe the nature of the journey that needs to be undertaken. The concern here is with planning the business transformation.
- *Managing the migration.* How do we manage the migration from the existing organization form to a new form? The concern here is with the change management process which seeks to ensure the successful transition from the old form to the new form. A particularly difficult area to tackle here is an organization's ability to incorporate information systems/ information technology (IS/IT) developments successfully where these involve significant business change.

A recurring problem faced by any organization engaging in redesign is determining an appropriate approach. Perhaps it is too ambitious to expect an existing method to be comprehensive enough to deal with all the issues involved. All organizations are different and changing an organization's form is more complex than simply identifying core processes and leveraging IT as many of the articles imply. The critical issue is to address broader themes such as culture, management development, IS/IT development, skills, reward systems, etc. These notions are complex, however, and do not subscribe to neat techniques but need to be managed carefully.

Traditionally, we have aligned IT with the business strategy, without much consideration to people issues or the organizational capability to deliver (Galliers, 1991). Macdonald (1991, 1993) provides a useful model highlighting interrelationships between the business strategy, IS/IT and organizational processes. While checking for alignment of these variables and identifying issues, he outlines the topography but fails to provide any help in reaching the required destination.

It is much easier to embellish the characteristics of the organization of the 1990s than to define clear frameworks to achieve these characteristics. What we do not have is a road map to translate these aspirations into a workable design. Additionally, the road map needs to identify potential hazards and obstacles that are likely to be encountered en route and how these are to be dealt with.

Figure 17.3 illustrates some of the problems faced by an organization attempting to move from a current form to a new one. There are many forces which will drive it off course and it is essential that these are managed in order successfully to achieve the desired goal.

A key point is that, even when we identify the destination, the challenge is to negotiate the journey. Any route planning needs to explicitly address these issues. Questioning an organization's fundamental approach to the way that it does business can be risky and may confront too many entrenched interests

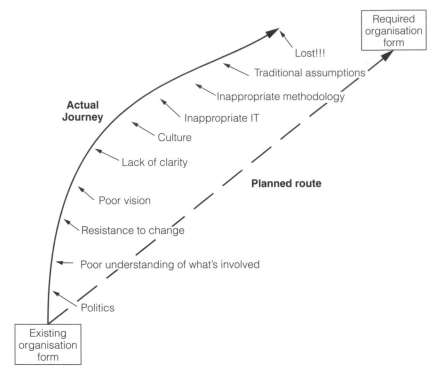

Figure 17.3   *Roadblocks and obstacles to a new organization*

among managers and employees to be worth doing unless an organization is in dire trouble. By then a complete overhaul is often too late to be of much use. It is often difficult to put across the idea that a successful organization should radically reconsider how it does business, however.

The issues can be fundamental and might include inappropriate IS/IT, management myopia, resistance, poor vision, etc. The stakes are high as is the need to manage them well particularly as many of them are central to people's value systems, such as power, politics and rewards. The characteristics of the new organization form, as described earlier, have a significantly different emphasis than those required by traditional forms, e.g. flexibility, process oriented, fast cycle response. In planning the migration we believe a fundamentally different paradigm should be used for managing this transition.

We have continually failed to provide an integrating framework to help in coordinating change and uncertainty. This uncertainty requires continual learning on the part of the organization both in terms of its destination and how to get there. A new multifaceted approach which integrates business strategy, IS/IT, organization design and human resources is needed.

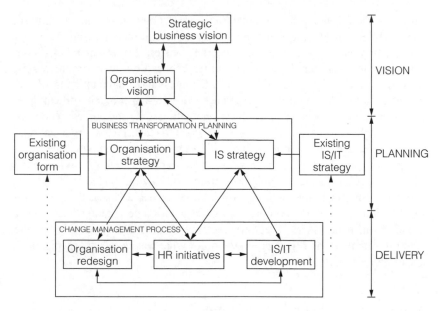

Figure 17.4 *Business transformation framework*

In Figure 17.4 we present a framework for business transformation which we have found useful when approaching issues associated with the migration towards a new organizational form. This framework expands on the model of IS/IT strategy formulation popularized by Earl (1989), Galliers (1991) and Ward *et al.* (1990) and incorporates organizational and implementation issues. It is structured around the triumvirate of vision, planning and delivery with considerable iteration between planning and delivery to ensure that the required form is being met.

The underlying premise of this framework questions the traditional sequential IS/IT planning model where business strategy drives IS strategy which determines the organization's IT strategy. It incorporates an organization's ability to deliver fundamental business change, recognizing that increasingly this change is being enabled by IT.

Vision

The requirement for a clear business vision is well known and espoused by many scholars on strategy. However, equally important is a vision of the organization form that is necessary to deliver and support the achievement of that strategy. This organizational vision needs to be more than the traditional structural perspective of centralization, differentiation and formalization.

Rather, it should define the organizational form CSFs in relation to culture, teamwork, empowerment, skills, reward systems and management style.

We define two types of visioning: business vision and organization vision. While business vision remains as currently practised by many organizations, the organization vision identifies the attributes and characteristics of the organization to achieve this business vision. Grand Metropolitan, for example, has an organization vision based on organizational competencies which are crucial to deliver its strategies. They believe that managerial and organizational competencies are more enduring and difficult to emulate than, what they call, 'the traditional structural strategies' of a conglomerate such as product portfolio, production sites and acquisition strategies. Having looked at the organizational CSFs for home banking, Midland Bank decided that their existing organization was not an appropriate vehicle for a home banking/telebanking organization, hence First Direct was set up. Acting 'independently' of the parent it articulated an organization vision of what was required organizationally to deliver this new service.

Business transformation planning

Business transformation planning demands two key activities: planning the organization strategy and developing an information systems strategy which facilitates this strategy but which is also closely aligned to business requirements. The conventional IS/IT planning framework does not explicitly consider the organization's ability and capability to deliver the business strategy.

A key concern of business transformation planning is a critical evaluation and understanding of the existing organization's characteristics and capabilities of how the current IS/IT strategy is being used to support them. The gap between existing and required can then be determined. It is important to emphasize that the relationship between both the organizing strategy and the IS strategy is bi-directional.

Organization strategy

An organization strategy involves more than simply considering the arrangement of people and tasks: what we typically call structure. It incorporates all the characteristics of organizational form which are encapsulated in the CSFs articulated in the organization vision. This will include what is needed in terms of skills, styles, procedures, values and reward systems. The organization strategy operationalizes these notions and will become the blueprint for the change management process.

A number of approaches to understand and evaluate aspects of organizational form have been proposed by many authors. For example, Johnson

(1992) presents the cultural web as a means of assessing existing organization culture. The strategic alignment process of Macdonald is also useful in reviewing the alignment of strategy, organizational processes and IT.

It is important also at this stage to consider the opportunities which IT offers in relation to organizing work. Groupware, for example, greatly enhances team work and can lead to greater productivity. IT facilitates more customer-oriented service as the systems provide more comprehensive information. BT now has one point of contact with both business and personal customers. Queries can be dealt with more efficiently and work routed to the appropriate area where necessary. First Direct is only possible due to IT, which allows the telephone clerks to give almost immediate response to requests.

Distance effects are also minimized due to IT. People from diverse geographical locations can now work together in the same team creating the boundary-less corporation. Multinational corporations can adopt a more efficient horizontal structure. Technology is also blurring the distinction between organizations. With technology, business processes can now transcend traditional organizational boundaries. Strategic alliances and value added partnerships are becoming key strategies for many organizations and IT has a major role to play in facilitating the communication and coordination necessary to make these pay off.

Changing the way things are done will usually require investment in human resource initiatives in order to enhance team skills, customer service skills, information sharing and organization wide values. These can become critical barriers and deflect an organization in migrating to the new form.

IS strategy

Although the organization of the 1990s will be information-based, we believe that designing systems solely around information flows is flawed. The emphasis will not be on how tasks are performed (faster, cheaper, better) but rather in how firms organize the flow of goods and services through value-added chains and systems. Organizing around business processes permits greater focus on what the organization is trying to achieve and not on operationalizing objectives around existing activities.

IT has, for too long, been seen as a tool for improving efficiency and effectiveness. The new organizational shapes are dependent on the capability of information and communication technologies. EIS, for example, permit senior managers to delegate and decentralize while still maintaining overall control.

As mentioned above, aligning IS strategy with business strategy is only half the story. The IS strategy must also be compatible with how the business is organized to meet the business strategy. As a result of their research, Hayes and Jaikumar (1988) contend that acquiring any advanced manufacturing system is more like replacing an old car with a helicopter. By failing to understand and prepare for the revolutionary capabilities of these systems, they will become as much an inconvenience as a benefit – and a lot more expensive.

During the business transformation planning phase, the existing organization form and the existing IS/IT strategy will be reviewed and the transformation plans developed. The change strategy will be mapped out in terms of approaches to be used, the rate of change, how it is to be achieved, milestones and how the road-blocks and obstacles are to be negotiated. Of critical concern, is a clear statement of the final destination.

Change management process

Migration to the new form is a change process which implements the plans in the most appropriate way.

Organizational redesign

Organization redesign involves managing the migration to the new organizational infrastructure. In particular:

* the change from function to process orientation
* developing and implementing new ways of working
* redefining roles and responsibilities in line with the migration.

These must be closely aligned with human resource (HR) initiatives and IS/IT development.

Human resource initiatives

Central to the successful management change are the HR initiatives which are put in place. Many organizations try to accomplish strategic change by merely changing the system and structure of their organization. This is a recipe for failure. HR initiatives will be incorporated within the organization's overall HR strategy and will include education, management development programmes, training and reward structures. Probably one of the greatest barriers to the management of change is the assumption that it simply happens or that people must simply change because it is necessary to do so (Peppard and Steward, 1993).

HR development has a crucial challenging role to play in successfully 'orchestrating' strategic culture change (Burack, 1991). US Labor Secretary

Robert Reich recently urged American companies to treat their workers as assets to be developed rather than as costs to be cut.

Many barriers to change are not tangible, and although are propagated by organizations, they exist in the mind of the manager. Indeed, such an initiative would also contribute towards the learning capability of organizations, although there is a distinction between learning as an individual phenomenon and an organization's capability to learn by the systematization of knowledge.

Management needs to be taught new skills, particularly interpersonal skills and how to work in teams. New organizational forms also require managers to carry out new tasks and roles. The informate phenomenon identified by Zuboff (1988) increasingly requires empowerment and wider responsibility for decision-making to be given to organization members.

Changing technology places additional strains on management. Education for new technology is important for two reasons: (i) strategically, to give a strategic view of IT; and (ii) organizationally – it is arguable that the chief contribution of managers to the competitive nature of organizations will be thinking creatively about organizational change.

Motorola spends $120 million every year on education, equivalent to 3.6 per cent of payroll. It calculates that every $1 it spends on training delivers $30 in productivity gains within three years. Since 1987, the company has cut costs by $3.3 billion – not by the normal expedient of firing workers, but by training them to simplify processes and reduce waste. For example, the purchasing department at the automotive and industrial electronics group set up a team called ET/VT = 1 because it wanted to ensure that all 'elapsed time' (the hours it took to handle a requisition) was 'value time' (the hours when an employee is doing something necessary and worthwhile). The team managed to cut from 17 to six the number of steps in handling a requisition. Team members squeezed average elapsed time from 30 hours to three, enabling the purchasing department to handle 45 per cent more requests without adding workers (Henkoff, 1993).

Scott Morton (1991) contends that one of the challenges for an organization in the 1990s is understanding one's culture and knowing that an innovative culture is a key first step in a move towards an adaptive organization. Managers have a core set of beliefs and assumptions which are specific and relevant to the organization in which they work and are learned over time. The culture of the organization propagates many of the traditional assumptions which underlie organizations and also makes it extremely difficult to change. This is not something that is unique to organizations but is firmly based in a society which fosters individuality. Everyone tends to be pigeonholed from an early age and it is only to be expected that it be carried to working life. Management education itself promotes specialization by teaching functional courses.

Hirschhorn and Gilmore (1992) have identified four psychological boundaries which managers must pay attention to in flexible organizations: *authority* boundary, *task* boundary, *political* boundary, and *identity* boundary. Let us briefly explore each of these.

- *Authority*. In more flexible organizations, issuing and following orders is no longer good enough. The individual with formal authority is not necessarily the one with the most up-to-date information about a business problem or a customer need. Subordinates must challenge in order to follow while superiors must listen in order to lead.
- *Task*. In a team environment, people must focus not only on their own work, but also on what others do.
- *Political*. In an organization, interest groups sometimes conflict and managers must know how to negotiate productively.
- *Identity*. In a workplace where performance depends on commitment, organizations must connect with the values of their employees.

An innovative HR policy that supports organizational members as they learn to cope with a more complex and changing world is required. New criteria to measure performance are also needed. It is no use fostering cross-functional teams if evaluation and reward are based on individual criteria. Every manager, regardless of position or seniority, responds to the criteria by which he or she is evaluated, who conducts the review, and how it is conducted.

IS/IT development

The approach to IS/IT development needs to take cognizance of the business objective as described in the IS and organization strategies. Most of the perspectives discussed above depend on harnessing the power of IT to make it all possible. However, it is important that the overall business applications of which IT developments are part are owned by business management. This is because their key involvement in requirements definition, data conversion, new working practices, implementation and realizing the benefits.

IS/IT developments are not all the same and the approach adopted needs to be related to business objectives. Ward *et al.* (1990) propose the use of the applications portfolio which indicates appropriate management strategies, particularly in relation to financial justification, IS/IT management style, the use of packages, outsourcing, contractors and consultants. This portfolio approach makes more effective the use of the IT resource in relation to business requirements.

Delivering the IS strategy is traditionally seen as a purely technological issue. However, of key concern are the changes which accompany any IT implementation (Galliers, 1991). People issues are key reasons why many IT investments fail to realize benefits (Scott Morton, 1991). Involvement and ownership in the design and implementation are seen as critical for the success of any IT development. The training needs required for the new technology must be integrated when appropriate with the HR initiatives.

Conclusions

The traditional organization has been criticized by many writers on organization. Alternatives have been proposed but these merely represent a destination without a clear road map setting the direction rather than presenting a map and route to negotiate the obstacles to be encountered along the way.

In this chapter we have presented a framework to help organizations in planning and implementing their journey. This framework is constructed around the triumvirate of vision, planning and delivery with considerable iteration between all stages. This helps with the management of uncertainty and reconfirms the destination.

Crucial in the visioning stage are the critical success factors of the new organizational form which define the requirements of critical issues such as culture, teamwork, people, skills, structure, reward systems and information needs. This provided the basis for the gap analysis highlighting the nature of the journey to be undertaken and the subsequent delivery initiatives of HR, organization design and IS/IT. Central to our framework are the interactions between HR, organization design and IS/IT in a way that enables the delivery of the new organization form with its CSFs.

Fundamentally, we believe that managing the migration to the new organization form will require a significant amount of senior management time, energy and initiative. If this is not forthcoming because management is 'too busy', the likelihood of success is minimal. This must be the first paradigm to be broken.

References

Ansoff, H. I. (1979) *Strategic Management*, Macmillan, London.

Argyris, C. (1976) Single-loop and double-loop models in research on decision-making. *Admin. Sci. Quarterly*, **21**, 363–375.

Argyris, C. (1982) *Reasoning, Learning and Action: Individual and Organization*, Jossey-Bass, San Francisco.

Bartlett, C. A. and Ghoshal, S. (1990) Matrix management: not a structure, a frame of mind. *Harvard Bus. Rev.*, July–August, 138–145.

Bertalanfy, L. von (1956) General systems theory. *General Systems*, **I**, 1–10.

Bettis, R. A., Bradley, S. P. and Hamel, G. (1992) Outsourcing and industrial decline. *Acad. Manage. Exec.*, **6**(1) 7–16.

Burack, E. H. (1991) Changing the company culture – the role of human resource development. *Long Range Planning*, **24**(1), 88–95.

Burgelman, R. A. (1983) A process model of internal corporate venturing in a diversified major firm. *Admin. Sci. Quarterly*, **28**(2), 223–244.

Burns, T. and Stalker, G. M. (1961) *The Management of Innovation*, Tavistock Publications, London.

Business Week (1992) Learning from Japan. *Business Week*, 27 January, 38–44.

Butler Cox Foundation (1991) The role of information technology in transforming the business. *Research Report 79*, January.

Chandler, A. D. (1962) *Strategy and Structure: Chapters in the History of the American Industrial Enterprise*, The MIT Press, Cambridge, MA.

Charan, R. (1991) How networks reshape organizations – for results. *Harvard Bus. Rev.*, September–October, 104–115.

Davenport, T. H. and Short, J. E. (1990) The new industrial engineering: information technology and business process redesign. *Sloan Manage. Rev.*, Summer, 11–27.

Dean, J. W. and Susman, G. I. (1989) Organizing for manufacturable design. *Harvard Bus. Rev.*, January–February, 28–36.

deGeus, A. P. (1988) Planning as learning. *Harvard Bus. Rev.*, March–April, 70–74.

Drucker, P. F. (1988) The coming of the new organization. *Harvard Bus. Rev.*, January–February, 45–53.

Dumaine, B. (1989) What the leaders of tomorrow see. *Fortune*, 3 July, 24–34.

Earl, M. J. (1989) *Management Strategies for Information Technology*, Prentice-Hall, Hemel Hempstead, UK.

Emerson, H. (1917) The twelve principles of efficiency. *Eng. Mag.*, xviii.

Ernst, D. and Bleeke, J. (eds) (1993) *Collaborating to Compete: Using Strategic Alliances and Acquisitions in the Global Marketplace*, John Wiley, New York.

Galliers, R. D. (1991) Strategic information systems planning: myths, reality and guidclines for successful implementation. *Europ. J. Inf. Sys.*, **1**(1), 55–64.

Garvin, D. A. (1993) Building a learning organisation. *Harvard Bus. Rev.*, July–August, 78–91.

Griffin, J., Beardsley, S. and Kugel, R. (1991) Commonality: marrying design with process. *The McKinsey Quarterly*, Summer, 56–70.

Hamel, G., Doz, Y. L. and Prahalad, C. K. (1989) Collaborate with your competitors and win. *Harvard Bus. Rev.*, January–February, 143–154.

Hammer, M. (1990) Reengineering work: don't automate, obliterate. *Harvard Bus. Rev.*, July–August, 104–112.

Hayes, R. H. and Jaikumar, R. (1988) Manufacturing's crisis: new technologies, obsolete organisations. *Harvard Bus. Rev.*, September–October, 77–85.

Hayes, R. H., Wheelwright, S. C. and Clark, K. B. (1988) *Dynamic Manufacturing: Creating the Learning Organization*, The Free Press, New York.

Hedberg, B. and Jonsson, S. (1978) Designing semi-confusing information systems for organizations in changing environments. *Accounting, Organizations, and Society*, **3**(1), 47–64.

Henderson, B. D. (1979) *Henderson on Corporate Strategy*, Abt Books, Cambridge, MA.

Henkoff, R. (1993) Companies that train best. *Fortune*, 22 March, 40–46.

Heygate, R. and Brebach, G. (1991) Corporate reengineering. *The McKinsey Quarterly*, Summer, 44–55.

Hirschhorn, L. and Gilmore, T. (1992) The new boundaries of the 'boundaryless' company. *Harvard Bus. Rev.*, May–June, 104–115.

Johnson, G. (1992) Managing strategic change – strategy, culture and action. *Long Range Planning*, **25**(1), 29–36.

Johnson, R. and Lawrence, P. R. (1988) Beyond vertical integration – the rise of the value-adding partnership. *Harvard Bus. Rev.*, July–August, 94–101.

Kaplan, R. B. and Murdock, L. (1991) Core process redesign. *The McKinsey Quarterly*, Summer, 27–43.

Katzenbach, J. R. and Smith, D. K. (1992) Why teams matter. *The McKinsey Quarterly*, Autumn, 3–27.

Kochan, T. A. and Useem, M. (eds) (1992) *Transforming Organizations*, Oxford University Press, New York

Kotler, P. and Stonich, P. J. (1991) Turbo marketing through time compression. *J Bus. Strategy*, September–October, 24–29.

Krachenberg, A. R., Henke, J. W. and Lyons, T. F. (1988) An organizational structure response to competition. In *Advances in Systems Research and Cybernetics* (ed. G. E. Lasker), International Institute for Advanced Studies in Systems Research and Cybernetics, University of Windsor, Windsor, Ontario, pp.320–326.

Lawrence, P. and Lorsch, J. (1970) *Studies in Organization Design*, Richard D. Irwin, Homewood, IL.

Lorenz, A. (1993) BT versus the world. *The Sunday Times*, 16 May.

Lyons, T. F. Krachenberg, A. R. and Henke, J. W. (1990) Mixed motive marriages: what's next for buyer-supplier relationships? *Sloan Manage. Rev.*, Spring, 29–36.

Macdonald, K. H. (1991) Strategic alignment process. In *The Corporation of the 1990s: Information Technology and Organisational Transformation* (ed. M. S. Scott Morton), Oxford University Press, New York.

Macdonald, K. H. (1993) Future alignment realities. Unpublished paper.

Maslow, A. H. (1943) A theory of human motivation. *Psychology Rev.*, **50**, 370–396.

Maslow, A. H. (1954) *Motivation and Personality*, Harper, New York.

Mason, R. O. and Mitroff, I. I. (1981) *Challenging Strategic Planning Assumptions: Theory, Cases and Techniques*, Wiley, New York.

Mayo, E. (1971) Hawthorne and the Western Electric Company. In *Organisation Theory* (ed. D. S. Pugh), Penguin, Middlesex.

McClelland, D. (1976) Power as the great motivator. *Harvard Bus. Rev.*, May–June, 100–110.

Miles, R. and Snow, C. (1978) *Organization Strategy, Structure, and Process*, McGraw-Hill, New York.

Miles, R. and Snow, C. (1987) Network organizations: new concepts for new forms. *California Manage. Rev.*, Spring.

Miller, D. (1986) Configuration of strategy and structure: towards a synthesis. *Strategic Manage. J.*, **7**, 233–249.

Miller, D. (1987) The genesis of configuration. *Acad. Manage. Rev.*, **12**(4), 686–701.

Miller, D. and Mintzberg, H. (1984) The case for configuration. In *Organizations: A Quantum View* (eds D. Miller and P. H. Friesen), Prentice-Hall, Englewood Cliffs, NJ.

Mintzberg, H. (1973) *The Nature of Managerial Work*, Harper and Row, New York.

Mintzberg, H. (1979) *The Structuring of Organizations*, Prentice-Hall, Englewood Cliffs, NJ.

Mintzberg, H. (1991) The effective organization: forces and forms. *Sloan Manage. Rev.*, Winter, 54–67.

Mitroff, I. I. and Linstone, A. (1993) *The Unbounded Mind: Breaking the Chains of Traditional Business Thinking*, Oxford University Press, New York.

Nakamoto, M. (1992) Plugging into each other's strengths. *Financial Times*, 27 March.

Ohmae, K. (1989) The global logic of strategic alliances. *Harvard Bus. Rev.*, March–April, 143–154.

Ostrof, F. and Smith, D. (1992) The horizontal organization. *The McKinsey Quarterly*, **1**, 149–168.

Peppard, J. W. and Steward, K. (1993) Managing change in IS/IT implementation. In *IT Strategy For Business* (cd. J. W. Peppard), Pitman, London, pp.269–291.

Peters, T. and Waterman, R. H. (1982) *In Search of Excellence*, Harper and Row, New York.

Porter, M. E. (1980) *Competitive Strategy*, Free Press, New York.

Porter, M. E. (1985) *Competitive Advantage*, Free Press, New York.

Poynter, T. A. and White, R. E. (1990) Making the horizontal organisation work. *Bus. Quarterly (Canada)*, Winter, 73–77.

Quinn Mills, D. and Friesen, B. (1992) The learning organization. *Europ. Manage. J.*, **10**(2), 146–156.

Reich, R. B. (1987) Entrepreneurship reconsidered: the team as hero. *Harvard Bus. Rev.*, May–June, 77–83.

Rockart, J. F. and Short, J. E. (1989) IT in the 1990s: managing organization interdependencies. *Sloan Manage. Rev.*, **30**(2), 7–17.

Schwenk, C. R. (1988) A cognitive perspective on strategic decision-making. *J. Manage. Studies*, **25**(1), 41–55.

Scott, W. G. (1961) Organization theory: an overview and an appraisal. *Acad. Manage. Rev.*, April, 7–26.

Scott Morton, M. S. (ed.) (1991) *The Corporation of the 1990s: Information Technology and Organization Transformation*, Oxford University Press, New York.

Senge, P. M. (1990a) *The Fifth Discipline: The Art and Practice of the Learning Organization*, Doubleday/Currency, New York.

Senge, P. M. (1990b) The leaders new work: building learning organizations. *Sloan Manage. Rev.*, Fall, 7–23.

Senge, P. M. (1991) Team learning. *The McKinsey Quarterly*, Summer, 82–93.

Slevin, D. P. and Colvin, J. G. (1990) Juggling entrepreneurial style and organization structure: how to get your act together. *Sloan Manage. Rev.*, **31**(2), Winter, 43–53.

Smith, A. (1910) *The Wealth of Nations*, Dent, London.

Snow, C. C., Miles, R. E. and Coleman, H. J. Jr (1992) Managing 21st century network organizations. *Organization Dynamics*, Winter, 5–20.

Stalk, G. Jr (1988) Time – the next source of competitive advantage. *Harvard Bus. Rev.*, July–August, 41–51.

Stata, R. (1989) Organizational learning – the key to management innovation. *Sloan Manage. Rev.*, Spring, 63–73.

Taylor, F. W. (1911) *Scientific Management*, Harper, New York.

Thompson, V. (1961) *Modern Organizations*, Knopf, New York.

Venkatraman, N. (1991) IT-induced business reconfiguration. In *The Corporation of the 1990s: Information Technology and Organization Transformation* (ed. M. S. Scott Morton), Oxford University Press, New York, pp.122–158.

Ward, J., Griffiths, P. and Whitmore, P. (1990) *Strategic Planning for Information Systems*, John Wiley, Chichester, UK.

Weber, M. (1947) *The Theory of Social and Economic Organization*, Free Press, New York.

Zuboff, S. (1988) *In the Age of the Smart Machine: The Future of Work and Power*, Basic Books, New York.

Questions for discussion

1   How does the concept of organizational form differ from that of organizational strategy and structure as presented in the previous chapter by Karimi and Konsynski?
2   There is much talk today of achieving 'dynamic' and 'flexible' organizations. What does it mean to be 'dynamic' and 'flexible'?
3   Consider the six organizational forms discussed by the authors:
    – has any emerged as the dominant paradigm in the late 1990s?
    – are the forms mutually exclusive? What are some variants?
    – highlight the role of IT in each of the forms: what specific technologies are necessary to make the forms effective?
    – what are the impediments to the effective functioning of the forms?
    – what might be the appropriate IS strategy for the different forms?
4   What might be the role of IT in the human resource initiatives, mentioned by the authors as critical to the change management process?

18 Information Technology and Organizational Decision Making

The effects of advanced information technologies on organizational design, intelligence, and decision making

George P. Huber

This chapter sets forth a theory of the effects that computer-assisted communication and decision-aiding technologies have on organizational design, intelligence, and decision making. Several components of the theory are controversial and in need of critical empirical investigation. The chapter focuses on those technology-prompted changes in organizational design that affect the quality and timeliness of intelligence and decision making, as contrasted with those that affect the production of goods and services.

Introduction

This chapter draws on the work of organizational researchers, communication researchers, and information systems researchers to set forth, in the form of a set of propositions, a theory concerning the effects that *advanced information technologies* have on organizational design, intelligence, and decision making. The motivations for such a chapter are four.

One motivation concerns the need to reinvestigate and possibly revise certain components of organization theory. A large part of what is known about the factors affecting organizational processes, structures, and performance was developed when the nature and mix of communication technologies were relatively constant, both across time and across organizations of the same general type. In contrast, the capabilities and forms of communication technologies have begun to vary, and they are likely to vary a great deal in the future. For example, communication technology (or communication medium) is now a variable whose traditionally relatively constant range (from face-to-face at one extreme to unaddressed broadcast documents at the other, cf. Daft and Lengel, 1984, 1986) is being expanded by organizations to include *computer-assisted communication technologies* (e.g. electronic mail, image transmission devices, computer conferencing, and videoconferencing) that facilitate access to people inside and outside the organization with an ease that previously was not possible. Also, more sophisticated and more user-friendly forms of *computer-assisted decision-aiding technologies* (e.g. expert systems, decision-support systems, on-line management information systems, and external information retrieval systems) are in the late stages of development or early stages of implementation. Consequently, as the uses, capabilities, and forms of communication and decision-aiding technologies increase in their range, researchers must reassess what is known about the effects of these technologies because what is known may change. 'That is, new media impacts may condition or falsify hypothesized relationships developed by past research' (Williams and Rice, 1983, p.208). Thus, one motivation for setting forth propositions concerning the impact of advanced information technologies is to encourage investigation and debate on what the nature of organizational design, intelligence, and decision making might be when these technologies become more sophisticated and more widely used.

The second motivation is to take a step toward creating a theory of the effects that advanced information technologies have on organizations. *Advanced information technologies* are devices (a) that transmit, manipulate, analyze, or exploit information; (b) in which a digital computer processes information integral to the user's communication or decision task; and (c) that have either made their appearance since 1970 or exist in a form that aids in communication or decision tasks to a significantly greater degree than did pre-1971 forms. (For expanded discussion of the term *advanced information technologies*, see Culnan and Markus, 1987; Gibson and Jackson, 1987; Johansen, 1988; Rice and Associates, 1984; and Strassman, 1985a.) The need for such a theory has been exemplified in a review by Culnan and Markus (1987) and in a special issue of *Communication Research* (Steinfield and Fulk, 1987). In that special issue, the guest editors noted that, although there are many empirical findings concerning the effects of advanced information technologies on organizations, 'there has been little synthesis, integration, and development of theoretical explanations [and] that it is time for theory development and theory-guided research' (Steinfield and Fulk, 1987, p.479).

Together, the propositions in this chapter comprise a theory such as that called for by Steinfield and Fulk, but like any theory, it is limited. It includes

Table 18.1   *Dependent variables included in the theory (and the numbers of the propositions related to them)*

Design variables (subunit level)	Design variables (organizational level)	Design variables (organizational memory)	Performance variables
Participation in decision making (1)	Centralization of decision making (4, 5)	Development and use of computer-resident data bases (8)	Effectiveness of environmental scanning (10)
Size and heterogeneity of decision units (2)	Number of organizational levels involved in authorization (6)	Development and use of computer-resident in-house expert systems (9)	Quality and timeliness of organizational intelligence (11)
Frequency and duration of meetings (3)	Number of nodes in the information-processing network (7)		Quality of decisions (12)
			Speed of decision making (13, 14)

as dependent variables only (a) characteristics of organizational intelligence and decision making, such as timeliness, and (b) aspects of organization design associated with intelligence and decision making, such as the size of decision units. Further, within this still rather large set of dependent variables, the theory includes only those (a) that seem to be significantly affected by advanced information technology, (b) that are of interest to organization scientists or administrators, or (c) whose variance seems to have increased with the advent of advanced information technologies. The dependent variables included in the theory are shown in Table 18.1. Variables that are not included in the theory, but whose omission is briefly discussed, include horizontal integration, specialization, standardization, formalization, and the distribution of influence on organizational decisions.

As independent variables the theory includes only (a) the use of computer-assisted communication technologies and (b) the use of computer-assisted decision-aiding technologies. The theory does not encompass the use of computer-assisted production technologies or the use of transaction-enacting technologies such as computerized billing systems. (For ideas concerning the effects of advanced information technologies, broadly defined to include computer-assisted automation, on a broader set of organizational attributes, see Child, 1984, 1988; Gibson and Jackson, 1987; Strassman 1985a; Zuboff, 1984.) Finally, the theory does not explicitly address use of advanced information technologies for impression-management purposes such as those described by Sabatier (1978) and Feldman and March (1981).

The third motivation for integrating the work of organizational researchers, communication researchers, and information systems researchers is to help researchers in each of these fields become more aware of the existence, content, and relevance of the work done by researchers in other fields. Without such awareness, the efficiency of the research establishment is less, opportunities for synergy are lost, and progress in theory development is inhibited.

The fourth and last motivation is of practical, administrative importance. Advanced information technologies are becoming a pervasive aspect of organizations, but their relatively recent appearance and rapidly changing nature virtually guarantee that administrators and their advisors will not have experience as a guide in anticipating and planning for the impacts they may have. In the absence of experience, the value of theory is considerable.

It is important to note that the theory described here is not based on a great deal of directly applicable empirical research. There are two reasons for this. The first is that the components of organization theory that were drawn upon in developing the propositions were not validated under conditions in which decision and communication systems were computer assisted; consequently, they may not be valid for organizations that presently use a good deal of advanced information technology. The second reason is that many of the empirical studies that were drawn upon inductively in developing the propositions pertain to forms of technology that are not necessarily representative of the more sophisticated forms now in use or expected to be in use in the more distant future. (See Hofer, 1970; Pfeffer, 1978; Rice, 1980; Robey, 1977; Whisler, 1970, for brief reviews of some of these early studies, and Olson and Lucas, 1982, for some thoughtful speculations concerning the effects of advanced information technologies on a variety of organizational attributes and behaviors.) Thus, most propositions about the organization-level effects of advanced information technology must be viewed with some caution, whether derived from mature, but possibly outdated, organization theory or from recent, but perhaps soon-to-be outdated, empirical findings.

The above cautions notwithstanding, the propositions set forth are supportable to the degree necessary to be responsive to the motivations just noted, especially if the qualifications attendant to each proposition are seriously considered by users. In any case, these propositions can serve as a basis for the development of specific hypotheses.

Nature of advanced information technologies

What are the critical characteristics of advanced information technologies that might cause these technologies to have effects on organizational design, intelligence, and decision making different from the effects of more traditional technologies?

For purposes of discussion, characteristics of information technologies will be divided into two groups. *Basic characteristics* are related to data storage capacity, transmission capacity, and processing capacity. Advanced information technologies, largely as a result of their digital computer component, usually provide higher levels of these basic characteristics (Culnan and Markus, 1987, p.420; Rice and Associates, 1984, p.34). [No distinction is made in this definition or in this chapter between data (stimuli and symbols) and information (data conveying meaning as a result of reducing uncertainty).]

Characteristics of the second group I will call *properties*. Although the above basic dimensions are relevant to users, often it is the multidimensional configuration of the levels characterizing a particular technology that is most relevant for a particular task. Some authorities have considered these configurations when comparing advanced information technologies with traditional information technologies, and have made generalizations about the resultant properties of advanced information systems. Because these properties cause the use of advanced information systems to have effects such as those noted in this chapter, some of these generalizations are reviewed here. (See Culnan and Markus, 1987; Rice and Associates, 1984, especially chapter 2, for discussions of how these properties follow from the levels that the technologies attain on the basic dimensions.)

In the context of *communication*, these properties include those that facilitate the ability of the individual or organization (a) to communicate more easily and less expensively across time and geographic location (Rice and Bair, 1984), (b) to communicate more rapidly and with greater precision to targeted groups (e.g. Culnan and Markus, 1987; Sproull and Keisler, 1986), (c) to record and index more reliably and inexpensively the content and nature of communication events, and (d) to more selectively control access and participation in a communication event or network (Culnan and Markus, 1987; Rice, 1984).

In the context of *decision aiding*, the properties include those that facilitate the ability of the individual or organization (a) to store and retrieve large amounts of information more quickly and inexpensively; (b) to more rapidly and selectively access information created outside the organization; (c) to more rapidly and accurately combine and reconfigure information so as to create new information (as in the development of forecasting models or financial analyses); (d) to more compactly store and quickly use the judgment and decision models developed in the minds of experts, or in the mind of the decision maker, and stored as expert systems or decision models; and (e) to more reliably and inexpensively record and retrieve information about the content and nature of organizational transactions. (Discussions of these properties of computer-assisted decision-aiding technologies, richer in detail than space allows here, are contained in Sprague and McNurlin, 1986; Sprague and Watson, 1986; Zmud, 1983.)

Mistaken Impressions

It may be helpful to draw upon the above discussion of the basic characteristics and properties of information technologies to dispel some occasionally held, but mistaken, impressions. One such mistaken impression is that advanced information technologies are universally inferior or superior to traditional technologies. This impression is erroneous because the properties just delineated may be less important than other properties possessed by a more traditional technology. In addition, particular uses of the advanced technologies may have undesirable side effects (cf. Culnan and Markus, 1987; Markus, 1984; Zuboff, 1984). Further, traditional technologies often score higher with respect to acceptability, ease of use, and richness (cf. Culnan and Markus, 1987; Fulk *et al.*, 1987; Trevino *et al.*, 1987), or have scores that overlap on these properties with the scores of advanced information technologies. For these reasons, use of advanced information technologies will not eliminate use of traditional technologies. However, when the properties of advanced information technologies are useful for enhancing individual or organizational effectiveness, and when retarding forces such as those just noted are not potent, it is reasonable to believe that organizations will use the advanced technologies.

The availability of the advanced information technologies increases the communicating or decision-aiding options for the potential user, and thus in the long run, unless the selected technology is inappropriately employed, the effect is to increase the quality (broadly defined) of the user's communication or decision-making processes. Presumably, through experience or observation, organizational members learn which communication or decision-aiding technology is most likely to achieve their purpose, and then adopt it. Field studies, which will be cited later, verify this belief.

In a related vein, it is a mistake to view advanced information technologies solely as substitutes for traditional technologies. To the contrary, advanced information technologies are frequently used more as supplements and complements to traditional technologies, rather than as substitutes. For example, electronic mail is often used to confirm with text what was said in a phone conversation or to set up face-to-face appointments, and image transmission devices are often used to make available drawings that will be discussed after all the parties have had a chance to study them. Of course, people do substitute computer-assisted media for traditional media when it seems efficacious to do so. Overall, the effect of availability of user-friendly computer-assisted communication technology is to increase the range of options for the communicator. Presumably, through experience or observation, organizational members learn to choose communication technologies wisely. Evidence, which will be cited, indicates that this presumption is correct. An analogous discussion applies to computer-assisted decision-aiding technologies, but limits of space force its omission.

A final mistaken impression is that, although advanced information technologies may lead to rational outcomes (such as information that is more accurate and comprehensive or decisions that are more timely) in organizations characterized by strong adherence to a norm of economic rationality, these outcomes are unlikely in more highly politicized or power-driven organizations. In the absence of scientific evidence with which to develop the required contingency theory, three observations are offered. The first is that the external environments of many organizations are sufficiently competitive that, in order to survive, the organizations must adopt and properly use rationality-enhancing communication and decision-aiding technologies. If organizational politics interferes with such adoption or use, the marketplace or parent organization intervenes until universal conformance is achieved. Thus, in their time, the telegraph became a pervasive technology in railroads, the calculator in brokerage houses, and the radio in armies. In the organizations that survived, those managers whose proprietary inclinations caused them not to use the technologies to further organizational goals (such as timely delivery of freight, accurate and comprehensive information for investors, or effective coordination in battle) were evidently converted or purged. In essence, superordinates or organizations require subordinates or subunits to help them compete effectively or otherwise satisfy environmental demands, and if rational use of technology is necessary, it occurs in the long run, whatever the proprietary inclinations of the subordinates or subunits.

The second observation is that highly politicized or power-driven organizations also have highly competitive internal environments, and in such environments it is necessary for managers to maximize their own competitive effectiveness by appearing to satisfy the goals of resource controllers on an issue-by-issue basis. In these environments, technical or financial analyses are widely used to persuade the resource controllers that the manager's proposals best satisfy the resource controller's goals (Burgelman, 1982; Kelley, 1976; Shukla, 1982). Thus, even in organizations where power plays a significant role in resource allocation, so also do 'the numbers' (cf. Gerwin, 1979; Pfeffer and Moore, 1980; Sabatier, 1978; Shukla, 1982). Managers who do not employ the most appropriate technologies in developing and selling analyses are at a competitive disadvantage; they must adapt or lose out.

The third observation is that, in almost all organizations, effective fulfillment of organizational responsibilities contributes to the development and maintenance of a manager's reputation. Thus, aside from whatever a manager might do to negatively or positively affect the quality or timeliness of the design, intelligence, or decision making of superordinate units, he or she is likely to employ any communication or decision-aiding technologies that can contribute to his or her personal effectiveness or the effectiveness of his or her own unit (cf. Daft *et al.*, 1987).

Together, these observations suggest that even though power and politics influence organizational design, intelligence, and decision making, so too do information technologies; *for advancement of their own interests, organizational participants will use advanced information technologies in ways that increase their effectiveness in fulfilling organizational goals*. This fundamental assumption underlies many of the propositions included in the theory and seems to be validated in the studies referenced.

The propositions

The propositions are grouped for expositional purposes into four sections. The propositions in the first three sections portray the effects of advanced information technologies on organizational design, that is, the effects on (a) subunit structure and process, (b) organizational structure and process, and (c) organizational memory. Although these effects will most often result from evolved practices rather than from prior managerial intentions, I expect that in the future, as administrators and their advisors learn about whatever functional effects of advanced information technologies on organizational design and performance may accrue, more and more of the effects will be the outcomes of intentions. In the short run, however, many managers will probably continue to introduce advanced information systems in order to reduce the number of personnel, to increase managerial efficiency, or to imitate other managers. After the systems are implemented for these purposes, these managers or other organizational participants will sometimes see that the systems can accomplish other purposes and will adjust the organization's design to facilitate accomplishment of these purposes (e.g. by extending the scope of responsibility of an organizational unit that now has easier access to a broader range of information).

The propositions of the fourth section set forth the effects of advanced information technology on organizational intelligence and decision making. Some of these effects are direct and some occur indirectly through changes in design. [Organizational intelligence is the output or product of an organization's efforts to acquire, process, and interpret information external to the organization (cf. Porter, 1980; Sammon *et al.*, 1984; Wilensky, 1967). It is an input to the organization's decision makers.]

Each of these four sections contains specific suggestions concerning research that would seem to be useful for examining the validity and domains of particular propositions. The last section of the chapter contains more general recommendations for researchers in the areas of organization science and information systems.

Effects at the subunit level

The focus in this section is on those aspects of organizational design that ultimately affect organizational intelligence and decision making. For example, aspects of structure that affect the accuracy of communications or the timeliness of decisions are considered. The first three propositions of the section deal with variables generally thought of in the context of organizational subunits. The remaining six propositions deal with variables more associated with the design of the organization as a whole. (This distinction is made solely for expository purposes – the categorizations are not intended to have theoretical merit.)

Participation in decision making

In many organizational decisions, technical and political considerations suggest that the development, evaluation, or selection of alternatives would benefit from exchanges of information among a moderate to large number of experts or partisans. But communicating takes time and effort, and so the variety and number of participants is often narrower than *post hoc* analyses determine to be appropriate. Assuming that the time and effort involved in communicating are critical determinants of the number of individuals who become involved, *what is the effect of computer-assisted communication technology on the breadth of participation in decision making?*

Because computer assisted communication technologies can greatly reduce the effort required for those individuals who are separated in time or physical proximity to exchange information (cf. Hiltz and Turoff, 1978; Culnan and Markus, 1987; Special Report, 1988), it is probable that more people would serve as sources of information. Thus, we have the story where

> . . . a product developer sent a message to distribution lists that reach thousands of people asking for suggestions about how to add a particular new product feature. Within two weeks, he had received over 150 messages in reply, cutting across geographical, departmental, divisional, and hierarchical boundaries, almost all from people the product developer did not know. (Sproull and Keisler, 1986, p.1510)

And, of course, teleconferencing and other similar computer-assisted communication systems are useful for sharing information (Johansen, 1984, 1988; Rice, 1984).

In contrast, authorities have argued that computer-assisted communication technologies do not enable decision makers to obtain 'soft' information (Mintzberg, 1975), 'rich' information (Daft *et al.*, 1987), the 'meaning' of information (Weick, 1985), or information about sensitive matters. To the extent that this argument is correct, it would preclude the use of computer-assisted communication technologies where the need for such information is paramount. However, the circumstances where the arguments of these authorities are salient may be fewer than first thought. For example, the argument that computer-assisted technologies provide fewer cues than does face-to-face communication is valid, but it misses the fact that managers and other professionals usually choose the communication medium that fits the communication task (Daft *et al.*, 1987; Rice and Case, 1983; Trevino *et al.*, 1987). Thus, computer-assisted communication technology might still be used to exchange factual or technical information, whereas other media are used to elaborate on this information or to exchange other types of information.

The issue is not one of the technologies driving out the use of richer media, but rather of the technologies enabling communications that otherwise would be unlikely to occur. For example, Foster and Flynn (1984), Sproull and Keisler (1986), and others (Palme, 1981; Rice and Case, 1983) reported that the availability of electronic mail caused organizational participants to increase the overall amount of their communication; there was not a one-for-one trade-off between media. Overall, the preponderance of arguments and the available empirical evidence suggest that:

Proposition 1: Use of computer-assisted communication technologies leads to a larger number and variety of people participating as information sources in the making of a decision.

There will be exceptions to the relationship explicated in this and all propositions. A proposition states that across a large number of cases, *ceteris paribus*, there will be a tendency for the stated relationship to be observed. Extensive testing of hypotheses derived from the proposition will, eventually, identify any *systematic* exceptions to the relationship.

Further research is needed, of course, to determine (a) if the increase in participation is of practical significance; (b) if the increase in participation leads to higher quality decisions or better acceptance of decisions; (c) if the information includes 'hard' information, soft information, or both; and (d) if the decision process becomes more effective. (For reviews of the effects that computer-assisted communication technologies have on group behaviors, see Johansen, 1984, 1988; Rice, 1984. For a review of the behavioral effects of teleconferencing in particular, see Svenning and Ruchinskas, 1984.)

It is important to note that although organizational members tend to use the technologies that communicate their messages with timeliness and veracity (Trevino *et al.*, 1987), they also consider the social acceptance of the technology (Fulk *et al.*, 1987), the ease of use (Huber, 1982), and other attributes (Culnan and Markus, 1987).

Size and heterogeneity of decision units

In many situations, organizational subunits are responsible for developing, recommending, or selecting a proposal for action. Thus, aside from the many individuals who might participate in this process, there is usually one individual or one group of individuals who is formally accountable for the decision. Such an individual or group is referred to as a *decision unit* (Duncan, 1974).

What is the effect of computer-assisted communication technology on the size and heterogeneity of decision units? To answer this question, note that small groups provide more satisfying experiences for their members (Jewell and Reitz, 1981; Kowitz and Knutson, 1980), and that small groups are less costly in terms of human resources. Also note that homogeneous groups provide more satisfying experiences and, if they have the necessary expertise, accomplish decision-related tasks more quickly (Jewell and Reitz, 1981; Kowitz and Knutson, 1980). Finally, note that the discussion associated with Proposition 1 suggests that computer-assisted communication technologies can help decision units to become relatively smaller and more homogeneous by obtaining information beyond that obtainable using traditional communication media; both experts and constituency representatives can often make their knowledge and concerns available through electronic mail, teleconferencing, or videoconferencing. Cost considerations suggest that organizations will seek such efficiencies in their use of human capital. For example:

> You cannot afford to have an expert in very rare kidney disease on your team, just in case you might need him or her someday. . . . The technology allows you to have experts available electronically. (Strassman, 1985b, pp.22, 27)

What is the effect of computer-assisted decision-support technology, as contrasted with communication technology, on the size and heterogeneity of decision units? Sometimes experts can be replaced by expert systems and information keepers can be replaced by management information systems. To the extent that a decision unit can properly use the expert system for resolving some uncertainties, the expert need not be a member of the decision unit; therefore, the unit's size and heterogeneity will be decreased.

Research is needed, of course, to determine if these changes occur. They may not. For example, it may be that organizational aspirations will rise and information technologies will be used to acquire additional diverse information, information whose acquisition and interpretation will require approximately the same size face-to-face decision-group membership as is presently found. If the group's task involves less the acquisition of information than it does the routine processing of information, then the increase in the unit manager's span of control that is facilitated by increased internal communication capability may lead to an overall increase in unit size. It will be interesting to see if future studies can ascertain the net effect of the conflicting forces under various conditions. However, it seems that there are many situations where the increasing efficacy of the technologies and the need for efficient use of human resources will make valid the following:

> *Proposition 2: Use of computer-assisted communication and decision-support technologies leads to decreases in the number and variety of members comprising the traditional face-to-face decision unit.*

Thus, although Proposition 1 suggests that the total number and variety of *participants serving as information sources* are likely to increase with use of computer-assisted communication technologies, Proposition 2 suggests that the number and variety of *members within the traditional face-to-face decision unit* will decrease with use of either computer-assisted communication or decision-support technologies.

It was noted earlier that people consider multiple criteria when selecting communication media. Similarly, it is important to recognize that even though organizational members tend to choose decision aids and decision procedures that facilitate the making of timely and technically satisfactory decisions (Lee *et al.*, 1988; Sabatier, 1978), they also consider other criteria when making this choice (Feldman and March, 1981; Sabatier, 1978).

Meetings

Research confirms the everyday observation that completing an organizational decision process often takes months or years (Mintzberg *et al.*, 1976; Witte, 1972). Meetings are often used to speed up decision processes by creating situations where rate of decision-related information exchange among the key participants is generally higher than that which occurs outside of meetings. Meetings, whether *ad hoc* processes or co-joined with more permanent structures, such as standing committees, are an important component of organizational decision processes and occupy a good deal of the time of managers and other professionals.

What is or what will be the effect of computer-assisted communication and decision-support technologies on the time absorbed by meetings? Some arguments and evidence suggest these technologies will result in fewer meetings with no loss of progress in the overall organizational decision-making effort. For example, many times discussion is halted and another meeting scheduled because needed information is missing. On-line management information systems or other query-answering technologies, including expert systems, may be able to provide the information, avoiding the need to schedule a subsequent meeting. Also, electronic mail and other computer-assisted communication media sometimes can be used to access soft information that can be obtained only by querying people. Further, decision-support systems can sometimes be used within meetings to conduct analyses that provide new information with which to resolve disagreements about the significance of effects of different assumptions, and thereby allow progress to continue rather than forcing adjournment until subsequent staff work can clarify the effects and another meeting can be scheduled.

Reflection suggests that each of the technologies just mentioned as facilitating the completion of meetings can sometimes lead to the cancellation of meetings. That is, with the added communication and computing capabilities, organizational members can occasionally accomplish the task of the meeting before the meeting takes place. Finally, it seems that because group-decision support systems enhance information exchange, they contribute to the effectiveness of the meeting and, thus, may enable groups to complete their tasks with fewer meetings (Benbasat and Konsynski, 1988; Johansen, 1988).

In contrast, if managers and others involved in making organizational decisions believe that use of the technologies will result in more effective meetings, the availability of the technologies may encourage them to have *more* decision-related meetings than they would otherwise. In addition, electronic mail, decision support systems, and other information-sharing and generating technologies may facilitate mini-meetings. This might preempt the need for the larger, formal meetings, but the result might be more meetings in total. The outcome of the increase in technologically supported mini-meetings versus the decrease in traditional meetings is a matter for future empirical investigation. However, because such mini-meetings are likely to be shorter, and in view of the several preceding arguments, it seems reasonable to believe that on balance and across time:

Proposition 3: Use of computer-assisted communication and decision support technologies results in less of the organization's time being absorbed by decision-related meetings.

It is important to note that, because computer-assisted communication technologies facilitate participation in meetings by persons remote in time or geography, more people may ultimately participate in a meeting (see Kerr and Hiltz, 1982, and the discussion surrounding Proposition 1). In contrast, the mini-meetings that sometimes preempt the larger, formal meetings will typically involve fewer people. Because the net effects of these two phenomena are likely to be highly variable, no proposition is offered with *person-hours* as the dependent variable.

Validation of Proposition 3 would be a significant step in documenting the effect that computer-assisted technology has on organizational processes. It would be desirable to test this proposition for each technology separately. This may not always be possible, however, because many technologically progressive organizations will have a variety of technologies in place. (For a review of the effects of advanced information technologies on the overhead costs and benefits of technologically supported meetings, such as document preparation and meeting summaries, see Rice and Bair, 1984.)

Effects at the organizational level

Centralization of decision making

By enabling top managers to obtain local information quickly and accurately, management information systems reduce ignorance and help the managers to make decisions that they, otherwise, may have been unwilling to make (Blau *et al.*, 1976; Child and Partridge, 1982; Dawson and McLoughlin, 1986). Motivations for top managers to make decisions that address local, lower level problems might include lack of confidence in subordinates (Vroom and Yetton, 1973), desire to reduce stress (Bourgeois *et al.*, 1978), need for achievement (Miller and Droge, 1986), or concern that information about the organization's overall situation or about its policies be appropriately utilized (Huber and McDaniel, 1986). Thus, it seems likely that, on occasion, management information systems would cause decisions to be made at hierarchically higher organizational levels than if these systems were not available (cf. Carter, 1984). The opportunity to obtain contextual clarification with electronic mail and other computer-assisted communication technologies would amplify this tendency.

Conversely, electronic bulletin boards enable lower- and middle-level managers to stay better informed about the organization's overall situation and about the nature of the organization's current problems, policies, and priorities (cf. Fulk and Dutton, 1984) and, consequently, permit decisions made by these managers to be more globally optimal, rather than more parochial and suboptimal, as observed by Dawson and McLoughlin (1986). Further, computer-assisted communication technologies allow lower-level units to clarify information in a more timely manner. Thus, on some occasions it seems that computer-assisted communication technologies would cause decisions to be made at organizational levels lower than if such technologies were not available. Motivations that lead top managers to permit this practice include the desire to decrease the time for organizational units to respond to problems or the desire to provide autonomy for subordinates. Some evidence suggests that this downward shift in decision making occurs – after observing the implementation of networked personal computers in the General Motors' Environmental Activities Staff, Foster and Flynn (1984, pp.231–232) concluded that 'from the former hierarchy of position power there is developing instead a hierarchy of competency. . . . Power and resources now flow increasingly to the obvious centers of competence instead of to the traditional hierarchical loci.'

Therefore, *is the net effect of the use of computer-assisted communication and decision-support technologies to increase centralization or to decrease it?* Perhaps this is the wrong question. Together, the arguments in the previous two paragraphs suggest that computer-assisted and decision-support communication technologies, when used to provide most organizational levels with information that was formerly known to only one or a few levels, enable organizations to allow decision making to occur across a greater range of hierarchical levels without suffering as much of a loss in decision quality or timeliness, as would be the case if the technologies were not available. Which hierarchical level would actually make a particular decision would depend on the inclination and availability of the relevant decision makers at the various levels (Cohen *et al.*, 1972) or other idiosyncratic factors, as noted by Fayol (1949/1916) and Duncan (1973). Thus, given that the technologies can reduce the one-to-one correspondence between certain organizational levels and certain types of information, it is likely that:

Proposition 4: For a given organization, use of computer-assisted communication and decision-support technologies leads to a more uniform distribution, across organizational levels, of the probability that a particular organizational level will make a particular decision,

Corollaries to Proposition 4 are:

Proposition 4a: For a highly centralized organization, use of computer-assisted communication and decision-support technologies leads to more decentralization.

and

Proposition 4b: For a highly decentralized organization, use of computer-assisted communication and decision-support technologies leads to more centralization.

Propositions 4, 4a, and 4b follow from the arguments presented, but are not directly based on empirical studies. It may be that the forces implied in the arguments are weak relative to those that influence traditional practices. For example, advanced information technologies enable centralized organizations to become even more centralized without incurring quite the loss in responsiveness that would occur without their presence. Similarly, they enable decentralized organizations to operate in an even more decentralized manner. I believe that, on balance, the arguments preceding Propositions 4, 4a, and 4b will be the more predictive, but empirical studies may prove this judgment to be incorrect. Certainly, the propositions require empirical study.

It is important to emphasize that by increasing the hierarchical range across which a particular type of decision may be made without a corresponding loss in decision quality or timeliness, computer-assisted communication and decision-support technologies allow other decision-location considerations to be applied without prohibitive costs. Such considerations include political matters; adherence to organizational traditions, norms, or culture; and the preferred style of top managers. Because the relative influence of these considerations will vary from organization to organization it seems that:

> *Proposition 5: For a population of organizations, broadened use of computer-assisted communication and decision-support technologies leads to a greater variation across organizations in the levels at which a particular type of decision is made.*

Number of organizational levels involved in authorization

Consider the common situation where at least some conclusions of lower-level units about what actions should be taken must be authorized by higher-level units before being acted upon, and these are forwarded upward as proposals. In their study of the approval process for a research and development budget, Shumway *et al.* (1975) found that the organizational design caused seven hierarchical levels to be involved in the proposal authorization process. Because each hierarchical level requires time to process a proposal in addition to the time required to render its judgments, the more levels involved, the longer the process takes. Each corresponding increment in the duration of the approval process can, in turn, adversely affect both the timeliness of the authorized action and the enthusiasm with which the proposers carry out the action once it is authorized.

Why then do organizations commonly involve several levels in authorizations? Frequently, the answer is that each level in the hierarchy has knowledge or decision-specific information that qualifies it to apply criteria or decision rules that less well-informed lower-level units cannot apply (cf. Meyer and Goes, 1988). For example, each higher level in an organization tends to know more about organizationwide issues, needs, and resources, and more about the nature of currently competing demands for resources, than does its subordinate units. The greater the amount of such information needed, the greater the number of hierarchical levels that will be involved in the authorization process. (In some respects this is the basis for vertical differentiation.)

What is the likely effect of communication and decision-support technologies on the number of hierarchical levels involved in authorizing a particular decision? It seems that the technologies will cause a decrease in the number of hierarchical levels involved in authorizing a proposal because technologies such as management information systems, expert systems, electronic mail, and electronic bulletin boards make information more widely available. In some cases organizational levels can obtain information that was previously unavailable and, thus, they can apply criteria or decision rules that they previously were not qualified to apply. Consequently, because the technologies facilitate the vertical distribution of information and knowledge (understanding about how to use information), there is more commonality (less extreme differentiation) of information and knowledge across organizational levels. Therefore, except when information technologies are allowed to create a problem of information overload, a given organizational level is more likely to be qualified to apply more criteria and decision rules than it could without the technologies. Assuming that use of the technologies does not somehow cause the number of decision rules to increase greatly, it follows that:

Proposition 6: Use of computer-assisted communication or decision-support technologies reduces the number of organizational levels involved in authorizing proposed organizational actions.

Possible support for Proposition 6 is found in the observations of managers that use of information technology is associated with a decrease in the number of organizational levels (Special Report, 1983a, 1983b, 1984). The link between these observations and Proposition 6 is questionable, however, since the observed decreases could follow from decreases in the number of employees. Apparently few systematic studies have examined the relationship between the use of information technology and the number of organizational levels involved in decision authorization. This is unfortunate, because more sophisticated studies may find that the two variables (i.e. the increases in the use of advanced information technology and the reductions in the number of levels) are less causally related to each other than they are related to other variables (e.g. attempts to reduce direct labor costs). Thus, such studies may find that observed correlations between the use of advanced information technology and reduction in the number of middle-level managers or organizational levels have much less to do with the seeking of improved decision processes than they have to do with general reductions in the size of organizations when robots replace blue-collar workers and when computers replace clerical workers (cf. Child, 1984).

Number of nodes in the information-processing network

Decision-making individuals and units obtain much of the information used to identify and deal with decision situations through an information-processing network. The outer boundaries of the network are the sensor units that identify relevant information from either inside or outside the organization. (Examples of sensing units include market analysis, quality control personnel, radar operators, and accountants.) These units serve as information sources, and in many situations they pass on their observations in the form of messages to intermediate units closer to the ultimate user, the decision-making unit. Quite often these intermediate units are at hierarchical levels between the sensor unit and the decision-making unit.

The recipients of the sensor unit's message process the message and pass it on to a unit that is closer still to the decision-making unit. The information processing performed by such intermediate units ranges from straightforward relaying to elaborate interpreting. For a variety of reasons the number of such units – the number of nodes on the network path connecting the sensor unit to the decision unit – may be greater than warranted: 'Most managerial levels don't do anything. They are only relays' (Drucker, 1987, p.61).

Besides the unnecessary costs implied in Drucker's observation, each information-handling unit in the network path tends to contribute distortions and delays, as detailed by Huber (1982). For these reasons, top managers sometimes attempt to reduce the role and number of such units and to use computer-assisted technologies as alternative means for obtaining the information (Special Report, 1983a, 1983b, 1984). This reduces the workload used to justify the existence of these intermediate units and levels. Computers sometimes can be used to merge, summarize, filter, and even interpret information, thus eliminating clerical workers, managers, and the organizational units of which they are a part. These observations suggest that use of computer-assisted information processing and communication technologies would lead to the elimination of human nodes in the information processing network.

There is, however, a contrary argument. Elimination of intermediate nodes in the network results in an information overload on the decision unit. When the processing functions performed by intermediate information-processing units cannot be as efficiently or effectively performed with technology or changed practices, such as those suggested by Huber (1984) and Hiltz and Turoff (1985), the units will be retained. So, *do the aforementioned technologies actually decrease the number of nodes in the organization's information-processing network?*

Informal surveys (Special Report, 1983a, 1983b, 1984) have found correlations between the use of computer-assisted communication technology and decreases in the number of managers. However, as mentioned previously, these surveys did not determine the cause of the correlation, and it may be the result of concomitant reductions in the overall number of employees. Certainly, there is a need for more sophisticated, in-depth studies to determine the nature of the cause-effect links between the use of computer-assisted technology and the number of nodes in the information-processing network. On balance, however, it seems that in some instances reductions would take place. Thus,

Proposition 7: Use of computer-assisted information processing and com-munication technologies leads to fewer intermediate human nodes within the organizational information-processing network.

(Note that Proposition 7 deals with the number of intermediate nodes, Proposition 1 deals with the number of information sources, and Proposition 2 deals with the number of members in the traditional face-to-face unit.) If the network processes information across hierarchical levels, then a corollary of Proposition 7 is:

Proposition 7a: Use of computer-assisted information processing and com-munication technologies reduces the number of organizational levels involved in processing messages.

The last two propositions of this section deal with the design of the organization's memory. Designing the organization's memory is a novel idea to organizational scientists, but will become more familiar as organizational learning becomes a more mature area of study and as top management increases its emphasis on intellectual capital.

Effects on organizational memory

In their discussion of information search routines in organizational decision making, Mintzberg *et al.* (1976) distinguished between an organization's memory search and the active or passive search of its environment. *Memory search* refers to 'the scanning of the organization's existing memory, human or paper' (or, today, computer-resident) (Mintzberg *et al.*, 1976, p.255).

Everyday experience and some research suggest that the human components of organizational memories are less than satisfactory. For example, research shows that forecasts about the time necessary to complete organizational tasks are quite erroneous, even when such tasks have been carried out in the organization on many occasions. Kidd (1970), Abernathy (1971) and Souder (1972) studied the judgments of project completion times made by managers, and found them to be woefully inaccurate, even though the managers had a good deal of experience with similar projects. Given what is known about the many factors contributing to inaccurate learning and incomplete recall (Nisbett and Ross, 1980; Kahneman *et al.*, 1982) and to motivational distortions in sharing information (Huber, 1982), it is not at all surprising that the human components of organization memories are less than satisfactory.

The problem of poor memory is, however, much more complex than simple considerations of the deficiencies of humans as repositories of organizational information and knowledge might suggest. Everyday observations make clear (a) that personnel turnover creates great losses of the human components of an organization's memory; (b) that nonanticipation of future needs for certain information results in great amounts of information not being stored or if stored not being easily retrieved; and (c) that information is often not shared by organizational members. For at least these reasons, organizational information and knowledge frequently are less available to decision makers than they would wish.

What are the effects of computer-assisted communication and decision-support technologies on the nature and quality of organizational memory? One answer to this question follows from the fact that more and more organizational activities are conducted or monitored using computer-assisted technology. For instance, it is possible to obtain and maintain information about the times necessary to carry out many organizational activities just as readily as it is to obtain and maintain information about the financial expenditures necessary to carry out the activities (e.g. times necessary to fabricate certain products, to receive shipments, to recruit or train employees, or to deliver services). With sufficient foresight such information can be readily indexed and retrieved through computer technology (Johansen, 1988). Although much organizational knowledge is computer-resident at some point, its users often do not recognize its potential usefulness for future decision making.

Another type of useful computer-resident information is information that is exchanged across the organizational boundaries. In the future, smart indexing (cf. Johansen, 1988) or artificial intelligence will facilitate retrieval of this transaction information and will result in computer-resident organizational memories with certain properties, such as completeness, that are superior to the human components of organizational memories. Ongoing increases in the friendliness and capability of computer-based information retrieval systems suggest that today and even more so in the future:

Proposition 8: Availability of computer-based activity and transaction-monitoring technologies leads to more frequent development and use of computer-resident data bases as components of organizational memories.

Research is needed to understand what incentives are necessary for those organizational members whose actions produce the data to share it or to maintain its quality.

Since much of what an organization learns through experience is stored in the minds of its members, many organizations nurture members who are expert with respect to an intellectual task such as (a) diagnosing quality problems or equipment malfunctions; (b) learning the identities of extraorganizational experts, influence peddlers, resource providers, or other useful nonmembers; and (c) locating information or resources that cannot be located using official, standard sources. As the processes for eliciting knowledge, building expert systems (Welbank, 1983), and validating information (O'Leary, 1988) become standardized, organizations are creating computer-based expert systems using the knowledge of their own experts (Rao and Lingaraj, 1988; Rauch-Hindin, 1988; Waterman, 1986). These expert systems have properties such as accessibility, reliability, and 'own-ability', that are both superior to humans and useful as components of organizational memories. Thus, even though expert systems have properties that are inferior to human experts, it seems reasonable to believe that:

> *Proposition 9: Availability of more robust and user-friendly procedures for constructing expert systems leads to more frequent development and use of in-house expert systems as components of organizational memories.*

How do experts react when asked to articulate knowledge and, perhaps, their secrets, so that these can be incorporated into software that might diminish their importance? How do local managers react in such a situation when their influence and status, which are derived from this information or knowledge, is lessened by giving others the ready access to expert systems possessing much of this local information or knowledge? What incentives are appropriate and effective for motivating experts to explicate their knowledge so that it can be used without their future involvement? These are questions in need of investigation.

Propositions 8 and 9 suggest that certain advanced information technologies increase the range of memory components for an organization, just as other advanced information technologies increase the range of media with which the organization can communicate its information and knowledge.

Effects on other design variables

Before leaving this discussion of organizational design variables, it seems useful to comment on the effects of advanced information technologies on some design variables that have not yet been explicitly mentioned: (a) horizontal integration, (b) formalization, (c) standardization, and (d) specialization. *Horizontal integration*, important as it is, requires little additional comment. Since it refers to the use of communication structures and processes for facilitating joint decision making among multiple units or individuals, the effects are the same as those discussed in Propositions 1, 2, and 3, and, as will be seen, in Proposition 14.

Formalization is used to ensure adherence to standards, especially when behavioral norms cannot be counted on to provide the desired behavior. Thus, early in the adoption of any new technology, because the required norms have not had time to develop and to take hold, the level of formalization is often high. (Of course, very early in adoption, standards might not exist, so control might not be exercised through either norms or formalization.) As the new technology becomes familiar and 'ages', it seems reasonable to believe that the degree of formalization associated with it approaches the degree of formalization associated with the technology being replaced. Consequently, the long-term effect of new technology on formalization might be nil. Although advanced information technology greatly facilitates the recording and retrieval of information about organizational events and activities and, thus, makes control of behaviors and processes through formalization more viable, the use of advanced information technology for closely controlling intelligence development and decision making has not been reported in the literature, to my knowledge. This may be due to the frequent need for initiative and non-routine activities by those engaged in these processes (cf. Wilensky, 1967). (For a discussion of the use of advanced information technology for controlling other behaviors and processes in organizations, see Zuboff, 1984.)

Standardization is the reduction of variability in organizational processes. As noted earlier, advanced information technologies have greatly increased the range of communication and decision procedures. If organizational members can use discretion when choosing which information technology to use (and such discretion seems commonplace), the variation of technologies will increase, and standardization will decrease: This is so apparent that no proposition is needed.

With regard to *specialization*, advanced information technology can either lead to the addition of job categories (e.g. computer programmer) or the deletion of job categories (e.g. bookkeeper), and, therefore, will affect the degree of specialization within the organization. However, such specialities support, make operational, or become part of technologies. The increase or decrease in the variety of support personnel has little or no impact on intelligence or decision making, independent of the technologies. For this reason, *specialization* was not discussed as a design variable that affects organizational intelligence and decision making.

Propositions 1 through 9 describe the effects that advanced information technologies have on those aspects of organizational design that, ultimately, influence organizational intelligence and decision making. The next section deals with more direct effects of the technologies on organizational intelligence and decision making and, ultimately, on organizational performance in these areas. Of course the development of organizational intelligence and the making of decisions are organizational processes inextricably intertwined with an organization's design. The present conceptual separation of these processes from design is primarily for expository purposes.

Effects on organizational intelligence and decision making

This section sets forth two propositions dealing with information acquisition and then three propositions concerned with decision making and decision authorization.

Environmental scanning and organizational intelligence

To some degree, all organizations scan their external and internal environments for information about problems or opportunities. Yet sometimes managers do not learn about problems or opportunities in time to act with maximum effectiveness. In many cases the alerting message is delayed as it moves through the sequential nodes in the communication network. In other instances incumbents of adjacent nodes in the communication network have difficulty connecting across time, as in 'telephone tag'. *What is the effect of advanced information technologies on these impediments? What is the effect on information acquisition overall?* With regard to these questions, recall that the reasoning surrounding Proposition 7 suggested that the use of computer-assisted information processing and communications technologies leads to rifle-shooting of messages and ultimately to fewer intermediary nodes in the information processing network. This idea, in combination with the fact that the probability and duration of message delay and the probability and extent of message distortion are both positively related to the number of sequential links in the communication chain connecting the receiver to the information source, suggests that use of computer-assisted information processing and communication technologies would facilitate rapid and accurate identification of problems and opportunities.

A contrary line of reasoning exists, however. Since an important role of many information network nodes is to screen, package, and interpret messages, the use of advanced information technologies and the consequent elimination of nodes can result in an overload of irrelevant, poorly packaged, or uninterpretable messages. One study indicated that this danger may not be as serious as it appears. Hiltz and Turoff (1985) found that social norms and management practices tend to develop to reduce the problem to a level below what might be imagined. It is likely that computer-assisted technologies will be used to enhance information retrieval, especially from lower organizational levels and outside sources. Thus, on balance:

> *Proposition 10: Use of computer-assisted information processing and communication technologies leads to more rapid and more accurate identification of problems and opportunities.*

Use of these technologies can aid not only in the identification of problems and opportunities, but also in a wide variety of more focused probes and data acquisitions for the purpose of analysis. Recalling Mintzberg *et al.*'s (1976) *active search*, and Mintzberg's (1975) notion that managers require timely information, consider that computer-assisted information systems can bring facts to the organization's decision makers almost immediately after the facts occur (e.g. check-out scanners and commodities market data).

Together, technologically advanced systems for the acquisition of external information and the development of computer-enhanced organizational memories enable organizations to increase the range of information sources that the producers and users of organizational intelligence can draw upon. Thus, in summary:

> *Proposition 11: Use of computer-assisted information storage and acquisition technologies leads to organizational intelligence that is more accurate, comprehensive, timely, and available.*

This proposition is based on the assumption that the external information sources are accurate, comprehensive, timely, and available. Otherwise, garbage in, garbage out.

A matter of some interest is how inclined information users are to employ accessible sources, rather than those with the highest quality information (cf. Culnan, 1983; O'Reilly, 1982). How computer-assisted communications and information acquisition systems affect the trade-off between perceived accessibility and perceived quality, and the resultant information-seeking behavior, is an issue much in need of investigation.

Decision making and decision authorization

It is reasonable to believe that the quality of an organizational decision is largely a consequence of both the quality of the organizational intelligence (as implied in Proposition 11) and the quality of the decision-making processes. Further, the discussion associated with Propositions 1 and 3 (and perhaps other of the propositions related to organizational design) strongly suggests that, by facilitating the sharing of information, computer-assisted communication technologies increase the quality of decision making, and that by aiding in the analysis of information within decision units, computer-assisted decision-aiding technologies increase the quality of decision making. Thus, in helping with Propositions 1, 3, and 11:

> *Proposition 12: Use of computer-assisted communication and decision-support technologies leads to higher quality decisions.*

Because reducing the number of levels involved in authorizing an action will reduce the number of times the proposal must be handled (activities of a logistical, rather than a judgmental nature), it seems likely that:

Proposition 13: Use of computer-assisted communication and decision-support technologies reduces the time required to authorize proposed organizational actions.

Authorization as a particular step in the decision-making process has received little attention from organizational scientists (for exceptions, see Carter, 1971; Gerwin, 1979), and the time required for organizations to authorize action also has received little attention (for exceptions, see Mintzberg *et al.*, 1976; Shumway *et al.*, 1975). These topics are worthy candidates for study in general, and the potential effects of information technology seem to be especially in need of examination, given their probable importance and the total absence of systematic research on their effect on decision authorization.

Once a problem or opportunity has been identified, several types of activities are undertaken that might be more effective if undertaken using advanced information technology. For example, management information systems and electronic mail might enable decision makers to immediately obtain the information they seek when deciding what to do about problems and opportunities (see Proposition 11). Decision-support systems might enable decision makers or their assistants to analyze this information quickly (at least for some types of problems). Electronic mail and video- or teleconferencing might help decision makers obtain clarification and consensus without the delays imposed by the temporary nonavailability, in terms of physical presence, of key participants (see Proposition 1). Finally, forms of advanced information technology might reduce the time required to authorize proposed organizational actions (see Proposition 13). These facts suggest that:

Proposition 14: Use of computer-assisted communication and decision-support technologies reduces the time required to make decisions.

Available evidence supports this proposition:

For instance, managers in the Digital Equipment Corporation reported that electronic mail increased the speed of their decision making and saved them about seven hours a week (Crawford, 1982). Managers at Manufacturers Hanover Trust reported that electronic mail saved them about three hours a week, mostly by eliminating unreturned phone calls and internal correspondence (Nyce and Groppa, 1983). (Sproull and Keisler, 1986, p.1492)

However, studies employing casual self-report data need to be supplemented with more systematic studies, such as some of those noted by Rice and Bair (1984). Sophisticated studies may find that the actual reduction in time is marginal, and that the net benefit may be offset to some extent by the losses in decision quality that may follow from a reduction in the time spent cogitating, as noted by Weick (1985).

Toward a conceptual theory

Extensive organizational use of advanced information technologies is too new, and systematic investigation of their use is too limited, for a theory of their effects to have evolved and received general acceptance. As a result, the propositions set forth here were not derived from a generally accepted theory. Instead, they were pieced together from organizational communication and information systems research, extrapolating only when it seemed reasonable.

A *theory* may be defined as a set of related propositions that specify relationships among variables (cf. Blalock, 1969, p.2; Kerlinger, 1986, p.9). The set of propositions set forth in this chapter, related to one another (at the very least) through their possessing a common independent variable, advanced information technology, passes this definitional test of a theory. Yet, more is expected from a theory, such as a framework that integrates the propositions.

If other connecting relationships can be found to link them, perhaps the propositions of this chapter can serve as building blocks for the development of a less atomistic, more conceptual theory. The result would, of course, be quite tentative, in that the propositions require additional substantiation and in that any one author's connective framework must be subjected to review, critique, and discussion across an extended period before gaining general acceptance. As a step in the development of a conceptual theory of the effects of advanced information technologies, the following concepts and constructs are offered. The constructs summarize and the concepts connect ideas that were mentioned previously but served a different purpose at the time.

Concept 1: Advanced information technologies have properties different from more traditional information technologies. *Availability of advanced information technologies* (Construct A) extends the range of communication and decision-making options from which potential users can choose. On occasion a technology will be chosen for use, and when chosen wisely – such that the chosen technology's properties better fit the user's task – use of the technology leads to improved task performance. This reinforcement in turn leads to more frequent *use of advanced information technology* (Construct B).

Concept 2: Use of advanced information technologies (Construct B) leads to more available and more quickly retrieved information, including external information, internal information, and previously encountered information, and thus leads to *increased information accessibility* (Construct C). Concept 2 follows from Propositions 1, 4, and 7 through 11.

Concept 3: Increased information accessibility (Construct C) leads to the *changes in organizational design* (Construct D). Concept 3 follows from Propositions 1 through 7.

Concept 4: Increased information accessibility (Construct C), and those *changes in organizational design* (Construct D) that increase the speed and effectiveness with which information can be converted into intelligence or

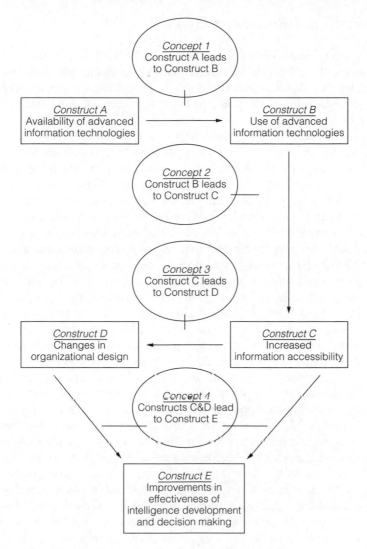

Figure 18.1   *Conceptual theory of the effects of advanced information technologies on organizational design, intelligence, and decision making*

intelligence into decisions, lead to organizational intelligence being more accurate, comprehensive, timely, and available and to decisions being of higher quality and more timely, decisions that lead to improvements in *effectiveness of intelligence development and decision making* (Construct E). Concept 4 follows from Propositions 11 through 14.

These constructs and concepts are summarized in Figure 18.1.

Summary and Recommendations

In the form of propositions and their corollaries, this chapter sets forth a theory concerning the effects that computer-assisted communication and decision-aiding technologies have on organizational design, intelligence, and decision making. Subsequently, the propositions were connected with constructs and concepts, and from these a more conceptual theory was developed.

Some boundaries on the original theory (here called *the theory*) were delineated early in the chapter. The theory is, nevertheless, a candidate for elaboration and expansion. For example, it was not possible, within the space available, to extend the scope of the theory to include propositions having to do with the effects of advanced information technologies on the distribution of influence in organizational decision making (see Zmud, in press). Examination of some relevant literature makes clear that numerous propositions would be necessary because (a) the technologies may vary in their usefulness for generating the particular types of information used by decision participants having different sources of influence, (b) the technologies may vary in their usefulness for enhancing the image or status of participants having different organizational roles, and (c) the technologies may vary in their usefulness to different types of participants as aids in the building of decision-determining coalitions. Certainly, the theory is a candidate for elaboration and expansion, just as it is a candidate for empirical testing and consequent revision.

The process used to generate the propositions comprising the theory included drawing on components of established organization theory and on findings from communication and information systems research. Specific suggestions were made, with respect to many of the propositions, about matters in need of empirical investigation. In addition to these specific suggestions, three somewhat more global recommendations are in order. The first is directed to any researchers exploring the effects of advanced information technologies. In this chapter, different forms of advanced information technology were discussed by name (e.g. electronic mail) yet the propositions were stated in general terms. This latter fact should not obscure the need to specify more precisely the particular technology of interest when developing hypotheses to be tested empirically. As more is learned about the effects of computer-assisted communication and decision-support technologies, it may be found that even subtle differences count (cf. the discussion by Markus and Robey, 1988). Even if this is not so, as researchers communicate about these matters among themselves and with administrators, it behooves them to be clear and precise about what it is that they are discussing.

The second suggestion, directed to organizational researchers, is to believe (a) that information technology fits within the domain of organization theory and (b) that it will have a significant effect on organizational design, intelligence, and decision making. Organization researchers, in general (there are always welcome exceptions), may not believe that these technologies fit within the domain of organization theory. This would be an erroneous belief. Organization theory has always been concerned with the processes of communication, coordination, and control and, as is apparent from the research of communication and information systems researchers (Culnan and Markus, 1987; Rice and Associates, 1984), the nature and effectiveness of these processes are changed when advanced information technologies are employed. Organizational researchers also may not have recognized that organizational designs are, at any point in time, constrained by the capability of the available communication technologies. Two of the infrequent exceptions to this important observation are cited by Culnan and Markus (1987):

> Chandler (1977) for example, argues that the ability of the telegraph to facilitate coordination enabled the emergence of the large, centralized railroad firms that became the prototype of the modern industrial organization. Pool (1983) credits the telephone with the now traditional physical separation of management headquarters from field operations, and in particular with the development of the modern office skyscraper as the locus of administrative business activity. (p.421)

Also, Huber and McDaniel (1986) state that:

> Without telephones, corporations could not have become as large as they have; without radios, military units would be constrained to structures and tactics different from those they now use; without computers, the processes for managing airline travel would be different from what they are. Any significant advance in information technology seems to lead eventually to recognition and implementation of new organizational design options, options that were not previously feasible, perhaps not even envisioned. (p.221)

Since information technologies affect processes that are central to organization theory, and since they also affect the potential nature of organization design (a principal application of organization theory), a corollary of this second global recommendation is added: Organizational researchers should study advanced information technology as (a) an intervention or jolt in the life of an organization that may have unanticipated consequences with respect to evolved organizational design, (b) a variable that can be used to enhance the quality (broadly defined) and timeliness of organizational intelligence and decision making, and (c) a variable that enables organizations to be designed differently than has heretofore been possible. (A review of recent discussions of emerging organizational and interorganizational forms [Borys and Jemison, 1989; Luke *et al.*, 1989; Miles and Snow, 1986; Nadler and Tushman, 1987] suggests that use of computer-assisted communication technologies can enhance the usefulness of such designs, requiring, as many will, communication among dispersed parties.)

The third global research recommendation is directed toward information systems researchers. It is straightforward. As is easily inferred by observing organizational practices, much information technology is intended to increase directly the efficiency with which goods and services are produced, for example, by replacing workers with computers or robots. But organizational effectiveness and efficiency are greatly determined by the quality and timeliness of organizational intelligence and decision making, and these, in turn, are directly affected by computer-assisted communication and decision-aiding technologies and are also indirectly affected through the impact of the technologies on organizational design. Therefore, it is likely that administrators will ask information systems researchers to help anticipate the effects of the technologies. In addition, builders and users of computer-assisted communication and decision-aiding technologies generally do not explicitly consider the effects that the technologies might have on organizational design, intelligence, or decision making. Thus, information systems researchers should arm themselves with the appropriate knowledge by increasing the amount of their research directed toward studying the effects that advanced information technologies have on organizational design, intelligence, and decision processes and outcomes.

References

Abernathy, W. M. (1971) Subjective estimates and scheduling decisions. *Management Science*, **18**, 80–88.

Benbasat, I. and Konsynski, B. (1988) Introduction to special section on GDSS. *Management Information Systems Quarterly*, **12**, 588–590.

Blalock, H. M., Jr. (1969) *Theory Construction: From Verbal to Mathematical Formulations*, Prentice-Hall, Englewood Cliffs, NJ.

Blau, P. M., Falbe, C. M., McKinley, W. and Tracey, P. K. (1976) Technology and organization in manufacturing. *Administrative Science Quarterly*, **21**, 20–40.

Borys, B. and Jemison, D. (1989) Hybrid arrangements as strategic alliances: Theoretical issues in organizational combinations. *Academy of Management Review*, **14**, 234–249.

Bourgeois, L. J. III, McAllister, D. W. and Mitchell, T. R. (1978) The effects of different organizational environments upon decision and organizational structure. *Academy of Management Journal*, **21**, 508–514.

Burgelman, R. A. (1982) A process model of internal corporate venturing in the diversified major firm. *Administrative Science Quarterly*, **28**, 223–244.

Carter, E. E. (1971) The behavioral theory of the firm and top-level corporate decisions. *Administrative Science Quarterly*, **16**, 413–428.

Carter, N. M. (1984) Computerization as a predominate technology: its influence on the structure of newspaper organizations. *Academy of Management
Journal*, **27**, 247–270.

Chandler, A. D., Jr. (1977) *The Visible Hand: The Managerial Revolution in
American Business*, Harvard University Press, Cambridge, MA.

Child, J. (1984) New technology and developments in management organization. *OMEGA*, **12**, 211–223.

Child, J. (1988) Information technology, organization, and response to strategic challenges. *California Management Review*, **30**(1), 33–50.

Child, J., and Partridge, B. (1982) *Lost Managers: Supervisors in Industry
and Society*, Cambridge University Press, Cambridge, MA.

Cohen, M. D., March, J. G. and Olsen, J. P. (1972) A garbage can model of
organizational choice. *Administrative Science Quarterly*, **17**, 1–25.

Crawford, A. B., Jr. (1982) Corporate electronic mail – a communication-
intensive application of information technology. *Management Information
Systems Quarterly*, **6**, 1–14.

Culnan, M. J. (1983) Environmental scanning: the effects of task complexity
and source accessibility on information gathering behavior. *Decision Sciences*, **14**, 194–206.

Culnan, M. J. and Markus, L. (1987) Information technologies: electronic media
and intraorganizational communication. In *Handbook of Organizational
Communication* (eds F. M. Jablin *et al.*), Sage, Beverly Hills, pp.420–444.

Daft, R. L. and Lengel, R. H. (1984) Information richness: a new approach to
managerial information processing and organizational design. In *Research
in Organizational Behavior* (eds B. M. Staw and L. L. Cummings), JAI
Press, Greenwich, CT, pp.191–233.

Daft, R. L. and Lengel, R. H. (1986) Organizational information requirements,
media richness, and structural design. *Management Science*, **32**, 554–571.

Daft, R. L., Lengel, R. H. and Trevino, L. K. (1987) Message equivocality,
media selection and manager performance: implications for information
systems. *Management Information Systems Quarterly*, **11**, 355–368.

Dawson, P. and McLaughlin, I. (1986) Computer technology and the redefinition of supervision. *Journal of Management Studies*, **23**, 116–132.

Drucker, P. (1987) Advice from the Dr. Spock of business. *Business Week*,
28 September, 61–65.

Duncan, R. B. (1973) Multiple decision-making structures in adapting to
environmental uncertainly. *Human Relations*, **26**, 273–291.

Duncan, R. B. (1974) Modifications in decision structure in adapting to
the environment: some implications for organizational learning. *Decision
Sciences*, **5**, 705–725.

Fayol, H. (1949/1916) *General and Industrial Management* (Constance Storrs,
trans.), Pitman, London.

Feldman, M. and March, J. (1981) Information in organizations as signal and symbol. *Administrative Science Quarterly*, **26**, 171–186.

Foster, L. W. and Flynn, D. M. (1984) Management information technology: its effects on organizational form and function. *Management Information Systems Quarterly*, **8**, 229–236.

Fulk, J. and Dutton, W. (1984) Videoconferencing as an organizational information system: assessing the role of electronic meetings. *System, Objectives, and Solutions*, **4**, 105–118.

Fulk, J., Steinfield, C. W., Schmitz, J. and Power, J. G. (1987) A social information processing model of media use in organizations. *Communication Research*, **14**, 529–552.

Gerwin, D. (1979) Towards a theory of public budgetary decision making. *Administrative Science Quarterly*, **14**, 33–46.

Gibson, C. F. and Jackson, B. B. (1987) *The Information Imperative*, Heath, Lexington, MA.

Hiltz, S. R. and Turoff, M. (1978) *The Network Nation: Human Communication via Computer*, Addison-Wesley, Reading, MA.

Hiltz, S. R. and Turoff, M. (1985) Structuring computer-mediated communication systems to avoid information overload. *Communications of the ACM*, **28**, 680–689.

Hofer, C. W. (1970) Emerging EDP patterns. *Harvard Business Review*, **48**(2), 16–31, 168–171.

Huber, G. (1982) Organizational information systems: determinants of their performance and behavior. *Management Science*, **28**, 135–155.

Huber, G. (1984) The nature and design of post-industrial organizations. *Management Science*, **30**, 928–951.

Huber, G. (1988) Effects of decision and communication technologies on organizational decision processes and structures. In *Organizational Decision Support Systems* (eds R. M. Lee *et al.*), North-Holland, Amsterdam, pp.317–333.

Huber, G. and McDaniel, R. (1986) Exploiting information technology to design more effective organizations. In *Managers, Micros, and Mainframes* (ed. M. Jarke), Wiley, New York, pp.221–236.

Jewell, L. N. and Reitz, H. J. (1981) *Group Effectiveness in Organizations*, Scott, Foresman, Glenview, IL.

Johansen, R. (1984) *Teleconferencing and Beyond*, McGraw-Hill, New York.

Johansen, R. (1988) *Groupwave: Computer Support for Business Teams*, Free Press, New York.

Kahneman, D., Slovic, P. and Tversky, A. (eds) (1982) *Judgment Under Uncertainty: Heuristics and Biases*. Cambridge University Press, Cambridge, UK.

Kelley, G. (1976) Seducing the elites: the politics of decision making and innovation in organizational networks. *Academy of Management Review*, **1**, 66–74.

Kerlinger, F. N. (1986) *Foundations of Behavioral Research*, Holt, Rinehart and Winston, New York.

Kerr, E. B. and Hiltz, S. R. (1982) *Computer-Mediated Communication Systems: Status and Evaluation*, Academic Press, New York.

Kidd, J. S. (1970) The utilization of subjective probabilities in production planning. *Acta Psychologica*, **34**, 338–347.

Kowitz, A. C. and Knutson, T. J. (1980) *Decision Making in Small Groups: The Search for Alternatives*, Allyn and Bacon, Boston, MA.

Lee, R. M., McCosh, A. and Migliarese, P. (1988) *Organizational Decision Support Systems*, North-Holland, Amsterdam.

Luke, R. D., Begun, J. W. and Pointer, D. D. (1989) Quasi firms: strategic interorganizational forms in the health care industry. *Academy of Management Review*, **14**, 9–19.

Markus, M. L. (1984) *Systems in Organizations: Bugs and Features*, Pitman, Marshfield, MA.

Markus, M. L. and Robey, D. (1988) Information technology and organizational change: conceptions of causality in theory and research. *Management Science*, **34**, 583–598.

Meyer, A. D. and Goes, J. B. (1988) Organizational assimilation of innovations: a multilevel contextual analysis. *Academy of Management Journal*, **31**, 897–923.

Miles, R. and Snow, C. (1986) Organizations: new concepts for new forms. *California Management Review*, **28**(3), 62–73.

Miller, D. and Droge, C. (1986) Psychological and traditional determinants of structure. *Administrative Science Quarterly*, **31**, 539–560.

Mintzberg, H. (1975) The manager's job: folklore and fact. *Harvard Business Review*, **53**(4), 49–61.

Mintzberg, H., Raisinghani, D. and Théorêt, A. (1976) The structure of 'unstructured' decision processes. *Administrative Science Quarterly*, **21**, 246–275.

Nadler, D. and Tushman, M. L. (1987) *Strategic Organization Design*, Scott, Foresman, Glenview, IL.

Nisbett, R. and Ross, L. (1980) *Human Inference: Strategies and Shortcomings of Social Judgment*, Prentice-Hall, Englewood Cliffs, NJ.

Nyce, H. E. and Groppa, R. (1983) Electronic mail at MHT. *Management Technology*, **1**, 65–72.

O'Leary, D. E. (1988) Methods of validating expert systems. *Interfaces*, **18**(6), 72–79.

Olson, M. and Lucas, H. C. (1982) The impact of office automation on the organization: some implications for research and practice. *Communications of the ACM*, **25**, 838–847.

O'Reilly, C. A. (1982) Variations in decision makers' use of information sources: the impact of quality and accessibility of information. *Academy of Management Journal*, **25**, 756–771.

Palme, J. (1981) *Experience with the Use of the COM Computerized Conferencing System*, Forsvarets Forskningsanstalt, Stockholm, Sweden.

Pfeffer, J. (1978) *Organizational Design*, AHM, Arlington Heights, IL.

Pfeffer, J. and Moore, W. L. (1980) Power in university budgeting: a replication and extension. *Administrative Science Quarterly*, **19**, 135–151.

Pool, I. de Sola (1983) *Forecasting the Telephone: A Retrospective Assessment*, Ablex, Norwood, NJ.

Porter, M. E. (1980) *Competitive Strategy: Techniques for Analyzing Industries and Competitors*, Free Press, New York.

Rao, H. R. and Lingaraj, B. P. (1988) Expert systems in production and operations management: classification and prospects. *Interfaces*, **18**(6), 80–91.

Rauch-Hindin, W. B. (1988) *A Guide to Commercial Artificial Intelligence*, Prentice-Hall, New York.

Rice, R. E. (1980) The impacts of computer-mediated organizational and interpersonnel communication. In *Annual Review of Information Science and Technology*, Vol. 15 (ed. M. Williams), Knowledge Industry Publications, White Plains, NY, pp.221–249.

Rice, R. E. (1984) Mediated group communication. In *The New Media* (eds R. E. Rice and Associates), Sage, Beverly Hills, CA, pp.129–154.

Rice, R. E. and Associates (1984) *The New Media*, Sage, Beverly Hills, CA.

Rice, R. E. and Bair, J. H. (1984) New organizational media and productivity. In *The New Media* (eds R. E. Rice and Associates), Sage, Beverly Hills, CA, pp.185–216.

Rice, R. E. and Case, D. (1983) Electronic message systems in the university: a description of use and utility. *Journal of Communication*, **33**, 131–152.

Robey, D. (1977) Computers and management structure. *Human Relations*, **30**, 963–976.

Sabatier, P. (1978) The acquisition and utilization of technical information by administrative agencies. *Administrative Science Quarterly*, **23**, 396–417.

Sammon, W. L., Kurland, M. A. and Spitalnic, R. (1984) *Business Competitor Intelligence: Methods for Collecting, Organizing, and Using Information*, Wiley, New York.

Shukla, R. K. (1982) Influence of power bases in organizational decision making: a contingency model. *Decision Sciences*, **13**, 450–470.

Shumway, C. R., Maher, P. M., Baker, M. R., Souder, W. E., Rubenstein, A. H. and Gallant, A. R. (1975) Diffuse decision making in hierarchical organizations: an empirical examination. *Management Science*, **21**, 697–707.

Souder, W. E. (1972) A scoring methodology for assessing the suitability of management science models. *Management Science*, **18**, B526–B543.

Special Report (1983a) A new era for management. *Business Week*, 25 April, 50–64.

Special Report (1983b) How computers remake the manager's job. *Business Week*, 25 April, 68–76.

Special Report (1984) Office automation. *Business Week*, 8 October, 118–142.

Special Report (1988) The portable executive. *Business Week*, 10 October, 102–112.

Sprague, R. H. and McNurlin, B. C. (1986) *Information Systems Management in Practice*, Prentice-Hall, Englewood Cliffs, NJ.

Sprague, R. H. and Watson, H. J. (1986) *Decision Support Systems: Putting Theory into Practice*, Prentice-Hall, Englewood Cliffs, NJ.

Sproull, L. and Keisler, S. (1986) Reducing social context cues: electronic mail in organizational communication. *Management Science*, **32**, 1492–1512.

Steinfield, C. W. and Fulk, J. (1987) On the role of theory in research on information technologies in organizations: an introduction to the special issue. *Communication Research*, **14**, 479–490.

Strassman, P. (1985a) *Information Payoff: The Transformation of Work in the Electronic Age*, Free Press, New York.

Strassman, P. (1985b) Conversation with Paul Strassman. *Organizational Dynamics*, **14**(2), 19–34.

Svenning, L. and Ruchinskas, J. (1984) Organizational teleconferencing. In *The New Media* (eds R. E. Rice and Associates), Sage, Beverly Hills, CA, pp.217–248.

Trevino, L. K., Lengel, R. and Daft, R. L. (1987) Media symbolism, media richness, and media choice in organization: a symbolic interactionist perspective. *Communication Research*, **14**, 553–574.

Vroom, V. H. and Yetton, P. W. (1973) *Leadership and Decision-making*, University of Pittsburgh, Pittsburgh, PA.

Waterman, D. A. (1986) *A Guide to Expert Systems*, Addison-Wesley, Reading, MA.

Weick, K. E. (1985) Cosmos vs. chaos: sense and nonsense in electronic contexts. *Organizational Dynamics*, **14**(2), 50–64.

Welbank, M. (1983) *A Review of Knowledge Acquisition Techniques for Expert Systems*, Martlesham Consultancy Services, Ipswich, UK.

Whisler, T. (1970) *Impact of Computers on Organizations*, Praeger, New York.

Wilensky, H. L. (1967) *Organizational Intelligence*, Basic Books, New York.

Williams, F. and Rice, R. E. (1983) Cummunication research and the new media technologies. In *Communication Yearbook 7* (ed. R. N. Bostrom), Sage, Beverly Hills, CA, pp.200–225.

Witte, E. (1972) Field research on complex decision-making processes – the phase theorem. *International Studies of Management and Organization*, **2**, 156–182.

Zmud, R. W. (1983) *Information Systems in Organizations*, Scott, Foresman, Glenview, IL.

Zmud, R. W. (in press) Opportunities for manipulating information through new technology. In *Perspectives on Organizations and New Information Technology* (eds J. Fulk and C. Steinfield), Sage, Beverly Hills, CA.
Zuboff, S. (1984) *In the Age of the Smart Machine*, Basic Books, New York.

Reproduced from Huber, G. P. (1990) A theory of the effects of advanced information technologies on organizational design, intelligence, and decision making. *Academy of Management Review*, **15**(1), 47–71. Reprinted with permission of the publishers, Academy of Management, Pace University, New York.

Questions for discussion

1   Consider the author's classification of technology into the basic characteristics of data storage, transmission, and processing capacity, and properties of communication and decision aiding. Would you add anything to this classification?
2   Consider your experience with electronic mail and compare this to the propositions. Does email increase participation? If yes, what are the results of such increased participation? Does email enable 'communication that otherwise would be unlikely to occur'. Does email increase 'information sources' but decrease the 'size of the decision unit'? Does email change the number of meetings held or the nature of meetings?
3   The author suggests that decision-aiding technologies will lead to greater centralization in companies that were decentralized and greater decentralization in centralized companies. Discuss how the opposite might occur. What have your experiences been?
4   The author states 'because the technologies facilitate the vertical distribution of information and knowledge, there is more commonality of information and knowledge across organizational levels'. What are some barriers to this?
5   The author considers the influence of IT on certain organization processes, what are some other organizational factors, beyond the scope of the current chapter, that IT has shaped?
6   If the propositions in the chapter are correct, what are the implications, if any, for organizational performance?

19 Information Technology and Organizational Culture

Understanding information culture: integrating knowledge management systems into organizations

D. E. Leidner

Knowledge management initiatives to help organizations create and distribute internal knowledge have become important aspects to many organizations' strategy. The knowledge-based theory of the firm suggests that knowledge is the organizational asset that enables sustainable competitive advantage in hypercompetitive markets. Systems designed to facilitate knowledge management (knowledge management systems) are being implemented in an attempt to increase the quality and speed of knowledge creation and distribution in organizations. However, such systems are often seen to clash with corporate culture and, as a result, have limited impact. This chapter introduces a framework for assessing those aspects of organizational culture that are likely to be the source of implementation challenges. In so doing, it associates various organizational subunit cultures with different information cultures, and presents a series of propositions concerning the relationships among individual, organizational, and information cultures.

1 Introduction

When asked about why the organization was building a worldwide Intranet and knowledge management system, the Chief Knowledge Officer of a large multinational consulting firm replied: 'We have 80 000 people scattered around the world that need information to do their jobs effectively. The information they needed was too difficult to find and, even if they did find it, often inaccurate. Our Intranet is meant to solve this problem' (Leidner, 1998). Roughly a decade ago, case studies of organizations implementing executive information systems (EIS) suggested that a major reason behind these systems was a need for timely, accurate, and consistent information and to help managers cope with the problem of information overload (Rockart and DeLong, 1988; Houdeshel and Watson, 1987). And although a goal of management information systems (MIS) was to provide relevant information for managerial control and planning, MIS were unable to provide timely, complete, accurate, and readable data of the type executives needed for strategic decision making. Even earlier, in 1967, Ackoff notes that 'I do not deny that most managers lack a good deal of information that they should have, but I do deny that this is the most important information deficiency from which they suffer. It seems to me that they suffer from an overabundance of irrelevant information'. Interestingly, in 1997, Courtney *et al.* state that 'omitting the unimportant information [from corporate intranets] may be as important as concentrating on the important. The mere availability of "information" may have a distracting effect. . . .'. Is information systems' history repeating itself over and over again in a continuous cycle of providing more information in greater detail in a more timely manner in a more graphical format, yet forever doomed to be providing 'too much irrelevant' information while leaving the important information 'too hard to find'? Or, is it that each time progress is made on one front, new forms of barriers to the impact of IS are encountered? Alternatively, has the real culprit in IS's seeming failure to impact organizational effectiveness not yet been discovered?

Recommended approaches to helping ensure that information systems result in organizational improvements have included structuring information systems requirements analysis (Yourdan and Constantine, 1978), involving users in analysis (King and Rodriguez, 1981; Ives and Olson, 1984), attempting to link IT to the business strategy (Pyburn, 1983), and improving change agentry skills (Markus and Benjamin, 1996). The latter is reproduced in this collection as Chapter 6. All of the approaches merit consideration, as do contingency theories which would suggest that the success of information systems (IS) in an organization depends upon the proper fit of IT to the organization's structure and design. Yet despite the prescriptive advice, information-based systems still seem to fail to live up to expectations and often fail to provide the dramatic improvements in organizational effectiveness for which they are designed (Lyytinen and Hirschheim, 1987; Mowshowitz, 1976).*

---

* The term 'information-based' is meant to distinguish systems designed to provide managers with information from systems designed to improve communication (such as GSS and electronic mail) and systems designed to improve transactions (such as MRP and ERP).

Moreover, there appears to be almost a crisis in the image of IS in organizations, with such problems as high CIO turnover, executives not recognizing the strategic importance of IS, and declining top management commitment to large IS investments.

This chapter offers a new exegesis to the reasons why information-based systems appear to be encountering the same problems repeatedly despite significant advances in planning and implementation methodologies and theories, as well as in the technology itself: an incongruity with corporate culture. The chapter posits that information systems implementation efforts must take into account corporate culture when designing the plan for change; if not, such systems might produce results, some anticipated others not, but the systems will fall way short of providing the major improvements expected in most large systems implementation efforts.

This chapter first traces briefly information-based systems advancements and the dominant organizational paradigms used to investigate the organizational effects of IS, and will then examine current developments in information-based systems, namely knowledge management systems. It will show how these systems in particular call for a new paradigm of interpretation, that of organizational culture theory. It will introduce the notion of information culture in the context of knowledge management systems and will present a brief overview of the relevant work on organizational culture. The chapter offers the existence of information culture as a framework for assessing those aspects of organizational culture that are likely to be the source of implementation challenges. Propositions will be offered concerning the relationship between organizational subunit culture and information culture and these will be tied to managerial prescriptions on managing the implementation of knowledge management systems.

2 Advances in information systems

Information systems can be classified in several ways, including according to their broad function, to the organizational function they serve, to the underlying technologies, or to the organizational level at which they are used (Laudon and Laudon, 1997). Here, we will consider information systems by broad function since much of the IT literature focuses on particular systems classified in this manner, such as decision support systems, expert systems, and electronic mail. In particular, we are interested in systems designed to provide information to managers and professionals at any organizational level. Hence, we will focus primarily on MIS and EIS (as both systems aim to supply managerial information) and knowledge management systems (a new line of systems oriented to providing professionals and managers unstructured information).

2.1   MIS and the structuring of organizations

As noted in Somogyi and Galliers (1987) in Chapter 1, as firms began to computerize in the 1950s, the first applications were in the area of transaction processing. Transaction processing systems are computerized systems that perform and record the daily routine transactions necessary to the conduct of business such as payroll, sales order entry, shipping, order tracking, accounts payable, material movement control (Laudon and Laudon, 1997). These systems were designed to facilitate data collection and to improve the efficiencies of organizational transactions. Soon thereafter, with advances in programming languages, databases, and storage, systems oriented toward providing performance information to managers emerged (Somogyi and Galliers, 1987). MIS are computer-based information systems that provide managers with reports and, in some cases, with on-line access to the organization's current performance and historical records. MIS primarily serve the functions of planning, controlling, and decision making at the management level. Generally, they condense information obtained from transaction processing systems and present it to management in the form of routine summary and exception reports.

Simon (1977) predicted that computers, namely MIS, would recentralize decision making, shrink line organizational structures, decrease the number of management levels, and result in an increase in the number and size of staff departments. It was believed that information technology would enable greater centralization of authority, clearer accountability of subordinates, a sharper distinction between top management and staff, and the rest of the organization, and a transformation of the planning and innovating functions. The organizational theory used to evaluate the effect of MIS on organizations was contingency theory of organizational structure, technology, and the environment. Research prior to 1970 indicated that IT provided a means of collecting and processing large amounts of data and information, thus enabling a small number of persons effectively to control authority and decision making; hence, IT was said to facilitate centralization (Klatzky, 1970; Whisler, 1970; Stewart, 1971). Research after 1970 seemed to find that IT, by enabling organizations to gather and process information rapidly, facilitated decentralizing decision making (Carter, 1984; Foster and Flynn, 1984; Dawson and McLaughlin, 1986). For example, Carter (1984) felt that as the extent of computer utilization increased in subunit applications, the locus of decision-making authority would become more decentralized in the organization, and the division of labor as reflected by functional diversification, functional specialization and functional differentiation would increase. Carter found in her study of newspaper organizations that as computers become the predominant technology, upper management was released from the day-to-day encumbrances of centralized decision making, fostering a decentralized organizational structure. In other cases IT appeared to have had no effect when changes were expected (Franz *et al.*, 1986). Considering the weak relationships found when using technology as an independent variable, other researchers employed technology as a moderator variable between the environment and structure, or as a dependent variable. Robey (1977) found that IT supported an existing decentralized structure in organizations with uncertain environments but that in more stable environments, IT strengthened a centralized authority structure.

In summary, early research on the impact of IT, namely MIS, on organizations focused on the effect of IT on organizational structures. The results were highly mixed, leading to an emergent imperative which argued that the particular effects of IT were dependent on a given organization's context and, hence, were not predictable or systematic across organizations. An alternative perspective was that certain inherent limitations of MIS prevented predictable improvements to organizational effectiveness. Among the limitations of MIS are that they have highly limited analytical capabilities, they are oriented almost exclusively to internal, not environmental or external, events, and that the information content is fixed and not tailored to individual users (Laudon and Laudon, 1997).

2.2 DSS, EIS and organizational decision making

Decision support systems (DSS) and executive information systems (EIS) aimed to provide what MIS were unable to: specific online information relevant to decision makers in a flexible format. DSS are interactive model-oriented systems, and are used by managers and knowledge workers, analysts, and professionals whose primary job is handling information and making decisions (Keen and Morton, 1982; Sprague and Carlson, 1982). DSS assist management decision making by combining data, sophisticated analytical models, and user-friendly software into a single powerful system that can support semi-structured or unstructured decision making (Keen and Morton, 1982; Sprague and Carlson, 1982). DSS tend to be isolated from major organizational information systems and tend to be stand-alone systems developed by end-user divisions or groups not under central IS control (Hogue, 1987). EIS are computer-based information systems designed to provide managers access to information relevant to their management activities. Originally designed for senior managers, the systems quickly became popular for managers at all levels. Unlike DSS which are tied to specific decisions and which have a heavy emphasis on models, EIS focus on the retrieval of specific information, particularly daily operational information that is used for monitoring organizational performance. Features distinguishing EIS from such systems as MIS and decision support systems include a non-keyboard interface, status-access to the organizational database, drill-down analysis capabilities (the incremental examination of data at different levels of detail), trend analysis capabilities (the examination of data across desired time intervals), exception reporting, extensive graphics, the providing of data from multiple sources, and the highlighting of the information an executive feels is critical (Kador, 1988; Mitchell, 1988). Whereas the traditional focus of MIS was on the storage and processing of large amounts of information, the focus of EIS is on the retrieval of specific information about the daily operational status of an organization's activities as well as specific information about competitors and the marketplace (Friend, 1986).

Huber (1990) advanced a theory of the effects of advanced decision- and information-providing technologies, such as DSS and EIS, on organizational decision making. While he also made propositions concerning the effect of such systems on organizational design and structure, the dominant paradigm for examining the organizational effects of information technology was turning towards decision making. Huber and McDaniel (1986) argued that decision making was the most critical management activity and that the effectiveness of IS rested more in facilitating organizational decision making than enabling structural responses to environmental uncertainty. A wide body of research emerged examining organizational decision making and the decision-making consequences of IS. However, most of the IS literature focused on the individual level of analysis, which was reasonable given that DSS were designed in most cases for individual decision makers, and most of the EIS research also supported individual rather than organizational improvements.*

While some of Huber's propositions have been substantiated (Leidner and Elam, 1995; Molloy and Schwenk, 1995), the organizational level effects have received little substantiation and have been overshadowed by the individual level effects (Elliott, 1992). Moreover, research on DSS showed that decision makers used the tools in such a manner as to reduce time, but not necessarily to increase quality (Todd and Benbasat, 1991), but in the cases where the systems did appear to increase quality, the decision makers seemed not to perceive subjectively this improvement (Le Blanc and Kozar, 1990). Empirical evidence has shown that EIS enable faster decision making, more rapid identification of problems, more analysis before decision making, and greater understanding of the business (Leidner and Elam, 1995; Elliott, 1992). Evidence also suggests that EIS allow single- and double-loop learning (Vandenbosch and Higgins, 1996). Other promises for EIS, which have not been empirically substantiated, involved helping companies cope with

---

* Group Decision Support System (GDSS) research examines the impact of GDSS on groups; however, GDSS are less about information provision than they are about providing tools for brainstorming and structuring group meetings. Hence, the term GSS (group support system) is commonly used to refer to IT designed to facilitate communication in groups.

reduced staff levels (Applegate, 1987; Applegate and Osborn, 1988), substantial monetary savings (Holub, 1988), power shifts and a change in business focus (Applegate and Osborn, 1988), and improving service (Holub, 1988; Mitchell, 1988; Kador, 1988). Interestingly, these promises sound reminiscent of the promises that were made for MIS and that are now being made for Intranets, as will be discussed later.

Among the most serious challenges to EIS implementation involved overcoming information problems, namely organizational subunits feeling ownership of information that was suddenly being accessed by senior managers who previously had relied on these subunits to summarize and analyze their own performance in periodic reports. Such ownership problems led to system failure in some cases, when subunits consciously and covertly altered data to be more favorable to the unit and thereby rendered the EIS inaccurate (Leidner, 1992). Other weaknesses of EIS are the difficulty of pulling information from multiple sources into a graphical PC-based interface, justifying the costs of the systems given the unclear payoff, and ensuring that the information remains relevant as the needs of managers changes (Leidner, 1992). In summary, DSS and EIS research adopted an organizational decision-making paradigm as a reference theory for determining the organizational impacts of these systems. While the systems have well-documented individual level benefits, the organizational level benefits have been less lucid.

2.3 Knowledge management systems and organizational culture

A new line of systems based on web technology has emerged which compensates for some of the limitations of EIS, namely the difficulty of integrating information across platforms. These systems return control for information content to organizational subunits, hence bypassing some of the informational problems encountered with EIS, yet also require active participation of users not only in the design process, but also in the process of information provision. Corporate intranets are private web-based networks, usually within a corporation's firewalls, that connect employees to vital corporate information. They let companies speed information and software to employees and business partners (Thyfault, 1996; Vidal *et al.*, 1998). The primary incentive is their ability to provide 'what computer and software makers have frequently promised but never actually delivered: the ability to pull all the computers, software, and databases that dot the corporate landscape into a single system that enables employees to find information wherever it resides' (Cortese, 1996). While there is a business case for the value of intranets, there is little proof of the economic value of such systems (Rooney, 1997).

Among the most lauded potential applications of intranets is the provision of tools for knowledge management. Knowledge includes the insights, understandings, and practical know-how that employees possess. Knowledge management is a method of systematically and actively managing ideas, information, and knowledge of employees. Knowledge management systems refer to the use of modern information technologies (e.g. the Internet, intranets, extranets, browsers, data warehouses, software filters and agents) to systematize, enhance, and expedite intra- and inter-firm knowledge management (Alavi and Leidner, 1998). Knowledge management systems (KMS) are intended to help organize, interpret, and make widely accessible the expertise of an organization's human capital to help the organization cope with turnover, rapid change, and downsizing. KMS are being built in part from increased pressure to maintain a well-informed, productive workforce.

The concept of systematically coding and transmitting knowledge in organizations is not new – training and employee development programs have served this function for years. The integration of such explicit knowledge involves few problems because of its inherent communicability (Grant, 1996). Explicit knowledge is that knowledge which is transmitted in formal systematic language (Nonaka, 1994). It is externally documented tacit knowledge (Brown and Duguid, 1991). It is declarative and procedural knowledge which can be divorced from the context in which it is originally created and transferred to various other contexts with little if any modification. Advances in information technology have greatly facilitated the integration of explicit knowledge through increasing the ease with which explicit knowledge can be codified, communicated, assimilated, stored, and retrieved (Huber, 1991). However, what has in the past proved elusive – that context-dependent knowledge obtained by professional workers (referred to as 'tacit knowledge' [Nonaka, 1994]) – is the focus of KMS. Figure 19.1 classifies knowledge creation into tacit and explicit, based on Nonaka (1994).

Nonaka focused on knowledge creation, although the knowledge management process must give equal attention to knowledge storage, knowledge distribution, and knowledge integration in order to achieve significant organizational improvements (Alavi and Leidner, 1998). Indeed, the major challenge of tacit knowledge is less its creation than its integration (Grant, 1996; Davenport, 1997a); such knowledge is of limited organizational value if it is not shared. With KMS, it is not sufficient that users use the system, they must actively contribute their knowledge. This is a large departure from previous information systems where user involvement was needed primarily at the analysis and design phase, not the content provision phase. Moreover, such systems make information readily available at a low cost across functions and business units, hence implying the capacity for an integration of information even if the functions and units themselves remain unintegrated.

While there is not yet empirical evidence of the organizational impacts of KMS, preliminary descriptive research suggests that KMS may require a change in organizational culture and that the values and culture of an organization have a significant impact on the learning process and how effectively a company can adapt and change (Sata, 1989). Respondents in the Alavi

From

Tacit   to   Explicit

Tacit	Socialization	Internalization
to		
Explicit	Externationlization	Combination

Figure 19.1 *The knowledge-creation process (From Nonaka, 1994)*

and Leidner (1998) study suggested that the information and technology components of knowledge management constituted only 20 per cent of the challenge, whereas overcoming organizational cultural barriers accounted for the major part of effective knowledge management initiatives. Similarly, over half the respondents in Skyrme and Amidon (1997) recognize that corporate culture represents the biggest obstacle to knowledge transfer, and a similar proportion believe that changing people's behaviors represents the biggest challenge to its continuing management.

Junnarkar and Brown (1997) suggest that knowledge managers interested in the role of IT as an enabler of knowledge management should not simply focus on how to connect people with information but how to develop an organizational environment conducive to tacit knowledge sharing. Similarly, Newman (1997) sees information hoarding behavior resulting from perceptions of the strategic value of information. His modified Johari Window (see Figure 19.2) provides a view of when individuals are likely to cooperate and when they are unlikely to do so.

Poor communication between people can be a major barrier to learning. In many organizations, information and knowledge are not considered organizational resources to be shared, but individual competitive weapons to be kept private (Davenport, 1997b). Organizational members may share personal knowledge with a certain trepidation – the perceived threat that they are of less value if their knowledge is part of the organizational public domain. Research in organizational learning and knowledge management suggests that some facilitating conditions include trust, interest, and shared language (Hanssen-Bauer and Snow, 1996), fostering access to knowledgeable members (Brown and Duguid, 1991), and a culture marked by autonomy, redundancy, requisite variety, intention, and fluctuation (Nonaka, 1994).

Hence, in understanding the potential impact of KMS on organizations, it is first necessary to understand the cultural implications of such systems. We

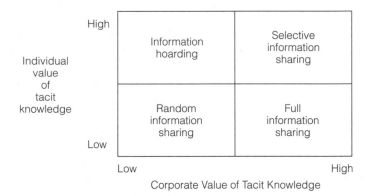

	Known to you	Known to others
High strategic impact	Protect and develop	Cooperate
Low strategic impact	Share	Ignore

Figure 19.2   *The Johari Window (From Newman, 1998)*

High

Individual value of tacit knowledge	Information hoarding	Selective information sharing
	Random information sharing	Full information sharing

Low

Low   High

Corporate Value of Tacit Knowledge

Figure 19.3   *Information culture matrix*

would argue that the division of knowledge creation into tacit versus explicit, while interesting, does little to advance our understanding of the users' view of the knowledge or information included in KMS. The Johari Window of knowledge sharing likewise does not explicitly deal with the users' view of their own knowledge (except to classify apparent knowledge as 'high or low in strategic value', although it is unclear if this is of value to the individual, organization, or both). If we consider the user as a contributor of information to the KMS, we can think of information as having a certain value to the user as an individual asset and a certain degree of value as a corporate asset. This is depicted in a simple matrix in Figure 19.3.

According to Figure 19.3, we would expect certain individuals to share knowledge willingly, others to hoard knowledge, others to be indifferent (labeled random sharing), and others to engage in selective sharing. Moreover, it should be noted that certain types of knowledge will be viewed differently than other types of knowledge. For example, explicit knowledge such as a company training manual is unlikely to be perceived as valuable as an individual asset. However, the very type of knowledge that KMS are designed to amalgamate – tacit knowledge such as lessons learned on a project – is likely to be the type of knowledge with the greatest potential for being viewed as an individual asset. One could try to classify various categories of knowledge into the four quadrants; for our propositions, we will consider the primary challenge of knowledge management to be that of fostering the sharing of tacit knowledge.

Based on the above discussion and Figure 19.3, we would venture the following propositions:

> *Proposition 1. Individuals perceiving their tacit knowledge to be high in individual value and high in corporate value will engage in selective sharing, sharing that knowledge which might bring recognition and reward to them but concealing that knowledge which might be successfully used by others with no reward for them.*
> *Proposition 2. Individuals perceiving their tacit knowledge to be high in individual value and low in corporate value will engage in information hoarding, choosing to avoid sharing their knowledge but attempting to learn as much as possible from others.*
> *Proposition 3. Individuals perceiving their tacit knowledge to be low in individual value and high in corporate value will engage in information sharing, sharing freely with others for the benefit of the organization.*
> *Proposition 4. Individuals perceiving their tacit knowledge to be low in individual value and low in corporate value will engage in random sharing, sharing freely when their knowledge is requested but not consciously sharing otherwise.*

In determining the factors that might influence information culture (i.e. the perceptions on the value of tacit knowledge to the individual and to the organization), an understanding of corporate culture is in order. This will be discussed in Section 3.

2.4   Summary

New classes of information systems for managers and professionals are continuing to emerge, yet the perennial problem of obtaining systematic benefits from such systems remains. IS researchers have attempted to explain the impact of IS on organizations by considering the effect of IS on organizational structure and decision making. The former line of research led to mixed findings and the latter, findings more at the individual than organizational level. With the changes in systems, summarized in Table 19.1, the role

Table 19.1 *Summary of information-based systems*

	MIS	DSS	EIS	KMS
Purpose	Provide summarized performance reports to management	Provide tools, models, and data for aid in decision analysis	Provide online access to real-time financial and operational information	Provide online access to unstructured information and knowledge throughout the organization
Users	Managers at various levels	Analysts and middle managers	Senior and middle managers	Professionals and managers throughout an organization
Role of users	Participation in design	Participation as designer, active user	Participation in design, active user	Participation in design, active user, content provider
Information strategy	One-for-all	One-for-one	One-for-one	Anyone, anytime, anywhere
Interpretive framework	Organizational structure	Organizational decision making	Organizational decision making	Organizational culture

MIS = management information systems; DSS = design support systems; EIS = executive information systems; KMS = knowledge management systems.

of the user has progressed from involvement in system design (MIS), to in many cases system designer (DSS), to interactive system user (EIS), to information content provider (KMS). This shift in the role of the user requires a concomitant shift in our conceptualization of information systems with less emphasis on the 'systems' aspect and more on the 'information' aspect, namely the users' view of information as an individual or corporate asset. Information has been classified according to its accuracy, timeliness, reliability, completeness, precision, conciseness, currency, format, accessibility, and perceived usefulness (Delone and McLean, 1992). Previous systems' design focused on these aspects as the foundation of information quality. What is missing is an understanding of the information culture issue. As we have seen, the latest class of systems requires far greater activity of users in not just information requirements processes, but in supplying information for the system.

Moreover, we seem to have moved from a 'one-for-all' to a 'one-for-one' to an 'anyone anytime anywhere' information provision strategy as we have advanced from MIS to DSS and EIS, to KMS. The latter strategy requires greater horizontal and vertical integration of information in an organization. It is arguable that the potential impact of systems is greater when a larger part of the organization is affected, such as with systems integrated organization-wide, or even across organizations. Yet the greater the required integration, the greater the potential implementation difficulties. As the degree of horizontal integration increases, we would expect structural constraints. For example, enterprise-wide systems are transaction-based systems which most effectively operate in environments with horizontal coordination. In organizations where little horizontal coordination existed, i.e. where units were highly decentralized, we would expect greater implementation challenges than in already centralized organizations. Likewise, vertical integration is expected to pose control challenges. In loosely formalized organizations, for example, email systems would not be expected to pose threats to power distributions (in that employees can easily communicate upward without hesitation), but in rigidly formalized organizations, the possibility of lower level employees by-passing individuals in the hierarchy via electronic communication might create difficulties. Systems requiring both vertical and horizontal integration will create the greatest cultural challenges for organizations (Figure 19.4). We will next examine organizational culture and its implication for KMS implementation.

3 Organizational culture and its implication for KMS

Schein (1985) defines organizational culture as 'the set of shared, taken-for-granted implicit assumptions that a group holds and that determine how it perceives, thinks about, and reacts to its various environments'. Burack (1991) defines culture as the 'organization's customary way of doing things and the

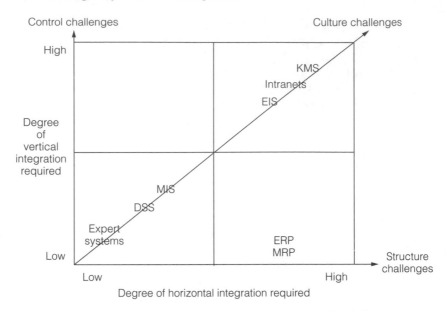

Figure 19.4   *Systems and organizational integration (KMS = knowledge management systems; EIS = executive information systems; MIS = management information systems; DSS = design support systems)*

philosophies and assumptions underlying these', and Johnson (1992), as 'the core set of beliefs and assumptions which fashion an organization's view of itself'. These are similar to Hofstede's (1980, 1991) definition of national culture as the 'collective programming of the mind that distinguishes one group of people from another'. Culture is hence viewed as a shared mental model which influences how individuals interpret behaviors and behave themselves, often without their being aware of the underlying assumptions. Schein (1985) states that the members of a culture are generally unaware of their own culture until they encounter a different one.

Culture is manifested in rituals and routines, stories and myths, symbols, power structures, organizational structures, and control systems (Johnson, 1992). Whereas a wealth of inconclusive contingency research examines the appropriate structure and technology in various environments to maximize organizational effectiveness, we are only now beginning to see research aimed at determining the contribution of organizational culture to organizational effectiveness. Part of the reason for this has been the difficulty of categorizing and measuring organizational cultures. Furthermore, there may have been an unstated view that cultures evolve and are beyond the control of organizational decision makers; hence, research focused on more malleable constructs such as structure, technology and decision making processes.

In the organizational culture literature, culture is examined either as a set of assumptions or as a set of behaviors. Behaviors, or norms, are a fairly visible manifestation of the mental assumptions, although some argue that the behaviors should be considered 'organizational climate' and the norms, as comprising organizational culture.* We will present a brief discussion of both the values and behavioral perspectives of culture.

3.1 The value view

Denison and Mishra (1995) studied the impact of organizational culture on organizational effectiveness and looked for a broad set of cultural traits that were linked to effectiveness in various environments. Denison and Mishra suggested that, from a values perspective, culture could be thought of as including degrees of external versus internal integration and tradeoffs of change and flexibility with stability and direction. They classified cultures as being adaptability oriented, involvement oriented, mission oriented, or consistency oriented. Their classification is drawn from Quinn and Rohrbaugh's (1983) value set which argued that organizations focus to various degrees internally or externally, and, in terms of structure preferences, have tradeoffs in stability and control versus flexibility and change.

Denison and Mishra found that in two of four organizations studied, organizational effectiveness appeared to be tied to consistency and mission, yet the cases also seemed to support the idea that involvement oriented cultures led to organizational effectiveness. In a survey, Denison and Mishra found that mission and consistency, traits of stability, predicted profitability, whereas involvement and adaptability, traits of flexibility, predicted sales growth.

Chatman and Jehn (1994) argue that organizational cultures within a given industry tend to deviate very little; in other words, they argue that the environment dictates to a certain extent cultures in organizations (at least for organizations that survive in the industry). A problem with Denison and Mishra's study is its inability to consider the effect of the environment on cultures, given that there was not sufficient industrial variation in the sample. Thus, we are unable to deduce if the environment might have influenced their findings.

Hofstede *et al.* (1990) examined culture both in terms of values and behaviors. In terms of value, they found that organizational culture was tied to the national culture dimensions identified by Hofstede (1980) and reflected preferences for centralized versus decentralized decision making (power distance), preferences for the degree of formalization of routines (uncertainty avoidance), degree of concern over money and career versus family and

---

* See Denison (1996) for a thorough review of the subtle differences between culture and climate.

cooperation (masculinity/femininity dimension), and degree of identification with the company and preference for individual versus group reward systems (collectivistic/individualistic dimension). When the authors eliminated the effects due to nationality, the value differences between organizations were primarily dependent upon subunit characteristics rather than overall membership in the organization. Hence, the authors concluded that organizational subunits were the more appropriate level of analysis for organizational culture study. Moreover, they found that behaviors were a better means of distinguishing subunit cultures than were value systems.

3.2   The behavioral perspective

Although popular literature insists that shared values represent the core of organizational culture, the empirical data from Hofstede *et al.* (1990) showed that shared perceptions of daily practices formed the core of organizational subunit culture. The behavioral dimensions isolated by the authors were:

1   *Process vs. results oriented*. This dimension refers to a focus on improving the means by which organizational goals are achieved (process) as opposed to a focus on the attainment of goals.
2   *Employee vs. job oriented*. Employee orientation suggests a concern for people, whereas a job orientation refers to a concern over performing tasks effectively.
3   *Parochial vs. professional*. A parochial orientation suggests that individuals are loyal to their organization, whereas a professional orientation suggests that individuals are loyal to their profession.
4   *Open vs. closed system*. This dimension describes the communication climate in the subunit.
5   *Loose vs. tight control*. The control dimension reflects the degree of internal structuring, with loose organizations having few written or unwritten codes of behavior and tight organizations having strict unwritten and written policies.
6   *Normative vs. pragmatic*. Pragmatic units are market driven and customer oriented, whereas normative units are product oriented. Interestingly, some units were found to be pragmatic but not results oriented (i.e. a goal of improving customer service might not imply a goal of improving the bottom line).

The process/results, parochial/professional, loose/tight, and normative/pragmatic were found to relate partly to the industry, confirming Chatman and Jehn's (1994) conclusion that industry or environmental factors more generally affect organizational cultures, whereas the employee/job orientation

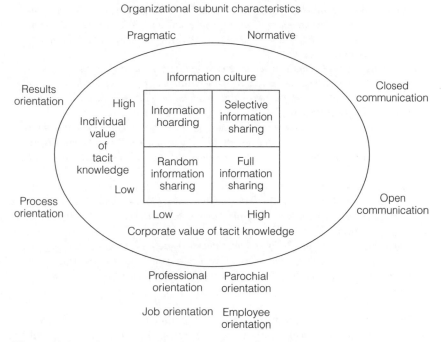

Figure 19.5 *Subunit and information culture relationship*

and open/closed system were more determined by the philosophy of the founders and senior managers. These latter dimensions might therefore be more malleable.

In considering the possible influence of the behavioral dimensions of subunit culture on information culture, one dimension in particular appears more relevant to predicting the quality of the knowledge contributed to a system rather than to predicting the value placed on the knowledge. Specifically, loose versus tight control might influence whether individuals follow organizational rules and procedures about sharing knowledge but would not necessarily influence their beliefs about whether the knowledge was properly theirs or the organization's and, hence, might influence the quality of the knowledge they elected to contribute to a system but would not likely influence their attitude about the value of that knowledge to them or the organization. We therefore do not include this dimension in predictions about the influence of subunit culture on information culture. If we map the remaining dimensions into Figure 19.4 to form Figure 19.5, we might expect that certain of these subunit cultural behaviors would tend to foster the view of tacit knowledge as an individual asset, whereas others would encourage viewing tacit knowledge as a corporate asset.

Proposition 5. Individuals in subunits characterized by a results orientation will view tacit knowledge largely as an individual asset, whereas individuals in subunits characterized by a process orientation will view tacit information less as an individual asset.

Proposition 6. Individuals in subunits characterized by a professional orientation will view tacit knowledge less as a corporate asset, whereas individuals in subunits characterized by a parochial orientation will view tacit knowledge more as a corporate asset.

Proposition 7. Individuals in subunits characterized by an open communication culture will view tacit knowledge less as an individual asset, whereas individuals in subunits characterized by a closed communication climate will view tacit knowledge more as an individual asset.

Proposition 8. Individuals in subunits characterized by a pragmatic culture will view tacit knowledge less as a corporate asset, whereas individuals in subunits characterized by a normative culture will view tacit knowledge more as a corporate asset.

Proposition 9. Individuals in subunits characterized by an employee culture will view tacit knowledge more as a corporate asset, whereas individuals in subunits characterized by a job orientation will view tacit knowledge less as a corporate asset.

The above propositions are intended to predict the possible influence of subunit cultural factors on information culture. A final consideration will be the dimension of culture at the individual level, as discussed next.

3.3　Individual cultures

Although Hofstede *et al.* (1990) discount the utility of considering culture at the individual level, others propose that individual level cultures interact either synchronously or disharmoniously with organizational culture (Patterson *et al.*, 1996; Chatman and Barsade, 1995). Chatman and Barsade (1995) examined individual level culture in organizations using the individualistic/collectivistic dimension of culture which has been the topic of extensive communication research at the individual level of analysis (Gudykunst *et al.*, 1996).

Individualism versus collectivism was first identified by Hofstede (1980) as a dimension distinguishing national cultures. Individualism is the preference for a loosely knit social framework in society in which individuals are supposed to take care of themselves and their immediate family as opposed to collectivism in which there is a larger in-group to which is given unquestioning loyalty (Hofstede, 1980). Individualism is related to a low-context communication style wherein individuals prefer information to be stated directly and exhibit a preference for quantifiable detail, whereas collectivism is related to a high-context communication style in which individuals prefer to draw inferences from non-explicit or implicit information (Hall, 1976;

Gudykunst, 1997). In individualistic cultures, the needs, values, and goals of the individual take precedence over the needs, values, and goals of the in-group. In collectivistic cultures, the needs, values, and goals of the in-group take precedence over the needs, values, and goals of the individual (Gudykunst, 1997; Hofstede, 1980). Research suggests that those who are associated with individualistic values tend to be less concerned with self-categorizing, are less influenced by group memberships, and have greater skills in entering and leaving new groups than individuals from collectivist cultures (Hofstede, 1980; Hall, 1976). Individualistic values are associated with preferences for individual rewards (or a norm of justice, meaning that an individual is rewarded according to his/her input rather than a norm of equality in which all individuals who work as a group are rewarded equally) (Gudykunst and Ting-Toomey, 1988).

Earley (1994) argued that organizations could also be thought of as being dominantly individualistic or collectivist. Organizations encouraging individuals to pursue and maximize their goals and rewarding performance based on individual achievement would be considered as having an individualistic culture, whereas organizations placing priority on collective goals and joint contributions and rewards for organizational accomplishments would be considered collectivist (Chatman and Barsade, 1995).

On an individual level, Chatman and Barsade (1995) propose that workplace cooperation – the willful contribution of employee effort to the successful completion of interdependent tasks – is as much dependent on individual culture as organizational culture. They suggest that individuals with cooperative dispositions place priority on working together with others towards a common purpose, while persons with a low cooperative disposition place priority on maximizing their own welfare irrespective of others. Cooperative persons are more motivated to understand and uphold group norms and expect others to cooperate, whereas individualistic people are more concerned with personal goals and expect others to behave in like manner. Chatman and Barsade (1995) proposed that people who have a high disposition to cooperate and who work in a collectivistic organizational culture will be the most cooperative, while people who have a low disposition to cooperate and who work in an individualistic culture will be the least cooperative. This may suggest that individualistic cultures are results oriented and tend to be closed, whereas cooperative cultures are process oriented and tend to be open. It might be that cooperative people in a cooperative culture could be more willing to share tacit knowledge than individualistic individuals in a cooperative culture or cooperative individuals in an individualistic culture. When mapped into Figure 19.4, we would expect the following influence of individual culture on information culture (Figure 19.6).

If we consider the relationship between individual level culture, subunit culture, and information culture, we propose the following:

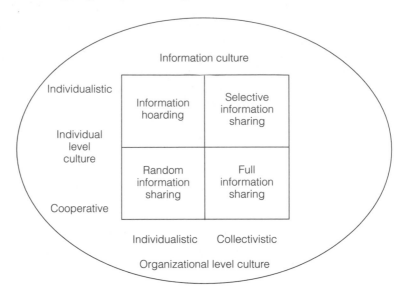

Figure 19.6   *Individual culture's relationship to information culture*

Proposition 10. Individualistic individuals in collectivistic organizational subunits will engage in selective sharing of tacit knowledge.
Proposition 11. Cooperative individuals in collectivistic organizational subunits will engage in full sharing of tacit knowledge.
Proposition 12. Individualistic individuals in individualistic organizational subunits will engage in hoarding of tacit knowledge.
Proposition 13. Cooperative individuals in individualistic organizational subunits will engage in random sharing of tacit knowledge.

3.4   Summary

This section has presented a brief summary of organizational subunit cultures and has made propositions concerning the relationship of subunit culture and individual culture with the information culture discussed in Section 2. The propositions, in abbreviated form, are summarized in Table 19.2.

The above propositions reflect an organizational imperative – that organizational factors, in this case organizational subunit and individual culture, influence the successful implementation and use of knowledge management systems. It is also conceivable that KMS will affect organizational cultures (a technology imperative). There is evidence that as systems integrate information vertically and horizontally, organizational cultures are altered. For example, in the case of EIS, it has been found that by virtue of the fact that top managers are viewing detailed daily information previously viewed in monthly

Table 19.2 *Summary of propositions*

Nature of Proposition	Proposition number	Proposition (abbreviated)
Information culture	1	Individuals perceiving their tacit knowledge as high in individual and corporate value will engage in selective sharing of tacit knowledge.
	2	Individuals perceiving their tacit knowledge as high in individual and low in corporate value will engage in information hoarding.
	3	Individuals perceiving their tacit knowledge as low in individual and high in corporate value will engage in full sharing.
	4	Individuals perceiving their tacit knowledge as low in individual and corporate value will engage in random sharing.
Organizational subunit culture influence on information culture	5	Results, as opposed to process, oriented subunits will foster a view of tacit knowledge as an individual asset.
	6	Parochial, as opposed to professional, oriented cultures will foster a view of tacit knowledge as a corporate asset.
	7	Closed, as opposed to open, subunit communication climates will foster a view of tacit knowledge as an individual asset.
	8	Normative, as opposed to pragmatic, oriented cultures will foster a view of tacit knowledge as a corporate asset.
	9	Employee, as opposed to job, oriented cultures will foster a view of tacit knowledge as a corporate asset.
Individual and organizational culture influence on information culture	10	Individualistic individuals in collectivistic cultures will engage in selective sharing of tacit knowledge.
	11	Cooperative individuals in collectivistic cultures will engage in full sharing of tacit knowledge.
	12	Individualistic individuals in individualistic cultures will engage in hoarding of tacit knowledge.
	13	Cooperative individuals in individualistic cultures will engage in random sharing of tacit knowledge.

or weekly reports in a summarized fashion, all levels in the organization take notice of the information being tracked by the senior managers and alter their behavior in such a manner as to focus on the measures being examined by the top managers. In some cases, this was part of a planned attempt to help focus the attention of employees on the factors considered most critical by the top managers (Carlsson *et al.*, 1996). Over time, the underlying values might shift to be become consistent with the new behavior. KMS are being implemented in a time of increasing global competition and the need to be 'flexible'; as such, part of the implementation goal may be directed toward enabling a more flexible, adaptable culture. In this case, by implementing the system and inculcating desired sharing behaviors, over time the organizational culture may itself become more open, flexible, and employee oriented. However, this chapter purports to evaluate the constraints posed by organizational culture on the implementation of KMS, rather than the potential long-term consequences of KMS on organizational culture. The latter interesting question is left for future research.

4   Implications and conclusion

It can be argued that the first step in developing an implementation plan is understanding where barriers might be encountered and why. The above analysis is intended to help evaluate where and why such barriers might exist when implementing KMS. Several strategies for KMS implementation have been suggested: one strategy is to include information of high value such as corporate directories which make users comfortable with, and dependent upon, the corporate intranet. Another is education on the need and potential of such a system to improve individual productivity and customer service. Another commonly used strategy is providing rewards and incentives, such as bonuses, based on the amount and quality of knowledge one contributes. The strategy used to implement KMS should be tied to the organizational subunit culture. For example, individuals in reward-oriented subunits might respond well to incentive systems, whereas individuals in process-oriented subunits might require greater education and training on the benefits of such a system. Furthermore, changes in reward systems will do little to change the information culture; in which case, at most, we would expect that subunit cultures which foster a view of knowledge as a high individual asset (results-oriented, professional-oriented subunits) will be able to encourage selective information sharing but not the full sharing of the most valuable of tacit knowledge. To obtain full sharing in subunits that are results oriented, closed, professional oriented, and job oriented, the change management plan might need to focus first on changing the culture and only secondly, on implementing the system. It would be misleading to think that the system would encourage full sharing in organizations where the information culture ran contrary to such sharing, just as it has been found that electronic mail systems do not encourage greater communication among subunits with infrequent, irregular communication (Vandenbosch and Ginzberg, 1997). However, in organizations with cultures that foster the attitude of tacit knowledge as primarily a corporate asset, it would be expected that KMS could be implemented with little resistance.

This chapter has taken the view that organizational effectiveness in the highly competitive global environment will depend largely on an organization's capacity to manage individual employee knowledge. We have argued that knowledge management systems will be important computer-based information system components to such effectiveness, but that the success of these systems will depend on an appropriate match with organizational subunit and individual culture. We have offered propositions in an attempt to provide a framework for understanding where potential incongruity between these new IS and organizational culture might exist.

One way to consider the advances of information-based systems in organizations is to consider the dominant organizational theory underlying the assumptions of the need for information. The era of MIS can be thought to correspond to the organizational theory termed the 'information processing view of the organization'. This view posited that organizations process information to reduce uncertainty – the absence of information, and to reduce equivocality – the existence of multiple and conflicting interpretations about an organizational situation (Daft and Lengel, 1986). According to this view, information systems are needed to help organizations understand the environment and make appropriate plans in response. As DSS and EIS came into vogue, so was the information-processing view of the firm replaced with the decision-making view of the firm espoused by Huber and McDaniel (1986) wherein decision making was seen as the most critical managerial activity. This view placed the primary purpose of IS as supporting organizational decision makers by providing tools, timely information, and ready access to important operational and financial information. More recently, it is being argued that the most critical organizational activity is creating, sharing, and utilizing the knowledge that resides in employees (Nonaka, 1994). To understand the potential organizational effect of systems designed to harness knowledge, it is argued that the traditional paradigms of structure and decision making are insufficient, but a perspective incorporating organizational culture is needed.

The major intent of this chapter has been to encourage thinking about the important topic of current IS and its relationship to organizational culture, rather than to offer a complete set of guidelines on implementing KMS or evaluating the effectiveness of KMS in given organizational cultures. It is hoped that the reader leaves with a framework for assessing the potential conflicts resulting from cultural factors that may arise with the implementation of knowledge management systems, and can use the frameworks proposed herein to guide thinking on potential implementation strategies.

References

Ackoff, R. L. (1967) Management misinformation systems. *Management Science*, **14**(4), 147–156.

Alavi, M. and Leidner, D. (1998) Knowledge management systems: emerging views and practices from the field. Working paper, University of Maryland.

Applegate, L. M. (1987) Lockheed-Georgia Company: executive information systems. *Harvard Case (9-187-147)*, Harvard Business School, Boston, MA.

Applegate, L. M. and Osborn, C. S. (1988) Phillips 66 Company: executive information systems. *Harvard Case (9-189-006)*, Harvard Business School, Boston, MA.

Brown, J. S. and Duguid, P. (1991) Organizational learning and communities-of-practice: toward a unified view of working, learning, and innovation. *Organization Science*, **2**(1), 40–57.

Burack, E. (1991) Changing the company culture – the role of human resource development. *Long Range Planning*, **24**(1), 88–95.

Carlsson, S., Leidner, D. E. and Elam, J. J. (1996) Individual and organizational effectiveness: perspectives on the impact of ESS in multinational organizations. In *Implementing Systems for Supporting Management Decisions* (eds. P. Humphreys *et al.*), Chapman and Hall, London.

Carter, N. M. (1984) Computerization as a predominate technology: its influence on the structure of newspaper organizations. *Academy of Management Journal*, June, 247–270.

Chatman, J. A. and Barsade, S. G. (1995) Personality, organizational culture, and cooperation: evidence from business simulation. *Administrative Science Quarterly*, **40**, 423–443.

Chatman, J. and Jehn, K. (1994) Assessing the relationship between industry characteristics and organizational culture: how different can you be? *Academy of Management Journal*, **37**(3), 522–553.

Cortese, A. (1996) Here comes the Intranet. *Business Week*, 26 February, 76–84.

Courtney, J., Crosdell, D. and Paradice, D. (1997) Lockean inquiring organizations: guiding principles and design guidelines for learning organizations. *Proceedings of the 1997 America's Conference on Information Systems*, http://hsb.baylor.edu/ramsower/ais.ac.97/papers/courtney.htm.

Daft, R. L. and Lengel, R. H. (1986) Organizational information requirements, media richness and structural design. *Management Science*, **32**(5), 554–571.

Davenport, T. H. (1997a) Knowledge management at Ernst and Young, 1997. URL: http://knowman.bus.utexas.edu/E&Y.htm.

Davenport, T. H. (1997b) Some principles of knowledge management. URL: http://knowman.bus.utexas.edu/kmprin.htm.

Dawson, P. and McLaughlin, I. (1986) Computer technology and the redefinition of supervision: a study of the effects of computerization on railway freight supervisors. *Journal of Management Studies*, **23**, 116–132.

Delone, W. H. and McLean, E. R. (1992) Information systems success: the quest for the dependent variable. *Information Systems Research*, March, 60–95.

Denison, D. (1996) What IS the difference between organizational culture and organizational climate? A native's point of view on a decade of paradigm wars. *Academy of Management Review*, **21**(3), 619–654.

Denison, D. and Mishra, A. (1995) Toward a theory of organizational culture and effectiveness. *Organization Science*, **6**(2), 204–223.

Earley, P. C. (1994) Self or group? Cultural effects of training on self-efficacy and performance. *Administrative Science Quarterly*, **39**, 89–117.

Elliott, D. (1992) Executive information systems: their Impact on executive decision making. Doctoral dissertation, The University of Texas at Austin, May.

Foster, I. W. and Flynn, D. M. (1984) Management information technology: its effects on organizational form and function. *MIS Quarterly*, December, 229–236.

Franz, C., Robey, D. and Koeblitz, R. (1986) User response to an online IS: a field experiment. *MIS Quarterly*, **10**(1), 29–44.

Friend, D. (1986) Executive Information Systems: successes, failures, insights and misconceptions. *D55-86 Transactions* (ed. J. Fedorowicz), 35–40.

Grant, R. M. (1996) Prospering in dynamically-competitive environments: organizational capability as knowledge integration. *Organization Science*, **7**(4), 375–387.

Gudykunst, W. B. (1997) Cultural variability in communication. *Communication Research*, **24**(4), 327–348.

Gudykunst, W. B., Matsumoto, Y., Ting-Toomey, S., Nishida, T., Linda, K. S. and Heyman, S. (1996) The influence of cultural individualism-collectivism, self construals, and individual values on communication styles across cultures. *Human Communication Research*, **22**, 510–543.

Gudykunst, W. B. and Ting-Toomey, S. (1988) *Culture and Interpersonal Communication*, Sage, Newbury Park, CA.

Hall, E. T. (1976) *Beyond Culture*, Anchor Books/Doubleday, Garden City, NJ.

Hanssen-Bauer, J. and Snow, C. C. (1996) Responding to hypercompetition: the structure and processes of a regional learning network organization. *Organization Science*, **7**(4), 413–437.

Hofstede, G. (1980) *Culture's Consequences*, Sage, Beverly Hills, CA.

Hofstede, G. (1991) *Cultures and Organizations: Software of the Mind*, McGraw-Hill, London.

Hofstede, G., Neuijen, B., Ohayv, D. D. and Sanders, G. (1990) Measuring organizational cultures: a qualitative and quantitative study across twenty cases. *Administrative Science Quarterly*, **35**, 286–316.

Hogue, J. T. (1987) A framework for the examination of management involvement in decision support systems. *Journal of Management Information Systems*, **4**(1).

Holub, A. (1988) What happens when info regarding the quality of a bank's services becomes visible. *EIS Conference Report*, **1**(4), 1–2.

Houdeshel, G. and Watson, H. J. (1987) The MIDS system at Lockheed-Georgia. *MIS Quarterly*, **11**(1) March, 127–140.

Huber, G. P. (1990) A theory of the effects of advanced information technologies on organizational design, intelligence, and decision making. *Academy of Management Review*, **15**(1), 47–71.

Huber, G. (1991) Organizational learning: the contributing processes and the literatures. *Organization Science*, **2**(1), 88–115.

Huber, G. P. and McDaniel, R. R. (1986) The decision-making paradigm of organizational design. *Management Science*, **32**(5), 572–589.

Ives, B. and Olson, M. (1984) User involvement and MIS success: a review of research. *Management Science*, **30**(5), 586–603.

Johnson, G. (1992) Managing strategic change – Strategy, culture and action. *Long Range Planning*, **25**(1), 28–36.

Junnarkar, B. and Brown, C. V. (1997) Re-assessing the enabling role of IT in knowledge management. *Journal of Knowledge Management*, **1**(2), 142–148.

Kador, J. (1988) ESSs keep execs in control. *Planner*, **11**(2), 10–14.

Keen, P. G. W. and Scott Morton, M. S. (1982) *Decision Support Systems: An Organizational Perspective*, Addison-Wesley, Reading, MA.

King, W. and Rodriguez, J. (1981) Participative design of strategic DSS. *Management Science*, **27**(6), 717–726.

Klatzky, S. R. (1970) Automation, size, and the locus of decision making: the cascade effect. *Journal of Business*, **43**, 141–151.

Laudon, K. and Laudon, J. (1997) *Essentials of Management Information Systems*, 2nd edn, Prentice-Hall, Englewood Cliffs, NJ.

Le Blanc, L. A. and Kozar, K. A. (1990) An empirical investigation of the relationship between DSS usage and system performance: a case study of a navigation support system. *MIS Quarterly*, **14**, 263–277.

Leidner, D. E. (1998) Personal interview.

Leidner, D. E. (1992) Reasons for EIS failure: an analysis by phase of development. Working paper, Baylor University, TX.

Leidner, D. E. and Elam, J. J. (1995) The impact of executive information systems on organizational design, intelligence, and decision making. *Organization Science*, **6**(6), 645–665.

Lyytinen, K. and Hirschheim, R. (1987) Information systems failures –
a survey and classification of the empirical literature. *Oxford Surveys in
Information Technology*, **4**, 257–309.

Markus, M. L. and Benjamin, R. (1996) Change agentry – the next IS frontier.
MIS Quarterly, **20**(4), 385–408.

Mitchell, P. (1988) An EIS is good for you. *EIS Conference Report*, **1**(4), 4.

Molloy, S. and Schwenk, C. (1995) The effects of IT on strategic decision
making. *Journal of Management Studies*, **32**(5), 283–311.

Mowshowitz, A. (1976) *Information Processing in Human Affairs*, Addison-
Wesley, Reading, MA.

Newman, V. (1997) Redefining knowledge management to deliver competitive advantage. *Journal of Knowledge Management*, **1**(2), 123–128.

Nonaka, I. (1994) A dynamic theory of organizational knowledge creation.
Organization Science, **5**(1), 14–37.

Patterson, M., Payn, R. and West, M. (1996) Collective climates: a test of
their sociopsychological significance. *Academy of Management Journal*,
28(6), 1675–1691.

Pyburn, P. (1983) Linking the MIS plan with corporate strategy. *MIS Quarterly*, June, 1–14.

Quinn, R. E. and Rohrbaugh, J. (1983) A spatial model of effectiveness
criteria: towards a competing values approach to organizational analysis.
Management Science, **29**(3), 363–377.

Robey, D. (1977) Computers and management structure: some empirical
findings re-examined. *Human Relations*, **30**, 963–976.

Rockart, J. and DeLong, D. (1988) *Executive Support Systems: The Emergence of Top Management Computer Use*, Dow-Jones-Irwin, Illinois.

Rooney, P. (1997) Imposing order from chaos. *INTRANETS*, **2**(8), Computerworld Supplement.

Sata, R. (1989) Organizational Learning – the key to management innovation.
Sloan Management Review, Spring, 63–74.

Schein, E. (1985) *Organizational Culture and Leadership*, Jossey-Bass, San
Francisco, CA.

Schein, E. (1996) Culture: the missing concept in organization studies.
Administrative Science Quarterly, **41**, 229–240.

Simon, H. A. (1977) *The New Science of Management Decision*, Prentice-
Hall, Englewood Cliffs, NJ.

Skyrme, D. J. and Amidon, D. (1997) *Creating the Knowledge-Based Business*, Business Intelligence Limited, London.

Somogyi, E. K. and Galliers, R. D. (1987) Applied information technology: from data processing to strategic information systems. *Journal of
Information Technology*, **2**(1), 30–41. Reproduced in Galliers, R. D. and
Baker, B. S. H. (eds.) (1994), *op cit.*, under the title Information technology
in business: from data processing to strategic information systems, 9–27.

Sprague, R. H. and Carlson, E. D. (1982) *Building Effective Decision Support Systems*, Prentice-Hall, Englewood Cliffs, NJ.

Stewart, R. (1971) *How Computers Affect Management*, MIT Press, Cambridge, MA.

Thyfault, M. E. (1996) The intranet rolls in. *Information Week*, **564**(15), 76–78.

Todd, P. and Benbasat, I. (1991) An experimental investigation of the impact of computer-based decision aids on decision making strategies. *Information Systems Research*, June, 87–115.

Vandenbosch, B. and Ginzberg, M. J. (1996/97) Lotus notes and collaboration: plus ça change. *Journal of Management Information Systems*, **13**(3), 65–82.

Vandenbosch, B. and Higgins, C. (1996) Information acquisition and mental models: an investigation into the relationship between behavior and learning. *Information Systems Research*, June, 198–214.

Vidal, F., Saintoyant, P. Y. and Meilhaud, J. (1998) *Objectif Intranet: Enjeux et Applications*, Les Editions d'Organisation, Paris.

Whisler, T. L. (1970) *The Impact of Computers on Organizations*, Praeger Publishers, New York.

Yourdan, E. and Constantine, L. L. (1978) *Structured Design*, 2nd edn, Yourdan Press, New York.

Questions for discussion

1   Do you agree or disagree with the assumption that culture is an important impediment (or facilitator) of effective IT implementation? What are some situations you have experienced that confirm or disconfirm this assumption?

2   Consider the likely reaction of colleagues you have worked with to a system such as KMS. What type of reaction would you expect? What types of incentives would be necessary to encourage information sharing?

3   Consider the assumption that KMS will only be effective if full information sharing occurs. Do you agree or disagree with this assumption? What would be the characteristics of an effective KMS?

4   Consider the organizational culture of organizations where you have worked. How important was culture to your satisfaction, motivation, and job performance? Which aspects of culture were most important? Which aspects of culture would be most important toward ensuring the success of systems such as KMS?

20 Information Technology and Organizational Performance

Beyond the IT productivity paradox

L. P. Willcocks and S. Lester

Despite the massive investments in Information Technology in the developed economies, the IT impact on productivity and business performance continues to be questioned. This chapter critically reviews this IT productivity paradox debate and finds that an important part, but by no means all, of the uncertainty about the IT payoff relates to weaknesses in measurement and evaluation practice. Based on extensive research by the authors and others, an integrated systems lifecycle approach is put forward as a long term way of improving evaluation practice in work organizations. The approach shows how to link business and IT/IS strategies with prioritizing investments in IT, and by setting up a set of interlinking measures, how IT costs and benefits may be evaluated and managed across the systems lifecycle, including consideration of potential uses of the external IT services market. An emphasis on a cultural change in evaluation from 'control through numbers' to a focus on quality improvement offers one of the better routes out of the productivity paradox. Improved evaluation practice serves to demystify the paradox, but also links with and helps to stimulate improved planning for management and use of IT, thus also reducing the paradox in practical terms – through the creation of greater business value.

Introduction

The history of numerous failed and disappointing Information Technology (IT) investments in work organizations has been richly documented. (Here IT refers to the convergence of computers, telecommunications and electronics, and the resulting technologies and techniques.) The 1993 abandonment of a five year project like Taurus in the UK London financial markets, in this case at a cost of £80 million to the Stock Exchange, and possibly £400 million to City institutions, provides only high profile endorsement of underlying disquiet on the issue. Earlier survey and case research by the present authors established IT investment as a high risk, hidden cost business, with a variety of factors, including size and complexity of the project, the 'newness' of the technology, the degree of 'structuredness' in the project, and major human, political and cultural factors compounding the risks (Willcocks and Griffiths, 1994; Willcocks and Lester, 1996). Alongside, indeed we would argue contributing to the performance issues surrounding IT, is accumulated evidence of problems in evaluation together with a history of general indifferent organizational practice in the area (Farbey *et al.*, 1992; Strassman, 1990). In this chapter we focus firstly on the relationship between IT performance and its evaluation as it is expressed in the debate around what has been called the 'IT productivity paradox'. A key finding is that assessment issues are not straightforward, and that some, though by no means all, of the confusion over IT performance can be removed if limitations in evaluation practice and measurement become better understood. From this base we then provide an overall conceptualization, with some detail, about how evaluation practice itself can be advanced, thus allowing some loosening of the Gordian knot represented by the IT productivity paradox.

'What gets measured gets managed' – the way forward?

The evaluation and management of IT investments is shot through with difficulties. Increasingly, as IT expenditure has risen and as the use of IT has penetrated to the core of organizations, the search has been directed towards not just improving evaluation techniques and processes, and searching for new ones, but also towards the management and 'flushing out' of benefits. But these evaluation and management efforts regularly run into difficulties of three generic types. First, many organizations find themselves in a Catch 22 situation. For competitive reasons they cannot afford not to invest in IT, but economically they cannot find sufficient justification, and evaluation practice cannot provide enough underpinning, for making the investment. Second, for many of the more advanced and intensive users of IT, as the IT infrastructure becomes an inextricable part of the organization's processes and structures, it becomes increasingly difficult to separate out the impact of IT from that of other assets and activities. Third, despite the high levels of expenditure, there is widespread lack of understanding of IT and Information Systems (IS – organizational applications, increasingly IT-based, that deliver on the information needs of the organization's stakeholders) as major capital assets. While senior managers regularly give detailed attention to the annual expenditure on IT/IS, there is little awareness of the size of the capital asset that has been bought over the years (Keen, 1991; Willcocks, 1994). Failure to appreciate the size of this investment leads to IT/IS being under-managed, a lack of serious attention being given to IS evaluation and control, and also a lack of concern for discovering ways of utilizing this IS asset base to its full potential.

Solutions to these difficulties have most often been sought through variants on the mantra: 'what gets measured gets managed'. As a dominant guiding principle more – and more accurate – measurement has been advanced as the panacea to evaluation difficulties. In a large body of literature, while some consideration is given to the difficulties inherent in quantifying IT impacts, a range of other difficulties are downplayed, or even ignored. These include, for example:

- the fact that measurement systems are prone to decay
- the goal displacement effects of measurement
- the downside that only that which is measured gets managed
- the behavioural implications of measurement and related reward systems, and
- the politics inherent in any organizational evaluation activity.

In practice, counter evidence against a narrow focus on quantification for IT/IS evaluation has been gathering. Thus some recent studies point to how measurement can be improved, but also to the limitations of measurement, and areas where sets of measures may be needed because of the lack of a single reliable measure (Farbey *et al.*, 1995). They also point to the key role of stakeholder judgement throughout any IT/IS evaluation process. Furthermore some published research studies point to the political-rational as opposed to the straightforwardly rational aspects of IT measurement in organizations. For example Lacity and Hirschheim (1996) provide an important insight into how measurement, in this case benchmarking IT performance against external comparators, can be used in political ways to influence senior management judgement. Currie (1989) detailed the political uses of measurement in a paper entitled 'The art of justifying new technology to top management'. Additionally, there are signs that the problems with over-focusing on measurement are being recognized, albeit slowly, with moves toward emphasizing the demonstration of the value of IS/IT, not merely its measurement. Elsewhere we have argued for the need to move measurement itself from a focus on the price of IT to a concern for its value; and for a concomitant shift in emphasis in the measurement regime from control to quality improvement (Willcocks and Lester, 1996).

These difficulties and limitations in evaluation practice have become bound up in a widespread debate about what has been called the IT productivity paradox – the notion that despite large investments in IT over many years, it has been difficult to discover where the IT payoffs have occurred, if indeed there have been many. In this chapter we will address critically the overall sense that many have that despite huge investments in IS/IT so far, these have been producing disappointing returns. We will find that while much of the sense of disappointment may be justified, at the same time it is fed by limitations in evaluation techniques and processes, and by misunderstandings of the contribution IT can and does make to organizations, as much as by actual experience of poorly performing information systems. The focus then moves to how organizations may seek to improve their IT/IS evaluation procedures and processes. Taking into account the many limitations in evaluation practice continuing to be identified by a range of the more recent research studies, a high level framework is advanced for how evaluation can and needs to be applied across the systems lifecycle. The chapter also suggests that processes of evaluation, and the involvement of stakeholders, may be as, if not more, important than refining techniques and producing measurement of a greater, but possibly no less spurious, accuracy.

The IT 'productivity paradox' revisited

Alongside the seemingly inexorable rise of IS/IT investment in the last 15 years, there has been considerable uncertainty and concern about the productivity impact of IT being experienced in work organizations. This has been reinforced by several high profile studies at the levels of both the national economy and industrial sector suggesting in fact that if there has been an IS/IT payoff it has been minimal, and hardly justifies the vast financial outlays incurred. Two early influential studies embodying this theme were by Roach (1986) and Loveman (1988). A key, overarching point needs to be made immediately. It is clear from reviews of the many research studies conducted at national, sectoral and organization specific levels that the failure to identify IS/IT benefits and productivity says as much about the deficiencies in assessment methods and measurement, and the rigour with which they are applied, as about mismanagement of the development and use of information-based technologies. It is useful to chase this hare of 'the IT productivity paradox' further, because the issue goes to the heart of the subject of this chapter.

Interestingly, the IT productivity paradox is rarely related in the literature to manufacturing sectors for which, in fact, there are a number of studies from the early 1980s showing rising IT expenditure correlating with sectoral and firm-specific productivity rises (see Brynjolfsson and Hitt, 1993; Loveman, 1988). The high profile studies raising concern also tend to base their work mainly on statistics gathered in the US context. Their major focus, in fact, tends to be limited to the service sector in the US. Recently a number of studies question the data on which such studies were based, suggesting that the data is sufficiently flawed to make simple conclusions misleading (Brynjolfsson, 1993). It has been pointed out, for example that in the cases of Loveman (1988) and Roach (1986) neither personally collected the data that they analysed, thus their observations describe numbers rather than actual business experiences (Nievelt, 1992).

Still others argue that the productivity payoff may have been delayed but, by the mid-1990s, recession and global competition have forced companies to finally use the technologies they put in place over the last decade, with corresponding productivity leaps. Moreover, productivity figures always failed to measure the cost avoidance and savings on opportunity costs that IS/IT can help to achieve (Gillin, 1994).

Others also argue that the real payoffs occur when IS/IT development and use is linked with the business reengineering (BPR) efforts coming onstream in the 1990s (Hammer and Champy, 1993). However, recent UK evidence develops this debate by finding that few organizations were actually getting 'breakthrough' results through IT-enabled BPR. Organizations were 'aiming low and hitting low' and generally not going for the radical, high-risk reengineering approaches advocated by many commentators. Moreover there was no strong correlation between size of IT expenditure on reengineering projects, and resulting productivity impacts. In business process reengineering, as elsewhere (see below), it is the management of IT, and what it is used for, rather than the size of IT spend that counts (Willcocks, 1996b).

Bakos and Jager (1995) provide interesting further insight, as they argue that computers are not boosting productivity, but the fault lies not with the technology but with its management and how computer use is overseen. They question the reliability of the productivity studies, and, supporting the positive IT productivity findings in the study by Brynjolfsson and Hitt (1993), posit a new productivity paradox: 'how can computers be so productive?'

In the face of such disputation Brynjolfsson (1993) makes salutary reading. He suggests four explanations for the seeming IT productivity paradox. The first is measurement errors. In practice the measurement problems appear particularly acute in the service sector and with white collar worker productivity – the main areas investigated by those pointing to a minimal productivity impact from IT use in the 1980s and early 1990s. Brynjolfsson concludes from a close examination of the data behind the studies of IT performance at national and sectoral levels that mismeasurement is at the core of the IT productivity paradox. A second explanation is timing lags due to learning and adjustment. Benefits from IT can take several years to show through in significant financial terms, a point also made by Strassman

(1990) in arguing for newer ways of evaluating IS/IT performance at the organizational level. While Brynjolfsson largely discounts this explanation, there is evidence to suggest he is somewhat over-optimistic about the ability of managers to account rationally for such lags and include them in their IS/IT evaluation system (Willcocks, 1996a).

A third possible explanation is that of redistribution. IT may be beneficial to individual firms but unproductive from the standpoint of the industry, or the economy, as a whole. IT rearranges the share of the pie, with the bigger share going to those heavily investing in IT, without making the pie bigger. Brynjolfsson suggests, however, that the redistribution hypothesis would not explain any shortfall in IT productivity at the firm level. To add to his analysis one can note that in several sectors, for example banking and financial services, firms seemingly compete by larger spending on IT-based systems that are, in practice, increasingly becoming minimum entry requirements for the sector, and commodities rather than differentiators of competitive performance. As a result in some sectors, for example the oil industry, organizations are increasingly seeking to reduce such IS/IT costs by accepting that some systems are industry standard and can be developed together.

A fourth explanation is that IS/IT is not really productive at the firm level. Brynjolfsson (1993) posits that despite the neoclassical view of the firm as a profit maximiser, it may well be that decision-makers are, for whatever reason, often not acting in the interests of the firm: 'instead they are increasing their slack, building inefficient systems, or simply using outdated criteria for decision-making' (p.75). The implication of Brynjolfsson's argument is that political interests and/or poor evaluation practice may contribute to failure to make real, observable gains from IS/IT investments. However, Brynjolfsson appears to discount these possibilities citing a lack of evidence either way, though here he seems to be restricting himself to the economics literature. Against his argument however, there are in fact frequent study findings showing patchy strategizing and implementation practice where IS is concerned. (for an overview see Willcocks *et al.*, 1996). Furthermore, recent evidence in the IT evaluation literature suggests more evidence showing poor evaluation practice than Brynjolfsson has been willing to credit (see Ballantine *et al.*, 1996; Willcocks and Lester, 1996).

It is on this point that the real debate on the apparent 'IT productivity paradox' needs to hinge. Studies at the aggregate levels of the economy or industrial sector conceal important questions and data about variations in business experiences at the organizational and intra-organizational levels. In practice, organizations seem to vary greatly in their ability to harness IS/IT for organizational purpose. In an early study Cron and Sobol (1983) pointed to what has since been called the 'amplifier' effect of IT. Its use reinforces existing management approaches dividing firms into very high or very low performers. This analysis has been supported by later work by Strassman

(1990), who also found no correlation between size of IT expenditure and firms' return on investment. Subsequently, a 1994 analysis of the information productivity of 782 US companies found that the top 10 spent a smaller percentage (1.3 per cent compared to 3 per cent for the bottom 100) of their revenue on IS, increased their IS budget more slowly (4.3 per cent in 1993–4 – the comparator was the bottom 110 averaging 10.2 per cent), thus leaving a greater amount of finance available for non-IS spending (Gillin, 1994).

Not only did the the top performers seem to spend less proportionately on their IT; they also tended to keep certain new investments as high as business conditions permitted while holding back on infrastructure growth. Thus, on average, hardware investments were only 15 per cent of the IS budget while new development took more than 50 per cent, with 41 per cent of systems development spending incurred on client/server investment (Sullivan-Trainor, 1994). Clearly the implication of this analysis is that top performers spend relatively less money on IS/IT, but focus their spending on areas where the expenditure will make more difference in terms of business value. An important aspect of their ability to do this must lie with their evaluation techniques and processes. Nievelt (1992) adds to this picture. Analysing database information on over 300 organizations he found empirically that IT as a coordinating, communicating and leveraging technology was capable of enhancing customer satisfaction, flattening organizational pyramids and supporting knowledge workers in the management arena. At the same time many organizations did not direct their IT expenditure into appropriate areas at the right time, partly because of inability to carry out evaluation of where they were with their IT expenditure and IT performance relative to business needs in a particular competitive and market context.

Following on from this, it is clear that significant aspects of the IT productivity paradox, as perceived and experienced at organizational level, can be addressed through developments in evaluation and management practice. In particular the distorting effects of poor evaluation methods and processes need close examination and profiling; alternative methods, and an assessment of their appropriateness for specific purposes and conditions need to be advanced; and how these methods can be integrated together and into management practice needs to be addressed.

Investing in information systems

In the rest of this chapter we will focus not on assessing IT/IS performance at national or industry levels, but on the conduct of IT/IS evaluation within work organizations. As already suggested, IT/IS expenditure in such organizations is high and rising. The United States leads the way, with government statistics suggesting that, by 1994, computers and other information technology made up nearly half of all business spending on equipment – not including the billions spent on software and programmers each year. Globally, computer and telecommunications investments now amount to a half or more of most large firms' annual capital expenditures. In an advanced industrialized economy like the United Kingdom, IS/IT expenditure by business and public sector organizations was estimated at £33.6 billion for 1995, and expected to rise at 8.2 per cent, 7 per cent and 6.5 per cent in subsequent years, representing an average of over 2 per cent of turnover, or in local and central government an average IT spend of £3546 per employee. Organizational IS/IT expenditure in developing economies is noticeably lower, nevertheless those economies may well leapfrog several stages of technology, with China, Russia, India and Brazil, for example, set to invest in telecommunications an estimated 53.3, 23.3, 13.7, and 10.2 billion dollars (US) respectively in the 1993–2000 period (Engardio, 1994).

There were many indications by 1995, of managerial concern to slow the growth in organizational IS/IT expenditure. Estimates of future expenditure based on respondent surveys in several countries tended to indicate this pattern (see for example Price Waterhouse, 1995). The emphasis seemed to fall on running the organization leaner, wringing more productivity out of IS/IT use, attempting to reap the benefits from changes in price/performance ratios, while at the same time recognizing the seemingly inexorable rise in information and IT intensity implied by the need to remain operational and competitive. In particular, there is wide recognition of the additional challenge of bringing new technologies into productive use. The main areas being targetted for new corporate investment seemed to be client/server computing, document image processing and groupware, together with 'here-and-now' technologies such as advanced telecom services available from 'intelligent networks', mobile voice and digital cellular systems (Taylor, 1995). It is in the context of these many concerns and technical developments that evaluation techniques and processes need to be positioned.

Evaluation: a systems lifecycle approach

At the heart of one way forward for organizations is the notion of an IT/IS evaluation and management cycle. A simplified diagrammatic representation of this is provided in Figure 20.1. Earlier research found that few organizations actually operated evaluation and management practice in an integrated manner across systems lifecycles (Willcocks, 1996a). The evaluation cycle attempts to bring together a rich and diverse set of ideas, methods, and practices that are to be found in the evaluation literature to date, and point them in the direction of an integrated approach across systems lifetime. Such an approach would consist of several interrelated activities:

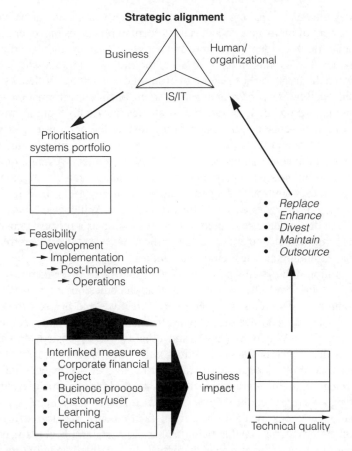

Figure 20.1 *IT/IS evaluation and management cycle*

1 Identifying net benefits through strategic alignment and prioritization.
2 Identifying types of generic benefit, and matching these to assessment techniques.
3 Developing a family of measures based on financial, service, delivery, learning and technical criteria.
4 Linking these measures to particular measures needed for development, implementation and post-implementation phases.
5 Ensuring each set of measures run from the strategic to the operational level.
6 Establishing responsibility for tracking these measures, and regularly reviewing results.
7 Regularly reviewing the existing portfolio, and relating this to business direction and performance objectives.

A key element in making the evaluation cycle dynamic and effective is the involvement of motivated, salient stakeholders in processes that operationalize – breathe life into, adapt over time, and act upon – the evaluation criteria and techniques. Let us look in more detail at the rationale for, and shape of such an approach. In an earlier review of front-end evaluation Willcocks (1994) pointed out how lack of *alignment* between business, information systems and human resource/organizational strategies inevitably compromised the value of all subsequent IS/IT evaluation effort, to the point of rendering it of marginal utility and, in some cases, even counter-productive. In this respect he reflected the concerns of many authors on the subject. A range of already available techniques were pointed to for establishing strategic alignment, and linking strategy with assessing the feasibility of any IS/IT investment, and these will not be repeated here (for a review see Willcocks, 1994). At the same time the importance of recognizing evaluation as a process imbued with inherent political characteristics and ramifications was emphasized, reflecting a common finding amongst empirical studies.

The notion of a systems portfolio implies that IT/IS investment can have a variety of objectives. The practical problem becomes one of *prioritization* – of resource allocation amongst the many objectives and projects that are put forward. Several classificatory schemes for achieving this appear in the extant literature. Thus Willcocks (1994) and others have suggested classificatory schemes that match business objectives with types of IS/IT project. Thus, on one schema, projects could be divided into six types – efficiency, effectiveness, must-do, architecture, competitive edge, and research and development. The type of project could then be matched to one of the more appropriate evaluation methods available, a critical factor being the degree of tangibility of the costs and benefits being assessed. Costs and benefits need to be sub-classified into 'for example' hard/soft, or tangible/intangible, or direct/indirect/inferred, and the more appropriate assessment techniques for each type adopted (see Willcocks, 1994 for a detailed discussion). Norris (1996) has provided a useful categorization of types of investments and main aids to evaluation, and a summary is shown in Table 20.1.

After alignment and prioritization assessment, the *feasibility* of each IS/IT investment then needs to be examined. All the research studies show that the main weakness here have been the over-reliance on and/or misuse of traditional, finance-based cost-benefit analysis. The contingency approach outlined above and in Table 20.1 helps to deal with this, but such approaches need to be allied with active involvement of a wider group of stakeholders than those at the moment being identified in the research studies. A fundamental factor to remember at this stage is the importance of a business case being made for an IT/IS investment, rather than any strict following of specific sets of measures. As a matter of experience where detailed measurement has to be carried out to differentiate between specific proposals, it may well

Table 20.1 *Types of investment and aids to evaluating IT*

Type of investment	Business benefit	Main formal aids to investment evaluation	Importance of management judgement	Main aspects of management judgement
Mandatory investments as a result of:				
Regulatory requirements	Satisfy minimum legal requirement	Analysis of costs	Low	Fitness of the system for the purpose
Organizational requirements	Facilitate business operations	Analysis of costs	Low	Fitness of the system for the purpose. Best option for variable organizational requirements
Competitive pressure	Keep up with the competition	Analysis of costs to achieve parity with the competition. Marginal cost to differentiate from the competition, providing the opportunity for competitive advantage	Crucial	Competitive need to introduce the system at all. Effect of introducing the system into the marketplace. Commercial risk. Ability to sustain competitive advantage
Investments to improve performance	Reduce costs	Cost/benefit analyses	Medium	Validity of the assumptions behind the case
	Increase revenues	Cost/benefit analyses. Assessment of hard-to-quantify benefits. Pilots for high risk investment	High	Validity of the assumptions behind the case. Real value of hard-to-quantify benefits. Risk involved

Table 20.1 *(continued)*

Type of investment	Business benefit	Main formal aids to investment evaluation	Importance of management judgement	Main aspects of management judgement
Investments to achieve competitive advantage	Achieve a competitive leap	Analysis of costs and risks	Crucial	Competitive aim of the system. Impact on the market and the organization. Risk involved
Infrastructure investment	Enable the benefits of other applications to be realized	Setting of performance standards. Analysis of costs	Crucial	Corporate need and benefit, both short and long term
Investment in research	Be prepared for the future	Setting objectives within cost limits	High	Long-term corporate benefit. Amount of money to be allocated

Source: Norris (1996).

be that there is little advantage to be had not just between each, but from any. Measurement contributes to the business case for or against a specific investment but cannot substitute for a more fundamental managerial assessment as to whether the investment is strategic and critical for the business, or will merely result in yet another useful IT application.

Following this, Figure 20.1 suggests that evaluation needs to be conducted in a linked manner across systems development and into systems implementation and operational use. The evaluation cycle posits the development of a series of *interlinked measures* that reflect various aspects of IS/IT performance, and that are applied across systems lifetime. These are tied to processes and people responsible for monitoring performance, improving the evaluation system and also helping to 'flush out' and manage the benefits from the investment. Figure 20.1 suggests, in line with prevailing academic and practitioner thinking by the mid-1990s, that evaluation cannot be based solely or even mainly on technical efficiency criteria. For other criteria there may be debate on how they are to be measured, and this will depend on the specific organizational circumstances.

However there is no shortage of suggestions here. Taking one of the more difficult, Keen (1991) discusses measuring the cost avoidance impacts of IT/IS. For him these are best tracked in terms of business volumes increases compared to number of employees. The assumption here is that IT/IS can increase business volumes without increases in personnel. At the strategy level he also suggests that the most meaningful way of tracking IT/IS performance over time is in terms of business performance per employee, for example revenue per employee, profit per employee, or at a lower level, as one example – transactions per employee.

Kaplan and Norton (1992) were highly useful for popularizing the need for a number of perspectives on evaluation of business performance. Willcocks (1994) showed how the Kaplan and Norton balanced scorecard approach could be adapted fairly easily for the case of assessing IT/IS investments. To add to that picture, most recent research suggests the need for six sets of measures. These would cover the *corporate financial perspective* (e.g. profit per employee); the *systems project* (e.g. time, quality, cost); *business process* (e.g. purchase invoices per employee); the *customer/user* perspective (e.g. on-time delivery rate); an *innovation/learning* perspective (e.g. rate of cost reduction for IT services); and a *technical* perspective (e.g. development efficiency, capacity utilization). Each set of measures would run from strategic to operational levels, each measure being broken down into increasing detail as it is applied to actual organizational performance. For each set of measures the business objectives for IT/IS would be set. Each objective would then be broken down into more detailed measurable components, with a financial value assigned where practicable. An illustration of such a hierarchy, based on work by Norris (1996), is shown in Figure 20.2.

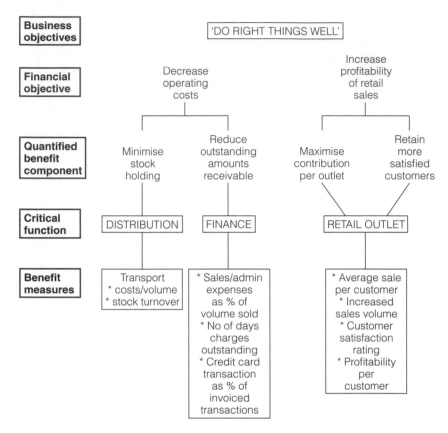

Figure 20.2   *Measureable components of business objectives for IT/IS (Adopted from Norris, 1996)*

Responsibility for tracking these measures, together with regular reviews that relate performance to objectives and targets are highly important elements in delivering benefits from the various IS investments. It should be noted that such measures are seen as helping to inform stakeholder judgements, and not as a substitute for such judgements in the evaluation process.

Some detail can be provided on how to put metrics in place, monitor them and ensure benefits are delivered. The following schema is derived from work by Peters, (1996) and Willcocks and Lester (1996). Projects were found to be managed well, and often over-performed their original appraisal, where a steering group was set up early in a project, was managed by a senior user manager, and represented the key operating functions impacted by the IT/IS. The steering group followed the project to a late stage of implementation

Performance variables \ Benefits manager	Sales manager	Purchasing manager	Accts payable supervisor	Warehouse manager	Production scheduler	Production supervisor
Orders/man day	E					
No. of suppliers		E				
Invoices/man day			E			
Finished inventory	S			E	S	
Stock out occurrence	S				E	
Slow movers leadtime	S					E

Figure 20.3 *Assigning responsibility for delivering benefits of IT/IS implementation (E = executive responsibility; S = support) (Based on Peters, 1996)*

with members frequently taking responsibility for delivering benefits from parts of the IT/IS implementation. Project benefits need to be incorporated into business area budgets, and individuals identified for monitoring performance and delivering benefits. Variables impacted by the IT/IS investment were identified and decomposed into a hierarchy based on key operating parameters necessary to deliver the benefit. A framework needs to be established for clearly identifying responsibilities for benefits (Figure 20.3). Peters (1996) suggests that the information on responsibilities should be published, and known to relevant parties, and that measures should be developed to monitor benefits at the lowest level of unit performance. We would add that links also need to be made between the individual's performance in the assessment role and his/her own appraisal and reward.

The steering group should regularly review the benefits gained, for example every three months, and also report less frequently to the IT/IS strategy steering group, with flushing out of IT/IS benefits seen as an essential extension of the strategic review process, not least in its capacity to facilitate more effective IT/IS implementation. What is clear in this scheme is that measurement that is business – not solely technical efficiency – focused plays an important part in evaluation but only in the context of appropriate processes in place operated by a wide range of motivated stakeholders.

Completing the cycle: existing and future investments

One all too often routinized phase of review is that of *post-implementation* (see Figure 20.1). Our own research suggests that this is one of the most neglected, yet one of the more important areas as far as IS evaluation is concerned. An advantage of the above schema, in practice, is that post-implementation evaluation arises naturally out of implementation assessment on an ongoing basis, with an already existing set of evaluators in place. This avoids the ritualistic, separated review that usually takes place in the name of post-implementation review (Kumar, 1990 – detailed discussion on how to perform an effective post-implementation review cannot be provided here, but see Norris, 1996).

There remains the matter of assessing the ongoing systems portfolio on a regular basis. Notoriously, when it comes to evaluating the existing IS investment, organizations are not good at drop decisions. There may be several related ramifications. The IT inheritance of 'legacy systems' can deter investment in new systems – it can, for example, be all too difficult to take on new work when IT/IS staff are awash in a rising tide of maintenance arising from the existing investment. Existing IT/IS-related activity can also devour the majority of the financial resources available for IS investment. All too often such failures derive from not having in place, or not operationalizing, a robust assessment approach that enables timely decisions on systems and service divestment, outsourcing, replacement, enhancement, and/or maintenance. Such decisions need to be based on at least two criteria – the technical quality of the system/service, and its business contribution – as well as being related back to the overall strategic direction and objectives of the organization (see Figure 20.1).

A further element in assessment of the ongoing systems portfolio is the relevance of external comparators. External benchmarking firms – for example RDC and Compass – have already been operating for several years, and offer a range of services that can be drawn upon, but mainly for technical aspects of IT performance. The assessment of data centre performance is now well established amongst the better benchmarking firms. Depending on the benchmarking database available, a data centre can be assessed against other firms in the same sector, or of the same generic size in computing terms, and also against outsourcing vendor performance. Benchmarking firms are continually attempting to extend their services, and can provide a useful assessment, if mainly only on the technical efficiency of existing systems. There is, however, a growing demand for extending external benchmarking services more widely to include business, and other, performance measures – many of which could include elements of IT contribution (see above). Indeed Strassman (1990) and Nievelt (1992) are but two of the more well known of a growing number of providers of diagnostic benchmarking methodologies that help to locate and reposition IT contribution relative to actual and required business performance. It is worth remarking that external IT benchmarking – like all measures – can serve a range of purposes within an organization. Lacity and Hirschheim (1996) detail from their research how benchmarking services were used to demonstrate to senior executives the usefulness of the IT department. In some cases external benchmarking subsequently led to the rejection of outsourcing proposals from external vendors.

This leads into the final point. An increasingly important part of assessing the existing and any future IT/IS investment is the degree to which the external IT services market can provide better business technical and economic options for an organization. In practice, recent survey and case research by the authors and others found few organizations taking a strategic approach to IT/IS sourcing decisions, though many derived economic and other benefits from incremental, selective, low risk, as opposed to high risk 'total' approaches to outsourcing (Lacity and Hirscheim, 1995). The Yankee Group estimated the 1994 global IT outsourcing market as exceeding $US49.5 billion with an annual 15 per cent growth rate. As at 1995 the US market was the biggest, estimated to exceed $18.2 billion. The UK remained the largest European market in 1994 exceeding £1 billion, with an annual growth rate exceeding 10 per cent on average across sectors. Over 50 per cent of UK organizations outsourced some aspect of IT in 1994, and outsourcing represented on average 24 per cent of their IT budgets (Lacity and Hirscheim, 1995; Willcocks and Fitzgerald, 1994).

Given these figures, it is clear that evaluation of IT/IS sourcing options, together with assessment of on-going vendor performance in any outsourced part of the IT/IS service, needs to be integrally imbedded into the systems lifecycle approach detailed above. Not least because an external vendor bid, if carefully analysed against one's own detailed in-house assessment of IT performance, can be a highly informative form of benchmarking. Figure 20.1 gives an indication of where sourcing assessments fit within the lifecycle approach, but recent research can give more detail on the criteria that govern successful and less successful sourcing decisions.

In case and survey research Willcocks and Fitzgerald (1994) found six key factors (see Figure 20.4). Three are essentially business related. Firstly, IT can contribute to *differentiating* a business from its competitors, thus providing competitive advantage. Alternatively an IT activity/service may be a commodity, not distinguishing the business from a competitor in business offering and performance terms.

Second, the IT may be *strategic* in underpinning the firm's achievement of goals, and critical to its present and future strategic direction, or merely useful. Third, the *degree of uncertainty about future business environment and needs* impacts upon longer term IT needs. High uncertainty suggests in-house sourcing as a better option. As Figure 20.4 suggests the preferred

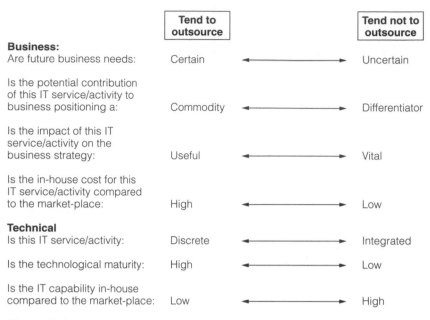

Figure 20.4   *Criteria for making sourcing decisions*

option where possible, is to outsource useful commodities in conditions of certainty about business requirements across the length of the contract. Three technical considerations are also important. It is unwise for an organization to outsource in a situation of low *technology maturity*. This exists where a technology is new and unstable, and/or where there is an existing technology but being applied in a radically new way, and/or where there is little relevant in-house experience with the technology. Next, *the level of IT integration* must influence the sourcing decision. Generally we found it preferable not to outsource systems/activities that are highly integrated with other parts of the technical platform, and/or that interface in complex ways with many business users who will be impacted significantly by the service. Finally, *where in-house capability is equivalent to or better than that available on the external market*, there would seem to be a less pressing need to outsource the IT service/activity.

Making sourcing decisions, in practice, involves making trade-offs among the preferences suggested by these factors. In addition, we note six reality checks that need to be borne in mind before deciding on a specific sourcing option:

• Does the decision make economic sense?
• How does the decision fit with the rate of technological change?

- Are there issues around ownership when transferring people and assets?
- Is a suitable vendor available?
- Does the organization have the management capability to deliver on the decision?

Will significant human resource issues arise – during the change process, and subsequently for in-house and vendor staff?

Outsourcing is defined as the commissioning of third party management of IT assets/activities to required result. This does not exclude another way of using the market, of course, namely 'insourcing' – where external resources are utilized in an organization under in-house management. There is also an option to have long or short term contracts with suppliers. In situations of high business uncertainty and/or rapid technological change shorter term contract are to be preferred. We also found, together with Lacity and Hirschheim (1995), that selective rather than total outsourcing (80 per cent or more of IT budget spent on outsourcing), tended to be the lower risk, and more successful option to take.

In more detailed work, we found outsourcing requiring a considerable cultural change on evaluation. Before outsourcing any IT, the more successful organizations measured everything in a three to six month baseline period. This enabled them to compare more accurately the in-house performance against a vendor bid. It also prefigured the setting up of a tighter evaluation regime with more detailed and accurate performance measures and service level agreements. In cases where an in-house vendor bid won, we found that the threat of the vendor bid actually galvanized the in-house staff into identifying new ways of improving on IS/IT performance, and into maintaining the improvement through putting in place, and acting on the output from, enhanced evaluation criteria and measures. This brings us full circle. Even where an organization does not outsource IT, our case evidence is that increasingly it is good practice to assess in-house performance against what a potential vendor bid might be, even if, as is increasingly the case, this means paying a vendor for the assessment. By the same token, benchmarking IT/IS performance against external comparators can also be highly useful, in providing insight not only into in-house IT/IS performance, but also into the efficacy of internal evaluation criteria, processes and the availability or otherwise of detailed, appropriate assessment information.

Conclusion

There are several ways out of the IT productivity paradox. Several of the more critical relate to improved ways of planning for, managing and using IT/IS. However, part of the IT productivity paradox has been configured out of difficulties and limitations in measuring and accounting for IT/IS performance.

Bringing the so-called paradox into the more manageable and assessable organizational realm, it is clear that there is still, as at 1996, much indifferent IT/IS evaluation practice to be found in work organizations. In detailing an integrated lifecycle approach to IT/IS evaluation we have utilized the research findings of ourselves and others to suggest one way forward. The 'cradle to grave' framework is holistic and dynamic and relies on a judicious mixture of 'the business case', appropriate criteria and metrics, managerial and stakeholder judgement and processes, together with motivated evaluators. Above all it signals a move from 'control through numbers' assessment culture to one focused on quality improvement. This would seem to offer one of the better routes out of the productivity paradox, not least in its ability to link up evaluation to improving approaches to planning for, managing and using IT. As such it may also serve to begin to demystify the 'IT productivity paradox', and reveal that it is as much about human as technology issues – and better cast anyway as the IT-management productivity paradox, perhaps?

References

Bakos, Y. and Jager, P. de (1995) Are computers boosting productivity? *Computerworld*, 27 March, 128–130.

Ballantine, J. *et al.* (1996) Information systems/technology evaluation practices: evidence from UK organizations. *Journal of Information Technology* (forthcoming).

Brynjolfsson, E. (1993) The productivity paradox of information technology. *Communications of the ACM*, **36**(12), 67–77.

Brynjolfsson, E. and Hitt, L. (1993) Is information systems spending productive? *Proceedings of the International Conference in Information Systems*, Orlando, December.

Cron, W. and Sobol, M. (1983) The relationship between computerization and performance: a strategy for maximizing the economic benefits of computerization. *Journal of Information Management*, **6**, 171–181.

Currie, W. (1989) The art of justifying new technology to top management. *Omega*, **17**(5), 409–418.

Engardio, P. (1994) Third World leapfrog. *Business Week*, 13 June, 46–47.

Farbey, B., Land, F. and Targett, D. (1992) Evaluating investments in IT. *Journal of Information Technology*, **7**(2), 100–112.

Farbey, B., Targett, D. and Land, F. (eds) (1995) *Hard Money, Soft Outcomes*, Alfred Waller/Unicom, Henley, UK.

Gillin, P. (ed.) (1994) The productivity payoff: the 100 most effective users of information technology. *Computerworld*, 19 September, 4–55.

Hammer, M. and Champy, J. (1993) *Reengineering The Corporation: A Manifesto For Business Revolution*, Nicholas Brealey, London.

Kaplan, R. and Norton, D. (1992) The balanced scorecard: measures that drive performance. *Harvard Business Review*, January–February, 71–79.

Keen, P. (1991) *Shaping the Future: Business Design Through Information Technology*, Harvard Business Press, Boston.

Kumar, K. (1990). Post-implementation evaluation of computer-based information systems: current practices. *Communications of the ACM*, **33**(2), 203–212.

Lacity, M. and Hirschheim, R. (1995) *Beyond the Information Systems Outsourcing Bandwagon*, Wiley, Chichester.

Lacity, M. and Hirschheim, R. (1996) The role of benchmarking in demonstrating IS performance. In *Investing in Information Systems: Evaluation and Management* (ed. L. Willcocks), Chapman and Hall, London.

Lacity, M. Willcocks, L. and Feeny, D. (1995) IT outsourcing: maximize flexibility and control. *Harvard Business Review*, May–June, 84–93.

Loveman, G. (1988) An assessment of the productivity impact of information technologies. MIT management in the nineties. *Working Paper 88–054*. Massachussetts Institute of Technology, Cambridge.

Nievelt, M. van (1992) Managing with information technology – a decade of wasted money? *Compact*, Summer, 15–24.

Norris, G. (1996) Post-investment appraisal. In *Investing in Information Systems: Evaluation and Management* (ed. L. Willcocks), Chapman and Hall, London.

Peters, G. (1996) From strategy to implementation: identifying and managing benefits of IT investments. In *Investing in Information Systems: Evaluation and Management* (ed. L. Willcocks), Chapman and Hall, London.

Price Waterhouse (1995) *Information Technology Review 1994/5*, Price Waterhouse, London

Roach, S. (1986) *Macrorealities of the Information Economy*, National Academy of Sciences, New York.

Strassman, P. (1990) *The Business Value of Computers*, Information Economic Press, New Canaan, CT.

Sullivan-Trainor, M. (1994) Best of breed. In *The Productivity Payoff: The 100 Most Effective Users of Information Technology* (ed. P. Gillin), *Computerworld*, 19 September, 8–9.

Taylor, P. (1995) Business solutions on every side. Financial Times Review: *Information Technology*, 1 March, 1.

Willcocks, L. (ed.) (1994) *Information Management: Evaluation of Information Systems Investments*, Chapman and Hall, London.

Willcocks, L. (ed.) (1996a) *Investing in Information Systems: Evaluation and Management*, Chapman and Hall, London.

Willcocks, L. (1996b) Does IT-enabled BPR pay off? Recent findings on economics and impacts. In *Investing In Information Systems: Evaluation and Management*, Chapman and Hall, London.

Willcocks, L. and Fitzgerald, G. (1994) A business guide to IT outsourcing. *Business Intelligence*, London.

Willcocks, L. and Griffiths, C. (1994) Predicting risk of failure in large-scale information technology projects. *Technological Forecasting and Social Change*, 47, **47**(2), 205–228.

Willcocks, L. and Lester, S. (1996) The evaluation and management of information systems investments: from feasibility to routine operations. In (1996). *Investing In Information Systems: Evaluation and Management* (ed. L. Willcocks), Chapman and Hall, London.

Willcocks, L., Currie, W. and Mason, D. (1996) *Information Systems at Work: People Politics and Technology*, McGraw-Hill, Maidenhead, UK.

Reproduced from Willcocks, L. and Lester, S. (1996) Beyond the IT productivity paradox. *European Management Journal*, **14**(3), June, 279–290. Reprinted by permission of Elsevier Science.

Questions for discussion

1   What is the IT productivity paradox? Does it actually exist in your view, and if so, to what extent is it sectorally based? Do you believe it will remain a problem in, say, 5 years' time?

2   Why is the evaluation and management of IT investment 'shot through with difficulties'? And what's wrong with the maxim 'what gets measured gets managed'?

3   Critically evaluate the IT/IS evaluation and management cycle introduced in this chapter. How might it be adapted so as to be integrated in an ongoing IS planning process?

4   Reflect on the question of the evolution and management of different types of IT investments mentioned in this chapter, and the 'stages of growth' concept introduced in Chapter 2. How might evaluation and management of IT evolve from one stage to another?

5   Managing benefits are highlighted as a critical success factor by the authors. Reflect on the differing roles an IT steering committee, individual executives and managers might take in dealing with stock-outs for example.

6   The authors introduce the issue of sourcing IT services. Why might outsourcing IT services require 'a considerable cultural change on evaluation'? Reflect on issues introduced in Chapter 18 when considering this question.

Author index

Abernathy, W. M., 505, **516**
Ackoff, R. L., 36, 53, 58, 524, **546**
Ajzen, I., 357, **364**
Akerlof, G. A., **422**
Alavi, M., 530, **546**
Allen, C. D., 140, **152**
Amidon, D., 531, **549**
Andersen Consulting, **265**
Anderson, A., 240
Anderson, R. E., 151, **152**
Andrews, K. R., 61, **81**
Andrews, R., **82**
Ang, J. S. K., 82, **363**
Ansoff, H. I., 61, 81, 456, **481**
Anthes, G. H., 401, **422**
Anthony, R. N., 61, **81**
Applegate, L. M., 528, **546**
Argyris, C., 136, **152**, 377, **390**, 469, **481**
Arhur Andersen & Co., **241**
Arnold, P., 376, **391**
Arthur D. Little, **390**
Ash, N., 22, 24
Athos, A. G., 39, 40, **60**, 368, **392**
Avison, D., 26, **28**

Back, 530
Badrii, M. A., 208, **213**
Baets, W. R. J., xv, **xvii**, 292, **293**, 428, **430**
Bair, J. H., 491, 500, 511, **520**
Baker B. S. H., xi, **294**, **549**
Baker, F. T., 7, **19**
Baker, M. R., **520**
Bakos, J. Y., 297, 298, **324**, 398, 400, **422**, 555, **570**
Baliga, B. R., **450**
Ball, L., 188, 189, 213
Ballantine, J., 556, **570**
Bancroft, N. H., 139, **152**
Barki, H., 357, **364**
Barney, J. B., **294**
Baroudi, J., 65, **83**

Barrett, S., **450**
Barsade, S. G., 540, 541, **546**
Bartels, R. W., **185**
Bartlett, C. A., 433, 434, 439, **450**, 470, **481**
Basche, J., **450**
Bashein, B. J., 132, 42, **152**
Bastian, R. C., **160**
Batelaan, M. V., 369, 372, 374, 375, 387, **390**
Beardsley, S., **482**
Beasly, J. E., 317, **327**
Beath, C. M., 130, 140, 146, **152**, 265
Beer, M., 374, 376, **390**
Beers, M. C., 372, 387, **390**
Begun, J. W., **519**
Bell, C. H., 368, **391**
Benbasat, I., 26, **28**, 32, 36, **58**, 297, 299, 300, **325**, **327**, 330, 355, **365**, 499, **516**, 528, **549**
Bender, D., 316, **325**
Benjamin, R. I., **xvii**, 21, 27, 123, **146**, **152**, **154**, **184**, **185**, 293, 297, 298, 300, 325, 376, 377, 388, **390**, 398, **424**, 444, **452**, 524, **550**
Benson, R. J., **83**, **289**, **364**
Bertsch, B., 372, 376, 384, 387, **390**
Bettis, R. A., 459, **482**
Bettman, R. J., 296, 301, 302, 304, 313, 315, **325**
Bhabuta, L., 31, 36, 37, 39, **58**
Bjorn-Andersen, N., 136, **153**
Blalock, H. M., Jr., 512, **516**
Blau, P. M., 500, **516**
Bleeke, J., 460, **482**
Block, P., 132, 133, 143, **152**
Blumenthal, S. C., 69, **81**
Blunt, J., 21
Boddy, D., 141, 146, 147, **152**
Boland, R. J., **28**, **58**, **363**
Bolwijn, 464
Boone, M. E., **120**

Borys, B., 515, **516**
Bostrom, R. P., **213**, **521**
Bouman, W., 388, **390**
Bourgeois, L. J. III, 500, **516**
Bowers, J. L., 234, **241**
Bowman, B., 233, **241**, 296, 315, **325**
Boynton, A. C., 217, 238, 240, **241**
Bradley, S. P., **482**
Brancheau, J. C., 188, 189, 190, 192, **213**, **214**, **215**, 240, **241**, **243**, 298, 300, **325**, 364
Breback, G., 467, **483**
British Computer Society, **58**
Broekstra, G., 368, **390**
Brooks, R. F. Jr, 6, **19**
Brown, C. V., 531, **548**
Brown, J. S., 530, **546**
Brynjolfsson, E., 398, **422**, **429**, **430**, 554, 555, 556, **570**
Buchanan, D., 141, 146, 147, **152**
Buckingham, R. A., 27, **28**
Buitendam, A., **153**
Bullen, C. V., 240, **241**
Burack, E. H., 478, **482**, 535, **546**
Burgelman, R. A., 470, **482**, 493, **576**
Burn, J., 188, 195, 196, **213**
Burns, T., 463, **482**
Bushoff, G., 368, **390**
Bushoff, R., 368
Buss, M., 442, **451**
Butler Cox Foundation, 273, 281, **289**, 467, **482**
Butler, B., 400, **423**
Buzzard, S. H., 118
Buzzell, R. D., 317, **325**

Cafasso, R., 21, **24**
Calhoun, K. J., 334, 336, **363**
Carey, D., 188, **213**
Carey D. R., 118, **119**
Carlson, E. D., 11, **20**, **549**
Carlson, W. M., **265**, 527
Carlsson, S., 544, **546**
Carlyle, R. E., 442, 443, 447, **451**
Caron, J. R., 368, 378, **390**
Carrico, S. R., 299, 302, 304, **326**, 447, **451**
Carter, E. E., 511, **516**
Carter, N. M., 500, **517**, 526, **546**
Case, D., 496, **520**
Cash, J. I. Jr., xvi, **xvii**, 36, 38, **58**, 291, **293**, 296, 298, 299, 300, 302, **325**

Champy, J., 368, 372, 374, 375, 376, 387, 388, **391**, 402, 405, **423**, 555, **570**
Chan, Y. E., 62, **82**, 333, **363**, 368, **390**
Chandler, A. D., 433, 439, **451**, 457, **482**, 515, **517**
Charan, R., 464, **482**
Chatman, J. A., 537, 538, 540, 541, **546**
Cheney, P., 418, 421, **423**
Chepaitis, E. V., 200, 201, 202, 204, **213**
Cheung, H. K., 196, **213**
Child, J., 489, 500, 502, **517**
Clark, K. B., 469, 470, **483**
Clark, T. H., 400, 401, 403, 419, **423**
Clarke, R., 406, 408, 409, **422**
Clemons, E. K., **265**, 291, **293**, 297, 298, **325**, 398, 416, 421, **422**
Coase, R. H., 398, 400, **423**
Codd, E. F., 8, **19**
Cohen, 304, 420, 421, **423**, 501, **517**
Coleman, H. J. Jr., 462, **485**
Coleman, T., 281, **289**
Colvin, J. G., **485**
Compeau, D., 130, **152**
Connoly, T., **153**
Conrath, D. W., 79, **82**, 330, 331, **363**
Constantine, L. L., 524, **550**
Cooper, R., 374, 376, 377, **390**
Copeland, D. G., 291, **293**, 301, **325**
Cortese, 529
Courtney, J., 524, **546**
Crane, D. B., 444, **451**
Crawford, A. B., Jr., 511, **517**
Cresap, McCormick, and Paget Co., 332, 338, **363**
Cron, W., 316, **325**, 556, **570**
Crosdell, D., **546**
CSC Index, **213**, 368, 375, 376, 384, 385, **390**
Culnan, M. J., 488, 491, 492, 495, 496, 510, 515, **517**
Cummings, L. L., **326**
Cummings, T. G., 27, **28**, 135, **152**
Currie, W., 553, **570**, **572**
Cuyvers, L., **266**

Daft, R. L., 488, 493, 495, 496, **517**, **521**, 545, **546**
Danziger, J. N., 234, **241**
Das, S., 330, **363**
Davenport, T., 27, **28**, 142, 144, 146, **153**, 293, 368, 372, 373, 374, 376, 384, 387,

390, 391, 402, 405, 418, **423**, 467, **482**, 530, 531, **546**, **547**
Davidson, E. J., 139, **153**
Davidson, W. H., 388, **391**
Davis, G. B., 195, **214**, **241**, **265**, 300, **325**
Dawson, P., 500, **517**, 526, **547**
de Geus, A. P., 234, **241**, 470
De Gros, J. L., **213**
De Laat, P. B., 375, 376, **392**
De Leeuw, A. C. J., 375, 377, **392**
De Vries, E., 388, **390**
Dean, J. W., Jr., 143, **153**, 464, **482**
Deans, P. C., 188, **213**
Dearden, J., **119**
Dekeleva, S., 208, **213**
Delone, W. H., 535, **547**, **549**
DeLong, D., 103, **120**, 524
Denison, D., 537, **547**
Dertouzos, M. L., **184**
Dexter, A. S., **28**, **58**, 208, **213**, **325**
Dexter, I., 28
Dickinson, C., Jr., **325**
Dickson, G. W., 188, **213**, 240, **241**, 300, **325**
Dixon, J. R., 376, **391**
Dixon, P. J., **185**
Doll, W. J., 334, **363**
Donaldson, H. M., 118, **119**
Dooley, R. E., 298, **325**
Doz, Y. L., **451**, **452**, **482**
Dranzin, R., 369, **393**
Drew, S., 368, **391**
Droge, C., 500, **519**
Drucker, P. F., 462, 463, **482**, 504, **517**
Drury, A., **28**, **58**, 300, **325**, **326**
Duck, J. D., 376, 377, **391**
Duguid, P., 530, 531, **546**
Dumaine, B., 467, **482**
Duncan, R. B., 497, 501, **517**
Dunkle, D. E., **119**
Dunphy, D., 377, **391**
Dutton, W., 500

Earl, M. J., 26, 27, **28**, 31, 33, 34, 35, 36, 39, 44, **58**, **59**, 63, 67, 68, 69, 80, **82**, 85, 101, 132, **153**, 157, **159**, 216, 217, 233, **242**, 276, 278, **289**, 330, **363**, 368, 374, 378, **391**, 475, **482**
Early, P. C., 541, **547**
Eccles, R. G., **153**, 444, **451**
Edwards, B. R., 27, 38, 49, **58**, 69, **82**, 85, 101, **294**, **364**, 368, **391**

Edwards, C., 371
Eijckelhoff, M., 368, **390**
Ein-Dor, P., 204, 211, **213**
Eisenstat, R. A., 374, 376, **390**
Elam, J. J., 428, **430**, 528, **546**, **548**
Elliot, D., 528, **547**
Emerson, H., 456, **482**
Emery, J. C., **184**
Engardio, P., 558, **570**
Engelhoff, W., 433, **451**
Ernst & Young, 273, **289**
Ernst, D., 460, **482**

Fagundes, J., **214**
Falbe, C. M., **516**
Farbey, B., 159, 278, 289, 552, 553, **570**
Farrell, C., 433, **452**
Farwell, D., 135, 146, **153**, **155**
Fayol, H., **517**
Feeny, D. F., 27, **28**, **29**, **58**, **59**, 69, **82**, 85, 101, 132, **153**, 291, 292, **294**, 356, **364**, **571**
Feldman, M., 489, 498, **518**
Festinger, L., 107, **119**
Fielder, K. D., 429, **430**
Fishbein, M., 357, **364**
Fitzgerald, E. P., 63, 70, **82**
Fitzgerald, G., 26, **28**, 567, **572**
Fjeldstad, O., 432, 443, **453**
Flynn, D. M., 496, 500, **518**, 526, **547**
Foster, L. W., 496, 500, **518**, 526, **547**
Franz, C., 527, **547**
Freeman, J., 368, **392**
French, W. L., 368, **391**
Frenke, K. A., **451**
Friedman, A. L., 126, 130, 133, **153**
Friend, D., 528, **547**
Friesen, B., 469, 470, **484**
Fritz, M. B., 293, **294**
Fry, L. W., **547**
Fuerst, W. L., **294**
Fulk, J., 488, 492, 500, **518**, **521**

Gale, B. T., 317, **325**
Gallant, A. R., **520**
Galliers, R. D., xi, xv, xvii, 3, **19**, 20, 26, **28**, 31, 33, 34, 35, 37, 39, 41, 46, 50, 54, 55, 57, **58**, **59**, **60**, 63, **82**, 101, 159, 208, **213**, **215**, 220, 240, **242**, 293, **294**, 330, 331, **364**, 428, **430**, 473, 475, 480, **482**, 526, **549**

Gallupe, B. R., **155**
Garvin, D. A., 469, **482**
Gash, D. C., 130, **154**
Gerf., V. G., **184**
Gerstein, M., 297, **326**
Gerwin, D., 493, 511, **518**
Ghoshal, S., 433, 434, 439, **450**, **451**, 470, **481**
Gibbons, M., 428, **430**
Gibson, C. F., 26, **28**, 31, 32, 33, **59**, 103, **119**, 326, 488, 489, **518**
Gillin, P., 555, 557, **570**, **571**
Gilmore, T., 480, **483**
Ginsberg, A., 296, **326**
Ginzberg, M. J., 545, **550**
Glaser, B. G., 241, **242**
Glassburn, A. R., 118, **119**
Gluck, 36, **59**
Goes, J. B., 502, **519**
Goldstein, R., **28**, **58**, 300, **325**
Goodhue, D. L., 234, **242**, 447, **451**
Goodman, S. E., 200, **213**
Goslar, M. D., **213**
Gotterbarn, D., **152**
Graeser, V., **160**
Grant, R. M., 530, **547**
Greenwood, R., 368, 369, **391**
Greiner, L. E., 26, **28**, 36, **59**
Griffin, J., 464, **482**
Griffiths, C., 272, **289**, 552, **572**
Griffiths, P., 26, **29**, **60**, **83**, 157, **160**, 274, 475, 480, **485**
Grindley, K., 159, 272, **289**
Grinzberg, M. J., 545, **550**
Groppa, R., 511, **519**
Grosch H. R. J., 4, **19**
Grover, V., **154**, 159, 368, 374, 375, 376, 377, 378, 384, 385, **391**, 429, **430**
Gruber, W. H., 216, 222, **243**
Gudykunst, W. B., 540, 541, **547**
Gunton, T., 26, **28**
Gurbaxani, V., 398, **423**

Hackathorn, R. D., 234, **242**
Hall, E. T., 540, 541, **547**
Hall, G., 371, 374, 375, 376, 377, 384, 385, 388, **391**
Hambrick, 102, **119**, **294**, **327**
Hamel, G., 371, 384, **390**, 460, **482**
Hamilton, S., 31, **59**

Hammer, M., 144, **153**, 368, 371, 372, 374, 375, 376, 384, 387, 388, **391**, 402, 405, **423**, 467, **482**, 555, **570**
Hannan, M., 368, **392**
Hansen, J. V., 444, **451**
Hanssen-Bauer, J., 531, **547**
Hardaker, M., **159**
Harman, P. E., 118, **119**
Harrigan, K. R., **451**
Harris, R., 188, 189, **213**
Harrow, J., **290**
Hartog, C., 189, **214**, 240, **242**
Hartwick, J., 357, **364**
Hassan, S. Z., 200, **214**
Hayes, C., 400, **423**, 469, 470, 475, **483**
Hedberg, B., 469, **483**
Heineke, J., 376, **391**
Henderson, B. D., 457, **483**
Henderson, J. C., 62, 63, 68, 70, 81, **82**, **153**, 217, 234, 240, **242**, 292, **294**, 330, 333, **364**, 368, 372, 384, **392**
Hendricks, J. A., 159, **160**
Henke, J. W., 464, **483**
Henkoff, R., 479, **483**
Herbert, M., 189, **214**, 240, **242**
Heskett, J. A., 374, **393**
Hess, C. M., 398, 400, **423**
Heygate, R., 375, 376, 377, 384, **392**, 467, **483**
Heyman, S., 540, **547**
Higgins, C., 528, **550**
Hill, N. C., 444, **451**
Hiltz, S. R., 495, 499, 504, 509, **518**, **519**
Hin Keung, 196
Hinings, C. R., 368, 369, **391**
Hirschheim, R. A., 26, 27, **28**, 31, 36, 38, 39, 49, **58**, **59**, 132, **153**, **363**, 524, **549**, 553, 567, 569, **571**
Hirschhorn, L., 116, 119, 480, **483**
Hitt, L., **429**, **430**, 554, 555, **570**
Hochstrasser, B., 274, **289**
Hodgson, G. M., 398, 421, **423**
Hofer, C. W., 490, **518**
Hoffer, J. A., 189
Hofstede, G., 536, 537, 538, 540, 541, **547**, **548**
Hogue, J. T., 527, **548**
Holland Systems Corporation, **265**
Holland, C., xv, **xvii**, 293, 294
Holub, A., 529, **548**
Hopstaken, B. A. A., 67, **82**

Horovitz, J., 332, **364**
Hosoda, M., **266**
Houdeshel, G., 524, **548**
Huber, G. P., 428, 441, **451**, 496, 500, 504,
    505, 515, **518**, 528, 530, 545, **548**
Huberman, A. M., 336, **364**
Huff, S. L., 62, **82**, 195, **214**, 333, 363, 368,
    390
Huizing, A., 388, **390**
Humphreys, P., **546**
Huse, E. F., 27, **28**, 135, **152**

Iacono, C. S., 146, **153**
IBM Corporation, **242**, **265**
Igbaria, M., 197, **214**
Index Group, 330, **364**
Inmon, W. H., 234, **242**
Iramon, W. H., 442, 445, **451**
Islei, G., **29**, **294**
Ives, B., 31, **59**, **265**, 291, **294**, 297, 298,
    305, **326**, 333, **364**, 418, 421, **423**, 524,
    548
Izzo, J., 298, **326**

Jackson, B. B., 103, **119**, 488, 489, **518**
Jaeger, A. M., **450**
Jager, P., 555, **570**
Jaikumar, R., 475, **483**
Jamieson, M., 281, **289**
Janson, M. A., **213**
Janssens, G. K., **266**
Janz, B. D., 190, **214**
Jarhe, M., **518**
Jarvenpaa, S., 293, **294**, 305, **326**, 333, **364**,
    368, 369, 378, **390**, **393**, 402, 418, **423**
Jehn, K., 537, 538, **546**
Jemison, D., 515, **516**
Jenkins, M., 406, 408, 409, **422**
Jeong, S. R., 368, 374, 375, 376, 377, 378,
    384, 385, **391**
Jewell, L. N., 497, **518**
Jick, T. D., **28**, **153**
Johansen, R., 488, 495, 496, 499, 506, **518**
Johansson, H. J., 368, 372, 373, 374, 384,
    387, **392**
John, D. A., **185**
Johnson, D. G., **152**
Johnson, G., 69, **82**, 475, **483**, 536, **548**
Johnson, R., 460, **483**
Johnston, H. R., 292, 299, 302, 305, **326**,
    398, **423**, 439, 447, **451**

Jonsson, S., 469, **483**
Judd, C. M., 378, **392**
Junnarkar, B., 531, **548**

Kador, J., 528, 529, **548**
Kahneman, D., 505, **518**
Kambil, A., 411, **423**
Kanter, R. M., 27, **28**, 125, 140, **153**, 298,
    325
Kaplan, R. B., 373, 374, 375, 387, **392**, 467,
    483, 563, **571**
Karawan, K. R., **213**
Karimi, J., 234, 238, **242**, 428, 442, 448, **451**
Kasper, G., 418, 421, **423**
Katz, M. L., 419, **423**
Katzenbach, J. R., 140, 462, **483**
Kearney, A. T., 272, **289**
Keen, P. G. W., 11, **19**, **119**, 142, **153**, **184**,
    297, 298, **326**, 442, 445, 446, 447, **451**,
    527, **548**, 553, 563, **571**
Keil, M., 124, 130, 138, 145, **153**
Keisler, S., 491, 495, 496, **521**
Kelley, G., 493, **518**
Kelly, G. G., **215**
Kelly, M. L., 118, **119**
Kemerer, C. F., 398, 400, **423**
Kennedy, H. E., 118, **119**
Kerlinger, F. N., 512, **519**
Kerner, D. V., **265**
Kerr, E. B., 499, **519**
Kettinger, W. J., **154**, 368, 374, 375, 376,
    377, 378, 384, 385, **391**
Khandwalla, P. N., 368, **392**
Kidd, J. S., 505, **519**
Kidder, L. H., 378, **392**
Kim, J. S., 376, **391**
Kimbrough, S. O., 297, **325**
King, J. L., 26, **28**, 32, **59**, **119**, 300, **326**,
    432, 442, 450, **451**, **452**
King, W. R., 62, 64, 68, 70, 79, **82**, **83**, 220,
    233, 237, 240, **242**, **243**, **264**, **266**, 299,
    326, 448, **452**, 524, **548**
Kirkpatrick, 470
Kirsch, **242**
Kiudorf, E., **213**
Klatzky, S. R., 526, **548**
Kleijne, D., **82**
Knight, K., 441, **452**
Knoll, K., **294**
Knutson, T. J., 497, **519**
Kochan, T. A., **364**, **392**, 428, **430**, 469, **483**

Koeblitz, R., **547**
Kokuryo, J., 406, 410, 418, **424**
Konsynski, B. R., 36, 38, **58**, 291, **293**, 297, **325**, 428, 432, 439, 442, 443, 444, **450**, **452**, **453**, 499, **516**
Kor, R., 376, **393**
Koster, E., 388, **390**
Kotler, P., 466, **483**
Kotter, J. P., 103, **119**, 375, 376, 377, 388, **392**
Kowitz, A. C., 497, **519**
Kozar, K. A., 528
Krachenburg, A. R., 464, **483**
Kraemer, K., 26, **28**, 32, **59**, 102, **119**, 300, **326**
Kranendonk, A., 67, **82**
Krippendorff, K., 303, **326**
Kugel, R., **482**
Kumar, K., 566, **571**
Kumpe, 464
Kurland, M. A., 494, **520**
Kwamoto, L., **153**
Kwon, T. H., 26, **28**

Laast-Laas, J., **213**
Lacity, M. C., 26, 27, **28**, **29**, 132, **153**, 553, 567, 569, **571**
Lambert, R., 428
Land, F. F., 15, **19**, **28**, 46, **59**, **159**, **289**, **570**
Lane, D. C., 69, **82**
Lane, J. P., **119**
Langford, H., 46, **59**
LaPlante, A., 21, **24**
LaRovere, R. L., 200, **214**
Lasker, G. E., **483**
Lasswell, S. W., 118, **119**
Laudon, J. P., 70, **82**, 525, 526, 527, **548**
Laudon, K. C., 70, **82**, **185**, 525, 526, 527, **548**
Laughlin, R. C., 369, **392**
Lawrence, P. R., 133, **153**, 398, **423**, 457, 460, **483**
Le Blanc, L. A., 528, **548**
Learmonth, G., **265**, 291, **294**, 297, **326**
Leben, J., 444, **452**
Lederer, A. L., 63, **82**, 217, 220, 222, 233, 238, 240, **243**, **264**, 270, 330, 331, 334, 336, **363**, **364**
Lee, D., **153**, **155**
Lee, H. G., 400, 401, 403, 419, **423**
Lee, R. M., **518**, 519

Leidner, D. E., 293, **294**, 429, **430**, 524, 529, 530, 531, **546**, **548**
Leitheiser, R. L., **213**, **241**, **325**
Lengel, R. H., 488, **517**, **521**, 545, **546**
Lester, S., 159, **160**, 278, 281, 287, **290**, 429, 552, 553, 556, 564, **572**
Levinson, E. A., 123, **152**, 376, 377, 388, **390**
Lewin, K., 104, **119**
Lincoln, T., 159, **160**
Linda, K. S., 540, **547**
Lindsey, D., 418, 421, **423**
Lingaraj, B. P., 507, **520**
Linstone, A., 470, **484**
Lockett, M., **28**, **59**
Lorenz, A., 466, **483**
Lorsch, J., 457, **483**
Loveman, G., 554, **571**
Lu, M., 433, **452**
Lucas, H. C., 490, **519**
Luke, R. D., 511, **519**
Lyons, T. F., 464, **483**
Lyytinen, K., 524, **549**

Ma, L., 196, **213**
MacDonald, H., 368, **392**
Macdonald, K. H., 473, **483**
Maher, P. M., **520**
Maier, S. F., 420, 421, **423**
Majchrzak, A., 124, **153**
Malone, T. W., xv, **184**, 398, **424**, 444, **452**
Mantz, E. A., 78, **82**
March, J., 489, 498, **517**, **518**
Markus, M. L., 27, 102, **119**, 124, 130, 132, 133, 138, 145, **152**, **153**, **154**, 374, 376, 377, **390**, 488, 491, 492, 495, 496, 514, 515, **517**, **519**, 524, **549**
Marshall, P. H., 3, **19**
Martin, J., **265**, 444, **452**
Martin, M., 21, **24**
Maslow, A. H., 456, **483**, **484**
Mason, D., 273, **290**, **572**
Mason, R. O., 470, **484**
Massimb, M. N., 419, **424**
Mata, F. J., 291, **294**
Matsumoto, Y., 540, **547**
Mattay, S., **82**, **363**
Mayo, E., 456, **484**
McAllister, D. W., **516**
McClelland, D., 456, **484**
McComb, D., **185**
McCosh, A., **519**

McCubbrey, D., **185**
McDaniel, R., 500, 515, **518**, 528, 545, **548**
McFadden, F. R., 189
McFarlan, F. W., 36, **59**, 65, **82**, **265**, **266**, 274, **289**, 291, **294**, **325**, 432, 439, 444, 450, **452**
McGregor, D. M., 115 116, **119**
McHenry, W. C., 200, **213**
McHugh, P., 368, 372, 373, 374, 384, 387, **392**
McKeen, J. D., **155**
McKenny, J., **59**, 274, **289**, 291, **293**, 301, **325**
McKinley, W., **516**
McKinsey, 26, 39
McLaughlin, I., 500, **517**, 526, **547**
McLean, E. R., **24**, 264, 535, **547**
McLuhan, M., 187
McNurlin, B. C., 491, **521**
McWhinney, W., 129, **154**
Mead, T., 442, **452**
Meilhaud, J., 529, **550**
Meindl, J. R., 296, 301, 304, 313, **327**
Mendelow, A. L., 222, 233, 240, **243**, **264**, 330, 331, 333, 336, **364**
Merali, Y., **213**, **364**
Meyer, A. D., **120**, 502, **519**
Migliarese, P., **519**
Miles, M. B., 336, **364**
Miles, R. E., 368, 369, 371, **392**, **452**, 458, 464, **484**, **485**, 515, **519**
Millar, V. E., 240, **243**, 275, **289**, 291, **294**, 297, 299, 314, **327**
Miller, D., 457, **484**, 500, **519**
Miller, P., 159, **160**
Mink, J., 388, **390**
Mintzberg, H., 61, 69, **82**, **83**, 222, 234, 238, **243**, 368, 369, **392**, 457, 458, 469, **484**, 495, 498, 505, 510, 511, **519**
Mishra, A., 537, **547**
Mitchell, P., 528, 529, **549**
Mitchell, T. R., **516**
Mitroff, I. I., 470, **484**
Molloy, S., 429, **430**, 528, **549**
Mookerjee, A. S., 433, 443, 446, **452**
Moore, W. L., 103, **120**, 493, **520**
Moskowitz, R., **265**
Mowshowitz, A., 524, **549**
Moynihan, T., 216, 234, **243**
Mulligan, P., 376, **391**
Mumford, E., 139, **154**
Murdock, L., 373, 374, 375, **392**, 467, **483**

Nadler, D., 515, **519**
Nakamoto, M., 460, **484**
Nance, W. D., 130, **154**
Narasimhan, S., **294**
Nechis, M., **213**, **325**
Nelson, K. E., 413, **424**
Neo, B. S., 422, **424**
Neuijen, B., 537, 538, 540, **548**
Newman, V., 531, **549**
Niblock, E. G., 331, **365**
Niederman, F., 188, 189, 192, 240, **243**, 330, **364**
Nievelt, M. C. A., 374, **392**, 555, 557, 566, **571**
Nijziel, R., 368, **390**
Nisbett, R., 505, **519**
Nishida, T., **547**
Nolan, R. L., 26, **28**, 31, 32, 33, 36, 39, **59**, 60, 198, 300, **326**
Nonaka, I., 530, 531, 545, **549**
Noria, N., 433, **451**
Norris, G., 560, 563, 566, **571**
North, J. B., 118, **120**
Norton, D. P., 31, 374, 375, 387, **392**, 563, **571**
Norusis, M. J., 378, **392**
Nyce, H. E., 511, 519

O'Callaghan, R., 432, 442, 443, **452**
O'Leary, D. E., 507, **519**
O'Leary, T., 159, **160**
O'Reilly, C. A., 510, **519**
Ohayv, D. D., 537, 538, 540, **548**
Ohmae, K., 428, **430**, 460, **484**
Oliehoek, M., 388, **390**
Oliver, I., 46, **59**
Olsen, J. P., **517**
Olson, M. H., 316, **327**, 490, **519**, 524, **548**
Ong, D., 286, **289**
Orgad, M., **213**
Orlikowski, W. J., 64, **83**, 126, 130, **154**, 429, **430**
Osborn, C. S., 529, **546**
Osher, H. M., **185**
Ostrof, F., 465, 466, **484**
Oz, E., 151, **154**

PA Consulting Group, 278, **289**
Palme, J., 496, **520**
Palvia, P. C., 187, 188, 195, 196, 197, 201, 202, 205, 206, 209, **214**

Palvia, S. C., 187, 188, 195, 196, 197, 201, 202, 205, 206, 209, **214**
Paradice, D., **546**
Parker, M. M., 62, 63, 68, 69, 70, 81, **83**, 282, 285, **289**, 330, **364**
Parsons, G. L., **265**, 298, **326**
Partridge, B., 500, **517**
Pascale, R. T., 39, 40, **60**, 368, **392**
Patterson, M., 540, **549**
Pattison, E. M., **28**
Payn, R., 540, **549**
Peircy, N., **58**
Pels Rijcken, L., 388, **390**
Pendlebury, A. J., 368, 372, 373, 374, 384, 387, **392**
Pennings, J. M., **153**
Peppard, J., 368, 371, **391**, 428, 478, **484**
Perrolle, J., **152**
Pervan, G. P., 191
Peters, G., 276, **289**, 564, 565, **571**
Peters, T. G., **393**, 458, 470, **484**
Pettigrew, A. M., 27, **29**, 64, **83**
Pfeffer, J., 296, **326**, 490, 493, **520**
Phelps, B. D., 419, **424**
Pilger, D. R., 118, **120**
Pine, B. J., 374, **393**
Pinto, J. K., 375, 377, **393**
Piore, M. J., **184**
Plesums, C. A., **185**
Pointer, D. D., **519**
Pool, I. De Sola, 515, **520**
Porter, M. E., 62, **83**, 240, **243**, **265**, 275, **289**, 291, **294**, 297, 299, 314, **327**, 373, **393**, 428, **430**, 431, 432, 433, 434, 450, **452**, 460, **484**, 494, **520**
Powell, W., 444, **452**
Power, J. G., **518**
Poynter, T. A., 466, **484**
Prahalad, C. K., 371, 384, **391**, **451**, 452, **482**
Premkumar, G., 67, 70, 79, **83**, **264**
Price Waterhouse, 278, **290**, **364**
Prusak, L., **153**
Pyburn, P., **59**, 331, 334, 524, **549**

Quillard, J. A., **242**, 447, **451**
Quinn Mills, D., 469, 470, **484**
Quinn, J. B., 233, 234, 238, **243**, **393**
Quinn, R. E., 537, **549**

Rackoff, N., **265**
Raghunathan, B., 333, 334, **364**

Raghunathan, T. S., 220, 237, 240, **243**, 333, 334, **364**
Raisinghani, D., **519**
Rao, H. R., 507, **520**
Rao, K. V., 188, 195, **214**
Rauch-Hindin, W. B., 507, **520**
Rayport, J. F., 293, **294**
Reddi, S. P., 398, **422**
Reich, B. H., 297, 299, 300, **327**, 330, 355, 356, **365**
Reich, R. B., 462, **485**
Reisman, H., 297, **326**
Reitz, H. J., 497, **518**
Reponen, T., **28**
Rhee, H. S., **294**
Ribbers, P. M. A., 26, 61
Rice, R. E., 488, 490, 491, 495, 496, 500, 511, 515, **520**, **521**
Ricks, D. A., **213**
Roach, S., 554, 555, **571**
Robey, D., 130, 133, **154**, **213**, 429, **430**, 490, 514, **519**, **520**, 527, **547**, **549**
Roche, E. M., 200, **214**
Rockart, J. F., 69, **83**, 103, **120**, 141, 146, **154**, 158, **160**, **184**, **185**, 240, **241**, **242**, 298, 300, **325**, **327**, 447, **451**, 464, **485**, 524, **549**
Rodriguez, J., 524, 548
Rogers, E. M., 27, **29**, 125, 132, 140, 142, **154**
Rohrbaugh, J., 537, **549**
Romanelli, E., 291, **294**, 318, **327**
Romero, V., 447, **452**
Rooney, P., 529, **549**
Rosenthal, J., 371, 374, 375, 376, 377, 384, 385, 388, **391**
Ross, L., 505, **519**
Roth, N. L., 132
Row, M. C., 291, **293**, 298, **325**, 398, **422**
Rubenstein, A. H., **520**
Ruchinskas, J., 496, **521**
Runge, D. A., 297, 298, **327**
Ruohonen, M., 69, **83**
Rymer, J., 20, **24**

Saaksjarvi, M., 69, 79, **83**
Sabatier, P., 489, 493, 498, **520**
Sabel, C., **184**
Saintoyant, P. Y., **550**
Sakar, M. B., 400, **424**
Salancik, G. R., 296, 301, 304, 313, **327**

Sambamurthy, V., 330, **365**
Sammon, W. L., 494, **520**
Sampler, J. L., 368, 378, **391**
Sandalls, W. T., Jr, 331, **365**
Sanders, G., 537, 538, 540, **548**
Sarhan, M. E., 413, **424**
Sata, R., 530, **549**
Sauer, C., 26, **29**, 293, **294**
Sauvant, K., 442, **453**
Saxena, K. B. C., 196, **213**
Schein E. H., 27, 104, 108, **120, 185**, 535, 536, **549**
Schlesinger, L. A., 374, **393**
Schmitz, J., **518**
Scholes, K., 69, **82**
Schwartz, R. A., 420, 421, **423**
Schwarz, R. M., 27, **29**, 125, 135, 136, **154**
Schwenk, C. R., 68, **83**, 429, **430**, 470, 528, **549**
Scott Morton, M. S., 11, 69, **83, 185**, 273, **290, 325**, 428, **430**, 467, 479, 480, **485**, 527, **548**
Scott, W. G., 456, **485**
Segara, A., 159, **160**
Segev, E., **213**
Sein, M., **152**
Selig, G. J., **453**
Semler, R., 140, **154**
Senge, P. M., 469, 470, **485**
Sethi, V., 63, **82**, 217, 220, 222, 233, 238, 240, **243, 264**, 270
Sexton, T. L. **160**
Shank, R., 331, **365**
Shapiro, C., 419, **423**
Sherman, S., 140, **154**
Shonk, J. H., 374, **393**
Shore, B., 211, **214**
Short, J. E., 368, 376, 378, **391**, 402, **423**, 464, 467, **482, 485**
Shuff, R. F., 118, **120**
Shukla, R. K., 493, **520**
Shumway, C. R., 502, 511, **520**
Sifonis, J. G., 70, **82**, 217, 234, **242**, 333, **364**
Silver, M. S., 129, **154**
Simon, H. A., 526, **549**
Simpson, K., **294, 364**
Sinclair, D., 368, **393**
Sinclair, S. W., **264**
Sitkin, S. B., 132, **154**
Skyrme, D. J., 531, **549**

Slevin , D. P., 375, 377, **393, 485**
Slovic, P., **518**
Smith, A., 456, **485**
Smith, D. K., 465, 466, **483, 484**
Smith, E. R., 378, **392**, 400, **424**
Smith, J., **185**
Smits, M. T., 26, 61, 81, **83, 101**
Snow, C. C., 368, 369, 371, **392, 452**, 458, 459, 462, 464, **484, 485**, 515, **519**, 531, **547**
Sobkowick, R., 49, **60**
Sobol, M., 316, **325**, 556, **570**
Soden, J. V., **264**
Soh, C., 138, **154**
Somogyi, E. K., xvii, 20, **60**, 526, **549**
Souder, W. E., 505, **520**
Spearing, L., **213, 364**
Spector, B., 374, 376, **390**
Spitalnic, R., 494, **520**
Sprague, R. H., 11, **20**, 491, **521**, 527, **549**
Sproull, L., 491, 495, 496, 511, **521**
Stace, D., 377, **391**
Stalk, G. Jr, 466, **485**
Stalker, G. M., 463, **482**
Stallings, W., 444, **453**
Stanton, M. A., 144, **153**, 368, 375, 376, 388, **391**
Stata, R., 469, **485**
Staw, B. M., **326**
Stein, B. A., **28, 153**
Steinfield, C., 400, **424**, 488, 496, **518, 521**
Steward, K., 478, **484**
Stewart, N. S., 118, **120**
Stewart, R., 526, **550**
Stigler, G. J., 404, **424**
Stoddard, D. B., 368, 369, 376, 378, **391**, **393**, 402, 418, **423, 424**
Stonich, P. J., 466, **483**
Strassman, P. A., 125, 132, 142, **154**, 278, 280, **290**, 488, 489, 497, **521**, 552, 555, 556, 566, **571**
Strauss, A. L., 241, **242**
Subramani, M., **153**
Sullivan, C. H. Jr., **60**, 240, **243, 266**, 333, **365**
Sullivan-Trainor, M., 557, **571**
Susman, G. I., 464, **482**
Sutherland, A. R., 26, 37, 39, 41, 54, 55, **59**, **60**, 101
Sutherland, D. J., 118, **120**
Svenning, L., 496, **521**

Sviokla, J. J., 293, **294**, **335**
Swanson, K., **185**
Synott, W. R., 216, 222, **243**

Targett, D., **159**, **289**, **570**
Tavakolian, H., 429, **430**
Taylor, F. W., 456, **485**
Taylor, P., 558, **571**
Teng, J. T. C., 368, 374, 375, 376, 377, 378, 384, 385, **391**, 429, **430**
Theeuwes, J. A. M., 68, 69, 70, **83**
Théorêt, A., **519**
Thomas, A. B., 102, **120**
Thompson, V., **485**
Thorelli, H. B., 398, **424**
Thyfault, M. E., 529, **550**
Tigre, P. B., **214**
Ting-Toomey, S., 540, 541, **547**
Todd, P. A., 146, **155**, 528, **550**
Tofler, A., 12, **20**
Torkzadeh, G., 334, **363**
Toyne, B., **213**
Tracey, P. K., **516**
Trainor, H. E., **83**, **289**, 298, **364**
Trauth, E., 146, **153**
Treacy, M. E., 103, **120**, 297, 298, **324**, 372, **393**
Trevino, L. K., 492, 496, **517**, **521**
Tully, C. J., **28**
Turban, 23, **24**
Turoff, M., 72, **83**, 495, 504, 509, **518**
Tushman, M. L., 291, **294**, 318, **327**, 515, **519**
Tversky, A., **518**

Ulrich, W. A., **265**
Useem, M., **364**, **392**, 428, **430**, 469, **483**

Vacca, J. R., **265**, **266**
Van de Ven, A. H., 369, **393**
van der Poel, K. G., 26, 61, 81, **83**
van der Zijden, F. A. P., **82**
Van Heck, E., 411, **423**
Vandenbosch, B., 528, 545, **550**
Vantrappen, H., 372, **393**
Venkatachalam, A. R., 211
Venkatraman, N., 62, 68, 81, **82**, **214**, 217, 240, **242**, 292, **294**, 330, 333, **364**, **365**, 368, 372, 384, **392**, 462, **485**
Vidal, F., 529, **550**
Vitale, M. R., **265**, 297, 298, **326**, 439, **451**

von Bertalanfy, L. 457, **481**
von Simpson, E. M., 146, **155**, **185**
Vrakking, W. J., 375, 376, 377, **393**
Vroom, V. H., 500, **521**

Wade, J., 371, 374, 375, 376, 377, 384, 385, 388, **391**
Waema, T., 62, 65, 80, **83**
Walleck, A. S., **59**
Walsham, G., 62, 65, 80, **83**
Walton, R. E., 130, 139, **155**, 273, **290**
Wang, P., 195, 196, 197, **214**
Warbelow, A., 406, 410, 418, **424**, 432, 439, 443, **452**, **453**
Ward, B. K., **159**
Ward, J., 26, **29**, **60**, 63, **83**, 157, **160**, 475, 480, **485**
Warketin, M. E., **363**
Waterman, D. A., 507, **521**
Waterman, R. W., **393**, 458, 470, **484**
Watson, H. J., 491, **521**, 524, **548**
Watson, R. T., 188, 189, **214**, **215**
Weber, B., 416, 421, **422**
Weber, M., 456, **485**
Webster, J., **152**
Weggeman, M., 376, **393**
Weick, K. E., 496, 511, **521**
Weill, P. 316, **327**
Weir, M. 139, **154**
Weiser, M., **185**
Weitz, B. A., 296, 301, 302, 304, 313, 315, **325**
Welbank, M., 507, **521**
Welch, M., 12, **20**
West, M., 540, **549**
Wetherbe, J. C., **24**, 190, 192, 200, **213**, **214**, **241**, **243**, **265**, 298, 300, **325**, **364**
Whang, S., 398, **423**
Wheeler, W. A., 368, 372, 373, 374, 384, 387, **392**
Wheelwright, S. C., 469, 470, **483**
Whisler, T., 490, **521**, 526, **550**
Whitcomb, D. K., 420, 421, **423**
White, R. E., 466, **484**
Whitmore, P., **60**, **83**, 475, 480, **485**
Whittington, R., 27, **29**
Wiersema, F., 372, **393**
Wijnen, G., 375, 376, **393**
Wildschut, E., 372, 387, **390**
Wilensky, H. L., 494, 508, **521**

Willcocks, L. P., 26, 27, **29**, 159, **160**, 272, 273, 278, 281, 285, 287, **290**, **294**, 552, 553, 555, 556, 558, 560, 564, 567, **571**, **572**
Williams, A. W., 400, **424**
Williams, F., 488, **521**
Williams, G., 12, **20**
Williams, R., 372, 376, 384, 387, **390**
Williamson, O., 405, 420, **424**
Wills, L. A., 317, **327**
Wilson, T. D., 67, **83**, 272, **290**
Winslow, C., **153**
Wiseman, C., **265**, 297, **327**
Witte, E., 498, **521**
Wybo, M. D., **242**
Wyman, J., **325**

Yates, J., xvii, vii, **184**, 398, **424**, 444, **452**
Yetton, P., **294**, 500, **521**

Yin, R. K., 335, **365**
Young, D., 273, 401, **424**
Yourdan, E., 524, **550**

Zachman, J. A., 69, **83**
Zahra, S. A., **363**
Zairi, M., 368, **393**
Zammuto, R., 439, **453**
Zani, W. M., 240, **243**
Zigli, R. M., 206, **214**
Zmud, R. W., 26, **28**, 217, 238, 240, **241**, 330, **365**, 491, 514, **521**, **522**, 524
Zorkorczy, P. I., **59**, 159
Zuboff, S., xvi, **xvii**, 114, 115, **120**, **184**, 469, 479, **485**, 489, 492, 508, **522**
Zupancic, J., 208, **213**
Zviran, M., 292, **294**, 331, 333, 356, **365**

Subject index

Action research, 146
Advertising and circulation, 310
Airline industry, 439, 442
Allied Dunbar, 281
Advanced economies/nations, 189–195, 209
Aerospace industry, 218
American Airlines, 194, 281, 321
American Express, 322
American Hospital Supply Co., 194
Andersen Consulting *see* Method/1
Apple Macintosh, 178, 180
Applications (portfolio) *see* Information
    systems development
Artificial intelligence (AI), 16, 506
Association for Computing Machinery
    (ACM), 151
Association for Information Systems (AIS), 151
Audit *see* Information systems evaluation
Australian Meat & Livestock Corporation,
    407, 408, 415, 416

Backlog *see* Information systems
    maintenance
Balanced Scorecard, 562
Banking *see* Financial services sector
Batch systems, 2, 5
Baxter Travenoll, 319
Benchmarking, 566
    see also Information systems evaluation
Bergen Brunswig, 319
Board of directors *see* Top management
Brainstorming, 250
British Airports Authority, 284
British Telecom, 177
Budgets *see* Information systems costs/
    expenditure
Business acquisitions *see* Strategic alliances
Business analyst, 49, 50, 144
Business (inc. technological) environment,
    xii, xiii, xvi, 6, 10, 11, 15, 25, 61, 62,
    63, 64, 65, 67, 68, 74, 81, 84, 96, 109,

117, 131, 158, 161–186, 187–215, 238,
    253, 291, 371, 427–430, 493, 537, 569
Business Information Analysis and
    Integration Technique (BIAIT), 253
Business Information Characterization Study,
    253
Business network redesign, 462
Business processes (redesign/reengineering),
    xii, 22, 64, 65, 81, 111, 114, 116, 131,
    133, 136, 139, 142, 144, 145, 148, 158,
    170, 180, 181, 182, 251, 252, 258, 262,
    292, 331, 367–396, 402, 405, 467, 468,
    469, 555
Business Systems Planning (BSP), 69, 79,
    159, 221, 240, 251, 252, 258
Business strategy/strategic planning/
    visioning, xii, xiii, 18, 26, 27, 36, 61,
    62, 64, 65, 67, 68, 70, 71, 73, 74, 80,
    96, 116, 148, 194, 198, 211, 217, 224,
    225, 230, 233, 234, 238, 249, 251, 256,
    261, 262, 264, 273, 281, 291, 295–328,
    329–366, 428, 434, 435, 437, 438, 439,
    457, 473, 475, 476
alignment/link with IS strategy, xii, xiv,
    18, 26, 34, 38, 47, 51, 58, 61, 64, 65,
    68, 69, 75, 77, 79, 80, 81, 84, 86, 88,
    92, 95, 96, 99, 100, 158, 159, 170, 182,
    192, 193, 198, 204, 209, 216, 217, 219,
    220, 224, 226, 233, 238, 240, 249, 250,
    252, 263, 264, 273, 274, 276, 278, 282,
    284, 291–293, 295–328, 329–366
Business transformation *see* Organizational
    transformation

Canadian life assurance, 292, 330, 348, 354
Case study research, 61–84, 125
CATS systems, 407, 408, 413, 414, 415, 416
Change agent, 27, 104, 107, 108, 109, 110,
    114, 117, 118, 123–155
Change management (strategy), xi, xii, xiii,
    25, 27, 63, 67, 76, 102–122, 123–155,

158, 164, 179, 180, 182, 279, 286, 293,
   368, 369, 371, 372, 375, 378, 386, 388,
   404, 428, 479
Chemical industry, 218
Chief executive officer (CEO), xii, xiv, 27,
   40, 43, 80, 81, 86, 99, 100, 102–122,
   125, 135, 139, 142, 216, 218, 227, 228,
   230, 256, 257, 262, 291, 295, 298, 301,
   302, 304, 305, 339
Chief information officer (CIO), xiv, 38, 40,
   49, 53, 62, 71, 74, 75, 78, 79, 81, 84,
   85, 87, 90, 96, 97, 99, 124, 125, 131,
   134, 135, 138, 141, 142, 144, 162, 165,
   169, 171, 172, 178, 179, 180, 181, 182,
   188, 189, 193, 194, 199, 205, 216, 217,
   222, 224, 225, 226, 227, 228, 230, 233,
   256, 340, 341, 344, 352, 355
Chief knowledge officer (CKO), 523
Citibank, 320
Client-server, 21, 75, 131, 136, 137, 141,
   449, 557, 558
CODASYL, 8
Common Market *see* European Union
Communications technology *see*
   Telecommunications
Competitive advantage *see* Strategic IS under
   Information systems
Compuserve, 192
Computer-assisted decision aiding
   technologies, 488, 491, 496, 498, 501,
   502, 506
   see also Decision support systems (DSS)
Computer-assisted design (CAD), 98
Computer-assisted software engineering
   (CASE), 13, 168, 178, 179, 182, 194,
   195, 199, 200, 208, 228, 253, 282
Computer conferencing *see* Teleconferencing
Computer Science, 151, 234
Contextualism, 64, 65
Cost-benefit analysis *see* Return on
   investment
Costs *see under* Information systems
Cotton industry, 418
Credit authorization, 442
Credit card processing, 310
Critical Success Factors (CSFs), 130, 138,
   158, 182, 219, 221, 222, 223, 240, 253,
   276, 278
Cross functional teams, 464
Culture *see under* Organizational and/or
   Globalization/global issues

Curricula *see* Information systems education/
   training
Customer Resource Life Cycle, 253
Cybernetics, 175

Data (architecture), 8, 10, 22, 52, 87, 89,
   172, 174, 177, 183, 192, 200, 202, 204,
   228, 234, 251, 257, 258, 259, 447
   administration, 48, 259
   analysis techniques, 8, 9, 11, 189, 251, 253
   centre *see under* Information
   communications, 21, 74
   dictionary, 9, 168, 251, 253
   resource management, 32, 252
Data Resources, 192
Data service industries, 442
Database(s), 9, 10, 11, 17, 23, 32, 33, 130,
   161, 166, 169, 170, 171, 176, 183, 189,
   192, 193, 206, 229, 249, 250, 251, 252,
   258, 259, 262, 448
   design, 10, 253
   management systems (DBMS), 8, 9, 174
Data processing, 1–4, 18, 72, 73, 310
   function *see* Information systems function
   manager
   personnel/skills *see* Information systems
      personnel/skills
Datasolve, 273
Decision making/processes, xiii, xvi, 10, 11,
   16, 22, 71, 73, 125, 142, 168, 180, 181,
   273, 428, 487–522, 528
Decision support systems (DSS), 16, 49, 50,
   52, 54, 73, 116, 135, 168, 172, 173,
   511, 527, 528, 534, 535, 536, 545
Delphi method, 72, 253
Department of Defense, 125
Desk top computers/computing *see* end-user
   computing and/or personal computers
Disconfirmation, 105–107
Distributed systems/processing, 163
Documentation *see under* Information systems
Double-loop learning *see* Organizational
   learning
Dow Jones, 192
Dupont, 134
Dutch flower/florist industry, 407, 408, 411,
   415, 416

EDS, 121
Education/training *see under* Information
   systems

Electronic bulletin boards, 500
Electronic commerce/markets, xii, xv, 23,
    170, 292, 293, 397–425
Electronic data interchange (EDI), xv, 23, 68,
    86, 98, 175, 176, 462
    see also Inter-organizational systems
Electronic mail (email), 17, 23, 105, 161,
    165, 171, 173, 174, 176, 496, 498, 511
Electronic point of sale (systems) (EPOS),
    281
Electronics industry, 218
End-user computing, 13, 17, 19, 49, 163,
    168, 193
    see also under Information systems
Ends/Means Analysis, 253
Ethics, 131, 136, 148, 149, 150, 151, 183
European Union, 72
Evaluation *see under* Information systems
Executive Information Planning (EIP), 159
Executive information systems (EIS), 10, 11,
    16, 32, 52, 54, 69, 103, 116, 171, 173,
    174, 201, 203, 284, 488, 498, 500, 524,
    526, 527, 528, 529, 534, 535, 536, 542
Expert systems, 16, 73, 174, 200, 260, 282,
    497, 507
    see also Knowledge (management)
    (systems)
Explicit knowledge *see* Knowledge
    (management) (systems)

Federal Express, 318, 319
Finance Director, 228
Financial planning/strategy, 62, 89, 227, 261
Financial Services sector, 218, 273, 302, 305,
    306, 308, 309, 314, 315, 419, 442, 446
Finnish paper industry, 439
Focus Groups, 253
Food and drink industry, 218

General Electric, 321
General Motors, 24, 121
Global information management strategy,
    444–450
Globalization/global issues/systems, xiii, 158,
    170, 187–215, 431, 433, 441–444, 449,
    537, 544, 553
Government (policy), 209, 210, 211, 212
    see also Public sector
Graphics, 173
Grosch's Law, 4
Grounded Theory, 241

Group (decision) support systems (G(D)SS)
    see Groupware
Groupware, 130, 135, 137, 138, 148, 171,
    173, 470, 499, 558

Hawthorne effect, 109
High performance teams, 463
Holland Systems Corporation, 159, 251
Homogeneous groups, 497
Hong Kong Tradelink, 442
Hotel/lodging industry, 435, 437
Human resources management (HRM)/
    strategy/function, 62, 63, 138, 139, 150,
    201, 478

IBM, 4, 7, 8, 74, 159, 168, 169, 180, 240,
    251
Image processing, 17, 22, 172, 481, 558
Index Group, 258
Informate, 114, 115, 116, 117
Information, xvi, 13, 62, 63, 67, 84, 111,
    113, 116, 158, 170, 174, 175, 182, 189,
    192, 204, 314, 355, 488, 495, 498
    centre, 17, 49, 57, 163
    overload, 174, 503, 524
    requirements/needs/problem definition, 4,
        5, 6, 9, 14, 15, 18, 44, 45, 46, 47, 74,
        76, 97, 121, 132, 133, 141, 145, 169,
        174, 189, 194, 196, 198, 199, 203, 204,
        212, 225, 226, 233, 250, 251, 257, 272,
        274, 278, 279, 284, 285, 287, 288
    resources manager/ment, 49
    strategy/plan, xi, xii, xiii, xiv, 25, 26,
        61–84, 253, 274, 535
Information economics approach, 274,
    282–286
Information Engineering, 159, 221, 228, 234,
    251, 253
Information management (IM) strategy, xi,
    xii, 25, 27, 85–101, 217
Information Quality Analysis, 253
Information systems (IS), 10, 11, 16, 32, 69,
    284
    costs/expenditure, 2, 4, 5, 6, 12, 21, 22,
        32, 38, 43, 44, 67, 70, 74, 75, 76, 78,
        89, 90, 93, 95, 97, 111, 113, 114, 117,
        123, 124, 128, 129, 131, 139, 145, 146,
        158, 164, 165, 167, 170, 180, 182, 183,
        184, 194, 222, 227, 261, 271–298, 299,
        301, 304, 306, 310, 316, 552, 553, 554,
        557, 558, 560, 561, 562

development, xiii, xvii, 2, 3, 5, 6, 7,
13–16, 18, 19, 20, 26, 32, 43, 44, 45,
46, 48, 50, 57, 70, 75, 77, 78, 88, 89,
96, 97, 124, 133, 135, 139, 146, 158,
162, 163, 168, 169, 170, 177, 178, 183,
184, 189, 192, 193, 194, 199, 201, 204,
206, 208, 222, 223, 226, 227, 228, 230,
239, 250, 251, 252, 253, 256, 257, 258,
259, 262, 263, 557, 558, 560, 563
participative approaches, 18, 57, 139, 199,
200, 357
structured methods, 7, 46
documentation, 6, 69, 74, 75, 76, 177,
258
education/training, 21, 27, 38, 44, 47, 96,
98, 107, 126, 130, 137, 138, 142, 146,
147, 148, 149, 150, 200, 201, 202, 203,
207, 222, 251, 258, 260
evaluation/benefits/audit, xii, 37, 44, 48,
61–84, 97, 99, 111, 113, 122, 129, 131,
132, 134, 145, 146, 157, 159, 167, 182,
210, 217, 219, 220, 222, 227, 228, 237,
240, 252, 254, 261, 271–298, 315, 552,
553, 559, 563, 564, 565, 566,
failure(s), xiii, 26, 42, 47, 100, 124, 130,
133, 134, 198, 306
feasibility *see* Information systems
development
function/organization/management *see also*
Chief information officer (CIO), xii,
xvii, 2, 6, 8, 11, 12, 17, 18, 21, 26, 27,
32, 36, 37, 38, 39, 40, 41, 45, 46, 47,
48, 49, 50, 51, 57, 69, 70, 74, 75, 76,
78, 85–101, 126, 131, 132, 134, 135,
136, 138, 139, 140, 144, 145, 146, 151,
158, 162, 163, 165, 170, 171, 174, 175,
181, 182, 192, 193, 196, 197, 198, 209,
218, 225, 226, 227, 228, 230, 239, 250,
260, 261, 285, 330, 555, 559
implementation, xiii, xiv, xvii, 21, 26, 27,
42, 45, 47, 49, 78, 97, 102, 111, 117,
124, 128, 130, 133, 137, 159, 165, 175,
179, 216, 217, 221, 222, 224, 228, 230,
231, 236, 238, 239, 240, 249, 252, 253,
254, 255, 257, 258, 259, 264, 274, 288
management issues, xi, xiii, 26, 99, 158,
187–215
maintenance, 7, 12, 14, 15, 44, 45, 54, 86,
177, 178, 203, 204, 207
packages, 13, 42, 43, 44, 75, 76, 91, 135,
182, 194, 203, 204

personnel/roles/skills, xiii, 3, 4, 6, 9, 11,
13, 17, 20, 26, 27, 38, 42, 44, 45, 47,
48, 49, 51, 52, 54, 57, 70, 75, 87, 97,
123, 124, 132, 133, 138, 142, 144, 145,
146, 147, 148, 150, 175, 178, 181, 182,
193, 196, 197, 198, 199, 200, 203, 204,
207, 252, 253, 260, 285
planning/planners, xi, xii, xiii, 17, 25, 26,
27, 33, 34, 36, 44, 46, 48, 50, 57, 63,
69, 70, 71, 74, 75, 96, 157–160,
161–186, 216–248, 249–270, 330, 331,
333
portfolio (applications) *see* Information
systems development
prototypes/prototyping, 15, 88, 96, 141,
182, 184, 194
resistance/threats, xvi, 147, 179, 199, 222,
258, 279, 280, 286
security, xvi, 21, 22, 47, 78, 89, 91, 97,
174, 199, 204, 209
specification *see* Information requirements
strategic IS, xi, xv–xvii, 1–24, 38, 51, 52,
53, 54, 61, 63, 73, 75, 78, 91, 94, 96,
100, 117, 181, 192, 194, 198, 203, 208,
216, 217, 219, 220, 225, 228, 236, 237,
238, 239, 250, 262, 275, 278, 280, 281,
282, 297, 298, 299, 300, 301, 304, 305
strategy/policy, xi, xii, xiii, 17, 18, 25–28,
31–60, 63, 89, 91, 97, 100, 157, 158,
197, 198, 205, 209, 212, 216–248, 249,
254, 261, 276, 291, 347, 367–396, 477
users/clients, 5, 7, 12, 13, 14, 15, 17, 18,
19, 21, 38, 44, 45, 47, 48, 49, 71, 76,
88, 90, 124, 125, 128, 129, 130, 131,
132, 137, 139, 140, 141, 142, 143, 144,
147, 151, 164, 166, 167, 168, 171, 174,
178, 181, 182, 194, 196, 199, 203, 209,
221, 222, 224, 225, 227, 228, 229, 231,
237, 238, 239, 241, 250, 251, 252, 279,
286, 287, 288, 357
Information technology (IT), 12–13, 18, 19,
73, 77, 81, 138, 158, 161–186, 210,
488, 490, 491, 492, 493, 494, 525
convergence, 13, 17, 73
developments, xiv, xv, xvii, 1–24, 25, 47,
480, 481
director *see* Chief information officer
function/management *see* Information
systems function/organization/
management
impacts *see under* Organizational

infrastructure/architecture, xvi, 21, 27, 38,
    43, 64, 69, 70, 74, 75, 76, 78, 86, 142,
    144, 146, 158, 162, 165, 166, 167, 169,
    171, 174, 175, 177, 180, 181, 182, 189,
    193, 199, 209, 217, 221, 228, 230, 234,
    239, 250, 251, 252, 276, 282, 428,
    431–453
  investments *see* Information systems costs/
    expenditure and/or evaluation/benefits
  and organizational transformation/change
    see under Organizational
  maturity (models) *see* 'Stages of growth'
    concept
  productivity paradox, 428, 551–572
  scanning/forecasts, 67, 77, 84, 97, 161–186
  strategy/policy/planning/visioning, xi, xii,
    25, 27, 102–122, 171, 192, 193, 200,
    211, 217, 301, 337, 342, 348, 349, 352,
    354
Innovation, 107, 125, 131, 132, 140, 143,
    262, 284
Insourcing *see* Sourcing
Insurance industry, 61–84, 218
Integrated systems digital network (ISDN),
    21, 444
Internet/Intranet, 23, 524, 529, 536
Intelligent knowledge-based systems (IKBS)
    see Expert systems
International issues *see* Globalization/gobal
    issues/systems
Inter-organizational design/systems, 34, 38,
    53, 116, 170, 182, 439, 440, 462
    see also EDI

Japanese used-car dealer network (Aucnet),
    407, 408, 409, 410, 415, 416
Joint Application Development (JAD), 136,
    148
Just-in-Time, 466

Knowledge (management) (systems), 116,
    124, 172, 429, 494, 509, 510, 511, 523,
    529–545
    see also Expert systems
Knowledge Ware, 159, 253

Lap top computers *see* Personal computers
Leadership (style), 140, 197, 256, 257, 263,
    376, 385
Legacy systems (*see also* IS maintenance),
    18, 172, 179, 566

Lifecycle (system) *see* Information systems
    development
Local area network (LAN) *see* Networks
Logistics, 405, 412
London Stock Exchange, xiii
    Taurus System, xiii, 552
Lotus Notes, 130

Machine lubricant industry, 434
Mainframe computers, 5, 9, 21, 74, 76, 136,
    137, 167, 169, 194
Management of change *see* Change
    management strategy
Management information systems (MIS)
    see Executive information systems (EIS)
    and Information systems
Management Science, 3, 11, 12
Manufacturing (strategy), 62, 273, 276
Marine engine lubricant industry, 434
Market intelligence, 409
Marketing strategy, 62
Massachusetts Institute of Technology (MIT),
    179
McKesson, 321
Media industry, 198
Mergers & acquisitions *see* Strategic
    alliances
Merrill Lynch, 194, 281, 320
Method/1, 159, 221, 240, 251, 253
Methodology *see* Information systems
    development
Micro computers *see* Personal computers
Mini computers, 5
Multimedia, 20, 23, 418

Networks, 17, 21, 22, 68, 72, 74, 76, 89, 98,
    115, 116, 164, 165, 166, 167, 173, 182,
    193, 194, 195, 199, 200, 251, 260, 310,
    445, 446
Nolan Norton Company *see* 'Stages of
    growth' concept
Normalization *see* Data analysis techniques

O&M, 3
Office automation, 12, 13, 49, 69, 74, 75, 98,
    163, 199
Oil industry, 218, 302, 305, 306, 308, 309,
    314, 315
Operating systems, 168, 193
    see also Information technology
    infrastructure/architecture and Unix

Operational/operations reaearch (OR), 3
Oracle, 206
Organizational
  Behaviour/Theory, 146, 456, 457, 515, 526
  change/transformation, xiv, 10, 17, 116,
    117, 133, 144, 145, 162, 178, 182, 193,
    368, 372, 428, 475, 476
  competitiveness/performance, xiii, xiv, 19,
    70, 71, 76, 79, 131, 132, 142, 145, 146,
    249, 282, 293, 301, 315, 316, 317, 367,
    368, 369, 382, 551–572
  see also Competitive advantage
  coordination, 440, 444
  culture/politics/power, xiii, xvi, 10, 67, 68,
    76, 93, 96, 102, 116, 117, 158, 170,
    178, 179, 182, 183, 202, 203, 204, 234,
    273
  decision making *see* Decision making
  design (OD)/structure/forms, xiii, 27, 68,
    125, 135, 136, 137, 138, 139, 143, 150,
    151, 368, 369, 371, 372, 374, 376, 388,
    431–453, 454–486, 507, 508, 526, 527
  environment *see* Business (inc.
    technological) environment
  impact/role of IS/IT/ISS, xiv, 4, 10, 17,
    27, 61, 64, 65, 69, 70, 74, 77, 78, 79,
    81, 84, 112, 113, 114, 116, 123, 124,
    126, 127, 129, 133, 142, 146, 162, 175,
    179, 180, 285, 288
  intelligence *see* Knowledge (management)
    (systems)
  learning/memory, 69, 74, 80, 173, 180,
    193, 209, 229, 230, 234, 239, 288, 289,
    469, 470, 505, 506, 507, 528
  strategy *see* Business strategy/strategic
    planning/visioning
Outsourcing *see* Sourcing

Packages *see under* Information systems
Pastoral industry in Australia, 406, 407
Performance measures *see* Critical Success
    Factors (CSFs) and evaluation/benefits
    under Information systems
Personal/portable computers (inc. lap top
    computers), 12, 15, 74, 131, 163, 166,
    169, 173, 174, 178, 180, 197, 204, 206,
    260, 281
Petroleum industry *see* Oil industry
Portfolio Management, 253
Printing/publishing industry, 275, 302, 305,
    306, 308, 314, 315

Problem definition *see* Information
    requirements/problem definition
Process Quality Management (PQM), 159
Programming/programmer, 3, 9, 16, 43, 45,
    46, 48, 50, 141, 169, 193, 203
  languages, 194, 204
  COBOL, 3, 253
  FORTRAN, 3
  Fourth generation (4GLs), 13, 208
  Object oriented, 194, 199
  PASCAL, 7
  support environments *see* CASE
Project management, 5, 6, 48, 147
PROplanner, 159, 251
Public sector, 86

Quality (assurance), 15, 38

Raychem Corporation, 256–262
Requirements analysis *see* Information
    requirements
Resistance *see under* Information systems
Retail iudustry, 198, 218, 273, 302, 305, 306,
    308, 309, 314, 315
Return on investment (RoI), 48, 52, 67, 79,
    88, 113, 117
  see also Information systems benefits/
    evaluation
Return on Management, 280, 281
Risk, 272, 273, 275, 279, 280, 285, 286,405,
    552

Satellites, 310
Scientific American, 161
Senior management *see* Top management
Services sector, 218
'Seven S' concept, 26, 39, 40, 41, 54
Silicon chips, 12
Singapore Tradenet, 442
Single-loop learning *see* Organizational
    learning
Small & Medium-Sized Enterprises (SMEs),
    179
Societal impacts of IT, xvii
Society for Information Management (SIM),
    151, 189
Socio-technical approach/systems, 142
Software engineering, 5
Sourcing, 26, 43, 124, 128, 130, 132, 134,
    135, 138, 140, 169, 181, 193, 194, 201,
    459, 461, 462, 567, 568, 569

Specification *see* information requirements
Spreadsheets, 171, 173
'Stages of growth' concept (inc. IT maturity), 26, 31–60, 158, 198, 209, 253, 300
Stakeholder perspective, xii, 61, 62, 69, 71, 72, 76, 77, 80, 81, 136, 144, 159, 181, 216–248, 257, 261, 286, 288
Standards/standardization, 8, 70, 78, 98, 117, 131, 137, 139, 143, 145, 165, 167, 169, 182, 195, 199, 203, 204, 207, 443, 446
Steering committees, 69, 75, 227
Strategic IS (planning) *see* under Information systems
Strategic advantage *see* Competitive advantage
Strategic alliance(s), 53, 54, 70, 72, 73, 74, 75, 76, 78, 121, 460, 461, 477
Strategic management/planning *see* Business strategy/planning
Strategic Information Management
  scope of book, xi, xii, xiii
  students' use of book, xiii
Strategy Set Transformation, 253
Success factors *see* Critical Success Factors (CSFs)
Survey research, 62, 78, 79, 80
SWOT analysis, 69, 74, 77
Systems analysis/design, 3, 6, 9, 45, 48, 49, 50, 149
  (*see also* IS development)
Systems approach, 457
Systems Development Life Cycle (SDLC) *see* Information systems development
Systems dynamics, 175
Systems programmer/programming, 9

Tacit knowledge *see* Knowledge (management) (systems)
Taurus System *see* London Stock Exchange
Technological determinism, 27, 90, 126, 280
Telecommunications, 12, 13, 17, 69, 72, 75, 138, 158, 161, 162, 164, 166, 168, 169, 177, 193, 194, 195, 200, 204, 205, 228, 249, 251, 276, 481, 491, 496, 498, 501, 502, 506
Teleconferencing, 116, 174, 511

Text processing (systems), 17
Theory X, Theory Y, 115, 116
Top management (inc. top management support/involvement in IS projects/strategy), 38, 47, 48, 54, 58, 61, 62, 64, 68, 71, 73, 74, 76, 77, 78, 79, 80, 84, 85, 89, 90, 94, 96, 97, 100, 103, 106, 115, 116, 124, 129, 140, 144, 150, 159, 162, 170, 178, 181, 188, 193, 197, 198, 201, 202, 208, 209, 216, 218, 219, 220, 221, 222, 223, 225, 229, 231, 233, 234, 238, 241, 250, 251, 253, 254, 256, 257, 258, 259, 260, 261, 264, 271, 273, 285, 298, 299
Transaction cost analysis, 405, 420
Transaction processing (systems), 5, 10, 11, 69, 135, 170, 171, 198, 203, 506, 526
Trans-border data flows, 443
Transportation industry, 198, 218
Trust/confidence, 76, 98, 125, 132, 133

Underdeveloped/developing countries, 205–208, 209
United Airlines, 194, 321
United States meat industry, 413
Unix, 167, 169, 180, 184
Users *see under* Information systems

Value added network (VAN) *see* Networks
Value chain (analysis), 221, 240, 250, 252, 253, 275, 276, 373, 432, 433, 439, 444, 448
Video conferencing, 23, 138, 183, 511
Virtual reality, 23
Voice mail/processing (systems), 17, 138, 161, 165, 172, 173, 183

Wholesale industry, 198
Wide area network (WAN) *see* Networks
Windows, 178
World Bank, 200
World wide web (WWW), 23, 135, 138, 400, 529

Xerox, 173

Year, 2000 problem, xiii